For the President
Personal and Secret

Correspondence Between
Franklin D. Roosevelt and
William C. Bullitt

ORVILLE H. BULLITT, EDITOR

With an Introduction
by George F. Kennan

Revised Index
AUGUST 1973

HOUGHTON MIFFLIN COMPANY
BOSTON

Index

Malvy, Louis Jean, French, Minister of Interior, 292

Mandel, Georges Jeroboam Rothschild, French, Minister for Colonies 1938, Minister Interior 1940, 168, 174, 204, 318, 425, 434, 441, 462, 473, 479, 492, 524–525

Marshall, General George C., Chief of Staff United States Army 1939, Ambassador to China 1945, Secretary of State 1947, 559–560, 606; army preparedness, 342; on Middle East, 535, 550

Masaryk, Thomas G., Czechoslovakia President 1920–1935, 375

Maxwell, Russell L., Major General, Chief of United States Military Mission in North Africa, 534, 542

McIntire, Vice Admiral Ross T., White House Physician 1934–1945, 398

Memel, German occupation, 331, 332

Mendès-France, Pierre, French Deputy, 473

Messersmith, George S., Minister to Austria 1934, Assistant Secretary of State 1937, 124, 125

Miklas, Dr. Wilhelm, Austrian President, 101; defies Hitler, 255

Milch, Field Marshal Erhard, German, Inspector General Luftwaffe, 313

Moley, Raymond, Professor of Government, Barnard College, Adviser to President Roosevelt, 32; at Economic Conference, 34, 35

Molotov, V. M., Russian, Commisar Foreign Affairs 1939, 60, 66, 67, 93, 341, 576, 587; becomes Foreign Affairs Commissar, 340

Monick, Emmanuel, French, Secretary General to Resident General, Morocco, Governor, Bank of France, 184–185, 188–189, 201, 205, 299

Monnet, Jean, French, Allied Maritime Transport Council 1918, Deputy Secretary General, League of Nations 1919–1923, Chairman Franco-British Supply Council, 1940–1943, Monnet Plan 1947, European Common Market 1955, 93, 318, 326, 334, 336, 353, 355, 371, 389, 390; meets Lindbergh, 276; allied purchasing committees, 299–300, 302, 377, 379–380, 383, 392, 397

Moore, R. Walton, Virginia State Senate 1887–1890, United States Congress 1919–1931, Assistant Secretary of State 1933, Counselor State Department 1937, xlii, 38, 39, 44, 59, 78, 85–86, 92, 122, 131, 133, 157, 176, 195, 205, 206; on Welles, 214, 513

Morgenthau, Henry, Jr., Secretary of the Treasury 1934–1945, 142, 345, 434, 452; Russian recognition, 40, 42, 57; credit to China, 279; sales to France, 302–303, 391, 392; French debt, 318, 336, 353

Moscicki, Ignacy, President of Poland 1926–1939, 123, 126

Mowrer, Edgar, War Correspondent, Author, 212, 214

Munich Pact, 255–256, 287, 296; Hitler breaks, 305

Murphy, Robert, Counselor of Embassy, Paris 1937–1940, President's Personal Representative North Africa 1942, Ambassador to Belgium 1949, Ambassador to Japan 1952, 298, 368, 390, 441, 477, 505; on Bullitt in Paris, 168, 397, 403, 404, 475, 476; in North Africa, 565

For the President
Personal and Secret

President Roosevelt says good-bye to Ambassador Bullitt,
November 1933.

For the President
Personal and Secret

Correspondence Between

Franklin D. Roosevelt and

William C. Bullitt

ORVILLE H. BULLITT, EDITOR

With an Introduction
by George F. Kennan

Illustrated with photographs

19 BOS   TON 72

HOUGHTON MIFFLIN COMPANY

FIRST PRINTING   V

Introduction
by George F. Kennan

THE RANKS of American diplomatists have included, over the decades, many unusual people. Among the most striking of those of this century, both in his virtues and in his weaknesses, was the man whose letters to President Franklin Roosevelt and others make up the bulk of this volume. Brilliant, well-educated, charming, self-confident, and sophisticated, William C. Bullitt was in many ways singularly well fitted for the life and function of diplomacy. These qualities enabled him to render on many occasions services of exceptional value. Other qualities, on the other hand — a nature both impatient and impulsive, a contempt for the normal bureaucracy of foreign affairs, and a highly personalized concept of his role in government and his relationship to official Washington — were less useful to a diplomatic career and tended to limit, in time if not in substance, what he was able to accomplish. What he did accomplish was, however, far from negligible; his successive diplomatic positions afforded him unique insights into the Europe of the middle and late 1930s; and the record of his activities and reactions, as embodied in these letters, represents an important contribution to the history of the period.

When President Franklin Roosevelt, meeting Bullitt for the first time in 1932, welcomed him as a political follower and admirer, put him to work as a traveling observer and adviser on foreign affairs, and then, in 1933, sent him as the first American Ambassador to the Soviet Union, all this must have come to the younger man as a species of miraculous fulfillment. For some years past he had lived his life restlessly, aimlessly, in the consciousness of unusual abilities but without any fully satisfying purpose or professional dedication. Long years of residence and travel abroad had given him not only a good knowledge of the main European languages but also a familiarity with the European and Levantine scenes for which, to that point, he had found no very useful application. His first personal experience with diplomacy — a mission to Russia, in 1919, on orders of the Secretary of State and with the encouragement of Colonel Edward M. House and Lloyd George — had ended in disappointment and disillusionment. President Wilson had shown himself indifferent to the results of the mission, and had declined to receive him. Lloyd George had publicly denied him.

Now, fourteen years later, in Franklin Roosevelt — debonair, daring, riding the wave of success, and sharing to the full his own impatience with the mundane routine of traditional diplomacy — Bullitt found a President after his own heart, and one, above all, who had need of him, recognized his qualities, and was anxious to use him. Everything in Bullitt's life seemed to have prepared him for this moment. Single, financially independent, and elsewhere uninvolved, he had no ties, professional or personal, that could interfere with this new service. He was free to give it his total dedication — and did.

Bullitt's first regular tour of diplomatic duty — in Moscow, from 1933 to mid-1936 — was dramatic, exciting, and enjoyable — enjoyable not only for him but for those of us who were fortunate enough to be members of his staff. It ended, however, in frustration. The Soviet leaders had promised him, as he understood it, and promised him precisely as a *quid pro quo* for the diplomatic recognition now accorded to them, that they would cease subversive propaganda and other activity directed against the United States, permit the building of an American Embassy on the Sparrow Hills overlooking the Moscow River, and make arrangements for currency exchange that would permit an American Embassy to function without the humiliating necessity of resorting to the black market for its roubles. None of these promises was fulfilled; and Bullitt was not long in spotting the reason why. When these promises had been so freely given, in the autumn of 1933, the danger of Japanese aggression against the Soviet Far East had seemed, in Moscow, to be very great. By mid-1934, when the Embassy was fully established, this danger seemed largely to have passed.

Bullitt could not seriously blame himself for this turn of events. He had done his job in Moscow with verve and enthusiasm; and he was conscious of having done it well. It was not his fault if he had been deceived. But the experience left a deep imprint on his political opinions. From now on Stalin and the members of his entourage would appear to him, not inaccurately, as a group of ruthless political operators, secretive and conspiratorial in method, cynical and untrustworthy, ideologically committed against the West, unresponsive to good will and generous gestures on the part of others. This image would color his political attitudes for years to come; and it would not be without effect, ultimately, on his relations with the President.

Noteworthy among Bullitt's dispatches from this period are two, condensations of which are included in this volume, written in the spring of 1936 shortly before his final departure from Russia. The first of these (of March 4, 1936) was a composite dispatch, made up of excerpts from the dispatches of an American envoy who had represented the United States government in St. Petersburg some eighty years earlier — passages that were no less accurate with relation to Soviet Russia than they had been with relation to the Russia of the 1850s. The second, written some weeks later (April 20, 1936), gave the views at which Bullitt had arrived after two years at the Moscow post and which he carried away with him when he moved to Paris. It reflected a judgment on the world-revolutionary proclivities of the Soviet leaders that would be relevant only in small part, if at all, to the situation of the 1970s; but the advice for dealing with the Russians with which the dispatch ended, stressing as it did the need for patience and steadiness and urging a straightforward, honest and open approach, reflected the discipline of two years' experience, and remains as sound today as when it was written.

Bullitt's next post — Paris — was much more congenial to him, and offered a far better field for the unfolding of his constructive abilities than did the Moscow of the beginning of the purges. In Paris, he felt at home. The French responded to his qualities of mind and temperament. No American Ambassador could have had closer and more intimate relations than did he with the statesmen of the capital to which he was accredited. None could have kept an American President better informed of their hopes, plans, and reactions. Bullitt was justifiably proud of these personal connections, and of the quality of the services they enabled him to render to his government.

At the time when he arrived in France — in the autumn, that is, of 1936 — the dice that determined the circumstances of the outbreak of war three years later had already, though few understood this, been largely cast. German rearmament was outstripping the defense efforts of the Western democracies. Hitler's success in reoccupying the Rhineland earlier that year had revealed the fatal weakness and indecision of the Western governments. These failings were just then finding further confirmation in the experiences of the Spanish Civil War. There was now nothing to stop Hitler from undertaking the subjugation, and the incorporation into his Reich, of Austria and the Sudeten-German regions of Czechoslovakia. Stalin, seeing clearly the writing on the wall, recognizing the failure of his earlier efforts to induce the French and British to stand up to Hitler and thus spare Russia the necessity of an ultimate confrontation with Nazi power, was already delicately changing course with a view to putting himself in a position to make a deal with Hitler when the dreaded moment came. He would continue, of course, to string the French and British along to the end — partly in order to have an anchor to windward, partly because he needed his dealings with them as a means of putting pressure on the Germans. But he was now without illusions as to what they might do for him. The nonaggression pact of 1939, still three years off, was already in the cards.

No one could say that Bullitt failed to keep Washington well informed of this situation. Repeatedly, he warned of the forthcoming German moves against Austria and Czechoslovakia. He correctly portrayed the vacillations of French policy in the face of the likelihood of these moves. He came, finally, in early 1938, to the correct conclusion that the French would not fight to save their Czechoslovak allies. The Poles, he also predicted (and at a very early date), would be of no use in such a contingency: they had nothing against a German domination of central Europe to the south of themselves. And almost alone among prominent political figures in western Europe at that time, Bullitt wholly discounted the possibility of any voluntary help from the Russians.

Even prior to his appointment to France he had warned that dis-illusionment, flowing from the growing evidence that France and England could not be brought to take the initiative in opposing Hitler by force of arms, might well cause Soviet attention to turn to the possibilities of a rapprochement with the Nazis.

In the face of so unpromising a situation, the only hopes one could entertain were desperate ones. Bullitt himself, no more able than anyone else to live without hope, entertained just such a one during 1936 and 1937. It was the hope of a Franco-German rapprochement and collaboration. If the notion sounds strange today, he must be forgiven for it. He recognized it as a forlorn hope; but the alternative, as he also recognized, was another world war. The final personality of Hitlerism, as it was to emerge during World War II, had at that time not yet become fully ap-parent. Goering, with whom Bullitt talked at length in Novem-ber 1937, professed to desire good relations with France, as did other Nazi leaders; and such was the nature of the German inferi-ority complex with relation to that country (as also to England) that such impulses did not seem wholly implausible. Nor could one be certain, in the circumstances of that day, that such a rela-tionship between Germany and France, linked — as Bullitt hoped it would be — with schemes for a joint Franco-German leadership in the unification of Europe, would not exert a moderating influ-ence on the Nazi regime and serve to mitigate its tendency to in-ternal excesses.

Whatever the reasons, this hope was an unreal one; and by the beginning of 1938 Bullitt had himself come to accept its unreal-ity. From now on he could do little more than to remind Wash-ington periodically of the imminence of war, to urge it to free it-self from the shackles of the Neutrality legislation, and to bespeak its help for France in the building up of her military strength.

One is obliged to note, as a certain weakness in this otherwise excellent record of analysis, the extraordinary dislike and distrust for the British which marked Bullitt's feelings at that time. It was an animus which found a certain justification in the well-known deficiencies of British policy in those years, but it was car-ried further than the situation warranted; and Bullitt himself, ob-serving at a later date the magnificence of the British performance during the war, came to correct and probably — one senses — to regret it.

As the shadows of war descended upon France in 1939 and 1940, Bullitt remained at his post and did what little he could to mitigate the measure of the advancing catastrophe. He was subsequently reproached for allegedly encouraging the French to hope for American military help against the German attack. The record embodied in this volume will alone suffice to show (and the official records would support the conclusion) how unjust was this charge. Time after time, he warned the French that while they might count on America's sympathies, they must not count on her armed assistance. He did, on the other hand, contrive to demonstrate, in many ways that will not soon be forgotten in France, both his own devotion to that country and the feelings of admiration and friendship that Americans generally have always entertained for it.

Bullitt's reporting from this period gives a unique and historically important picture of the day-by-day reactions of the French leaders, as the successive blows fell upon them. It mirrors with vivid accuracy the general confusion and lack of realism that prevailed in their counsels. But it is characteristic of him that he never lost his faith in the common people of France. Repeatedly, he expressed his admiration for the unity, the willingness, and the determination with which they would, he felt, be prepared to meet the German challenge if called upon to do so. And if these hopes seemed then to be belied by the extraordinary military and civil collapse of the spring of 1940, he saw this rather as a dreadful failure of leadership than as a sign of national inadequacy.

Bullitt's reports from the period just before and during the German attack reflected the almost grotesque exaggeration of German air power and distortion of the relative capabilities existing in this respect that marked at that time the calculations of the French leaders and of many others in the Allied camp. He had no means of detecting and challenging this error. No more than anyone else, therefore, does he appear to have recognized that the French and British probably had a superiority in the number of planes all along, that the greater part of those the French had were never used, and that the French air force actually ended up, at the time of the surrender, with more planes on hand than they had had at the beginning of the war. All this being so, it is perhaps not surprising that he bombarded Washington, in those critical days, with proposals, one more frantic than the other, relating for the most part to the supposed urgent need of the French for American planes — proposals which were almost always behind the surge of events and served, in at least one instance, to irritate the President intensely.

When the German troops approached Paris, Bullitt decided, against the wishes of official Washington, to remain in the city. He took this decision in spite of the fact that he had alarming visions of what would occur when the capture of the city took place. (These visions were fortunately deprived of substance through the courtesies shown him by the German commander and the excellent discipline of the German combat forces when they first appeared on the Parisian scene.) The decision was admittedly a difficult and debatable one. He was given wide credit in French circles for having contributed importantly to the saving of the capital. Others felt, however, that he could have been more useful in remaining at the side of the French governmental leaders after their departure from Paris, helping them to preserve unity in the face of the military collapse.

Bullitt's experience during the capture of Paris was a dramatic climax to his tour of duty as Ambassador to France. It was not, however, the last service he was to render in that capacity. Visiting, shortly thereafter, the regime then in process of establishment at Vichy, he wrote, on July 1, 1940, from the nearby Bourboule, one of his most informative and historically important dispatches, based on lengthy talks he had had with Pétain, Darlan, and Chautemps. This dispatch stands as a uniquely authentic portrayal of the mentality and calculations of the Vichy leaders as they embarked on their tragic political venture.

The remainder of Bullitt's official career, while not devoid of interesting experiences, was anticlimactic. One has the impression that his relations with the President had begun, for some reason, to be undermined by the time he returned to the United States, in late July 1940. He failed, in any case, to receive the appointment he had been led to expect as Secretary of the Navy.

The President's decision to appoint Admiral William D. Leahy as diplomatic representative to the Vichy regime, taken without consultation with Bullitt and behind his back, led to a sharp exchange over the telephone between FDR and the outraged ex-Ambassador. And when, in April 1941, he went to the President demanding the removal of Under Secretary of State Sumner Welles, on the basis of documentary material concerning the latter's private life which he then produced for the President's edification, he unquestionably dealt to his relationship with FDR a blow from which it was never fully to recover. Welles was a close personal friend of the Roosevelt family. The President never fully forgave Bullitt for what he regarded as an uncharitable personal vendetta — a vendetta pursued not just in this one highly unpleasant interview in the White House but in statements to other people which were not long in reaching the Presidential ears. The historian stands helpless before this unpleasant difference; for if the zeal with which Bullitt pursued the regrettable matter seems, in retrospect, excessive, and from his own standpoint imprudent, the touchiness of the President in his reaction, and his stubborn reluctance to confront the situation as a problem of governmental security, seems equally difficult to explain.

Relations between the two men were not interrupted entirely and at once. In November 1941, the President sent Bullitt on a mission of information to North Africa and the Middle East — a mission which, to judge from the letters and reports contained in this volume, he performed very well indeed. But the recommendations submitted on the basis of this visit were disregarded; and when, a few weeks later, the President tried to persuade him, despite this evident rejection of his earlier recommendations, to undertake a second journey of observation to that part of the world, Bullitt's suspicions were aroused, and his patience exhausted. It seemed clear that the President had no desire to use him for any important purpose, but was concerned, rather, to keep him at a distance from Washington. On April 20, 1942, deeply hurt, he submitted his resignation from the position of personal representative of the President, which he had held since the termination of his ambassadorship to France, and told the President he would seek other work. And when, a year and a half later, the reluctant

President finally saw himself obliged, by an abundance of unpleasant gossip for which he surely held Bullitt responsible, to consent to Welles's departure from the governmental service, the breach between the two men was past healing.

There was, from that time on, no suitable place for Bullitt either in FDR's personal entourage or (since the President had a long arm) anywhere else in the governmental service. In late 1943 he was encouraged by the President (again, one senses, as a means of removing him from the foreign political scene) to run for mayor of Philadelphia. It was, for Bullitt, a wholly incongruous sort of undertaking; and when, as might have been expected, it ended in failure, this was really the end. Secretary of State Hull approached the President two or three times in early 1944, urging that some suitable assignment be found for Bullitt, but he found the President sullenly and adamantly opposed. Bullitt then applied to the Secretary of War, Mr. Henry Stimson, with the request that some sort of employment be found for him in active military service. This, too, was declined — in deference, no doubt, to the President's wishes. Thus rebuffed in his desire to be of service to his own country during the war, Bullitt turned, in the end, to his French friends. Here he was given a hearty and generous welcome — and by none other than General Charles de Gaulle in person. Commissioned a *commandant* in the French Army and attached to the staff of General de Lattre de Tassigny, he served actively in this capacity, often in combat and happy in the experience, for the duration of the war. In the last days of hostilities, he suffered, most unfortunately, an automobile accident which left him semicrippled for the remainder of his life; and this, plus a great bitterness over his earlier treatment and the disregard for his views — particularly his views about Russia — precluded further governmental service.

There remains to be mentioned only the long and remarkable letter that Bullitt addressed to FDR early in 1943. The President, in the autumn of 1942, had inquired his opinion on the problems of civil administration in territories about to be liberated by American forces. In the last of three communications responding to this request (January 29, 1943), Bullitt set forth at length his views on wartime strategy generally. He predicted with startling accuracy the situation to which the war would lead if existing policies continued to be pursued. He warned against placing any reliance on Russian good will. He urged the President to use, before it was too late, the great influence he still then had with a view to bringing Stalin to a specific renunciation of all conquests and annexations in Europe. He pleaded for an Anglo-American war strategy identical with that which was shortly to be advocated by Churchill — an attack, that is, on the "soft underbelly of the Axis" and an advance up through central Europe, with a view both to cutting the Germans off from their access to the Balkans and to saving the peoples of that area from being taken under Russian political control. This letter, supplemented by further and shorter communications sent in May and in August of that year, had no counterpart, so far as this writer is aware, as a warning of that date to the American President of the effective division of Europe which would ensue if the war continued to be pursued on the basis of the concepts then prevailing. And while, as in the case of so many other penetrating glimpses into the political future, the accuracy of the prophetic insight was superior to the practicality of the proposed alternatives (Bullitt's scheme would have complicated greatly the remainder of the war, not to mention the intense unhappiness and bewilderment it would have spelled for the American military authorities), the letter was unique in the insights it brought to the logic of the wartime developments. It deserves a place among the major historical documents of the time.

If Bullitt's letters to the President were, as this volume will show, stimulating, imaginative, and full of ideas, the same cannot be said of FDR's letters to him. It was no doubt the part of wisdom in the President not to reveal his thoughts in letters which were, for the most part, dispatched abroad and might easily find their way, by the vicissitudes of politics and war, into the wrong hands. His responsibility, after all, was a greater one than that of his Ambassador. Still, such is the level of triviality in these brief Presidential notes — the superficiality, the forced and often unsuccessful humor, the studied avoidance of every serious subject — that they do not reflect very happily on the qualities of the author. Granting the delicacy of his position and the likelihood that his numerous personal interviews with Bullitt were more informative, it is hard to believe that a more serious man would not have found something of greater moment to say in reply to letters discussing so many matters of profound importance. One reader, at least, comes away confirmed in the suspicion that to the extent Franklin Roosevelt had qualities fitting him for the great responsibilities he bore over those years of wartime leadership, these were primarily qualities of temperament, not of the intellect.

And what of Bill Bullitt himself? Here, I must permit myself a personal note. I liked him, admired him, and never lost, to his dying day, a certain feeling of sympathy and solicitude for him — not even when I was included among those many friends against whom, in his last sad years, he turned the point of a bitter pen. Like many others, he bore within himself, I always thought, the seeds of his own misfortune.

I recall with particular vividness one conversation with him, in 1933, as we were on our way to Russia for the presentation of his credentials. It was on the S.S. *President Harding,* then struggling through a succession of heavy winter gales. I was laid up with a cold. He came in one afternoon, sat on my bunk, and talked to me with that charm which was peculiarly his own. It was our first really personal conversation and I was naturally curious about the character of this brilliant and fast-moving man who had so suddenly become my immediate superior. I carried away from the talk an impression of enormous charm, confidence, and vitality. But I also had an impression of quick sensitivity, of great egocentricity and pride, and of a certain dangerous freedom — the freedom of a man who, as he himself confessed to me on that occasion, had never subordinated his life to the needs of any other human being.

I see Bill Bullitt, in retrospect, as a member of that remarkable group of young Americans, born just before the turn of the century (it included such people as Cole Porter, Ernest Hemingway, John Reed, and Jim Forrestal — many of them his friends) for whom the First World War was the great electrifying experience of life. They were a striking generation, full of talent and exuberance, determined — if one may put it so — to make life come alive. The mark they made on American culture will be there when many other marks have faded. But in most of them there seems to have been a touch of the fate, if not the person, of the Great Gatsby. Like Edna Millay, they burned their candles at both ends. The civilization of the 1930s and 1940s was not strong enough to support their weight. They knew achievement more often than they knew fulfillment; and their ends, like those of Bullitt himself, tended to be frustrating, disappointing, and sometimes tragic.

Although Bullitt was a writer, too, it was into the vessel of public affairs that he poured, primarily, his enthusiasm and his unquestionable longing to be of service to his country and his time. The record of that effort, of which this volume represents a major portion, deserves its place in the annals of American diplomacy.

Appreciation

WITHOUT THE GENEROUS permission of my brother's daughter Anne, many of the letters in this book could not have been published. She not only made them available, but arranged her father's files for my assistance and ready reference, which entailed countless hours of work on her part. She also gave me much valuable advice and many suggestions as to the contents of the book. My first and deepest thanks go to her.

Our cousin, Orville Horwitz, Professor of Medicine at the University of Pennsylvania, a distinguished physician and scholar, and a true and loyal friend to my brother and me, contributed immeasurably with advice and encouragement. His intimacy with my brother helped with many details and I owe him a great debt.

Professor George F. Kennan of the Institute for Advanced Study has not only contributed the Introduction to this book, but has permitted me to use quotations from his own works. Above all he has been of inestimable help in the sound advice which he has given, and the many hours he has allowed me to impose on him, providing information and suggestions from his vast first-hand experience and knowledge of this period of history. To him go my deepest thanks.

The major part of the Roosevelt-Bullitt correspondence was most courteously furnished me by the Franklin D. Roosevelt Library, Hyde Park, and all of the correspondence with the Honorable R. Walton Moore, together with letters and documents of Louis D. Wehle, Esq., and Sumner Welles came from the same source. I am grateful for the cooperation and help which I received at all times from the directors of the library, Dr. James E. O'Neill and Mr. J. C. James.

I would like to make special acknowledgment to the consulting editor, Dr. James V. Compton, Professor of History at San Francisco State College, knowledgeable in the events of this era. Dr. Compton spent many weeks editing the final manuscript, suggesting additional historical material and giving me much valuable advice. It was a pleasure to work with him after many months of solitary effort. His enthusiasm for the letters was stimulating and I shall always be grateful to him.

Elting E. Morison, Professor of History and American Studies, Yale University, most courteously reviewed the manuscript and I am indebted to him for undertaking this task. Since I am not an historian myself, his work was of inestimable value in contributing to the accuracy of my statements. It gives me pleasure to express my appreciation of his kindness.

Honorable Loy W. Henderson, Chargé d'Affaires in Moscow in the early days and future Ambassador, very kindly studied the manuscript and gave me the benefit of his advice on certain incidents in the book on which he had a firsthand knowledge. He remained a lifelong friend of my brother's.

Honorable Robert D. Murphy has been of assistance in permitting quotations from his book, and Admiral Roscoe H. Hillenkoetter has provided interesting accounts of the time he spent as Naval Attaché in the embassy in Paris. I thank them both.

I burdened M. Guy LaChambre of Paris with a great deal of correspondence and he was more than generous in his advice and his interest as a devoted friend of my brother's.

Mme. La Maréchale de Lattre de Tassigny wrote me several letters about my brother and kindly allowed me to quote from articles which she had published about him.

I acknowledge with thanks the courtesy of the National Archives and Records Service, Washington, in furnishing many documents from their files.

The family of the Honorable R. Walton Moore authorized me to use many of his letters. I am thankful for their kindness. Mrs. Louis B. Wehle furnished me with information about her husband and allowed me to use whatever letters or quotations from his book appear in the text. I am indebted to her for her help.

Transcripts of Crown-Copyright Records in the Public Record Office, London, appear by permission of the Controller of H. M. Stationery Office. This office promptly and graciously furnished me with copies of their files, from which quotations have been used in the text. I wish especially to thank Mr. R. F. Monger for his courtesy to me.

The letters from the Edwin M. House Collection, Yale University Library, and quotations from the Henry L. Stimson Papers appear through the courtesy of the Yale University Library.

Premier Daladier's letters appear through the courtesy of his sons John and Pierre Daladier.

Through the kindness of Madame Christiane Paul Reynaud and Madame Colette Dernis I am privileged to use letters from M. Paul Reynaud and I thank them for their courtesy.

Quotations from *Ambassador Dodd's Diary,* edited by William E. Dodd, Jr., and Martha Dodd, were made with permission of the publishers, Harcourt Brace Jovanovich, Inc.

Among others who have contributed helpful information are Albert Speer of Heidelberg, Professor Henri Laugier of Paris, Mr. David Irving of London, Mr. Edward H. Sims of Editor's Copy Syndicate, South Carolina, and M. André Chamson, Member of l'Académie Française. I thank Dr. Beatrice Farnsworth for permission to publish extracts from her book.

I wrote to Mr. Andrei A. Gromyko, Soviet Minister of Foreign Affairs, asking for any information from his files pertaining to my brother's relations with his predecessor, Maxim M. Litvinov. The reply which I received was that no documents about my brother could be found. They would have made interesting reading.

I again had the good fortune to have Mrs. Barbara Rex as an editor. Her comments were always valuable and pungent. Her interest and encouragement over many months were invaluable. Mrs. Patricia T. Davis also edited most of the manuscript and gave me many helpful suggestions. To both of them I express my sincere thanks.

Miss Mary H. Raitt, researcher, was of great assistance in securing documents from various government files in Washington.

I can not properly acknowledge my debt to all the staff of the library of the University of Pennsylvania, where much of the work on this book was done. They were always eager to be of help and took endless trouble in searching out information which I never would have found otherwise. I consulted them constantly and they made my work a pleasure.

Mrs. Maurice E. Green did an enormous amount of secretarial work, and once more Miss Cecelia C. Bavolek typed hundreds of pages of manuscript from my very bad handwriting. I thank them both for all they have done.

My wife must frequently have been bored with all my talk about the book, but she never showed it and always made excellent suggestions. She had been through it before, and I am constantly grateful for her patience and interest. She did express one wish: "Please don't start another book." I may disappoint her.

Orville H. Bullitt

Preface

THIS BOOK, although it contains many documents of historical interest, does not purport to be either a history or a biography. It is a selection from the correspondence between two men who played important parts in world affairs during the critical years from 1932 to 1945. I have included some letters of others and also certain messages already published by the government in *Foreign Relations of the United States,* in order to provide information not contained in the Roosevelt-Bullitt documents. Mr. Roosevelt's life and background are familiar, but my brother's training for foreign affairs is not generally known. I have, therefore, given a brief sketch of his life up until the time he first worked with Mr. Roosevelt, together with a more complete account of his work at the Versailles Peace Conference in 1919. This event had a profound effect on his future career and influenced his opinions on diplomacy.

For the sake of clarity I have referred to him as "Bill" in any passages where I am expressing my own ideas, but where he is referred to in the historical sense I have used "Bullitt."

The reader will note that almost all of Bill's telegrams to the President were sent through the State Department, whereas his letters went directly to the White House. At the same time, Bill was making voluminous written reports to the State Department on the same subjects. There is a vast amount of such documents. There are also important letters to, and from, Honorable R. Walton Moore, who at different times was Assistant Secretary of State, Acting Secretary of State, and Counselor to the State Department. Judge Moore had served in Congress with Secretary of State Cordell Hull and they were warm friends.

Mr. Hull describes Judge Moore thus: "Head of the Virginia bar for years, he was a person of unusual ability and high purpose, a profound student of both domestic and international affairs, and possessed character and patriotism of the highest order." During Bill's period as Ambassador to Russia it was Judge Moore, together with Robert F. Kelley, Chief of the Division of Eastern European Affairs, who kept in touch with him. Judge Moore was also a personal friend of Bill's, having been a friend of Father's in his youth.

It was through Louis B. Wehle that Bill first came into close contact with Mr. Roosevelt. Mr. Wehle, a nephew of Justice Brandeis's, was a prominent New York lawyer and had been a friend of the President's from their earliest days. He had ready and immediate access to the President.

The Roosevelt letters are all in a very personal vein, with practically no diplomatic instructions. Bill returned to the United States from time to time and talked intimately and at great length with the President on foreign affairs. They would discuss policy decisions and when Bill returned to his post he knew exactly what the President had in mind. If there were any doubts or questions that arose later the President was almost always careful to have instructions sent to Bill through the State Department. During the years at the Paris embassy there were frequent telephone calls.

Mention must be made of one other important individual whose name appears frequently. Carmel Offie, a foreign service officer, was with my brother from his first days in Moscow in 1934 up until the time of his death in 1967. Bill often told me how he had cabled the State Department: "Send me a secretary who can stand me and stand Russia." At times both of these requirements were trying, but no one could have had a more loyal friend than Mr. Offie. He was literally indispensable; he not only helped with Bill's work at any hour of the day or night, but he also lived in Bill's house and ran the entire establishment in an efficient and extraordinarily economical manner. The letters will show Mr. Offie's intimacy with the leading people of the world, an intimacy which still exists.

I have included, between letters, the significant events that were occurring at the time. These notes are purposely brief: the great interest lies in the letters themselves, and I have attempted not to disturb the flow of the correspondence.

In certain cases I have used the carbon copies of Bill's original telegrams, which were furnished to me by his daughter, Anne. A few words are different in some of the documents in the government files, but in no way are the meanings of the telegrams changed. Mr. Offie, who typed the originals, tells me that the slight discrepancies probably came about in the decoding in Washington.

The names of all important individuals mentioned, if not identified in the text, will be found in the index. Deletions in some of the letters have been made to eliminate extraneous comments and repetition, as well as certain personal remarks about living persons.

Orville H. Bullitt

May 1972

Contents

Illustrations

President Roosevelt says good-bye to Ambassador Bullitt, November 1933, *frontispiece.*

following page 242

Bullitt arriving in Moscow, March 1934, with Anne.
Bullitt meets President Kalinin, December 1933.
Anne and Bullitt. Moscow, 1935.
Leaving Elysée Palace after presenting credentials, October 13, 1936.
At his desk in the Embassy, Paris. The pictures behind Bullitt show Judge Moore, Thomas Jefferson, and Cordell Hull.
Château St. Firmin, Chantilly.
Léon Blum with Bullitt at Chantilly, 1936.
Bullitt with the Duke and Duchess of Windsor.
Bullitt and Daladier.
Bullitt and Orville H. Bullitt return from France, July 1940.
FDR, Miss Marguerite LeHand, and WCB at Hyde Park, July 22, 1940, for a report on the fall of France.
FDR's note of December 2, 1941.
At the London Conference, July 1942.
Entering Marseilles, August 1944.
General Marshall, de Lattre, Bullitt, October 1944.
Eisenhower and Bullitt, October 1944.

Chronology

July	Spanish Civil War begins.
	Austro-German agreement.
August	Bullitt appointed Ambassador to France.
Ootober	Bullitt presents credentials in Paris.
November	Rome-Berlin Axis.
	German-Japanese Anti-Comintern pact.
	Roosevelt in Buenos Aires.

1937

January	Roosevelt begins second term as President.
May	New Neutrality Act.
	Chamberlain becomes Prime Minister.
	Supreme Court reform proposed.
July	Japan advances into China.
September	Mussolini visits Germany.
November	Italy joins the German-Japanese Anti-Comintern pact.
	Bullitt in Warsaw and with Goering in Berlin.
December	Japanese sink U.S. gunboat *Panay*.

1938

February	Ribbentrop becomes German Foreign Minister.
	Eden resigns as Foreign Minister.
	Halifax appointed Foreign Minister.
March	Hitler occupies Austria.
	Sudeten, Czechoslovakia, agitations begin.
April	Daladier succeeds Blum as French Premier.
	Anglo-Italian agreement.
May	Czech Army mobilizes.
September 15	Chamberlain sees Hitler at Berchtesgaden.
September 22	Chamberlain sees Hitler at Godesberg.
	French partial mobilization.
September 28	British fleet mobilized.
September 29–30	Four-power agreement.
October	Poles occupy Teschen district in Czechoslovakia.
November 2	Hungary obtains southern Slovakia and part of Ruthenia from Czechoslovakia.
December	Franco-German declaration of friendship.

1939

March	Germans occupy Prague, Czechoslovakia.
	Lithuania cedes Memel to Germany.
March	Civil War ends in Spain.
April	Italians seize Albania.

	Anglo-French guarantee of Greece and Rumania.
	Hitler denounces Anglo-German naval pact.
	Hitler denounces German-Polish nonaggression pact.
	Conscription in England.
	Litvinov dismissed; Molotov Foreign Minister.
	Anglo-Turkish agreement.
May	Pact of Steel signed in Berlin between Germany and Italy.
June	Japanese blockade British at Tientsin.
August	Anglo-French-Soviet talks begin August 12.
	Anglo-French-Soviet talks broken on August 21.
August 23	German-Soviet pact.
	Chamberlain personal appeal to Hitler.
	Japan abandons Anti-Comintern pact.
August 24	Anglo-Polish agreement signed.
August 26	Daladier personal appeal to Hitler.
September 1	Poland invaded by Germany.
September 3	Britain and France declare war on Germany.
September 29	Poland surrenders.
November 4	Arms embargo repealed.
November 30	Russia attacks Finland.
December 14	Russia expelled from League of Nations.
1940	
March 12	Finland surrenders.
March 21	Reynaud succeeds Daladier as Premier of France.
April 9	Germany invades Norway and Denmark.
May 10	Germany invades Belgium and Holland.
	Chamberlain resigns; Churchill appointed Prime Minister.
May 28	Belgium surrenders.
	Evacuation of Dunkirk.
May 29	American pilots deliver planes to Canada.
June 10	Italy declares war on England and France.
June 14	Germans enter Paris.
June 16	Reynaud resigns. Pétain becomes Premier.
June 22	France signs armistice with Germany.
June 28	Soviet annexes Bessarabia and northern Bukovina in Rumania.
July	British attack French fleets in Africa.
	Vichy Government breaks relations with England.

	Russia absorbs Lithuania, Latvia, and Estonia.
	Battle of Britain begins.
August 18	Bullitt speaks at Independence Hall.
September 5	United States supplies Great Britain with fifty destroyers and obtains leases on naval bases.
November 7	Bullitt resigns as Ambassador to France.

1941

January	Roosevelt begins third term.
March 11	New Lend-Lease Bill.
March 31	Germans under Rommel attack in Africa.
June 22	Germany attacks Russia.
July 7	United States forces land in Iceland.
August 14	Churchill meets Roosevelt in Newfoundland and drafts Atlantic Charter.
November 22	Bullitt appointed Ambassador and personal representative of President to visit British in Egypt.
November 24	United States forces in Dutch Guiana.
December 7	Japan attacks Pearl Harbor.
December 8	Great Britain declares war on Japan.
December 11	Germany and Italy declare war on United States.

1942

April 20	Bullitt resigns as Ambassador and personal representative.
June 22	Bullitt becomes Assistant to the Secretary of the Navy.
August 12	Churchill meets Stalin in Moscow.
November 4	British defeat Rommel at El Alamein.
November 8	Invasion of North Africa.

1943

January 17	Casablanca Conference: Roosevelt, Churchill, and de Gaulle.
February 2	Germans defeated at Stalingrad.
May 12	Churchill goes to Washington.
July 10	Invasion of Sicily.
July 25	Mussolini arrested.
August 11	Quebec Conference: Roosevelt and Churchill.
September 2	Invasion of Italy.
September 8	Italy surrenders.
October 13	Italy declares war on Germany.
November 23	Roosevelt, Churchill, and Chiang Kai-shek meet in Cairo.

November 28   Teheran Conference: Roosevelt, Churchill, and Stalin.

1944
June 6   Invasion of France.
Bullitt joins French Army in Algiers.
August 15   French Army lands in south of France.
August 24   Paris freed.
September 13   Churchill and Roosevelt meet at Quebec.
October 9   Churchill and Eden meet Stalin in Moscow.

1945
January   Roosevelt begins fourth term.
February 7   Yalta Conference: Roosevelt, Churchill, and Stalin.
April 12   Roosevelt dies.
April 28   Mussolini's assassination.
April 29   Hitler's suicide.
May 7   Germany surrenders.
July 17   Potsdam Conference: Truman, Churchill, Atlee, and Stalin.
July 20   Bullitt returns to America.
August 14   Japan surrenders.

Biographical Foreword

THE LETTERS in this book run the whole gamut from the frivolous to the intensely serious. William Christian Bullitt served President Roosevelt as Ambassador to Russia after we recognized that country in 1933, and in 1936 he became Ambassador to France. This collection starts in 1932 and continues through the fall of France in 1940 and the war years. While some of the letters are to friends or colleagues in the State Department, the greatest number passed between President Roosevelt and Bullitt. Typical of the intimate relationship which existed between the two men are the following extracts.

THE WHITE HOUSE
WASHINGTON

Dear Bill:

. . . I am very proud that my Ambassador has rented the Park and the Great Château of Chantilly. May the ghost of the Great Condé haunt you and upset the canoe when you pull a water party on the great waterway. Tell Offie that I count on him to prevent you from spending more than ninety per cent of your capital in the next few years.

As ever,
FDR

EMBASSY OF THE
UNITED STATES OF AMERICA

Norman Davis was kind enough to inform me or, I hope, misinform me, with regard to your point of view. He made it sound as if you thought God had laid Woodrow Wilson's mantle upon you, and were about to take on your shoulders, or rather those of the people of the United States, all the pains of the world.

I don't believe this is so; but for Gawd's sake remember that Woodrow Wilson, as a collapsed ex-President, used to lie in bed thinking of the text, 'By their fruits ye shall know them'; and recalling that the fruits he could report to St. Peter were war and the Treaty of Versailles. Blessings and keep your shirt on.

Bill

Few of these letters have been previously published. They range from an account of Stalin kissing Bullitt to the successful efforts of the Russians to repudiate the promises they gave Roosevelt when he offered to recognize the Soviet. The letters from France are full of intimate details of the leading figures of the time: the efforts of the French to obtain help from America when the war began and the way certain French leaders endeavored to continue the war from Africa. There is remarkably prophetic material on what would happen in Europe if the Russians were allowed to reach Berlin, and throughout a lightness of touch appears even in the most important communications.

Bill, three years my senior, was born in Philadelphia on January 25, 1891, and attended the De Lancey School in that city. He was successful from childhood, winning various scholastic prizes at school, and at camp, where he was elected "best camper."

I fully realize the difficulty of writing objectively of one's brother. Of course Bill had weaknesses, which should be pointed out, as well as his abilities. Like all brothers, Bill and I had our fights. He once told a story of how I had chased him with a meat cleaver, although, he said, if the house was on fire we worked together. This was told before Philadelphia's Union League as an example of the need for cooperation between Republicans and Democrats in wartime. The fact that it was a baseball bat and not a meat cleaver did not change the point, and of course I could never run fast enough to catch him.

Sometimes his ever-active imagination would lead him to improve a good story, yet when it came to facts, he stuck grimly to them.

When we were both young there was a constant and energetic

flow of conversation at the dinner table, each of us wanting to express himself. It was also at meals that we first learned French, which Mother spoke to us, and my chief recollection of the language is being corrected or scolded with a sharp "Tu m'as compris!" Bill's later long residence in France led him to speak the language fluently. He was also proficient in German, having lived with a family in Munich as a young man, and he spent many months in Vienna in later life.

Bill was of medium height, well built and well coordinated. As a young man he had wavy brown hair and I suppose was very handsome, though later in life he was almost completely bald.

At Yale he was elected to Phi Beta Kappa, was an editor of the *Yale News,* and president of both the Dramatic Association and the Debating Association. He was voted the "most brilliant" member of his class and was the first man tapped for the Senior Society of Scroll and Key. This popularity, combined with his natural exuberance, built up his self-assurance and of course contributed to the ease with which he made friends. He had great ability to hold, and interest, any gathering, from five to five thousand people.

After graduating from Yale, he attended Harvard Law School for one year, but did not feel he could reconcile himself to the law, although Father wanted him to be a lawyer.

In 1914 Bill had his first sight of Russia. Father had died in March and in August Mother and Bill were in Moscow when war was declared. On the way home they stopped in Berlin and London. While in London he tried to become a war correspondent and obtained a letter from the *New York Times* asking him to write for them. But although our uncle, Colonel Ronald Brooke, introduced him to Sir Ian Hamilton, a leading figure in the Army, the War Office refused his request. He went on to Paris, where with his usual dramatic flair he hung out an American flag from the window of our grandmother's apartment, shortly after her death in France.

Bill now had a firsthand impression of the failure of diplomacy and the complete futility of war. In each of these capitals the people had been fed with the same propaganda for the defense of the homeland and denial of being the aggressor. In every country the same patriotic fervor existed. Today it is hard to picture the flag waving, the cheering crowds, and the sense of chivalry with which these young men were marching to their death. I was in Munich at the time and recall how deeply I was moved by the sight of the German soldiers. Later I was in Southampton in England and staying in a hotel with the young, untrained British officers of the first hundred thousand "contemptibles" on their way to France. On each side it was a crusade.

When Bill returned to America he sought work in which he could put his ideas before the public, and as he had always enjoyed writing he turned to a newspaper, the Philadelphia *Public Ledger,* where he was first assigned the task of covering the news in police stations. He soon began to submit editorials, some of which were printed, and in the short space of six months was made an associate editor of the paper. In December 1915 he received his first big opportunity. Henry Ford felt that he might be able to persuade the warring governments in Europe to arrive at terms of peace. He chartered an ocean liner, the *Oscar II,* and took with him many prominent people of similar opinion. Bill's articles home, written in an amusing satirical vein, received front-page, double-column space. The headlines read: JOY RIDING TO PEACE, BUMPING THE BUMPS WITH FORD'S PARTY; STORY OF THE MODERN SENTIMENTAL JOURNEY TOLD WITH DUE REGARD FOR TRUTH-FUL RECORD OF SUNDRY FAMILY JARS; THREE STUDENTS, ONE CLERGY-MAN GREET PARTY WHEN OSCAR II DOCKS AT CHRISTIANA [Oslo]. The finale of the trip came with a dispatch headed FORD ON LINER FOR UNITED STATES; BROKEN DOWN BY WORRY. Before he left the party Bill wired home that he "had been nuts for weeks."

In the spring of 1916 Bill married Aimée Ernesta Drinker, daughter of Dr. and Mrs. Henry S. Drinker, whose father was then president of Lehigh University. Ernesta was a striking beauty with dark hair, brilliant eyes, and a slender figure. Her portrait, by Cecelia Beaux, is owned by the Metropolitan Museum in New York City. She had a quick wit and was a fluent conversationalist. In *Family Portrait,* her sister Catherine Drinker Bowen gives an excellent description of Ernesta.

In May the newly married couple left for Europe. The *Ledger* had assigned Bill as a special correspondent to report on the situation in Germany and Austria. This was Bill's first entrance into the field of foreign affairs. He took with him letters of introduction to many important figures and interviewed both Count Tisza in Vienna and von Jagow in Berlin. Bill and Ernesta were gone five months, and later Ernesta wrote a book about the trip entitled *An Uncensored Diary*.

In Bill's account of his interviews, there is no reticence in the questions he asked Tisza and von Jagow. With Count Tisza he was direct in asking what Austria wished to do with Serbia, to which Tisza replied he did not wish to lay his hand on the table. Did Austria think of making a separate peace? The answer, a categorical no. When the note to Serbia was sent did not Austria expect war? Austria knew that Serbia must accept it unless Russia supported her. Did Austria talk over the note first with Germany? Count Tisza left it to Bill to draw his own conclusion. It was a long interview between the representative of a great empire and a twenty-five-year-old reporter, and very few definite answers were forthcoming.

A few days later in September, Bill asked similar questions of von Jagow in Berlin. But here the diplomat interviewed the reporter, asking why the United States wanted England to win the war, why was Wilson not neutral, etc. Von Jagow did say, however, that he had no hand in preparing Austria's note to Serbia, and only saw it at eight o'clock on the night it was presented.[1]

The trip included Belgium and Poland, and wherever he went he met many of the government officials, a habit which he was to follow throughout his career. He had no hesitancy in asking for introductions, and no timidity in presenting them.

On his return to the United States Bill worked for a short time for the Committee of Public Information, which supplied war items to the press on news released by the State Department. In 1917 he was placed in charge of the Washington office of the Philadelphia *Public Ledger*. As a reporter he naturally interviewed the well-known figures in Washington, among whom was Colonel Edward M. House, President Wilson's friend, confidant, and adviser. Over the years Colonel House became an intimate friend of Bill's, and the correspondence between them shows great mutual admiration, House signing his letters "Affectionately" and telling

Bill that the information on foreign affairs which he furnished was sometimes the best he received.

In December 1917, Bill began working in the State Department Western European Division under Joseph C. Grew, analyzing information from Germany and Austria, and the State Department requested that he not be inducted into military service. Bill's military career was to come a quarter of a century later.

Bill's first mention of Russia is in February 1918, in a letter to Colonel House in which he says, "I have passed over the question of the recognition of the Bolsheviki, because I know little at first hand of Russia." In the same letter he later says, "But it is obvious that no words could so effectively stamp the President's address with uncompromising liberalism as would the act of recognizing the Bolsheviki."

The horrors of the Russian Revolution had shocked the world. The murder of the Czar and his family, the killing and exile of countless thousands, and the appropriation of all property had turned Europe and the United States against the new regime. Bill was completely out of sympathy with these methods, but felt we must try to find a modus vivendi with this new government. While most statesmen were predicting the fall of the Bolsheviks, Bill thought they would remain in power and that our government should recognize this as a fact.

In February 1918, he wrote, "I wish I could see Russia with as simple an eye as Reed. [John Reed served for a time as director of revolutionary propaganda for the Bolsheviks. He was a radical leader, journalist, poet, and author of *Ten Days That Shook the World*.] I am unable to win through the welter of conflicting reports about the Bolsheviki to anything like a solid conviction."

During his entire life Bill never had a sense of inferiority in his personal relations, and always felt that he could meet anyone, no matter what his position, on an equal footing. He was not conceited about this, but simply had a sense of complete assurance about handling any situation which might arise. He had great respect for the dignity of the individual. He formed rapid and strong attachments and was bitterly disappointed when such acquaintances did not live up to the high standards which he expected of them. When this happened he would break the friendship with little compunction. More frequently, however, he was oblivious to time, distance, and adversity in his loyalty to those for whom he was a friend in need.

To Bill most decisions were either black or white; he had very little use for compromise in his character. Something was right or wrong, and he seldom chose the middle ground. This characteristic led to his break with Woodrow Wilson and later with Roosevelt. His advice, in most instances, was good and often prophetic to both these men. When they failed to accept his most vital and strongly held convictions he left them, to their detriment and his own. They could have used his knowledge and he could have continued an interesting and useful life.

There is no doubt that Bill was a controversial person, often being described as a Bolshevik, a Fascist, and later a warmonger and an appeaser. Actually, he was in effect conservative, with a deep feeling for the rights of man and an intense dislike for the rigidity of the ruling classes and of the status quo. He was frequently intolerant of others. His quick mind grasped essentials readily and he had little patience with those of a slower wit.

Bill had a distinct bias against the British that went back to his childhood, when England was engaged in the Boer War in South Africa. His sympathies were all with the Boers. His sense of identification with his ancestors imbued him with the spirit of resistance to Great Britain and his heroes were the leaders of the Revolution. In later years his betrayal by Lloyd George undoubtedly increased his dislike of the British and led him to mistrust their diplomacy. He was often sharply critical of the British for their attitude in several situations, but on many occasions readily acknowledged their tremendous contribution to world peace during the period of their supremacy of the seas, and admired frequently the high quality of their elite, but simultaneously decried the status of the general public. The British Government was fully aware of Bill's antagonism, and in the files of the British Foreign Office are such handwritten statements as: "Evidently a very dangerous intriguer." [2] The British Ambassador in Washington, Sir Ronald C. Lindsay, wrote to Sir John Simon: "In general I should say that he likes Englishmen, but hates the English. Really he suffers from that most tiresome of American diseases, namely an inferiority complex, and he would dearly love to destroy the moral superiority of the British!" [3] This is perhaps the only time in his life when Bill was accused of having an inferiority complex.

There is no doubt that he unjustly misjudged the British on several occasions, and it was not until after the fall of France in 1940 that he came to appreciate their courage.

In the many articles and comments of historians about him there are places where it is obvious that the writer was not possessed of all the facts. As an example, Bill was accused of encouraging the French to believe that if they declared war on Germany the United States would immediately join them. The hitherto unpublished letters in this book will show that the opposite was the case. For fifteen years before his association with President Roosevelt, Bill studied foreign affairs and knew the leading figures in world political and diplomatic circles. He was of inestimable value to Roosevelt. He was aware of the intricate details, the conditions and aspirations of various foreign governments, and the personalities of the leading statesmen of Europe.

Because Bill was strongly emotional and romantic, some of his letters to the President may sound like blatant flattery. However, he really felt profoundly what he wrote. I can remember one evening at home during the war when he and Judge R. Walton Moore, the Acting Secretary of State, discussed the President. They finally agreed that the only person they could really compare him to was Christ. I am sure that both of them were sincere.

Bill was an excellent host and a brilliant conversationalist, able to stimulate his guests to give their best. He had such a wide acquaintance that he could mix statesmen, diplomats, authors, musicians, and artists all at the same table with a happy result. He had no time for "society" but liked to have six or eight guests, so that the conversation could flow freely.

Bill enjoyed music, especially Mozart and Wagnerian opera. At his farm in Massachusetts he frequently had a chamber music quartet, after dinner with a few friends. He sang well, and many evenings at home he and Mother, who played the piano, would sing duets, some of which her mother had composed.

Bill had the good fortune to have dealt with two generations of statesmen. At the end of World War I these included Woodrow

Wilson, Lenin, Lloyd George, Asquith, and Clemenceau. Later his dealings were with Stalin, Roosevelt, Churchill, de Gaulle, Pétain, Goering, and others too numerous to mention. For a time he was a neighbor in Taiwan of Chiang Kai-shek and counted Eamon De Valera among his friends. He had an equally wide acquaintance among the arts, literature, and science, including such men as Einstein, Picasso, Matisse, Anatole France, Bernard Shaw, Sinclair Lewis, Rubinstein, and many others.

It was at the home of Madame Marie Cuttoli on the Rue Babylone in Paris that Bill met the intellectual, artistic, and cultural life of the French capital. She, with her husband, president of the Senate, continued the great tradition of the French salon in her apartment filled with works of art.

Except for the occasional parties which he gave while he was an Ambassador, Bill lived quite simply. He never maintained a large establishment, being perfectly happy on his farm in Massachusetts or in a modest rented house or apartment in Europe or Washington. He loved the country and enjoyed long walks, swimming in the pond, or simply looking at the White Mountains, the view of which stretched for almost fifty miles from the terrace of his farm. Although he liked people and an interchange of ideas, he could be perfectly happy alone and often solitude was one of his great pleasures.

Much has been written about Bill's wealth, and I would like to clarify this point. One article said that our grandfather John C. Bullitt was one of the ten wealthiest men in the country, reputed to be worth between ten and fifteen million dollars, a huge fortune in 1902. This is an amusing story for, as a matter of fact, by the time Bill inherited anything from this mythical estate it amounted to about $6000 a year. When Mother and Father died, Bill also inherited relatively modest amounts from them. Bill was never rich as the public imagines Ambassadors to be, but he was always comfortably off, which enabled him to travel and make many strong and valuable friendships all over the world. He took no interest in the acquisition of money and once wrote to me, "I don't know anything about investments and I have no idea what you are holding now in the way of stocks or bonds or what is in my account."

His thoughts on money did extend to sharing the wealth, at

least with me. He and I went to Europe when I was seventeen and I remember the last day in our cabin on the ship. Bill said, "You know Father wanted us to have the same amount of money, so I think we should both empty our pockets onto the bed and then divide it." Of course he had spent his. Later, when in France, he never had anything less than a gold piece to pay the taxis. In a letter thirty-five years later, asking us to join him in Paris, he wrote, "If you do, I promise you that I will have nothing but hundred dollar bills and thousand franc notes so that you will have to pay for everything in the customary manner!"

Actually, he was extremely generous and never owed me a penny.

Romantic, vigorous, at times almost flamboyant, reticence was not part of Bill's character. To me, much of the publicity he received was distasteful, and after *The New Yorker* ran an article about him I wrote him my feelings: "The only thing left is for you to stand at Broad and Chestnut Streets and brush your teeth in public." The articles continued, as he was a public character.

Even at the time of his death in 1967 the flamboyant headlines continued. Bill was always given headlines, and whether the story was accurate did not seem to make any difference. In a Philadelphia newspaper ten days after he died a headline appeared: BULLITT BECAME CATHOLIC HOURS BEFORE HE DIED.[4] The account stated that a prominent Philadelphia priest had flown to Paris and given him the last rites of the Church. The newspaper did not check the story with me and since I had been with him at the hospital, I was able to refute the statement. The priest had never even been in Paris at the time. The next day the headline read: PRIEST SAYS BULLITT STORY WAS INCORRECT. The priest issued a formal denial and Bill was buried from Holy Trinity Episcopal Church in Philadelphia, which we had all attended in our youth.

Some articles told of the kinship Bill felt with William Christian of the Isle of Man, who was hanged as a rebel, and with Fletcher Christian, who led the mutiny on the *Bounty*. Bill would talk of his relationship with "Grandma" Pocahontas, Patrick Henry, Lawrence Washington, Thomas Walker (the guardian of Thomas Jefferson), and various others. A recent unorthodox member of the family was Lady Astor, who had such an exciting and controversial career in Parliament. She was Nancy

Langhorne; our grandmother was Therese Caldwell Langhorne. Most of these families had opposed oppression and Bill identified himself with them.

In order to understand Bill's character, which these letters reveal so clearly, one must realize the profound influence his forebears had upon him and his development. Certainly he had them constantly in mind. These men and women were alive to him and had a real bearing on his actions.

The Bullitt family was originally French Huguenot, Joseph Boulet having come to Maryland from a small town near Nîmes in 1685. (Bill was made an honorary citizen of Nîmes in 1937.) Boulet encountered considerable anti-French feeling from the British colonists, and with typical French practicality anglicized his name to Bullitt.

In 1784 the family settled near Louisville, Kentucky. Alexander Scott Bullitt married the daughter of his neighbors William Christian and Anne Henry Christian, sister of Patrick Henry. Grandfather John C. Bullitt as a young man of twenty-four was sent to Philadelphia by a Louisville bank to collect a debt. He liked the city and remained there, establishing a law office. Keenly concerned with good government, he drafted the first city charter, which was presented in the state legislature by his son, William C. Bullitt, a Democrat. Father, however, a lawyer by profession, did not continue in political life and later engaged in supplying smokeless "Pocahontas" coal to the Navy and the transatlantic steamship lines.

Mother's grandfather, Jonathan Horwitz of Berlin, was an eminent Hebrew scholar who came to America in the late 1700s. He married Deborah Andrews and was graduated in medicine from the University of Pennsylvania. He practiced in Baltimore and, abandoning Judaism, joined the Grace Protestant Episcopal Church. His son Orville, a prominent member of the Baltimore bar, married Maria R. Gross, daughter of Dr. Samuel D. Gross of a long line of Lutherans. Dr. Gross, the most distinguished surgeon of his day, was Professor of Surgery at Jefferson Medical College. Thomas Eakins's masterpiece shows him in his operating room. A great deal of Bill's brilliance and charm was undoubtedly inherited from this side of the family.

I have sometimes felt that playing the part of the knight in

The Knight of the Burning Pestle at Yale had given Bill a picture of a Quixotic character helping the helpless. At other times it seemed that the words of Patrick Henry, "Give me liberty or give me death," came into his thoughts and governed his actions.

He and I kept in close touch with one another. He always told me his opinions without reserve and I was kept informed of what he was doing.

Bill was a devoted brother.

[O N E]

The Early Years

1

State Department and Versailles Conference

1917—1932

Bullitt's Trip to Russia
Treaty with Lenin
Break with President Wilson

DURING 1918 BILL WROTE many memorandums suggesting means
of dealing with Trotsky, at that time holding joint power with
Lenin in Russia, but his views did not receive support from either the President or Secretary of State Lansing. In December
Bill became a member of the staff of the American Commission to
Negotiate Peace and sailed to Europe with President Wilson and
his staff. He had been appointed Chief of the Division of Current
Intelligence Summaries, and it was his duty to furnish daily the
latest political and military information to each of the commissioners. He began by giving them written accounts, which
quickly became too burdensome for these busy men to read. The
method was changed and every morning Bill visited each commissioner for twenty minutes, some in their offices, some at breakfast,
and even in their bedrooms. He brought them up to date on the
latest news of importance that might enter into their discussions.

In January 1919, Bill wrote to Colonel House suggesting the
advisability of sending missions from England, France, and the
United States to examine conditions in Russia. As the American
members of the mission he suggested Judge Learned Hand, Raymond Fosdick, and William Allen White, with himself as "general bootblack." No such missions were appointed, but on February 18, 1919, Bill was ordered to Russia by Secretary Lansing. In

view of the confused accounts of his trip to Russia and the report that he even went on his own initiative, I give the text of the order:

AMERICAN COMMISSION TO NEGOTIATE PEACE

18 February 1919

Sir:

You are hereby directed to proceed to Russia for the purpose of studying conditions, political and economic, therein, for the benefit of the American Commissioners plenipotentiary to negotiate peace, and all American diplomatic and consular officials are hereby directed to extend to you the proper courtesies and facilities to enable you to fulfill the duties of your mission.

I am, sir, your obedient servant,
Robert Lansing
Secretary of State of the United States of America

A somewhat similar letter bespeaking the proper courtesies and facilities was given to him by Joseph C. Grew, secretary of the commission.

Bill's own words at this time were, "About that time I was working particularly closely on the Russian affairs . . . on the day that Colonel House and Mr. Lansing [both American commissioners] first asked me to undertake this mission to Russia, I was dining at Mr. Lloyd George's apartment to discuss Russian affairs with his secretaries." He added, "It was decided that I should go at once to Russia to attempt to obtain from the Soviet Government an exact statement of the terms on which they were ready to stop fighting." [1]

On the trip to Russia, Bill was accompanied by the author and Communist sympathizer, Lincoln Steffens, and Captain W. W. Pettit of military intelligence, who would act as interpreter and a secretary. Steffens said, in part: "On the train to London Bullitt showed penciled on a sheet of paper the seven items which Philip Kerr [Prime Minister Lloyd George's private secretary and later Lord Lothian — with whom Bill remained throughout his life on friendly and intimate turns] had given him as the terms for the Bolsheviki to agree to . . . Colonel House had proposed, Lloyd George had planned the visit; and Bullitt's instructions came from House and from the British Prime Minister. And the British paved our way. They had reserved our places on trains and boats and at the London hotel. When we called for our tickets on the boat to Norway they were delivered to us 'all paid.' British consuls met and speeded us through Norway, Sweden and Finland."

Mr. Kerr stated to Bill that he had discussed the matter with both Lloyd George and Balfour (British foreign secretary) and at one point offered a British destroyer for the trip.

During the week in which Bill was in Russia he conferred with Lenin, Chicherin, the People's Commissar for Foreign Affairs, and Litvinov, former Soviet Ambassador to London. His comment at this time on Lenin was: "He is a very striking man — straightforward and direct, but also genial and with a large humor and serenity. There is already a Lenin legend. He is regarded almost as a prophet." [2]

On March 14 he received from the Soviet Foreign Office a peace proposal which the Russians agreed to accept provided it was approved by the Allies before April 10. He also commented that in his opinion the proposal was open to further negotiations by the Russians. In brief, the Bolsheviks proposed that all military operations close in Russia and Finland for a two-week armistice; to permit all existing de facto governments to remain in full control of the territories occupied by them in the former Russian Empire and Finland until the people in those territories decided on a change; that the economic blockade by the Allies be raised and trade relations re-established; that the Soviet governments of Russia would have free access to the railways and ports of the former Russian Empire and Finland. They further proposed free entry into Allied countries by citizens of the Soviet Republics and the right of sojourn provided they did not interfere in the domestic politics. Nationals of the Allied countries were to have free entry to the Soviet Republics, the right of sojourn and free circulation in Russia, also provided they did not interfere in domestic affairs. There were to be an interchange of official representatives enjoying full liberty and immunity, between the Allied and associated governments; the giving of a general amnesty to all political opponents, offenders, and prisoners, including all Russians who had fought in or otherwise aided the armies opposed to the Soviet governments; the release and repatriation of all prisoners of war and all nationals held in Russia, the Allies to do the same; all Allied and associated troops to be withdrawn from Russia; armies of the Soviet and anti-Soviet governments in Russia and Finland to be reduced to a peace footing. Finally, the Soviet and other governments set up in the former Russian Empire and Finland would recognize their responsibility for the financial obligations of the former Russian Empire.[3] This proposal to be valid until April 10, 1919. The Executive Council of the Soviet government formally endorsed these suggested terms.

This is a summary of the principal terms of the Bolshevik Government's offer, which Bill negotiated with Lenin and presented to the American commissioners and the British. Colonel House wired him congratulations for what he had accomplished. Bill also asked Colonel House to show to Lloyd George the telegrams from Russia (sent from Finland), in order that he might be kept fully informed. Colonel House sent the telegrams to both Lloyd George and Mr. Balfour. In view of what has taken place in Russia, and the relations of the great powers with Russia since that date, it is difficult to understand the atmosphere of the Versailles Conference, which summarily dismissed these proposals and actually never discussed them at its meetings.

Lenin had offered to accept a proposal from the Allied governments embodying terms which today seem almost utopian in view of what Soviet policy became. Had these proposals been accepted by President Wilson and Lloyd George, they might have given us a different world than that in which we live today. Bill was probably the only representative of any great power who ever negotiated on foreign affairs with both Lenin and Stalin.

George F. Kennan, a member of the original staff in the Embassy and later Ambassador to Russia, says in his *Memoirs:* "He [Bullitt] had returned with Soviet proposals which were not ideal but which did offer the most favorable opportunity yet extended, or ever to be extended, to the Western powers for extracting themselves with some measure of good grace from the profitless involvement of the military intervention in Russia and for the creation of an acceptable relationship to the Soviet regime. He had been shabbily treated — disowned, in fact — on his return,

by Wilson and Lloyd George. Both had ignored his proposals
and had publicly denied, explicitly or implicitly, all responsibility for his journey." [4] Lincoln Steffens noted that "this gay boy
[he was then twenty-eight] did a man's work, soberly, sanely,
shrewdly — even wisely after we got to Moscow. There was no
more swank then." [5]

In connection with this offer, Louis Fischer in his autobiography writes of an evening with Rakovsky, who was Prime Minister
of Soviet Ukraine. Rakovsky showed Fischer a letter from Chicherin about Bill's trip. He spoke of the importance of the decision the Bolsheviks had made because they felt that otherwise the
blockade would be increased and that the Allies would send arms
to the forces opposing the Soviet. Chicherin also said that the
Bolsheviks felt they would not get big concessions from the Paris
conference, but that Bill hoped to carry it through.[6]

Bullitt had been described at this time as having "one outstanding talent: despite his age he was able to gain the confidence
of men in the highest positions. He disposed of just the right
mixture of prudence and gall to get away with things more timid
men would not attempt and more reckless men fail to bring off." [7]
"Bullitt was the perfect person to carry out House's plan. It was
essential that the Soviet Government believe that he represented
the Allies and equally essential for the Allies to be able to deny
ever having heard of him . . . House gave Bullitt written instructions and through the British made arrangements for transport." [8]
In his diary House wrote, "I am delighted with the way things
are going."

In 1966 historian John M. Thompson wrote about the trip,
"The Soviet leaders gave up a good deal, the terms proposed containing more concessions than the West has been able to extract
from the Soviet Government from that day to this." He went on
to say, "The proposals Bullitt brought back from Moscow provided a reasonable basis on which to negotiate such a
settlement." [9]

Unfortunately when Bullitt returned to Paris President Wilson
was ill, and although a copy of Bullitt's report was delivered to
Wilson's house he never discussed it with Bullitt. However, Bullitt immediately met for an entire day with the American commissioners, Messrs. Lansing and White and General Bliss, who ex-

pressed the opinion that it was highly desirable to attempt to bring about peace on the basis of the report. Colonel House was also in favor of the proposal. However, the report was never presented to the peace conference.

The news of Bullitt's trip leaked out and a storm broke in both Parliament and Congress. Bullitt was called to testify before a Senate committee and in London a series of questions was asked in Parliament. In America the President was silent; no one asserted that Bullitt had gone with orders from the Secretary of State. Although Bullitt had several conversations with the British before leaving, Lloyd George repudiated him. Bullitt had actually breakfasted with Lloyd George on his return from Russia. Also present were General Smuts, Sir Maurice Hankey of the British secretariat at Versailles, and Philip Kerr. At the conclusion of the meal, Lloyd George urged Bullitt to make public his report on the conditions in Russia in order to enlighten public opinion. President Wilson, however, vetoed the proposal. Bullitt gave to Lloyd George, in the presence of the others, the official Russian proposals. Therefore Lloyd George's later repudiation was, to say the least, an extraordinary action.[10]

In response to a question in Parliament, asking the Prime Minister for a statement on approaches to the British Government by any person who had received representations from the existing government in central Russia, Mr. Lloyd George replied: *"We have had no approaches at all.* [My italics.] Constantly there are men coming and going to Russia of all nationalities, and they always come back with their tales of Russia. But we have made no approach of any sort. I have only heard reports of others having proposals . . . I think I know what my right honorable friend refers to. There was some suggestion that a young American had come back from Russia with a communication. It is not for me to judge the value of this communication, but if the President of the United States had attached any value to it he would have brought it before the Conference, and he certainly did not." [11]

In Bullitt's own words, "It was a most egregious case of misleading the public, perhaps the boldest that I have ever known . . . So flagrant was this that various members of the British Mission called on me . . . and apologized for the Prime Minister's action in the case." [12]

Winston Churchill made an interesting comment on this episode. He said, "Both the Prinkipo proposals and the study of the military and diplomatic possibilities having been reduced to nullity, the Americans with the assent of Mr. Lloyd George sent a certain Mr. Bullitt to Russia on February twenty-second. He returned to Paris in a week or two with proposals for an accommodation from the Soviet Government in his pocket . . . The Soviet proposals to Mr. Bullitt . . . were treated with general disdain, and Mr. Bullitt himself was *not without some difficulty disowned by those who had sent him.*" [13] (My italics.)

Lenin's own words on this meeting, as quoted by John Silverlight in *The Observer,* were: "When we proposed a treaty to Bullitt a year ago, a treaty which left tremendous amounts of territory to Denikin and Kolchak, we proposed this treaty with the knowledge that if peace were signed, those Governments could never hold out." [14]

In the files of the British Foreign Office are the questions asked in Parliament together with the suggested answers by the ministers. Colonel Wedgwood asked the Prime Minister "whether the Report on their visit to Russia by Mr. Lincoln Steffens and Mr. Bullitt has been communicated to his Majesty's Government . . ." The draft of the reply is: "The answer to the first part of the Honorable and Gallant member is in the negative." [15]

Philip Kerr (later Lord Lothian, British Ambassador to the United States), at that time confidential secretary to Lloyd George, wrote from the peace conference in Paris to the Foreign Office: "Some time in February, Mr. Bullitt, who was on the staff of the American Commission to Negotiate Peace . . . told me that he contemplated making a rapid visit to Russia with the object of finding out what the local conditions were and what was the real attitude of the Soviet Government towards the Allies and the question of peace. He asked my opinion of this project, and I told him, as my personal opinion, that I thought it would be a good plan to get first hand information from Russia. Thereafter I saw Mr. Bullitt several times and we discussed, always in a perfectly unofficial manner, the possible basis of a settlement with Russia. [Kerr proceeds at some length to state his conditions for a settlement as he told them to Bullitt.] When he returned he immediately came to see me and gave me copies of his report together with the proposal of the Soviet Government. Mr. Bullitt had an interview with the Prime Minister during which the Prime Minister cross-examined him closely in regard to conditions in Russia, and the attitude and personalities of the Bolshevik leaders . . . I append a copy of Mr. Bullitt's 'proposals' for reference. P. H. Kerr." [16] The propsals enclosed cover five pages.

A member of the Foreign Office commented on this letter, "Mr. Kerr's apologia is not very convincing: it is, however, interesting to have an authentic copy of the Bullitt proposal; it strikes me that Mr. Kerr's previous unofficial conversations with Mr. Bullitt must have influenced the proposal which was brought away from Russia. I am afraid that Mr. Shortt's speech in the debate of the 9th of April in the House of Commons is rather vitiated by this memorandum, which admits that Mr. Kerr received immediately the Soviet Government's proposal and that Mr. Bullitt had an interview with Mr. Lloyd George. Mr. Shortt had said 'so far as the latest information I can get from Paris is concerned, no such proposals are before the British delegates . . . I do not believe for a moment, from the information I have, that there is really any Lenin negotiation as a suggestion brought to Paris at all. I believe the whole story is of German manufacture for the purpose of making the people of other countries believe that the Bolshevik is really a peaceable, civilised, reasonable person.' " There are comments by Foreign Office officials on this memorandum: "It's the result of having two Foreign Offices. One directed by the Secretary of State, the other by Mr. Philip Kerr." "The allegation that the draft was in Kerr's handwriting is serious and no doubt more will be heard of it in the Press and in the House of Commons." [17] In the House of Commons Mr. Bonar Law stated that "we had nothing to do with these people." At a later date Mr. Law told the House that "he adheres to his statement that it [the Bullitt testimony] is a tissue of falsehoods." [18]

On the morning of July 28, 1919, the *Daily Herald* in London, under the heading TERMS PREMIER SENT LENIN, published the story of the negotiations and said: "Not only did William Bullitt bring back from Russia a proposed basis for peace, but [in boldface type] that proposal was in reality an acceptance of a draft taken by him to Russia. That draft was in the handwriting of Mr. Philip Kerr — Mr. Lloyd George's principal private secretary."

There followed several paragraphs headed MR. LLOYD GEORGE'S TERMS, which ended with these questions: "Then Mr. Lloyd George, after Bullitt had returned, and reported to him as well as to President Wilson, pretended that he knew nothing about the whole matter, and that he had only vaguely heard about Bullitt's mission. WHY? Well, that is not perhaps very important. What is important is this — WHY not peace now on Mr. Lloyd George's own conditions, which Lenin has accepted?"

The press in London would not be silenced and almost two months later was still questioning the good faith of the government as witnessed by an editorial from the *Morning Post* of September 19, 1919: "We now have the official admission, issued by the Press Association, that 'some young American' about whom there was a suggestion 'breakfasted with Mr. Lloyd George and naturally had a private conversation with him.' This statement appeared after the first semi-official denial, in which Mr. Bullitt's statements were described as 'a tissue of lies' . . . He [Bullitt] carried to Russia suggestions as to the proposed terms of peace, given to him by Mr. Philip Kerr. The inference is, in fact, that Mr. Lloyd George was unofficially negotiating with the Bolsheviks through Mr. Bullitt. Again we await an explanation, and also an explanation of the Prime Minister's previous explanation given to Parliament."

This whole sordid and shabby exposition of the dealings of Prime Minister Lloyd George and of the statements made by him and the members of his government in the House of Commons left a mark on Bullitt which it was to take over twenty years to erase. This episode should be kept in mind when reading his letters to Roosevelt wherein he sometimes violently expresses his distrust of British diplomacy and the dependability of their statements.

On May 17, 1919, Bullitt presented his resignation as a member of the staff and in his letter to President Wilson he said, in part, "Russia, 'the acid test of goodwill' for me as for you, has not even been understood. Unjust decisions in regard to Shantung, the Tyrol, Thrace, Hungary, East Prussia, Danzig, the Saar Valley, and the abandonment of the principle of the freedom of the seas *make new international conflicts certain.* [My italics.] It is my conviction that the present League of Nations will be power-

less to prevent these wars, and that the United States will be involved in them by the obligations undertaken in the covenant of
the League and in the special understanding with France.
Therefore the duty of the Government of the United States to its
own people and to mankind is to refuse to sign or ratify this unjust treaty, to refuse to guarantee its settlements by entering the
League of Nations, to refuse to entangle the United States further
by the understanding with France." [19]

When Bullitt returned to the United States, he was summoned
to a meeting of the Committee on Foreign Relations of the
United States Senate on September 12, 1919. The senators present were Messrs. Lodge (chairman), Brandegee, Fall, Knox,
Harding, and New. Bullitt was closely questioned on his trip to
Russia and the opinions of the commissioners on the League of
Nations, particularly Secretary of State Lansing. He was strongly
criticized for divulging their views in opposition to the treaty,
and there is no doubt that this testimony provided Senator Lodge
considerable support in his successful fight against the United
States's becoming involved in the League of Nations.

Colonel House, as a memento of the conference and of Bullitt's
services, gave him an original draft of the League of Nations charter with annotations in President Wilson's handwriting.

Bullitt's action in resigning gives a good indication of his character. An idealist with a strong feeling for the romantic, he liked
to dramatize his purpose. Although his knowledge of world affairs was great and his advice on foreign affairs was often prophetic, he was not willing to compromise, a necessary ingredient
in all important dealings with others. He made friends easily
among all strata of society from Kings, Presidents, and Prime
Ministers to farmers, mechanics, and laborers, but once he was disappointed in another's character or deeds he would never return
to the former intimacy. His letter to Lady Astor clearly explains
his action:

Dear Nancy:
. . . I am not at all surprised that you were horrified at my testimony. Yet I am certain that if you had been in my place you would
have done just what I did — only more . . . I had a definite choice:
Either I could take refuge behind "I have forgotten" and "I have

not the documents" or I could speak the truth, and the whole truth. I knew well that if I did give a full account of the Russian business I should be hated bitterly by three fourths of the persons who had called themselves my friends. I knew that I should throw away any chance for a normal, advancing, political career — such as most of your friends will have. I knew that if I skimmed diplomatically over the surface of the truth in my testimony I should continue to enjoy the comparative goodwill of nearly everyone of importance. I knew also that, if I skimmed, my testimony would have no effect whatsoever in helping to end the murder by starvation and disease of the millions of Russians, who were being killed by the blockade — conducted by your government and assented to by mine. I thought that if I told the full truth, sparing no one — least of all, my own self — I might hasten the lifting of the blockade . . . I believe the blockade will be lifted and that peace will be made with Russia a little sooner because I let go the whole truth to the Senate. Therefore the dowagers and diplomats who are mewing for my blood do not disturb me.[20]

William C. Bullitt

In a memorandum of a later date he speaks of the Senate hearing:

"In May, 1919, I resigned from the American Commission to Negotiate Peace and took two positions which were, at that time, highly unpopular: I expressed the opinion that the Polish Corridor, the Hungarian settlement and various other provisions of the peace treaties would prepare for the world not peace but war. I added that, whether one liked it or not, the Soviet Government would remain in power and that peace should be made with it on the extraordinarily favorable terms Lenin was then ready to accept.

". . . To criticize the Treaty of Versailles was to be called "a pro-German," which at that time was the equivalent of "traitor," and to advocate peace with Russia was to be denounced as a Bolshevik. If one *knew* the realities of the situation one had to choose between sacrificing temporarily the good opinion of one's fellows or sacrificing one's own self-respect. I felt sure that I was right about both the Treaty of Versailles and about Russia, and I felt it was my duty to do what I could to inform American public opinion in regard to the realities of the situation. I took the unpopular course and the consequences.

"The Senate, when it is considering a peace treaty or any other treaty, like a court has the right to subpoena anyone and to compel the production of any paper in the possession of anyone. After my return to America, I was summoned by the Committee on Foreign Relations of the Senate. When I took the stand I was asked for many documents and much information.

"To lie to the constitutional representatives of the American people in a matter of great national importance is not in my tradition. It never occurred to me not to tell the truth. There are, however, many men who have been raised in a different tradition, and the documents the Senate drew from me unfortunately exposed various statesmen in various countries in a not altogether favorable light. It was especially unfortunate that certain documents should have shown that a distinguished British statesman had been somewhat frugal in his use of truth when addressing the House of Commons. There was naturally considerable criticism. But the men most intimately concerned, President Wilson and Colonel House, had no criticism to make. Recently Dr. Cary Grayson, who was with Wilson day and night, assured me explicitly, after refreshing his memory by re-reading his exhaustive diary, that never once did Wilson, even in the privacy of his bedroom, criticize my action; and Colonel House said to me at the time, "If I had been as young as you are, I should have done exactly what you did." He remained, and is today, my intimate friend." [21]

Most historians of this period now agree on the importance of the treaty with Lenin that Bullitt brought to Paris. His action in presenting all the details to the Senate committee was in keeping with his idealistic approach as to what would make a better world. There is no question that this testimony divulging conversations with Secretary Lansing and other commissioners was to jeopardize his future career, and for many years he was under a cloud of suspicion.

2

Introduction to the Governor

1932—1933

Meeting with Roosevelt
Preinauguration Trips to Europe for Roosevelt

FOR THE NEXT thirteen years Bill dropped out of public affairs, but much of this period he used to enlarge his acquaintance with foreign statesmen, as he lived a large part of the time in Europe. In 1920 he and Ernesta bought a run-down apple farm near Ashfield, Massachusetts. The house was an old one and they renovated it, making the barn hayloft into a huge living room, ideal for music. The stable became two bedrooms, which together with four in the old house provided ample room for the many visitors who came to stay. These visitors ranged from an automobile mechanic to foreign statesmen and diplomats.

In 1923 he and Ernesta were divorced. That same year he married Anne Moën Reed, the widow of John Reed and daughter of Hugh Moën and Anne Fiennes Moën of San Francisco. She used the pen name of Louise Bryant. She was extremely talented, and striking-looking, with dark hair and large luminous eyes. She had great charm, was an established journalist and foreign correspondent, and author of *Six Red Months in Russia, Mirrors of Moscow,* etc. When Reed was ill in Moscow and Louise was unable to reach him by normal means of travel, she cut off her hair and, disguised as a boy, shipped as a seaman on a freighter. She arrived in Moscow before his death, which was apparently from typhus.

Reed is buried in Red Square by the wall of the Kremlin. Bill and Louise rented the seventeenth-century house of the famous Kyöprülü family on the Bosporus. They remained there until moving to Paris the following year where their only child, Anne, was born.

It was during the years in Paris that Bill acquired complete fluency in French and made so many French friends. He developed a remarkably good taste in wines and became known as quite a connoisseur.

While staying on the Bosporus and in Paris he wrote his only published novel, *It's Not Done,* which appeared in 1926 and went to twenty-four printings. It created a furor in Philadelphia at the time, as that city was obviously the locale and most of the characters were easily recognized. He castigated the social life and satirized the aims and ideals of the rich. The book also dealt with sex, which in those days was usually treated as almost nonexistent. The book aroused considerable controversy and Bill was criticized by the social elements of the city. He did not accept the standards and conventions of the environment in which he had been raised, and he was again branded a nonconformist.

Bill continued his correspondence with Colonel House. House wrote that he hoped Bill would join him in the south of France, and Bill asked Colonel House to lunch with him, the Turkish Ambassador, and the former Turkish Prime Minister, Kemal. Later Colonel House wrote that he would like to come to the farm at Ashfield to stay.

Bill and Louise continued to live in Paris but spent the summers at the farm in Ashfield, making additions to the old house. The marriage ended in divorce in 1930, and Bill was awarded custody of their daughter, Anne. Following a long and tragic illness, Louise died in 1936.

In October 1930 Bill was in Vienna to begin a book about President Wilson with Sigmund Freud. He had just been staying at Schloss Salem, where Princess Max of Baden gave him all the files of Prince Max, former Prime Minister of Germany, to examine. Bill read the most important papers, including the minutes of the German cabinet meetings from September 1918 until the armistice on November 11. Bill commented: "The Kaiser, it is clear from his letters to Prince Max, had not the slightest ability to comprehend the facts which faced him."

Bill again spent the winter of 1931 in Vienna, having passed through London and talked with Ramsay MacDonald, George Lansbury, leader of the opposition, and other members of the government. He obtained what he describes as "direct information" that the Soviet would endure any provocation rather than go to war with Japan. Bill's absorption in foreign affairs is shown in a letter written with his usual self-confidence to Colonel House at this time. "I made arrangements in London to have any question whatever asked in the House of Commons." House immediately telephoned this news to Roosevelt as being of great importance. From Paris he reported the government felt sure that Hitler would become Chancellor.

As early as December 1931, Colonel House wrote to Bill that he wanted to show a letter of Bill's to Mr. Roosevelt, who was then governor of New York State. House wanted Roosevelt to know how valuable Bill would be to him on foreign affairs, if he should become President. At that time Bill was again in Vienna working with Freud, but the book about Wilson was not to be published until the winter of 1966, shortly before Bill's death. His reply to Colonel House says, "I should be glad to have you show Roosevelt my letter and I hope you will, as you suggest, let him know that I might not be altogether useless. My acquaintance with him in Washington was so slight that I should have to come into contact with him *de novo*." (This letter disposes of the many statements that Bill knew Roosevelt well in the war year of 1918.) By April Bill and Freud had finished the book and agreed to lay it aside and then review it later.

It was not until 1939, when Freud was in London, that they finally agreed on the completed text, and also decided not to publish it until after Mrs. Wilson's death. When the book came out in 1966 some critics implied that Freud had not worked on it. By that time Bill was too sick to refute these statements. There are pages of handwritten manuscript by Freud and frequent corrections by him in the typed copy, and his signature appears at the end of each chapter.

In a letter of April 1932, Bill asked Colonel House if it would be worthwhile to return home by way of Berlin, Moscow, and other capitals, or should he wait until November? House replied that he should wait until after the election in November, and this was the genesis of a trip that was to cause a furor in the United States Senate, with demands for Bill's arrest.

There is a vivid description of Bill's emotional side by author Eugene Lyons, who met him in Moscow that summer: "Sentimental to the core, Bullitt felt he could not leave Moscow without placing flowers on the grave of his friend John Reed, whose widow, Louise Bryant, he married some time after Reed's death. Reed's ashes were buried on Red Square . . . being surrounded by an iron fence . . . There was the eternal problem of obtaining a propusk, a permit to go behind the fence. George Andreytchine . . . finally elicited the propusk.

"Early one morning, Bullitt, Andreytchine and I drove to Red Square. Two of us watched from the distance while Bullitt, carrying a large wreath, walked solemnly toward Reed's grave. We saw him place the flowers on the stone and stand there with bowed head for many minutes. When he returned to the car, tears were rolling down his cheeks and his features were drawn with sorrow." [1] When Bill arrived in Moscow in 1933 as Ambassador, with Anne, they immediately went to the grave to lay a wreath on it.

In September 1932 Bill moved to New York and began working in Roosevelt's campaign headquarters preparing material for speeches. He notes the almost complete lack of money for the campaign. In general the complaint was that the large donors did not believe that Roosevelt could provide leadership. Bill again said, "I do not know enough about Mr. Roosevelt to be able to make any suggestions."

Louis B. Wehle writes of the summer of 1932: "I proposed to him [Bullitt] that he and I formulate the principles for an agreement of recognition between the United States and the U.S.S.R. In the course of doing so we ironed out such differences as there were between us. Whatever Bullitt's original thoughts may have been about the possibilities of the Soviet system when it and Bullitt were both young, he had clearly become thoroughly disillusioned by the development of the U.S.S.R. under Stalin. He condemned it and every part of it; and he now understood the extent of the Soviets' subversive activities in the United States during his long absences.

"We agreed that the first and overriding condition of recognition must be the pledge of the Soviet Government that it would refrain from any and all activities in the United States, or elsewhere, aimed against our institutions. That condition was carried a year later as the opening and chief paragraphs of the letter of November 16, 1933, from Maxim Litvinov to Roosevelt on which American recognition was based. The letter was formulated by top officers in the State Department on the core of Bullitt's draft, and the terms of recognition were negotiated by Bullitt as Special Assistant to the Secretary of State in meetings with Litvinov, who had been his 1919 vis-à-vis at Moscow."

Mr. Wehle goes on to tell of Bill's renewed acquaintance with Roosevelt in these words: "On August 13 [1932], I wrote to Roosevelt saying that Bullitt had returned from Europe, where he had close association with leading statesmen in Italy, France, Germany, Russia and England, and that he had seen a number of them recently. I added that Bullitt was distinctly conservative on any proposal to cancel debts owing by Europe, and could be useful on foreign affairs during the campaign. I urged that Roosevelt see him. Campaign trips and crowded days between them prevented this until, on September 30th, I had a wire setting October 5th at Albany for a meeting. In that first talk the two men became warm friends. There was a certain community of social background, as well as a temperamental congeniality heightened by the fact that both were brilliantly and boldly intuitional . . . Bullitt had the capacity for prodigious, sustained toil, for critically selecting relevant facts, and for resolving them into a plan for action. Yet he could swiftly and vividly make available to Roosevelt his scholarship in history and also his familiarity with Europe and its current leaders. They made an ideal team . . . When I saw Roosevelt on October 7th in Albany, he was as pleased about the meeting as Bullitt had been." [2]

Mr. Wehle also helped to enlist the support of Colonel House; he felt it would demonstrate that the Wilsonian sector of the Democratic party had forgiven Bullitt's 1919 course at Paris and

Washington. It was Mr. Wehle who brought about the association of the two men.

Bullitt's first letter from Governor Roosevelt was dated September 12, 1932, and was a formal note accepting his service in the Presidential campaign in connection with foreign policy. In his letter to Colonel House Bullitt said, "I heard the Topeka speech . . . All the Patrick Henry blood in me applauded . . . I suspect you've picked another man who will make a big dent in the world."

The correspondence between Roosevelt and Bullitt now begins, slowly and with formality, but gradually increasing in warmth, feeling, and freedom as each came to know and admire the qualities in the other.

YALE CLUB

VANDERBILT AVENUE AND FORTY-FOURTH STREET

NEW YORK

14 September 1932

My dear Governor Roosevelt:

I heard your Topeka speech this afternoon over the radio in Headquarters, and I want to thank you for making it. It was the most inspiriting address that I have heard since Wilson's speeches in 1918. You not only said the right things but also said them with a 1776 spirit. That is the thing I care most about in American life and that is what we need in the White House.

Enclosed is my cheque for a thousand dollars. I wish I could send more, but I have no more to send. Please use the cheque in any way you see fit.

Please also use me in any way you wish. I should of course be delighted to work with you on your return from your western trip, as you suggest in your letter of Sept. 12. Will you ask your secretary to let me know at the Yale Club on what date you wish to see me?

I have been working for the past two weeks in the research department at Headquarters turning out answers to requests for information, and I am now preparing a memorandum on foreign policy which might perhaps be of some service if you should wish to make an address on foreign affairs. Mr. Hoover's foreign policy has been as inept as his domestic administration, and I think you could, if you wished, point that out in an address as stirring as your address of today.

My heartiest good wishes and sincerest hopes that I may soon address you as Mr. President.

Yours very respectfully,
William C. Bullitt

An amusing comment on this contribution of a thousand dollars is supplied in the diary of Ambassador Dodd, later our representative in Berlin: "Bullitt is the heir to a great fortune and was known as a liberal contributor to the Roosevelt campaign in 1932. My gift was $25." [3]

A Republican campaign pamphlet spoke of Bullitt as "the gilded beneficiary of a spendthrift trust . . . who made a $25,000 contribution to the Democratic campaign fund."

I remember one of Bill's first assignments at the Roosevelt headquarters. He telephoned me that Governor Roosevelt was being accused of being a spender and raising the New York State debt. Would I, as a banker, please give him the answer? Although at that time I was a supporter of Mr. Roosevelt's, I am afraid I was able to give him very little reassurance on this question.

After the election Mr. Wehle suggested that Bullitt, on his own initiative and resources, make a trip to England and the Continent. There he would obtain information on the chances of reconciliation between France and Germany, and what the foreign governments expected to do about the installment due December 15 on their debts to the United States. It would be Bullitt's private venture and he was to go "purely on his own." [4] Great discretion had to be used, as neither he nor Roosevelt could represent our government. The Logan Act provided for a fine of five thousand dollars and imprisonment up to three years for any private citizen who, without our government's permission, conducted conversations with any foreign government about any matters affecting the two governments. This trip, and one two months later, had violent repercussions in the Senate and the press. Bullitt sailed for England on November 19 and sent all his reports to Mr. Wehle, who in turn delivered them to Mr. Roosevelt. They had a simple code of about only fifty words, mostly first names of our family and people Bill knew. There is a certain humor in the code. Debt payment was "Bill"; debt was "Orville." Bill's first letter to Wehle, dated December 3, was twelve pages long, giving a complete account of the conversations with many leaders in England and France. A few of the telegrams were:

LONDON NOVEMBER 28
CONSULTANT NEW YORK

CONVERSATION COVERING MANY SUBJECTS WITH PHILIP [McDonald] THIS MORNING SO INTIMATE THAT I CONSIDER IT UNWISE TO CABLE STOP OSWALD [Chamberlain] AND OTHERS OPPOSE BILL [debt payment] STOP DECISION THEREFORE SOMEWHAT DOUBTFUL STOP MY OWN OPINION BILL [debt payment] WILL BE PAID STOP PHILIP [McDonald] URGED ME TO KEEP IN CLOSE TOUCH WITH HIM AND ARRANGED DIRECT PRIVATE COMMUNICATION SO THAT IF YOU DESIRE INFORMATION ANY QUESTION AM NOW IN POSITION TO OBTAIN IMMEDIATE REPLY

BULLITT

PARIS DECEMBER 2
CONSULTANT NEW YORK

CONVERSATIONS TODAY VALENTINE [Herriot] STOP ALSO PERMANENT OFFICIALS FOREIGN OFFICE STOP ALSO AMBASSADOR BERENGER NOW PRESIDENT SENATE COMMITTEE FOREIGN AFFAIRS STOP VALENTINE [Herriot] AND ALL OTHERS FAVOR BILL [debt payment] BUT FACE ALMOST UNANIMOUS OPPOSITION CHAMBER STOP HORTENSE [France] ENTIRELY UNINFORMED FACTS ABOUT ORVILLE [debt] STOP DEEPLY HOSTILE BILL [debt payment] ON GROUND HERBERT [unidentified] INSISTED MORATORIUM FOR PAUL [Germany] STOP NOW REFUSES STOP SAME HORTENSE [France] STOP VALENTINE [Herriot] LIKELY TO FALL NINTH WHEN BILL [debt payment] WILL BE DEBATED STOP VALENTINE [Herriot] CONSIDERING PROPOSING BILL [debt payment] BE PAID BUT WITH ANNOUNCEMENT STOP HORTENSE [France] INSISTS BILL [debt payment] BE DEDUCTED FROM CARGO [lump sum settlement] . . . STOP WITH LUCK AND PERSONAL ASSURANCE FROM PHILIP [McDonald] I BELIEVE HE CAN WIN STOP IF YOU URGENTLY WISH WILL ALTER PLANS AND VISIT PHILIP [McDonald] VALENTINE [Herriot] GENEVA TUESDAY

BULLITT

BULLITT   DECEMBER 3, 1932

FORTY-SIX RUE DE PONTHIEU

PARIS

IF YOU CAN PERHAPS ASSIST VALENTINE [Herriot] GETTING NECESSARY
PERSONAL ASSURANCE I URGE YOUR GOING GENEVA STOP ALSO TELL
HENRI [unidentified] THAT I PERSONALLY URGE HIM ARRANGE IMMEDI-
ATE PUBLICITY ORVILLE [debt] FACTS INTERPRETING US
                                        CONSULTANT [Wehle]

In an eleven-page memorandum of this trip Bullitt recorded
his talks with a dozen or more of the leaders of Germany and
noted: "Hitler is finished — not as an agitator or as leader of an
aggressive minority, but as a possible dictator. His finish is due to
Hindenburg. The old man has absolutely refused so long as he is
alive to have Hitler as Chancellor . . . Hitler's influence is wan-
ing so fast that the Government is no longer afraid of the growth
of the Nazi movement."

One month later Hitler became Chancellor.

Wehle forwarded all Bullitt's cables and letters to Roosevelt
and advised him that if any news leaked out he would do best "by
ignoring criticism." Wehle communicated the information to
Colonel House, together with a suggested program for handling
the war debts. Wehle sent Roosevelt's further instructions to Bullitt, who came home December 16, having first been to Berlin.
He met with Wehle and Roosevelt on the twenty-seventh and
made a full report.[5]

Wehle reports on this evening that, "When Bullitt was away
for a few minutes, I said to Roosevelt, 'There is your man for
Paris.' Roosevelt replied that Bullitt would be immensely useful,
but that he could not appoint him because of a prior commitment. 'Well, if we should recognize Russia, he would by all odds
be your best man as the first ambassador.' With this Roosevelt
agreed." [6] Later Colonel House suggested him for the Paris post.
Bullitt went back to Europe on January 15, 1933.

On this trip the newspapers carried headlines that ROOSEVELT
SECRET AGENT IS REPORTED IN LONDON. (Roosevelt was not inaugurated until March.) Bullitt continued to make regular reports,
this time to Roosevelt at Warm Springs and not in code.

On account of the publicity Bullitt canceled the remainder of his trip and returned from Berlin to Paris February 10. Hitler had become Chancellor on January 30, and in February Japan left the League of Nations.

On February 2 the question was raised in the Senate. Senator Robinson: "Who is this man Bullitt? London and Paris dispatches state Bullitt described himself in those capitals as the representative of President-elect Roosevelt, despite Roosevelt's denial that Bullitt or anyone else was representing him . . . I think the State Department should immediately apprehend him." Senator Glenn: "I do not suppose he could be Colonel House in disguise?" [7] One headline read, SENATOR DEMANDS BULLITT ARREST AS FAKE ENVOY.

In November 1932 Chancellor von Papen of Germany had resigned and President Hindenburg had appointed General Schleicher to succeed him. The Communists were increasing in power and Germany was torn by strikes and fighting in the streets between Nazis and Communists. Papen was able to persuade Hindenburg that he should put the responsibility on Hitler's shoulders. Adolf Hitler became Chancellor of Germany on January 30, 1933.

FRANKLIN D. ROOSEVELT

HYDE PARK, DUTCHESS COUNTY

NEW YORK

January 13, 1933

Dear Bill:

I am delighted that you find it possible to go to Europe AGAIN. Please be sure to take note of my addresses so that we may keep in constant touch with each other.

Always sincerely yours,
Franklin D. Roosevelt

Copy made February 18 of letter still undelivered to Governor Roosevelt.

Louis B. Wehle

YALE CLUB

VANDERBILT AVENUE AND FORTY-FOURTH STREET

NEW YORK

14 January 1933

Dear Governor:

I have just 'phoned Miss LeHand to ask her please to be sure that

no word about my present trip escapes to the public. I did this because I was horrified this afternoon when Colonel House told me
that he was going to let a news agency know that I was leaving on
what was said to be an important mission for you.

I warned the Colonel with the utmost vehemence that publicity
would greatly handicap me on this trip and he promised me that he
would say nothing to anyone; but he left me with the unpleasant
impression that he had perhaps already been indiscreet and that
publicity might result. I have not told the Colonel why I am going
nor have I given him the slightest inkling of your instructions, and
I feel that you yourself should control absolutely any publicity in regard to my movements. Personally, I should consider any publicity
highly undesirable.

I am giving this note to Louis Wehle, with the request that he
should deliver it into your hands, and he has been kind enough to
agree to do so.

Good luck till we meet again.

Yours always sincerely,
William C. Bullitt

Wehle sent Bullitt a cable on February 14 in which he said
that he had not yet delivered the letter to Governor Roosevelt
but would do so in a couple of days. He further said: "My opinion is that the man will stand by you through action of the kind
he intimated to you before you left."

This letter was not delivered to the President until February
18 with the accompanying note from Wehle.

New York
February 18, 1933

Dear Frank,

I am delivering to you Bill Bullitt's note to you of January 14th,
written by him before he sailed to be handed to you if any publicity
should develop about his trip. He then feared it would come the
next day. After it broke from the other side I had no safe way to
get the note to you. To my mind it may well indicate the source of
the leak.

Yours always,
Louis

MEMORANDUM

LeHand
Warm Springs
Georgia

22 January 1933

I spent yesterday alone with MacDonald at Chequers. He was deeply impressed by your good will and asked me to express to you his profound personal appreciation and his desire to cooperate with you in every way.

I outlined your general position emphasizing that a lump sum settlement was impossible, that the entire principal must be paid, that the return of England to the gold standard was essential to any settlement by a reduction of interest. MacDonald said that he would be delighted to reach an agreement on that basis but said he would have great difficulty in persuading his colleagues to agree to return to gold immediately. He indicated, however, that he considered such a settlement possible . . .

MacDonald gave me his word of honor that England has no secret understanding with Japan, either written or verbal. On my insistence, MacDonald said he personally was ready to promise that the British Government would see to it that no British banker should extend financial assistance to Japan. He added, however, that he must communicate with Chamberlain before making this promise formally as loans might already have been promised. I shall attempt to obtain an absolute pledge from him today.

. . . He expressed serious fear of future attacks by Germany and asked the surprising question: "Would Roosevelt object to a considerable increase in the British Fleet?" I replied that I had never discussed that specific question with you but that you were definitely on the side of a further reduction in armaments and repeated some of the remarks you had made to me in regard to planes, submarines, mobile guns, etc. He remained astonishingly skeptical in regard to the value of limitation agreements.

In the matter of the reconciliation of France and Germany after a long discussion in which I moved very delicately, expressing extreme skepticism, MacDonald said: "Our policy is now to reconcile France and Germany." He had apparently forgotten what he had said to me in regard to this question last December. I, therefore, took him at his word and said: "You would then consider it in line with your policy if the United States should do what seemed possible in the way of promoting their reconciliation?" He replied: "We could have no possible objection to America attempting to reconcile them." When he had made this definite statement, I said, somewhat formally, that I would cable his statement to you and that if we should act in accordance with it and make any move to bring together France and Germany we should consider we were acting in accordance with the expressed desire of the British Government. MacDonald stiffened a bit but could do nothing else than assent. He did so, obviously somewhat reluctantly but definitely. The preservation of this record seems important . . .

A German representative here says Hindenburg would greatly value a simple friendly greeting from you to be delivered when I go to Germany. Will you cable one or shall I compose one? Good luck.

Bullitt

LEHAND   PARIS
WARM SPRINGS   JANUARY 26 [1933]

TODAY HELD TWO INTIMATE CONVERSATIONS WITH BONCOUR STOP YOUR GOOD WILL TOWARD FRANCE HAS MOVED HIM AND HE HOPES BY FOLLOWING PLAN WE DECIDED ON THAT IT WILL BE POSSIBLE TO OBTAIN PAYMENT DUE LAST DECEMBER STOP SHORTLY AFTER INAUGURATION HE EXPECTS TO ASK HERRIOT TO GO TO AMERICA OSTENSIBLY ON LECTURE TRIP BUT IN REALITY TO HAVE CONFIDENTIAL TALK WITH YOU STOP THIS WOULD BEGIN FEBRUARY TWENTY-FIRST STOP IN CASE THE BONCOUR MINISTRY SHOULD FALL A NEW GOVERNMENT WOULD ADHERE TO THIS PROJECT STOP HE GAVE DEFINITE PROMISE THAT NO LOAN WOULD BE GIVEN TO JAPAN STOP I AM LEAVING FOR GERMANY TOMORROW

BILL

LEHAND   BERLIN
WARM SPRINGS   JANUARY [30 OR 31, 1933]

HAVE HAD TALK WITH BÜLOW * AND NEURATH † STOP THE LATTER EXPECTING REMAIN AS MINISTER OF FOREIGN AFFAIRS IN THE NEW GOVERNMENT OR ELSE HINDENBURG WILL EMPOWER HIM TO CARRY THROUGH THE POLICIES OF DECEMBER OUTLINE STOP FULL RELIANCE CAN BE PLACED ON FRENCH AND GERMAN SUPPORT FOR RETURN OF ENGLAND TO

* Permanent Under Secretary for Foreign Affairs.
† Foreign Minister.

GOLD STANDARD STOP RECENT PUBLICITY HAS MADE CONVERSATION WITH OTHERS DANGEROUS STOP AM GOING TO AUSTRIA TOMORROW

BILL

ROOSEVELT "SECRET AGENT" IS REPORTED IN LONDON
By William Hillman
(Copyright 1933, by Universal Service, Inc.)

LONDON, Jan. 24 — William C. Bullitt, Woodrow Wilson's representative on a special mission to Russia in 1919, has been in London several days on a secret mission in which he is declared to be acting as the "emissary" of President-elect Roosevelt.

Bullitt, it is learned, visited Chequers, Prime Minister MacDonald's official country residence, Saturday, and No. 10 Downing Street, MacDonald's town residence, yesterday.

In the same authoritative quarter which declared Bullitt is the emissary of Roosevelt, it was declared the American told a prominent British statesman that Roosevelt favors a reduction of the British war debt by 80 per cent.

British officials are declared to have been advised from an important quarter that Bullitt's mission must not be made known to the Washington State Department. For this reason they are said to be puzzled as to his exact status.

In his London hotel last night Bullitt refused to be seen.

WASHINGTON, Jan. 25 (INS) — A demand that President-elect Roosevelt immediately tell the nation whether William C. Bullitt is representing him in Europe and whether he favors an 80 per cent reduction in war debts was voiced in the Senate this afternoon by Senator Robinson, Republican, of Indiana.

He charged that Mr. Roosevelt, by encouraging debt conferences with the debtor nations, was deliberately flaunting the policy laid down by Congress.

46 Rue de Ponthieu
Paris
7 February 1933

Dear MacDonald:

I am deeply sorry that I can not say good-bye to you before leaving for home. In view of the demands of Senator Robinson — the Republican Robinson — it is impossible. That fantastic report in the London papers stimulated him to demand not merely an investigation of my present trip in Europe but also that I should be arrested and prosecuted under the Logan act, which provides, I am told, that any American holding conversations with a member of a foreign government with a view to influencing the action of that government in a matter in dispute with the Government of the United States should be imprisoned for three years!

You and I know that my attempts to influence you, to date, have been confined to the purchase of that Sultana's dressing gown! But the Senators don't know that, and one should not blame them too much for being excited by that wild story. Did you ever discover who started it?

It now seems to be generally understood in America that we met merely as old friends; but if I should go home by way of England someone would certainly begin again to let his imagination work. We might confine our conversation to reminiscences of days together in Turkey or Switzerland or Paris but the result would be the same, more wild publicity . . .

To you, as always, my sincere friendship, and every good wish for your health and happiness.

Good luck and good-bye.

Bullitt

The debts owed by foreign governments to the United States in the summer of 1933 were as follows:

	Principal	*Interest*
France	3,900,000,000	77,000,000
Great Britain	4,500,000,000	197,000,000
Italy	2,000,000,000	2,750,000
Russia	337,000,000	144,000,000

Sir Ronald Lindsay, British Ambassador to the United States, on January 30, 1933, reported to the Foreign Office: "Mr. Roosevelt mentioned Bullitt to me incidentally. He said he had known him in the past years and saw him sometime ago. Learning he was going to Europe and knew the Prime Minister he had said to him he would be glad to hear anything he could find out about the situation but Bullitt was in no way his representative. He showed that he knew precisely what Bullitt's movements are. Roosevelt seemed rather shamefaced. I imagine he is in an equivocal position." [8]

Personal and Confidential   1811 Walnut Street
                                                     Philadelphia, Pa.
                                                     [Undated]

Dear Ramsay:

I promise you that if you were "very desirous indeed" of another talk with me, I was even more anxious to have another talk with you. And I wish that I could be with you today at Chequers. Since I can not be, I shall try to let you know by this letter how the land lies.

You will already have heard from Lindsay that his exposé of the point of view of the British Government produced an exceedingly bad impression. There is not the slightest chance of progress if your Government adheres to that point of view. You will remember that I warned you that while Roosevelt desired the closest collaboration with England he would insist on a true cooperation and would never accept a collaboration similar to the collaboration between the automobile and the chauffeur — with England in the driver's seat. If any one of your associates believes that the United States can be forced to accept such a role, he is mistaken. The end of the road Lindsay outlined is not acquiescence by the United States but default by Great Britain. The consequences are not pleasant to contemplate. But we are convinced that in the long run we should be able to bear them better than you could . . .

I write you this letter, dear Ramsay, with the utmost seriousness. You will agree, I think, that in all the years we have known each other I have never misled you. I am not misleading you now. Roosevelt has gone to the limit of possibility. He desires the most intimate collaboration between England and the United States in all the fields of world affairs. It is now for England to say whether or not she desires to collaborate with the United States.

Every good wish to you and strength for the fight.

                              Yours always sincerely and affectionately,
                                                     William C. Bullitt

William C. Bullitt, Esq.   104 East 65th Street
Yale Club   New York City
New York   Feb. 23, 1933

Dear Bill:

I have your letter asking whether I thought the recent publicity regarding your trip to Europe would make your appointment as Ambassador to Paris inadvisable.

On the contrary I believe it would be helpful rather than otherwise for the reason that it shows the American public how wide your acquaintance is in Europe, and how many of the leading statesmen who are now in power are your friends.

I am sure the Governor would find it a comfort at this time to have a loyal friend like you at such an important post. You are in sympathy with his plans and will know better than anyone how best to carry them out.

Affectionately yours,
Edward M. House

Personal and Confidential   15 Dupont Circle
4 March 1933

Dear Mr. President:

. . . I know how occupied you are by the domestic situation and I am sorry to have to call to your attention a question of foreign relations. I have refrained from doing so for the past two days but I feel that it is my duty to let you know without further delay that Claudel on March 2nd and 3rd communicated to me verbally a most important project for working out the problems of the Economic Conference, Debts, etc. (I at once reported to Secretary Hull.)

Briefly, Claudel proposed that you should summon the Economic Conference to Washington not later than April 15th, and that you should announce in your summons that debts would be discussed at the same time as the questions on the agenda of the Economic Conference. He promised that if you should do so, *France would make the December 15th payment at once.* He expressed absolute conviction that the Conference would be a success and that agreement could be reached on all fundamentals before June 15th, although he thought that a brief moratorium (6 months perhaps) might be needed as bait to obtain conclusion of the matter. He pointed out in great detail how the British might be isolated and forced to agreement, and asked me if possible to arrange for him to see you Monday or Tuesday.

I should add that Claudel presented the project as his own. But it seemed to me that it was in reality an official proposal of the French Government presented in this manner in order that the French Government might be free to assure the British that France had made no official proposal to me. The following facts convince me of this: Claudel said that the French Government would *certainly approve* of the project. He kept glancing at cables on his desk while he made his proposals. It was on his own initiative, not mine, that he sent for me three times in two days and talked for hours most insistently. Moreover, he proposed, when I was lunching with him on March 3rd, that I should at once use the transatlantic phone to talk with Léger, the new permanent director of the Quai d'Orsay, and ask any questions I felt were necessary for a clarification of the proposals. He added that Léger was ready to answer on the phone any question I personally might ask, including the question of the meaning of Daladier's impending visit to MacDonald. (As to this, I replied that I could not take the responsibility of phoning Léger without specific orders from you, since I did not know whether or not I should have any post in your administration and could not create the impression in France that I was acting as a future member of the government.)

Shall you have time to see Claudel on Monday or Tuesday? Would you care to have me give you a summary of his arguments before you see him? It took him about six hours to present them to me; but I think you could get everything essential out of him in about thirty minutes, if we should first spend ten minutes preparing the matter. If you should wish to discuss the matter with me, I shall of course be at your disposal at any time, day or night.

My heartiest congratulations and every good wish to you.

Yours respectfully and devotedly,

William C. Bullitt

On April 19, 1933, the President announced to the press that the United States had gone off the gold standard as a measure to counteract the severe deflation which had increased since his inauguration.

Harold Ickes in his diary gives an account of the decision to abandon the gold standard: "One night Bullitt was at the White House and found the President in the long corridor on the second floor . . . He asked Bullitt what he thought ought to be done and Bullitt said that we ought to go off gold. Then Senator Key Pittman came in and his opinion was asked. He said, 'Go off gold.' Raymond Moley was the third who came in and gave the same advice. There followed Secretary of the Treasury Woodin and the President waved cheerfully at him and said, 'Hello, Will, we have just gone off gold.' Woodin, taken aback, said: 'Have we?' " 9

Not long after this I spent the evening with Bill, Francis Biddle (later to be attorney general), and three or four others, one of whom I did not know. They were praising this act and I became more and more annoyed, especially in view of Roosevelt's campaign talks on maintaining the value of the dollar. I finally went around the circle, starting with Bill, whom I told that he had no right to an opinion as he had never even been able to balance his checkbook. Francis Biddle received similar treatment, but when I reached the stranger I was gloriously defeated. I said, "As for you, sir, if you only read the newspapers you would know how wrong you are." It was Henry Luce, publisher of *Time* and *Life*.

3

Assistant to Secretary of State

1933

London Economic Conference
Negotiations for Recognition of Russia

ON APRIL 20, Bullitt was formally appointed a Special Assistant to the Secretary of State. His first assignment was to prepare for the World Monetary and Economic Conference, which was to convene in London in June. In late April preliminary talks with Ramsay MacDonald, the British Prime Minister, took place in Washington. These meetings continued the conversations which Bullitt had had with him in the preceding months in England. When the conference met in London, Bullitt acted as Executive Officer of the American delegation. From the outset Mr. Cordell Hull experienced difficulties and said that "the strain of trying to build something at the conference with inadequate materials was wearing me down." Added to his difficulties were the actions of Raymond Moley, whom the President sent to act as liaison with Washington.

Mr. Hull was extremely sensitive about the publicity attendant on Moley's arrival, the press intimating that he had proved incapable of handling the situation.

CLARIDGE'S HOTEL

Personal and Confidential   London
To Be Destroyed after Reading   June 13, 1933

Dear Mr. President:

I was sure that you would understand the urgency of the cable which Cox and I sent you in our ultra-confidential code on June eleventh. Your return cable to Hull was perfect and arrived just in time to ease a situation which had become critical. The Secretary was in a condition which can only be described as "complete collapse" and had written his immediate resignation to be telegraphed to you. I have rarely seen a man more broken up, and his condition was reflected in that of Mrs. Hull, who literally wept all night. I did what I could to soothe the Secretary and told him that I was going to cable you on my own responsibility. I hope you will not mind my taking similar action in the future if the situation should again become critical in this way or in some other. Your cable to the Secretary eased the tension and put him for the moment, at least, in a more cheerful state of mind. I think he will go forward now like a good soldier . . .

Every good wish to you and apologies for transmitting this sort of news. I feel as obliged to let you know completely everything that is going on with the same frankness that I should if we were together in Washington. Good luck to you and a good holiday.

Yours devotedly,
William C. Bullitt

Moley's private conversations came to a head when he cabled the President an agreement he had negotiated for the stabilization of currencies. This the President vigorously rejected.

Hull was also having his troubles with MacDonald, who called him aside one day and "spoke to me like a schoolmaster lecturing his pupil. 'Do you know,' he said, 'that it is not customary to issue press statements at a conference like this? It just isn't done.' I retorted, 'It's no more unusual than for the chief of another delegation to go over my head and follow after and confer directly with a subordinate [Moley] of mine.' " [1]

Very Private and Confidential   10 Downing Street
Whitehall
July 10th, 1933

Dear Mr. Bullitt:

The Prime Minister has asked me to pass on to you, quite unofficially, a hint that these manifestos which are being issued from American sources about the work of the Conference are doing everybody concerned a good deal of harm. I am to add that when we are in a Conference in Europe we do not issue manifestos; we put our

ideas before the Conference, and that if the manifesto idea were to
be begun at international conferences no negotiation would be possible at all. The Prime Minister has had various representations
from important delegates on the subject and he has done his best to
smooth things down. He knows that the matter is a subject of considerable resentment in private talk.

Yours very sincerely,
Rose Rosenberg
(Secretary to the Prime Minister)

Claridge's
London
July 8, 1933

The President
The White House

Dear Mr. President:

  . . . On Tuesday morning, July 4, MacDonald had agreed with
the gold countries that the Conference should be adjourned, leaving
some sort of an undefined committee or committees behind and that
you should be blamed for the abandonment of the Conference.
MacDonald had promised to put through this dissolution at the
Bureau meeting scheduled for six o'clock. When we got wind of the
project, Hull sent me out to persuade MacDonald to adjourn the
Bureau meeting until the following day. I argued with the Prime
Minister for an hour, but could not budge him and the only way of
saving the situation was for Hull to intervene at the outset of the
Bureau meeting.

  As usual, I went with Hull to the Bureau meeting and had the
satisfaction of seeing him do a beautiful piece of work. The French,
and indeed all the gold standard countries, came in roaring for
blood. MacDonald opened the meeting with a speech that pinned
responsibility for the breakdown of the Conference on your message
and then read the proposals for adjournment of the Conference.

  Hull got up at once and asked MacDonald a series of questions in
regard to the actual situation and future work of the Conference.
MacDonald, being unable to answer any of the questions which
Hull had asked him, hemmed and hawed and even giggled a little
in his embarrassment, and sat down after showing clearly that he
was completely confused — which was just what Hull had intended.

  The Secretary rose again and with great dignity pointed out that
to take responsibility for the adjournment of a conference which
had been called to relieve the sufferings of the world was unjusti-
able, unless the actual situation and future plans were entirely clear.

He said that, of course, the other representatives in the Bureau were much less well-informed than the Prime Minister himself, the President of the Conference, and since the Prime Minister's mind seemed entirely unclear it must be realized that the minds of all the other Delegates were even more unclear and it was essential that time should be taken for consideration of the whole matter. He concluded by suggesting that the Bureau should adjourn without further debate until the following day.

The Secretary's speech made a deep impression on everyone present. Bonnet became bright purple with rage and Jung was scarlet, and it was clear that the Secretary had carried the majority of the Bureau with him. Chamberlain and Bennett supported the Secretary strongly and in spite of the speeches of Bonnet and Jung, the meeting of the Bureau was adjourned until Thursday.

At the Thursday meeting of the Bureau, the Secretary again got to his feet at the first moment and made a really fine simple address on the need for continuing the Conference. We had, of course, received your telegrams, saying you wanted the Conference to go on, and had lined up all the nations we could for continuance. Ishii followed Hull in support of our position and Bennett, Chamberlain and the Swedish Minister of Finance and a Chinese representative all made strong speeches supporting Hull. The gold countries and Spain were solid in opposition. Bonnet finally threatened flatly to leave the Conference at once and MacDonald appointed a committee of six to attempt to reconcile the difficulty: Hull, Chamberlain and Bennett on our side; Bonnet, Jung and Colijn, the Dutch Prime Minister, on the other. I went with Hull and we had an extremely stiff three-hour fight before we obtained the agreement to continue, with which you are already familiar. The Secretary's sincerity and distinction of character have at last begun to impress everyone impressionable. Bonnet is, of course, beyond reach. He is as cooperative as a rattlesnake . . .

I am more than ever convinced that we can do little in Europe and should keep out of European squabbles and that our future lies in the Americas and the Far East.

Apologies for the length of this letter and every good wish.

> Yours devotedly,
> William C. Bullitt

The conference continued to limp along for another three weeks and on July 27 Hull delivered his closing address. Although the conference had not succeeded, Hull told the delegates, "There are after all only two ways of reaching international agreement. One is by imposing one's will by force — by war. The other is by persuasion — by conference . . . We cannot falter. We will not quit. We have begun and we will go on." [2]

During the remainder of the summer Bullitt worked on the various questions involved in the recognition of Russia. The question of the relations between the United States and Soviet Russia now became of increasing importance. After the American Revolution, Catherine the Great of Russia was fearful of the effect that Republicanism might have on her country and was hesitant in granting recognition. Once relations were established, however, they were cordial during the nineteenth century. At the time of the Russo-Japanese War in 1904 many Americans became concerned over a possible conflict of interest in the Far East. After the Bolshevik Revolution in 1917 the shoe was on the other foot, and Americans were loath to recognize the new Communist government. In addition to the ideological differences objections were raised not only to the confiscation of American property and the failure of the new government to recognize Russia's debts, but also to the lack of freedom of religion.

Russia pressed for recognition and some Americans favored it, both because of potential trade and also on account of the rising power of Japan. President Roosevelt believed that an attempt should be made to normalize relations between the two great countries and so advised the State Department.

On this question Bullitt assisted Judge Moore, who was advising Secretary of State Hull on the most important points to be covered. Secretary Hull in his *Memoirs* said: "In some respects we stood to gain more than Russia by a restoration of diplomatic relations. Without relations, the Russians were probably much better informed about conditions in America than we were about the situation in Russia . . . Moreover, it was easier for Russians to do business in the United States without diplomatic protection than it was for Americans to do business in Russia . . . William C. Bullitt, an intimate friend of the President and my special assistant, was in close touch with the Soviet representatives here. A brilliant person, well versed in international affairs, he was particularly friendly toward Russia and was an ardent proponent of recognition. He so expressed himself to the President and to me." [3]

Germany, as a condition of the Locarno pact, had joined the League of Nations, but in October 1933 Hitler withdrew from the League and the disarmament conference which was then taking place.

Secretary Hull now instructed Judge Moore and Bullitt to each prepare a memorandum on the terms under which the United States might consider the recognition of the Russian government. In the following memorandum Bullitt gives his views.

Memorandum for the Secretary October 4, 1933

Dear Mr. Secretary:

Pursuant to our conversation of this afternoon:

Whatever method may be used to enter into negotiations with the Soviet Government, it seems essential that formal recognition should not be accorded except as the final act of an agreement covering a number of questions in dispute. Before recognition and before loans, we shall find the Soviet Government relatively amenable. After recognition or loans, we should find the Soviet Government adamant. Among the chief agreements which, in my opinion, must be reached before recognition are the following:

1. Prohibition of communist propaganda in the United States by the Soviet Government and by the Comintern.

2. Protection of the civil and religious rights of Americans in Russia which are inadequately protected under current Russian practice (e.g. "economic espionage").

3. Agreement by the Soviet Government that the act of recognition shall not be retroactive to the foundation of that government (which is the usual practice), but shall take effect only from the day on which it may be accorded. This is essential to protect both our Government and many citizens and corporations from suits for damages.

By negotiation before recognition, we should also attempt to obtain an agreement in regard to the repayment of the loans of the Government of the United States to the Kerensky Government, a waiver of Russian counter claims based upon our Vladivostok, Archangel and Murmansk expeditions; also some sort of provision for the settlement of claims of American nationals and corporations for property, goods and cash seized by the Soviet Government.

There are of course scores of other questions involved in resuming normal relations with Russia. Our position would be strongest, I believe, if all these questions, whether of a legal, economic or financial nature, should be handled as a unit in one global negotiation, the end of which would be signature of the agreements and simultaneous recognition.

Yours very respectfully,
William C. Bullitt

The negotiations with the Russians began October 11, 1933, and were conducted in an extremely cautious and arms-length manner with Skvirsky (representative of Amtorg, the Russian trade organization in America). Bullitt kept careful notes of these meetings, realizing the importance of a full record of any dealings with Russia.

THE WHITE HOUSE
WASHINGTON

Confidential   October 10, 1933
Memorandum from the President
For the Secretary of State

I have your suggested draft and I have made a sort of combination of yours and mine, which I think now covers the whole subject.

If you approve will you O.K. the procedure we discussed. Bullitt would go to Morgenthau's office and there show to the gentleman in question an unsigned carbon copy of this draft, with the request that in complete confidence a suggested draft of reply be received from the gentleman's headquarters. On receipt of this, if it is satisfactory, the formal letter or telegram would go forward over my name.

FDR

H. M., Jr., goes away Wed. noon. [Handwritten.]

THE WHITE HOUSE
WASHINGTON

October 10, 1933

My dear Mr. President:

Since the beginning of my Administration, I have contemplated the desirability of an effort to end the present abnormal relations between the hundred and twenty-five million people of the United States and the hundred and sixty million people of Russia.

It is most regrettable that these great peoples, between whom a happy tradition of friendship existed for more than a century to their mutual advantage, should now be without a practical method of communicating directly with each other.

The difficulties that have created this anomalous situation are serious but not, in my opinion, insoluble; and difficulties between great nations can be removed only by frank, friendly conversations. If you are of similar mind, I should be glad to receive any representatives you may designate to explore with me personally all questions outstanding between our countries.

Participation in such a discussion would, of course, not commit either nation to any future course of action, but would indicate a sincere desire to reach a satisfactory solution of the problems involved. It is my hope that such conversations might result in good to the people of both our countries.

I am, my dear Mr. President,

> Very sincerely yours,
> Franklin D. Roosevelt

Mr. Mikhail Kalinin
President of the All Union Central Executive Committee
Moscow

> Moscow
> October 17th, 1933

My dear Mr. President:

I have received your message of October tenth.

I have always considered most abnormal and regrettable a situation wherein, during the past sixteen years, two great republics — the United States of America and the Union of Soviet Socialist Republics — have lacked the usual methods of communication and have been deprived of the benefits which such communication could give. I am glad to note that you also reached the same conclusion.

There is no doubt that difficulties, present or arising, between two countries, can be solved only when direct relations exist between them; and that, on the other hand, they have no chance for solution in the absence of such relations. I shall take the liberty further to express the opinion that the abnormal situation, to which you correctly refer in your message, has an unfavorable effect not only on the interests of the two states concerned, but also on the general international situation, increasing the element of disquiet, complicating the process of consolidating world peace and encouraging forces tending to disturb that peace.

In accordance with the above, I gladly accept your proposal to send to the United States a representative of the Soviet Government to discuss with you the questions of interest to our countries. The Soviet Government will be represented by Mr. M. M. Litvinov, People's Commissar for Foreign Affairs, who will come to Washington at a time to be mutually agreed upon.

I am, my dear Mr. President,

Very sincerely yours,
Mikhail Kalinin

Mr. Franklin D. Roosevelt
President of the United States of America
Washington, D.C.

DEPARTMENT OF STATE
THE SECRETARY

Confidential   October 11, 1933
Memorandum for the Secretary

Dear Mr. Secretary:

In accordance with instructions received from yourself and the President, I went to Mr. Henry Morgenthau, Junior's office this morning at 10:35. Mr. Morgenthau introduced me to Mr. Boris E. Skvirsky and I delivered to him an unsigned carbon copy of the draft letter. Before giving the copy to Mr. Skvirsky, I had the following understanding with him:

1. That there should be absolutely no publicity of any sort in regard to this matter.

2. That in case the reply should not be satisfactory, the copy I had handed him should be burned up or buried in the Soviet archives.

3. That he should transmit the text by his most private code to Moscow and should obtain a draft of reply to be communicated to me as soon as received.

4. That on receipt of a satisfactory reply he would receive a signed original of the copy.

5. That no publicity whatever should be given to the proceedings by the Soviet Government, but that the President should control the

time and form of any publicity, and that he would inform the Soviet Government as to the hour of any announcement in the United States.

Mr. Skvirsky was obviously much moved by the text of the copy, read it extremely slowly, and, after collecting himself, said:

"This, if I understand it correctly, means preliminary negotiations and not recognition."

I replied: "That is precisely what it means."

He said: "You know that my Government has several times refused to enter into preliminary negotiations."

I told him I was aware of that. He said that his Government had insisted invariably on direct conversations following recognition. I replied that conversations could not be more direct than between representatives of the Soviet Government and the President himself; that such negotiations must precede any further steps. Mr. Skvirsky promised to send the text of the copy at once and said that he hoped to have a reply by Friday.

Yours very respectfully,
William C. Bullitt

Read and approved by the Secretary — Oct. 11, 12:45 P.M.

DEPARTMENT OF STATE
THE SECRETARY

Confidential
Memorandum of Conversation with Mr. Boris E. Skvirsky
Sunday, October 15, 1933, at 7:45 P. M.

Mr. Skvirsky called at my apartment and said that he had received a cable from Litvinov saying "Draft letter entirely acceptable." He asked me if we desired any further communication before handing him the formal letter. I replied that it had been clearly understood that he should hand us a draft reply before he received our formal letter and that he would not receive our formal letter until such a reply had been received and approved by the President. He said he quite understood that that had been our agreement in the first place and he would cable Litvinov at once not to be so sparing of words, but to send him a draft of the Soviet reply. He said he hoped to have it by Tuesday . . .

Mr. Skvirsky asked me for my opinion in regard to what representatives the Soviet Government should send over. I told him that I thought it would be most improper for me to express any opinion as

to such representation. He then volunteered the information that
he thought Litvinov himself would probably come. He left at about
eight o'clock to cable to Moscow.

I communicated the above information to the President at 9:55,
Sunday night, to the Secretary, the Under Secretary, and to Judge
Moore on Monday.

W.C.B.
William C. Bullitt

DEPARTMENT OF STATE
THE SECRETARY

Memorandum for the Secretary   October 19, 1933

My dear Mr. Secretary:

I saw Mr. Skvirsky yesterday afternoon at five o'clock. He said
that "direct relations" was a closer translation of the Russian text he
had received than "regular relations," and that he could therefore
make the alteration to "direct relations" without further communication with his Government. He handed me a new text with "direct
relations" replacing "regular relations," which I took to the President. The President considered that the phrase "direct relations"
was satisfactory, signed the original of his message to Kalinin and directed me to deliver it to Skvirsky. I delivered it to Skvirsky at 8
P.M., and received from him a signed text and a covering note.

The President asked me to keep all these papers and to deliver
them to him personally at the White House at two o'clock Friday afternoon. The President said that he would announce the exchange
of letters at his regular press conference at four o'clock, Friday afternoon, October 20, and would make it clear to the newspapermen
that this was not recognition and would request them to see to it
that their stories should give no basis for headlines involving the
word "recognition."

Yours very respectfully,
William C. Bullitt

DEPARTMENT OF STATE
THE SECRETARY

Memorandum for the Secretary   October 24, 1933

My dear Mr. Secretary:

Mr. Skvirsky called at my apartment early this morning and informed me that Litvinov would be accompanied by only two per-

sons: Ivan Divilkovsky, his personal secretary, and Konstantin Umansky of the Press Department of the Soviet Foreign Office. Mr. Skvirsky said that Litvinov had not yet decided which boat to take, but expected to arrive on Monday, November 6 . . .

Mr. Skvirsky then said that he felt it would be extremely undesirably if any demonstration of either "White Russians" or Communists should take place on Litvinov's arrival. He said that he felt sure the Communists would not organize a demonstration, but he was disturbed about the "White Russians" and asked if it would be agreeable to our Government if Mr. Litvinov should be taken off his steamer by a cutter at Quarantine, which would land him at the Baltimore & Ohio station in Jersey City. I told him that this idea seemed sensible to me and that I would take up the matter at once. Mr. Skvirsky added that the Soviet Government would wish to hire a private car to bring Mr. Litvinov to Washington and I told him that this matter could be discussed later and arrangements made privately, so that a demonstration might not take place in Jersey City. Mr. Skvirsky asked me if I could let him have a reply to these questions today, as Mr. Litvinov expects to leave Moscow on Thursday.

Yours very respectfully,
William C. Bullitt

DEPARTMENT OF STATE
ASSISTANT SECRETARY

November 10, 1933

Memorandum as to the Russian Conversations

When the conversations between Secretary Hull and Mr. Litvinov began last Thursday it was fairly apparent from the start that the latter's idea of establishing normal relations is to obtain unconditional recognition, and then an effort to follow to remove all serious difficulties by negotiations. He did not seem to have in mind the possibility that our Government, warned by what has occurred in the cases of other governments, and responsive to an American public demand, would require pledges concurrent with and as a basis or condition of recognition . . .

On Friday the discussion was more specific. We stressed the importance of protection being afforded our nationals relative to the profession and practice of their religion, and likewise the importance of safeguards being provided against propaganda and also the importance of a definition of what constitutes economic espionage, and there was mention of the importance of assuring just treatment of our nationals who may be charged with the commission of crime. We, of course, have all along been convinced that we should receive satisfactory agreements not simply in the way of telling us what is the Soviet law, with which we are tolerably familiar, but which will go beyond that law, it being conceded by Mr. Litvinov that there are quick processes by which this can be done if the Soviet Government is willing to do it. But he was insistent that he is not prepared to promise any protective measures in addition to those afforded by the present law, the interpretation and administration of which he admits are dependent upon the conceptions of individual courts and officials. Running through his talk was the idea above stated that recognition should be granted outright and then our nationals must be content with the rights and liabilities fixed by existing law. He urged that the fact that we would be officially represented in Russia would go far in guaranteeing proper treatment.

1. *As to religion.* He in effect rejected our agreement proposal by amending it so as to conform to the present Soviet law and of this the President has been fully advised.

2. *As to propaganda.* He was very resolute in declining to make any agreement that would place the Soviet Government under the responsibility of limiting the activities of the Third International and at the same time he did not hesitate to say that it is the purpose of that organization to affect conditions in other countries including the United States.

3. *As to espionage.* When he was reminded that under the present Soviet law regulations may be issued and not known to our nationals, the violation of which may constitute a crime, he admitted that such is the case, but was unwilling to enter into any agreement to protect our nationals against being penalized for violating regulations which may never have been brought to their attention.

4. *As to crimes.* He, of course, was compelled to admit that the Soviet law places persons charged with crime in a more uncertain and precarious situation than English and American law and that it is possible summarily to punish an alleged offender without trial even by shooting him, but he said that the fact that American nationals had not been severely dealt with heretofore is sufficient indication, without any change in the law that they will not be thus dealt with hereafter.

He was explicitly asked whether it is his position that in case recognition is granted our government and our nationals will have nothing on which to rely except the Soviet law as it is and as it may become and that he can not add to or detract from that law by any agreements and this question he answered categorically in the affirmative . . .

Incidentally it may be noted that where a condition connected with recognition is broken the act of recognition is not revoked but the same end is reached by withdrawing the official representatives from the government that is in default.

R. Walton Moore

Confidential   [Undated.]
W. Bullitt
Please speak to me about this. FDR

Recognition will inevitably bring sincere charges that the United States Government is making friends with a government avowedly an enemy of God and a persecutor of religion.

Man has a right to worship God according to the dictates of his conscience. The truth of this principle has been recognized throughout the history of our country, in its laws and traditions.

For these reasons, it is suggested that the following points be contended for:

1. Freedom of conscience be guaranteed in Russia for all Russian citizens and foreigners.

2. The free exercise, both public and private, of religion and worship be guaranteed. This agrees with the declaration made by the Russian delegate Chicherin at the International Economic Conference, held at Genoa, April–May, 1922.

3. Liberation be given to those imprisoned on account of religion.

4. Consequently, that there be a cessation of persecution and propaganda against God in Russia and elsewhere, and that freedom be given to ministers of religion to exercise their ministry in Russia.

A promise from the Soviet Government, in writing, would be the surest guarantee that the above mentioned points would be allowed and observed. It would be highly desirable to obtain such a promise prior to negotiations for recognition.

THE WHITE HOUSE
WASHINGTON

Memo for W.B.

As I have tried to make very clear:

1. My original letter said "discussion to reach a satisfactory solution of the *problems* involved" also "all questions outstanding between our countries."

2. That certain questions which I have at great length explained to Mr. Litvinov *must* be so clearly stated that the announcement will satisfy at least a majority of our people.

These are:

1. *Assurances* against propaganda.

2. *Assurances* for freedom of worship by Americans in Russia including right to have their own clergy.

3. Assurances for public trial and notice of arrest.

4. As to debts, claims and counterclaims. These are clearly one of the "outstanding questions" in regard to which a "satisfactory solution" must be reached. A mere agreement to discuss them in the future does not fulfill this.

All this is so clear that I honestly think that Mr. Litvinov should come to an agreement, especially in view of the excellent corroborating reply from M. Kalinin.

Yours,

[A handwritten memo.]   Franklin D. Roosevelt

DEPARTMENT OF STATE

WASHINGTON

November 15, 1933

My dear Mr. President:

Litvinov and I continued to argue for two hours on the subject of debts and claims. I finally managed to shake him a bit by telling him that the Johnson Bill, forbidding loans to countries in default on their indebtedness to the Government of the United States, was certain to be passed in January and that if the Soviet Government should make any absurd offer of settlement such an offer would surely be turned down by Congress and the Soviet Government would be unable to obtain one penny of credit from either the Government or any private corporation or individual in the United States, or their agencies abroad.

I urged Litvinov not to fix the lower figure at $50,000,000, as his Government would surely insist that that should be accepted as the maximum figure once the sum had been stated. He finally asked, "What sum would you consider might be acceptable to Congress?" and added, "You will, of course, say $150,000,000." I replied, "No, I will say nothing. I cannot predict what Congress will do, but the President can predict very exactly what Congress will do, and you should address that question to him."

Litvinov proposes to ask you that question when you meet at 2 o'clock.

Litvinov added that he would say to you that he had entire confidence in your fair-mindedness, and he was sure that when you looked at the facts about our loan to the Kerensky Government and found that the money had been spent for the most part by Bakhmetieff buying supplies for Kolchak's army, you would agree that the Soviet Government should not be obliged to assume liability for money used by its enemies.

The fact is that two-thirds of this Kerensky loan was telegraphed at once to Kerensky's Government and used fighting the Germans.

Litvinov added that the private claims had been so padded that $50,000,000 he considered would be a fair settlement of all claims and debts. This is, of course, absurd, and I think you should endeavor forcibly to get him to fix at least $100,000,000 as the lower limit . . .

I shall stop at your office at ten minutes before two, in case you should wish to draw up a final plan of campaign.

Yours devotedly,
William C. Bullitt
Special Assistant to the Secretary
P.S. I think we were a bit too gentle with him this morning.
W.C.B.

As a result of the meeting with the President on November 15, Litvinov wrote a letter the following day giving the Russian promises if recognition was accorded by the United States. The statements were definite and left no room for doubt as to what the Soviet's future actions would be vis-à-vis the United States.

Washington
November 16, 1933

My Dear Mr. President:

I have the honor to inform you that coincident with the establishment of diplomatic relations between our two Governments it will be the fixed policy of the Government of the Union of Soviet Socialist Republics:

1. To respect scrupulously the indisputable right of the United States to order its own life within its own jurisdiction in its own way and to refrain from interfering in any manner in the internal affairs of the United States, its territories or possessions.

2. To refrain, and to restrain all persons in government service

and all organizations of the Government or under its direct or indirect control, including organizations in receipt of any financial assistance from it, from any act overt or covert liable in any way whatsoever to injure the tranquillity, prosperity, order, or security of the whole or any part of the United States, its territories or possessions, and, in particular, from any act tending to incite or encourage armed intervention, or any agitation or propaganda having as an aim, the violation of the territorial integrity of the United States, its territories or possessions, or the bringing about by force of a change in the political or social order of the whole or any part of the United States, its territories or possessions.

3. Not to permit the formation or residence on its territory of any organization or group — and to prevent the activity on its territory of any organization or group , or of representatives or officials of any organization or group — which makes claim to be the Government of, or makes attempt upon the territorial integrity of, the United States, its territories or possessions; not to form, subsidize, support or permit on its territory military organizations or groups having the aim of armed struggle against the United States, its territories or possessions, and to prevent any recruiting on behalf of such organizations and groups.

4. Not to permit the formation or residence on its territory of any organization or group — and to prevent the activity on its territory of any organization or group, or of representatives or officials of any organization or group — which has as an aim the overthrow or the preparation for the overthrow of, or the bringing about by force of a change in, the political or social order of the whole or any part of the United States, its territories or possessions.

I am, my dear Mr. President,

Very sincerely yours,
Maxim Litvinov
People's Commissar for Foreign Affairs
Union of Soviet Socialist Republics

On receipt of this letter Mr. Roosevelt wrote to Litvinov on the same day with regard to religious freedom. Litvinov immediately delivered a lengthy reply stating that the Soviet Union would accord to the nationals of the United States:

1. The right to "free exercise of liberty of conscience and religious worship" and protection "from all disability or persecution on account of their religious faith or worship."

2. The right to "conduct without annoyance or molestation of any kind religious services and rites of a ceremonial nature."

3. "The right and opportunity to lease, erect or maintain in convenient situations" churches, houses or other buildings appropriate for religious purposes.

4. "The right to collect from their co-religionists . . . voluntary offerings for religious purposes."

5. Right to "impart religious instruction to their children either singly or in groups or to have such instruction imparted by persons whom they may employ for such purpose.

"Nationals of the United States shall be granted rights with reference to freedom of conscience and the free exercise of religion which shall not be less favorable than those enjoyed in the Union of Soviet Socialist Republics by nationals of the nation most favored in this respect."

In further letters, all dated November 16, 1933, Litvinov wrote to the President giving assurances that Americans would have the same legal rights as the nationals of the most favored nation; agreement on the part of Russia that until a final settlement was made, not to enforce any decisions of courts for amounts due or claimed against American nationals or corporations; agreement to waive all claims arising out of the activities of United States military forces in Siberia after January 1, 1918.

At the conclusion of this correspondence the following was given to the press.

THE WHITE HOUSE
WASHINGTON

November 16, 1933

Joint Statement by the President and Mr. Litvinov

In addition to the agreements which we have signed today, there has taken place an exchange of views with regard to methods of settling all outstanding questions of indebtedness and claims that permits us to hope for a speedy and satisfactory solution of these questions which both our Governments desire to have out of the way as soon as possible.

Mr. Litvinov will remain in Washington for several days for further discussions.

THE WHITE HOUSE

WASHINGTON

November 15, 1933

2:45 P.M.

Mr. Litvinov, at a meeting with the President, the Acting Secretary of the Treasury, and Mr. Bullitt, made a "gentleman's agreement" with the President that over and above all claims of the Soviet Government and its nationals against the Government of the United States and its nationals, the Soviet Government will pay to the Government of the United States on account of the Kerensky debt or otherwise a sum to be not less than $75,000,000 in the form of a percentage above the ordinary rate of interest on a loan to be granted to it by the Government of the United States or its nationals, all other claims of the Government of the Union of Soviet Socialist Republics or its nationals to be regarded as eliminated.

The President said that he believed confidentially that he could persuade Congress to accept a sum of $150,000,000, but that he feared that Congress would not accept any smaller sum. Mr. Litvinov then said that he could not on his own authority accept any such minimum, as his Government had already stated that it considered this sum excessive. Mr. Litvinov said that he had entire confidence in the fair-mindedness of the President and felt sure that when the President had looked into the facts he would not feel that a sum greater than $75,000,000 was justified. So far as he personally was concerned, and without making any commitment, he would be inclined to advise his Government to accept $100,000,000 if the President should still consider such a sum fair.

Mr. Litvinov agreed to remain in Washington after resumption of relations and to discuss with Mr. Morgenthau and Mr. Bullitt the exact sum between the limits of $75,000,000 and $150,000,000 to be paid by the Soviet Government.

FDR

Washington
November 22, 1933

My dear Mr. President:

On leaving the United States I feel it a great pleasure respectfully to convey to you my feelings of high esteem as well as gratitude for the many tokens of attention and friendship you have been good enough to show me during my stay in Washington.

I also wish hereby to thank the whole Executive and its various organs for their courtesies and cares.

I avail myself of this opportunity to express once more my firm conviction that the official linking of our two countries by the exchange of notes between you, Mr. President, and myself will be of great benefit to our two countries and will also be conducive to the strengthening and preservation of peace between nations towards which our countries are sincerely striving. I believe that their joint efforts will add a creative factor in international affairs which will be beneficial to mankind.

Believe me to be, my dear Mr. President, with the best wishes for the well being of yourself, your family and of your great country,

Yours very sincerely,
Maxim Litvinov
People's Commissar for Foreign Affairs
Union of Soviet Socialist Republics

TWO

The Moscow Embassy

1933–1936

4

Ambassador to the Soviet Union

NOVEMBER 1933

Russia Recognized
Bullitt Appointed Ambassador
Short Trip to Moscow
Dines with Stalin
Seeks an Embassy

WILLIAM PHILLIPS, then Under Secretary of State, has written the final story of recognition in these terms: "Following the Cabinet dinner and musicale on November 16, the President asked me to join him in his study. There a group which included Litvinov, Secretary of the Treasury Harry Woodin, Henry Morgenthau, Jr., William C. Bullitt and myself awaited the President. Secretary Hull had already left for a Pan American Conference in Montevideo. The President joined us at eleven o'clock and read the exchange of notes together with the various enclosures which had been agreed upon during the preceding days. Litvinov made a few objections that were finally overcome. Although the documents were dated November 16, actually the signing did not take place until fourteen minutes past one o'clock on the morning of the seventeenth. The President was elated and we all celebrated with quaffs of what was almost the last of prohibition beer. He detained me for a moment after the others had departed and asked my opinion of Bullitt, who was then a special assistant to Secretary Hull. He was friendly to the Russians and had been of great assistance in the negotiations. I praised his help and left the President with the impression that he would receive the appointment as Ambassador to Russia, which did occur a few days later." [1] Prior to his departure Secretary Hull had agreed with the President that Bullitt would be the first Ambassador to Soviet Russia.

On November 18 the newspapers carried the news of recognition of Soviet Russia and of Bullitt's appointment as Ambassador. Telephone communications with Russia over short-wave radio were inaugurated by Litvinov in a conversation with Moscow the same day. The headlines read: SOVIET PACT HELD BULLITT TRIUMPH. However, some members of the family did not feel the same way, and my father's brother, Archdeacon James F. Bullitt, was also given front-page coverage with: BULLITT'S UNCLE SAYS SOVIET DEAL DISGRACES UNITED STATES. He called the Soviet Union "a country which is beyond the pale — a pariah among nations," and added, "Russia will keep no promises with us."

One comment of a member of the staff of the British Foreign Office on this new appointment of Bullitt was: "I think Mr. Bullitt may do less harm in Moscow than in Washington, though he is the kind of man who does harm anywhere." [2] The British Ambassador in Washington reported: "He may be regarded as thoroughly untrustworthy, and completely unscrupulous where there is a question of taking his objective." [3]

Within two weeks Bullitt sailed for Russia.

Bullitt arrived in Russia on the eleventh of December, 1933, and on this, his first visit as Ambassador, he only remained until the twentieth. The correspondence with Roosevelt now begins in all its volume, and as many have written that Mr. Hull was often overlooked and not consulted, his own words should tell of this relationship. In his memoirs he says: "I am convinced that the President was completely frank with me . . . Several of our ambassadors, particularly Bullitt in Moscow and later Paris, Kennedy in London, and Davies in Moscow and later Brussels, who were old friends of his, had the habit of writing to him direct, over my head. While it is always inadvisable for ambassadors and ministers to carry on a correspondence with the President which includes discussion of important questions of policy — a fact I deprecated in my talks with Mr. Roosevelt — I do not recall any instance of any consequence in which the views and course of the State Department were seriously interfered with by the practice . . . Mr. Roosevelt never sought, so far as I am aware, to push upon me the views stated in their personal letters, save in some rare instances such as Bullitt's desire to remain in Paris when the French forces were evacuating it in 1940. Usually the President passed these letters on to me and also told me of any oral conversations he might have had with the ambassadors. Then, if I asked him a question, he was quick to respond on any point he had overlooked or possibly reserved." [4] The reader will again note that almost all telegrams to the President were routed through the State Department.

Wehle makes a comment on Roosevelt's relations with Hull which is revealing: "To him [Roosevelt] a moment of boredom was a desperate ordeal. He often preferred to consider foreign relations with Walton Moore, counselor of the State Department, or Sumner Wells or others who came to the point quickly, instead of with Cordell Hull, who had a rare quality of wisdom but was given to building up his case fact by fact and reason by reason. His mind was sure to range ahead of any slow speaker's." [5]

At this time there was great apprehension on the part of both Russia and China of an attack on the mainland by Japan. The Japanese, under control of the military party, had been strengthening their forces for some years. An undeclared war on China began in July 1937 and Japan carefully avoided going to war with Russia. Had they landed in 1933 at Vladivostok, on the east coast of Russia, they might have achieved the easy victory they obtained in the war of 1904.

Secretary of State	Paris
Washington	Dated December 24, 1933
Triple Priority	Rec'd 12:25 P.M. 25th
576, December 24, 7 P.M.	

Strictly Confidential for the President, the Acting Secretary and Assistant Secretary Moore from Bullitt

Owing to lack of codes in Moscow and the undesirability of sending this message from Berlin I have felt obliged to delay transmission until today.

Litvinov on Thursday December 21 asked me to convey to you in strictest confidence the following information.

He said that his Government was "under great pressure" from France to join the League of Nations and asked me if the Government of the United States would have any objection. I replied that as I had no codes I could not consult my Government in regard to this matter but that I had no hesitation in saying on my own behalf that I believed the Government of the United States would have no objection.

I then asked Litvinov to tell me the reason for this possible reversal of Soviet policy. He replied that the French had asked the Soviet Government to make a "regional agreement" for defense against attack by Germany, each party to declare war on Germany if Germany should declare war upon the other. He said that the Soviet Union considered an attack by Japan this Spring so probable that it felt it must secure its western frontier in every way; that he did not fear an immediate attack by either Poland or Germany but that if the probable war with Japan should drag on for two years he anticipated a joint attack by Poland and Germany, acting in concert with Japan. He added that he knew preliminary conversations looking forward to this eventuality had already taken place between Japan, Germany and Poland. Therefore the Soviet Government although still wishing to keep its hands free and not join the League of Nations felt that it must pay this price if necessary to obtain the agreement from France . . .

Attack by Japan upon the Soviet Union is regarded as certain by all members of the government and communist party with whom I talked in Moscow. Stalin introduced the chief of staff Egorov to me as "the man who will lead our army victoriously against the Japanese when they attack us" . . .

I repeatedly emphasized to all with whom I talked that the United States had no intention whatsoever of getting into war with Japan but that our participation in any Far Eastern difficulties would be confined to the use of our moral influence to maintain peace. Nevertheless the Soviet Union is so anxious to have peace that it is obvious that even our moral influence is valued very highly by the Soviet Government. It is difficult to exaggerate the cordiality with which I was received by all members of the Government including Kalinin, Molotov, Voroshilov and Stalin. Especially noteworthy is the fact that Stalin who until my arrival had never received any ambassador said to me "at any moment, day or night, if you wish to see me you have only to ask and I will see you at once."

[Note: Remainder of telegram pertains to housing, etc.]

Personal and Confidential   On board steamship *Washington*
January 1, 1934

My dear Mr. President:

In addition to the report of my trip to the Union of Soviet Socialist Republics which I shall submit to the Secretary of State, I should like to set down for your own eye some of the more intimate episodes.

Paris

We passed through Paris on December 8 and Herriot turned up unexpectedly at the railroad station to bid me good-bye. We walked the platform together for a half hour. Herriot asked me to convey to you his warmest personal wishes and to tell you that when he had been asked to become President du Conseil before the post was offered to Chautemps he had replied, "I will become President du Conseil on condition that you pay the defaulted installments of the debt to the United States and that you make arrangements immediately for a debt settlement." He added that he was determined never to become President du Conseil again until France was ready to meet her obligations. I asked him if that would not indefinitely postpone his return to power. He replied that much would depend on the attitude of the United States, that many of the leading politicians in France were most uneasy about the present situation, but that Daladier and others were able to argue that the United States had accepted the default without protest; that France was saving a considerable amount each year by not paying, and that nothing should be done unless it were shown that continued default would produce unpleasant consequences. I asked him what he advised. He said, "Tell the President that he must in some way show his disapproval of the French action and adopt some measures which will show France that she has something to lose by continuing her default." Herriot is supporting Chautemps and the Chautemps Cabinet looks more secure than it did when it was first formed.

Berlin

On my way through Berlin on December 9 I lunched with Dodd who asked me please not to take Flack permanently for the Embassy in Moscow, as he was the only person in the Embassy competent to deal with economic matters. I avoided seeing any officials of the German Government, but "Putzi" Hanfstaengl, Hitler's intimate assistant, called on me and talked in his customary irrational manner, saying among other things, "Of course you and I know that the Jews make all wars and are the sole beneficiaries of all wars." I disagreed. The most fantastic thing which has happened in Germany lately is the christening of the new military academy "Ernst Roehm Kadetten Erzieungs Anstalt." In view of the revelations about Roehm, the English equivalent would be the renaming of Sandhurst "Oscar Wilde Institute." *

U.S.S.R.

. . . We reached Moscow on Monday, December 11, where I was met at the station by Troyanovsky, Divilkovsky, Florinsky and a number of other officials. We were taken to the Hotel National, where the American flag was suspended over the entrance. The apartment reserved for me was the same which I was occupying with my mother when Austria sent her ultimatum to Serbia. [1914]

I had a long talk with Litvinov, then set out to look at houses . . .

The two houses which the Government offered us were (1) the Supreme Court Building, (2) the house of the Central Executive Committee.

The Supreme Court Building is a huge pile of medieval style which might do well for a jail or a German Embassy, but would produce deep gloom in any American and would require a half million dollars worth of repairs.

The house of the Central Executive Committee was constructed in 1914 by a merchant who traded vodka for furs. It is cheerful and only minor repairs are necessary to make it habitable, but it con-

---

* Ernst Roehm, a member of the Nazi party even before Hitler, had been one of Hitler's strongest supporters. He became head of the Brown Shirts, storm troopers. In the spring of 1934 there was increasing unrest in Germany against Hitler's actions. In June President Hindenburg told Hitler that unless the situation improved he would turn over the government to the Army. Hitler saw all his plans for power disappearing. In a hastily called meeting with Goering and Himmler they persuaded him — and it probably took little persuasion — that Roehm was the leader of a movement to unseat him. On June 30, 1934, after a stormy interview with Hitler, Roehm was arrested and immediately murdered on Hitler's orders.

The reference to Oscar Wilde is because Roehm was also a homosexual.

In this same purge Hitler killed the former Chancellor of Germany, General Schleicher, and his wife in their own home.

tains only five bedrooms and the living rooms are small with the exception of a colossal center hall. A new dining room is being built at one side of the house, so that temporarily there is no dining room. Nevertheless, this house is the best available. It is, of course, entirely inadequate to house our entire staff and offices.

I suggested that two small adjoining buildings should be given to us. On investigation we discovered that they were being occupied as living quarters by about 200 people, about eight to a room. That, it appears, is the normal congestion in Moscow at the moment. In 1914 Moscow was an overcrowded city of 1,250,000. There has been practically no building since and Moscow is today a city of nearly 4,000,000 . . .

It is, of course, impossible to keep codes in a hotel and until our joint office-building-residence is completed the code room and a number of auxiliary offices will have to be established in the house of the Central Executive Committee in which I shall live. As my family consists of Anne alone, I shall be glad to have living with me there temporarily some of the secretaries, keeping for myself only one room and one additional room. After May 1 it will probably prove best to have all the offices (except my own) and the code room located in the office-residence building.

On Wednesday, December 13, at noon, I presented my credentials to Kalinin at the Kremlin . . .

I had a delightful conversation with Kalinin after presenting my credentials. I had never met him and I had thought from all that I had read that he was a simple-minded old peasant, but he is far from simple-minded. He has a delightful shrewdness and sense of humor. He asked me to say to you that he was following with the closest attention everything that you were doing in America, and that he and everyone else in Russia considered you completely out of the class of the leaders of capitalist states; that it was clear to them all that you really cared about the welfare of the laboring men and the farmers and that you were not engaged in protecting the vested rights of property.

Kalinin said that he hoped that I would travel in every part of the Union of Soviet Socialist Republics, and I told him that I should be delighted to do so, but that the Union of Soviet Socialist Republics was a continent rather than a country and that I feared I should be restricted to Moscow and Leningrad unless I could cover it by airplane. He told me that I could go any place I might wish in the entire Union by plane. I replied that I should perhaps be able to arrange to have a plane of my own in Moscow for trips if he would permit me to use it without restrictions. He answered that there would be no restrictions whatever on my movements . . . Even the party press of the Communist Party which hitherto has been uniformly hostile to Ambassadors unearthed remarks of Lenin about me from his "Testament" and various speeches. Apparently he really liked me and expressed his liking many times. In view of Lenin's present position in Russia, which is not unlike that of Jesus Christ in the Christian church, this is a bit like having the personal endorsement of the Master recorded in St. Mark. Divilkovsky, for example, said to me, "You cannot understand it, but there is not one of us who would not gladly have his throat cut to have had such things said about him by Lenin" . . .

There was one [building site] which was not offered to us, but which we offered to ourselves: a bluff covered with beautiful woods containing a lake overlooking the river and the whole city of Moscow in the center of the great city park. It is a situation which suggests Monticello, and I can conceive of nothing more perfect for an American Embassy than a reproduction of Monticello in that setting with houses for the entire staff of both consulate and embassy arranged along the sides of the property. We were not modest in our demands, but asked for the entire bluff containing some fifteen acres of ground. The Moscow Soviet continued to offer us other building sites, any one of which would be adequate but none of which compared in interest or beauty to this site.

[There was considerable correspondence with the State Department about the new Embassy and its design, but nothing materialized.]

. . . That night Litvinov, with whom I had previously had several meals in private, gave me a formal dinner to which nearly all the members of the Government were present. It was a superb banquet with food and wines of a quality that no one in America would dare to serve nowadays, and many toasts were drunk to you and to me and to the United States . . .

It is unnecessary to record the whole series of dinners and conversations with the members of the Government that I had, but there are two, at least, which are worth noting:

On Tuesday, December 19, I had a long talk with Grinko, who is the People's Commissar for Finance, and arranged with him to handle the knotty problem of obtaining roubles in a manner which will be satisfactory to us. I am absolutely opposed to the smuggling of roubles in our diplomatic pouch . . . I am opposed to handling this matter of rouble exchange except in an honorable and above-board manner and I am sure that we can make a satisfactory arrangement with Grinko.

I sat next to Grinko at a number of dinners and banquets and managed to establish a friendly personal relationship with him which I think will be very helpful in the coming months. Incidentally, we agreed to enter into a personal competition with Litvinov as umpire. On the first day of June, 1934, we are to compete to see whether he speaks English better than I speak Russian, and I venture to suggest that a suitable prize for the winner would be a bronze mint medal with your own head on it, if one exists. I hope you will agree.

On Wednesday, December 20, Voroshilov, supreme commander of both the army and navy, had invited me to dine with him in the Kremlin, and Litvinov had told me that Stalin would be at the dinner. I had had several talks with Voroshilov, who is one of the most charming persons that I have ever met. He has an immense sense of humor and keeps himself in such perfect physical condition that he looks like a man of 35. He told me that he was especially anxious to have a full equipment of American military, naval and air attachés in Moscow. I replied that it was not our custom to have air attachés. He then asked if it might not be possible to have as Assistant Military Attaché and Assistant Naval Attaché men who were experts of the first water in aviation, as he hoped that he could obtain much good advice from our representatives. I told him that I would bring this matter to the attention of our Government when I reached Washington. It is obvious that our representatives in the Soviet Union today can have a really immense influence. If you wish, our military and naval men can play the part of an advisory military mission. If we send men who will be absolutely on the level with the Soviet Government and will refrain from spying and dirty tricks of every variety we can establish a relationship which may be very useful in the future.

This will also be true of our diplomatic representatives. There has been practically no social or intellectual intercourse between the diplomats in Moscow and the members of the Soviet Government . . . The men at the head of the Soviet Government today are really intelligent, sophisticated, vigorous human beings and they cannot be persuaded to waste their time with the ordinary conventional diplomatist. On the other hand, they are extremely eager to have contact with anyone who has first-rate intelligence and dimension as a human being. They were, for example, delighted by young Kennan who went in with me.

The dinner at Voroshilov's was carried out with great formality. His military aide called for me with his motor and conducted me through lines of soldiers to Voroshilov's residence in a palace in the Kremlin. There I found awaiting me Mr. and Mrs. Voroshilov, Stalin, Kalinin, Molotov, Litvinov; Egorov, Chief of Staff; Mejlaouk, member of the Five Year Plan Commission; Piatakov, Assistant Commissar for Heavy Industry; Kouibychev, President of the Five Year Plan Commission; Kaganovitch, Assistant Commissar for Heavy Industry; Ordjonikidzé, Member of the Revolutionary War Council; and the following men from the Foreign Office: Krestinski, Karakhan, Sokolnikov, and Ambassadors Troyanovsky and Dovgalevsky.

Litvinov said to me as I looked over the room, "This is the whole 'gang' that really runs things — the inside directorate." I was introduced to Stalin after I had shaken hands with Kalinin and Molotov, but made no effort to continue conversing with him before dinner, considering it best to let him come to me in his own good time. He drifted to one side of the room and I to the other . . .

The first impression Stalin made was surprising. I had thought from his pictures that he was a very big man with a face of iron and a booming voice. On the contrary, he is rather short, the top of his head coming to about my eye level, and of ordinary physique, wiry rather than powerful. He was dressed in a common soldier's uniform, with boots, black trousers and a gray-green coat without marks or decorations of any kind. Before dinner he smoked a large underslung pipe, which he continued to hold in his left hand throughout dinner, putting it on the table only when he needed to use both knife and fork. His eyes are curious, giving the impression of a dark brown filmed with dark blue. They are small, intensely shrewd and continuously smiling. The impression of shrewd humor is increased by the fact that the "crow's feet" which run out from them do not branch up and down in the usual manner, but all curve upward in long crescents. His hand is rather small with short fingers, wiry rather than strong. His mustache covers his mouth so that it is difficult to see just what it is like, but when he laughs his lips curl in a curiously canine manner. The only other notable feature about his face is the length of his nostrils. They are unusually long. With Lenin one felt at once that one was in the presence of a great man; with Stalin I felt I was talking to a wiry Gipsy with roots and emotions beyond my experience.

After we had consumed a tremendous hors d'oeuvre, consisting of every conceivable kind of caviar and crab and other Russian delicacy and every conceivable kind of vodka and other aperitif we sat down. I was placed at Madame Voroshilov's right at the center of one of the long sides of the table. Stalin was at her left. Immediately opposite her was Voroshilov with Kalinin on his right and Molotov on his left. Litvinov was on my right and on Stalin's left was Egorov, the Chief of Staff.

As soon as we had settled ourselves at the table Stalin rose, lifted his glass and proposed a toast "To President Roosevelt, who in spite of the mute growls of the Fishes dared to recognize the Soviet Union." Everyone drained his glass to the bottom and sat down again with considerable laughter at Stalin's reference to Ham Fish. I then proposed the health of President Kalinin and thereupon a series of toasts was begun which continued throughout the entire meal. The next one was Molotov's to me in which he proposed "The health of one who comes to us as a new Ambassador but an old friend."

After the tenth toast or so, I began to consider it discreet to take merely a sip rather than drain my glass, but Litvinov, who was next to me, told me that the gentleman who proposed the toast would be insulted if I did not drink to the bottom and that I must do so, whereupon I continued to drink bottoms-up. There were perhaps fifty toasts and I have never before so thanked God for the possession of a head impervious to any quantity of liquor. Everyone at the table got into the mood of a college fraternity banquet, and discretion was conspicuous by its absence. Litvinov whispered to me, "You told me that you wouldn't stay here if you were going to be treated as an outsider. Do you realize that everyone at this table has completely forgotten that anyone is here except the members of the inner gang?" That certainly seemed to be the case.

Stalin proposed my health several times and I did his once and we had considerable conversation across Madame Voroshilov. Toward the end of the dinner Stalin rose and proposed the health and continued prosperity, happiness and triumph of the American Army, the American Navy, the President and the whole United States. In return, I proposed a toast "To the memory of Lenin and the continued success of the Soviet Union."

There was a great deal of talk about the probability of an attack by Japan. Stalin, on introducing Egorov to me, said, "This is the man who will lead our Army victoriously against Japan when Japan attacks," and proposed a toast to Egorov and the Red Army in the same terms. Just before the meal ended Stalin rose again and turning to me said, "There is one thing I want to ask of you. The second line of our railroad to Vladivostok is not completed. To complete it quickly we need 250,000 tons of steel rails at once. They need not be new rails. Your rails are so much heavier than ours that the rails you discard are good enough for us. Your railways, I understand, are reequipping themselves and will have many old rails to dispose of immediately. Cannot you arrange for us to purchase the old rails? I do not ask that they should be given to us, but only that our purchase of them should be facilitated." I replied that I should be glad to do anything I could in the matter and asked where the rails should be delivered, to which Stalin replied, "Vladivostok." I then asked who in America would make the arrangements for their purchase and he replied, "Bogdanov." Stalin then said, "Without those rails we shall beat the Japanese, but if we have the rails it will be easier."

After dinner we adjourned to an adjoining drawing room and Stalin seized Piatakov by the arm, marched him to the piano and sat him down on the stool and ordered him to play, whereupon Piatakov launched into a number of wild Russian dances, Stalin standing behind him and from time to time putting his arm around Piatakov's neck and squeezing him affectionately.

When Piatakov had finished playing, Stalin came over and sat down beside me and we talked for some time. He said he hoped that I would feel myself completely at home in the Soviet Union; that he and all the members of the Government had felt that I was a friend for so long, that they had such admiration for yourself and the things you were trying to do in America that they felt we could cooperate with the greatest intimacy. I told him that you sincerely hoped that war might be prevented in the Far East and that the Soviet Government might work out its great experiment in peace. He said, "I know that that is what President Roosevelt wants and I hope you will tell him from me that he is today, in spite of being the leader of a capitalist nation, one of the most popular men in the Soviet Union."

Stalin was feeling extremely gay, as we all were, but he gave me the feeling that he was speaking honestly. He had by this time made the impression on me of a man not only of great shrewdness and inflexible will (Lenin, you know, said of him that he had enough will to equip the entire Communist Party), but also possessed of the quality of intuition in extraordinary measure.

Moreover, like every real statesman I have known, he had the quality of being able to treat the most serious things with a joke and a twinkle in his eye. Lenin had that same quality. You have it.

As I got up to leave, Stalin said to me, "I want you to understand that if you want to see me at any time, day or night, you have only to let me know and I will see you at once." This was a most extraordinary gesture on his part as he has hitherto refused to see any Ambassador at any time.

. . . After I had said good-bye to Voroshilov and the others, Stalin went to the door of the apartment with me and said, "Is there anything at all in the Soviet Union that you want? Anything?" There was one thing I wanted, but I hesitated to ask for it, as Litvinov had told me that the Moscow Soviet had definitely decided it would not give us the building site in the center of the town's park, and that a map would be submitted to me showing that the new canal would run through the property. Therefore I first said, "Everyone has been more than kind to me and I should hesitate to ask for anything in addition, except that the intimate relations we have begun tonight may continue." Whereupon, Stalin said, "But I should really like to show you that we appreciate not only what the President has done, but also what you yourself have done. Please understand that we should have received politely any Ambassador that might have been sent us by the Government of the United States, but we should have received no one but yourself in this particular way." He seemed moved by a genuinely friendly emotion. Therefore, I thanked him and said that there was one thing that I should really like to have, that I could see in my mind's eye an American Embassy modelled on the home of the author of the Declaration of Independence on that particular bluff overlooking the Moscow River, and that I should be glad to know that that property might be given to the American Government as a site for an Embassy. Stalin replied, "You shall have it." Thereupon, I held out my hand to shake hands with Stalin and, to my amazement, Stalin took my head in his two hands and gave me a large kiss! I swallowed my astonishment, and, when he turned up his face for a return kiss, I delivered it.

This evening with Stalin and the inner circle of the Soviet Government seems almost unbelievable in retrospect, and I should have difficulty in convincing myself that it was a reality if I had not on returning to my hotel awakened my secretary and dictated the salient facts to him. Moreover, the next day shortly before my departure Litvinov told me that Stalin had given orders to the Moscow Soviet that the property in the park should be ours if we wished to have it.

I had a long and very important conversation with Litvinov on the morning of December 21 in regard to which I cabled you briefly on my arrival in Paris.

Litvinov began by saying that he wanted to have a serious talk with me and asked me whether the Government of the United States would have any objection to the Soviet Government joining the League of Nations. I replied that as I had no codes I could not communicate with my Government, but speaking for myself I could say without hesitation that the Government of the United States would have no objection.

I then asked Litvinov why the Soviet Government was considering such a reversal of its established policy. He said that the Soviet Government was under great pressure from France to join the League, that he and all other members of the Soviet Government considered an attack by Japan in the spring so probable that everything possible must be done to secure the western frontier of the Soviet Union from attack; that he did not fear an immediate attack by Germany or Poland or both combined, but that he knew that conversations had taken place between Germany and Poland looking toward an eventual attack on the Soviet Union if the Soviet Union should become embroiled in a long war with Japan; that he feared that a war with Japan might drag on for years and that after a couple of years Germany and Poland combined might attack the Soviet Union, Poland with the hope of annexing the Ukraine and parts of Lithuania, and Germany with the hope of annexing the remainder of Lithuania as well as Latvia and Estonia. France had offered to make a defensive alliance with the Soviet Union providing that if either party were attacked by Germany the other party should at once declare war on Germany, but France felt that this could be done only within the framework of the League of Nations because of the difficulties caused by the Locarno agreements, and that in order to obtain this defensive alliance with France it would be necessary for the Soviet Union to enter the League.

I asked Litvinov how an alliance of this sort could be reconciled with the Covenant of the League and he said that it would be brought before the League as a "regional understanding." I told him that there seemed to me to be a considerable region separating France and Russia and he said that the proximity of both to Germany was a sufficient excuse. I pointed out that Russia had no common border with Germany, but he said with a laugh that Germany was quite close enough to make an agreement a "regional understanding." I asked him if he considered it probable that the Red Army would march against Germany to support France. He said he considered that it would be easy compared with the difficulty of getting the French Army to march against Germany to support the Soviet Union . . .

Litvinov said that it would be very important if it should be possible to obtain assurances from France and Great Britain and the United States that loans or credits would not be given to the Japanese Government for war purposes. I told him that I had good personal reason to believe that such assurances might be obtained. He expressed extreme skepticism. I did not go into the details of the matter, but assured him that he could take it from me personally that there might be such a possibility.

I had in mind, of course, the assurances which I obtained last January from Neville Chamberlain, representing the British Government on the one hand, and from Paul-Boncour, representing the French Government on the other hand. You will remember that Boncour gave a verbal assurance that the Japanese would receive no loans or credits in France for war purposes and Chamberlain gave me an aide-memoire which I turned over to you (which is doubtless in your most personal file at the present moment), which indicated that the British Government would not allow any money to be loaned by English banks to Japan except for ordinary commercial purposes . . .

Litvinov's entire preoccupation at the present time is the preservation of peace in the Far East. I am convinced that there is almost nothing that the Soviet Union will not give us in the way of commercial agreements, or anything else, in return for our moral support in preserving peace.

Litvinov gave a tremendous reception for me on the next afternoon, December 21, and that evening we left for Paris . . .

I reached Paris on Christmas eve, December 24. Claudel telephoned me from Brussels, where he is Ambassador, and said he wanted to have a talk with me. I saw him on December 27. He had just spent the morning with Boncour and Hymans and I asked him to give me an account of French intentions with regard to Germany, which he did with his customary frankness.

Claudel said that France would continue to oppose all German rearmament; that when the Disarmament Conference reassembled on January 21 France would bring forth a plan of disarmament which Germany would not accept. I suggested that Germany would simply go on rearming and asked what France would do in that case. He replied that France would do absolutely nothing, that France had such confidence in the new fortifications that she was convinced that Germany could not attack her and that when Germany had made herself strong enough to attack France's allies France would await the German attack and would then attack Germany from the rear. I said to him that this seemed to me a method of allowing Germany to dominate the Continent of Europe, whereupon he replied that the French Government realized that it was very dangerous, but that the opinion of France was absolutely pacifist at the moment; that no sanctions would be supported by the country; and that there was nothing to do but to rely on Germany to behave with her customary idiocy and arouse the people of France and the whole of Europe.

I subsequently had many conversations in Paris and found that this feeble procedure is the one which will probably be pursued by the French Government . . .

Thursday, December 28, I had lunch with de Tessan, Under Secretary for Foreign Affairs . . .

De Tessan insisted that I should have tea with Boncour at the Quai d'Orsay, which I did. Boncour seemed somewhat disturbed but not so upset as de Tessan and said that French public opinion was absolutely unprepared to make any debt settlement whatsoever, that there must be a new "fact." I told him that the French Government had only itself to blame for the situation and must take the consequences. He began to talk about approaches and I told him that no approaches were possible; that if he had anything to say to you on this subject, or any other of primary importance, he should say it directly through de Laboulaye and through no one else . . .

In conclusion:

1. It is obvious that the French Government will do nothing in the way of settling the debts unless we give French opinion a severe jolt, as suggested by Herriot.

2. Talks on my way home with Prittwitz and Scheffer and others in Berlin convinced me that the German Government will continue its policy of talking like a lamb and arming feverishly in the belief that within two years Germany will be stronger than France.

3. It is obvious that the Soviet Government values so highly the

moral support it may receive from the United States in the matter of preventing war with Japan that there is almost nothing we may not ask for and obtain at the present time.

It was a good trip, unmarred by a single unpleasant incident.

Blessings on you for the New Year.

Yours devotedly,
William C. Bullitt

THE WHITE HOUSE
WASHINGTON

January 7, 1934

Dear Bill:

It is clear to me that the unusual difficulties presented by the problem of establishing an Embassy and Consulate in Moscow require unusual treatment. You will be more or less in the position of Commander Byrd — cut off from civilization and I think you should organize your expedition as if you were setting out on a ship which was to touch no port for a year.

Your chief physical problems will be:

1. Lodging.
2. Transportation.
3. Supplies.
4. Health.
5. Recreation.

1. It seems evident that no permanent solution of the housing problem can be reached except by the construction of our own buildings for both Embassy and Consulate and for lodging the staffs. I am glad that you were able to obtain the offer of the site in the Moscow city park and I agree that nothing could be more appropriate than a reproduction of Monticello on that site with auxiliary buildings and lodgings arranged around the sides of the property . . .

2. As your residence will be twenty minutes on foot from the office building and as there are no taxicabs in Moscow, it seems to me essential that the Government should provide at least two automobiles for the use of the staff when engaged on official business.

3. The problem of supplies will obviously be the most difficult one and it seems to me that you should establish a commissary department either under an expert Naval Quartermaster acting under the directions of the disbursing officer or directly under the disbursing officer. You should take in with you all typewriters and other

office machines and supplies which may conceivably be necessary and should concentrate in the hands of the commissary all purchases of food and other supplies which it may be necessary to purchase in Moscow or to import from Poland or Latvia.

I agree that we should under no conditions smuggle roubles in our diplomatic pouch and that American officials should have no dealings with the Black Bourse in Moscow. I heartily approve of your proposal that consular fees in the U.S.S.R. should be charged in roubles at a rate to be fixed by ourselves which should approximate the rate in Warsaw and Harbin, and that the roubles thus acquired by the consulate should be delivered to the members of the staffs of the Embassy and Consulate, at their option, in place of dollars, up to a proportion of their salaries to be determined by yourself — perhaps one-tenth of each salary to be so payable. I hope you will be able to work out with Mr. Grinko the question of supplying any further roubles that may be necessary as indicated in your report.

4. It seems to me essential that you should take with you as a member of your Embassy staff a surgeon from either the Army, Navy or Public Health Service, and that he should take with him a full supply of hospital requisites. You should, I think, set up a small operating room and a room for non-contagious patients and an isolation ward for contagious diseases. I understand that the shortage of medicines is such in Moscow that major operations are now done under chloroform instead of ether and that there are no hospital facilities except those provided by the public wards of the Russian hospitals. I do not wish either our representatives or their families to have to go into these public wards or pesthouses in case of illness.

5. It seems to me highly desirable that an effort should be made to provide the Embassy and Consular staffs with a certain amount of American recreation. You will probably find it possible to arrange tennis courts for the summer somewhere and for the winter I suggest that (if it is possible to work the matter out) the Government should supply you with a radio so constructed as to be able to receive the news broadcasts from America, a talking picture machine and a Victrola. I understand that the Russians are very much interested in pictures of American industrial life and it seems to me that such pictures should offer an easy method of developing the social contacts with the members of the Soviet Government which you should cultivate.

In addition to the points enumerated above, it seems to me essential that all our diplomatic, consular, military and naval representatives in the U.S.S.R. should be forbidden to indulge in spying of any kind and should be instructed to cultivate the frankest and most direct relations with the members of the Soviet Government. You will, of course, warn all the members of the staff of both Embassy and Consulate in Russia that they will be spied upon constantly and that they should be on their guard against communicating at any time official secrets of any kind to anyone.

In selecting the staff of the Embassy and Consulate it seems to me desirable that you should take no one who is not a native-born American citizen and that insofar as possible you should take men who speak Russian or who have an exceptional facility in learning foreign languages and that you should require all members of your staff who do not speak Russian to begin at once to study it seriously.

As you will be thrown into extraordinarily close contact with all the members of your little community, you should exercise exceptional care in selecting men of congenial character and should keep a weather eye out for uncongenial wives.

Good luck to you.

FDR

The Beginning of Disillusionment

JANUARY—JUNE 1934

Debt Negotiations with Russia
Difficulties Arise
Embassy Housed

BULLITT RETURNED home early in January 1934 and, along with Alexander A. Troyanovsky, the Soviet Ambassador to the United States, was guest of honor on January 24 at a large dinner of the American Russian Institute in New York. Bullitt had previously spoken before the Chamber of Commerce in Philadelphia on January 19. In this speech he warned that excessive credits should not be granted to foster trade with Russia, but that we should take goods from them as well. "There are few products produced in the United States for which there is not some demand in the Soviet Union . . . We want no more of the strange financing of foreign sales which took place during the 1920s, and produced the result that we found we had given away our products when we thought we had sold them."

On March 7 he returned to Russia, and he already found that the Russians were putting a different interpretation on the terms of recognition and Secretary Hull said: "The misunderstanding is so wide that perhaps it would be best to bring all commercial and financial relations to a standstill until it can be clarified." [1]

Memorandum   March 5, 1934
For the Secretary

We are carefully watching for provable instances of the violation of Litvinov's promise to the President to prevent communist activities being projected from Russia and conducted in the United States with the encouragement or approval of the Soviet Government. Already there is pretty definite evidence of two or three such violations and as soon as more are discovered in the near future the facts will be brought to your attention to be dealt with by you in such manner as you may deem best.

R. Walton Moore

From a review of the correspondence and the memorandums it would appear that most major questions, with the exception of the exact amount of the Russian debt to the United States, had been settled. In connection with the debt the President's memorandum of November 15, 1933, makes it clear that Litvinov said he would personally recommend a figure of $100,000,000 and that the President would endeavor to have the Congress accept an amount of $150,000,000. In a letter to the President on November 16, Litvinov agreed that Russia would waive all claims against the United States for the activities of the United States military forces in Siberia. At a later date, January 1934, the Americans claimed they were due interest on the Russian debt, which the Russians refused to agree to. In March, Mr. Hull told the new Russian Ambassador that Litvinov was now offering an entirely different version of the debt settlement from anything the United States thought they were discussing, to such an extent that until it was clarified it might be better to stop all commercial transactions between the two countries.

Litvinov's letter of November 16 to the President is also of great importance in view of the meeting in Moscow in July 1935 of the Third International. This letter gave it as the fixed policy of the Russian government to "refrain from interfering in any manner in the internal affairs of the United States," and also to refrain from "any agitation or propaganda having as an aim . . . the bringing about by force of a change in the political or social order" of the United States. They further agreed "to prevent the activity on its territory of any organization or group which has as an aim . . . the bringing about by force of a change in, the political or social order of the whole or any part of the United States."

A year and a half later this pledge would appear to have been forgotten.

It was, of course, impossible for the President to keep in daily touch with the events occurring in Russia, and these letters show the method worked out between Judge Moore and Bullitt to keep Mr. Roosevelt informed of the most essential matters.

TELEGRAM

This telegram must be closely paraphrased before being communicated to anyone.

Secretary of State   Moscow
Washington   Dated March 14, 1934
11, March 14, 11 P.M.   Rec'd 10:47 P.M.
Strictly Confidential

One. Litvinov who is still ill received me in his bedroom this afternoon. He told me that Chiang Kai-shek had stopped the negotiations with the Soviet Union for a pact of non-aggression because of fear of the Japanese. He asked if the President might be inclined to propose a pact of non-aggression between the United States, the Soviet Union, Japan and China. I replied that I had no intimation that the President had any such intention. Litvinov said that he was less apprehensive of an immediate Japanese attack than he had been in December but that the Japanese Government might be overthrown and replaced by extreme Fascist Government which might decide to attack the Soviet Union. He still regards the situation as extremely serious.

Two. He asked me whether or not the United States intended to recognize Manchukuo and I replied that we had no such intention.

BULLITT

TELEGRAM

MARCH 17, 1934

AMEMBASSY
MOSCOW
YOUR 13, MARCH 15, 1 A.M.

FOR YOUR INFORMATION PRESIDENT IS CONVINCED THAT THE PROPOSAL RELATIVE TO DEBTS AND CLAIMS WHICH YOU ARE DISCUSSING WITH LITVINOV IS REASONABLE BUT HE IS WILLING TO GIVE CONSIDERATION TO

ANY NOT VITAL MODIFICATIONS INSISTED UPON BY LITVINOV WHICH YOU
MAY RECOMMEND.

YOU MAY INFORM LITVINOV THAT THE PRESIDENT EXPRESSLY STATES
THAT HE HAS NEVER HAD ANY THOUGHT OF A DIRECT LOAN TO THE SO-
VIET GOVERNMENT AND THAT THERE IS NOT THE SLIGHTEST POSSIBILITY
OF SUCH A LOAN BEING MADE . . .

KELLEY

461.11/394

It did not take long for the Soviet to create "misunderstandings." Stalin had told Bullitt that America should have the
land chosen for an Embassy. However, on March 25, 1934, the
Moscow Soviet told Bullitt the United States could only have the
eastern half of the land — this, in spite of the fact that the agreement had been confirmed in writing by the Russian Ambassador
and that the House of Representatives had voted the money based
on this promise. The eastern part of the land lay below the level
of a road and was thoroughly unsuitable for building.

The discussion continued for a year and a half and in September 1935 Mr. Hull finally suggested that the funds proposed for
building in Moscow be used for construction in certain unhealth-
ful missions in Central America. To this Bullitt replied: "I favor
heartily transfer Moscow building funds to construction at un-
healthy posts in Central America." [2]

March 19, 1934

My dear friend:

I have been giving very careful attention to the matters in which
you are interested. I believe that reply has been made to all of your
despatches. Those pertaining to the Russian debts, I have brought
to the attention of the President and they have received his approval. He was very much astonished that Litvinov should talk
about a direct loan to the Soviet, which, the President says, was
never discussed and which he speaks of as impossible not only because he does not favor it, but because it would not receive the sanc-
tion of Congress. The wire to you this morning shows that unless
the Soviet makes a satisfactory debt adjustment proposal, trade between that country and the United States may disappear. In view of
Litvinov's attitude some people on the inside are beginning to think
that his principal desire when he was here was to obtain recognition

without much regard for what would follow relative either to debts or commercial transactions and I have no doubt that you are correct in assuming that he is now a good deal influenced by the satisfactory arrangements he is working out with Sweden and other governments . . .

I see Mr. Troyanovsky infrequently and am satisfied that his activities here will be largely of a window dressing variety, with a reference to Moscow of everything of any real importance.

The President is furnished all of your despatches but under my understanding with Miss LeHand there are brought to his attention all of those which can not be finally dealt with by this Department and the replies thereto. These go into what he calls his "Bullitt File" . . .

Very truly your friend,
R. Walton Moore

Bullitt was particularly fortunate in having with him in Moscow some outstanding men. Chief among these was George F. Kennan, Ambassador to Russia in 1952, who spoke Russian; Loy W. Henderson, formerly stationed in Riga and subsequently Chief of the Division of Eastern European Affairs in the State Department and later Ambassador to Iraq, Iran, and India; Charles E. Bohlen, who became Ambassador to Russia in 1953 and to France in 1962; John C. Wiley, later Ambassador to Estonia; Elbridge Durbrow, who became Ambassador to Vietnam; Lieutenant Roscoe H. Hillenkoetter, later Admiral in command of U.S.S. *Missouri;* and Carmel Offie. The offices were established on two floors of the Hotel Savoy and the Ambassador's home, Spaso House, was over two miles distant, with no telephone switchboard. By the end of 1934 the Embassy had moved to permanent quarters in the center of town.

Bullitt's daughter, Anne, has written the following description of Spaso House: "As I remember it, Spaso House had been built by a Russian vodka merchant who was shot by his son in the front hall at the beginning of the Revolution. It was a Russian Victorian pomposity, badly proportioned and cold, enormous with no room for anything. It was built around a central ballroom with a glass dome like the Capitol, so I could crawl from my bedroom and lie on the floor upstairs and watch between the marble balustrade what was going on below, like Voroshilov and Bud-ënny doing Russian dances after polo.

"Everything was marble, floors and walls and all; very convenient for keeping rabbits indoors. It had been used by some commissars for entertaining, and they added an enormous dining room in red marble, incorporating the hammer and sickle in the Corinthian columns. With all this, there was only one small room to the right of the ballroom where one could sit downstairs, and that had a hideous fireplace. The servants used to skate around the ballroom with rags tied to their feet to wax it."

Bullitt was followed closely by the Russian Secret Service whenever he left the house, and he and his daughter played hide and seek with them, counting it a point gained when the spies could be eluded. He was also convinced that all the rooms in his house as well as those in the Chancery had to be constantly checked for "bugging" with microphones, for which he had on his staff a United States naval expert.

Personal   April 10, 1934
Dear Bullitt:

Before this reaches you, I will put before the President your recent despatches and the replies thereto, and have no doubt that he will direct what further communications shall be sent to you.

It is now quite apparent that Litvinov when he was here was not serious about any phase of the negotiation except recognition, and that he is now indifferent to all the assurances he gave in respect to other phases. It seems to me the only thing that would incline him to take a more reasonable attitude is the possibility of Japan knowing that the relations between our government and his have become strained, and conceivably may be terminated. You are better able than I to form an opinion as to what would be the effect of intimating to him that we may not construct an embassy building and that we consider the future relationship in every way doubtful. It will, however, be up to the President to instruct how far we shall go in communicating with you. Meantime, I think you are very wise in holding up arrangements to establish consulates and in every other direction avoiding an outlay that may prove not only unprofitable but useless . . .

Very sincerely your friend,
R. Walton Moore

Secretary Hull's advice to Bullitt was: "Since you were present at all conversations with Litvinov in Washington you are perhaps in better position than anyone else to understand how perfectly indefensible is his present attitude. Approve your idea of refraining from any further suggestion for time being unless it is invited by Litvinov and you can be confident there will be no negotiations here with Troyanovsky." [3]

On April 13, 1934, the President signed the Johnson Act. This act forbid the floating of loans in the United States by any foreign nation which was in default in the payment of its war debts to the United States. Finland was the only nation which paid its debt in full.

Moscow
Personal and Confidential   Easter Day, 1934
                                                 [4-13-34]

My dear Mr. President:

I have not burdened you with letters because I know you get too many from ambassadors. But I wish so much that I could talk with you tonight that I am seizing the excuse of a couple of matters that cannot go into despatches to the Department in order to give myself the sensation that I am not utterly cut off from you.

First — a pardon, which would not only give me a deep personal satisfaction but also would greatly strengthen our position in Moscow.

George Andreytchine has been appointed by the Foreign Office to look out for all the wants of this Embassy. He saves our tempers and almost our lives two or three times a day. He is one of the loveliest human beings I have ever known — a sort of Jack Reed in Macedonian terms. Some day he should be the Soviet Ambassador in Washington. He has been a close friend of mine for years and his feeling for the United States is deep and genuine.

Andreytchine was born in 1894 in Macedonia. He came to America before the war and joined the I.W.W. In August 1918 Judge Landis, in Chicago, sentenced him to twenty years hard labor in Leavenworth for anti-war propaganda. He was the editor of a paper in the Bulgarian language called "Worker's Thought." He was *not* charged with any overt act.

Andreytchine was in Leavenworth from August 1918 to June 1919, when he was released on bail pending an appeal to the Supreme Court of the United States. In April 1921 his sentence was confirmed by the Supreme Court. He jumped his bail and escaped to Russia.

In Moscow, Andreytchine served in the Foreign Office and at other government jobs. Trotsky was his intimate friend, and when Trotsky was exiled Andreytchine was imprisoned in Siberia. About two years ago he was released. Since then he has been acquiring gradually the position to which his brain and personality entitle him. He is deeply anxious to be pardoned, and I can think of no other act which would cost us so little and win so much good will here for you and for me . . .

Moscow has turned out to be just as disagreeable as I anticipated. The honeymoon atmosphere had evaporated completely before I arrived. As Wiley says, "The Japanese have let us down badly." The Russians are convinced that Japan will not attack this spring or summer and, as they no longer feel that they need our immediate help, their underlying hostility to all capitalist countries now shows through the veneer of intimate friendship. We shall have to deal with them according to Claudel's formula of the donkey, the carrot, and the club.

In addition to the "misunderstandings" about the extra interest on credits, there have been similar "misunderstandings" about the property on which we expect to build our Embassy, the obtaining of paper roubles, the payment of consular fees in paper roubles, repairs to the Embassy residence, and apartments in the office building. The only effective way of dealing with this general attitude, I believe, is to maintain the friendliest possible personal relations with the Russians but to let them know clearly that if they are unwilling to move forward and take the carrot they will receive the club on the behind. For example, the next time I discuss the payment of debts and claims with Litvinov, I shall allow him to derive the impression that if the Soviet Union does not wish to use the credits of the Import-Export Bank the Japanese Government will be eager to use the facilities of the Bank to finance large purchases from certain American heavy industries.

The bright spot in the murky sky is the Embassy staff. The men I selected in Washington have turned out to be both able and filled with the finest spirit. We have had to have secretaries of Embassy and clerks answering the front doorbell and carrying furniture, and they have done so as a matter of course without complaint. I am delighted with every man on the staff.

But I am a bit homesick. It is a new sensation for me and it arises from a very happy thing. In many years I have not had the sensation that I had a home, but in this past year you and Mrs. Roosevelt and Miss LeHand have made me feel that I was a member of the family, and the thing I miss so much is the afternoons and evenings with you in the White House. I am much too fond of you all.

Take good care of yourself. Good luck, and the Lord be with you!

Yours always,
William C. Bullitt

George Andreytchine later became a delegate to various international conferences, including the Versailles conference. He eventually died in a Bulgarian Communist prison.

There was a mass of correspondence at this time concerning the efforts to have Russia live up to its agreement when recognition was given. There are no direct letters from the President, all his communication with Bullitt being conducted through Mr. Moore.

THE WHITE HOUSE
WASHINGTON

April 23, 1934

Dear Bill:

Just a line in haste (because of the omnipresent Congress) to tell you that we should love to have young Litvinov spend the night at the White House. You can tell him I will show him my ships and stamps personally.

In regard to your bail-jumping roommate, I am sending that part of your letter in confidence to the Attorney General and I will let you know if we can do anything about it. Perhaps if we collected the amount of the bail the Government might feel that the offense had been at least in part expiated!

Missy and I thought you sounded just a bit homesick. In any event, we miss you a lot and I do hope you will have easier sledding this spring. It is fine that your staff is working out so well.

Some day soon I shall write you about the general situation here. It sounds worse but it is only a case of poison ivy and the patient will soon be cured.

As ever yours,
FDR

Hon. William C. Bullitt
American Embassy
Moscow

THE WHITE HOUSE

WASHINGTON

May 21, 1934

Dear Bill:

I enclose the correspondence in regard to the Andreytchine case — your little playmate. Please use in your discretion and return to me for my files.

Sorry we cannot accomodate him for the moment!

As ever yours,

FDR

Hon. William C. Bullitt
American Embassy
Moscow

The Ambassador in the Soviet Union (Bullitt)
to the Secretary of State

Moscow, April 13, 1934 — 1 P.M.

Your telegram No. 42, April 12, 1 P.M. Rubinin's trip ostensibly is to familiarize himself with the United States. His real purpose is to give Troyanovsky an intimate view of Litvinov's position with regard to the matter of debts and claims and to bring back to Moscow firsthand information as to the position of the Government of the United States.

I am informed unofficially but I think reliably that Troyanovsky has reported that he is in a helpless position being unable successfully to interpret the assurances which Litvinov gave in Washington or to contest the position taken by the Department.

I feel sure that Rubinin has not been empowered to enter into any negotiations but merely to give and receive information. Nevertheless I attach great importance to his receiving a swift impact.

Bullitt

Mr. Moore, who was Acting Secretary of State, wired Bullitt on April 23 that he had reviewed the entire situation with the President, who agreed with Bullitt that the next move should come from Litvinov. The President, he said, "has entire confidence in you and you are at liberty in your own tactful way to intimate to Litvinov how the relations of the two countries may be unfortunately affected by failure to agree."

Personal   May 8, 1934

My dear Mr. Bullitt:
. . . I make a point of showing the President all of your important despatches, and having his approval of the more important despatches that are sent you. I have no difficulty in seeing him by way of Miss LeHand's office . . .
Speaking very personally, I think the President is most anxious that an agreement should be reached, and will take a very liberal view of any proposal you can extract from Litvinov . . .

Affectionately your friend,
R. Walton Moore

THE WHITE HOUSE
WASHINGTON

May 9, 1934

Dear Bill:
. . . I get a lot of chuckles out of the scraps that you and Litvinov have. Keep up the good work!

As ever yours,
FDR

Hon. William C. Bullitt
American Embassy
Moscow

Mr. Roosevelt obtained great pleasure and relaxation from the occasional trips he made at sea and in July 1934 he embarked on a cruiser for a trip to Hawaii. The ship stopped en route at Haiti, St. Thomas and St. Croix in the Virgin Islands, Cartagena, Colombia, Panama, and Hawaii. The trip took over a month and at each stop he made a brief address, of no political significance, simply expressing the good wishes of the United States.

THE WHITE HOUSE
WASHINGTON

May 14, 1934

Dear Bill:
I am heartbroken about the Hawaiian trip but a decision had to

be made now on account of the cruiser and also in order to make other preparations.

I was ganged! Your dear old Far Eastern Division, plus the Assistant Secretaries, the Under-Secretary and the Secretary, felt that if you came I would have to have Grew and Johnson also, in order apparently to accord equal importance to Russia, Japan and China. That being decided by them, they felt that a gathering of this kind would be almost a Far Eastern Pacific conference and would create such a stir that there might be real discussion and speculation at a time when they want to avoid just that.

With much reluctance I yielded, though I am not in a happy frame of mind about it and still believe that you and I could have had our little party in Hawaii without bringing on a World War! However, there is one consolation — the foregoing of the Hawaiian trip gives you a much better excuse to run back here this fall.

After this wild-eyed Congress goes home I will be able to pay more attention to dispatches and you might also write me the real lowdown on what happens at your parties with the Russian foreign office at 3 A.M.

We all miss you much. Take care of yourself.

As ever yours,
FDR

Hon. William C. Bullitt
American Embassy
Moscow

Personal and Confidential   Moscow
May 18, 1934

My dear Mr. President:

I have just received a telegram from the Secretary of State informing me that you think it would be inadvisable for me to meet you in Hawaii.

I am deeply sorry that I shall not see you. I should like to hear the sound of your voice and be with you for a few days. I don't like being so far away from you.

I am sure also that I need to know your point of view on this Russian business, and I think it might be worthwhile for you to have a firsthand report from me. I have a feeling that together we might be able to devise a method of settlement. I realize, however, that my chief regret is simply the human one that I shall not see you.

I shall, I think, have my little girl come to meet me by way of

Leningrad — not by way of the Far East — and shall put her in school here and plan to remain here without vacation until you want to see me.

We are all still in good health and spirits but snowed under with work. Every detail of life for the entire staff has to be the subject of negotiations with the Foreign Office. Every detail with regard to the building of the new Embassy, also. I find that I keep going about fifteen or sixteen hours a day and make little progress.

The so-called debt negotiations at the moment are hopeless. The Soviet Union has taken an absolutely decided position and will, I believe, maintain that position for some time. Litvinov was so delighted by your invitation to his son, which I received just before his departure for Geneva, that he talked amicably and seemed ready for concessions; but when I called on Krestinsky to attempt to obtain the concessions I was met by a flat refusal even to discuss the matter on the basis of the Department's draft agreement.

The Foreign Office has promised me a reply within a couple of days in regard to our establishing a consolidated Embassy and Consulate here. There is one point which I hope you will keep in mind in case this relatively minor matter should have to be brought to your attention: If the Consul General and/or any other Consul becomes a Secretary of Embassy, it must be clearly understood that his position is no different from that of any other Secretary of Embassy; that he is under the orders of the Ambassador exactly as other Secretaries, and that one set of reports — not separate Embassy and consular reports — goes to the Department. Nothing could be more disastrous than to have an Embassy in which the Ambassador had control over only one-half of his Secretaries. I believe that the establishment of a consolidated office is desirable but only if that office has one boss.

No furniture for my house has yet arrived from the Department so that I have had to give up all idea of entertaining this spring. As the Department has also been unable to deliver any wire screening, we are, however, entertaining considerable numbers of flies and mosquitoes. I thank God daily that I picked the staff so carefully. The physical discomforts would make life hellish if all the men were not such good pioneers.

Take good care of yourself and don't forget that in Moscow there is a fellow who is very fond of you.

Yours permanently,
William C. Bullitt

ASSISTANT SECRETARY OF STATE
WASHINGTON

May 21, 1934

Dear Mr. President:

Attached is a telegram from Bullitt received this afternoon. Even if you should approve the proposal mentioned in the first paragraph of payment of $100,000,000 in settlement of debts, it does not seem that without the sacrifice of our interests the proposal mentioned in the concluding sentence of the second paragraph could be seriously considered. Perhaps the telegram requires only an acknowledgement, but should you think differently, I will be glad to see you at any time at your convenience.

Yours very sincerely,
R. Walton Moore

Enclosure: As stated.

I agree with you and Bullitt. Suggest telling him so. FDR [In President's handwriting.]

Moscow
June 14, 1934

Dear Mr. President:

A courier has just brought your letters of May 9, 14, and 21. I am deeply grateful to you for your letter about the Hawaiian trip. I really miss seeing you and hearing the sound of your voice.

You may be sure that if there should be another 3 A.M. party in the Kremlin I will write you privately. I got word from the Kremlin a few days ago that Stalin had chided his intimates for not seeing more of me. They replied that the lack of such parties had been my fault and not theirs. They have all entertained me lavishly and as yet I have not been able to have one of them in the house. That sort of party requires at least one door that can be closed and kept closed, and I still have the privacy of the information clerk in the Grand Central Station.

Within two weeks, however, I expect to have the Chancery out of my house and the dozen boys who are boarding here safely in the Mokhovaya building. Moreover, I hope to have a dining room table and some living room furniture. I shall then try to make up for lost time.

Fair winds and a smooth sea to you both for your Hawaiian trip and thereafter.

Yours affectionately,
Bill

6

Attempts at Friendship

JUNE—DECEMBER 1934

Russians Learn Polo
Russia Joins League of Nations
Bullitt Crosses Russia to Japan and China

BULLITT'S DAUGHTER, ANNE, now ten years old, had spent the winter at school in the United States and in June went to Moscow to stay with her father for the summer. She arrived at Helsinki and Bullitt flew to Leningrad on his way to meet her.

TELEGRAM

LENINGRAD VIA WASHINGTON   JUNE 24 [1934]

THE PRESIDENT, CARE HON. M. H. MCINTYRE
HOTEL NELSON POUGHKEEPSIE NY

PLANE LANDED UPSIDE DOWN BUT WE EMERGED RIGHTSIDE UP STOP TRUST
NONE HAS REPORTED TO YOU THAT WE ARE DEAD STOP WE ARE BOTH UN-
SCRATCHED STOP GOOD LUCK FOR YOUR TRIP

BULLITT

[The pilot of this plane, Lieutenant Thomas D. White, became Chief of Staff of the United States Air Force in 1957.]

Moscow
June 29, 1934

Dear Judge Moore:

Your letter of June 4th reached me just a few minutes ago on my return from Leningrad. That trip to meet Anne, which began somewhat inauspiciously, ended delightfully and we had three charming days in Leningrad.

The plane accident was very terrifying to the people on the ground watching us alight, but I regret to say that I was unable to get a single accelerated heartbeat out of it. The engine behaved as if the gasoline supply had been exhausted, but examination showed that there were thirty gallons left in the tank and the only explanation either White or I can contrive is that the feed-pipe was stopped by dirty gasoline. Methods of fuelling planes here are primitive in the extreme. There are no pumps and cans of gasoline are simply poured in by hand, which makes it possible always that a certain amount of dirt will enter the tank. White made an extraordinarily skillful landing.

We were just at the edge of a hummocky marsh cut across by deep ditches. He had to land between the ditches, on a tiny patch of marshy land, with only a hundred feet of altitude in which to maneuver. He did a quick side-slip, straightened the plane out and brought her down with somewhat of a thud necessarily in the marsh. The landing speed of the plane is about sixty miles an hour and we had the good fortune to roll a short distance before the wheels got definitely caught in the marsh and we went over. The Soviet officials who were waiting to receive me got a magnificent scare, as I doubtless should have had had I been on the ground and not in the plane. They came racing across the marsh, falling on their noses, to pick out the dead man, but by the time they arrived we had loosed our belts and climbed out and received them as if we were quite in the habit of landing upside down.

. . . I suspect that Litvinov has not reported to Stalin with any accuracy our side of the dispute about claims and indebtedness and I have in the past few days seen to it that other gentlemen who have access to Stalin should be informed as to our point of view. I hope that your task in Washington may be made somewhat easier as a result.

During my absence in Leningrad it was possible to move most of the staff into the Mokhovaya and to bring some furniture into my house, so that I now have at least the beginnings of a living room and can invite the Soviet leaders here. I expect to have a number of peaceable evenings with various Commissars during the next two weeks and shall try to impress upon them the desirability of coming to an agreement . . .

Good luck to you and every good wish.

Yours affectionately,
William C. Bullitt

"The dispute about claims" to which Bullitt referred went back to the First World War and the Bolshevik Revolution in 1917, when Russia asked Germany for an armistice. On March 3, 1918, in the Treaty of Brest-Litovsk, Russia surrendered to Germany, thus taking a powerful ally out of the war. Certain elements in Russia refused to surrender and the Russian Volunteer Army was formed, civil war following. America, France, England, and Japan had sent enormous amounts of munitions to Russia and the Soviet Government refused payment. These supplies were in the north of Russia and in the east at Vladivostok. To save them from falling into the hands of Germany and to support the Volunteer Army, the Allies landed troops at Vladivostok in Siberia and Archangel in northwestern Russia. Some 60,000 gallant Czech soldiers who had been in the Red Army had already seized Vladivostok and a large part of the Trans-Siberian Railroad. A long, bitter, and fruitless struggle followed and it was not until almost a year after Germany's defeat that the Allied forces withdrew from Archangel and Murmansk on October 12, 1919. A few months later the troops were withdrawn from western Siberia. It was the damage to Russia done by these troops of the Allied forces in 1918 to which Litvinov was referring.

The view of the State Department about the negotiations is summed up in a letter of Judge Moore's to Bullitt on July 9, 1934: "I can tell you that if Mr. Troyanovsky is to be trusted, which I believe is the case, he will feel as much disappointed as the rest of us in the event he does not receive authority to continue the debt negotiations here. Several times recently he has indicated to me his hope and belief he will soon receive instructions to that effect. But perhaps Litvinov, who seems to be without any conscience whatever, is deceiving him just as he deceived the President and yourself when he was here and precisely as he has ignored all of his promises in his conversations with you at Moscow."

Moscow
August 5, 1934

My dear Mr. President:
I hope you had as good a time in Hawaii as we expected to have. I regretted not seeing you every day of your trip.

Jean Monnet, one of my closest French friends, who has just spent six months advising the Chinese Government on financial reorganization, passed through Moscow a few days ago and gave me a creatively intimate picture of China and Japan. He is definitely of the opinion that the Japanese can be handled in such a way as to settle Eastern questions by peaceful means and I should like to spend a couple of weeks in China and Japan trying to verify his observations.

When our Hawaiian meeting was "spurlos versenkt," you suggested that you would want me to come back this autumn. If you still want to see me you might order me to report in Washington for a conference about December 1 and to come by way of the East. I could leave Vladivostok about October 15 and be in Washington by December 1st with the latest Far Eastern and Russian information. Do let me know soon how you feel about such a trip as I shall not make any plans to leave here until I know your personal wishes.

I have not been able to get anywhere with Litvinov and, while maintaining very cordial personal relations with him, have tried to build a backfire in the Kremlin by way of Voroshilov and Karakhan.

As a means to develop close relations with Voroshilov I imported a lot of polo equipment and have taught the Red Army Cavalry to play the game. We play every other day on a broad plain. The game at the outset had a number of unusual features not provided at Meadowbrook. All the ponies were sixteen-hand stallions who savaged each other and the riders whenever they came to close quarters, and on the first day a Mongolian soldier with an undeveloped genius for the game carried the ball in a bee-line three miles cross country before he could be stopped! The polo has brought not only myself but our military men into the closest relations with the Red Army leaders and has been most useful.

As you know, I have also started baseball here and that has helped to bring us into intimate relations with the Moscow Soviet.

We have had dozens of indications lately that Stalin, Voroshilov and Molotov are most anxious to develop really friendly relations with us and I think the most important thing I can do at the moment is to get my feeble Russian into shape to have conversations with them about various matters without the aid of an interpreter. I got word from the Kremlin the other day that all the leaders of the Government, including Stalin, would be glad to see a great deal more of me than they have been seeing and in the end I think we shall be able to beat down Litvinov's resistance. I do not expect any immediate results, however, as Litvinov is about to leave Moscow for a two months' holiday and Stalin is leaving for a cure in the Caucasus.

Do you know that our pet courier service has been stopped and also that the Comptroller General has snarled in scarlet tape the payment of Moscow salaries in gold and that we are all rapidly going bankrupt? I have had no explanation from the Department with regard to stopping the courier service which is, of course, absolutely essential to this mission. I am sending my own couriers now to Berlin but our funds are too limited to keep this up long. The exchange equalization is also vital for us here and I should be most grateful if you would give the Comptroller General a graceful but swift kick.

I am really too eager to see you all. The summer here has been delightful with plenty of polo, baseball, tennis and swimming in the late afternoons but the sun is already beginning to leave us and Washington is beginning to look more alluring than ever.

My very best wishes to Mrs. Roosevelt and Miss LeHand, and the hope that I may see you all soon.

Yours permanently,
William C. Bullitt

Moscow
July 11, 1934

My dear Litvinov:

I think those polo teams will be in form to put on a game that will be at least amusing by the 24th of this month. Would you care to come on that day? If so, I shall try to get hold of both Voroshilov and Budënny and we shall have a gay afternoon. If you should really like to see a game as you indicated, I would be delighted if you could lunch with me before the match and go out to the field with me. If this should be convenient for you I will try to get Voroshilov and Budënny as well.

With every good wish, I am

Yours very sincerely,
William C. Bullitt

THE WHITE HOUSE
WASHINGTON

August 14, 1934

Dear Bill:

I am back again after a perfectly heavenly cruise. I wished that you were in Hawaii with us. It was too lovely.

I am a little late in telling you but I was glad that you and Lieutenant White landed right side up in the plane. That was a very close call. Your cable was a joy.

We are prepared to recommend you highly as a moving picture actor and, as far as I can tell, your Russian is perfect!

I am anxious to hear all that has happened. Do write.

We go to Hyde Park the twenty-fourth and I will be back here after Labor Day.

The construction of the new building is in process and working here is much like working in a boiler factory!

Are you coming back this fall? I have not had a chance to have any conversations on the Russian debt situation but expect to before I leave.

My best to you.

As ever,
FDR

Hon. William C. Bullitt
American Embassy
Moscow

THE WHITE HOUSE
WASHINGTON

August 29, 1934

Dear Bill:

I think it is a fine idea for you to come back via the Far East where you will be able to get at least a cursory view of things in Siberia, Manchuria, China and Japan.

My present plan is to go to Warm Springs about the middle of November and stay until about December fifth. The White House office will not be ready much before then. Meanwhile things are in a mess, as the whole lower part of the White House is turned over to executive business.

I have not seen Troyanovsky since you returned but everybody likes him at the State Department and I am very certain terms could be arranged if he had a more free hand.

It is grand about the Polo and the Baseball. By the way, as an expert I want to compliment you again on your excellent Russian in that picture. All you need to do now is to swallow some lubricant just before starting to speak. It will give you the necessary speed-up! I do not need to warn you against too many lubricants!

I will not tell you about our trip except that it was a magnificent party and helped the general scheme of things in Central and South America and also in Hawaii — nor will I prognosticate about our economic future over here.

All the big guns have started shooting — Al Smith, John W. Davis, James W. Wadsworth, du Pont, Shouse, etc. Their organization has already been labeled the "I CAN'T TAKE IT CLUB."

Keep up the good work. We will all be happy to have you back again.

As ever yours,
FDR

Hon. William C. Bullitt
American Embassy
Moscow

Moscow
September 8, 1934

Dear Mr. President:

I was delighted to get your letter of August 14, and even more to get that cable. Thank God, I shall see you all again before Christmas.

I am sorry that the State Department was not able to get anywhere with Troyanovsky. I hoped that a discussion of specific trade deals might lead to a settlement.

The answer, I think, is that the Russians have had so much success lately that they are feeling exceedingly cocky. The harvest, which at one time looked catastrophic, was so revived by continuous rains that it will be good, and the Russians are convinced that if the Eastern Locarno should fail, France and Czechoslovakia will at once enter an alliance with the Soviet Union. The Government, therefore, feels that its back will be protected by France from attacks by either Poland or Germany in case Japan should decide to go after the maritime provinces.

Furthermore, the Government believes that Japan will not attack either this autumn or next spring and that by next summer the Red Army in the Far East will be so strong that Japan will not dare to attack.

The maintenance of really friendly and intimate relations with us, therefore, seems to the Russians much less important than it did when Litvinov was in Washington. If a Japanese attack should again seem likely, or if we should begin to develop any sort of a real understanding with Japan, it would not take the Soviet Government very long to discover that our demands with regard to debts and claims were most reasonable.

I cannot tell you how glad I shall be to see you.

This place is fun but I often wish I were with you in Washington. Good luck till we meet and a large embrace to the entire White House.

Yours permanently,

Bill

Personal and Confidential   Moscow
                                                    September 8, 1934

Dear Judge Moore:

I have just received your letter of August 13, and your cable of yesterday announcing that "efforts to reach an agreement with Troyanovsky have failed" . . .

I continue to believe that provided we can work out the physical details, we should go ahead with the construction of our new Embassy no matter how unaccomodating we may find the Russians at the moment. Unless all signs are deceptive, Moscow will become with each year an increasingly important point in international relations. Moreover, it is almost impossible to imagine a situation which would cause us to have exceedingly bad relations with the Soviet Government for the simple reason that the two countries have no major conflicting interests . . .

I am convinced that the chief obstacle both to a successful conclusion of the negotiations with regard to debts and claims and to the establishment of really frank and friendly relations between our two Governments is Litvinov himself. He has, as you know, thrown out of the Foreign Office recently both Sokolnikov and Karakhan — strong men who were very friendly to the United States, and seems to believe that he can afford not to make any effort to maintain warm relations between the Soviet Union and the United States. My guess is, from many slight indications I have had in conversations with him, that he is convinced that we will not enter into any special agreements with the Soviet Union directed against Japan or obliging us to take any action in the Far East and that he believes further that in case of war between Japan and the Soviet Union we would inevitably be drawn in on the side of the Soviet Union, and that it would make no difference whether our relations with the Soviet Union prior to such an event were warm, tepid or cold. His entire attitude is based on the belief that any real rapproachement between the United States and Japan is impossible. If he were to think for one minute that we might establish really good relations with Japan he would, of course, be scared to death . . .

Good luck to you until we meet — and after.

Yours affectionately,
William C. Bullitt

To Miss LeHand: You may like to read this, which came today and show it to the President.

R. Walton Moore   10/23/34

Personal and Confidential   Moscow
                                                    October 6, 1934

Dear Judge Moore:

. . . I talked with Litvinov yesterday and found him rather pulverized. He pretended that this was entirely due to the experiences he had had in Geneva which had made him feel that no nation in Europe really wanted to maintain peace enough to do anything effective to preserve it. I suspect also that he had been thoroughly kicked around the Kremlin on the previous day. The Russians hated entering the League of Nations and did so only as a preliminary step to a defensive agreement with the French and I suspect that the French, having got the Russians into the League, are now cooling off. One rather amusing little incident took place in our conversation yesterday when Litvinov said that he thought there would be no point in talking with Troyanovsky unless I were able to remain in Moscow for two or three weeks of conversations. I asked him why conversations should take so long a time as the only thing which was needed to obtain an agreement in principle was for him to say that he would give up the idea of a loan or an unrestricted credit. He replied, without giving any reasons, that he felt that two or three weeks of conversations would be necessary. I had been informed privately beforehand that Stalin would not return to Moscow until about the first of November so I said, "What you mean is that the Government will be in the Caucasus for the remainder of the month." He grinned broadly and nodded.

Usually when I see Litvinov our conversations are most belligerent, in fact, we frequently swear at each other but yesterday Litvinov took all my harsh words (expletives omitted) as if he were a broken spirited creature. He would not alter his position and indeed intimated he could not until he had talked with Stalin but I had the impression that the fight had gone out of him. On the other hand, I feel that he still under-estimates completely the influence that the United States can have in preserving peace in the Far East and that he is personally putting no energy whatever behind the work of achieving agreement. Fortunately, Voroshilov is putting a great deal of energy into this job and Litvinov positively quivered when I brought Voroshilov's name into the conversation. In the calls which I shall make during the next few days before my departure I shall attempt to prepare further the ground for Troyanovsky and if he acts as energetically as you seem to think he will act, I believe that he may be able to carry the day.

I was very anxious to fly to Vladivostok but decided that it was foolhardy and shall, therefore, take the train. I shall, in all probability, go to China via Korea and Tientsin, avoiding completely the territory of Manchukuo. If I go that way I shall land at Tientsin and go thence to Peiping, Nanking and Shanghai. I shall sail from Shanghai on November 27 on one of the *Dollar Line* boats, arriving in Seattle on December 11. I shall be in Washington presumably on December 15 . . .

> Yours affectionately,
> William C. Bullitt

Bullitt and Offie left Moscow on October 10, 1934, across the Trans-Siberian Railroad to Vladivostok. He reported to Secretary Hull on the condition of the railroad, noting that it had been double tracked to a point well to the west of Vladivostok. In his opinion it was at this point that the Russians expected to meet any attack by the Japanese. He notes that "Among the passengers on the train were Lice." Bullitt arrived in Japan on October 23, where he had a talk with the Emperor, whom he describes as having difficulty in speaking, "but when he listens he has a keen and understanding eye and a thoroughly alive and intelligent smile." He also saw several of the government officials but "All these conversations were so polite and formal in nature that they contained nothing of interest." In Tokyo he had a long talk with the Soviet Ambassador, Constantin Yurenev, who warned him not to underestimate the Japanese fleet, for they believed it was then actually stronger than our fleet, and they were convinced that ship for ship, man for man and officer for officer, the quality of their fleet was so superior that inferiority in numbers would count for little. Later in China he was to hear the same story. From Japan they went to Shanghai, where he saw T. V. Soong, Chiang Kai-shek's brother-in-law, and various other officials. On November 15 he reached Peiping, where he discussed possible Japanese advances into China, and then went on to Nanking, where the talks were about Communist activities supported by the Russians in China. In Nanking he had three important talks with Chiang Kai-shek.[1]

On December 14, 1934, Bullitt submitted a lengthy memorandum to the Secretary of State of his talks with Chiang Kai-shek covering a period from November 21 to 23. The talk turned largely on Chinese-Soviet relations and the mutual threat of Japanese aggression. Although the Chinese had sent a military mission to Moscow, no proposals had been made for any cooperation between the two countries. Chiang felt there could be no cooperation with Russia until the Communist movement in China had been crushed, but he felt the leaders of the movement were men of character who were able military commanders. If the Japanese advanced into Inner Mongolia, Chiang intended to declare war and resist with all his forces. A Japanese attack on North China would provoke the same reaction.

With regard to our Pacific fleet, Chiang felt that this fleet, operating in Far Eastern waters, would be of the greatest aid to China, and he felt the only reason the Japanese had withdrawn from Shantung was the strength of the American fleet at that time. They discussed the opium traffic and the general expressed his intention of suppressing it within five years. They then discussed China's relations with Russia, and Chiang asked Bullitt to let the Russians know that if they would play fair with China he would do everything possible to cooperate. Chiang further desired to work out a system of exchange of goods with the United States on a barter basis, with particular reference to the Chinese need for the development of its railroads.

All of these talks took place with Mme. Chiang Kai-shek acting as the interpreter.

7

Inside European Diplomacy

JANUARY—MAY 1935

Saar Plebiscite
Conscription in Germany
French-Russian Pact

DURING 1933 HITLER had made increasing demands for members of the Nazi party to be included in the Austrian Government. Chancellor Dollfuss of Austria was also faced with threats from the Socialist party, which had created its own army. Dollfuss sought the help of Italy and succeeded in obtaining from her a statement that the "normal conditions of independence and peaceful life must first of all be secured." On February 12, 1934, the Austrian Government broke the Socialist party in street fighting in Vienna. On February 17, the British, French, and Italian governments made a joint declaration on Austrian independence.

On June 14, Mussolini and Hitler met for the first time in Venice. Mussolini's first comment was: "I don't like his looks." Hitler gave Mussolini some hope of the relaxing of Nazi activities. However, the Nazis increased their plotting and on July 25 they broke into the Chancellor's office and murdered Dollfuss.

This action gained them little, as the Austrian President Miklas acted promptly and appointed his Minister of Justice, Dr. Schuschnigg, as Chancellor. The Austrian Army remained loyal and Mussolini promised Italian support, which he fulfilled by sending three divisions to the border. Hitler had failed.

In the summer of 1934 Hitler was having increasing difficulties at home. The right-wing parties and the industrialists were demanding a halt in the radical changes he was making in the government, and some were seriously concerned about the increasing persecution of the Jews. Counterplots were arising within the Nazi party which resulted in Hitler's purge of June 30 of some of the leaders, including Roehm and General Schleicher. It may very well be that in order to distract attention from his difficulties at home, Hitler ordered the murder of Dollfuss.

Bullitt arrived at Seattle on December 11 and went directly to Washington to report to the President. He was ill with a virus infection in January and early February.

THE WHITE HOUSE
WASHINGTON

February 6 [1935]

Dear Bill,

So glad to hear you still have a nose and a jaw and a smile — all three are essential in our business — But do forget the whole crew of Bolshies and Career Men (same idea) until they let you out of hock minus the bacilli — In other words the delousing in China was apparently badly done — If this second attempt fails I shall turn you over to the Army Medical Corpse — Best of luck and give me ring Sat. or Sunday —

As ever,

FDR

Ambassador Bullitt
Private Observation Ward
Somewhere
[A handwritten letter.]

HOSPITAL OF THE UNIVERSITY OF PENNSYLVANIA
PHILADELPHIA

9 February 1935

Dear Mr. President:

It was like no one but your own self to take the trouble to telephone as you did this morning. And your letter, which arrived when I was feeling like a poisoned pup, was the perfect emetic.

You are an angel as well as a President, and the best proof I know of how dumb old Uncle Henry Adams was when he wrote, "A friend in office is a friend lost."

But, after all, he was speaking of Republicans — there were no Democrats in office.

I am really grateful to you.

Yours to the finish,
Bill

After his illness Bullitt went to Florida and did not sail for Europe until March 22, 1935. Although he was still Ambassador to Russia he stopped in Paris and had some important talks. The "Jesse" referred to in the next letters was Ambassador Straus, whom Bullitt kept fully informed on all these conversations, and the reader will note that the letters were typed in the American Embassy.

EMBASSY OF THE
UNITED STATES OF AMERICA

Personal and Confidential   Paris

April 7, 1935

Dear Mr. President:

I wish I could sit down with you this evening for a long gossip in the White House. I should like to have another look at you and there is so much to write that fifty pages could not contain a full description of the facts and fantastic projects that have been poured into my ears since I reached Paris. The whole of Europe is concentrating in and on Paris these days and the statesmen and diplomatists without exception seem to be neurasthenic. I find myself in a condition of Buddhistic calm compared to everyone I meet. The people at the top have even lost all sense of the ridiculous. For example, yesterday afternoon I called at the house of a French friend and there were André Geraud (Pertinax) of the "Echo de Paris" and the Soviet Ambassador, Potemkin, seated together in one large chair with their arms around each other whispering intimacies. Inasmuch as there is no human being who hates the Soviet Union more deeply than Pertinax and no one who has been distrusted more than Pertinax by the Soviet Government . . . the spectacle seemed to be a good sample of the unreality which underlies all the diplomatic combinations now being made.

The one fortunate element in the situation from our point of view is that no one expects the United States to become involved in any way whatsoever. Comert said to me last night that when the American Ambassador appears at the Quai d'Orsay everyone has the same feeling as if the Dalai Lama had dropped in. The French and

all the others feel that there will not be the slightest chance of drawing us into the war which they now regard as inevitable. As nearly
as I can gather the present situation is the following:

Eden went too far in his conversations in Moscow to please the
British Government although he pleased the Soviet Government immensely. He had a heart attack in Cologne and may be out of the
picture for some time. He may not even be able to go to Stresa. His
conversations in Warsaw were a flat washout. Pilsudski was apparently enjoying one of his periodic relapses and was too ga-ga to
reply intelligently to any of Eden's questions. Beck, I am told, was
not more satisfactory and still remains obsessed by his dislike of
France. (In this connection I have heard from two reliable sources
the following statement: General Weygand is reported to have said
that when Beck was Polish Military Attaché in France, he was given
access to many of the secrets of the French Army. The French General Staff became suspicious of him and after giving him certain important papers sent to him an agent who pretended to be acting for
a foreign power. The agent bought from Beck exact copies of the
documents handed to Beck in strictest confidence by the French
General Staff. The French General Staff had Beck recalled immediately. It is alleged that this episode is the basis of Beck's hostility to
France. Whether the story is true or not it is at least interesting to
know that it is believed in the French Foreign Office.)

The relations of France and the Soviet Union seem to be the following:

Flandin does not want the alliance. Laval does not want it.
Flandin is entirely ready to let the Germans expand to the east as a
method of avoiding war in Western Europe. Nevertheless, the
French Government will probably be pushed into the conclusion of
the alliance in the form of an agreement for mutual assistance in
case of aggression, tied into the mechanism of the League of Nations. Titulescu has been the prime mover in drawing together the
Russians and the French. The Russians a couple of weeks ago demanded that the French put up or shut up, intimating strongly that
if France did not do so the Soviet Union would begin to develop as
close relations as possible with the German Reichswehr which has
always been, as you know, pro-Russian and anti-French. The Quai
d'Orsay then prepared a text which was entirely unsatisfactory to
the Russians and Potemkin then called on Laval with an extremely
harsh statement from Stalin. Titulescu then began running back
and forth between the French and the Russians as he said to me, "I
represented France with the Russians and the Russians with the

French, and there is now a text in preparation at the Quai d'Orsay which will provide that in case of aggression against either France or the Soviet Union the matter shall first be referred to the Council of the League of Nations. If the Council declares unanimously against the aggressor either France or the Soviet Union, as the case may be, will place its forces totally at the disposal of the other. If the Council of the League should not be unanimous the Powers will recover their liberty of action and France and the Soviet Union will place their forces unreservedly at each other's disposal." This, of course, amounts to an alliance but is so camouflaged by the League of Nations declaration that the French people will accept it. There is, however, the additional point that adherence to such an agreement will be open to all nations on the continent including Germany.

It is confidently believed in Paris that Czechoslovakia will at once enter a similar agreement with the Soviet Union and that Italy may also. It is hoped that Rumania and Yugoslavia and even Poland finally may be persuaded to join.

Laval has promised to leave for Moscow on the 20th and will have to sign something definite there. The above seems to be the inescapable minimum. How unhappy he is about the matter may be judged from the fact that Titulescu told me yesterday that Madame Laval had said to him at least once a day for the past week, "You are driving my husband to destruction."

The possibility, which we discussed before I left, that Hungary might follow the example of Germany and introduce conscription and thus precipitate a march by the Rumanians and the Czechs to Budapest seems to be definitely eliminated . . .

I am going to spare you an attempt to replace an evening of conversation by a letter. There are a thousand facts and statements that I should like to pour in your ear. For example, the Soviet Ambassador here told me that the Soviet Consul in the Yemen, whom he knew intimately and knew to be an absolutely accurate informant, had let him know recently that through the Yemen were coming streams of enormous packing cases from Japan addressed to Addis Ababa and labeled "Pianos." He was not certain as to the exact type of munitions contained therein.

Wiley writes me from Moscow that there is every prospect that the Soviet Foreign Office will continue to be as disagreeable as possible both personally and officially. If the French alliance or pact of mutual assistance, as you prefer, should go through the Soviets will be cockier than ever and I may find it difficult to send back as much information as heretofore. I shall, however, endure any such situation with considerable equanimity.

Dodd wrote me from Berlin asking me to stop off for a conversation with him and I shall stop between trains just long enough to find out what he wants. Cudahy telephoned that it was absolutely essential that I should stop in Warsaw and I shall spend twenty-four hours with him, reaching Moscow on April 13. The conversations which I have had in Paris have made me more than ever certain that your present policy of keeping out of this mess now and hereafter is the only one consistent with the interests of the United States. We can do nothing now that will really help and any commitments we make will tend to produce our involvement from the beginning in the ultimate conflict. To say nothing, do nothing, and carry a large cannon seems to me the only policy for us to pursue. I do not expect any conflict in the near future. When it does come, provided we stay out of it, we shall be in good shape to help reconstruct what remains of Europe.

Bless you for your kindness to me when I was in America and for your friendship. It means a great deal.

Yours permanently,
William C. B.

P.S. . . . I have been trying to avoid seeing Laval as I have not wanted Jesse to feel that I was butting into his cow pasture, and turned down politely three suggestions from his subordinates that I should see him. Tonight in my absence Laval *personally* phoned and got Offie and said he insisted on seeing me tomorrow morning. So I shall have to see him and as he will certainly tell me the whole story I shall be in the highly embarrassing position of having to prepare a telegram with Jesse. But he is a good fellow and will not, I think, go prima donna. His white spat brigade will, however, be delivered of kittens all over the office floor.

Love to all,
Bill

EMBASSY OF THE
UNITED STATES OF AMERICA
Personal and Confidential   Paris
April 7, 1935

Dear Judge Moore:

Just a line to thank you for your kindness to me when I was in Washington and to give you the Parisian atmosphere . . .

I have never known a more disagreeable atmosphere in Paris. The German rearmament is throwing into pretended friendships men and nations who cordially distrust and detest each other . . .

The general situation seems to be this: Europe is superficially and temporarily united by fear of Germany. The only exceptions are Hungary and Poland. There is a small group in France that believes this temporary cohesion should be taken advantage of and that France should move actively against Germany; but the French people have never been more completely pacifist than they are today and any aggressive action by France is out of the question.

The Franco-Russian alliance in the form of a pact for mutual assistance, under the aegis of the League of Nations will, I believe, go through.

. . . People in France are by no means disposed to agree to declare war on Germany if there should be a minor incident of a military nature between Germany and the Soviet Union but would be willing to promise to fight in case of a real war. The French have no illusions about the Russians and do not expect any real help from the Soviet Union. If they make the alliance, they will make it merely because they are afraid that, if they do not, the Soviet Government will turn to Germany. They expect the Reichswehr to increase its control over Hitler and they know that the Reichswehr has always been in favor of an attack not on the Soviet Union but on France. They seem to believe that the mere formulation of a mutual assistance agreement with the Soviet Union will keep the Soviet Union out of Germany's arms.

My own feeling is that the Soviet Government will make the mutual assistance pact with the French and then begin to flirt with Germany as well as France and succeed in getting Germany and France bidding against one another for Soviet support, and that the only country which will derive any real benefit from the present maneuvers will be the Soviet Union.

I could write you fifty pages detailing the schemes and counter schemes which are being proposed in Paris by governments all the way from England to Rumania. It seems useless to do so as they all seem the gestures of impotent diplomatists in the face of inevitable tragedy. There is an air of unreality and almost silliness in the whole complex of maneuvers. Thank God we are standing aloof. We can do absolutely nothing to help. Any action of ours would, I believe, merely tend to make it certain that we would be involved from the beginning in the conflict which is coming. I hope to

Heaven that you, the Secretary, and the President will continue to turn deaf ears to the pleas of those well-intentioned but relatively ignorant persons who want us to involve ourselves in the mess. There is, fortunately, no sign here that anyone expects the United States to intervene in any way by either word or act. The general French attitude is that there is a war coming and that it is only natural that the United States, in view of the fact that its sole harvest from the last war was a crop of disillusionment, should remain completely aloof.

A letter from Wiley informs me that my reception in Moscow will probably be extremely cool and that I shall find it much more difficult than in the past to maintain the intimate contacts which have been useful to us from the point of view of information. I shall do the best I can but should not be surprised if I were unable to supply you with as much advance information as I have been able to in the past . . .

I find that almost everyone that I meet is very much more excited about the general situation than I am. The present Nationalist movement in Germany has, in my opinion, been inevitable since the terms of the Treaty of Versailles were imposed. Only a nation without courage could have endured that Treaty and the Germans, whatever their other shortcomings, have courage. I do not expect any immediate or early outbreak of hostilities. Hungary, Titulescu informed me, has given formal promises not only to the Rumanian Government but to the British that no attempt will be made to imitate Hitler and reintroduce conscription, so that for the moment at least we shall not see Rumanian troops marching toward Budapest.

Very competent observers who have been in Vienna recently tell me that there is considerable chance that Austria, as a result of internal pressure not external, will go Nazi this summer and the French expect the Italians to march into Austria if that should happen. I find it difficult to believe that if the change in the Austrian Government should come by the free action of the Austrian people, the Italians would dare to march in. To do so would be to begin a war on very doubtful moral grounds indeed. I do not, therefore, feel that there will be any early outbreak of hostilities but the statesmen and diplomatists of Europe are in such a neurotic state of mind that anything is possible . . .

Every good wish to you and to your sisters.

Yours affectionately,
William C. Bullitt

EMBASSY OF THE
UNITED STATES OF AMERICA

Paris

April 8, 1935

Dear Mr. President:

You will, I fear, think that your remark that you really wanted me to write to you is going to produce an endless flood of letters when you see this in addition to the pages I wrote you yesterday. I want simply to explain to you developments flowing from that P. S.

It was indeed Laval who phoned last night and I saw him this morning. I reported at once to Jesse Straus and you will unquestionably have seen the telegram which Jesse dictated as a result of my reports on conversations with Titulescu, Laval and Potemkin.

Laval said that he would reach Moscow on the 25th and would sign the mutual assistance pact on that date or on the 26th. I asked him if he would remain in Moscow for the fêtes of the first of May and he said that he would not as the French people would consider that he should not participate in a revolutionary celebration! It is a long way from 1789!

Laval said that the definitive text of the pact was not yet established but that he was working on it. He added that he had had some hesitation about concluding the agreement because, in his opinion, the Soviet Army was essentially a force for keeping down the Russian people and handling internal problems and could not operate effectively outside the Soviet Union. He added that his military advisors, however, believed the Soviet air force had a certain value . . .

He then asked me what policy I thought the Russians would follow. (This question seemed to me to be the cause of his insistence on seeing me.) I replied that the Russians would doubtless follow the example of France and attempt to develop close relations with Germany. He said that he thought the agreement would place the Soviet Union in a very favorable position to bargain between France and Germany. I replied that I agreed that Russia would be in the happy position of being able to wait for the offers of the highest bidder . . .

We talked about lots of other things of minor importance and he displayed a really surprising cordiality throughout our conversation.

Potemkin, the Soviet Ambassador in Paris, confirmed today at luncheon all the statements that Laval had made and said in addition that he was discussing with Laval a subsidiary pact which would be adopted shortly after the pact of mutual assistance. Potemkin said that this subsidiary agreement would provide for immediate declaration of war by the Soviet Union and France in the case of flagrant aggression by Germany . . . Potemkin said also that after the signature of the mutual assistance agreement by France and the Soviet Union, the Soviet Union would sign immediately a similar mutual assistance agreement with the Czechoslovaks. Both Potemkin and his staff were in a triumphant state of mind . . .

My own opinion is that the Soviet Union will be the single great beneficiary of the agreement described above. Neither Germany nor Japan will dare to attack the Soviet Union, and France and Germany will be compelled to begin to bid high for Soviet assistance . . .

It is obvious, of course, from all of these maneuvers and counter maneuvers that no one in Europe is any longer thinking of peace but that everyone is thinking furiously about obtaining as many allies as possible for the next war. As each day passes I become more convinced that our only sane policy is to stay just as far as possible outside the mess. In this connection it was interesting at luncheon today at the Soviet Embassy to see the reaction of a large table full of guests which included French cabinet ministers and former ministers. Rosenberg, who is now the Soviet assistant secretary at the League of Nations and was formerly Soviet Chargé d'Affaires in Paris, called across the table to me and said that he felt that the United States should participate actively in the present negotiations and asked me why the United States was remaining so aloof. To a silent table I delivered a short oration which, if I may say so, was worthy of yourself. At the end of the discourse everyone, including the French cabinet ministers, said, "You are perfectly right. No one can expect the United States to involve itself in the events which are approaching."

During the course of [the] luncheon I said to the Soviet Ambassador that of course the mutual assistance agreement with France was just an old-fashioned alliance camouflaged by a smear of League of Nations paint for the benefit of the French people. He said, "You are quite right." I then said that I felt the only weak point in the whole project was Austria, that I was informed on good authority that there was a considerable possibility that Austria, not from external pressure but from internal force, would go Nazi this summer . . .

Excuse me if I have burdened you too greatly. Good night and the Lord be with you.

Yours permanently,
Bill

On March 9, 1935, Hitler defied the sixteen-year-old Versailles Treaty and announced the formation of the Luftwaffe, the German Air Force. One week later, on the sixteenth, he decreed universal conscription for the new German Army, setting the number of divisions at a figure far higher than even his generals had hoped for. The French immediately raised the length of service in their army to two years and the seeds of a new war were well sown. The Nazi actions were a clear violation of the peace treaty, which was the cornerstone of the League of Nations. Hitler invited the British Foriegn Minister, Sir John Simon, to Berlin on March 24 and announced to him that the German Air Force, which had been training secretly, was already the equal of that of England.

Parliament was shocked by this disclosure and Stanley Baldwin, accepting the blame, stated: "It is the responsibility of the Government as a whole, and we are all responsible, and we are all to blame." [1] Although the British immediately undertook construction they never believed that, in the next four years, they were able to obtain parity with the Germans.[2]

The impotent Council of the League of Nations met in the middle of April to discuss the German breach of its obligation. Nineteen countries voted to make a formal protest to Germany, but as usual no country was willing to take action. Hitler had won another bloodless victory.

EMBASSY OF THE
UNITED STATES OF AMERICA

Personal and Confidential   On train enroute to Moscow
                                         from Warsaw, April 12, 1935

Dear Mr. President:

John Cudahy, with whom I have spent the past twenty-four hours in Warsaw astonished me this morning by saying that he had only one wish in life: to be appointed Minister to Ireland. He is anxious to get out of Poland as he has had more than enough of the physical disorder of Eastern Europe. It occurred to me at once that this wish of Cudahy's might be the key to a happy solution of your diplomatic appointment problems . . .

In my opinion Cudahy would make an admirable Minister to Dublin. He loves to hunt and is a very attractive fellow of the type that the Irish like and his private life is as blameless as the Pope himself could desire.

. . . I had a long talk in Berlin night before last with Lipsky, the Polish Ambassador, and one last night with the Under Secretary of Foreign Affairs in Warsaw. I am convinced not only from these conversations but from every other piece of evidence I have been able to get in Paris and elsewhere that there is no secret agreement or alliance between the Poles and the Germans, and that the basis of Polish policy is and will remain refusal to make any agreement permitting either German or Russian forces to set foot on Polish soil under any circumstances . . . In Poland the hatred of Russia and the fear of the ultimate power of Russia, is greater than the fear and hatred of Germany. The Poles are convinced that so long as Hitler is in power the German drive will be toward annexing to Germany those portions of Europe which are inhabited predominantly by Germans and not toward the acquisition of any Slav territory . . .

Good luck and love to you all.

Yours permanently,
Bullitt

In Moscow on May 2, 1935, Pierre Laval on behalf of France signed an agreement of mutual assistance with the Soviet Union. The Franco-Soviet pact was not definitely binding on either party in case of German attack, and therefore only had small advantages. It did help Laval in obtaining the support of the French Communists in his defense program and his establishing a two-year term of army service. The pact was drawn for a five-year period.

Shortly thereafter a similar pact was signed between the Russians and Czechoslovakia.

The British had recently discovered another violation of the Versailles Treaty by Hitler. Under the treaty the Germans were limited to four battleships and six cruisers of no greater than ten thousand tons apiece. The two latest ships were of twenty-six thousand tons each and were fast battle cruisers and commerce raiders. The ships must necessarily have been begun shortly after Hitler's accession to power in 1933. Rather than take any action against Germany under the League of Nations, England, without consulting France or the League, entered into a naval pact with Germany whereby the new German Navy was not to exceed one third of the British fleet. England also permitted the building of German submarines — a right explicitly denied under the Versailles Treaty — to a strength 60 per cent of that of the British submarine force. This allowed Hitler openly to build submarines and he, of course, had no intention of holding to any such ratio.

Many of the members of the League of Nations were shocked by this Anglo-German naval agreement, and it further impaired the usefulness of the League.

THE WHITE HOUSE
WASHINGTON

April 21, 1935

Dear Bill Buddha:

The batch from Paris is grand. All the news makes me think that your old buddy Laval does not like your Vatican, as he has apparently postponed that weekend visit to Moscow. What a mess it all is! You, too, seem pessimistic and I think you are right, though one gets curious slants the other way.

Sir Stafford Cripps lunched with me — he evidently has some fairly close German connections — and he does not think Germany will be ready for five years and will, in the meantime, wiggle out of any actual war. Also he told me, with a straight face, that Hitler does not feel he can count on the German people to back him up in a war. I asked him if he was playing the role of a Haldane * and he laughed it off.

I hope you are not being ostracized by the "information givers" at Moscow, though I gather that no European Capital in the present confusion cares a continental damn what the United States thinks or does. They are very unwise in this attitude.

Things here are going better. I had a very successful cruise with Vincent.†

We have offered Norway to Biddle and I think he will take it. Armour will go to Canada.

After all the howls and squawks the Social Security Bill passed the House with only thirty-three votes against it. Before I get through I shall get the Senate to adopt a decent cloture rule. Even Senators can become nationally unpopular!

---

* Viscount Haldane, Lord Chancellor 1912–1915, withdrew from political activity in World War I because of German affinities.

† Vincent was Vincent Astor.

It is Easter day — pouring and raw. I suppose you are out sleighing in a samovar! Pin a rose on Lenin when you attend the May first celebration. He is a great man because dead!

As ever yours,

FDR

Honorable William C. Bullitt
American Embassy
Moscow

P.S. I never worry about your health mentally but I do worry about you physically. Therefore, do take care of yourself. Why not try one of the French or Italian "cures" this summer? They are wonderful for sleep and for internal and external cleaning. Also, you would be nearer the war than in Moscow!

THE WHITE HOUSE
WASHINGTON

April 26, 1935

Dear Bill Buddha:

Alas, for the first time in your life you are too late! We have offered Ireland to Owsley. In any event, I would not like to take Cudahy away from Warsaw at this particular time because I think he is doing a good job.

What a shame that you missed Litvinov in Warsaw and could not travel with him in his compartment to Moscow!

As ever yours,

FDR

Honorable William C. Bullitt
American Embassy
Moscow

8

A Russian Murder and a Polish Funeral

MAY—JUNE 1935

Bullitt Gives a Party
Murder of Kirov
Goering and Bullitt at Pilsudski's Funeral

THE GREAT PURGES, which convulsed Soviet life from 1935 to 1938, were particularly severe on the leading men of Russia. It has been estimated that the party central committee lost 70 per cent of its membership. In addition, the majority of the highest officers in the army and many of the lesser ones were purged, to say nothing of the thousands of trade union officials, intellectuals, and party members.

Stalin attributed this gruesome act to supposed plots of counterrevolutionaries, especially from German sources, but it was evident that it arose from his own paranoid suspicions of those who surrounded him. He later is supposed to have told Churchill that one "cannot make an omelet without breaking eggs." This blood bath, together with the farce of the show trials, contributed to the disillusionment of the foreign admirers of the Soviet system and added to the disheartening atmosphere in which Bullitt had to work during his service in Moscow.

Personal and Confidential   Moscow
                                                          May 1, 1935

Dear Mr. President:

I have just come back from the May Day parade on the Red Square. It has been a great show with tanks galloping across at 60 miles per hour and new pursuit airplanes at 400 kilometers p.h. Stalin came late and left early due, I was told, to a last minute hitch in the negotiations with the French. It was also noticeable that when he walked the short space from the Kremlin wall to Lenin's tomb he held a handkerchief to his face. He may really, after all, be a bit frightened as indicated in the very confidential despatch I am sending by this pouch which I have asked the Secretary to send over to you.

Physically, Moscow is a pleasanter place than this time last year. The subway has been completed. Blocks of old buildings have been turned into streets and squares, and the paving of the streets has been improved. Emotionally, however, Moscow is by no means so pleasant a place. The terror, always present, has risen to such a pitch that the least of the Muscovites, as well as the greatest, is in fear. Almost no one dares have any contact with foreigners and this is not unbased fear but a proper sense of reality. The chief engineer of the Amo works, now the largest producers of trucks in the world, has just spent eight months in jail because he ventured to call on the Latvian Minister, a very old friend of his. Every single acquaintance, even the most casual, of the Japanese language students in Leningrad, has been exiled. The only real friend of this Embassy, George Andreytchine, whom I asked you to pardon last year, is in the Lyublianka prison awaiting either death or exile. The only decent guide in the Soviet Union who took my cousin, Marshall, and his family around the country last year and is a thoroughly good friend of mine, has been exiled. Everyone who has had any contact with the Japanese Embassy, even down to the tailor, has been exiled. And the three not-too-awful dentists of the town suffered the same fate, leaving members of the American Embassy hanging on to temporary fillings!

It is extraordinarily difficult to preserve a sweet and loving exterior under the circumstances. I can, of course, do nothing to save anyone. In fact, *strictly between ourselves,* I got a message from Andreytchine, sent by grapevine from the OGPU Lyublianka prison, asking me for God's sake to do nothing to try to save him, if I should, he would certainly be shot.

The Russians still dare to come to my house for large entertainments when there can be no possibility of private conversation. There was a good turnout for the ball I gave on the 23rd of April. Litvinov came with his wife and eldest daughter. It was an astonishingly successful party, thoroughly dignified yet gay. Everyone happy and no one drunk. In fact, if I can believe the letter I got from the British Ambassadress and many verbal messages, it was the best party in Moscow since the revolution. We got a thousand tulips from Helsingfors and forced a lot of birch trees into premature leafage and arranged one end of the dining room as a collective farm with peasant accordion players, dancers, and all sorts of baby things, such as birds, goats, and a couple of infant bears about the size of cats. We also had pleasant lighting effects done by the best theater here and a bit of a cabaret. It was really great fun and the Turkish Ambassador and about twenty others remained until breakfast at eight . . .

Do you remember our bet of one red apple or whatever (I have forgotten what) as to the scene of the first outbreak of war? You picked Europe and I picked the Far East. I am beginning to be inclined to think that you will probably turn out to be right as usual. The Austrian situation seems to contain all the elements of a major explosion while the Far Eastern situation is momentarily quiet. The long range outlook everywhere is about as bad as can be and the worst of it is that we can do nothing whatever to stop the march of events. The economic basis of Germany and Japan is such today that neither nation has any future, except a continuously diminishing standard of living, unless it can acquire new sources of raw materials and new markets. The Japanese line is obvious. My guess is that Hitler has decided that the German line of advance shall be down the Danube and not toward the Ukraine, although if he is blocked in his economic domination of Central Europe and the Balkans he will certainly try to turn toward the Ukraine.

I see no way that we can achieve anything by attempting to stop the march of events — horrible as it is — except our own involvement in war and I hope that you will turn a very deaf ear to the songs of the sirens who must be keeping you awake nights with their music. I saw that Stimson had donned the mermaid's tail and there must be a thousand others whose hearts are better than their heads.

There is nothing very gay to report from Moscow except an incident that happened the other day when, on the completion of a tremendous new hospital at Gorki, aviators were sent up to take pictures from the air for propaganda purposes. When they came down and the pictures were developed, the hospital turned out to be the most perfect German swastika! The architect was immediately exiled and new wings are being built feverishly.

I wish I could hear the sound of your voice.

Bless you.

Bill

THE SECRETARY OF STATE
WASHINGTON

May 16, 1935

My dear Mr. President:

At the request of Ambassador Bullitt I enclose, as of possible interest, a highly confidential despatch from Moscow regarding the Kirov murder.

Mr. Bullitt has especially requested that the despatch be treated as secret, since the position of the Lithuanian Minister in Moscow might be gravely compromised if the source of the information contained in this despatch should become known to the Soviet Government.

Faithfully yours,
Cordell Hull

Enclosure:
Despatch

Sergei Kirov, head of the Communist Party in Leningrad, was often thought of as the successor of Stalin. He disapproved of the ruthless action of Stalin in imprisoning and killing those who were opposed to him. Kirov was murdered in Leningrad on December 1, 1934. The following letter gives an intimate picture of the intrigues of the Russians and the emotional basis on which many decisions were founded.

No. 552   Moscow
Subject: The Kirov Murder   April 26, 1935
Strictly Confidential — for the Secretary
The Honorable Secretary of State
Washington

Sir:

I have the honor to report certain highly confidential information with regard to the Kirov murder.

You will recall that when I had the honor and pleasure of discussing the Kirov case with you personally in Washington I expressed the opinion that the reports then in the Department and the explanation of Ambassador Troyanovsky did not give an intimate or altogether credible account of the affair, and promised you to attempt to discover the underlying facts when I returned to Moscow.

On the evening of April 17 from Mr. Baltrusaitis, the Lithuanian

Minister, I obtained an explanation of the affair which seems to me to come close to the truth and, indeed, may be entirely accurate.

(Mr. Baltrusaitis enjoys a unique position in the Soviet Union. He has been a resident of Moscow for more than forty years. Before the Revolution he became one of the leading poets of Russia — his works being written not in Lithuanian but in Russian. When Litvinov was in Washington, I asked him if there were anyone in the diplomatic corps in Moscow of particular value. He replied that there was only one man, Baltrusaitis, who knew Russia intimately . . .

On reaching Moscow, therefore, I cultivated an intimacy with Mr. Baltrusaitis which I have found of value on many occasions. Our relations are extremely friendly and he seems to have no hesitation in telling me anything that he knows. In the past I have found the information which he has given me to be correct and the story he told me regarding Kirov was supplemented by such a wealth of detail and such assurances of absolute accuracy that I felt it contained the kernel of the Kirov mystery.)

Mr. Baltrusaitis said that Nikolaiev, the murderer of Kirov, had been for a long time a special agent of the OGPU. His place of activity was, in the main, Leningrad. He said that Kirov had been sent to Leningrad for an "executive education," and added that Kirov had been given almost independent authority in the Leningrad Oblast in order to prepare him to assume at a later date the dictatorship of the Soviet Union. He asserted that Stalin had decided definitely that Kirov should be his successor and commented that Kirov, whom he (Baltrusaitis) had known personally, was very much the same type of human being as Stalin and was trusted implicitly by Stalin.

Mr. Baltrusaitis went on to say that Kirov had fallen in love with the wife of Nikolaiev and that Nikolaiev, although he cared about his wife, had consented to a liaison between her and Kirov in order to further his own career . . .

Mr. Baltrusaitis said that in spite of Nikolaiev's subservience to Kirov he had not received the promotions to which he considered himself entitled and finally had become enraged with Kirov, considering that Kirov had purchased his wife and had not paid the price. The shooting of Kirov, Mr. Baltrusaitis insisted, was a crime commited by Nikolaiev in a moment of passionate and uncontrollable rage.

Mr. Baltrusaitis then described the scene which took place in Stalin's apartment in the Kremlin when Yagoda, Chief of the OGPU (who is now called Commissar for Internal Affairs), called on Stalin after the murder. He asserted that Stalin, as Yagoda walked into the room, moved toward him with a hand outstretched as if to take him by the throat, calling out, "This time you have bitten off more than you can chew." He said that Stalin at that moment had been under the impression that Yagoda had procured the murder of Kirov by his agent Nikolaiev.

Mr. Baltrusaitis asserted that Yagoda had been intensely terrified, but, perceiving at the same moment that Stalin himself seemed terribly shaken, had preserved sufficient presence of mind to defend himself and to accuse Yenukidze, Secretary of the Central Executive Committee, a personal enemy of his, of responsibility for the murder because he had once protected Nikolaiev from arrest by the OGPU . . .

As a result, Yenukidze was dismissed as the Secretary of the Tsik and sent to be Governor of the Trans-Caucasus. All members of the office force of the Tsik inside the Kremlin were exiled. In addition, all Yenukidze's particular friends in the Kremlin were exiled, including the two immediate subordinates of Pedersen, Commandant of the Kremlin. In addition, all members of the so-called "secret guard" of fanatical young Communists in the Kremlin were exiled . . .

Mr. Baltrusaitis then asserted that the story of a plot of former followers of Trotsky and Zinoviev to murder Kirov, Stalin, et al, was a fabrication by Yagoda for the purpose of protecting himself from Stalin's wrath, eliminating his personal enemies, and getting rid of all possible leaders for the discontented Communist youth. Mr. Baltrusaitis said that he knew of his own knowledge that many of the younger members of the Communist Party were now dissatisfied with Stalin's regime and were as eager to revolt against the present government as their predecessors had been to revolt against the Czar.

Mr. Baltrusaitis stated further that Yagoda had played on Stalin's personal fears of assassination in a most subtle and able manner. For example, Mr. Baltrusaitis asserted that Stalin receives his meals from the kitchen of the Kremlin hospital restaurant in containers and that Yagoda, shortly after the murder of Kirov, had placed six OGPU agents in the kitchen to watch the cooks and that since that time Stalin had received all his containers sealed with the seal of the OGPU to protect him from poison.

Mr. Baltrusaitis said further that since Kirov's murder Stalin had become inordinately suspicious of everyone around him with the exception of Voroshilov and Molotov . . .

The arrest and exiling of innocent human beings in all quarters of the Soviet Union continues apace. Mr. Baltrusaitis asserted that everyone in the slightest degree distasteful to the Soviet Government in Leningrad had already been arrested and asserted that a card of individual exile numbered Leningrad 21,000 had come to his attention. (From another wholly reliable source I have the information that a Leningrad card of exile with entire family numbered 7,000 has been seen.)

The arrests in Moscow are still in progress. As I have already reported to the Department the only two fairly competent dentists in Moscow have been exiled recently and the fear of arrest is so great that the Muscovites now do not dare to have any contact with foreign embassies.

In this connection it may be of some interest to the Department to know that Mr. George Andreytchine, who last year was assigned to work out the physical difficulties of the American Embassy by the Foreign Office and was of invaluable assistance to us, was seized some weeks ago by the OGPU. He is, I am now informed, *most privately,* in the Lyublianka prison and may be shot or exiled. Among the charges against him is the accusation that although he saw constantly the American Ambassador to the Soviet Union he was unable to influence the Ambassador to take a more favorable view of Soviet policy.

Respectfully yours,
William C. Bullitt

THE WHITE HOUSE
WASHINGTON

June 3, 1935

Dear Bill:

I have been a long time in writing to you but, as you undoubtedly know, we have had much excitement here due to the decision of the Supreme Court. However, the fact remains that the principles of NRA must be carried on in some way.

As usual I was much interested in your letter to me and also the dispatch which the Secretary of State let me read. That was a fascinating story. Do write me often.

The Ball sounds magnificent but I hope you will not have to

have another one very soon again — at least not until you are quite well.

I have been much interested in hearing from Missy the story of ————. You must be glad to have her on her way back to America.

We were all quite worried at the reports in the paper about your illness in Warsaw and are delighted to hear from Judge Moore that you had gone on to Vienna to be looked over. Do let us hear what the Doctors in Vienna said and for heaven's sake do as they tell you. I hope they have been able to make you more comfortable.

As ever yours,
FDR

Honorable William C. Bullitt
American Embassy
Moscow

Personal and Confidential   Moscow
                                                        June 3, 1935

Dear Mr. President:

Now that I have returned to the status which Queen Victoria used to refer to as that of a "common Duke," I think I ought to give you an account of my experiences during my elevation to the rank of your Special Representative.

To get to Pilsudski's funeral on time was not easy. I received the Secretary's telegram Thursday morning (May 16) and had to be in the church in Warsaw at nine on Friday morning and there were no regular trains or planes available. I got a plane and flew from Moscow to Minsk, noting with stupefaction the improvement in conditions throughout White Russia. The fields were extraordinarily well-planted and there were hundreds of new apple orchards beautifully tended, each tree with its trunk neatly whitewashed. Minsk, the traditional garbage heap of the Jewish pale, was clean and contained one enormous Government office building which would not have been out of place in Washington. The reports that my plane had a crash in Minsk were a pure invention. The flight was as easy and comfortable as could be. I then crossed the frontier by train and the Poles had waiting for me Pilsudski's private car which they hooked onto a train that got to Warsaw an hour before the ceremonies began.

The Polish Government was obviously delighted that you should have sent a Special Representative (only Crosby, our Chargé d'Affaires seemed somewhat miffed), and went out of its way to place me at the top of the procession by using a pleasant twist of the French diplomatic alphabet. I was the representative of "Amerique, États-Unis d'," and not "États-Unis d'Amerique." That put me for all the ceremonies next to Goering who, as representative of "Allemagne," had place No. 1.

Goering swept into the Warsaw cathedral late as if he were a German tenor playing Siegfried. He has the usual German tenor proportions. He is at least a yard across the bottom as the crow flies! In an attempt to get his shoulders out as far as his hips he wears two inches of padding extending each one. It is useless. The shoulders just won't go that far. He is nearly a yard from rear to umbilicus, and as he is not even as tall as I am and encases himself in a glove-tight uniform, the effect is novel. He must carry with him a personal beauty attendant as his fingers, which are almost as thick as they are short, carry long, pointed, carefully enamelled nails and his pink complexion shows every sign of daily attention. His eyes pop wildly as if he were either suffering from a glandular derangement or still taking cocaine. His lips are as thin as those of an infant. When he was 250 pounds lighter he must have been a blond beauty of the most unpleasant sort. He is really the most appalling representative of a nation that I have ever laid eyes on. He made me feel that the Germans will achieve nothing but a series of national disasters until they cease to take the *Niebelungenlied* seriously.

Goering stole the show from the moment he entered the cathedral, and it became not Pilsudski's funeral but Goering's great first-act entrance. Throughout the march from the cathedral to the aviation field — three hours in a drizzling rain — I walked behind the young Siegfried who struck poses every time a camera appeared.

The crowds that lined the streets were impressive. They were absolutely silent and did not even stir. At the field the troops marched past the coffin to the beat of a drum. The silence was more impressive than any music. That night we took the train for Cracow and the next day the march was repeated, ending at the Wawel, the old hill castle of the Polish kings. The Catholic Church did itself proud by putting on a really beautiful service. It was rather long, however, and Goering went to sleep.

Afterward, President Moscicki held a reception for the representatives of the various nations and asked me to thank you personally for having sent a Special Representative for the occasion. The next day I had luncheon at the Potockis' with Pétain. He and Laval had been treated throughout as if they were unwelcome cousins from the country and Laval was sore; but the old man was in great form. He is seventy-nine but after luncheon he kept a crowd of about thirty persons in screams of laughter for a half hour with an account of his attempts to avoid ice water on his visit to the United States during prohibition.

As Vienna is only two and one-half hours by plane from Cracow, I thought I might as well fly down and consult a decent doctor and did so. My last Cracow view was of a regiment turned out to do the honors as I got into the plane.

The visit to Vienna was a colossal success. Professor Luger spotted the difficulty immediately. It appears that the streptococcus is now entirely out of my body but that it took with it about one-half the sugar in my blood. The result was that my blood pressure when I reached Vienna was exactly one hundred, that of a new-born babe! Hence the exhaustion.

It is difficult to believe, but four days of sunlight and plenty of chocolate in Vienna raised my blood pressure from 100 to 130 and I returned to Warsaw feeling quite alive.

When I was in Vienna I saw Schuschnigg and Berger-Waldenegg, the Foreign Minister, and scores of Austrians whom I have known for years. Messersmith arrived just before I did and I had a number of long talks with him. The most interesting conversation I had was with an old friend of mine who for some years has been one of the secret leaders of the Austrian Nazis. He confirmed everything which I gathered from our own representatives and all the Viennese with whom I talked.

No one in Austria really likes the present Government. Schuschnigg is a colorless, bloodless, young man who resembles a tight-lipped young priest in civilian clothing. He wears a gold cross hanging from one buttonhole and the old Greek sign for Jesus Christ in the other. On a small table just in front of his desk stands a large crucifix with a silver Christ and two candles. He is the representative of the Catholic Church and does nothing without consulting Cardinal Innitzer. That means that he will do nothing especially foolish but also that he can not catch the imagination of a nation in the twentieth century.

Berger-Waldenegg, the Foreign Minister, is an orderly bureaucrat who reminded me of Burian, the first Austrian Foreign Minister I ever saw at that desk in the Ballhaus.

In addition to the support of the Catholic Church the Government has the support of the Jews of Vienna, including the bankers who are scared to death of a Nazi Government. Moreover, the remnants of the Christian-Socialist Party which used to control all the farmers of the country give a lukewarm support.

Starhemberg doesn't like Schuschnigg much but is not inclined to clash with him immediately. Starhemberg, it appears, has not been taking his politics too seriously lately and has been devoting his larger energies to a series of charming young ladies. Schuschnigg is frankly a monarchist. I asked him when he thought the Emperor would return and he replied that the matter had not yet come up in serious form, that it might be twenty years, that it might be in ten years, and it might be in one. Starhemberg is not too anxious to have the Hapsburgs return. An old friend of mine told me that he had been talking with Starhemberg on this subject a few days before my arrival and Starhemberg had said, "Why should I or Austria want to have the *nouveau riche* Hapsburgs back again? My people were good enough to defend Austria for centuries before the Hapsburgs were ever heard of." The spirit of the Philadelphia Club is also international.

The financial situation in Austria has improved out of all reason and the general economic situation is improving. The Nazi boss whom I have known so well in the past that I feel able to vouch for the sincerity of the statement, stated that he did not anticipate any Nazi *putsch* this summer or for a "very long time thereafter." He said that all the public leaders of the Nazis were either in jail or beyond the frontiers, that all the Nazi centers had been smashed, that Hitler was sending few funds, only enough to keep together small nuclei, and that the Government at the moment had all the cannons and machine guns, the decisive factors. Temporarily, therefore, the Austrian structure seems secure although it would collapse at a moment's notice if any of the supporting beams should be withdrawn. If Mussolini withdraws his support, it will surely go. If Starhemberg should get really angry with Schuschnigg there would, of course, be a collapse, but if the present planks in the structure hang together there is no chance of the Government being overthrown by a Nazi explosion. I was much surprised to reach this conclusion as all the news I had received here and in Warsaw had led me to believe that the position of the Austrian Government was threatened by internal Nazi explosion. Incidentally, Messersmith holds the same opinion that I do and he is no fool.

When I returned to Warsaw I had lunch along with Beck and his wife. The lady, who is a charmer, left us immediately after the meal and we had a good talk. From Beck and from many other persons in Poland I got the following bits of information: Before Pilsudski's death it had been arranged that as soon as the new constitution, which gives dictatorial powers to the President, should take effect, Moscicki, who is now President, should resign and be replaced by one of Pilsudski's chief assistants. Pilsudski had not indicated which one he would choose but the general opinion was that it would be General Smigly-Rydz, now Inspector General of the Polish Army . . . The Poles are sincere patriots and unless Moscicki should collapse physically or make some big mistakes, I think that Beck, Smigly-Rydz, and the rest will be content to work under and through him. Beck assured me that this would happen and so did many others.

I am more convinced than ever that there is no secret agreement between Poland and Germany. The Polish Army is definitely anti-German and I can not find in Beck a trace of real pro-Germanism. His whole policy is based on the determination never to allow the foot of a German or Russian soldier to be placed on Polish soil and never to permit airplanes of either power to fly over Polish territory. That is not pro-Germanism but plain common sense.

I said this to Litvinov when we travelled together from Warsaw to Moscow. (Incidentally, our late guest in Washington was most affable and invited me to join him in his private car for the trip, which I did.) Litvinov replied that while he agreed that there was no written agreement between Poland and Germany he believed that Beck's unwillingness to enter into a pact of mutual assistance with the Soviet Union was based on the hope that within the next few years Japan would attack the Soviet Union and that Poland would then be able to annex sections of the Ukraine and also would participate in a joint German-Hungarian-Polish demolition of Czechoslovakia. That seems to me pure Bolshevik propaganda. As Litvinov and I were in the same car we talked for many hours about everything in heaven and earth and were finally reduced to playing a Russian card game, the central feature of which is a cork in the middle of the table which one tries to slap before one's opponent.

Litvinov is a quick slapper.

I wish I could transfer myself to Washington by radio for an evening of talk with you. A volume of typewriting would be needed to cover all I have to tell you. And I would like to hear your voice again.

Good luck and every good wish.

Yours always,

Bill

Hermann Goering was one of the aviation heroes of World War I in Germany, where he was commander of the renowned Richthofen Fighter Squadron. After the war he moved to Munich, where he met Hitler in 1921, and by 1922 had been made the leader of the storm troopers, or Brown Shirts. He continued his close association with Hitler until the end. He rose in power to become Minister of the Interior of Prussia, which supervised the police, Minister of Aviation and General, then Field Marshal, which made him the highest military officer, Economic Dictator of the Reich, and finally in 1939 Hitler named him as his successor. At the postwar Nuremberg trials he was able to cheat the hangman by swallowing poison.

THE WHITE HOUSE
WASHINGTON

June 21, 1935

Dear Bill:

Your letter of June third proves (a) that your sense of humor is completely intact and (b) that by this token your physical well-being must be vastly improved.

What a grand picture that is of that Goering person! If you get a figure like his I will order a special uniform for you and send you to all official funerals.

I am interested in what you say about the chocolate diet. I had always supposed that a liquor diet and a sugar diet were practically synonymous from the point of view of chemical result but evidently I am wrong!

Breck Long has been here and he, too, is much encouraged because what he feared was something serious turned out to be a mere stomach ulcer. In spite of this he is still pessimistic about the future of Europe!

I am off to the New London Races and am much afraid that your damn Elis will sweep the river.

Do not get too high a blood pressure. If you can keep it at that of a newborn babe, perhaps you will live three score years and ten longer!

We miss you. Good luck!

As ever yours,
FDR

Honorable William C. Bullitt
American Embassy
Moscow
U.S.S.R.

P.S. I take it the small growth on your spine will develop eventually into wings! [This was a small lesion which Bullitt had removed.]

P.P.S. Yes Yale done it doggone it. [Handwritten.]

9

The Third International Congress
and Disappointment

JULY—DECEMBER 1935

Propaganda by Third International
Possible Break in Relations
Italy Attacks Abyssinia
Neutrality Act

THE THIRD INTERNATIONAL CONGRESS, held in Moscow in July and August 1935, was a revealing and significant gathering of world Communist Party leaders. The determining factor throughout was undoubtedly the international situation and the dangers inherent in this situation for the Soviet state.

The principal results of the Congress were substantial, and it demonstrated the overwhelming degree to which the international Communist movement had become dominated by the Soviet party. It was clear from the speed with which the delegates adopted the new line on behalf of their parties that Stalin was determined to snuff out any dissension and forestall the threat of any rival power within the international organization.

The Congress adopted the stratagem of the Popular Front. Communist parties throughout the world were now instructed to make common cause not only with non-Communist elements on the left, but with liberal and even conservative forces, as well. The one credential required for Comintern benediction was opposition to Nazism and Fascism.

Earl Browder, the general secretary of the American Communist Party, attended the conference, along with many other Americans. Under Browder's leadership they embraced the new tactic enthusiastically. Communism was now proclaimed to be twentieth-century Americanism. The *Daily Worker* expressed approval of everything from the New Deal to baseball, and Browder announced in a speech that even J. P. Morgan would have been welcomed into the fold. The process reached its ultimate expression in the dissolution of the American Communist Party during the war, a decision for which Browder was to pay with expulsion after 1945. The party, however, was reformed later in the same year.

Personal and Confidential Moscow
July 15, 1935

Dear Mr. President:

This letter should reach you before the issue raised by the impending congress of the Third International in Moscow becomes acute. As I cannot have a talk with you, I am going to bore you by writing you what I would say if I were with you in the White House.

I am engaged in attempting to keep the congress off the subject of the U.S.A. by exuding gloom and expressing my personal opinion that the congress may produce the severance of diplomatic relations. I think I shall be successful in reducing somewhat the activities of the congress with respect to the United States but have almost no hope that I can forestall violation, at least technical, of the last article of Litvinov's propaganda pledge to you.

Some people in Washington will doubtless want to break relations even if the violation is merely technical; but I can hear you roar with laughter over the idea of breaking relations on the basis of a mere technical violation of Litvinov's pledge. Indeed, if the Soviet Government should lean over backwards to avoid offending the United States, I suppose that you will wish to ignore the congress altogether. If the violation should be merely technical and if you should feel that we cannot ignore it, I think we should confine our action to an oral protest by me to Litvinov, a simultaneous withdrawal of the exequaturs [authorization of a consul by a foreign government] of the Soviet Consuls in New York and San Francisco and a tightening of our liberal policy of giving visas to the United States to Soviet officials.

If we should take these steps the Soviet Government would retaliate by making the position of this Embassy as difficult as possible and might very well pretend that our reluctance to issue visas makes it impossible for the Soviet Government to carry out its intention to purchase thirty million dollars worth of goods in the United States this year. And I shall probably get no news at all from Litvinov or any communist for some time.

If the violation should be not technical but gross and insulting, I suspect that you will feel obliged to break relations. If we should not, the Soviet Government would be convinced that it could break its pledges with impunity and would feel free to direct actively the American communist movement. The results of a break in relations, I think, would be: 1. Reduction of Soviet purchases in the United States. 2. A long period without relations, since, if we break on the ground that the Soviet Government has not kept its pledges, it will be most difficult later to say that we consider its pledges trustworthy. 3. The loss of an observation post in Moscow. 4. An increased chance that Japan will attack the Soviet Union. 5. A considerable decrease in the prestige of the Soviet Union and a weakening of its present ascending influence.

(Parenthetically, it occurs to me that if we break with the Soviet Union it would be a pleasant gesture to ask the Finns to take charge of our interests here. We could not trust any great power. The Finns have more influence than the Norwegians or the representatives of any other minor power. And they paid their debts.)

If the violation should fall between the two extremes and be neither technical nor gross and insulting (and I think it will fall between the extremes) it will be most difficult to decide what to do.

Whatever we do, we should do promptly — instantaneously, if possible . . .

I hope most heartily that all this may blow over and that our relations may continue. The Soviet Union is quite likely to become involved in war, both in the Far East and in Europe, during the next few years and it seems honestly desirable to have diplomatic representation here.

I apologize for this solemn screed. You will know exactly what to do without advice. In a few minutes I shall write Judge Moore the above solemnities.

Every possible good wish to you all.

Yours affectionately,
William C. Bullitt

At this time Bullitt's health had recovered sufficiently for him to feel the need for the outdoors and exercise. The following telegram and letters show his friendship for and lack of hesitation in imposing on Wehle. They also indicate Wehle's intimacy with the President, whom he always wrote to as Frank.

Moscow
May 11, 1935

Dear Louis:

I should have written you before if there had been anything of interest to write. There still isn't but I am writing to you now just to let you know that I am still alive. At that I am less alive than I should like to be.

We have had snow or cold rain nearly every day since I have been here and I haven't been able to get any of the exercise or fresh air that I need and still feel like a dead fish. I take to my bed at 7:30 each evening exhausted and into the bargain have to rest after luncheon. As soon as I can get some sun and fresh air I think I shall pull out of the depression, although I admit that that may be a Hoover hope.

If anything of interest develops I will let you know at once. Meanwhile, you will know that I still consider you as my guardian angel even though I don't send you a daily missive to that effect.

I asked Bukharin the other night about fishing in the Caucasus. He said that the streams were small, not more than twenty-five feet across at the most and that the trout were usually about twelve inches long. That means a small rod. He said that they would take almost any kind of fly. Kelley expects to reach Moscow about the 15th of September and if all goes well we shall go to the Caucasus at that time. If Kelley does not come I don't think I will make the trip. Could you keep in touch with him and if he finally decides to come pick up the rod for me at Abercrombie & Fitch or anywhere else you choose.

Love to you all.

Yours permanently,
Bill

July 26, 1935

Dear Bill:

There's no doubt about it: I do miss you. So much is happening here and elsewhere that calls for appraisals and policies; and, anyway, even if they didn't —

Did you ever receive the three tennis racquets I bought for you from Feron's about two months ago? And were they satisfactory?

This afternoon I'm getting the trout rod tackle and flies for you at Abercrombie & Fitch and having our acquaintance there — Mr. Fitzmaurice, ship them straight down to Kelley.

I had an hour with the President one late afternoon in the early days of July, swimming in his pool, where we had plenty of opportunity to chat about various things and affairs. He seemed much pleased with you, as Ambassador and otherwise, and laughed over the long letter you had written recently about some happenings outside of the Soviet Union when you were on a trip. Judge Moore had already told me of it with equal gusto. I expect to see it before long, because Missy also told me about it and was going to send it to me.

My best to Offie.

Let me know, if there's anything I can do for you.

Yours always,
Louis B. Wehle

P.S. Answer about the tennis racquets.

On July 28, Harold Denny in the *New York Times* reported that direct orders were going from the Communist International to work within the American labor unions and endeavor to create a united proletarian front of industrial workers and farmers. The report also suggested that American church property be seized to help the unemployed.

DEPARTMENT OF STATE
ASSISTANT SECRETARY

Memorandum for Miss LeHand   August 1, 1935

I think the President should see this. I am having put in convenient form all the information we are receiving with reference to the proceedings of the Communist International, now in session at Moscow, with the thought that when the meeting ends, our Government may wish to make a vigorous representation to the Soviet Government through Mr. Bullitt. It is already very clear that Litvinov's pledge has been violated, and that when we have the full picture, there can be little doubt of it appearing that the violation has been very complete.

R. Walton Moore

Personal and Confidential   Moscow
                                                                                    July 15, 1935

Dear Judge Moore:

  . . . Some of the Bolsheviks feel quite violently about the meeting of the Communist International. A few evenings ago Karl Radek was at my house for a dinner and dance that I was giving in honor of the Italian Ambassador who is about to leave for Berlin. I said to Radek in a most friendly way that I hoped he and his friends in the Third International would not raise such hell at the communist congress that they would compel us to break relations. I never saw a man grow more instantaneously and violently angry. He sprang up and said, "We have lived without the United States and we can continue to live without the United States. We shall never allow you to dictate to us what we may do or what we may not do in Moscow." I replied that Litvinov had made certain formal promises on the subject whereupon Radek stalked away.

  It is unquestionable that in spite of Litvinov's note to the President a lot of the Communist International members intend to disregard the propaganda pledge at the first favorable opportunity. I do not, however, believe that they will consider the present moment a favorable opportunity. They are much too worried about the general international situation. It is, however, perfectly clear that to speak of "normal relations" between the Soviet Union and any other country is to speak of something which does not and will not exist. All the diplomatic representatives here, myself included, are increasingly being placed in the position of representatives of the capitalist enemy . . .

  Whatever we do, we should do promptly — instantaneously if possible. I think we should avoid at all costs the usual practice of writing a large pontifical note of protest. The Soviet Government would merely answer by a larger, more pontifical and intensely insulting note and we cannot compete with the Bolsheviks in invective . . .

  I hope that the Bolsheviks may show some common sense and not compel us to do any of these things but they have been so dumb in the handling of their relations with the United States that I should not be surprised by any action that they may take . . .

Every possible good wish to you and your sisters.

Yours affectionately,

William C. Bullitt

A British Embassy official in Moscow commented on Bullitt's life at this time in a gossipy letter, part of which said: "He [Bullitt] has promoted a very decent clerk [Offie], an Italian American of Cuban origin [untrue] to be an attaché and this wretched young man puts up with being at his beck and call all day and all night, for if he has an idea during the night he calls for his attaché to take down a draft. He gets up in the morning at any hour between five and seven and takes the unfortunate fellow for a walk with him.

"He has had installed in the Embassy a super Western Electric movie apparatus and has an electrician on his staff to work it who receives from the U.S. Government a salary of £600 per annum (I understand some other Embassies now have cinemas). He has just received 500 cases of stores for the winter months." [1]

One wonders to what use the Foreign Office put this news.

Moscow

August 3, 1935

Dear Mr. President:

I wish I could be in the White House with you this evening to talk about the Congress of the Communist International and several thousand other subjects.

The emotions of the Congress in deciding to cooperate with the Socialists and bourgeois Democrats in a fight against Fascism are, of course, on all fours with the emotions of the tiger when he went out for that historic ride with the young lady of Niger. The Communists feel sure they will come back from the ride with the Socialists and Democrats inside.

As I have no knowledge of the reaction of American public opinion or your own feelings, and as I wrote you solemnly on July 15, 1935, I shall await a word from you before again bursting into song.

I shall not, however, spare you two strange bits of news.

Justice Van Devanter lunched with me a few days ago. We had a delightful conversation in the course of which, although he was careful not to tell tales out of school, he indicated apropos of the T.V.A. that, while he considered it constitutional for the Government to sell electricity which might be generated from dams erected to improve navigation, he considered it unconstitutional for the Federal Government to sell electricity generated by a dam built for the specific purpose of generating and selling electricity!

The other bit of news which will, I think, raise your hair as high as it raised what remains of mine, was the discovery of the fact that our confidential despatches, letters, and even most secret cipher tables of our confidential codes are being sent to Riga by a pouch that goes calmly through the open mail via Nazi Germany!

The duplication of seals has certainly not become a lost art in Germany since the World War and I think we may assume safely that the Germans now have all our confidential codes except the special one I have in Moscow.

You will remember that I spoke to you some months ago about the Department's habit of sending cipher tables in the open mail and that we tried then to have the practise stopped.

However, the administration of the Department of State has been for so many years in the hands of people who are without knowledge of the world or comprehension of human guile that I feel that it will be impossible to handle secret matters in a secret way until you decide that a 1935 Foreign Service is just as essential as a 1935 fleet and ordain a full reorganization and reconstruction, on the solid ground that a Merrimac-Monitor Department and Foreign Service, in 1935, is dangerous. It is.

Incidentally, if the Bolsheviks should become so violent before this Congress is over that you decide to break relations, please let me have a personal and strictly confidential intimation well in advance so that I can send out of the country by courier our code books, confidential despatches, and telegrams before our Soviet friends grab them. They are entirely capable of behaving like Bolsheviks.

God bless you and good luck, and apologies for putting so much unpleasantness in one letter.

Yours affectionately,
William C. Bullitt

Bullitt was often concerned about the secrecy of his messages to Roosevelt and the possibility that the Germans were obtaining information from them. We now know that Hitler probably did read Bullitt's messages, which were decoded by the Germans and placed in Hitler's hands within one or two days.* A ledger was kept by the German Foreign Office of the cables, but unfortunately only a few of the actual documents survive, and none of these are Bullitt's cables to the President. However, the Germans had the American code, and as we read the "Secret and Confidential" messages it is interesting to speculate on Hitler's reaction and what plans he made in the light of the inner knowledge he no doubt had of American diplomacy.

THE WHITE HOUSE
WASHINGTON

August 14, 1935

Dear Bill:

I wish I could have been acting as the butler when the eminent Justice lunched with you.† I probably would have spilled the soup down his neck!

In regard to that other piece of news about the confidential matters going through the open mail from Riga through Germany, I will say nothing about it until you tell me whether you have taken it up with the State Department or not — for I do not want them to think that you are telling tales out of school! Let me know.

Since you wrote on August third, there is no violent news of *your* Congress so I take it I shall not have to send an ambulance for you.

My Congress is also less violent and I think that in time it will be wholly well again!

I am glad you are not here this week. I should probably pull the hair on the top of your head! Why don't you find out the Russian secret of becoming hirsute?

Many thanks for remembering that I am a stamp collector. There was no sign that your letter had been opened.

I miss you much.

As ever yours,
FDR

Hon. William C. Bullitt
American Embassy
Moscow

---

* I am indebted for this information to author David Irving of London, who has been engaged for several years in compiling a major biographical work on Hitler.

† The eminent Justice was one of the "nine old men" of the United States Supreme Court.

On the fourteenth of August Mr. Hull wired Bullitt some of the reasons why the United States Government considered that the Communist International was breaking the Soviet promises to the United States. The *Daily Worker,* the organ of the Communist Party in the United States, published a message from the International urging the *Daily Worker* to become an agitator and organizer of the workers' struggle and to become the standard-bearer for the masses of the American working class. The Red International of Labor Unions had dealt with the problem of organizing revolutionary elements within the American Federation of Labor, and of the task of the conquest of the majority of the working class. Hull also objected to the representatives of the American Communist Party, Earl Browder and William Weinstone, participating in the proceedings. He considered these and other examples to be violations of Litvinov's letter to the President of November 16, 1933.[2]

On August 25 the *New York Times,* in an article by Walter Duranty, reported: RUSSIANS ARE MUTE ON PROTEST BY U.S., BUT STUPEFACTION AND ANGER ARE BELIEVED TO BE THE REACTION OF SOVIET. Bullitt had presented to the Russian Government one of the strongest notes of protest in diplomatic history as a result of the proceedings of the Congress of the Communist International. The note had to do with interference in the internal affairs of the United States in violation of the Soviet pledge of November 16, 1933. Such phrases as "most emphatic" and "flagrant violation" were used, and the statement was made that if the Russians did not take appropriate steps to prevent such action in the future, the development of friendly relations would inevitably be precluded and the United States "anticipated the most serious consequences." Bullitt took the unusual step of giving the American correspondents a copy of the note immediately after his call on Krestinsky, Acting Commissar for Foreign Affairs.

Charles E. Bohlen made the following comment on the upshot of the meeting of the International: "The Soviet Government, as was its practice, refused to accept any responsibility for the activities of the Communist International . . . This led, on Bullitt's recommendation to the exchange of some bad-tempered notes between the two governments. It was not long before these and other disappointments produced a very marked change in the attitude of Ambassador Bullitt, who was for the rest of his life a consistent, and at times violent opponent of the Soviet Union." [3]

Bullitt's letters show that he was becoming increasingly disillusioned with the Russian Government. The President and he had worked out an agreement with Litvinov before the United States recognized the Soviet Government. At that time they had every reason to believe that this agreement meant what it said and would be adhered to by both parties. As the Russians kept putting obstacles and different interpretations on the various clauses, both men gradually lost faith in the sincerity of the Soviet Government. Bullitt became more and more unhappy under this situation until he finally asked to be moved to another post.

At this time Bullitt finally worked out with Litvinov a minor trade agreement whereby the Russians would buy $30,000,000 of American goods in the following year, which was more than double the previous year. There were no reciprocal concessions by the United States on tariffs. [4]

THE WHITE HOUSE

WASHINGTON

September 26, 1935

Dear Bill:

I am off today in an effort to get a little rest, which we all need.

A box of apples has just arrived from your farm and we are all looking forward to eating them. I have written Mr. Hartwell.

I am sorry that you still do not feel your usual healthy self — for Heaven's sake do pay attention to the Doctors and get yourself in condition for a busy 1936. We need you.

I hear you have been running a full-fledged hospital at the Embassy — you were lucky to miss Senator Lewis' illness!

I know you have been having a bad time in many ways.

Thank you for the postcards from Warsaw. I am delighted to have them.

Affectionately,

FDR

Honorable William C. Bullitt
American Embassy
Moscow
U.S.S.R.

On the ninth of November, Bullitt lunched with Litvinov, and for once the conversation did not turn to debts or the activities of the Communist International. Litvinov told Bullitt that he was sure the British had decided to eliminate Mussolini and that Mussolini knew he was beaten. He went on to say that he thought the British would blockade the Suez Canal when they thought it necessary, and that in the end Mussolini would commit suicide. When the British had finished Mussolini they would finish Hitler, and they would work with the French and never with Hitler. He felt sure Japan planned the domination of China, but would not attack the Soviet Union.[5]

The Ambassador in the Soviet Union   [Bullitt]
to the Secretary of State

Moscow
November 9, 1935 — 10 P.M.

. . . Litvinov said that he wished he had been in Moscow when I had presented our note of protest against the actions of the Third International. He then asserted that he had an entirely clear conscience; that I must know that he had said to the President that he could not be responsible for the Third International; and that the President had replied that he would hold the Soviet Union to its pledge only in case of important injury to the interests of the United States.

I replied that my memory was entirely different: that I recalled that he had said he could make no promises about the Third International, but that the President had told him that he would hold him to strict accountability with regard to the Third International and that he, Litvinov, had subsequently signed the pledge. He replied that he had made his statement to the President after signing the pledge.

As this statement made his position even weaker, and as the conversation was growing acrimonious, I suggested that a discussion of present relations might be more valuable than further remarks about the past. Litvinov then made it clear that the Soviet Government would not in any way restrain the activities of the Communist International in the United States or the Soviet Union, or of American Communists connected with the Communist International in the Soviet Union. He expressed with his customary cynicism the view that there was no such thing as friendship or "really friendly" relations between nations . . .[6]

Bullitt

On October 3, 1935, Mussolini opened his campaign for the annexation of Abyssinia without declaring war. In retrospect the position of the great powers seems extraordinary. France and Britain were so intent on retaining his good will for any possible joint opposition to Hitler that they took no steps. In Churchill's own words, "It was felt undesirable at that moment to warn him [Mussolini] off Abyssinia, which would obviously have very much annoyed him."[7] The Assembly of the League of Nations by a vote of fifty to one resolved to take action against Italy. That action consisted in sanctions which were completely ineffective in preventing the rape of this defenseless nation by a fellow member of the League.

One result of the Ethiopian conflict was the resignation of Sir Samuel Hoare as Foreign Minister of Great Britain and the appointment of Anthony Eden. Hoare had drawn up a pact for the partition of Abyssinia with Pierre Laval of France. This document shocked the House of Commons and seriously endangered the Baldwin Government, but the Cabinet would not accept the Hoare-Laval proposals and Hoare was discredited.

On December 9, 1935, the United States, Great Britain, France, Italy, and Japan met for the London Naval Conference. The Italian-Ethiopian war was in progress and Japan had denounced the Washington naval limitation of 1921 and demanded parity with Great Britain and the United States. In January the Japanese refused to join in any further discussion until this demand was met. When the other powers voted against parity Japan withdrew from the conference on January 15, 1936. While the conference was still in session in March, Hitler had thrown down his challenge by occupying the Rhineland. The treaty finally provided no agreement on overall tonnage, as, without Japan, such a provision would have been meaningless. It did call for a limitation on the size of battleships, guns, aircraft carriers, and submarines. Also, the different signatories were to give one another their annual programs of construction.

Bullitt returned to Washington on December 12 to report to the President and there is no further correspondence until he returned to Moscow in February 1936.

As the war clouds gathered in Europe, the Neutrality Acts of 1935 to 1937 became the most visible symbol of the controversy which raged right down to Pearl Harbor, between isolationist and interventionist forces over the direction of American foreign policy. A substantial body of opinion had become convinced by this time that the American entry into World War I had been a mistake whose repetition must at all costs be avoided. Also, the Depression had pushed foreign affairs well down on the list of priorities in the popular mind.

The isolationist mood was more pervasive than is frequently believed and President Roosevelt, keenly aware of the power of public opinion, found it necessary to temper his internationalist instincts.

The Neutrality Acts were really an attempt to prevent a recurrence of World War I by closing off those loopholes in the neutrality of 1914 to 1917 through which, it was alleged, the country was dragged into that earlier conflict. Roosevelt, never very enthusiastic about the acts, nevertheless signed them in the face of overwhelming evidence of popular support for them. The Administration tactic was then to struggle for maximum Presidential discretion in the interpretation of the acts, with the hope of eventual repeal of the more restrictive features.

The Neutrality Acts prevented the sale of any completed implements of war to foreign countries, but did allow products of a general nature and of agriculture to be carried in American ships to belligerent nations. In other words, component parts could be supplied but would then have to be assembled by the purchaser.

Henry Morgenthau, Jr., noted in his diary on February 2, 1936, a wise decision of the President. He was having tea with the President and Miss LeHand and was discussing the spending program. The talk turned to the appointment of the Director of the Budget. They discussed several names but could come to no conclusion. Miss LeHand brought up the possibility of Bill Bullitt and the President replied, "No, no, he is all wrapped up in international diplomacy and knows nothing about this." [8] He never made a better decision, as Bill would hardly have known the difference between red and black ink.

10

Leaving Russia

FEBRUARY—OCTOBER 1936

Hitler Occupies Rhineland
Bullitt Leaves Russia
Interviews von Neurath
Ambassador to France

THE YEAR 1936 began with clouded skies for the democracies.
Mussolini had completely overrun gallant but powerless Ethiopia; the Russians, while appealing for collective security against
Fascist aggression at the League of Nations, were, with the purges
now in high gear, dashing any remaining hopes for a democratic
development within the Soviet Union; and above all Hitler was
on the march. He was vigorously rearming and openly defying
France and England. On March 7 the German Foreign Minister
proposed to the British, French, Italian, and Belgian governments
a twenty-five-year pact to limit air forces, a nonaggression pact,
and above all the demilitarization of both sides of the Rhine. On
the same day this proposal was made, Hitler's troops were entering the principal cities of the Rhine. He thus violated the Treaty
of Versailles and the Locarno Treaty. Neither England nor
France took any action against this preliminary step of aggression,
although it is now clear that Hitler would have had to withdraw
promptly had he been faced with a strong stand, backed by the
military superiority of the French at that time.

On October 4, 1925, an international conference had been held
at Locarno, in Switzerland. The countries participating were
Britain, France, Germany, Italy, and Belgium. The results were:
a treaty of mutual guarantee between the powers which pledged
the signatories to stand together against any aggression on the

part of one signatory against the other; a series of arbitration treaties between Germany and France, Belgium and Germany, Germany and Poland, and Germany and Czechoslovakia, if either of them were attacked.

Personal and Confidential   Moscow
                                                    February 22, 1936

Dear Mr. President:

In order to spare you a solemn Cook's tour across Europe, I am going to confine this letter to disjointed fragments.

1. London. Our little friend, the King, is spending his weekends at the Fort Belvedere end of Windsor Great Park, not the Windsor Castle end! I had an invitation from a charming Maryland lady but had to move on to Moscow before the date fixed.

There is something like a willful hysteria in London. In order to make sure that the increased military and naval estimates will encounter no opposition, the fear of Germany is being played up deliberately and the most commonplace remark at every lunch and dinner table is to the effect that within three years England will have to choose between making war on Germany or permitting Germany to dominate Czechoslovakia, Austria, Hungary, and Rumania preparatory to an attack on the Soviet Union. Strangely enough, all the old anti-Bolshevik fanatics like Winston Churchill are trumpeting this Bolshevik thesis and are advocating an entente with the Soviet Union!

2. Paris. There is a rising wave of feeling that France should not go to war with Germany to save either Czechoslovakia or the Soviet Union:

Hence the stubborn opposition to ratification of the Franco-Soviet Treaty of Mutual Assistance . . .

3. Berlin. I stopped in Berlin only between trains and had a talk with Dodd, who is still somewhat under the weather.

As you know, my close friend, Attolico, is now Italian Ambassador in Berlin. He had just come from Rome where he had seen a great deal of Mussolini. I therefore pricked up my ears considerably when he suggested most seriously, as I cabled the Department, that the time was approaching when you might intervene with a "Hoare-Laval proposal with modifications favorable to Italy." I have no doubt that the Foreign Offices of both Britain and France, as well as Mussolini, would be delighted to have you take the onus of proposing such a settlement. The English could then throw up their hands in holy horror and say that you had forced them to accept an immoral compromise. I felt so sure that you would not rise to that bait — and hook — that I did not pursue Attolico's suggestion. But I warn you it was serious and you may hear more of it.

4. Warsaw. I saw a large number of Poles in Warsaw, including Beck, the Foreign Minister, with whom I had a long and intimate conversation. The Poles have not deviated from their determination not to allow a single Russian or German soldier to set foot on Polish soil. But, on the other hand, I gathered from Beck that Poland would offer no resistance, either physical or diplomatic, to a German attack on Czechoslovakia. Beck emphasized the closeness of the relations between Poland and Hungary and I gathered the impression that he would be glad, rather than otherwise, to see Germany control Austria and Bohemia, and to see Hungary walk off with Slovakia, while Poland got "frontier rectifications" in the Teschen district.

Needless to say, all the way from London to Moscow the chief topic of conversation was the dangerous situation of Czechoslovakia. The Czechoslovak position is made somewhat more desperate by the fact that nobody in Europe likes Czechs, to say nothing of Czechesses, whose piano legs and aversion to soap are notorious from one end of the continent to the other.

Cudahy was in Paradise when I told him that D. V. the Auld Sod was his. He is eager to come home to campaign and promises 3,000,000 Polish votes! *

5. *Moscow.* Russia, as usual, is looking up. The improvement in physical conditions is striking even after so short an absence as mine. The people are certainly better fed and clothed than at any time since the Revolution. And the Moscow Street Cleaning Department today puts that of New York to shame. In spite of the perpetual snows, you can see the asphalt on every street.

Litvinov greeted me in an unusually amiable manner. The day of my arrival I had an ordinary tea and movie at my house, and both he and Madame Litvinov, Marshal Budënny, and a host of army officers and government officials turned up to bid me welcome. It means absolutely nothing from the political point of view but it does mean, I believe, that Stalin has told Litvinov to be more polite to this Mission.

Stalin's latest imitation of Le Roi Soleil is to dictate in the field of music and drama. Recently he went to see a modern Soviet opera and a modern ballet which had been praised by the critics as the su-

---

* John Cudahy had just been transferred to Dublin as American minister to Ireland from his post as Ambassador in Warsaw.

preme achievements of the human race. In the ballet Georgians were shown to be drunk. Stalin at once caused ukases to be issued damning all the musicians and producers who have been heralded for the past few years by the Soviet press as demi-gods. The result is that half the artists and musicians in Moscow are engaged in having nervous prostration and the others are trying to imagine how to write and compose in a manner to please Stalin . . .

By the time you get this letter I shall be engaged in waiting for that cryptic telegram from you. I warn you that from the fifteenth of March to the first of April, I shall be at the office each day from 7:30 A.M. forward to open personally all messages.

Bless you and good luck.

> Yours always,
> Bill

Edward VIII succeeded his father, King George V, on January 20, 1936, and abdicated the throne on December 10, 1936. After his abdication the former King assumed the title of Duke of Windsor and was married to Mrs. Wallis Simpson of Baltimore, Maryland. (The charming Maryland lady mentioned in Bullitt's letter is undoubtedly the future Duchess of Windsor.) They took up residence at Paris, where Bullitt was to see them frequently in future years, as he had in the past.

Personal and Confidential   Moscow
                                                        February 22, 1936

Dear Judge Moore:
 . . . Life in Moscow is somewhat quieter and more restricted than ever, as a considerable number of the chiefs of mission have collapsed in one way or another and there is little or no entertaining. The Polish Ambassador has had a complete nervous breakdown and the British Ambassador did not seem far from one when I saw him the other day and he said, "I feel like a prisoner pacing my garden between banks of snow unable to escape."

Our own Embassy is almost the only cheerful spot in the town . . .

I had a delightful stay with Cudahy who, much to my displeasure, slipped into the Soviet Union before my arrival and went bear shooting. He had arranged his own trip through Intourist. The result was that he got up far to the north beyond Vyatka and was carted from one primitive village to the other without food or de-

cent lodging and never saw hide nor hair of a bear! His opinion of
the Soviet Union is somewhat lower than ever . . .

Yours permanently,
William C. Bullitt

The Neutrality Act of August 31, 1935, was due to expire on
February 29, 1936, and the President and Secretary Hull had
been studying means of altering some of its provisions. On January
3, 1936, the President delivered his message to Congress in
which he said: "We decline to encourage the production of war
by permitting belligerents to obtain arms, ammunition or implements
of war from the United States; we seek to discourage the
use by belligerent nations of any and all American products calculated
to facilitate the prosecution of a war in quantities over and
above our normal exports to them in time of peace." A bill was
introduced by Pittman in the Senate and McReynolds in the
House which would increase the discretion of the President in
applying the arms embargo. The bill met with violent opposition
from the isolationists and from those who wanted to increase exports
to belligerents. The isolationist sentiment in the country
had greatly increased since the first Neutrality Act was passed.
The bill was never reported out of the Senate committee. Instead,
the existing act was extended until May 1, 1937, with three
amendments. These forbade loans or credits to belligerents,
made mandatory the existing discretionary power of the President
to extend the arms embargo to additional states becoming involved
in a war, and exempted from application of the act any
American republic at war with a non-American nation.

Personal and Confidential   Moscow
March 4, 1936

Dear Mr. President:

Roy Howard has just blown through Moscow like a healthy wind
and I hope that when he calls on you in Washington you will tell
him what a great little fellow he is.

Before he arrived I had arranged for him to interview Stalin and
on the night of his arrival he was given a dinner by Doletsky, the
head of Tass, at which a lot of prominent Bolsheviks were present.
When he rose to reply to a toast he made a speech which was so
perfect that it might have been made by yourself.

This is the first time within my knowledge that any prominent American has talked like an American to the Bolsheviks. The usual run of businessmen who come here think that they will get somewhere by licking the Bolshevik boots. Howard, on the contrary, told the Bolsheviks that while there had been no country in the world that had regarded their experiment with more sympathy than the United States, they could not expect our friendship so long as they continued to interfere in our internal affairs. He did it politely and beautifully and it would have done you good to have seen the shocked expressions on the faces of the more fanatical Bolsheviks — like Radek and that filthy little squirt, Umansky, who is about to go to America to replace Skvirsky.

In the course of Howard's conversation with Stalin, which lasted three and one-half hours, he told the Dictator that he was certain as a newspaper man, that any repetition of Soviet interference in American internal affairs would produce a break in diplomatic relations. Umansky was interpreting and Howard said that when Umansky had to translate that remark his face looked "like a spanked baby's butt."

Howard is really a great fellow and it pleased me immensely to discover that his support of you was based on real friendship.

Incidentally, Howard would make a startling but superb Ambassador of the United States to Great Britain. The King, at least, would love him. You will recall the King's thrice repeated remark to me about his wish to see America represented in London by Americans, not imitation Englishmen . . .

I felt sure that Stalin's readiness to receive Howard was not due primarily to any love for my beautiful eyes or his desire to improve relations with the United States, but because he wished to make an announcement about Outer Mongolia. I told Howard that before he saw Stalin and Howard asked the appropriate question. Stalin came out with the blunt announcement that the Soviet Union would fight if the Japanese should invade Outer Mongolia.

The Bolsheviks at the moment are extremely confident about their position in the world. Their most recent information from Paris indicates that the Franco-Soviet Pact will be ratified by the French Senate. The Soviet-Czech Pact which, as you know, does not come into effect until the Franco-Soviet Pact has been ratified will then exist also; and they expect confidently that a Soviet-Rumanian Pact will then be concluded . . .

I have got to the bottom of the delay in the conclusion of the Soviet-Rumanian Pact. There is no serious dispute; but both Titulescu and Litvinov are Oriental bargainers of the Levantine–rug vendor type and each one feels it is his duty to haggle until the customer leaves the shop. They understand each other perfectly, however, and each one knows that the rug is going to be sold.

The Bolsheviks are still engaged in talking about the imminence of German aggression against the Soviet Union, and their present disposal of their military forces on the western frontier gives a clear indication of the line of German advance they fear. I have been informed most confidentially that they have now sixteen divisions in the Kiev-Odessa military district; that is to say, the Rumanian border; six in the White Russian district and only three in the Leningrad area.

There are, in addition, six divisions in the triangle, Moscow-Kiev-Kharkov, for support of the sixteen that are closer to the Rumanian border.

This distribution of forces indicates clearly that the Council of People's Commissars is of the opinion that if German attack is to be expected it is to be expected by way of the line Czechoslovakia, Hungary and Rumania.

I can not find anyone in Moscow who believes any longer that the Germans may try to march on the Soviet Union by way of Lithuania and Latvia although Stalin made a remark about attack via the Baltic States to Howard. In that region the railroad communications would be so poor and the front so narrow that it would be impossible for the Germans to follow the classic route of invasion via Vilna. As Vilna is in the hands of the Poles and as Pilsudski had the political cleverness to have his heart buried there, it is almost impossible for the Poles to let the Germans through by that route . . .

It is, therefore, clear that unless the Germans have the cooperation of the Poles they can not make an attack on the Soviet Union with any hopes of success. I am absolutely convinced that the Poles today will not permit the Germans to send an army through Poland. This Polish attitude might conceivably change if the Germans should be able to annex Austria and overwhelm Czechoslovakia, but I believe that even in that case the Poles would refuse to allow the foot of a German soldier to be placed on Polish soil. They would be damned fools if they did allow that and they are no longer such idiots as they were in the 18th century . . .

As I said to you in Washington, we are, in my opinion, back where we were before 1914 when the familiar and true remark was, "Peace is at the mercy of an incident." The recent Japanese incident might have touched off war. It appears, on the contrary, to have strengthened the possibility of peace; but a new incident in Europe or Asia can loose the whirlwind . . .

Before you get this letter I hope I shall have received that wire from you. In any event, the Lord be with you and good luck.

Yours affectionately,

Bill

THE WHITE HOUSE
WASHINGTON

March 16, 1936

Dear Bill:

It is good to get yours written on Washington's Birthday. I am glad you were able at least to stop in so many Capitols.

Meanwhile, since a week ago, the fat is in the fire again. What a thoroughly disgusting spectacle so-called civilized man in Europe can make himself.*

I fear I cannot send you any message until I get back April fourth. The Secretary has left and I go on the nineteenth. Many foundations have been laid.

Our All American Conference is coming well and I think it will be held in September. The Secretary stands so well in South America that already they are talking of erecting statues to him. Pretty good for a Democratic Administration and a great fellow!

As ever yours,

FDR

Honorable William C. Bullitt
American Embassy
Moscow

Personal and Confidential

Moscow
March 30, 1936

Dear Judge Moore:

. . . The Soviet Government is engaged once more in exiling people on a grand scale and the only thing one can do for one's friends and acquaintances is to avoid seeing them. As a result, one is depen-

---

* This paragraph probably refers to Hitler's occupation of the Rhineland on March 7.

dent on contact with the diplomatic corps and the higher officials of the government.

The stories which are reaching us from Leningrad sound unbelievable. The British Vice Consul there reports that 150,000 persons have been exiled from the city and 500,000 from the Leningrad Oblast. In Moscow the OGPU is now carrying out arrests every night. I know, personally, of three recent cases. In each case, at 2 A.M. the secret police appeared, entered the apartment, took all papers, sealed whatever room contained books, and removed the head of the family. Since the disappearances, wives and children have been unable to get any information as to whether fathers or husbands are alive or dead. In each case, these persons were without question loyal to the Soviet regime but belonged before the Revolution to the middle or upper classes.

I have just noted the Department's instruction No. 639 of February 25, 1936 (signed by you) with regard to the despatch on Soviet housing which was signed by Henderson. I confess that I do not think the characterization of Soviet housing is exaggerated or prejudiced. It is undignified largely because the subject is undignified. The mess is unbelievable; and from an artistic point of view, as well as a physical, the most accurate adjective to describe it is the vulgar one, "lousy." There is absolutely nothing that the Soviet Union can teach us or any civilized nation in the way of housing.

Litvinov is due to arrive tomorrow and I shall then presumably be able to telegraph a report of some interest. So nearly as I can discover, Litvinov went to Paris with orders to push the French to extreme intransigence. The fundamental aim of the foreign policy of the Soviet Union is to keep Europe divided, and the Soviet Government can be counted on to do anything necessary to maintain a hearty hatred between France and Germany.

The German action has, however, caused a great deal of worry here. As you know, Monsieur Alphand, the French Ambassador in Moscow, was the chief architect of the Treaty of Mutual Assistance between France and the Soviet Union. He is in a state of extreme depression and apprehension, and the Bolsheviks are at the moment, looking on life almost as pessimistically.

The point is this: The existence of the demilitarized zone did not give France and Belgium much additional security against German attack. If Germany had wished to attack France and Belgium, it would have taken only a day and a half to send troops across the demilitarized zone. But the demilitarized zone made it extremely easy for France to attack Germany in defense of her allies and satellites in Central and Eastern Europe.

The prospect which is troubling the French and Russians is that within a year Germany will have constructed fortifications on her French and Belgian frontiers comparable to the French "Maginot Line." After such fortifications have been constructed, it will be impossible for France to attack Germany unless she is ready to contemplate an initial loss of a million men. An attack by Belgium will be totally out of the question.

As a result, France will have to decide whether to give up her power and prestige in Central Europe or face the most horrifying casualty lists. Both the French Ambassador and the Russians, as well as my humble self, feel that the Quai d'Orsay will do everything possible to maintain the French position in Central Europe even though it means war of this nature. But we all feel that the French people will be deeply unwilling to face such casualties on behalf of Austria, Czechoslovakia, Poland, or the Soviet Union.

In other words, if Germany constructs fortifications on the French frontier, she will be comparatively safe from French interference in any designs she may have on Austria and Czechoslovakia (to say nothing of the countries to the east) and will be able to establish a completely dominant position in Central Europe.

A great deal will depend on the skill with which Hitler handles his diplomatic maneuvers. It is conceivable, though not likely, that he will behave with sufficient arrogance and stupidity to arouse even the pacific French to a readiness for war. The Russians will, of course, do everything possible to push the French toward war.

Everything that I have written above will probably sound silly by the time it reaches you because of new propositions by Hitler which, I understand, are due tomorrow . . .

Anne's school was flooded and she is now in Philadelphia but apparently the damage was not fatal and Mrs. Bement hopes to have the school in order soon, so that before this letter reaches you Anne will doubtless be in Deerfield once more . . .

We are still having snowstorms daily and there is no sign of Spring. Russia is a good country for pine trees, St. Bernard dogs, and polar bears, and I must say frankly that I long to be at home again. At this minute, by a miracle, I have America on the radio!

My best wishes to your sisters and as always my deepest friendship.

Yours affectionately,
William C. Bullitt

Before leaving Moscow permanently Bullitt dispatched two lengthy cables to the Secretary of State containing his view of the Soviet Government and what should be American policy in the future.

Extracts from these messages are:

Bullitt to the Secretary of State   Moscow
No. 1436   March 4, 1936
Sir:

I have the honor to submit herewith certain personal observations on conditions in this country.

I believe that what follows presents an accurate picture of life in Russia in the year 1936, but a regard for truth compels me to admit that the remainder of this despatch was written not by myself but another American envoy, The Honorable Neil S. Brown of Tennessee, in his despatches to the Secretary of State in the years 1851, 1852, and 1853. Plus ça change, plus c'est la même chose.

This is a hard climate, and an American finds many things to try his patience, and but few that are capable of winning his affections. One of the most disagreeable features that he has to encounter, is the secrecy with which everything is done. He can rarely obtain accurate information, until events have transpired, and he may rely upon it, that his own movements are closely observed, by eyes that he never sees. The Russian mind seems naturally distrustful, and this is especially so with the Government officials. Everything is surrounded with ceremony, and nothing is attainable, but after the most provoking delays . . .

I had a good deal during last winter to try my patience, for the Government possesses in an exquisite degree, the art of worrying a foreign representative without giving him even the consolation of an insult. The position as an Ambassador here is far from being pleasant. The opinion prevails, that no communication, at least of a public nature, is safe in the Post Office, but is opened and inspected as a matter of course. Hence those Legations that can afford it, maintain regular couriers, and never send anything by mail. The opinion also prevails, that Ministers are constantly subjected to a system of espionage, and that even their servants are made to disclose what passes in their households, their conversations, associations, et cetera. Of all this I have had no positive evidence, but I believe there is some foundation for such charges . . .

Secrecy and mystery characterize everything. Nothing is made public that is worth knowing. You will find no two individuals agreeing in the strength of the army and navy, in the amount of the public debt, or the annual revenue. In my opinion it is not intended these things should be known.

Respectfully yours,
William C. Bullitt

Bullitt to the Secretary of State   Moscow
No. 1537   April 20, 1936
Sir:

. . . Today Stalin considers it sound strategy to support democratic forms of government in countries in which communism is still weak; but the meaning of that support was displayed by Dimitrov at the Comintern Congress in August, 1935, when he pointed out that at the moment the cause of communism could be promoted best by use of the tactics of the Trojan horse and warned his communist comrades that they were not good communists if they felt that it was indecent or unduly hypocritical to become the collaborators and pretended friends of democrats in order to the better eventually to lead those democrats to the firing squad . . .

There is no doubt whatsoever that all orthodox communist parties in all countries, including the United States, believe in mass murder. Moreover, the loyalty of a believing communist is not to the nation of which he is technically a citizen but to his faith and to the Caliph of that faith. To such men the most traitorous betrayals are the highest virtues . . .

Yet it must be recognized that communists are agents of a foreign power whose aim is not only to destroy the institutions and liberties of our country, but also to kill millions of Americans. Our relations with the Soviet Union, therefore, involve questions of domestic policy which can not be answered except on the basis of a careful estimate of the strength of world communism and the reality or unreality of its threat to our liberties and lives.

Moreover, the time is not distant when the Soviet Union will become a dangerous factor in the field of international trade. The Soviet Government has not the slightest intention of abandoning its monopoly of foreign trade. It is attempting to make itself as self-sufficient as possible and it will use its monopoly of trade ruthlessly to undersell and injure its enemies and to assist its friends. It will not, in good faith, enter into any international agreements which have as their object improvement of the general economic condition of the world. It will, on the contrary, try to produce as much chaos as possible in the economies of capitalist countries in the hope that misery may beget communist revolution . . .

The secret police and the army are better fed, housed, and entertained than any other portion of the population. Their loyalty to the Soviet regime is unquestionable. And there is no longer reasonable doubt as to the strength of the Red Army. It numbers today nearly a million and a half men. Its material equipment in artillery, airplanes, and tanks is abundant in quantity though deficient in quality. It can not undertake offensive operations due to the fact that the railroads are still inadequate for the peacetime needs of the country and to the equally important fact that there are literally no modern highways in the entire Soviet Union. But on the defensive, the Red Army would fight hard, well and long.

The only actual threat to the Soviet Union is the Japanese. All Litvinov's propaganda trumpetings to the contrary, the Soviet Government knows very well that Germany can not be in a position to make war on the Soviet Union for many years. Every feasible route for German attack leads across Polish territory and the whole basis of Polish policy is never to permit the foot of either a German or a Russian soldier to be placed on her soil.

The Japanese threat is actual. But the Japanese have so bungled their relations with the Mongols, and the strength of the Soviet Far Eastern Army has increased so fast, that the Russians today are confident that a Japanese attack would end in destruction of the Japanese Army . . .

The chief weakness of the Soviet State today is, indeed, the inefficiency of the bureaucracy. The communist form of State requires a bureaucracy of exceptional ability. The Russians have always been and are bad bureaucrats. In consequence, extraordinary numbers of Jews are employed in all the Commissariats. Only one out of each sixty-one inhabitants of the Soviet Union is a Jew; but twenty of the sixty-one Commissars and Vice-Commissars are Jews.

What then should be the policy of the United States with regard to the Soviet Government and the world communist movement?

We should not cherish for a moment the illusion that it is possible to establish really friendly relations with the Soviet Government or with any communist party or communist individuals.

We should maintain diplomatic relations with the Soviet Union because it is now one of the Greatest Powers and its relations with Europe, China, and Japan are so important that we can not conduct our foreign relations intelligently if we do not know what is happening in Moscow. Moreover, in spite of all efforts to conceal the truth from foreigners, it is possible to obtain in Moscow considerable information as to the Soviet Union and the world communist movement.

We should use our influence quietly to oppose war in the Far East between the Soviet Union and Japan not only because of our moral opposition to war but also because, if there is a war, someone may win it. In case the Soviet Union should win, a Communist China would be inevitable. In case Japan should win, China would be completely subjected to Japan.

We should instruct our diplomatic representatives in Europe to use all opportunities in personal conversations to point out the danger to Europe of the continuation of Franco-German enmity and to encourage reconciliation between France and Germany.

We should attempt to promote our trade with the Soviet Union by direct bargaining of the sort involved in our agreement of July 13, 1935. But we should have no illusion that our trade with the Soviet Union may ever be stable or permanent. It may be cut off for political reasons at any minute. Therefore, we should not make loans or give long-term credits to the Soviet Union and should advise American industrialists against putting in expensive machinery to produce for the Soviet market . . .

The keynote of our immediate relations with the Soviet Union should be patience. The communist movement in the United States today constitutes a potential danger but not an actual threat. We do not need to get excited about it. Our political relations with the Soviet Union are negative; but our trade is increasing. It is difficult to conduct conversations with the Soviet Foreign Office because in that institution the lie is normal and the truth abnormal and one's intelligence is insulted by the happy assumption that one believes the lie. But patience and diplomats exist for just that sort of difficulty.

We should neither expect too much nor despair of getting anything at all. We should be as steady in our attitude as the Soviet Union is fickle. We should take what we can get when the atmosphere is favorable and do our best to hold on to it when the wind blows the other way. We should remain unimpressed in the face of expansive professions of friendliness and unperturbed in the face of slights and underhand opposition. We should make the weight of our influence felt steadily over a long period of time in the directions which best suit our interests. We should never threaten. We should act and allow the Bolsheviks to draw their own conclusions as to the causes of our acts.

Above all, we should guard the reputation of Americans for businesslike efficiency, sincerity, and straightforwardness. We should never send a spy to the Soviet Union. There is no weapon at once so disarming and effective in relations with the communists as sheer honesty. They know very little about it.

Respectfully yours,
William C. Bullitt

In March Mr. Moore wrote to Bullitt that he had talked to the President about sending him to Paris as Ambassador, and two weeks later wrote, "Very confidentially, of course, I wish to ask you whether you would care to go to Rome in case Mr. Long should give up that post in the near future; to go to Rome with the prospect of going from there to Paris, in the event that Mr. Straus should quit. I believe there is a probability of Long, and a possibility of Straus retiring." In a later letter he told Bullitt he had suggested this to the President.

Bullitt's reply from Moscow was:

Personal and Confidential   Moscow
April 8, 1936

Dear Judge Moore:

. . . I have thought over carefully the highly confidential question you ask in your letter of March 19. Of course, I am ready to go anywhere and do anything that the President wants me to do; but I would honestly prefer to take a leave of absence without pay this summer and work in the campaign, rather than be appointed Ambassador to Italy, with the prospect of moving on later to Paris.

I know Italy well and I have talked over intimately with Breckinridge Long the diplomatic work in Rome. It doesn't seem to differ greatly from the work in Moscow. There are infrequent meetings with Mussolini. Long has, I think, talked with him only twice in three years. There are no negotiations of importance and there is a great deal of the sort of social life that I participated in with pleasure at the age of 17, and from which I have attempted to escape ever since . . .

London and Paris are the only two posts in Europe at which one can make one's human contacts mean something. What I would like beyond anything else at the present time is to work and work hard. Life in Italy would, of course, be extremely pleasant in contrast to the extremely unpleasant life here, and I should like the climate. But I do not feel that there would be any outlet for the energy which is, at the moment bursting within me . . .

Another consideration weighs heavily with me and is perhaps controlling: I want Anne to have an American education and I want to be with her or, at least, so close to her that I can see her every week. I should not hesitate to take Anne to Paris where there are good American schools; but she could not find an American education in Rome and I am certain that she would not be happy there. Paris, I should prefer infinitely to Rome. But as I said before, I will go cheerfully to any point where the President may think he would like to have me.

You will, I think, understand me without further explanation, as you know me thoroughly. The appeal that an ambassadorship has for most Americans leaves me completely cold. I had so much international social life as a child and young man that I know its emptiness as well as any American concerned with politics. It is perhaps a weakness not to care about prestige and position but I simply do not. The work to be done is the thing that counts.

I believe that your own view of life is so close to mine that you will understand fully. I must say also that I am very much in love with America. The problems of America are the things that interest me most and I like to be with my friends of whom, thank God, I now have a number in Washington and elsewhere at home.

Please do not think me ungrateful. I am conscious always of a deep sense of thankfulness for your friendship and the constant support you give me. I feel almost as if we had been roommates at the University of Virginia and that there is nothing to explain.

My thanks and every good wish.

Yours affectionately,
William C. Bullitt

Bill's reference to his international social life as a child was a bit far-fetched. Our grandmother and three of her four daughters lived in Europe: she and one daughter in France; another daughter, married to an Italian, in Rome; and the third daughter in London. In the summer they would all meet, usually in Switzerland, for a couple of weeks, and sometimes Bill and I would accompany Mother. We did meet some of their foreign friends, but it was in no sense the international social life as it is known today. Father would take a cure for gout at Carlsbad during these trips and apparently thought so little of the life there that in his will he expressed the hope that his children would not live abroad. He did not foresee where Bill's career would lead him. Bill did meet a number of important English people, in both the social and political life, when he stayed with a cousin at her country place.

On May 18, 1936, Bullitt talked with the German Minister for Foreign Affairs in Berlin. Von Neurath, the minister, was remarkably frank in what he said about German plans. He began with the statement that Germany would do nothing active until "the Rhineland had been digested" and until fortifications were built on the French and Belgian frontiers. Germany would restrain the Nazis in Austria and would not antagonize the Czechs. After the fortifications were built, "those countries will begin to feel very differently about their foreign policies and a new constellation will develop."

Von Neurath insisted that Hitler's deepest desire was to come to a real understanding with France and that this had also been the core of his personal foreign policy, but he did not see the slightest chance of bringing this about.

He was attempting friendship with Italy to keep Mussolini from attacking Austria, the Italian Army being largely mobilized on the Austrian frontier. The youth of Austria were turning to the Nazi party and its dominance was only a matter of time.

With regard to England he expressed regret that no friendship had been established between the two countries and he had just told Hitler that he expected shortly a statement from England that they could see no moral objection to the joining of Austrian Germans to the German Republic. He was prepared for this and had no intention of allowing the British policy to embroil Germany with Italy by producing a Nazi coup d'état in Austria.

Von Neurath spoke of Russia and said the hostility between Germany and the Soviet Union was absolutely irremovable. The Soviet believed the Nazis to be the one obstacle to the conquest of Europe by Communism.

The conversation continued at some length, covering the possible re-entry of Germany into the League of Nations, the situation in Czechoslovakia, Germany's need for colonies, and her internal situation.[1]

At the end of April 1936, Bullitt made a brief trip to Kovno, where he talked with Mr. Preston of the British legation. Mr. Preston gives a full account in a letter to the Foreign Office of Bullitt's views at this time when he was to leave the Soviet permanently. A brief summary of the letter will give Bullitt's ideas after over two years of association with the Soviet Government. Undoubtedly he reported similar remarks to Mr. Roosevelt in the White House. Bullitt felt the Russians had not abandoned the plan of world revolution and with their enormous natural resources and great industrial and military strength were a potential danger to peace and might eventually overrun Europe. The only country able to withstand them was Germany. He felt that war was not imminent with Japan. Bullitt felt that Mussolini was more dangerous than Hitler, as there was no telling what he would do next. He thought the time might come when Britain might have to support Germany in stemming the tide of Russia.[2]

The notes of various Foreign Office officials on this letter are: "I do not think Mr. Bullitt's views have great value," "I agree that the Soviet Union may one day be a grave menace to the capitalist world," and "Mr. Bullitt at least compliments us by allowing us a foreign policy." The summation is: "As the Secretary of State recently observed on another paper, 'nobody, not even Lady Astor, now takes Mr. Bullitt seriously.' "[3]

THE WHITE HOUSE

WASHINGTON

April 21, 1936

Dear Bill:

Your cables have been very amusing. I know how anxious you are to have some definite work and I hope to Heaven you will have it by the middle of May. You know, without my telling you, that these things move very slowly and this particular bit of work involves several changes. I can tell you this, however, that when the change is made you will pack up your furniture, the dog and the servants — where you will deposit them, we will have to tell you later.

As you may know, Louis Howe died on Saturday night and the

funeral services are held this afternoon. While we all feel a sense of great personal loss, we know that for him it must be a blessed release.

As ever yours,

FDR

George F. Kennan speaks of Bullitt's hopes and his disillusionment in these terms: "These hopes were quickly disappointed. This was, after all, the day of Stalin, not of Lenin. Bullitt soon became embittered over the behavior of the Soviet government in a whole series of questions. Increasingly, as the years 1934 and 1935 ran their course, he made himself the advocate of a hard line toward Moscow, a line which most of us in the embassy wholeheartedly supported but which FDR, caring little about the specific issues involved, had no intention whatsoever of adopting. Not only did he have no intention of adopting it, but since the mere recommendation of it reflected an outlook on Soviet-American relations that did not fit with the general orientation of his policy, he soon sidetracked Bullitt altogether as an advisor on Russian matters, no doubt blaming the deterioration of Soviet-American relations primarily on Bullitt's personal pique and impatience.

"Bullitt spent, as I recall it, little time in Moscow after the early months of 1935. In the summer of 1936, he resigned as ambassador to the USSR and was soon given the Paris post in its place. Throughout much of the latter part of 1935 and 1936 the Moscow embassy carried on under the experienced and competent direction of Loy Henderson as chargé d'affaires ad interim. By the end of 1936 it was developing, we felt, into one of the best-informed and most highly respected diplomatic missions in Moscow, rivaled only by the German, which was at all times excellent. We were in many respects a pioneer enterprise — a wholly new type of American diplomatic mission — the model and precursor of a great many missions of a later day. We were the first to cope seriously, for example, with the problems of security — of protection of codes and files and the privacy of intra-office discussion — in a hostile environment. For this purpose, Bullitt brought in a detachment of Marine sergeants, in civilian clothes. But we were also the first to take a primarily intellectual and scholarly attitude to our work. We endeavored to carry forward into our reporting work the same scholarly approach and standards that had previously been adopted in Riga. We were profoundly imbued with a sense of the importance, present and future, of Soviet-American relations. We thought it of the utmost importance that the nature of the Soviet regime be correctly analyzed and that sound approaches be worked out for dealing with it. Our work in Moscow proceeded under formidable technical and physical difficulties, occasioned largely by the various minor harassments we never ceased to suffer at the hands of the Soviet authorities; but this only made us the prouder of our achievement. We regarded ourselves as a lonely and exposed bastion of American governmental life, surrounded by a veritable ocean of official Soviet ill will; and we took pride in our accomplishments precisely because of all this adversity." [4]

These were the last letters from Russia, as Bullitt returned home on the fourth of June, thoroughly out of patience with the lack of good faith on the part of the men he was dealing with at the top of the Soviet Government.

Bullitt's career in Moscow has been summed up by Mr. Kennan in his *Memoirs:* "The late William C. Bullitt was, in my opinion, a fine ambassador. I believe I reflect the views of others beside myself among those then stationed in Moscow when I say that we took pride in him and never had occasion to be ashamed of him. One should bear in mind, as I say this, that there is no scrutiny more critical than that to which an ambassador at a foreign post is subjected at the hands of his reserved and outwardly respectful career associates.

"Bullitt, as we knew him at that time in Moscow, was charming, brilliant, well-educated, imaginative, a man of the world capable of holding his own intellectually with anyone, including such great intellects of the Communist movement as Radek and Bukharin, both of whom were then still around and had no objection to coming to the embassy to talk with him. He had an excellent knowledge of both French and German, which went far to compensate for his lack of knowledge of Russian. His was outstandingly a buoyant disposition. He resolutely refused to permit the life around him to degenerate into dullness and dreariness.

All of us who lived in his entourage were the beneficiaries of this blitheness of spirit, this insistence that life be at all times animated and interesting and moving ahead.

"His greatest weakness as a diplomatist (and it was the natural counterpart of his virtues) was impatience. He came to Russia with high hopes, and he wanted to see them realized at once. These hopes were not the result of any ideological sympathy for the Soviet regime; they reflected rather, if my own impression is correct, a certain overoptimism concerning the impressionableness of the Soviet leaders. Here Bullitt was no doubt betrayed by his earlier experience with Lenin. He had gone to Russia in February 1919, during the Paris Peace Conference, with the blessing of Colonel House and at least the tacit consent of President Wilson and Prime Minister Lloyd George. He had dealt there with Lenin and other Soviet leaders of that day.

"All this had occurred at a time when the attitude of the Soviet regime toward the United States had not yet congealed — when there was still considerable vacillation among the Soviet leadership — when that leadership still included a number of people not disinclined to view the United States as something less than an entirely imperialistic and negative force in world affairs. Such pro-American tendencies in Moscow naturally received a severe rebuff in the treatment accorded to Bullitt by the Western leaders. Bullitt had never forgotten this. On returning to Russia as ambassador in 1933 he had hoped, I suspect, that the approach to the Roosevelt administration, free of the prejudices of 1919, free of the rigidities of the Republican regimes that had intervened over the preceding twelve years, and prepared to correct insofar as it could the errors of that earlier day, would evoke a favorable response on the Soviet side." [5]

Bullitt remained in Washington for the rest of the summer and worked on the question of reorganizing the State Department, with particular reference to the foreign service. He also spent some time on the foreign aspects of Mr. Roosevelt's speeches to be given in the coming campaign.

[THREE]

The Paris Embassy
1936–1939

11

Paris at Last

Rome-Berlin Axis
Roosevelt Elected to Second Term
Attempts to Involve United States in Europe

BULLITT WAS APPOINTED Ambassador to France on August 25, 1936, and left for Paris at the end of September. For him it was a happy appointment to his second home. He knew the French so well and was apparently so much in their confidence that he was able to give the President the most intimate details of the thoughts and probable actions of the leading statesmen, both in office and in opposition. These letters will show a knowledge of the country which few diplomats have been able to report to their government. He was in direct personal touch with the President and his first transatlantic telephone call took place a few days after his arrival in Paris.

Jim Farley described the situation in this way: "Ambassador Bullitt was busy holding the hands of Daladier, Reynaud, Paul-Boncour, Blum and the rest. The Embassy was a bee-hive. All diplomatic messages from the State Department to continental embassies and legations funneled through the structure at the Ave. des Champs-Élysées and the Rue Boissy-d'Anglas. Bullitt dispatched couriers throughout Europe, as telephone and telegraph wires were known to be tapped. The Embassy had a direct wire to Washington through which Roosevelt and Bullitt maintained constant communication. From what I saw, Bullitt was closer than anyone in the diplomatic service to the President.

Bullitt's capacity for work impressed me tremendously." [1] Mr. Farley remained a close friend of Bullitt's until his death.

As an outsider, Juliusz Lukasiewicz, Polish Ambassador to France, speaks of the friendly relations between Premier Daladier and Bullitt. When Lukasiewicz was seeking assurances on the bombing of open cities, Daladier said that "the best thing would be if you got in touch with our friend Bullitt and asked him to clear up this really very vital question." [2] Although the letters will show this intimacy, the words of Guy La Chambre, French Minister of Air, are of interest: "In fact we sympathized the first day we met each other almost as if we had been brothers. He was so bold and so frank, indeed he was close to the leading figures in French political life."

Robert Murphy was Counselor of Embassy in Paris, and later Roosevelt's personal representative in Africa prior to and after the Allied landings. He was General Eisenhower's political adviser in Africa, first postwar Ambassador to Belgium, Ambassador to Japan, and Assistant Secretary of State. Murphy says of the next four years in Paris: "When World War II broke out I had been serving for three years with Ambassador Bullitt, a brilliant man with profound knowledge of Europe and its history. He was convinced that the European conflict would directly threaten the United States, so he felt his own role in the approaching tragedy was bound to be important [3] . . . Bullitt at times was in daily touch with our Ambassadors, such as Joseph Kennedy in London, Tony Biddle in Warsaw, and others in key posts. He felt he had a tacit mandate from Roosevelt to act as his eyes and ears in Europe. Bullitt drove his associates in the Embassy to maintain close and friendly relations with French statesmen and other leaders. Thus we made invaluable contacts, ranging from the extreme left of Maurice Thorez, Jacques Duclos and Marcel Cachin, through Léon Blum, Vincent Auriol, Pierre Cot, Gaston Bergery, Édouard Herriot, Paul Reynaud, Édouard Daladier, Camille Chautemps, Yvon Delbos, Jules Jeanneney, Georges Bonnet, Pierre Laval, Pierre-Étienne Flandin, Georges Mandel, Raymond Patenôtre, Albert Sarraut — even Marcel Déat and Colonel de la Rocque.[4]

". . . No emissary from any land ever got closer to French political life than Ambassador Bullitt, who had lived in France off and on since boyhood, spoke the language as if it were his own, and had warm friendships with men and women of all sorts. He had great influence upon French policy, judged personalities shrewdly, and used ingenuity in getting information and putting across his own ideas. Bullitt deserves great credit for bringing to his mission a dynamic imagination coupled with knowledge of internal French affairs. If he erred, it was on the side of yielding to a subjective approach, which carried him inside the French Government to an unheard-of-degree. An ambassador is usually well advised to remain close enough to local politicians to enjoy their confidence but to be sufficiently aloof to ensure against their assuming control of him. But this was an extraordinary situation which called for unorthodox methods. Bullitt had the advantage of access to intimate Cabinet information which was as important at this time to President Roosevelt as it was dear to Bullitt's own instincts, derived from his early career as a newsman. When war finally was declared, he had a good general idea of what was likely to happen. He was never an emotional interventionist but he was profoundly concerned about the security of the United States in case of a French-British defeat, which he feared. Bullitt was very critical of British policy under the Baldwin and Chamberlain governments, for much the same reasons that Churchill was. But Bullitt underestimated Churchill, thinking of him as a has-been, which was the general opinion at that time in England as well as in Europe.

"Ambassador Bullitt's relationship with President Roosevelt was remarkably intimate during his years in Russia and France. He often bypassed the Secretary of State and talked at length with the President by trans-Atlantic telephone. The two men threshed out matters of policy with no correspondence to record their discussions, particularly during those first eight months of World War II." [5]

Harold Ickes wrote: "Bullitt practically sleeps with the French Cabinet." [6] In 1940 he suggested to the President that Bullitt be made Secretary of War but: "He [the President] said, however, that he doubted whether he could take Bullitt from France because not only the officials there but the people depend so strongly upon his advice and sympathy." [7]

On October 13, 1936, Bullitt presented his credentials as American Ambassador to France to President Albert Lebrun at the Élysée Palace. He pledged himself to efforts to reinforce Franco-American friendship on the basis of loyalty to "liberty, democracy and peace." He also brought a message from the President to President Lebrun for the happiness and prosperity of France.

The political situation in France had been extremely unstable for a long time. Between the years 1932 and 1940 a dozen different Premiers (Présidents du Conseil) had been overthrown by the Parliament. Léon Blum held this position for the first eight months of Bullitt's service as Ambassador. Blum, who had never held a cabinet position before, formed a government in June 1936, composed of his own Socialist followers, the Radicals under Édouard Daladier, and the Communists led by Maurice Thorez. This coalition was given the name of Popular Front by Blum. The Communists were, of course, only interested in policies which would further Stalin's aims; the Radicals, who were not a powerful party and in spite of their name were more conservative than the Socialists, opposed the monetary and social reforms of Blum. By June 1937, the Popular Front was defeated.

Outside the government were powerful groups with Fascist aims or royalist tendencies. The principal ones were: the Action Française, whose storm troopers were called the Camelots du Roi, led by Maurice Pujot; opposed to them were the Jeunesses Patriotes, who were largely university students and had been formed into small groups for street fighting. There were also the Solidarité Française, formed by Coty the perfumer, and the Croix de Feu, led by Colonel de la Rocque, composed largely of war veterans. To disrupt public meetings and for rioting these groups would often combine, and in January 1934, the street fighting became serious, culminating in the bloody affray of February 6. Daladier had just become Premier as a huge mob gathered in the Place de la Concorde attempting to cross the Seine to storm the Chamber of Deputies. Fighting between the mob, the gendarmes, and the Republican and mobile guards also broke out in the streets on the Left Bank and even around the Élysée Palace. When the rioting was over many lay dead and there were hundreds of wounded. The following day Daladier resigned.

This rioting and bloodshed was to remain in the minds of the politicians, and the divisiveness of French political life with all its different factions should be borne in mind while reading Bullitt's accounts of his talks with government leaders.

Personal   Paris

October 5, 1936

Dear Mr. President:

The morning of my departure I telephoned you as I had promised. I telephoned from poor Jesse Straus' bedroom because after seeing him I felt certain that you would not have a chance to see him before the end, and he was eager to talk with you. But every time I called, the operator said that you were not available. I was sorry.

I didn't have anything to say except — good luck. I have nothing more to say now except that my reception was extraordinarily friendly, and that a series of conversations with old friends inclines me to believe that in Washington we have been much too pessimistic about the situation in France.

Our own stock is very high just now. The French are delighted by the cooperation you gave them in the matter of devaluation and the members of the government seem to be greatly pleased by my appointment. Léger, for example, said: "The best indication of the President's special friendliness for France is that he sent you here at this time."

Up to date there has been no unpleasant incident. Offie pretends that it is unsafe to walk on the Champs-Élysées; but he hasn't learned yet how sweetly and gently Frenchmen can riot.

Good luck for the remainder of the campaign and after.

Yours affectionately and always,

William C. Bullitt

Personal   Paris

October 5, 1936

Dear Judge Moore:

With reference to your telegram No. 386 of October 3, 1936, 1 P.M., Hampel is the Navy expert who picks out dictaphones. I want him here to inspect the Chancery and my house which have *never* been inspected. I should think a week would be sufficient. The Naval Attaché here informs me that he thinks he can get the Navy Department to order Hampel to Paris. If there is any hitch I will pay for his trip from my own pocket. Don't bother about the matter . . .

You will be pleased to learn that last night Offie was the guest of honor at Maxim's at a dinner given by the Marquis and Marquise de Polignac, who are the greatest snobs in France. Inasmuch as the Polignacs habitually ignore everyone from this Embassy, including the Ambassadors, I think you will agree with me that our child is already going fast and far. The Marquise herself drove him home at midnight!

Lebrun has been in the country and I have not, therefore, presented my letters of credence as yet. However, I have seen enough old friends to be convinced that we have been much too excited in Washington about the situation in France. It is not nearly so dangerous as it has appeared to be on the other side of the Atlantic.

I will write you fully and, I hope, more intelligently by the next pouch.

Good luck and every good wish.

Yours affectionately,
William C. Bullitt

THE WHITE HOUSE
WASHINGTON

October 20, 1936

Dear Bill:

This is a very hasty note to tell you how nice it was to hear from you yesterday on the telephone, and to thank you for the stamps which you sent. Incidentally, I do know where Touva is and what it is!

I did not see Jesse Straus before he died. The day I was to go there Mrs. Straus telephoned me to say that he was in a coma and two days later he died. I am happy that he did not know how sick he was.

The Western trip was almost too successful. Everything went well although we missed you on the speeches.

Good luck to you!

Affectionately,
FDR

Honorable William C. Bullitt
American Embassy
Paris
France

In October 1936, Count Ciano, the Italian Foreign Minister, met with the German Foreign Minister, Neurath, in Berlin to discuss Italian-German relations. As a result of these talks Ciano went to Berchtesgaden to talk with Hitler, who, cajoling him with flattery, painted a picture of the two countries conquering the continent and England. The result was the Rome-Berlin Axis. Mussolini's fatal tie to Germany was now official.

Personal and Confidential   Paris
                                                    October 24, 1936

Dear Mr. President:

It was bully to hear your voice on the phone although the connection was so bad that it made you croak like a bullfrog.

I was immensely distressed to hear that you might lose Vermont; but in compensation, I can inform you that you carried the American Club of Paris by one vote! As the American Club is composed largely of representatives of the biggest banks, oil companies, etc., who don't love you, I thought that showed a very healthy state of mind. Good luck and God bless you for the next four years . . .

There is so much political news to write that it is almost hopeless to begin. I got away to a good start with Blum. We lunched together at the house of an old friend of mine who is also an old friend of his, and I had a most intimate conversation with him. He looks exactly like the caricatures of him, and has the sort of quicksilver intelligence and the little fluttery gestures of the hyper-intellectual queer ones. He seemed to be deeply grateful for your collaboration in the monetary arrangements and was honestly delighted when I said to him, as you had told me to say, that you felt his task in France was very like the task that had faced you in America. He has taken the position that if the Communists refuse to support him he will not attempt to make a deal with the Right but will ask the dissolution of the Chamber of Deputies and new elections. The Communists know at the present time that new elections would mean an immense reduction in their vote and unless they get orders from Moscow to raise hell (orders based on Russian interests, not on French) they will, I think continue to support him and the government will continue in power for some time.

The aristocracy and upper bourgeoisie are just as dumb here as their opposite numbers in the United States. They show no sign of appreciating the fact that Blum is as conservative as anyone who can hold the situation together. If Blum were in for a four-year term as you were in 1933, I have no doubt that he could do a highly constructive job and that the internal situation in France would right itself rapidly. But as he has to maneuver daily to maintain his position and as no one in the country has any fundamental respect for his character — since there is no one who does not know why he was fired from the École Normale — he is not exactly a Rock of Gibraltar. The man the French need is a man who has both intelligence and a character that people can respect. But such a leader is utterly invisible at the present time. There is no one on the Right. People respect de la Rocque but believe that there isn't a sign of a brain in his head. Tardieu is utterly discredited. Mandel is regarded as an intensely clever fellow with no character whatsoever. Chautemps is considered a jelly fish with lots of common sense. Herriot's health has been failing and his position with it. Daladier is completely distrusted by everyone except Daladier. If there were a leader to the Right of Blum, even like old Poincaré, a coherent opposition on the Right might be developed. As it is, Blum is strong because of the weakness of his opponents.

I do not see any sign of the street fighting and general revolutionary activity that has been predicted so frequently in our press. The whole of France has been shocked by the civil war in Spain. The lower middle class, which in the last election in considerable measure voted Communist, doesn't want that sort of thing in France. There is, moreover, an extremely interesting movement developing of which you will hear more in the next couple of years among the Catholics. A really serious attempt is being made to organize a Catholic Liberal or Radical Party in the hope that it may be possible within the next year to form a majority consisting of Radical Socialists, Socialists and Catholic Radicals with the Communists excluded. That is a hopeful line.

I have talked with lots of men on the Right like Paul Reynaud and Mandel. They believe that they will be able to upset Blum and make a series of political deals which will produce the sort of government that France has suffered under for the past ten years. They might conceivably be able to form such a government but it could not last. The country is just as definitely on the Left as the United States was on the Left in 1933.

You have doubtless been reading reports of the so-called riots on the Champs-Élysées and elsewhere. They are very French riots, carried out in the most pleasant and almost theatrical spirit and are not to be taken seriously — at least not yet. People forget how politely Frenchmen can riot.

On the whole, I am optimistic as to the internal situation. But the position in foreign affairs is definitely bad. You may have seen the long telegram I sent referring to my conversation with Blum. From him and from a number of other conversations at the Quai d'Orsay, I gather that he intends to try through diplomatic channels to make a genuine effort to reach an understanding with Germany, in the first instance on economic matters and in the second on political matters. He will, I think, be badly represented in Berlin by François-Poncet, who said to me one of the last times I passed through Berlin that he was convinced there was no basis whatever for understanding between Germany and France and that in his proposals to the German Government he was merely building up material to be published in a white book to be issued when war broke out. Blum wants really to reach an understanding with Germany and the obvious line is through the French Ambassador in Berlin and Neurath, since Neurath has worked for years in the direction of Franco-German understanding. I don't believe François-Poncet will play ball in the way ball has to be played if results are to be produced.

Delbos, who is now Minister of Foreign Affairs, is a nice chap but no heavyweight. He follows the line of Léger and the old guard in the Quai d'Orsay. They are completely unconstructive at the moment, shocked by the action of Belgium, fearful that Rumania will slip into a position similar to that of Belgium and just plain frightened.

Beck's visit to Paris did not produce the increase in French confidence in him that he hoped it would produce. The French can not forget that when he was Polish Military Attaché in Paris, they threw him out for communicating official secrets of the French General Staff to Germany. I spent three hours with him when he was here and to my great surprise he said that he hoped he could visit the United States this summer. I am sure that you would be really interested in a talk with him. He has a subtle, if somewhat devious, mind and is unusually well informed with regard to political conditions in every country in Europe. I like him but I am about the only person alive who does . . .

I have just seen the *Havas* correspondent in Moscow, a chap named Gilles, who is perhaps the ablest of the correspondents there. He said that the harvest is definitely unsatisfactory and that the

Stakhanovite movement is not producing one half the results expected. He asserted that there was so much discontent in the country that Stalin had decided to eliminate any possible distinguished leaders around whom such opposition could gather. Hence the fate of Zinoviev, Kamenev, Radek, Sokolnikov, Pyatakov, and the rest. This does not sound unreasonable to me as I have heard the same thing from the Polish Ambassador here who was in Moscow when I was there and who still has intimate connections there. I have heard the same thing also from our Embassy in Moscow.

I have not yet started any reorganization of the Embassy. All the representatives of the Departments in that magnificent building, except Offie and myself, will be in such a state of dejection and fear on November 4th that we should be able to push them around with much less resistance than before your re-election has been celebrated. I have at least discovered that every clerk in the Embassy *without exception* is married to a foreign wife! This includes all the confidential code clerks.

Please don't forget that before you and Cordell leave Washington you must give Judge Moore the authority which he can have only if he is Under Secretary of State. A temporary position as Acting Secretary of State is no good . . .

Best wishes and may the Lord be with you.

Yours affectionately,
William C. Bullitt

The Stakhanov movement began in August 1935 and was named for a Donets coal miner who claimed to have mined 102 tons of coal in six hours. It was essentially a speedup of production methods involving higher work quotas and greater productivity of labor.

Bullitt had now moved into the Ambassador's residence at 2 Avenue d'Iéna at the corner of the Avenue Albert-de-Mun. There is a fine view over the gardens of the Trocadéro to the Seine with the Eiffel Tower in the background. The house is separated from the street by a courtyard with a porter's lodge and on one side is a small garden. It is an ostentatious, ugly, and uncomfortable dwelling. Three drawing rooms open on the side to the sunlight, but the small library is dark and ugly. An indication of the taste of the wealthy Frenchman who built it lies in some thirty different-colored marbles used in the floors and walls. There is a large dining room in the rear of the house for formal dinners. When necessity called for these large parties Bullitt would either have chamber music in the central drawing room after dinner or show moving pictures in the spacious hall on the second floor at the head of the grand staircase.

The house was always filled with flowers which the butler purchased in the early morning hours at the flower market in Les Halles. Bullitt had a magnificent wine cellar and was recognized as a good judge of wine.

It has recently been announced that the government will move the Ambassador's residence to the Rue du Faubourg St.-Honoré in a magnificent house formerly owned by the Baron Édmond de Rothschild. It is adjacent to the British Embassy and the Élysée Palace, with a handsome formal garden and extending to two and a half acres. It has the added advantage of being within a very short walking distance of the Embassy on the Place de la Concorde. This property will furnish a far more suitable abode for the representative of the United States than the old one, which was completely inadequate for large functions.

Bullitt also had a small apartment for many years, which he kept until his death. It was on the Rue de Ponthieu, near the Rond-Point of the Champs-Élysées. He loved it and I thought it was dreadful: a small living-dining room with an alcove for a bed, a tiny kitchen, and a small room for his Chinese manservant.

Personal and Confidential Paris
October 28, 1936

Dear Mr. President:

. . . The French and the Italians are both exceedingly anxious to borrow money in the United States now and will wish to make some sort of settlement in order to escape from the Johnson Act and open the American money market with the underlying thought that war is on the horizon; that the loans will never have to be paid because of war and that they can get a great deal of money for one or two comparatively small payments. We can not, of course, refuse a reasonable offer but I believe we should not accept anything less than a thoroughly reasonable offer. I believe that it is definitely in the national interest for us to have the capital which has now accumulated in the United States invested in the United States rather than loaned abroad to be lost in a new war. In other words, thanks to the Johnson Act, the debts *unpaid* are proving to be of considerable value to us.

You should receive this letter on Election Day and I will say now CONGRATULATIONS AND THE LORD BE WITH YOU.

Yours affectionately,

William C. Bullitt

TELEGRAM RECEIVED

SECRETARY OF STATE	PARIS
WASHINGTON	DATED NOVEMBER 4, 1936
1079, NOVEMBER 4, 8 P.M.	REC'D 3:51 P.M.
PERSONAL FOR MOORE	

THOMAS JEFFERSON HAS JUST PHONED ME TO SAY THAT ALEXANDER HAMILTON WALKED IN THIS MORNING AND ADMITTED THAT THE AMER-ICAN PEOPLE WERE TO BE TRUSTED AFTER ALL. CONGRATULATIONS AND LOVE. BILL.

[This refers to the President's re-election.]

Personal and Confidential   Paris

November 8, 1936

Dear Mr. President:

I am as happy as a proud father about the election! But you know that already, and I will not burden you any more with my emotions but will tell you about the reactions of the French.

The wave of enthusiasm in France which greeted your election was really phenomenal. No American President ever received such a tornado of praise. I enclose herewith the translations of articles which Herriot and Claudel wrote.

Blum came personally to express his congratulations. That is un-heard of. If you could have seen the manner of his coming, it would have done you good. At least you would have laughed. He entered the front door, flung his broad-brimmed black hat to the butler, his coat to a footman, leaped the three steps to the point where I was standing, seized me and kissed me violently! I stag-gered slightly; but having been kissed by Stalin, I am now immune to any form of osculation, and I listened without batting an eye to as genuine an outpouring of enthusiasm as I have ever heard.

You have, of course, received from de Laboulaye the resolution adopted by the Chamber of Deputies and the resolution of the town of Lannoy which claims to be the home of your ancestors. How many cities was it that claimed Homer?

The cause of this outburst is that the French regard you as a national leader who has succeeded in giving the lower classes a greater proportion of the national income without disturbing any of the ancient liberties. The French are all praying for such a man. Blum, himself, said to me that he felt his position had been greatly strengthened because he is attempting in his way to do what you have done in America. In addition, the French all feel that you have a genuine understanding of French civilization and a genuine liking for France, and that you will somehow manage to keep Europe from plunging again into war.

In every conversation that I have had, either with members of the French Government or the opposition, or ambassadors and ministers, or French statesmen who happen to be outside the government, like Herriot, I have attempted to elicit some statement of some constructive project for the prevention of war. I have never encountered such complete hopelessness. There is no feeling of crisis because no one believes that war is imminent; but there is a universal belief that Europe is drifting toward war and that no man on the continent has imagination enough to devise any method of reconciliation.

Every minister of a small European state who has yet called on me has expressed the hope that you might intervene, saying that if you did not, his country would certainly be destroyed by the inevitable conflict. I have asked how you could intervene, what you could do to prevent war, how you could be certain that anything you did would not produce a fiasco similar to the London Economic Conference. The reply invariably has been that no one in Europe can think of any way in which you can intervene effectively — but you might be able to think of some way yourself.

You are, in other words, beginning to occupy the miracle man position. And I am strongly reminded of the sort of hope that for a time was reposed in Woodrow Wilson. I wish I could talk out with you some evening in the White House the possibilities and impossibilities.

You would, I am sure, get nothing whatever from an *unprepared* conference of chiefs of state or prime ministers or foreign secretaries. The mess would be greater, because the conflict of interests would be greater, than at the London Economic Conference. On the other hand, I am not at all sure that you may not be able to do something which may have at least a fair chance of success.

You will remember in 1932, after your election but before your Inauguration, I had conversations with Schleicher and Neurath in Berlin and with Herriot and Boncour in Paris. It looked at that time as if something could be done to draw France and Germany together. You will remember also that all four of the gentlemen mentioned above felt that the essential thing would be quiet pressure and assistance from the United States acting through the American Ambassadors in Berlin and Paris.

In spite of the explosions of Mussolini, the nub of the problem of European peace is still — as it has been for so long — reconciliation between France and Germany. Ever since Hitler came into power everyone in France has assumed that reconciliation is impossible, and when I passed through Berlin last May, Neurath said to me that he felt there were fewer chances of reconciliation than ever before.

I don't believe that this is true. The essential thing the Germans must have, is the development of their economic relations with Central Europe and the Balkans. The French (or at least Blum and Delbos) have no objection to this. Indeed, it is perfectly obvious that whether the French want it or not, it will come to pass. It is in the logic of economic facts, for example, that Rumania should exchange her wheat and oil for German machines and construction material. Similarly, the Germans need the products of Yugoslavia, Hungary, Bulgaria, and Turkey, and those countries need German products. No one can invent any legitimate reason for trying to prevent this German economic development. The reason why so many people are afraid of it is because they fear that economic domination will lead to political domination and the realization of the old Berlin-to-Bagdad bloc.

I do not believe that political domination must necessarily follow economic domination and I believe that it may be possible to get together the French and the Germans on the basis of an economic agreement which would give the Germans a chance to develop Central Europe and the Balkans economically: provided such an agreement should be accompanied by an agreement with regard to limitation of armaments and a general revival of a feeling of European unity.

That sounds like a large order. It is a large order; but the events in Spain have made most people in most European countries realize that there is such a thing as European civilization which reposes on certain very old civilized principles that may be destroyed by war or Bolshevism. I do not mean that people are anxious to start a crusade against Bolshevism or that anyone (even Germany) intends to invade the Soviet Union, but I do mean that there is beginning to be a feeling that if the nations of Western Europe do not hang together, they will all hang separately.

If we can assist diplomatically in laying the basis for a reconciliation between France and Germany, I think we should help. If we get anywhere diplomatically and see a fair chance of success, you could then come forward with some tremendous public announcement. But I feel emphatically that you should not let yourself be persuaded to make some great gesture until you have prepared the ground with great care.

How can we prepare the ground? You can, of course, do much in any conversations you may have with the French and German Ambassadors in Washington and I shall be, I think, in a position to do whatever you want me to do here; at least so long as the present government remains in office. I have been astonished by the frankness with which Blum and Delbos have treated me and I have, of course, had a very confidential relationship with Léger for many years.

When Dodd leaves Berlin I think you should select your man for that post with extreme care. As Hitler does not speak anything but German any Ambassador of ours there who does not speak German *perfectly* will be useless. That qualification rules out most of the men who have been mentioned for the post. (Incidentally, Joe Davies' German is, I understand, lousy.*) I wish I had someone better to suggest, but I can think of no one better than Hugh Wilson, who has been for many years our Minister in Berne. His German is perfect and in spite of the fact that his connections are largely Republican and that his wife especially is no lover of the Democratic Party or you or myself, I can not think of anyone else who could begin to establish the really intimate and confidential relationship we need with the bosses in Berlin, which will be essential if we are to accomplish anything.†

* Joseph E. Davies succeeded Bullitt at the Moscow Embassy.
† Hugh Wilson was a distinguished career diplomat. He had wide experience, serving in the Argentine, Berlin, Vienna, and Tokyo. From 1927 he was Minister to Switzerland until he became Assistant Secretary of State in 1937. Appointed Ambassador to Germany in 1938, he brought to the position a thorough knowledge of the language, an objective point of view, and a calm and diplomatic personality which made him persona gràta at all his posts.

At the same time, I think you should signalize the arrival of Wilson or whoever replaces Dodd, by beginning at once to rebuild the Blucher Palace as the center of our activities in Berlin. As you know, we have owned the Blucher Palace for years and expected to house in it not only the Ambassador but also all the offices of the Embassy and Consulate General. As Dodd wanted to save money, he didn't want to take on any such establishment and held up the matter. Our Berlin establishment at the present moment would be an excellent one for Honduras. It is not a good stage setting for dealings with gentlemen who conceive of themselves as Parsifal and young Siegfried. And whether we like it or not, the Pure Fool and Goering are the bosses of Germany.

It is perhaps silly for me even to attempt to make suggestions of this sort in a letter. A discussion of all the whys and wherefores is so necessary that I may simply succeed in making you believe that I have lost whatever mind I ever possessed. However, it won't be useless if I can make you realize how intensely many people in Europe want you to do something about the European situation; and how inordinately difficult it is to do anything constructive, and how necessary to prepare the way. After all, it wouldn't have happened without John the Baptist.

I have lots of news to write you; but this letter is already so long that I shall only put in a few lines of it.

You probably saw the telegram in which I said that Blum had told me that he intended to replace de Laboulaye.

What actually happened was this: Blum said that he would like to see me at once and asked me to come to his own apartment on the Île St. Louis. I did and he said he had a highly indiscreet question to ask me. He said he had wished to withdraw de Laboulaye last Spring and his predecessors had wished to replace de Laboulaye for more than a year, and de Laboulaye had wished to be replaced. But Jesse Straus had informed him, as well as his predecessors, that it was absolutely essential to the interests of France that de Laboulaye should be kept in Washington so long as you were President, because he was such an intimate friend of yours that you would regard his removal as a personal affront. He wished to know if this was really the case because, while he would leave de Laboulaye in Washington if it were the case, he had received in the past week letters from three different men, all of whom he regarded as entirely reliable, informing him that both de Laboulaye and Madame de Laboulaye had made statements about him and the present government of France which were, to say the least, disloyal . . .

I replied that de Laboulaye had never made any such statements to me and that I thought he had conducted himself very satisfactorily as a career ambassador; that he was a very good friend of yours and that Madame de Laboulaye was a very good friend of Mrs. Roosevelt; but that I felt you would not consider it a personal affront if de Laboulaye should be replaced . . .

Putzi Hanfstaengl blew into Paris a couple of days ago and I had a talk with him night before last. He said that Goering will be made Reichskanzeler with Hitler retaining the superior position of Fuehrer. He prophesied that Rosenberg (the fellow who runs the anti-Russian propaganda and the plans for expansion to the East) will disappear from circulation during the next twelve months. He predicted that the rise of Goering would bring a very strong movement in Germany for rapprochement with the Soviet Union which would be opposed only by Hitler because of his religious conviction that the Bolsheviks are the children of Hell. Goering will be supported by the Reichswehr, the industrialists and Schacht . . .

I have, thank God, now completed all the obligatory speeches that I have to make. The last one was at the American Students and Artists Center, which is under the aegis of Dean Beekman of our noble church. The Latin Quarter religious audience has a somewhat peculiar odor of sanctity. While I was speaking, Offie was seated next to a very strange looking lady who kept pulling out of her pocket a quart bottle of Pernod and taking enormous swigs, while announcing to the lady on her right that when I had finished speaking, she intended to brain me with the bottle. The lady on her right, in whispers, argued with her that this would not be seemly. Finally, the absinthe drinking lady screeched out, "Can't you understand I'm in love with him?"!

. . . Good luck to you for your trip to South America and for all the years to come.

Yours affectionately,
Bill

THE WHITE HOUSE
WASHINGTON

November 9, 1936

Dear Bill:

It was good to get yours of October twenty-fourth on Election day and later to talk with you on the phone. I was delighted that you got into the American Club just in time to break the tie vote. Their vote was typical of thousands of representatives and employees of the big companies. They did not dare say out loud that they were going to vote for me for fear of offending the policy makers at the top. That was why the straw ballots were so deceptive.

In the New York Subway all through October people played a delightful game — Roosevelt buttons all the way downtown and then as the Wall Street station was approached a quick shift to Landon buttons to please the Boss.

Do I remember Elsie Hooper! A cousin of mine, by Jove. In fact, several cousins of mine! When I last saw her she looked like Buddha and I think had a sneaking suspicion that she was a reincarnation of said fat man!

The reports of the way the French received the election results were most interesting.

The Statue of Liberty exercises went off well, as did the unveiling of the Jusserand memorial seat in Rock Creek Park Saturday.

I am proceeding as fast as I can on certain matters in the Department but there is mighty little time between now and the time I sail on the seventeenth.

All well except that I need a week of sleep.

As ever yours,
FDR

Honorable William C. Bullitt
American Embassy
Paris
France

Personal and Confidential   Paris
November 24, 1936

Dear Mr. President:

The appended memorandum will give you the gist of a conversation I had with Monick but will not give you the odor of it. It is a subtle, and not altogether pleasant, odor which pervades every conversation I have in Paris whether with Frenchmen, Englishmen, Belgians, or Czechs. It is the emanation of a violent nervous desire to get us into the next war.

Everyone in France, including Blum and the British Ambassador, is convinced that war is about to arrive. Herriot, Claudel, and the more nervous representatives of the smaller countries, are convinced that war will come next Spring or Summer. Everyone is convinced that war will come by the Spring or Summer of 1938.

As you will see from the memorandum, I refused to listen to the details of Monick's scheme, and I have since refused to receive his project from a third party. I suspect that it involves not simply a debt settlement but also some vast scheme for economic and financial collaboration of the United States with England and France, designed to get us into close political collaboration as well.

We shall have to watch every agreement or other commitment with extreme care if we are to avoid slipping into a position from which there will be no retreat. I think that henceforth we should not accept any *"proposal in principle."* We ought to be willing to discuss specific detailed proposals but nothing else.

It will be difficult for me to make you realize the degree to which French Cabinet Ministers and representatives of all the countries of Europe in Paris talk as if they had within them the same phonograph record — playing the theme, "War is inevitable and Europe is doomed to destruction unless President Roosevelt intervenes."

Invariably I reply by asking how you can intervene effectively. Invariably the reply is, "We don't know, but the President must have some idea." Invariably I answer that I am reminded of the situation at the close of a Greek tragedy, when the difficulties become too vast to be handled by man and the *deus ex machina* appears to set everything right. I then remark that you are not a *deus* and that you have no authority to bend the rulers of Europe to your will, and that you are not going to send the American Navy and American soldiers to Europe.

Invariably the reply is, "That is quite right. There is no reason why you should send your armed forces again to Europe; but — "

Thereupon the conversation begins again; and once more it becomes obvious that our money, ships and men are the things that are wanted.

As the situation grows worse, you will hear much flattery about your moral prestige and your duty to western civilization.

The pressure of one sort and another will not be easy to handle.

I am informed reliably that the Muscovites themselves are about to begin a new drive to attempt to get our good will and that they will inaugurate it by covering Joe Davies with tons of the very best butter. They are disturbed by the recent Japanese-German agreement and are beginning to realize how foolish they were to give us the kick in the face which they delivered so light-heartedly when they made the American communists the stars of the Comintern Congress in the summer of 1935.

Incidentally, I am informed that they are re-inaugurating the propaganda, which they started at that time, to the effect that neither you nor the American Government cared in the least whether or not they directed the American Communist Party from Moscow; but that the protest we made at that time was due entirely to my ill temper. I understand that they have been attempting to get "The Nation" and "The New Republic" of New York to commence this line of attack on me and to start a campaign for close cooperation between the "democracies" of the United States and the Soviet Union!

I hope that you have instructed Joe Davies to be exceedingly cordial to the Bolsheviks but also to be absolutely adamant on the point of Russian interference in our internal affairs through control of the American Communist Party from Moscow. In the period ahead, we can not let either Mussolini, Hitler, or Stalin organize and direct groups of American citizens.

The war in Spain, as you know, has become an incognito war between the Soviet Union and Italy. The Spanish Ambassador here admitted to me a couple of days ago that the entire air force of the Madrid Government is composed of Russian pilots and Russian planes. He boasted that some of the Russian pursuit planes in Madrid had a speed of 510 kilometers per hour and admitted that the only hope of the Madrid Government was in the Russian planes and Russian arms. On the other hand, Franco's forces actually at the fighting front are composed almost entirely of Moors, and Italian and German aviators. Reports are that the German aviators are much better than the Italian. My own impression is that Mussolini has decided to put through Franco whatever the cost may be. I think that the cost will be very high.

I would not be surprised if Mussolini should be compelled to enlist a couple of Italian Army Corps in the Spanish Foreign Legion. I believe that before the Spanish Civil War is over it may bring Europe to the very edge of war. I believe, however, that war will not spring directly out of it. A situation may arise from it, however, which will give Hitler a chance to make some move against Czechoslovakia.

Czechoslovakia, clearly, is the next item on Hitler's menu.

If Hitler should send forces into Czechoslovakia the position of France, as well as Czechoslovakia, would become tragic. (No military man with whom I have talked believes that the Soviet air force can bring any effective aid to Czechoslovakia.) The French would have to decide whether or not to carry out the obligations of their treaty of alliance with Czechoslovakia.

The Quai d'Orsay would be all for carrying out those obligations but I am inclined to believe that the greater part of the country would be dead against carrying them out.

The Belgian Ambassador here is an able man of long experience. He said to me a few days ago that he was certain France would not march in support of Czechoslovakia. He predicted that France would first ask Belgium and England what they would do. He said that he was certain both his own country and England would refuse to do anything; that the French would then be faced with the problem of attacking Germany alone, unsupported, or allowing Czechoslovakia to be swallowed and denying their pledged word. He added that he was certain the French, under the circumstances, would not march.

I have, however, discussed the same eventuality with a number of Frenchmen, and they say that France would march, knowing perfectly well that, when France began to be beaten by Germany, England would have to come in on the side of France.

My own guess is that there would be a hair's breadth decision, and that no one can predict with certainty as to whether or not France would march in support of Czechoslovakia.

I do not want to worry you with more of this sort of speculation. The tragic fact is that no one in Europe today is putting any constructive energy whatsoever behind the idea of preserving peace. Everyone is spending every ounce of energy on preparing instruments of war. The nub of the situation remains the hostility between France and Germany. As I wrote you before, I see no sign of rapprochement. I should like to see us in a position to do what we can to help in Berlin and Paris if there should be a chance that they may come together. I shall keep my ears as wide open as possible, as well as my nostrils, to try to detect any faint trace of peace and shall let you know at once if I feel that there is anything we can do without involving ourselves in the horrors to come.

What those horrors will be, you can imagine. Pierre Cot, the French Air Minister, said to me a few days ago that, while he was going on building airplanes as fast as he could, he felt that the airplane race between France and Germany had now reached the point of absolute idiocy. He already had in his air force sufficient planes to destroy Berlin and Essen instantly. Goering already had enough planes to destroy Paris instantly. Neither of them had any means of defense against those planes. The destruction of cities and populations was inevitable. Incidentally, the French Government recently considered a proposal to supply the population of Paris with gas masks. It was found that the cost would be two billion francs. It was decided to let the population take its chances.

In all this intellectual chaos and impending doom, the underlying truth is that the development of the airplane has made Europe an absurdity. Last year, flying from Munich to Venice, I crossed Austria in fifteen minutes. When you and I were children, it took that long to drive from the Place de la Concorde to the Bois de Boulogne. These dinky little European states can not live in an airplane civilization. Today they have the alternative of submerging their national hatreds and national prides sufficiently to unify the continent or of destroying themselves completely and handing Europe over to the Bolsheviks. There is as yet no sign that there may be an outbreak of common sense.

I hope you are having a grand trip to South America.* My love and blessings.

Yours affectionately,
Bill

Enclosure: Memorandum as stated above.

MEMORANDUM FOR THE PRESIDENT

Your cable saying that I was right arrived at the right minute. Less than twenty-four hours later Monick called to see me. As I had your cable I could answer him categorically.

Monick began by saying that he understood I was taking steps to reopen the matter of the French debt to the United States.

I asked him to stop right there, and said that I had not taken any steps whatsoever to open the matter, and that I would not take any steps whatsoever.

I told him how Madame Claudel had telephoned asking me to come to see Claudel urgently; how Claudel had then proposed that he (Monick) should go to talk with you in Buenos Aires; and how I had squashed the idea.

I explained that Claudel had then asked me if I felt there was anything inadvisable in his continuing his newspaper campaign for payment of the debts and that I had replied that I saw nothing against it. Claudel had then said that he felt it advisable to get the cooperation of Madame Tabouis, who was at the moment the cleverest journalist in Paris, and had stated to me that he had intended to

---

* President Roosevelt arrived in Buenos Aires on November 30, 1936, on the cruiser *Indianapolis* to address the opening session of a conference of the American republics. He remained there two days.

ask Monick to see Madame Tabouis. I informed Monick Madame Tabouis had then repeated to me what Claudel had said to her, and that I had warned her that if she began a campaign in her paper that there was every likelihood that the impression would be created that I had started the campaign. I felt it was advisable, therefore, that any campaign should be started in another quarter and that, in any event, I would have nothing to do with the campaign.

I have explained to Madame Tabouis that while the American Government would be glad to consider any definite offer; that we would not play French internal politics and that so far as I was concerned I desired to be left out of any consultations as to what should and what should not be done.

I should, of course, be glad to serve as a channel of communication if Monsieur Blum desired to make an official offer of a debt settlement to me . . .

He replied, "Bon. That clears the ground. Now I should like to tell you exactly what I consider are the only possible principles on which we could pay the debts."

I replied that I did not wish to discuss any scheme. He said that there were merely certain principles he would like to state. Before doing so he would like to ask the question whether or not, from your point of view, it would be inopportune at the present time to open the question of the debts.

I replied that, of course, you wanted the debts to be paid and added that I saw no reason why the present time should be inopportune.

Monick said that he had asked this question because he had been in communication with the British on the question of reopening the debt negotiations and the British had informed him that they had received the impression from Washington that you would be averse to considering any debt offer at this time.

I replied that I thought this was a mistaken impression.

Monick then said that he would go on to state his principles which would be of a general nature . . .

[There follow six pages of Monick's proposal for debt settlement.]

William C. Bullitt

The Spanish Civil War, which raged from 1936 to 1939, was one of the most dramatic events of the interwar period. As in France, a coalition of center and left political forces in Spain in

1935 called itself the Popular Front. The Front won a substantial victory over rightist parties in the election of 1936 but found itself in difficulty almost at once. A Nationalist revolt broke out which drew its strength from the army, the Church, and the wealthier agricultural and industrial interests who had been aroused by the leftish program of the government.

An attempt by the leading powers to isolate and neutralize the war by international agreement soon proved a total farce as German and Italian arms and men poured in on the Nationalist side. The Republic attracted some Soviet aid and also the support of international brigades formed in various countries, including the Abraham Lincoln Brigade from the United States.

The Republic, however, much undermined by internal dissension, was finally overwhelmed by the superior force which the Axis powers were able to supply to the Nationalists. Francisco Franco was installed by them as the leader of Spain in March 1939.

During November Hitler had strengthened his international alliances by announcing the Rome-Berlin Axis, and signing an anti-Comintern pact with Japan.

These letters should put to rest for all time the stories that have been written saying that Bullitt encouraged the French to believe that if they went to war with Germany, America would come into the war and send troops to France. Throughout his correspondence he stressed that they could not expect such aid, and constantly said this to the French Government. In the words of the French Premier Paul Reynaud: "The press of Paris and that of Vichy said that Ambassador W. C. Bullitt had given hope to the French Government of American intervention to push it to war. I can testify to this point on the lying character of these allegations. Shortly before the war, I heard Mr. Bullitt say, in a group, in my presence, that we should not count on this intervention." [8]

Premier Camille Chautemps said about Bullitt: "He has been often criticized in America because people believed he had encouraged the French Government in a political attitude which was able to provoke war. I can positively state that such an accusation is entirely without foundation. The Ambassador, instead, at least during my time, told us again and again that, in the frame of mind of public opinion at that time, the United States would not take part in a European war. No doubt his feelings were strongly against Hitler and the Nazis. But he had the sense of responsibility as the American envoy and he never gave us any dangerous advice." [9]

Bullitt's position vis-à-vis the French Government is told by Forrest Davis and Ernest K. Lindley in *How War Came:*

"The American Ambassador, standing on such intimate terms with pre-war ministries that certain diplomatic wits insisted he should have a portfolio . . . Bullitt had diligently pursued the romantic pattern of American diplomatic behavior in France first traced by his fellow Philadelphian, Benjamin Franklin. Like Thomas Jefferson, he cultivated philosophers . . . like Franklin, Bullitt had an eclectic circle of friends, knew everyone, went everywhere on both banks, and 'meddled' heartily in French politics." [10]

There are numerous other accounts of Bullitt's French associations, but these examples give a picture of his unusual ability to inspire confidence with the leaders of the country to which he was accredited.

Personal and Confidential   Paris
                                                  November 29, 1936

Dear Judge Moore:

   . . . I want to write you today about several matters of "high policy."

The French, at the moment, are looking desperately for friends. There are a thousand signs (the details of which I shall spare you), that they have decided to attempt to develop the closest possible relations with the United States, having in the back of their minds the hope that when they become involved in the war which they regard as inevitable, the United States finally will come in on their side.

This may seem far-fetched to you, but I assure you it is true. If you should talk with the French Ambassador, unquestionably he would say to you that he knew the United States would never again send soldiers, ships and money to Europe, but you would probably be able to detect at the bottom of his mind the thing which is very evident here; to wit: the hope that by a series of small steps we may finally become involved as we became involved in 1917.

I am confident that so long as the President is in the White

House and the Secretary of State and yourself in the Department, we will not become involved; and I feel that it is our duty not only to ourselves, but also to the French to compel them to realize that if they count on us for the sort of support they got in 1917, they will not get it.

. . . (We should, I think, take a vow right now *never to accept anything "in principle,"* but only to discuss concrete detailed proposals.)

This confronts you in Washington and me in Paris with an extraordinarily delicate problem. We don't want to see France destroyed. We do have a fellow feeling for the democracies of England and France. We are sympathetic; but we have to be adamant when it comes to refusing the only sort of support that, in the last analysis, the French want. It will not be easy to avoid the building up in France of great hopes of American support; hopes which, in the end, inevitably will be destroyed. Unless we kill those hopes politely and affectionately, but ruthlessly, before they grow too great, then final destruction will give rise to enormous hatred of us here . . .

The answer at this point, invariably, is that the President since his reelection has great "moral authority." My reply invariably is that I am reminded of the great moral authority which Woodrow Wilson enjoyed before the Armistice. After the Armistice, it became immediately evident what that moral authority consisted of. His moral authority did not avail one whit to turn Clemenceau, Lloyd George and the other vultures at the Peace Conference from their meal. It did not avail because its only base in reality was the extreme need of England, France and Italy, so long as the war was on, for American ships, men and money. His moral authority was the moral authority which the rich man with a pocket full of money has over the starving beggar — nothing more.

I then point out that this is a somewhat extreme statement; that the President, like Woodrow Wilson, because his ideas are right and righteous, has a certain stature in the world; but that the authority this gives him, when it comes to practical matters of European politics with all the hatreds, jealousies and menaces involved, is impotent.

I then go on to say that the most unfriendly act that any friend of France can commit today is to let the French Government or the French people allow themselves to believe that they can by hook or by crook, by debt settlements or propaganda, or any other means get American troops again in Europe.

This, incidentally, is absolutely true. We can do France no worse disservice today than to allow her to base her security on an illusion of American support.

If you in Washington and I in Paris can, with friendship and sympathy, kill this hope of the French, we will preserve them from a deception which might finally be fatal to them, and we would save our country from French hatred.

I feel, therefore, that both of us should make it entirely clear to the French that, while we should be glad to have them settle their debt to us, they must be certain that they can not re-create the physical cooperation which existed when we went to war . . .

The additional question which you will have to consider and answer in Washington is what our government attitude is to be if the New York bankers start again to float foreign loans for billions in the United States. It is idle to pretend that the money which we may send abroad at the present time will be used for productive purposes.

It may be earmarked for productive purposes and may, indeed, be applied for productive purposes, but it will serve merely to release other government revenues in Europe for war purposes.

It is my honest opinion at the present time that unless we can prevent the flooding of enormous foreign loans, it is better for us to remain protected from them by the provisions of the Johnson Act. That is to say, to have the debts remain in default. I do not mean to say that I feel we should, for all future time or even for an indefinite time, refrain from large scale foreign lending, but I do mean that the danger of war in Europe during the next two years is so great that the comparatively ignorant American investor and country banker ought not to be let in again for the loss of American savings in Europe. We have adjusted ourselves to the non-payment of the debts and any payment on a large scale would be likely to upset considerably the balance of payments . . .

It may be that the horizon will clear during the next six months and if it should clear, foreign lending on our part might be good business, but I do not like the smell of it now. I know that I myself would not lend one penny today to any European Government and I don't see why it should be better business for any American than it would be for me . . .

My love to you and every good wish.

Yours affectionately,
William C. Bullitt

12

Inside Government Circles

DECEMBER 1936

Reconciling France and Germany

ALTHOUGH MR. ROOSEVELT WAS a consummate politician, he had
his peer in the chairman of the Democratic National Committee.
James A. Farley occupied this post from 1932 to 1940 and during
his tenure of office the President was elected and re-elected with
little difficulty. Mr. Farley was a member of the New York State
Assembly from 1923 and Mr. Roosevelt chose him as his campaign manager. From then on it was plain sailing until Mr. Farley, disapproving of a third term, resigned his office. Mr. Farley
has an amazing memory for names and faces and in any important
city in the country can instantly recall all his previous acquaintances. He built up a powerful organization which was certainly
not harmed by his acting as postmaster general from 1933 to 1940.

Personal and Confidential   Paris
                                                    December 7, 1936
Dear Mr. President:
   Jim Farley has just passed through Paris. I took him to the dog
races but did not lead him any further into the paths of iniquity so
that, if he returns to you a changed man, you must blame the result
on Ralph Strassburger and not on me. It was a delight to see him.
   In talking with Jim, I tried to convince him (and I believe I did)
that the situation in Europe today is too serious for him to suggest
the planting of dubs in diplomatic posts in order to repay them for

contributions to the campaign fund. Jim said that he agreed with me, and we went on to discuss how it might be possible for you to get rid of some of the men who are not fit to hold their present jobs as chiefs of mission in the present world crisis.

In the course of our discussion, it occurred to me and I suggested to Jim and now suggest to you, and shall suggest to Judge Moore, that it might be advisable for you to order him as soon as you get back from South America, to issue at once a circular instruction to all chiefs of mission reading as follows:

"Chiefs of mission are reminded that owing to the change in the date of Inauguration, their resignations should be in the hands of the President not later than January 15, 1937."

(Offie suggests that, as a result of this letter, I am likely to receive the only one of such instructions issued. Anyhow, I hereby submit my resignation.)

I suggest an instruction of this kind from Judge Moore to the chiefs of mission because I have no doubt that there are a number of men whom you wish to replace, but that you will find it highly unpleasant to ask for their resignations. If the reminder is sent out as a circular instruction by the Department of State, no one can resent receiving it because it would be addressed to all chiefs of mission without distinction. Then you would be able to get rid of misfits by a polite and hearty letter of thanks and praise . . .

If there is a chance to maintain peace in Europe during your next Administration, that chance lies in the small possibility that it may be possible to draw the French Government and the German Government closer together.

Blum, lunching with me alone a few days ago, said that he hoped to be able to inaugurate soon a movement for reconciliation with Germany based on the reduction of economic barriers, financial and economic collaboration and reduction of armaments. He said that he felt the active support and collaboration of the United States would be essential in any attempt to bring France and Germany together.

Another conversation on the same lines was one in which Delbos, the Papal Nuncio, and others participated. They said that Hitler two weeks ago had sent to Paris his "super-Ribbentrop," von Lersner, to say to the French Government, and to the leading French politicians outside the Government, that Hitler still desired most ardently to reach agreement with France. Von Lersner stated that Hitler felt the two countries were so far apart that they could not be brought together without the friendly assistance of the United States. He added that Hitler felt that Luther [German Ambassador] was not in close touch with our Government and that he should be replaced by someone closer to his intimate circle.

I have managed to establish entirely confidential relations with Blum and Delbos and can see them privately whenever I wish. (I am having lunch with Blum privately twice this week.) It should be possible for our ambassador in Berlin to establish the same sort of relationship with the heads of the Nazi Government in Berlin. It would be difficult but it could be done. If we had an Ambassador who could do that in Berlin, he and I could at least be of some assistance in bringing France and Germany together — nothing much is needed except some verbal assistance in erasing the lies each believes about the other — and in any event, we should be able to keep you fully informed with regard to the most intimate inner details of the European situation.

Dodd has many admirable and likable qualities, but he is almost ideally ill equipped for his present job. He hates the Nazis too much to be able to do anything with them or get anything out of them. We need in Berlin someone who can at least be civil to the Nazis and speaks German perfectly. The latter qualification is an absolute necessity as Hitler speaks only German and, unless I am mistaken, Goering speaks only German.

As I wrote you before, I can not think of any American so well qualified as Hugh Wilson for the Berlin job. He speaks perfect German and is on good terms with the Germans without being in the faintest degree pro-German or pro-Nazi. Unless you have someone up your sleeve, I think that you ought to send Wilson to Berlin . . .

Good luck and every good wish.

Yours affectionately,
Bill

TELEGRAM RECEIVED

This telegram must be closely paraphrased before being communicated to anyone.

Secretary of State	Paris
Washington	Dated December 1, 1936
1176, December 1, 6 P.M.	Rec'd 3:45 P.M.

Blum lunched with me alone today and I had an opportunity to repeat to him everything that I had said to Delbos with regard to the absolute determination of the United States to stay out not only of any wars on the continent of Europe but out of any engagements or commitments which might possibly lead to our involvement in wars.

I repeated what I had said to Delbos; to wit: that I should be a bad friend of France if I did not advise him against basing his foreign policy or any portion of it on the expectation that by debt payments or any other means of cultivating a pleasant atmosphere France could by hook or by crook get the United States to take the position which we took in 1917 . . .

Bullitt

Personal and Confidential   Paris
December 8, 1936

Dear Mr. President:

So many rumors are flying around about the imminence of revolution in France that it occurs to me you might like to have my guesses on the subject.

In my opinion, the only thing which could lead to a general revolutionary movement would be a general strike. I do not expect a general strike for the simple reason that I think the Communists know it would not be successful. The country would support a general strike in one circumstance only — as a final means to prevent a fascist coup d'état. The fascist movement in France has diminished almost to invisibility. If the Communists should attempt to pull off a general strike now, the country would react violently against them and the Army would intervene against them instantly.

Daladier, who is now Minister of War, has taken pains to send all members of Communist cells in the Army first to jail for sixty days and then to the eastern garrisons. He said to me a few days ago that he is now absolutely confident that he can rely on every division in the army to assist in breaking a general strike, and that he will not hesitate to act instantly. It seems to me, therefore, that any real revolutionary movement in this country for the present is most unlikely.

The stability of the present government is another matter. The Communists are attacking the government, which in theory they support, more violently even than the parties of the extreme Right. Blum very nearly resigned yesterday because of a violent attack on his foreign policy by the Communist leaders in the Chamber of Deputies. Daladier told me that he had urged Blum twenty times to cut loose from his Communist supporters and base himself on the Socialists, Radical Socialists and some of the Center Parties. Blum, however, has said to me that, if he does this, he knows his government will be pushed into taking a more and more conservative position until he will find himself opposing the factory workmen for whom and with whom he has worked all his life . . .

In this connection, it may interest you to know that both Blum and Delbos have promised me that if the charwomen, furnace men, orderlies, etc. of the American Hospital in Paris strike and occupy the Hospital again, as they did last June, they will be ejected at once . . .

If the law for compulsory arbitration should be successful, and if Blum should take a stiff attitude with respect to occupations of factories, confidence in France would return rapidly, and I should expect to see a rapid improvement in the economic and financial situation.

Delbos is terrified with regard to the possibility of a general European war emerging from the conflict in Spain. I do not agree with him because I believe that the Russians will not at this time dare to face war with Italy and Germany.

As I wrote you before, I am attempting to get out of the minds of the French the belief that they may count on us again to send our army, navy and money to Europe. I have, from time to time, felt like the lady who tried to sweep back the sea with a broom. The French want so much to believe that we shall do again what we did in 1917, that one is brushing back constantly a sea of hopes and wishes. I have made the point clear to all the members of the Government and all the other political leaders with whom I have come in contact, but it is impossible to restrain the comparatively ignorant and light-headed. Our friend, de Tessan, who is not over-burdened with brains, in a speech the other day said that he was convinced by his conversations with you that we would certainly, in case of need, do again what we did in 1917! He should be spanked and I shall spank him verbally when next we meet. But his attitude is characteristic of that of millions of Frenchmen . . .

I wish to Heaven I could have a talk with you tonight.

Anyhow, my love and good luck.

Yours affectionately,
Bill

TELEGRAM RECEIVED
This telegram must be closely paraphrased before being communicated to anyone.

Strictly Confidential

Secretary of State	Paris
Washington	Dated December 16, 1936
1261, December 16, 10 P.M.	Rec'd 9:40 A.M., 17th

Georges Bonnet called on me this afternoon. He said that Blum had offered him the post of Ambassador to the United States. He was reluctant to accept because of his interest in domestic politics. He and Blum had had recently long conversations the upshot of which was the following: They were convinced that there was great danger of an early war in Europe. The next eighteen months would be the crucial period. After eighteen months England would be rearmed. Then Germany would hesitate to attack France. To maintain peace during the next eighteen months Blum "dreamed" of creating a close collaboration between France, England and the United States. The three great democracies should first agree between themselves on a plan and should then offer it to Germany. The Plan should contain clauses dealing with (one) economic aid to Germany including the lowering of barriers to international trade and access to raw materials; (two) financial aid to Germany; (three) limitation of armaments.

If Germany could be convinced that the great democracies were standing shoulder to shoulder Germany would not dare attack in the next eighteen months. The situation now resembles the situation in 1914 with America today in the position England was in 1914. Germany would not have attacked in 1914 if she had known that England would come in. Germany would not attack today if she believed that America would come in . . .

I then said to Monsieur Bonnet that if I understood the project I felt that there was not the slightest chance that the United States would participate. I explained to him that while we were deeply and sincerely interested in the preservation of peace not only in the Western Hemisphere but also in Europe and the Far East, there were certain absolute limits beyond which we could not go. He and all other French statesmen must realize that the United States would not send troops, warships and money to Europe again to support France and England. He should also realize that we would not become involved in the political difficulties of Europe. I added that

the United States could collaborate in two fields: removal of barriers
to international trade and limitation of armaments . . .

Bullitt

Personal and Confidential   Paris
December 20, 1936

Dear Mr. President:

It was grand to hear your voice over the telephone. I heard you
as clearly as if you had been in the next room and it took me exactly two minutes to get through from the Embassy to the White
House. That is the result of the installation of direct telephone
communication between Paris and New York. If by any chance
you should ever wish to call me, tell the telephone operator at the
White House to put the call through to France direct, not via
England . . .

I am more convinced every day that the only chance of preserving
peace in Europe lies in the possibility that the French and the Germans may reach some basis of understanding. The new element
which has created this possibility is the fact that the bombing plane
has been developed to such a pitch of efficiency that the French
Government knows the Germans can destroy the city of Paris in 24
hours and the German Government knows the French can destroy
Essen and all the towns of the Ruhr in 24 hours. There is beginning to be a general realization, therefore, that war will mean such
horrible suffering that it will end in general revolution, and that the
only winners will be Stalin and Company.

For different reasons, the British, Italians and Russians are all opposed to Franco-German reconciliation. The only great Power
which favors it genuinely is the United States. Poland desires it ardently and so do all the small countries of Europe, except Hungary
and Bulgaria.

You will have seen from my recent cables that I have attempted
to do what I could, in a quiet way and without involving the
United States in the least, to encourage the idea of Franco-German
rapprochement. I think it might be most useful if, when you see de
Laboulaye and Luther, you should stress the idea that peace in Europe is purely a question of Franco-German reconciliation; that the
modern bombing plane has confronted Europe with the alternative
of unification or destruction and that we ardently desire to see
France and Germany reconciled.

If, on some occasion, you should have an opportunity to say to

Ronald Lindsay that we should be shocked if we should find that England was not genuinely doing everything possible to promote Franco-German rapprochement, it might be very helpful.

The British, of course, will say that they favor it and will do everything possible to sabotage it. But they may be less active if they think your eye is on them.

Delbos again this morning reiterated to me his remarks about Great Britain's absolute opposition to any concessions to Germany in the matter of colonies. As he pointed out yesterday to me, it was the frown of Britain which prevented France from following up Schacht's conversations with Blum.

Inasmuch as we can not involve ourselves directly in European politics, inasmuch as Great Britain, Italy, and the Soviet Union will do everything possible to prevent Franco-German rapprochement and inasmuch as the French and the Germans fear and suspect each other deeply, the chances are slim, but I feel that there is nevertheless a chance — the only chance.

If the Franco-German conversations should make some progress, there may come a moment when you could make a general declaration which would be most helpful. Meanwhile, I feel that the less we say about Europe the better. Above all, I hope that you will not let anyone persuade you into launching some scheme without previous consultation in the first instance with the French Government, and in the second, with the German and the British.

We can and should avoid the mistake that Hoover made when he launched his moratorium proposal without consulting the French in advance. That sort of thing produces over all Europe a sense that we are apt to do uncertain and unexpected things. Hitler and Mussolini have given the whole Continent the jitters by their unexpected explosions — we ought to be steady and should, I think, move only on firm ground after preparation and consultation.

During the past few days, I have taken the liberty of saying to Delbos, Bonnet and Monick that I knew you would never involve the United States in general commitments by the acceptance of proposals in the form of general principles. I enclose herewith a most secret document which will show you the reason for these declarations of mine. It is the memorandum on debt settlement which Monick prepared for the French Government.

You will perceive that he proposes to get us to accept certain general principles which would in fact involve us in the whole European tangle up to the hilt. He gave me the document himself under pledge of strict secrecy and I am sending it to no one except your-self. He elaborated on the ideas in the document and made it entirely clear that he hoped, via such a debt settlement, to get us to promise enormous economic and financial aid to France and Germany, and to involve ourselves in all the economic difficulties of Europe. Furthermore, he wished the scheme to be sprung on the Germans by a united front of England, France and the United States. I can not imagine a better way for us to start toward involvement in the next war than by accepting his proposal.

I do not know whether or not my conversations here in the past few days have killed the idea but I suspect that it will be brought up in one form or another at a later date.

I have been working unbelievably hard since I reached Paris, but I hope to get a bit of rest this week by spending Christmas in Algiers. The work is, of course, fascinating; but there is so much of it that one gets too tired to enjoy anything. When I come back after Christmas, I think I shall imitate you and inaugurate regular afternoon swims.

I wish to Heaven I could swim with you today. There is so much to talk about and all of it is interesting — tragically interesting.

My love to you and a Merry Christmas and a Happy New Year to Mrs. Roosevelt and all the family.

Yours affectionately,

Bill

13

The Tension Tightens

JANUARY—JUNE 1937

Limitation of Armaments
Chamberlain Prime Minister

In December the German Ambassador in Paris, Count von Welczeck, approached Bullitt, seeking his help in a reconciliation between France and Germany and stating that von Ribbentrop, the German Foreign Minister, wished to come to Paris to discuss the subject with Bullitt. Bullitt replied he was certain the French desired intensely an understanding with Germany and that direct conversations between the two were necessary. He was told that a previous talk had been most promising but that because of British opposition the matter was not followed up. Bullitt expressed the opinion that the American Government would heartily favor reconciliation. Bullitt was invited to go to Berlin but refused.

Personal and Confidential   Paris
                                             January 10, 1937
Dear Mr. President:

As Anne and I have just come from seeing the movie version of "Green Pastures," I feel sufficiently like that excellent negro God who was constantly on the verge of wiping mankind from the planet, to write you about the state of Europe.

I have thought and talked endlessly about ways and means of stopping the deluge which is approaching. I am still convinced that the only possible method of stopping it is through direct negotiations between Paris and Berlin. But I am not at all sure that such negotiations can succeed because I suspect that the Eastern frontiers of Germany fixed by the Treaty of Versailles remain just as inacceptable to Germany as the day they were decreed.

Philip Kerr, that is to say, Lord Lothian, spent the night before last with me. He is in close touch with the Germans and knows Hitler. He is convinced that Hitler will not accept peace except at the price of domination of Eastern and Central Europe and the Balkans (Russia excluded as not being part of Europe).

Kerr personally would like to see Germany get that domination and is absolutely opposed to any armed interference by England to prevent it. I do not know a single Frenchman, however, who is ready to accept such a solution. Those French who agree with Kerr in his diagnosis of the German attitude — like Mandel and many other politicians of the Right — draw the conclusion that any attempt to reach reconciliation with Germany through economic and financial concessions and limitation of armaments will merely strengthen Germany for the inevitable conflict. There is so much to be said for that point of view that it is difficult to argue against it except on the simple basis that to accept it is to render inevitable an early war, and that there *is* a small chance that it may be possible to reach a genuine reconciliation with Germany.

Last night I had an intensely interesting conversation with the Minister of Czechoslovakia who is Benes' right hand man. He has just returned from Prague and he tells me in the greatest confidence that Benes is attempting to get Rumania and Yugoslavia to support him in urging France to attempt to reach a direct understanding with Germany. He went so far as to say that Benes had decided that if France did not do this, Czechoslovakia would immediately start to make her own deal with Germany rather than wait to be crushed.

The crucial period will be the next eight months. Lothian told me that he had had a talk with Inskip just before leaving London and that Inskip had stated to him that Great Britain's air progress was much further advanced than anyone suspected and that in about six months Great Britain would be able to give a good account of herself in the air. On the other hand, Great Britain cannot put a single division on the continent at the present time — the only one available now is in Palestine — and if Germany makes war in the near future, Great Britain will be able to do little more than blockade Germany and use her airplanes for defense. The French army will be alone on the western front.

Blum and Delbos are still away on vacation and so is Vienot, the

Undersecretary of Foreign Affairs. The absence of these three men is the surest indication, as I said to Judge Moore over the telephone, that the French do not anticipate war arising from the present rumpus over Morocco. The conversation I had with Léger, which I telephoned in detail to the Department and assume that you saw, seemed to me to be equally convincing on this point.

The single circumstance that gives me much hope is that I hear constantly from people who have just come from Germany that the Germans are beginning to be a bit frightened by the forces now arrayed against them. They seem to have begun to realize that if they get into war against an immense coalition, the result will be the result of the Second Punic War rather than the result of the First. Germany will be cut to pieces.

Osusky, the Czech Minister, said that he and Benes had precisely the same idea that I have discussed with Blum and with many others here, to wit, that France should attempt to reach an agreement with Germany by direct negotiations which would couple, in one global agreement, limitation of armaments and economic and financial assistance.

Many of the French outside the Cabinet have the same idea in mind. Monick has just written two more colossal memoranda, copies of which I enclose. As you will see from them, he proposes the creation of international trusts, organized as the Suez Canal Company is organized, for the delivery of raw materials to countries that need them and for the placing of finished products.

It is, of course, an old scheme. I remember H. G. Wells suggesting something similar in about 1906. The difficulty is that the U. S. A. and other countries would have to supply credits to Germany and Italy for the purchase of the raw materials and then would have to allocate markets to Germany and Italy for the distribution of the finished products.

In other words, they would have to subsidize German competition with their own products in the world markets. I cannot imagine our country or any other taking very kindly to such a solution.

The only chance that I can see is the slim one that after François-Poncet has done some preliminary work, Blum will be able to take an enormously high ground and come out with a sweeping proposal for limitation of armaments and financial and economic peace on the continent. That is to say, some scheme which would be little short of the proposal for the unification of Europe.

He would have the fullest support of Poland and the Scandinavian States, Belgium, Holland, Czechoslovakia, Austria and all the smaller countries of Europe with the exception of Hungary and Bulgaria; but, as soon as he got down to details the squabbles would become bitter and success would be inordinately difficult to achieve.

It would be especially difficult because the Soviet Union and Italy would do everything they could obliquely to kill any such proposal. I am not certain what the British would do. Sir George Clerk talks as if the British would welcome real reconciliation. But there are many indications that the British want nothing of the sort. For example, read the enclosed clipping from the London *Times* of December 28, 1936.

I understand that the story emanated from the British Embassy in Paris. The British got worried because Marcel Knecht, Secretary General of the *Matin* went to Berlin on a plain mission of inquiry to find out if Germany might be in a mood to negotiate with France. The mere fact that old Bunau-Varilla sent Knecht put the British into such a state of mind that they shot a torpedo of this sort.

With every day that passes I become more convinced (if such a thing is possible) that the only policy for us is to stay as far out of the mess as possible. As I have written you before, if Blum does manage to start something that looks promising and if he should need the assistance of a word from you at a crucial moment, or some diplomatic non-entangling assistance, you might well help him. But we should not attempt to take the lead.

As I wrote to Judge Moore recently, we ought to make it clear that the United States, like God, helps those who help themselves.

I have heard from a large number of sources that the Germans are much disturbed because their relations with us are so bad and that they are thinking of replacing Luther at an early date.

George Bonnet will go to Washington as French Ambassador. You will, I think, dislike Bonnet. He is highly intelligent and well-versed in financial and economic matters but is not a man of character. You will remember that he was the head of the French delegation at the London Economic Conference and that he led the personal attacks on you until I scared him to death in a certain gay and historic scene. He now pretends to be a great friend, but he has a shifty eye.

As I told you over the telephone, we left Paris to spend Christmas in the Sahara and came back by way of Tunis. It was a lovely trip and Tunis and Algiers remind me of California in the year 1900. Incidentally, you may be interested to know that it has been discovered recently that it is possible to get water by artesian wells in almost any portion of the Sahara. My own guess is that the water table will sink rapidly if many of these wells are drilled but that remains to be seen.

Another thing which amused me in Algiers was the discovery that slavery still exists. Quantities of negros come from the Sudan to sell themselves and their families into slavery in Algiers. They have been used to the institution and like it. I talked to the French Administrator of the Sahara regions about it and he said there was nothing to be done. The negros were entirely free legally even after they had sold themselves but they preferred to regard themselves as slaves. They are as black as anthracite and their dress consists of a belt of skins of the small desert foxes!

The internal situation in France has improved definitely. There are lots of financial worries ahead but the feeling of the whole country is much calmer and less jittery than it was a few weeks ago, and the international outlook is somewhat less ominous.

But to return to "Green Pastures": this is a good time to build a large ark labeled "The United States of America." Henceforth, I shall think of you as Brother Noah.

Every good wish to you, Mrs. Noah, and Ham, Shem and Japhet.

Incidentally, do you know how the French Bible translates that Beatitude which goes: "Blessed are the meek and humble in spirit, for they shall inherit the Earth!" Well, sir, it is this: "Heureux sont les débonnaires, car ils hériteront la terre!"

Yours affectionately,

Bill

Personal and Confidential   Paris

January 17, 1937

Dear Mr. President:

When François-Poncet told me about his conversations in Berlin with regard to limitation of armaments, he said that the British had indicated they did not wish to enter into any agreement for limitation of armaments until the completion of their present program. He asserted that the discussions he had had in Berlin, therefore, had been on the basis of "no *new* programs."

It occurred to me at once that we might wish to come in on any general limitation of armaments scheme and that we might be greatly embarrassed if we had no program in being. I don't know what you are thinking of in the way of future armaments, but I feel that there is sufficient possibility that Poncet may have some success in Berlin to make it advisable for us to have some sort of a program announced . . .

> Yours affectionately,
>
> Bill

Bullitt kept up a great interest in what was happening in the United States and there are several letters discussing domestic questions. The next two letters give an indication of the sense of intimacy he and the President felt toward one another: Roosevelt apparently felt no displeasure at receiving suggestions from an Ambassador who had no business to offer such comment. The President always replied in a light vein to these letters and made up his own mind.

> Paris
>
> January 25, 1937

Dear Mr. President:

As I cannot be at the White House in person to make a chart indicating the routes on which you should sail the Ship of State, I am enclosing herewith one for your guidance. You will also note full indications as to the method by which the Federal Housing Program may be transferred effectively to the hands of the efficient beavers.

I hope this reaches you on your birthday. Anyhow, it brings you my love and every good wish.

> Yours always,
>
> Bill

> February 8, 1937

Dear Bill:

I am perfectly delighted with the chart which you sent me and any time I get off the course from now on, I shall put the blame directly on you! Thank you ever so much. It was good of you also to send me the cable on my birthday.

We are all delighted that you are coming home soon and I am looking forward to getting some real first-hand information. When do you plan to leave?

> Affectionately,
>
> FDR

Honorable William C. Bullitt
Ambassador of the United States
Paris, France

On Washington's Birthday, 1937, Bullitt spoke at the American Club in Paris and, without any doubt, what he said had been worked out carefully with the President. After a brief introduction, he stated: "We shall stay out of any war which may break out in the future as long as God permits." He then called for a reduction of trade barriers and the limitation of armaments.

The British Foreign Office wondered whether this was an invitation to France, England, and Germany to take concerted action and whether Bullitt might have discussed the matter with the French and even the Germans. Mr. Arthur Henderson was reported as proposing to ask the Prime Minister in the House of Commons whether the British Government was ready to collaborate with President Roosevelt on this program "as the best method of securing world peace." Their further comment was that the Foreign Office knew the Germans had been talking to the Americans and that they found Bullitt's remarks "quite nauseating." The final words are: "I should be inclined, therefore, to leave the matter severely alone." [1]

Thus the door was closed on one more possibility of negotiations between France, England, and Germany which might have resulted in a modus vivendi and the preservation of peace.

Bullitt returned to the United States in March. He spent a week in Warm Springs, Georgia, with the President and a few days in Washington and returned to Paris at the end of the month.

Paris
April 12, 1937

Dear Mr. President:

I wish you were in Paris today. All the trees and flowers are out and it is as lovely as any place this side of paradise. Everybody has spring fever, including the entire Government, the kind of spring fever that used to be treated by our ancestors with sulphur and molasses. No Frenchman is doing any work or even thinking any thoughts.

Blum and almost all his Cabinet are in the country picking primroses and those who are in town might just as well be on vacation because they are thinking about nothing except what a beautiful day it is.

As a result I have nothing startling to report except that Potemkin, the Soviet Ambassador, told me this morning that Litvinov has decided to attend the Coronation and is apprehensive with regard to the picture he will make in knee breeches! I was told that Litvinov had said to Stalin that he was worried about how his feet would look and that Stalin had replied that the thing he ought to be worried about was his face!

I had a long talk with Delbos, who intends to go ahead pushing the proposal for the withdrawal of volunteers from Spain, but has no hope of its being accepted. He said that the French Government has positive information that Franco's army is now composed of 60,000 Italians, 15,000 Moroccans and 15 to 20,000 Spaniards. The government forces are composed entirely of Spaniards with the exception of 6 to 10,000 foreigners. The International Brigade has borne that brunt of the fighting on the government side for so long that it has literally been shot to pieces. The withdrawal of foreign "volunteers," therefore, would mean almost no decrease in the government forces but would mean the withdrawal of about three-fourths of Franco's army. It is, therefore, inconceivable that Mussolini should accept any such proposal.

Delbos told me that Schmidt, the Austrian Foreign Minister, who will attend the Coronation, had arranged to have detailed conversations with him in Paris and with Eden in London, with regard to any support which France and England might be ready to give Austria. Delbos said that France could not guarantee to defend Austria by force from German aggression and that he was certain that England could not make any such promise. Delbos said he would have nothing better to suggest to Schmidt than that Austria should attempt to form a Danubian confederation with the other small Danubian States. This, in view of the opposition of Yugoslavia, is an impossibility; and Austria, it seems, is likely to be left hanging on the bough to be plucked at an appropriate moment by Hitler . . .

It was lovely to be with you in Warm Springs and I thank you from the bottom of my heart for being so perpetually kind to me.

Love to you and all the family.

Bill

On May 1, 1937, the President signed a new Neutrality Act, and this time there was no date of expiration named in the act. It provided among other things that goods from the United States sold to belligerents must be on a cash-and-carry basis. American ships could not carry supplies to belligerents and ownership of such goods must pass into foreign hands before they could leave the United States. There were also certain provisions with regard to assistance in the Spanish Civil War.

April 20, 1937

Dear Bill:

. . . I was surprised last Friday to be told by a representative of the Associated Press that the day before Senator Pittman had introduced a bill creating the office of Counselor in the State Department. Forthwith the newspapers commented by stating that the purpose is to enable the President to appoint Mr. Welles Under Secretary and appoint me Counselor. Enclosed is a sheet of the Congressional Record of yesterday which refers to the matter. Apparently, Mr. Welles has won his fight with the President and the Secretary, and it is desired that I shall win the consolation race. "Thus runs the world away!" I heard someone say that if Welles is to be Under Secretary, the logical thing would be to replace him as Assistant Secretary by his spokesman, Drew Pearson. They are two persons whom I hold in utter contempt . . .

Affectionately your friend,
R. Walton Moore

THE WHITE HOUSE
WASHINGTON

April 21, 1937

Dear Bill:

I am delighted to have your rural rhapsody of April twelfth and to know that the French Government has spring fever. Spring has come to Washington also and even the Senators, who were biting each other over the Supreme Court, are saying "Alphonse" and "Gaston" to each other.

Your wild flower simile applies to diplomacy I note, for you say that Austria "is likely to be left hanging on the bough to be plucked at an appropriate moment by Hitler." If he does pluck that apple and eats it, I hope it will have the effect of a green apple.

I, too, am influenced by this beautiful spring day. I haven't a care in the world which is going some for a President who is said by the newspapers to be a remorseless dictator driving his government into hopeless bankruptcy.

Take care of yourself and do not eat any sulphur and molasses. The spring fever should be kept with one as long as possible.

As ever yours,

FDR

Honorable William C. Bullitt
Ambassador of the United States
Paris, France

Personal and Confidential   Paris

May 5, 1937

Dear Mr. President:

This letter should reach you about the day you return to Washington. I hope you found a lot of vigor and endurance in the Gulf of Mexico because I have a lot to say.

1. For cat's sake put through Howland Shaw as Chief of Foreign Service Personnel. The morale of the Service is becoming more demoralized every day and nothing could turn the tide of discouragement so quickly and completely as his appointment.

2. You will remember that we discussed the possibility of sending Edgar A. Mowrer as Minister to Czechoslovakia. Unless I miss my guess, Czechoslovakia will be a post of the most vital importance during the next twelve months. The new policy of Belgium which will prevent France from using Belgian territory to attack Germany in case Germany should attack Czechoslovakia has increased greatly the chance that Germany will go after Czechoslovakia. We shall need at Prague a man who knows Germany and Czechoslovakia intimately and has guts.

Mowrer is admirably equipped, in my opinion, for the post . . .

3. You have perhaps seen the long telegram I sent with regard to my conversation with Van Zeeland. If not, you might find it worth reading. There is one thing that I hope you will remember when Van Zeeland calls on you. Belgium, at the present time, is the little brother of England. Van Zeeland is, to all intents and purposes, a representative of the British Government. You can count on anything you say to him being repeated to Chamberlain and you can count on his displaying an acceptance of all British points of view. I gathered from Van Zeeland that the British would take no initiative whatsoever with regard to his mission and would give him no active support, but would expect him to get the other countries of the world committed to something in advance which could then be served up to them for their acceptance or rejection.

4. Tom Lamont came to Paris a few days ago and in the course of a long conversation made one statement which I thought was of some interest. He said that he knew Chamberlain very well indeed and that he was somewhat disturbed about the manner in which Anglo-American relations might develop with Chamberlain as Prime Minister "since if it could be said that any Englishman was anti-American, Chamberlain was that anti-American Englishman."

It surprised me that Lamont should say such a thing but he presumably had some reason for his remarks.

I could extend the points in this letter to a thousand but I think this is a sufficient dose for one evening.

Blessings and good luck.

Yours affectionately,

Bill

In May 1937, Chamberlain became Prime Minister of England, succeeding Stanley Baldwin. He remained in office until May 10, 1940, the day on which the Germans attacked, without warning, Belgium and Holland.

Mr. Baldwin had helped to oust Mr. Lloyd George as Prime Minister in 1922. Mr. Bonar Law served as Prime Minister until early 1923, when ill health caused him to resign. Mr. Baldwin then took over the leadership of the Conservative party and was Prime Minister in 1923, again from 1924 to 1929, and from 1935 to 1937. He retired on his own volition with the praise of all parties.

Personal and Confidential   Paris

May 10, 1937

Dear Mr. President:

I have sent an enormous number of telegrams lately. But, as you were away, I assume that you have not seen any of them.

The general situation is this: Delbos and Blum are more or less in despair with regard to the possibility of keeping Austria and Czechoslovakia out of the hands of Germany. Hitler has the ball and can run with it in any direction he chooses. There never was a time when it was more essential for us to have an Ambassador in Berlin in real contact with the German Government.

I do not expect an immediate crash; but before next October we ought to be ready for anything. We ought to have an Ambassador and a staff in Berlin who can find out exactly what Hitler, Goering, Goebbels and the rest of the gangsters are thinking about. That means personal contact . . .

Meanwhile, I have a withdrawal of a recommendation to make, and with shame. I have just this day discovered what I had not learned in ten years of acquaintance with the Mowrers. Mrs. Edgar Mowrer is an English woman. I should be afraid of that in as tight a spot as Czechoslovakia. Mowrer is really exceptionally fitted for that post and I am sorry.

Blessings and good luck.

Yours affectionately,
Bill

May 20, 1937

Dear Bill:

. . . The President sent to the Senate yesterday the nomination of Mr. Welles for Under Secretary and me as Counselor, and I suppose that the appointments will be confirmed today. From what the President said to me yesterday, I am satisfied, as I can tell you very confidentially, that he had a pretty distinct preference. But I can understand the situation in which he was placed, having been Mr. Welles' schoolmate and in very close personal relations with him as shown by the fact that Welles was one of his wedding attendants. Not only was he embarrassed, but he had determined that appointees to this Department should be designated by the Secretary. I can also understand in what a sweat the Secretary has been involved for several months, in view of his disinclination to deal with the matter of appointments. All the water has now passed over the wheel except that I suppose there will be more or less doubt as to the division of duties of the two offices, and such questions as to who shall act as Secretary in the absence of the Chief. Mr. Welles is a heavy fighter, whereas in this business I have refrained from fighting, and it is not improbable that the particular question mentioned will be decided in his favor in spite of the fact that there is an Executive Order in effect that names me as Acting Secretary during the absence of the Secretary. I shall be content to let the future take care of itself without any effort to control it, and go along in exerting myself to the utmost to render useful service . . .

As I said to you this morning, Norman Davis the other day spoke of you as our outstanding representative.

The President looks well and none the worse for being a little thinner, and is in excellent spirits. The Court proposal is constantly on his mind, and that is what he began to discuss when I went into his office yesterday . . .

Affectionately your friend,
R. Walton Moore

The retention of Sumner Welles as Under Secretary of State led, many years later, to a distinct cooling of the intimate relationship between the President and Bullitt.

Mr. Welles had been a close personal friend of both Mr. and Mrs. Roosevelt for many years. He was a man of great ability, but with a cold manner. He had served in the State Department and had been appointed Ambassador to Cuba in 1933.

Personal and Confidential   Paris
May 28, 1937

Dear Mr. President:

I enclose herewith a photograph taken from my bedroom window. It is as good a description of Europe as any dispatch could be. You will note on the left, the eagle of the Nazis, on the right the cross of the Pope, and in the middle, the Bolshevik's hammer and sickle. The latter statue, incidentally, has a name in Paris. It is called, "Hurrying to the Lyublianka." (If you do not remember what the Lyublianka is, ask your friend ———. Her love, Steiger, is now interred there. You will certainly remember the gentleman she adored so because he used to knock her on the floor and jump on her stomach. For a New England girl, that was exciting.)

Paris has become a madhouse and each day about fifty persons appear with letters of introduction from the Secretary of State and Senators. I stack them together in colossal teas in accordance with your recommendation. I admit that I still give them champagne and caviar, as my self-respect continues to be more Virginian than the Whitelaw Reids, who, if I remember correctly your description, served their guests pink lemonade in the garden.

The American visitors aren't the worst of it. I had five royalties that I could not avoid at luncheon yesterday, and in addition, had to give cocktails to the brother of the Shah of Afghanistan!

The only one of the royalties who was thoroughly agreeable was a son of little Willy [Crown Prince of Germany]! His name is Friedrich von Preussen and he is a really nice boy. He is the white hope of the Hohenzollerns and left the luncheon table to go visit his grandpapa [the Kaiser] at Doorn.

The flood of visitors leaves me little time to do any real work and since the young men in the Embassy think they have fulfilled the whole duty of man when they have entertained each other at luncheon and dinner each day, we do not cover the town as well as I wish. I would have a lot of them transferred if there were any one better in the Service to bring here; but as Mr. Shakespeare remarked, "It's poor picking between rotten apples." As a matter of fact, by leaving out sleep entirely, I have managed to see very nearly everyone I should see.

I had one conversation of peculiar interest. Old George Lansbury, who recently spent three hours with Hitler, wrote me and asked if he could come to Paris for a conversation with me. As you know, we have been rather intimate friends for twenty years. He talked to me for about three hours and gave me the first coherent idea I have had of Hitler. He is convinced that there is no possibility of Hitler coming to any understanding with the Soviet Union and no possibility that he may let up on his persecution of the Jews; but he believes that Hitler wants to come to some understanding with England which will enable him to work out the economic future of Germany peacefully.

I have known George for so long that I do not take his judgments too seriously; but his detailed account of his conversation was rather impressive. Hitler received him in the simplest possible manner with his feet on the table while George put his up on the sofa and they went to it in a very direct way. Lansbury said, and I agree with him, that he felt that if the British Government would push hard at the present time for the reconciliation of France and Germany, economic rehabilitation and limitation of armaments, the Germans and the French would fall in line.

He then added that he did not believe the British Government would do anything of the sort. After his return from Berlin, he had had long conversations with Eden, Baldwin, Chamberlain, Hoare, et al. and he feared Britain's policy would be to continue to rearm to the hilt, to tell the Germans that Britain would be glad to come to an understanding with them, and to tell the French that Britain had no idea whatsoever of coming to an understanding with Germany.

I had a curiously interesting confirmation of this judgment of Lansbury's from two sources. Eden and Chamberlain said to Delbos that they were convinced that it was absolutely impossible to come to any understanding with Germany and that the great problem was to gain time by pretending to Germany that reconciliation between

Britain and Germany was possible. On the other hand, Eden told Beck whom he thinks (quite rightly) is apt to repeat to the Germans most of the things he hears, that Great Britain desires nothing so much as to reach understanding with Germany. In other words, while the British do not want war on the continent of Europe, they remain just as anxious as they have been all through their history to keep France and Germany from reaching any real understanding. So long as the British remain in that state of mind, I believe there is nothing that we can do to bring the continent together.

The situation in Austria continues to be puzzling. I believe that Hitler will not make any attempt to take over Austria so long as he has hopes that he may reach a friendly understanding with Great Britain; but the moment he becomes convinced that the British have been playing him for a sucker, I think he will act — probably via a revolt of the Nazis within Austria.

Your friend Tom Watson turned up day before yesterday in a state of depression as he is ashamed of our representation in the Exposition. However, I put him on his feet again by giving a luncheon in his honor at which he was smothered in princesses and duchesses.

Your baseball nine of Ambassadors who have been in London recently are now on their way to Paris. I expect to be able to keep this house open just long enough to entertain the lot. The gate of the Exposition which is at my front door is not yet finished. The day it is opened, I shall have to leave.

I have found the pleasantest country place in France to live in, a little château in the Park of the Great Château of Chantilly. The magnificent joke is that by renting the little château, I become the sole proprietor of the Park of Chantilly! I even have had it stipulated in the lease that I can swim in all the lake ponds and rivers, and can place an American Indian canoe on the great waterway which hitherto has been reserved for the Grand Condé and Louis XIV!

I am sure that this will meet with your approval. Incidentally, it will meet even more with your approval when I tell you that the total rental I pay is $1000 annually. This combination of grandeur and thrift has received the approbation even of Offie, so that I do not fear any objections from you.

Blessings and good luck.

Yours affectionately,
Bill

Personal and Confidential   Paris

June 2, 1937

Dear Judge Moore:

. . . Real work occasionally demands the whole of each twenty-four hours; for example, yesterday when the bombardment of Almería * by the Germans occurred, I had in the course of the day three conversations with Blum and two with Delbos and additional talks with the German and Belgian Ambassadors, to say nothing of two talks on the telephone with Washington. In addition there is the most enormous amount of representative work to be done. For example, on Memorial Day I had official ceremonies from 10 A.M. to 7 P.M., including two speeches. All this in the broiling sun, including parades. Then I had Blum at dinner . . .

The whole thing is too burdensome to be possible in the long run. I expect to escape from Paris on the 16th of June for a brief trip southward during which I shall inspect various consulates. The French Government is a bit upset by some letters that our Consul in Nice wrote recently and I want to investigate the facts personally before making any recommendations to the Department . . .

Bill

THE WHITE HOUSE
WASHINGTON

Confidential and Private   June 17, 1937

Dear Bill:

You may thank Mr. Theodore Spicer-Simson for the bronze medal and tell him that I am grateful to him for sending it and that I am glad to have it. Entre nous, although my name surrounds the head, the features suggest to me a cross between any two of the best known murderers you can think of.

Your friend, Tom Watson, has just been here and has described your situation as a neighbor of the Paris Exposition. By the way, when you said that Steiger is interred in the Lyublianka, did you mean that literally or is he merely interned?

I am not worrying greatly over your continued association with royalty. What gives me more kick is the thought of Litvinov appearing at the Coronation in short pants.

I am very proud that my Ambassador has rented the Park and

* Almería is a city on the southern coast of Spain.

the Great Château of Chantilly. May the ghost of the Great Condé haunt you and upset the canoe when you pull a water party on the great waterway.

Tell Offie that I count on him to prevent you from spending more than ninety percent of your capital in the next few years.

As ever yours,

FDR

Honorable William C. Bullitt
Embassy of the United States of America
Paris, France

Bullitt had rented a charming house in the park of the great château of Chantilly, twenty-five miles northeast of Paris, at the opposite end of the Grand Canal from the château. His house was dignified with the name of Château St. Firmin, named for a nearby village.

The grounds were originally designed by Lenôtre and Bullitt's house was built in 1776, a date he considered particularly appropriate. The lawn sloped down to the Grand Canal and in front of the house was a man-made waterfall, over which the small river la Nonette fed the canal. It was utterly peaceful and protected, as the park extended for hundreds of acres. Although countless Americans have visited Chantilly, there are probably very few who have ever seen St. Firmin. It was built for a member of the family of the Great Condé, who had inherited Chantilly in 1643, but Chantilly was destroyed during the Revolution and not rebuilt in its present form until the latter part of the nineteenth century. The entire vast property was given by the Duc d'Aumale to the Institut de France and it was from the Institut that Bullitt obtained a long-term lease at such a nominal rental. The house was in very bad repair and he obtained it on the basis of rehabilitating it and its outbuildings of stables and barns. Here he could walk in the miles of *allées* in the park and use his canoe. It was a perfect spot to retire to in order to get away from the pressure of work and visitors in Paris, and to have time to think objectively of the problems which were daily becoming more pressing.

The house itself was not large and could have graced any American suburb. It was beautifully proportioned, with large windows opening out onto the terrace. The drawing room had the original paintings on the panels of the wall and on the ground floor there were a library and dining room. A half dozen bedrooms completed the house.

14

Personal Diplomacy

JULY—DECEMBER 1937

Blum Ousted
Roosevelt Loses Supreme Court Fight
Rome-Berlin Anti-Comintern Pact
Bullitt Interviews Polish and German Foreign Ministers
Germans Prepare for War and Annexation of Austria

IN JUNE 1937, the government of Léon Blum was overthrown and Camille Chautemps became Premier and remained in power until March 1938. In July 1937, the Japanese began their attack on China, then under the government of Chiang Kai-shek. Bullitt reported France's position on July 30, 1937, to the Secretary of State by coded telegram:

According to Delbos the Italian position had been defined to the Chinese Ambassador in Rome, not to the Chinese Ambassador in Moscow. Delbos declines to discuss the position in the Far East. He said that in fact China was isolated though he was definitely opposed to an appeal by China to the League of Nations. The League of Nations today was a cipher and the only result of a Chinese appeal would be the cipher would become the shadow of a cipher. The League still had some utility in Europe and he did not wish to see it made ridiculous. He favored, on the other hand, an appeal by China to the signatories of the Nine Power Pact and had so stated to Koo yesterday. He was certain that at the present moment the Soviet Union would do nothing to aid China. Indeed he had just received a telegram from the French Ambassador in Nanking stating that Chiang Kai-shek was furious with the Russians. The Russians had led him to believe that they would support him and now had told him that they would do nothing. (I talked with the Soviet Ambassador in Paris this afternoon who expressed the opinion that his Government would do nothing whatsoever to assist China at the present time.) Delbos then said . . . It had been clearly understood at the time of the signing of the Franco-Soviet treaty of mutual assistance that France was not bound to take any action whatsoever in the case of conflicts arising in the Far East. Insofar as he could foresee the future the position that France would take would depend entirely on the position of England. France would not undertake alone to fight Germany and Italy. The position of France would be the same as her position in the Spanish affair. If England should wish to stand firmly by the side of France against Germany and Italy, France would act. If England should continue to hold aloof France could not act. France would never be caught in the position of having the Soviet Union as her only ally. Delbos went on to say that he felt the British were making a great mistake in attempting to curry favor with Mussolini at the present time . . . Delbos added that he feared the truth was that Great Britain had decided to recognize Franco's belligerency and to treat both Italy and Franco in an amiable manner in the hope that Mussolini might be reasonable. Delbos expressed the opinion that Mussolini would regard this new attitude on the part of England as a proof of weakness and that he would drive ahead in the Spanish affair in an even more unrestrained manner than in the past. The British in his opinion would like to see Franco win provided they could feel sure his victory would not mean Fascist domination of the Mediterranean. They were trying to get sufficient assurances from Mussolini and Franco to convince themselves that Franco's victory would not mean loss of their route through the Mediterranean.[1]

Personal and Confidential   Paris

July 5, 1937

Dear Judge Moore:

. . . The burdens of this post continue to be almost intolerable. It is literally true that I have obligatory duties for about sixteen hours a day, seven days a week. I can not keep up the pace and I do not believe that any other living human being can do it. I have just come to the decision that I will accept no invitations from organizations which desire to have the presence of the American Ambassador simply as a flower in their caps. You will doubtless hear that I have become a hermit. The fact will be that instead of attending some function given by the Daughters of the American Revolution,

I am having supper quietly with Chautemps or whoever happens to be Prime Minister or Foreign Minister at the time.

The tradition at this post that the American Ambassador must attend upwards of three hundred banquets and ceremonies a year was built up by American Ambassadors who spoke no French and did no real work and spent their entire time on functions. It is impossible to do real work here and handle the function side of life as well. I have no doubt that you will approve this decision. I still have a hoard of engagements for the next few months which I shall keep but I shall accept no new obligations . . .

Every possible good wish to you and good luck.

Yours affectionately,
William C. Bullitt

Personal and Confidential   Paris
July 23, 1937

Dear Mr. President:

I have a number of complaints to make with regard to your conduct.

1. You have infected my daughter, Anne, with a passion for stamp collecting and she now spends all her time, to say nothing of whatever funds she can wheedle out of her father, on stamps. She came back to the house a few days ago with the two stamps I enclose herewith. As she is already a true stamp collector, she had been careful to buy duplicates for herself. She wanted to know if you could tell off-hand which stamp was correct and thought that you would like to have the pair as a curiosity.

I am merely an agent for their transmission but I venture to express the hope, in the best diplomatic manner, that my daughter may recover.

2. Why did you never tell me what an astonishing youth Franklin, Jr., is? He and his bride dined with me the night they arrived and after dinner I had a chance to talk with him. I have never had a more interesting conversation with a boy of that age. Then, as he said he wanted to meet some of the heads of the French Government, I had a little luncheon for him at Chantilly which consisted of Chautemps, Blum and Delbos.

I must say the luncheon began rather well because Chautemps was so pleased to escape for a moment from his duties as Prime Minister that even before a cocktail, he turned somersaults on the lawn!

But the point is that Franklin, Jr., not only spoke excellent French but also had things to say which interested everyone. He is wise beyond his years and, in my humble opinion, as promising a youth as I ever saw.

Incidentally, Chautemps phoned me the same evening and said that he had never talked with a more intelligent or charming boy. You ought to feel just a little bit proud of yourself.

3. What the devil is Mr. Hoover's Ambassador to Brussels up to [Hugh Gibson, former Ambassador to Brussels and then Ambassador to Brazil]? He has now passed through Paris three times and has carefully avoided seeing me each time and his Belgian wife has been announcing to all and sundry that he is now to take up again his duties under the Hoover regime, which consisted of running the entire diplomatic service of the United States of America on the continent of Europe, representing the President at all conferences, etc.

You may or may not remember that it was your humble servant who, when everybody else wanted Gibson kicked out of the Service because he was Hoover's best friend, stood up for him and advised you to keep him in the Service. I have nothing personal against him but it seems to me bad ball when an Ambassador straight from headquarters does not cooperate to the extent of coming in even for a conversation. Gibson, of course, loves you, myself and all other Democrats in the same manner that Mr. Hoover does and I think that whoever sold you that baby as an ambassador in Europe was not especially wise.

I don't want you to do anything about this except to be damned careful not to put Brother Hoover in charge of the conduct of our relations with the European continent.

4. I hope you have written me before this in reply to my letter about Mrs. Tuck's offer to build and endow a school at Warm Springs. I enclose a recent letter from her and I hope that it will stir you to instant action if you have not already behaved as well-behaved Presidents and Grotonians should behave.

I shall close by telling you that your ex-boss, Josephus Daniels, who was at Chantilly with me yesterday and with whom I lunched today, is in great form and seems much younger than when he was Secretary of the Navy [1914]. He is a grand old man.

Blessings and good luck.

Yours affectionately,

Bill

Enclosure: Letter as stated above.

23 July 1937
Chantilly

Dear Mr. President:

Excuse me for sending you a handwritten letter. I don't want to dictate this — even to Offie.

I am deeply sorry about the result of the Supreme Court fight — sorry for the country and for you and all of us.* I am as sure today as I have always been that in your power to carry the country steadily and rapidly toward a fairer distribution of the national income lies our only chance to avoid the clash of classes and eventual crash of all we care about in America. And this seems to me a national disaster.

All the blind rich who hate you today will wring their hands and wish for you fifteen years hence — just as all the French who followed Clemenceau wish today that they had followed Wilson and written a real peace instead of the Treaty of Versailles.

You will laugh, I know, as you always do, and say, "Aren't human beings awful!" As I am less robust, I do not laugh. And I do not like it.

Anyhow, I want to tell you that you have been and are absolutely right. And in victory or defeat you are a very great man.

My love and deepest admiration.

Bill

On Sunday, July 31, 1937, President Roosevelt spoke to France by radio. The occasion was the dedication of a monument to the American dead at Montfaucon. This tiny village, on a hill overlooking the location of the American attack in the Argonne in September 1918, was a bitterly contested vantage point. The small church tower gave a commanding view of the surrounding country and, after its capture, was used by the Americans for artillery observation. Present at the ceremony besides Bullitt were the President of the French Republic, Marshal Pétain, and General Pershing. The copy of the speech has many changes in the President's handwriting, and is signed by him with the notation, "Original mailing copy — This was made from U.S.S. *Potomac* alongside wharf, at Quantico." Also in his writing is one para-

* Roosevelt had attempted, unsuccessfully, a reorganization of the Court in order to produce decisions more sympathetic to the New Deal.

graph reading: "To the preservation of this civilization American soldiers and sailors contributed their lives and lie buried on this and other battlefields. They died brothers-in-arms with Frenchmen. And in their passing America and France gained deeper devotion to the ideals of democracy." [2]

THE WHITE HOUSE
WASHINGTON

August 5, 1937

Dear Bill:

I am delighted that Anne has taken to the collecting of stamps. Tell her from me that this is an excellent way of saving the Bullitt family fortune. Starting with the year 1840, the value of stamps has increased on the average 3% a year. That means that the return on your money is better than you would get in any reputable savings bank in the United States — and having locked the cash up in stamps, Anne will have the assurance that you will not spend it on hiring the Palaces of the former monarchs of France! The latest inside information is that not content with having leased Chantilly for the summer of 1937, you are negotiating with the French Government for the lease of Versailles during the summer of 1938. I understand further that there are no bathrooms in Versailles but that you will provide them.

I have been looking at those two delightful ninety centime stamps and the only difference I can see is that M. Descartes had washed his face in one copy and had not in the other.

On further examination I see that "de" has been substituted for "sur." As if anybody cared!

It was grand of you to have Franklin meet the heads of the Government — and that he behaved himself well. It was a wonderful opportunity for him.

I am surprised at your colleague in Brussels. He is wholly entitled to talk with the King of the Belgians. I do my own discussing with Van Zeeland!

I am writing you about the school at Warm Springs as soon as I drag some information from the Manager of the Foundation.

The ceremonies at Montfaucon came through splendidly and your voice and what you said were excellent. I am glad to know, too, that my voice got through to all of you who were at the field.

All well on this Western Front in spite of what you read in the newspapers!

As ever yours,
FDR

Honorable William C. Bullitt
American Embassy
Paris, France

Personal and Confidential   Paris

September 7, 1937

Dear Mr. President:

. . . Your mother is in tremendous form. You might as well have asked me to stop the flow of Niagara as to have asked me to see to it that she did not accept a vast number of invitations. She is feeling exceedingly well and by her own wish goes out constantly. She is, of course, having an immense personal success. All the French love her and unlike the thirty-six Senators, Congressmen, and wives that are now with us, she speaks admirable French.

For the past two months I have had an unending flood of inescapable visitors to entertain and I now understand why all my predecessors fled from Paris during the summer.

Chantilly is lovely but over-run with visiting firemen and I am about dead.

Love to you all.

Yours affectionately,
Bill

In September events were beginning to move more rapidly in Europe, and Mussolini visited Hitler in Germany.

Hitler displayed Germany's military strength to Mussolini with parades, army maneuvers, factory visits, and a huge open-air meeting in Berlin with an estimated crowd of a million. Mussolini was duly impressed and became favorably disposed toward Germany.

Bill returned home at the end of September, bringing his daughter, Anne, to stay with my wife and me. In a letter to me he asked us to return to France with him in October and said, "If you do, I promise you that I will have nothing but hundred dollar bills and thousand franc notes so that you will have to pay for everything in the customary manner." He had not forgotten our trip of twenty-five years earlier!

While in Washington Bullitt made an address on October 6 over the radio to Versailles on the occasion of the dedication of a monument to General Pershing, the commander of the expeditionary force in World War I.

Personal and Strictly Confidential   Paris
                                                    November 2, 1937

Dear Mr. President:

I talked with Norman Davis at length on his arrival here and informed him as well as I could with regard to the point of view of the French Government; and he was kind enough to inform me or, I hope, misinform me, with regard to your own point of view. He made it sound as if you thought God had laid Woodrow Wilson's mantle upon you, and were about to take on your shoulders, or rather those of the people of the United States, all the pains of the world.

I don't believe this is so; but for Gawd's sake remember that Woodrow Wilson, as a collapsed ex-President, used to lie in bed thinking of the text, "By their fruits ye shall know them"; and recalling that the fruits he could report to St. Peter were war and the Treaty of Versailles.

There are a lot of people in America at the moment who are beginning to be ashamed of the idea of keeping the United States at peace. A number of times in Washington I heard the statement, "Well, I'd rather not be in the Government if the United States won't intervene in the Far East and the war which is coming in Europe." That sort of thinking seems to me the product of nothing but overgrown egotism on the part of men who are so old that they know they won't have to go out and die.

You may have seen a recent book of Bertrand Russell's which contains a brilliant analysis of the present international situation. Bertrand (who is in many ways an ass) holds as the one hope of the world the possibility that the United States will stay out of war in the Far East or in Europe and will have, at the end of the holocaust, a civilization intact and sufficient strength to pick up the pieces and put them together again.

I believe that it is a damned sight nobler to act on that line than to throw the United States again into war in order to produce again a peace worse than the present peace to end peace.

I apologize for this outburst; but when I listened to the fluff and fuzz of your edition of Benjamin Franklin's Mr. Bancroft talking about what you intended to do, I was moved on behalf of the U.S.A. — even though I didn't believe a word he said.

Blessings and keep your shirt on.

Yours affectionately,

Bill

Personal and Strictly Confidential   Paris

November 3, 1937

Dear Mr. President:

Strictly between you, myself and the angels, I have just had a letter from Judge Moore which leads me to believe that he is so acutely unhappy that he is about to resign. Inasmuch as he is the only man in the Department who sincerely and completely loves you and would gladly stand up against a wall and be shot to help you, I should hate to see that happen for your sake; and I should hate to see that happen for his sake as I am deeply fond of him.

As you know, Moore has been deprived of all his duties in the Department and has been removed from the Personnel Board. So nearly as I can discover, the only reason for the recent abolition of the Eastern European Division was because Moore supervised it and its abolition made it possible to encyst him completely as if he were a very dirty germ.

It would, I am sure, buck him up enormously if you could have him put back on the Personnel Board either as the representative of the Secretary of State on that Board or, if necessary, by having a small act passed in Congress to provide that the Counselor of the Department of State should be on the Personnel Board.

I am convinced that you won't have Moore long in Washington or indeed, on this earth, unless he is given something to do. His service as Acting Secretary of State during the Secretary's absence in South America was completely distinguished and to be reduced now to a post which is somewhat less than that of the negro messengers in the halls of the Department is necessarily very discouraging.

Needless to say, Moore is the one man in the entire Administration who is completely loved and respected by the House and the Senate and any act concerning him would pass unanimously.

Good luck and best wishes.

Yours affectionately,

Bill

Personal and Confidential Paris

November 4, 1937

Dear Mr. President:

I talked to the Duke of Windsor and his Duchess for several hours last night . . . He is much calmer and much more self-confident, and seems to be taking serious interest in housing and other problems connected with the life of the industrial workers. Incidentally, he drank almost nothing and is obviously intensely in love with his wife . . .

I am sorry that Mrs. Roosevelt will be on her speaking tour when the Windsors arrive and I explained to them both, as you ordered, that the tour had been arranged months in advance and could not be cancelled . . . Incidentally, the Duchess expressed at considerable length, and apparently with sincerity, a deep admiration for Mrs. Roosevelt, and I hope they may meet somewhere sometime while the Windsors are in the United States.

I am giving a dinner tonight in honor of the pair and if anything interesting occurs I'll get off another letter at once.

The most interesting thing last evening was when the Duchess remarked, in describing Hitler's intense interest in architecture, that the Führer had said to her: "Our buildings will make more magnificent ruins than the Greeks'." That seemed to me to be about as revealing psychologically as anything I have ever heard. The curse of the Germans is that they have swallowed the *Niebulungenlied* and do not recoil even before the *Götterdämmerung*.

Love to you all and good luck.

Yours affectionately,

Bill

THE WHITE HOUSE

WASHINGTON

November 11, 1937

Dear Bill:

It is a good sonnet — even in Provençal — but it does not hold a candle to the sonnet recently written to me by my fellow Americans, the Eskimos of Alaska.

Is the story printed in the Hearst papers true — that the Boulets of Nîmes are directly descended from the Pope Joan, who, I am given to understand, lived in that neighborhood? Compared to that the de Lannoy ancestry was plebeian!

It is all very well for you to send me Caleb Hyde's generous offer * but you sent no recommendation with it. What do *you* think? And what do you think Congress (which would have to accept the offer) would say to the additional cost of up-keep?

I have always thought that the house on the Avenue d'Iéna was a mistake and that the office building on the Place de la Concorde should have been so designed as to include the residence of the Ambassador. If that had been done it would have been obvious and proper to give the Ambassador a place at Versailles — but three establishments will look a bit steep to the Congressmen from Missouri, etc.

Meanwhile, I will talk with the Secretary about the offer — and you might tell Mr. Hyde that I am deeply appreciative but that a good many questions are involved, including that of Congress, and that I will let him hear from me in a short time.

As ever yours,
FDR

Honorable William C. Bullitt
American Embassy
Paris, France

Bullitt went to Warsaw on November 14 and spent three days talking with the Polish leaders. In particular, a conversation he had with Colonel Beck, the Polish Foreign Minister, was of interest. Beck felt sure that if Germany were to attack Czechoslovakia the French would remain passive, but Bullitt thought the French would immediately mobilize if such an event were to take place. Beck assured him that Poland would stand aside and not help the French to protect Czechoslovakia. Beck also told him that Hitler wanted good relations with Poland and would not permit the Germans in Danzig to cause any trouble.

From Warsaw Bullitt called on the German Foreign Minister, Baron von Neurath, in Berlin, who told him that there were no difficulties with France that could not be solved and that he could tell the French that the Germans only wanted the best possible relations with them.

Von Neurath said Germany had abandoned Alsace-Lorraine definitely and forever. One source of disagreement between the

---

* Mr. Hyde, a wealthy American, had offered his property at Versailles as a residence for the American Ambassador.

two countries was France's support of the Czechs, who were treating three and a half million Germans in Czechoslovakia as an inferior race. Von Neurath was more optimistic about a reconciliation with France than with England, which was being extremely stiff-necked about Germany's former colonies. He made it clear, however, that the German Government would not take the initiative insofar as peace was concerned.

Dr. Hjalmar Schacht spoke of the absolute necessity of doing something to produce peace and that the only way was by direct negotiations between France and Germany. Hitler was determined to have Austria. Bullitt's talk with General Goering was fully covered in a separate letter to the President.

While in Berlin, he was guest of honor at a dinner at the French Embassy.

Personal and Strictly Confidential   Paris

November 23, 1937

Dear Mr. President:

I am sending you herewith a copy of a despatch to the Department of State. You will find, I guarantee, the portion of it which deals with my conversation with General Goering, a source of amusement to say nothing of instruction. It was really an amazing conversation and I hated to have to put it into respectable form for the Department.

You will remember that when I was representing you at the funeral of Marshal Pilsudski, I had to sit and walk next to General Goering for three days and found him so repellent that I literally could not address a word to him. When I reached Berlin last Thursday I was horrified to discover that the Italian Ambassador there, Attolico, who is an old friend of mine, without the slightest suggestion from me and without obtaining my consent, had gotten in touch with Goering and told him that I was coming through Berlin and that Goering had said that he would like to see me. I was a bit staggered by the prospect but Attolico had put himself in such a position by arranging for the conversation that I could see no way out except an immediate attack of ptomaine poisoning. I at once informed Dodd and asked him if he thought the ptomaine poisoning advisable but he said that he thought it might be worthwhile to go and ask the General some questions.

As a result, I went to see Goering in his private residence. He has built for himself a house in the middle of a huge block of public buildings. You go in through the entrance of the old Herren House and after being marched by soldiers through endless halls and past endless sentries find yourself in a garden of four or five acres in the middle of which his house stands. Goering had provided an interpreter for the interview but as he had somebody with him and I had to talk with the interpreter for five minutes while waiting, and as the interpreter was properly impressed by the extreme fluency of my German, he said that he would like to inform the General that an interpreter could only be an encumbrance — so I saw the man alone.

His office is a big room with a huge oak table at one end; a table about fifteen feet long, six feet broad, and at least four inches thick. There were three chairs, all built in mammoth proportions and covered with cerise velvet, trimmed with gold. The chairs were so big that Goering looked rather less than the size of a normal man and, as you know, he strongly resembles the hind end of an elephant. In my chair I must have looked like some sort of animated flea.

The whole decor was obviously designed to reduce his bulk to normal and the feat was accomplished. He has also lost about thirty pounds since I saw him in Warsaw and looks more human. You will find that I jolted him a bit and he liked it. For any man who spoke good German and had some brains and bluntness it would, I think, be the easiest thing in the world to have a direct relationship with him.

In the account of the conversation which I am sending to the Department, I have left out, for obvious reasons, his reference to Dodd. After he had expressed to me his desire to have better relations with the United States he then said that he desired to say something to me which he hoped I would not resent. The matter was a delicate one. But he considered it simply disastrous that there should be no American Ambassador in Berlin. Neither he nor anyone else in the German Government could recognize Dodd as an American Ambassador. Dodd was too filled with venomous hatred of Germany to have any relations with members of the Government, and in fact did not exist.

Most of my conversation with Neurath was taken up by Neurath's remarks on the subject of Dodd which were far more violent than Goering's. Neurath said to me that as we had known each other well for so many years, he felt he had a right to speak to me frankly about a matter which he felt was doing a great injury to German-American relations and indeed to the general world situation.

I was perhaps aware that some weeks ago he had had the German Ambassador in Washington speak to Mr. Welles and say that the German Government could not have any further relations with Dodd and would be extremely relieved if he could be withdrawn from Germany; that the German Government did not wish to be pushed to asking for his withdrawal but would have to ask for it unless he should be removed. Neurath said that he desired to have better relations with the United States instead of worse relations and, therefore, did not wish to be compelled to ask for Dodd's withdrawal; but the fact was that the German Government could no longer tolerate his presence in Berlin and would in the near future ask for his withdrawal unless the American Government should withdraw him. He said that he hoped I understood and that my Government understood the reason for this attitude on the part of the German Government. Dodd was so consumed with hatred of the present regime in Germany that he never ceased in any conversation he might have with anyone to attack the German Government in any possible way. He was totally blind to such virtues as the German Government might have and magnified every fault. He had even spoken publicly against the German Government and the activities of his son against the German Government had been utterly outrageous.

I asked Neurath why he had spoken to me about this matter at the moment since presumably it had been arranged through conversation between Dieckhoff and Welles. He replied that Dieckhoff had informed him that the matter had been arranged; but that Dodd, on his return to Berlin, had stated to countless persons that although he had desired to resign the President had insisted on his returning to Berlin and that he expected to remain indefinitely. (I ascertained later through Dodd's similar statement to me and from his Counselor of Embassy to whom he had made the same statement, and from various other sources, that this was the line which Dodd had taken.)

Neurath went on to say that although Dodd had always been violently hostile to the leaders of the Nazi Government, he had for a long time maintained personal relations with him. However, at the present time, Dodd was treating him with the same contempt and hostility with which he was treating all other members of the Government and he could tell me flatly that he, Neurath, would in future refuse to have any relations whatsoever with Dodd.

I attempted to pass off this matter without further conversation and turned to another subject but before I left Neurath again returned to it and said, "I want to impress upon you once more that Dodd's presence in Berlin is intolerable and if he should not be withdrawn, in the near future we will be compelled to ask for his withdrawal."

Attolico, the Italian Ambassador, also spoke to me about Dodd's present attitude in Berlin, saying that he felt the United States could play an immense role in Berlin at the present time as the German Government was most anxious to have good relations with the United States and that a great opportunity to promote peace was being lost by keeping Dodd in Berlin.

I was not surprised that this statement should come from the Italian Ambassador but I was extremely surprised when the French Ambassador, François-Poncet, whom Dodd considers his good friend, said to me, "Bullitt, for Heaven's sake, get Dodd moved out of Berlin. He used to be bad as an Ambassador but now he is impossible. He even scolds me because I invite members of the German Government to my Embassy. And he embarrasses all of us ambassadors by taking the line that we should not be ambassadors to the Government to which we are accredited but should carry on a sort of holy crusade against National Socialism. He is conducting a personal crusade against the Nazi Government and has no patience with anyone who will not join him in that crusade, forgetting that a crusader against a particular government should be anything in the world except an ambassador accredited to that government."

Poncet went on to say that he felt that at the present time it might be possible for the United States to exercise great influence in Berlin in the direction of European peace, provided we had a really first-rate ambassador, and that he hoped ardently he would soon have an American colleague with whom he could work.

I have written you too much lately but you have brought it on your own head by telling me that you wanted me to write you more often. I have poured upon your unoffending head too many words of wisdom; but I have got the habit now and here are a few more.
 The situation today as I see it is the following:

Germany is increasing in military strength more rapidly than France and England combined. I have heard this statement repeatedly from military men in Paris and had it in Berlin from the French Military Attaché who is the great foreign expert on German armament. He said, for example, that at the present time Germany has between five thousand and six thousand planes ready for action.

The French have possibly less than two thousand. He said that the rate of increase in German armament would inevitably, in his opinion, continue to be greater than that of France and England combined unless England should introduce conscription at once.

The atmosphere in Berlin today is singularly like the atmosphere before 1914. The Germans are confident and cocky; sure that time is working for them; sure that they can get exactly what they want and determined to get it.

The Poles are convinced that this German estimate of their position is absolutely correct. Except in case of a direct attack on France — in which case, I believe, the Poles would respect their alliance and enter war against Germany — they will do nothing whatsoever to stop Germany's march.

The Russians, by general agreement even on the part of their protagonists in Paris, are completely out of the picture so far as Europe is concerned. All hope that they might help Czechoslovakia has been abandoned.

The Italians, fully aware that when Hitler has cleaned up Austria and Czechoslovakia, they will become mere German satellites, nevertheless are ready to accept this position because they hope that in return for their cooperation, Hitler may some day toss them Tunis and perhaps Algiers.

The French are at their wit's end, divided between the belief that it is better to have war now rather than let Germany take in the Germans of Czechoslovakia and their fear that they will be defeated in such a war by the combined efforts of Germany and Italy.

The British, so nearly as I can discover, are at the moment on the following line: They will finally, deviously, by silences and tacit approvals, as the lesser evil, permit Hitler to take Austria; take the Germans of Czechoslovakia and dominate Central Europe and the Balkans; relying on the possibility that when Hitler is firmly established on the Brenner Pass, Mussolini, in self-defense, will be compelled to swing into the French-British orbit. Furthermore, I believe the British are prepared to offer Hitler a colonial domain but no portion of their colonial domain. The colonial domain they will offer will be first, that of Portugal; then that of Belgium; and finally, if necessary, that of France.

I am less sure than I was a few weeks ago that France will actually go to the support of Czechoslovakia in case of a German attack. I still believe that France will do so but there is a considerable possibility that if the Germans begin their attack by a revolt of the Germans of Bohemia, the French will communicate at once with

London and ask if Great Britain will support France in defending Czechoslovakia and the British will reply by advising France to refer the matter to the League of Nations and adding that until the League has decided on appropriate action they will do nothing. This may prevent the French from taking any action until Germany has overrun Czechoslovakia. Under these circumstances, I should not be surprised to find Chautemps, in the course of the next few weeks, swinging to the view that it is better to make a spectacular effort to reach terms with Germany. He will unquestionably be opposed by the Quai d'Orsay whose only policy since 1919 has been to register German violations of the Treaty of Versailles in order to prepare a beautiful White Book to be published at the outbreak of the next war.

Chautemps, I think, will wish personally to enter into direct conversations with Germany and perhaps make the necessary concessions: In other words, to abandon Austria and the Germans of Czechoslovakia to Hitler. But he will know that his Government will fall if he tries to put this policy in practice. The Communists, on whose votes he depends for his majority, would throw him out and the French have, on the whole, that curious sort of a sense of honor which makes it possible for them to contemplate submitting to a German *fait accompli* with regard to Czechoslovakia but makes them unwilling to advise the Czechs to submit before a *fait accompli*.

This is not a promising picture but there is one element in it that is not altogether dreadful. The Russians have now apparently retired behind their swamps, and the fact is beginning to be recognized even in France that the eastern boundary of Europe is not the Ural Mountains but the swamps which extend from Finland, past Poland, to Rumania. To give up the Russian Alliance and admit that Germany, having lost the war, has won the final victory and will be henceforth the dominant factor in Europe, would be, I believe, today regarded as the part of wisdom by the vast majority of the people of France who think about international affairs. It is not today practical politics.

The only way that I can see that the growth of German strength, which I regard as inevitable, can be used for constructive instead of destructive purposes is by a general effort to make the giving of these concessions to Germany a part of a general plan of unification for Europe. I believe that we can have a considerable influence in bringing about such a result. I am not advising that we should get into the game ourselves or start again to play an active part in Eu-

238 : *The Paris Embassy*

ropean politics; but I was struck in Germany by the fact that I was told by everyone, not simply Nazis, but also Americans and also the ambassadors and ministers of half a dozen other nations that the Germans have the most profound desire to improve their relations with us and that we can influence them. We can certainly also influence the Italians. We do not have to do more than give them decent, simple advice of which every American would approve and to transmit from one nation to another the good things about each rather than transmitting the bad things.

I realize that all this may sound as if I had become a Pollyanna. I don't think I have. I admit that the chances are against peace and in favor of war, and I believe that the year 1938 will be decisive, but I think we ought to make the effort to preserve peace — just as quietly as possible.

Incidentally, François-Poncet, in saying to me that we could exercise an immense influence for peace in Germany, added, "For Heaven's sake, don't try to exercise your influence for peace by calling any general conference at the present time. It could only serve to emphasize differences and not to bring about reconciliation. The ground must be prepared carefully by regular diplomatic channels and in that your Government can play a great part." I agree.

Love and good luck.

Bill

Enclosure: Copy of Embassy's despatch dated November 23, 1937, entitled: "Visit of Ambassador Bullitt to Warsaw."

Bullitt was also in constant correspondence with Secretary Hull, reporting all matters of interest to him and receiving instructions from him. On November 23, 1937, he reported to Secretary Hull on the same subject. The contrast between the two reports is striking. One is like a Monet or Renoir painting, full of intimacy, dancing light, and shades of feeling, personalities being painted in broad strokes of the brush and detail left to the imagination. In the Hull letters the treatment is equally fine, but like an Andrew Wyeth, with every detail depicted.

His report contains no preamble of Goering's looks or office and in his account to the Secretary he begins bluntly: "Goering said that there was no direct conflict whatsoever today between Germany and France. Germany had given up entirely and forever the idea of regaining Alsace-Lorraine . . . In addition, the economic systems of France and Germany were completely complementary . . . The French had contributed so much to the culture of Germany and the Germans had contributed so much to the culture of France that as two civilized peoples who lived side by side they had a deep underlying esteem for each other . . . In addition, the French Government had indicated that it was prepared insofar as it was concerned, to return the German colonies which had been transferred to France by the Treaty of Versailles. There was, unfortunately, the proviso that France would only take this action if Great Britain were prepared to make a similar concession . . . So far as Germany was concerned, he could say with authority that Germany today was prepared to conclude at once *an offensive and defensive alliance with France* . . . I asked Goering if he meant that Germany was absolutely determined to annex Austria to the Reich. He replied that this was an absolute determination of the German Government . . . Germany would tolerate no solution of the Austrian question other than the consolidation of Austria in the German Reich . . . He said, 'There are schemes being pushed now for a union of Austria, Hungary and Czechoslovakia either with or without a Hapsburg at the head of the unit. Such a solution is absolutely inacceptable to us, and for us the conclusion of such an agreement would be an immediate *casus belli* . . . I asked Goering if the German Government was as decided in its views with regard to the Germans in Bohemia as it was with regard to Austria. He replied that there could be only one final solution to this question. The Sudeten Germans must enter the German Reich as all other Germans who lived contiguous to the Reich . . . Goering then added that the only other two considerable German racial groups which lie outside the borders of the German Reich, after the Germans of Austria and Bohemia had been included, would be the Germans of the South Tyrol who were now in the hands of Italy and the Germans in Poland. He did not feel that there was a sufficient number of Germans in Italy to warrant a major war . . . Goering went on to say that the idea that Germany had any ambitions to annex the Ukraine was pure nonsense."

They then discussed colonies, trade barriers, and American hostility to Germany. Goering spoke of the organization of German-Americans formed to protest against America's entering a new war. Bullitt replied to this: " 'You will understand that, if, as you have said, there are six million Germans in the United States today, who could be organized to influence the action of the United States government, there are a great many more than six million tree limbs on which to hang them.' Goering seemed to find this remark entirely reasonable." [3]

The conversation covered a wide range of other subjects and Bullitt's letter to Secretary Hull is thirty-two pages. It is an amazing document, as it gave the United States the complete plans of German aggression well in advance, and the source, the next in command after Hitler, was unquestionably official. Undoubtedly our State Department gave the details to the British and French, who had them four months before the annexation of Austria. It was a full ten months before Chamberlain and Daladier surrendered to Hitler at Munich. This letter can not fail to raise serious questions as to what those governments were doing in order to counteract the German plans. Munich should have been no surprise with such a forecast to study.

The State Department acknowledged this information with a letter which said in part: "You are considered as having been on leave of absence for six days from November 14 to 19, 1937, inclusive, which time is chargeable against your statutory leave of absence." The reward and encouragement of individual initiative.

Sumner Welles, however, on December 1 wrote to Bullitt: "Your conversation with Goering is one of the most important pieces of information which has reached the Department in many a month. I wish to the good Lord that during the past years we had been getting this type of information from Berlin."

Personal and Strictly Confidential   Paris
November 24, 1937

Dear Mr. President:

I have to report that, in accordance with your instructions, I delivered respectfully into the hands of His Royal Highness the Duke of Windsor your communication with photograph. The Duke was appreciative; but, on regarding himself as Prince of Wales, seemed somewhat depressed by his present appearance.

You would really like that boy now. He is much nicer than he has ever been . . . You will be glad to know that [the Duchess'] favorite bridge partner is Offie! . . .

I never believed you were about to mount a white charger but Cordell's friend, Norman, had assured me that just as soon as the Japanese should refuse to join the conference at Brussels you would launch a project for the effective quarantining of Japan by use of our Fleet in the Far East, and even more violent measures.

At this moment, when you are nursing the poison of a bad tooth in Washington and I am nursing the poison of a bad tooth in Paris, it seems to me that we both are in a position to appreciate that the slightest lowering of resistance is apt to produce bad results when there are germs around. You get so much cockeyed advice on foreign affairs that you have to keep your resistance to germs in that area particularly high. Norman simply made me fear for a moment that you had an international infected tooth.

The white charger reminds me that you are shortly going to have to decide who is to be the Chief of Cavalry. Colonel Joseph A. Baer, now at Headquarters of the Third Corps Area at Baltimore, is one of the two leading candidates. I don't know whether the other man is better than he is or not, but I can promise you that Baer, whom I know well, is absolutely first-rate.

In view of the remarks of Vandenberg on my visit to Tony Biddle, I have decided that my travels for the moment must be confined to the Bois de Boulogne. The United States Government on January 1st will owe me 107 days' holiday. I think I will take most of them in the spring rather than excite Vandenberg again by returning to see Anne for Christmas, and joining the homeward flight of Bingham, Davies, et al. I shall have Anne mount the S. S. *Europa* on December 16th and spend her Christmas holidays with me here.

I understand that people in America are rather excited because the French Government is digging arms out of various cellars in Paris. No one here is in the least excited. On my return from Warsaw no one mentioned the matter to me for forty-eight hours. I finally began to consider this somewhat peculiar and said to a lady at a ball at the Polish Embassy that I wondered why this was so. "Why," she said, "ever since the 6th of February, 1934, everyone in Paris has had a passion for collecting machine guns!"

I talked with the Minister of the Interior and the Chief of the Sûreté Générale today, and with Chautemps, Delbos and Bonnet on the subject yesterday. There wasn't a single one of them who had anything to add to the lady's comment!

You will understand the French attitude; but I can't imagine many other Americans comprehending it in the least.

Blessings.

Bill

Personal and Confidential   Paris
                                                      December 7, 1937

Dear Mr. President:

. . . I can not tell you how delighted I was to get the news of Hugh Wilson's appointment to Berlin.* I have felt like singing a *Te Deum Laudamus.*

As you will have gathered from the account of the conversations I had during a mere twenty-four hours in Berlin, it is not difficult to establish good conversational relations with the Nazi leaders, and Hugh Wilson should be able to give you the same sort of information from Berlin that I can send you from Paris. His appointment at this moment is especially well-timed. The Germans are anxious to get together with the French and the French are even more anxious to get together with the Germans, and Hugh and I, without seeming to move hand or foot, ought to be able to pour a lot of useful oil on the troubled waters. There are sufficient favorable elements in the present situation to make it possible to hope that, if they are nurtured with sufficient diplomatic skill, this coming summer may mark not the beginning of the destruction of Europe but the beginning of the construction of peace in Europe. I don't say that the result will necessarily be peace; but I do think that the chances for peace in Europe are increased definitely by your appointment of Hugh to Berlin, and I thank you profoundly.

I hope that you will advise Hugh to pass through Paris on his way to Berlin. The Germans will see nothing out of the way in that and I shall arrange for him to have long conversations with Chautemps, Delbos and the rest. His interest to the leaders in Berlin, indeed, will be considerably enhanced by his stay in Paris. Twenty-four hours here will be enough and there could be no possible criticism of that.

I have telegraphed so fully this past week that there is little to add. I think it might be most useful if on any occasion when you

* Ambassador Dodd resigned and Hugh R. Wilson succeeded him in December 1937.

Bullitt arriving in Moscow, March 1934, with Anne.

Soyquz Photo

Bullitt meets Président Kalinin, December 1933. At the right
is Maxim Litvinov. Behind Kalinin and Litvinov stand Bullitt's
aides George Kennan and Joseph Flack.

Anne and Bullitt, Moscow, 1935.

Leaving Elysée Palace after presenting credentials, October 13, 1936.

Photo by Charlie Phillips courtesy of Life *magazine.* © *Time Inc.*

At his desk in the Embassy, Paris. The pictures behind Bullitt
show Judge Moore, Thomas Jefferson, and Cordell Hull.

Château St. Firmin, Chantilly.

Léon Blum with Bullitt at Chantilly, 1936.

New York Times *Photo*

Bullitt with the Duke and Duchess of Windsor.

Bullitt and Daladier.

Bullitt and Orville H. Bullitt return from France, July 1940.

FDR, Miss Marguerite LeHand, and WCB at Hyde Park, July 22, 1940, for a report on the fall of France.

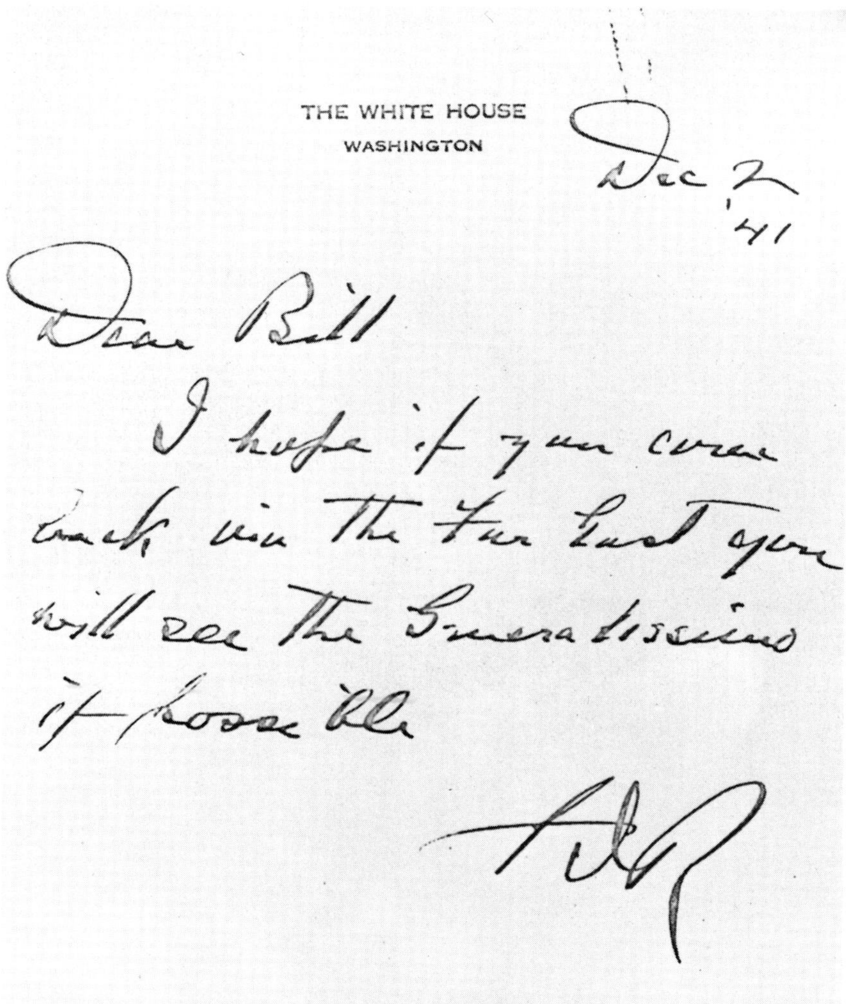

THE WHITE HOUSE
WASHINGTON

Dec 2
'41

Dear Bill

I hope if you come
back via the Far East you
will see the Generalissimo
if possible

FDR

Hon. Wm. C. Bullitt

FDR's note of December 2, 1941.

At the London Conference, July 1942.

Entering Marseilles, August 1944.

General Marshall, de Lattre, Bullitt, October 1944.

Eisenhower and Bullitt, October 1944.

see either the German Ambassador or the French Chargé d'Affaires, you would say that you are delighted to see that there has been an improvement in Franco-German relations. The French care tremendously about your opinion and the Germans care a lot also because to them America represents the great question mark. They are afraid that in spite of all our efforts to remain out of the next war, we shall be drawn into it as we were drawn into the last war. They want tremendously to diminish the chance that we may come in against them and, therefore, want to improve their relations with us, not realizing that diplomatic politeness would not affect our ultimate action or inaction in any way. Their desire to improve relations, however, may enable us to get out of them a lot of things we want . . .

Just before Norman Davis left Paris, he asked me my opinion with regard to the following proposal: that the United States, Great Britain and France should agree never to recognize any territorial conquests of Japan in China and never to permit any of their institutions or nationals to make any loans to Japan so long as Japan should remain in occupation of Chinese territory.

I told Davis that before answering any such question I should want to lie on my back and look at the ceiling for a number of hours while imagining all the possible consequences of such action. I remarked, however, that one objection occurred to me at once. The use of the words "ever" and "never" should be prohibited in American diplomacy. This applies especially to the Far East which is today a focal point of international conflict. I still believe, as I have for several years, that conflict between Japan and Russia is inevitable because of the position of Vladivostok as the geographical center of the Japanese Empire. I felt certain that we have no vital interests in the Far East any more than we have in Africa.

From me to you my opinion is this: we have large emotional interests in China, small economic interests, and no vital interests. The future is obscure; so obscure that I can not help recalling that the Kaiser persuaded T. R. to urge France to accept a conference in the Moroccan affair of 1905 by the argument that the destruction of the German Navy in a war would leave Great Britain and France free to partition China!

By 1914 T. R. must have thought that his fears about destruction of the German Navy leading to partitioning of China by Great Britain and France had been a rather lousy basis on which to determine policy.

There is no basis of policy more unreal or disastrous than the apprehension of remote future dangers. As our mutual friend, Euripides, wrote:

There be many shapes of mystery,
And many things God brings to be;
    Past hope or fear,
And the end men looked for cometh not,
And a path there is where no man thought,
    So hath it happened here.

The far-off bugaboo of complete Japanese domination of Asia and an eventual attack on us seems to me no basis whatsoever for present-day policy. The Japanese will have their hands full with China and the Soviet Union and their one hope will be to avoid war with us. I think, therefore, that for the foreseeable future we should watch events in the Far East but not participate in them if we can avoid participation. It seems to me that we should at the moment discourage any Americans from lending a penny to Japan — provided any are so idiotic as to want to — but I think our Government should do it on the quiet, without making any large announcements of policy or giving any pledges to that effect to France or England or anyone else.

I feel also that the more ships we add to our Navy the better. If the Japanese try to keep pace with our building it will diminish by just so much their resources for the domination of China . . .

I haven't seen your . . . friends, the Windsors, for some time but, from reports, I gather that they are winning friends daily in Paris. The ladies of France are captivated by the Duchess who dresses better even than they do . . .

Good luck for the tooth, Merry Xmas, a Happy New Year and my love to you and all the family.

                                                                    Bill

15

Reconciling France and Germany of No Avail

JANUARY—JUNE 1938

Difficulties of Reconciliation
Panay Incident
Ribbentrop Foreign Minister
Germans Occupy Vienna
Daladier Prime Minister
French Airplane Shortage
Trouble in Czechoslovakia

BULLITT PURSUED, at every opportunity, his idea of bringing about closer relations between France and Germany. In this he had a dual purpose. One was to avoid the chances of a new European war and the other was to thwart the plans of Russia for domination of Europe.

Gordon Craig and Felix Gilbert in *The Diplomats* speak of Bullitt's desire for a reconciliation between France and Germany in these terms: "To the extent that Bullitt had formulated a consistent and harmonious view about the situation in Europe, he permitted it to be dominated by his distrust of the Soviet Union . . . He had become convinced that the aim of the Soviet Government is, and will remain, to produce world revolution. The leaders of the Soviet Union believe that the first step toward this revolution must be to strengthen the defensive and offensive power of the Soviet Union. They believe that within ten years the defense position of the Soviet Union will be absolutely impregnable and that within fifteen years the offensive power of the Soviet Union will be sufficient to enable it to consolidate by its assistance any communist government which may be set up in Europe. To maintain peace for the present, to keep the nations of Europe divided, to foster enmity between Japan and the United States, and to gain the blind devotion and obedience of the communists of all countries so that they will act against their own governments at the behest of the Communist Pope in the Kremlin, is the sum of Stalin's policy. 'In order to counteract such a policy, the United States should instruct its diplomatic representatives in Europe to use all opportunities in personal conversations to point out the dangers to Europe of the continuation of Franco-German enmity and to encourage reconciliation between France and Germany' . . .[1]

"So great was his popularity, especially in government circles, that the wits dubbed him minister without portfolio in the kaleidoscope of French cabinets. And in this atmosphere Bullitt responded with affection, devotion, and trust." [2]

The policy of suspicion of Russia and rapprochement between France and Germany was not accepted by many at that time but Roosevelt relied on his ability to charm the Russians and to obtain his way with them and fortunately did not live to see the disillusionment of such a trustful approach.

Winston Churchill, however, had his usual clear view of the situation and in his inimitable phrases expressed his ideas: "If we could only weave Gaul and Teuton so closely together economically, socially, and morally as to prevent the occasion of new quarrels, and make old antagonisms die in the realization of mutual prosperity and interdependence, Europe would rise again. It seemed to me that the supreme interest of the British people in Europe lay in the assuagement of the Franco-German feud, and that they had no other interests comparable or contrary to that." [3]

In December 1937 Bullitt reported to Secretary Hull on the talks which were taking place between the French and Germans to adjust their differences. Georges Bonnet told Bullitt that it was important that the two countries be reconciled, but this would need the blessing of the United States. Bullitt replied that any such effort would have the approval of the United States. The same day the German Ambassador in Paris told Bullitt that Ribbentrop had ordered him to try and reach a full understanding with France, but that England, the Soviet Union, and Italy were all opposed to such a reconciliation. Bullitt also told the German Ambassador that the United States favored rapprochement. Later that day Bonnet proposed a plan whereby France,

England, and the United States draw up a plan for peace and then submit it to the German Government. Bullitt replied that there was not the slightest chance that the United States would participate. He stressed that the United States would not become involved in European politics and furthermore that the French statesmen must realize that, although the United States was deeply interested in the preservation of peace, it would not send troops, warships, and money to support France and England. The French continued to make proposals in an effort to draw the United States into European affairs. Berlin was also using the same tactics, asking President Roosevelt to call an international conference on the abolition of world trade barriers.[4] The efforts were put to a halt by Anthony Eden, who went to Paris to express England's views to Premier Léon Blum.

Five years previously, Bullitt had asked Ramsay MacDonald, Prime Minister of England: "Do you really want reconciliation between France and Germany or do you want them to remain friendly enemies?" MacDonald screwed up his left eye, nodded, and said: "That's exactly it. We do not want them to come to war but we do not want them to be friends!"

Paris

January 3, 1938

Dear Miss LeHand:

Antoine Pierre Marie, Duc de Lévis Mirepoix, an extremely well known French writer and historian, and what is more unusual, one of the few honest, authentic, legitimate and certified dukes that still exist in France, left for a tour of the United States the other day on the same boat as Anne. He is going to spend four months giving lectures all over the United States to gatherings organized by the Alliance Française. He called on me just before leaving and said, as everyone does, that he would like to see the President. I hope most heartily that the President will see him if he can.

The Duke looks more Lévis than Mirepoix, and perhaps the family foot slipped somewhere, but I can assure you that in spite of his looks he is a charming and intelligent gentleman and of real importance. The President may perhaps have read either his book, *Les Campagnes Ardentes,* which was crowned by the Académie Française, or his book, *François Ier,* which received the Prix Gobert. He has also written a number of highly successful and distinguished novels, notably *Le Papillon Noir, Le Seigneur Inconnu* and *Le Voyage de Satan*.

I told Lévis Mirepoix that he would, of course, have to have his request for an interview with the President presented by the French Embassy and he said that he had made all arrangements to have this done. He may not be in Washington for some time but I hope that whenever he does arrive, you will be able to dig this letter out of your memory and see that he has a glimpse of the gentleman whom I assume I am now to call the Commander-in-Chief.

Every possible good wish for the New Year.

Yours very sincerely,
William C. Bullitt

THE WHITE HOUSE
WASHINGTON

Memorandum for M. A. L.   January 13, 1938

Tell Bill that I shall be delighted to see his "Old Testament Duke" and that I am particularly anxious to meet him because on Christmas morning, having nothing else to do, I read by pure chance, before breakfast, his book *Les Campagnes Ardentes,* which was crowned by the French Academy, and his book *François I*^{er} which received the Prix Gobert. I was so much interested that after attending church I read those successful and distinguished novels —
Le Papillon Noir, Le Seigneur Inconnu and *Le Voyage de Satan.*

Tell Bill that these are not nearly as interesting as fifteen or twenty of his other books, which I trust Bill will read and memorize before he gets here in March!

FDR

GENERAL ORDERS

December 15, 1937

FROM: Commander-in-Chief
TO: The Ambassador of the U.S. to the French Republic
SUBJECT: Holiday

1. You are hereby directed, between the receipt of this letter and February first, to take a complete holiday for at least three weeks.

2. During such period you will carry on no official correspondence, see no officials, French or otherwise, on any official subject.

3. In other words, when I say holiday, I mean holiday.

FDR

Dear Commander-in-Chief:

Orders duly received and contents noted. Obedience, however, impossible due to absence of second in command who is in Switzerland taking care of his sinus as usual.

. . . As I wrote you before, I believe that there is a real chance to bring France and Germany closer together this year and I want to concert a lot of things with Hugh.

I was, of course, delighted at Joe Kennedy's appointment to London and I wish that I could have a talk with him before he goes to his post. There is a lot of information about the Embassy plumbing that he ought to have, and you and I are the only people I know who are sufficiently low-minded to discuss drains with him. You will, I assume, have Joe in Washington for several weeks before he leaves and I hope you will have a chance to remind him that: 1. The British Government has every code of our Embassy in London. (You will remember Ramsay MacDonald's statement to me that every message sent or received by our Embassy in London is decoded at once and is on the desk of the Cabinet Minister interested the following morning.) 2. It is highly improbable that the British Government has missed the opportunity to put the most efficient dictaphones in our new Chancery, which is in a building only part of which is rented by us. 3. There are probably dictaphones in the Ambassador's residence and certain members of the staff of the Embassy are undoubtedly members of the British Secret Service.

This is the kind of thing that the Department is apt to consider too low to discuss with an Ambassador but it is something that Every Young Man Ought To Know.

Salmon, the head of the code room in the Department, is an admirable fellow and he has a number of new coding devices which should be private for a few messages at least. I think you ought to advise Joe to have a long talk with Salmon and ask for some device which will enable him, in time of need, to send you really confidential messages. I also think you ought to have Joe take to London the best expert on picking out dictaphones that the Navy or Army can produce and have a thorough inspection made both of his house and his office.

It is extremely difficult, of course, to discover the damn things without tearing a house to pieces. For example, recently in Moscow the French Embassy was about to move into a new habitation which had been renovated by Russian labor. The day the French Ambassador was to move in, the ceiling of his office fell, revealing a magnificent series of dictaphones established in the walls and ceilings. You will recall the fishpole dictaphone that the Russians planted in the wall between Joe Davies' bed and the desk where he dictated all his telegrams. The British are not so crude as the Russians and an investigation might yield nothing. Nevertheless, I think it worthwhile to have one made.

Davies to Brussels was a stroke of genius. He can not do much harm there. And as there is almost no work to do he will be able to survive physically. As you doubtless know, Pletnev, the great Russian heart specialist, told him that his arteries were in such shape that any serious work would kill him.

If you have not yet picked the man to replace Davies in Moscow, I suggest that you take an extremely stable career officer. By all odds the best man, because of his knowledge of the Far East, would be MacMurray. He would doubtless hate to go there, as anyone else would, but I think he would be excellent and the long suffering staff in Moscow ought not to have to suffer the infliction of another Davies . . .

Your handling of the *Panay* sinking was masterly. To turn it from a *Maine* to a *Lusitania* was all that could be expected and you got more out of the Japanese than anyone here believed you could.

Henceforth, your chief job is going to be to maintain our national honor while avoiding involvement in war. The best way to do that, I think, is to be as wise as the serpent *before* the event, not after.

When Saint-Quentin comes to see you, you will face the quintessence of the Quai d'Orsay. He thinks the Treaty of Versailles was the best treaty that could be devised under the circumstances and that French foreign policy since that time has been intelligent. When I asked him if he saw any possibility of preserving peace, he said that he saw none. He did not feel that there was anything that France and England could or should do except wait. I said to him that this seemed to me not the policy of a statesman but the policy of an undertaker. He replied that after all human beings were so helpless in the face of events that all they could do was to bury the dead.

He is upright and honorable, and his point of view and that of Léger and the rest of the permanent officials of the Quai d'Orsay seems to me fatal. They have so much obstructive power that it is doubtful that Chautemps or Delbos or Blum or anyone else will be able to carry out a constructive policy in the face of their intelligent and well-informed negation.

I enclose the small word which I have sent to the Department on Saint-Quentin. I think it might be useful if you should say to him that the United States intends to stay out of any war which may start on the continent of Europe just as long as possible.

I am looking forward with the most intense eagerness to seeing you in March. There is so much to talk over each day that I wish that I could have a foot on each side of the ocean.

Blessings and good luck.

Yours affectionately,

Bill

The Japanese had been bombing Chinese cities, and our government had frequently warned them of the danger to the lives and property of American citizens. The climax came on December 12, 1937, when Japanese planes sank an American gunboat, the *Panay,* and three Standard Oil Company tankers on the Yangtze River near Nanking. It was a deliberate action, as the boats were all plainly marked with American flags painted on their decks. The survivors of the ships were machine-gunned, as was the sinking *Panay,* and Japanese even boarded the *Panay.* The incident was an extremely grave one and might have produced a break of relations, or even war with Japan.

Our government lodged a strong protest calling for an immediate apology and full payment for the damage. Furthermore, immediate steps were to be taken guaranteeing that no such action would again take place. The Japanese Foreign Minister, Hirota, immediately called on the American Ambassador, Joseph C. Grew, and offered the profound apology of the Japanese Government. The Japanese Ambassador in Washington also presented apologies to Secretary Hull. The Japanese Government accepted the American demands, apologized, paid for the damage, punished those involved, and gave assurances for the future.

Paris

January 20, 1938

Dear Mr. President:

You have doubtless followed with amusement the gyrations which resulted in the calling of Monsieur Chautemps to replace Monsieur Chautemps.

He has more common sense than any other French politician but I wish his present Ministry were a bit stronger. He and Delbos want to go ahead on the policy of reconciliation with Germany; but they are likely to be thrown out by the Communists and Socialists if they go far.

The curious thing about the "crisis" was that no one in France took it seriously. I have never heard so many roars of laughter from the leading politicians as during those days which were supposed to be critical.

When Herriot funked the Premiership, Central Europe went over the dam. Austria will fall into the hands of Germany, and France will do nothing except protest feebly. That, plus a prolongation of the present line in Rumania, will give Germany a controlling position in Central and Eastern Europe. If the Germans should have the common sense to refrain from violence in their dealings with Czechoslovakia, they should be able to get what they want without war.

That is, I know, a big IF, and I remember that everything was moving beautifully for Germany in 1914; but I feel that Hitler's present amiable attitude *vis-à-vis* France is based on the conviction that he will need to do nothing except be amiable in order to get what he wants in Central Europe. Incidentally, I believe that this outcome would be in line with the real policy of Neville Chamberlain and the instructions that he has given his Ambassador in Berlin. We may, therefore, see peace preserved by the simple process of England and France acquiescing in German domination over Central Europe.

I have spent too much time lately thinking of what you could do to help the chances of peace. I have come to the unpleasant conclusion that you can do nothing effective in Europe until you have an ambassador in Berlin and one in London who can discover for you what those Governments really want.

I remember talking over with you the idea that you might call a world conference in Washington to discuss international law. I feel now that, while such an appeal would be acceptable to American public opinion, it would seem an escape from reality to the rest of the world. It would be as if in the palmiest days of Al Capone you had summoned a national conference of psychoanalysts to Washington to discuss the psychological causes of crime.

Van Zeeland's report, which I have just read, seems cold porridge. It may have been a bit hotter before Neville Chamberlain recooked it but I find it difficult now to believe that it will excite the world.

I hope that you will consider with the utmost care the question of

Hugh Wilson's successor as Assistant Secretary of State. Two requirements are absolute: (1) He should be a New Dealer. (2) He
should know the difference between Budapest and Bucharest! . . .

I am leaving Paris tomorrow to spend three days in Lorraine, in
the course of which I shall have to make eleven speeches at official
functions and shall be decorated with an LL.D., by the University of
Nancy.

Blessings and good luck.

Yours affectionately,
Bill

The Foreign Minister of Germany, Baron von Neurath, had
held this post prior to the advent of Hitler, but now Der Führer
desired a more pliant occupant of the Foreign Office. On February 4, 1938, von Neurath resigned and his place was taken by
Joachim von Ribbentrop, who had been the German Ambassador
in London since August 1936. William L. Shirer has described
him as being: "Incompetent and lazy, vain as a peacock, arrogant
and without humor." He also quotes Goering's opinion of him as
an Ambassador: "When I criticized Ribbentrop's qualifications to
handle British problems, the Fuehrer pointed out to me that Ribbentrop knew 'Lord So and So' and 'Minister So and So.' To
which I replied, 'Yes, but the difficulty is that they knew
Ribbentrop.' " [5]

Bullitt's name was frequently mentioned in connection with
Pennsylvania politics. His distaste for such projects is clear from
the following letter.

Secretary of State   Havre
Washington   Dated February 25, 1938
Rush February 25, 11 A.M.   Received 11:20 A.M.

Personal and Confidential for the President
from Ambassador Bullitt

I could scarcely hear what you said on the telephone last night
and assume that you had equal difficulty in hearing me. I tried to
express to you my profound conviction that for me to leave the field
of foreign affairs at this critical moment in order to become Governor of Pennsylvania would be an abandonment of duty. There are
a number of men in our party who would make excellent governors

of Pennsylvania, notably Joe Guffey and Dave Lawrence. My entire interest at the present time is in devising ways and means to keep the United States out of the series of wars which are on the horizon; and, as I said to you and perhaps you heard, if I should be nominated today for the governorship and should receive a wireless informing me of the nomination, I should at once refuse by wireless.

I shall come to the White House as soon as possible after reaching New York and I hope that you will not permit the party to put itself in the position of being damaged by my refusal to run. I appreciate greatly the interest of Earle, Guffey and Stern but it seems to me a peculiarly inappropriate time for a man who is experienced in foreign affairs to desert them for domestic affairs.*

As I have told you often, I shall always be ready to do anything that you wish me; but I ask you to hear my views before making any decision. Love to you all. Bill.

Bullitt did not become the Democratic candidate for the governorship of Pennsylvania.

Bullitt arrived in America on March 3 for a short trip, the purpose of which was to report to Roosevelt. He still maintained a childhood faith in Philadelphia doctors and dentists, and one of the purposes of the trip was to have an infected tooth removed.

Under the date of May 1, 1938, Harold Ickes noted in his diary a talk he had with Bullitt: "He thinks that Italy will find Ethiopia a great financial burden. He thinks that Franco is bound to win in Spain, although the war will probably drag on longer than some people think . . . He believes that the Chamberlain government will maintain itself in Great Britain. He looks for German subjugation of Czechoslovakia. He commented on the fact that Hitler's timing had always been perfect; that he had moved from one objective to another, and so far obtained his ends without having to fire a gun. He thinks that Hitler will have his will on Czechoslovakia, not by invading it by armed forces, but by working through the very large German population in Czechoslovakia. The deed will be done in such a way that Russia and others will claim justification for not going to the aid of Czechoslovakia." [6]

* Joseph Guffey, David Lawrence, and George Earle were prominent figures in Pennsylvania politics. David Stern was publisher of the Philadelphia *Record*.

Bullitt gave Roosevelt all these views which forecast events to come.

Hitler was now beginning to move. Schuschnigg, the Chancellor of Austria, had opposed the Nazi efforts and on March 9, 1938, announced there would be a plebiscite on the thirteenth. On the eleventh, the Germans closed the frontier with Austria at Salzburg and mobilized an army corps at neighboring Munich. The same day Goering ordered Schuschnigg to cancel the plebiscite and resign from office. If he did not, the German Army would invade Austria. In the face of such a threat Schuschnigg tendered his resignation to President Miklas. With great courage the President refused to nominate a Nazi Chancellor. On Sunday, March 13, the German tanks entered Vienna followed by a triumphant Hitler. This was the death of the Austrian Republic, which was forthwith annexed to Germany.

The official Russian account, printed in Moscow, tells of this highhanded occupation of Austria in the following words: "Fascist Germany, with the connivance of Great Britain, France and the U.S.A. seized Austria in 1938 and Czechoslovakia in 1938–39." [7]

On April 10, Edouard Daladier succeeded Léon Blum (who had regained the position the previous month) as Président du Conseil in France and also assumed the offices of Minister of National Defense and Minister of War. Georges Bonnet became Foreign Minister.

Later in the month of March, with Hitler's approval, Konrad Henlein, the Nazi leader in the Sudeten region of Czechoslovakia, began his demands for autonomy for the districts bordering on Germany. Henlein made his statement in a speech in Carlsbad on April 24 and the British and French urged the Czechs to do everything possible to settle the question. In May, Henlein's supporters held demonstrations in favor of autonomy within the framework of Czechoslovakia. By May 17 the Czech Government began discussions with Henlein under the threat of German troops at their border. The Czech Army was partially mobilized on the twentieth and, unknown to the world, Hitler on the twenty-eighth ordered plans for military action to begin against Czechoslovakia the following October 2. This timetable was met without the use of the army because the humiliating Munich pact was signed on September 30, 1938, and the Czechs were given ten days to evacuate the Sudetenland.

Personal and Confidential   Paris

May 12, 1938

Dear Mr. President:

For four hours last night Guy La Chambre, the new French Minister for Air, gave me the low-down on the French air force. In spite of the fact that the Germans probably know as much about the French air force as La Chambre himself, I feel that I should not pass along anything by cable to the Department and shall, therefore, bury in my memory and yours what he had to say.

Briefly, the situation is this. The French General Staff estimates that at the present moment France must have for war with Germany a minimum of 2600 first-line planes. At the moment, France has 1500. The present French rate of production is about 45 a month. La Chambre has promised the General Staff to have 2600 first-line planes in condition for battle by next Spring.

The weakest hole in the French air force is the almost total lack of pursuit planes. La Chambre is interested in getting pursuit planes from America immediately. He has not yet signed his contract with Curtiss-Wright for the P-36s. Curtiss-Wright proposed to him first to deliver three hundred planes in the autumn of 1939, beginning their construction after the delivery of similar planes to the United States Army, using the same machinery, at a cost of $28,000 per plane. La Chambre has preferred to work out a contract for the delivery of 100 planes in April 1939 at a cost of $34,000 per plane. This will require the installation of additional machinery by the Curtiss-Wright people and there will be a supplementary contract providing that the French may purchase this machinery after the delivery of these planes and may request its delivery either in France or Canada, or anyplace else that the French Government may select.

La Chambre does not believe that it will be possible to set up factories operated on American lines in France as he feels that French industrialists and workmen are entirely incapable of using American methods at the moment. He may, however, set up in Canada a factory for Potez — the most successful of the French constructors — where American methods might be used, and the Curtiss-Wright machinery may be transferred to Canada.

I was shocked to discover that in spite of everything that I had said to de la Grange and that the Department of State had said to him, he had said to La Chambre, who incidentally is an especially fine young fellow aged about forty, that if Germany and France should go to war, you would certainly circumvent the Neutrality Act and would continue deliveries of planes to France. I told La Chambre that in case of war between France and Germany, public opinion in America would be overwhelmingly in favor of application of the Neutrality Act and that you would have no choice but to apply it and prevent the delivery of planes and munitions.

British plane production has fallen off terribly due to change in models and defective organization, so that at the present moment, British production is about eighty a month. The British, however, hope within six months to get their production up again to two hundred and fifty planes per month.

Meanwhile, the Germans are producing between three hundred and five hundred planes per month, and the bottleneck in Germany is no longer the production of planes but the training of pilots . . .

La Chambre expressed the opinion that the blow to French honor would be so great if Germany should march into Czechoslovakia that France would declare war. I employed Daladier's words, "With what?" in asking him to develop this thought. He said that the French General Staff at the present time admitted that it was impossible to attempt to attack Germany on the line of the Rhine between Switzerland and Strasbourg. Gamelin, however, believed that it was still possible to make a further attack on the "Siegfried Line," between Strasbourg and Luxembourg. The "Siegfried Line" was already a most formidable fortification. Within a year it would be as impregnable as the French Maginot Line. It was not yet impregnable and Gamelin had prepared plans for a frontal mass attack on the "Siegfried Line." Such an attack obviously would mean the most terrible French casualties and probably could be held by the Germans with one-third of the present German Army, leaving two-thirds free for operations elsewhere, since General Gamelin estimated that one soldier behind the present fortifications of the "Siegfried Line" would be worth four soldiers attacking.

I asked La Chambre if he did not feel that the Germans were so superior in the air that they might be able to drive the French completely out of the air after a few weeks of fighting. He admitted that this was a possibility but insisted that, even without an aviation force, the French Army could still attack.

La Chambre was rather contemptuous of the efficiency of the

Russian air force. He said that the Russians had killed every airplane engineer and constructor that they had. They had no new planes and the best that they had were their imitations of American models four or five years old. The imitations were not nearly as good as the originals and in addition the officers corps of the Russian air force had been annihilated so completely that he did not believe the Russian air force could be considered an effective fighting force in spite of the number of planes it contained. Moreover, he did not believe that the Russians would decide to make war on Germany to support Czechoslovakia.

Good luck.

Yours affectionately,

Bill

Guy La Chambre became a close friend throughout the rest of Bullitt's life. La Chambre was the finest type of Frenchman, tall and handsome and a man with whom one felt an immediate sense of sympathy and intimacy. He could be trusted implicitly and had a high sense of honor. His approach was straightforward, and he never withheld any inner secrets. La Chambre spoke perfect English. As he will be mentioned so often in these letters, the reader should have a brief account of his background.

At this time he was forty years old. He had served in the First World War and been decorated with the Croix de Guerre. At the age of twenty-two he was in the government of Aristide Briand, and at thirty was a deputy from his native Saint-Malo in Brittany. He had a large property there on the tidal river, the Rance, the view from his château being across his fields to the water. La Chambre became Under Secretary of State in five Administrations and was finally made Minister of Air in 1938. In May of 1940, when the Germans attacked, he joined the army as a captain. He was thoroughly familiar with all phases of the government and, of course, also knew the army. When France fell he was demobilized and joined Bullitt, going to the United States to help with American military aviation.

The Pétain Government issued a warrant for his arrest along with the arrest of other members of the former government. Although he could have remained in America, and despite the urgings of the President and Bullitt against his return, on the ground that the French Government of Pétain and Laval was a Nazi puppet government, he chose to return to France to face any charges against him. Promptly placed in jail, he remained there from September 1940 until April 1943, when he received provisional liberty and was finally rescued by the Maquis in June 1944. Madame La Chambre had accompanied him and lived in villages close to his places of confinement.

La Chambre had chosen possible death rather than have his loyalty to France questioned. When he left the United States, the President said to him, "I disapprove completely your decision, but I fully realize your feelings." After the war he served as mayor of Saint-Malo for eighteen years and directed the reconstruction of the city, which had been badly damaged in the fighting. He now lives in Paris, the south of France, and at Saint-Malo. He can well look back on a life devoted to his country and filled with actions showing a high sense of honor and duty.

THE WHITE HOUSE
WASHINGTON

[Undated.]

Dear Bill:

I was greatly interested in your letter of May 12 in regard to the condition of the French Air Force and its plans to purchase planes in this country. Do you think it possible that La Chambre can accelerate French production sufficiently to have 2600 first-line planes in condition for battle next spring? The 1500 already on hand, plus the 100 which the French are purchasing here, plus 45 per month for the next ten months would bring the figure only up to 1850. Where are the remaining 730 to come from? Unless further orders are placed in this country immediately, our factories, which already have almost as many orders as they can handle, could not manufacture for delivery in France by next spring any considerable fraction of that number. Do you think that the French monthly production of 45 can be materially increased in so short a time?

Since your letter was written, the French have closed their contract with Curtiss-Wright for 100 planes of the type P-36, deliveries to begin in November of this year and to be concluded in April 1939, and they have arranged with J. P. Morgan to effect cash payments. Saint-Quentin called at the State Department last week and outlined the plans of the two French air missions which are coming here to make trial flights and to supervise the production of the Curtiss planes. The State Department is asking War and Navy to treat these missions as liberally as possible. In fact, all along we have done everything we properly could to facilitate French purchases of planes in this country. The delays which have ensued have been due to their own dilatory methods of doing business and not to any lack of reasonable cooperation on our part. I do not believe, however, that we can, with propriety, permit the diversion to the French of P-36 planes already under construction under contract for our Army. To do so would contravene a wise policy of long standing to which no exceptions have been made since 1932. On general principles, I do not believe that we should permit the diversion to other governments of planes manufactured under contract for this Government unless the interests of our own national defense are directly involved, but should we in this case decide to make an exception as a friendly gesture to the French the result would probably be disadvantageous to the French themselves. The fact could not be kept secret. Everything of importance that happens in the aviation industry is known to everyone in the industry within a few weeks, and therefore sooner or later to the press. You can imagine what some sections of the press would do if they got hold of a story that we were actively aiding French rearmament to the extent of allowing planes constructed for our Army to be delivered to them. That would mean embarrassment to us, and in the long run to the French in their efforts to purchase arms in this country.

You did well to try to set La Chambre right on the question of the Neutrality Act. I hope that you cleared up any misconception which he may have had. As long as that act remains in effect, it would have to be applied to any major European war, and we could not conceivably connive at violations of the embargo provisions in favor of any particular power.

Affectionately yours,

FDR

[Untitled memorandum, evidently of telephone conversation.]

[Undated. Probably
May 9, 1938.]

You tell the President that today in the Sudeten area, for one reason or another there has been great disorder; that the Sudetens have been marching around with flags and there has been rioting and a large number of Sudetens have been shot and wounded by the troops and the police. At 5:30 the Sudeten leaders met and presented a 6-hour ultimatum to the Govt., which expires tonight at 11:30, that is to say in just about an hour and twenty minutes from now.

The fact is this: That the ultimatum to the Govt. demands the withdrawal of the Czech troops in the Sudeten area and demands also that the authority in the Sudeten region be put in the command of the mayors. It amounts to a withdrawal of Czech authority in the Sudeten region. The Czech Govt. has already rejected this ultimatum but has said that it does not consider negotiations closed. There is considered to be and there is considerable possibility that after the expiration of this ultimatum in an hour and 20 min., German troops may cross the Czech border, which means war.

The French Govt. has told the British that they should try to get the German Govt. into a conference right away to settle the question. There is no reply yet from the British but one is expected any minute. There is as yet no French mobilization. I wish you would tell the President that there is something which I would like to say personally and it is extremely difficult for me to dictate it because he alone knows the background . . .

(Can be reached at his home in the country, Chantilly 93.) It is important to have a word with him, no matter what time. We may have a complete blow-up within the next few hours.

Personal and Secret   Paris

May 20, 1938

Dear Mr. President:

I hope this letter will reach you before Europe blows up. At the moment, it looks to me as if the Czechs had decided that in the long run it would be better for them to have general war rather than give the Sudeten a sufficient autonomy to satisfy either Henlein or Hitler. They will shoot some Sudeten, and Hitler will march across the Czech frontier.

The question of whether or not all Europe shall go to war is, therefore, ceasing to be a question of finding a basis for compromise between the Czechs and Germany. It is becoming a question of whether or not France will march when the Germans cross the Czech frontier. Neither you nor I can decide that question for the French Government; but we can both have a certain amount of influence on the decision.

I feel that it would be an unspeakable tragedy if France, to support Czechoslovakia, should attack the "Siegfried Line" between Strasbourg and Luxembourg, which is the only point at which attack is considered possible by the French General Staff. As you know, French airplane production is now about 45 planes per month; British about 80 per month. The Germans, at worst, even when changing types, produce 300 per month and at best 500 to 600 per month. The French have no anti-aircraft artillery worth mentioning, and are just beginning to produce it. There are only thirty thousand gas masks available for the entire civilian population of France. The slaughter of the entire younger generation of France would be certain and every city in France could be levelled to the ground by German planes. The French, even under such circumstances, would hold out and the war would be a long one, involving England and all Europe. There could be only one possible result; the complete destruction of western Europe and Bolshevism from one end of the Continent to the other.

The chances are today that the French will carry out their pledge to Czechoslovakia as a matter of honor — whatever the cost. If you believe, as I believe, that it is not in the interest either of the United States or civilization as a whole to have the Continent of Europe devastated, I think we should attempt to find some way which will let the French out of their moral commitment.

I do not believe that any general appeal for peace by you at the present time would be effective. Today the governments of both Germany and Italy hate the United States so heartily that neither one would accept any such proposal as you were thinking of making last January. Moreover, there would not be time to summon representatives to Washington. Both Germany and Italy might, however, accept a specific proposal of a limited nature.

I am fully aware of all the objections to the suggestion which I am about to make. If you should act on it, you would be accused of involving the United States in European politics and sacrificing another small nation to Hitler. But I feel that when the people of the United States realize, as they soon will, that general war in Europe is imminent they will not only accept but will demand some action from you which may promise to stop it.

If and when a German march across the border of Czechoslovakia seems imminent, I think that you should take action of the following nature:

Call to the White House the Ambassadors of England, France, Germany, and Italy. Ask them to transmit to Chamberlain, Daladier,

Hitler and Mussolini your urgent invitation to send representatives at once to The Hague to attempt to work out a peaceful settlement of the dispute between Germany and Czechoslovakia. Add that, if the four governments desire, a representative of the United States will sit with them. You should also make a personal appeal of the sort that you know best how to make; referring to the fact that we are the children of all the civilizations of Europe, that just as we are grateful for Shakespeare, so are we grateful for Beethoven; that just as we are grateful for Molière, so are we grateful for Leonardo da Vinci, etc.; that we can not stand by and watch the beginning of the end of European civilization without making one last effort to stop its destruction; that you are convinced that the only result of general European war today would be an Asiatic despotism established on fields of dead.

After a general conversation with the four Ambassadors, you might reinforce your action by personal conversations with each Ambassador, stressing to the German Ambassador the fact that France will fight and England will fight, that war in Europe today can end only in the establishment of Bolshevism from one end of the Continent to the other, that your proposed conference will leave the Bolsheviks beyond the swamps which divide the Soviet Union from Europe and are Europe's real eastern boundary. I think that even Hitler would accept under such circumstances.

The conference in The Hague would probably have to recommend that a plebiscite be held in Czechoslovakia to determine the will of the different peoples of that country. If the Czechs should refuse to hold such a plebiscite, the French would have an escape from their desperate moral dilemma and general European war would be avoided.

You would be accused, or the man sent to The Hague as your representative would be, of selling out a small nation in order to produce another Hitler triumph. I should not hesitate to take that brick on my head and I don't think you should either if, thereby, you could avoid a general European war.

I could make this letter fifty pages long filled with explanations, but as between you and myself I feel no explanations are needed. You, at least, will know that I have not become either a cynic or a lover of Hitler. I have thought this matter over night after night and I am convinced that this highly unpleasant course is the one that we should pursue and the only one that offers a chance of success.

If you should consider that this proposal is sound, I think you should work out at once your statement to the Ambassadors in detail so that you can spring it at a moment's notice. The moment has not yet arrived, but it may soon.

It would be fatal, I believe, to communicate your intention to any government, including the British. They would at once relax their own efforts to reconcile the Czechs and Germans because they would feel that at last they were getting the United States tied up in European political problems. Furthermore, they would, in confidence, tell all their friends in Europe and you could certainly, in that event, count on refusals from Hitler and Mussolini.

You would, of course, make it clear to the people of the United States that your action was directed toward this one emergency and that you had no intention of involving the United States in all the disputes of Europe.

In addition, I believe that it would help immensely if you should call in St. Quentin and tell him that you hope France will not commit suicide and if you would authorize me to say the same thing for you to Daladier.

In any event, as soon as you have considered this suggestion, will you please send me a telegram containing one word, either "affirmative" or "negative."

I would give anything to be with you in the White House tonight so that we could talk over this proposal and all the objections and difficulties. I am aware of how intensely undesirable it is from a great many points of view; but I believe sincerely that it may be the only way to preserve from destruction the few shreds of civilization that remain in the world.

Please telegraph me as soon as you can.

Love and every possible good wish.

Bill

Bullitt had apparently not been told that Roosevelt, several months before, had wanted to call together in Washington the representatives of the European governments to find a way to compose their differences. The plan was first proposed in January 1938 by the Under Secretary of State, Sumner Welles, to the British Ambassador, who urged his government to accept the plan. Chamberlain was cold to the idea, but Anthony Eden tried to soften the blow to Roosevelt. As a result of Eden's efforts the British let Roosevelt know that while they welcomed his initiative they would not take any responsibility if it failed. Winston Churchill says of this suggestion of Roosevelt's: "To Britain it was a matter of life and death. No one can measure in retrospect its effect upon the course of events in Austria and later at Munich. We must regard its rejection — for such it was — as the loss of the last frail chance to save the world from tyranny otherwise than by war."[8] On February 20 Eden resigned.

16

France Awakens

JUNE—SEPTEMBER 1938

French Prepare for War
Sudeten Troubles
A Young Visitor
Lindbergh Visit
The Approaching Crisis

IN *The Diplomats,* edited by Craig and Gilbert, Bullitt was accused that "because he feared the Soviet Union, consistently underestimated the nature and imminence of the German threat during the summer of 1938," he "pictured the United States as the disinterested peacemaker who would bring together the contending factions of Europe." [1]

On the other hand, William Langer and S. Everett Gleason in *The Challenge to Isolation* give this picture of Bullitt: "Ambassador Bullitt's position in Paris was equally strong [as Ambassador Kennedy's] and probably more influential. In contrast to his colleague in London, Mr. Bullitt tended to be optimistic with respect to the role the United States could play and far from defeatist even with regard to the chances of the European democracies. A man whose experience in diplomacy went back to the First World War and whose interest in international affairs was extensive and keen, Mr. Bullitt could always be relied upon to keep himself exceptionally well posted and to pass every scrap of news to the President. In view of his imagination, courage and energy it was inevitable that, in the midst of the confusion and uncertainty, he should have played a central role in Parisian politics and diplomacy. He was on intimate terms with Premier Daladier, whom he greatly admired, but also received the confidences of Foreign Minister Bonnet and the high officials of the Quai d'Orsay. In a sense Mr. Bullitt transcended his particular assignment and served as an Ambassador at Large. Representatives of the lesser powers in Paris confided in him and sought his advice or assurance. Consequently his reports, crisp, direct and forceful, supplied a rich and varied fare of intelligence and interpretation, and make fascinating reading even after the passage of years.

"Ambassador Bullitt's views were as clean-cut as Mr. Kennedy's, but in many respects quite divergent. He detested the Nazi dictatorship, regarded it as a menace to Western civilization, and believed that if Hitler were not checked he would ultimately attempt to extend his power even to the New World. The effort to appease the Fuehrer, in his opinion, was entirely futile; therefore the only hope of salvation lay in taking a strong stand and uniting the forces in Europe opposed to the spread of Nazism. Mr. Bullitt had no extravagant conception of British and French military power and for that reason approved the efforts of the democracies to draw Soviet Russia into the peace front, despite his strong dislike and invincible distrust of the Communist regime." [2]

Personal and Confidential   Paris
                                                    June 13, 1938

Dear Mr. President:

Here at Chantilly this evening with the nightingales singing and the river pouring its white cascade below the still woods, I feel like a participant in the last days of Pompeii.

I have talked with General Gamelin, Chief of the French General Staff, twice this week and with General Réquin, who is in command of the French Army in the single area where attack on Germany remains possible — the "Siegfried Line" sector between Strasbourg and Luxembourg.

You probably knew Réquin as intimately as I did when he was in Washington during the war as representative of the French General Staff. A few nights ago at Chantilly he showed me the map which he carries in his breast pocket, even when he is absent from the front, on which he has marked the lines of French attack against the "Siegfried Line," and of possible German attack against France.

As I have cabled, public opinion in France has solidified to such an extent that if the German Army should cross the Czech frontier, France would mobilize at once and march against Germany. Gamelin is certain of this and so is Réquin, and there are few politicians who disagree.

Réquin, who will command the French troops, looks upon this prospect of a frontal attack on the "Siegfried Line" with absolute horror. He expects to be able to advance, especially in the Saar district, twenty or thirty miles before he is stopped. He said that the battle in that area would resemble the Battle of the Somme on a much larger scale. It would be direct frontal attack on fully prepared positions. The chief advantage of the French would be the possession of tanks which are far superior to the German tanks. The casualties of the attacking side, that is to say, the French, would be three to four times the casualties on the German side. "It means," he said, "the death of a race." The attack finally would be stopped and the armies would face each other in a deadlock. Gamelin agrees entirely with the foregoing estimate and both Gamelin and Réquin believe that the Germany Army could hold such an attack of the entire French Army with from one-third to one-half of the German forces.

Both Gamelin and Réquin agree that the German forces left free to attack Czechoslovakia would be sufficient to overwhelm the Czech armies in the course of two or three weeks at most. Meanwhile, both generals agree that German preponderance in the air would be such that Paris would be destroyed by air raids. They both feel that the French would continue to hold out on the Maginot Line and would wait for the pressure of the blockade — since they both assume that England would be in the war from almost the first day — to strangle Germany.

Gamelin is much more optimistic than Réquin in his estimate of the time that would be required for the blockade to reduce seriously Germany's power to fight. Gamelin insists that even though the Germans should be able to acquire full control of the Rumanian and Polish oil fields, and even though they have considerable stocks of petroleum on hand and are making synthetic fuel, the ability of the Germans to continue the war would diminish rapidly after approximately two years . . . He added that if Italy should enter the war on the side of Germany, the problem would be aggravated since Italy would be unable to obtain oil except from Poland and Rumania. He insisted that the Italians and Germans would have to have access to the oil of Iraq and Persia in order to continue to fight after two years. He was convinced that France and England could continue to resist that long, although both countries would suffer horribly from aerial bombardment.

Réquin is not nearly so confident that the oil factor would come into play so soon or that it would be so decisive, and is much more apprehensive than Gamelin that the civilian population of France and England might suffer a collapse of morale in the face of daily bombardments of the most horrible sort which would make the bombardments in Spain seem infantile by comparison. He expects a war of at least six years.

Gamelin insists that if Italy should come into the war, French forces in North Africa would be sufficient to take Libya almost at once and considers that the Italians in Ethiopia could be isolated and destroyed. He also believes that the Germans and Italians could be prevented from reaching Iraq and Persia. And he considers that no merchant ship of any country could use the Mediterranean.

The number of unpredictable factors is enormous. The French might jump at once on Spanish Morocco, which they believe they can take in a very few days. They would also probably despatch sufficient troops and munitions to wipe out Franco.

Poland remains in a tragic quandary. There would be an enormous sentiment in Poland for war with Germany, but there would be an equally enormous fear that if Poland should become involved in war with Germany, Russia would enter Poland from the east. The Polish Ambassador stated categorically to Gamelin in my presence two days ago that Poland positively would not march with France and positively would not declare war on Germany if France should go to war to defend Czechoslovakia. Moreover, the Poles and the Rumanians have both stated officially that if the Soviet Army should attempt to march across their territory to get to Czechoslovakia, both would declare war on the Soviet Union . . .

There is beginning to be a general conviction throughout Europe that the United States will be drawn into the war, if it starts, after a comparatively brief period. This conviction is helpful insofar as it may tend to diminish the readiness of Germany to go to war; but we shall find ourselves violently unpopular in both France and England when it becomes clear that we intend to maintain our neutrality. Day in and day out, I say to the French that, if war should come, the United States would declare immediate neutrality and the Neutrality Act would come into force at once. The answer invariably is, "Yes, we know that; but the Germans will behave in such a way that you will soon be drawn in."

I remain as convinced as ever that we should not permit ourselves to be drawn in. I believe that if war starts, the destruction on the Continent of Europe will be so great that, unless we are able to remain strong and relatively untouched, there will be no nation on earth left to pick up the pieces. If we should stay out, we could at least help to keep alive whatever human beings may remain alive in Europe.

You perhaps saw the telegram in which I gave an account of François-Poncet's intention to attempt to work out a settlement of the Czech-German dispute by direct negotiations between France, England and Germany — represented by himself, Henderson and Ribbentrop. His idea, which is the idea of the French Government, is that the Czechs should be compelled to grant full autonomy to the Sudeten geographic area and that Czechoslovakia should become a neutralized state, of the sort that Belgium was before 1914, its independence guaranteed by England, France and Germany. He said he had no great hope that it might be possible to succeed in this negotiation, but he could see no other way to avoid war.

I understand perfectly the dilemma in which Beneš finds himself.* All his life he has been an adventurer and a courageous one. He knows that if he grants autonomy now to the Sudeten Germans, the Sudeten some day will vote themselves out of Czechoslovakia and into Germany, and he will go down in history as the man who began the disintegration of the Czechslovak State. On the other hand, if he refuses to grant autonomy and makes only concessions which the Sudeten will reject and war comes, he will be the hero who resisted against great odds, and he will be able to fly at the last moment to the Soviet Union.

I have information from a number of reliable sources which indicates that Hodza and Krofta are much more inclined to make concessions to the Sudeten than Beneš.† Their view is that Czechoslovakia would be demolished by Germany and that, even if the allies of the Czechs should win the war, nobody would ever again be so silly as to put together Czechoslovakia in its present form. The most they could hope for would be a small Czech state. They are, moreover, inclined to believe, as most people in France are, that the war

* Eduard Beneš, President of Czechoslovakia, 1935–1938.
† Milan Hodza, Prime Minister of Czechoslovakia, 1935–1938. Kamil Krofta, foreign minister of Czechoslovakia, 1935–1938.

would inflict such suffering on all the civilian populations of Europe that communist revolutions would take place from one end of the Continent to the other. Neither Hodza nor Krofta is anxious to see his country a Czech Soviet Socialist Republic directed from Moscow.

This letter will, I am sure, seem to you unduly pessimistic. I can assure you that it gives a faithful picture of opinion and atmosphere here. I know no informed Frenchman who does not feel that he is living in the last days of his civilization which is so lovely and which he loves so much.

The only cheery bit of news I have to communicate concerns your new Ambassadress to Belgium.* She has taken a large house in Paris, ostensibly for one of her daughters, and is having it done over for her own occupancy. One of the boys who has just been yachting with her and her consort in the Black Sea came to Paris yesterday and informed me that she had said to him that she knew she would be bored by Brussels, so she had decided to spend *all* her time in Paris! War will, at least, save me from that. I don't know what else will, unless you tell the lady and gentleman that the Belgians will *expect* them to stay in Belgium, and that you will too.

I had Ickes and his little wife and Frances Perkins at dinner two nights ago. Mrs. Ickes is charming. How Ickes accomplished that is beyond me. I took the Ickeses from the door of their plane to my house in the country and then put them in a small hotel, so that they haven't been found by the reporters and have had a happy time. Frances Perkins seemed well and lively and I kept her smothered in orchids the day she was here.

If I cable you that the Germans are about to cross the Czech frontier, I hope that you will issue an immediate appeal to the British, French and Germans to meet at once at The Hague with a representative of the United States. You might be able to get a settlement on the basis of autonomy for the various minorities in Czechoslovakia, plus neutralization of Czechoslovakia and a guarantee of Czechoslovakia as an independent state by England, France and Germany. That might be the beginning of something like peace in Europe. At any rate, I can think of nothing else that you could do that would have the slightest chance of success, and we should not wash our hands by a pious and futile gesture.

* The Ambassadress to Belgium was Mrs. Joseph E. Davies, wife of the former Ambassador in Moscow.

I wish you could be here with me tonight. This place is so beautiful that you would forget even your stamps for an evening.

Blessings!

Yours affectionately,

Bill

THE WHITE HOUSE

WASHINGTON

June 25, 1938

Dear Bill:

Ever so many thanks for yours of the thirteenth. May God in His infinite wisdom prove that you are wrong. I know you share this hope with me.

All well but terribly rushed cleaning up.

As ever yours,

FDR

Honorable William C. Bullitt
American Embassy
Paris, France

The Polish Ambassador to France, Juliusz Lukasiewicz, was making every effort to prevent a conflict and was in close touch with Bullitt. Poland, however, was raising the question of the Polish minority in Czechoslovakia and felt that if the German minority there were given satisfaction the long-standing problem of the Polish minority would have to be dealt with. In a report of May 27, 1938, Lukasiewicz states: "Ambassador Bullitt told me that M. Bonnet had said in a talk with him that he did not entertain the thought that the United States might support the British and French *démarche* in Berlin, to which Ambassador Bullitt replied that he was definitely right. This confirms how little M. Bonnet needs to assert that a particular state is on the side of France." [3]

My own impression of Bonnet, after my first meeting him, was to ask Bill: "Do you have any confidence in what he says to you?" I felt immediately that he was using the most obvious flattery in talking to Bill, and only saying what he thought would ingratiate himself with Americans.

Lukasiewicz had been Ambassador in Moscow at the same time

as Bullitt and went to Paris in 1936, so that the two men had parallel careers for seven years, and were close friends. Lukasiewicz twice went to Washington as the representative of the Polish government-in-exile and Bullitt was able to introduce him to many American diplomatic and political figures. On the very first meeting one was attracted to Lukasiewicz. Handsome, a man of great charm and sincerity, he became a warm friend of Bullitt's. The friendship lasted until Lukasiewicz's tragic death in Washington in 1951. For ten years in poor health, without financial resources and no official position, he had continued the struggle for Polish independence.

During the summer of 1938 there were two visitors who spent some time at the Embassy, Joseph P. Kennedy, Jr., and John F. Kennedy, sent to Paris by their father, Joseph P. Kennedy, American Ambassador in London, to learn French. They spent about a week in Bullitt's house on the Avenue d'Iéna and then moved into an apartment that Mr. Offie had on the Rue de Rivoli. Of this trip by the future President and his brother, Mr. Offie says: "As I recall, they arrived in late June and stayed until the Munich crisis. They did not learn much French but they had a good time because we got them invited to various parties in the diplomatic corps where they could meet young ladies and it was there they formed some friendships which lasted as long as they lived. No one took them very seriously but just by being around the Embassy for a time each day they sat in with various officers of the Embassy and thereby learned a lot of what was going on. I remember Jack sitting in my office and listening to telegrams being read or even reading various things which actually were none of his business but since he was who he was we didn't throw him out."

Dear Mr. Ambassador:

Flew over yesterday from London. The Biddles are all you said they were, they couldn't be nicer. I wanted to write and to thank you for the wonderful time I had in Paris. You were awfully kind to put me up and that month ranks as just about the best I've ever put in. Offie sent over that letter of introduction to Franklin Gunther in Bucharest. Thanks a lot. Expect to stay here a few days then on to Russia. I hope I get a chance to get over to Paris at the end of this trip. Hope you're feeling better — I'm once more on my diet of red meat and red wine as Mrs. Biddle is another disciple, so am rapidly getting back into condition.

Best regards.
Jack Kennedy

[Handwritten.]

*Personal and Confidential*Paris

June 21, 1938

Dear Mr. President:

This is a very private letter which requires no answer.

Some days ago I received a telegram from Mrs. Roosevelt inform- ing me that Hall [Mrs. Roosevelt's brother] was coming to Paris and asking me to do anything I could for him.

This morning at 10 o'clock Bonnet told me that the Spanish Am- bassador had informed him that the Spanish Government could buy more than one hundred planes in the United States at once for im- mediate delivery to Spain via France and had berated him for agree- ing to the closing of the French frontier to military shipments. Bonnet added that the Spanish Ambassador had asserted that you personally had approved the sale of these planes to the Spanish Gov- ernment and that you were arranging for the evasion of the Neutral- ity Act involved in their shipment to France, knowing fully that their destination would be Spain. I expressed my skepticism to Bon- net and telegraphed the Department for immediate instructions, leaving out of my telegram, for obvious reasons, any indication that the Spanish Ambassador had alleged that you personally had ap- proved this deal. (See my telegram No. 970, June 21, 12 Noon.)

Shortly after I had sent this telegram, Hall telephoned to me, whereupon I invited him and his son to a ball. He said he wanted to talk to me at once. I asked him to come to the office this after- noon.

When Hall came in at 4:15 this afternoon, he said that he, acting through Harold Talbott of Cleveland, had managed to gather for the Spanish Government approximately 150 new and second-hand planes of various makes — all of which he specified. He said that he had discussed this transaction with you and that it had your entire approval. He stated that you and he and Jimmy had discussed all the details and that you had agreed to wink at the evasion of the Neutrality Act involved, because of your interest in maintaining the resistance of the Spanish Government against Franco, and on Monday, June 13th, had sent for Joseph Green, who is in charge of such matters in the Department of State, and had ordered him to permit the export of these planes and to accept such falsified papers as might be presented and not scrutinize the entire matter too carefully.

I expressed no opinion whatsoever to Hall with regard to these statements; but informed him that my instructions from the Department indicated that the policy of our Government was to oppose absolutely the giving of licenses for shipments of planes to Spain via France, and that I had had no intimation of any change in this policy. He replied that you had thought of writing to me; but that since he would arrive in Paris as quickly as a letter you had preferred to have him explain the matter to me by word of mouth.

I informed Hall also that the French Government had closed the frontier to Spain absolutely; that the French Government had a real hope that the volunteers might be withdrawn at last from both sides in Spain and that the British were pushing for an armistice pending the withdrawal of volunteers. I told him that I could not imagine a moment more unpropitious for an attempt to organize the shipment of planes to Spain in contravention of the wishes of the British and French Governments and our own Neutrality Act.

I also told Hall about the conversation I had had this morning with Bonnet (omitting mention of your name) and the telegram I had sent to the Department asking for instructions. He said he would come in to see me tomorrow morning and that he would telephone to Jimmy with great discretion this afternoon and say that the situation seemed to have changed since he had left America.

Shortly after Hall had left me, I received a reply to my telegram No. 970, June 21, 12 Noon, in two forms: First, a telephone call from Green, saying that there had been no change whatsoever in the opposition of our Government to the shipment of planes to Spain via France; that our Government was fully aware of the attempt that certain people were making to ship a large number of second-hand planes to Spain, and had definitely decided to refuse export licenses for the shipment of such planes. Later I received a telegram from the Department signed Welles, Acting, which confirmed Green's statements.

Tomorrow morning I shall show Hall the telegram signed by Welles.

I have not the slightest desire to know what lies behind this expedition of Hall's, and I am writing this letter for your own eye and no one else's, merely because I feel that since your name has been used by the Spanish Government in its conversations with the French Government, you ought to have a full account of the facts.

Good luck and every good wish.

Yours always,
Bill

On June 22 Charles A. Lindbergh arrived at the Hotel Crillon in Paris next door to the Embassy and called on Bullitt the following morning. He found the aviation in France in much worse shape than he had supposed and thought there were not enough military planes even to put up a show in case of war. His comment was, "Germany has developed a huge Air Force while England slept and France has deluded herself with a Russian alliance." [4] In September, Lindbergh, again in Paris, went out to dine at Chantilly with Bullitt and La Chambre, and expressed the opinion, after their conversation, that the French situation was desperate and that La Chambre apparently thoroughly understood the seriousness of their plight.[5] Bullitt now brought Jean Monnet in touch with Lindbergh and they all met at lunch with La Chambre to discuss means of buying aircraft in America and creating new factories. Lindbergh thought: "It would be better not to spend great sums in buying aircraft in America but to use the money in France in an attempt to bring back life to a corrupt and demoralized nation." [6] He went on to dine with Monnet and spent the night in the bedroom in the Ambassador's house, which he occupied in 1927 after his flight in the *Spirit of St. Louis*.[7] Conversations continued in the following days and Lindbergh agreed to consider plans for building factories in Canada. Such plants would not be subject to the Neutrality Act.

Personal and Confidential   Paris
                                                      July 19, 1938

Dear Judge Moore:

. . . I am not able to spend as much time as I should like with Anne because of the pressure here, which is almost unendurable during this season of summer tourists and official functions, but we do lots of things together. For example, she went with me when I was made an honorary citizen of Reims, and to see Howard Hughes and his companions take off for Moscow.

I am living at Chantilly altogether and only open the town house when I have to give some sort of official dinner or other function. The ball for the four hundred youngsters from Annapolis was really jolly. From every corner of Paris I have heard applause for the discipline, to say nothing of the good looks of the boys.

I don't like the general situation in Europe at all. I have reported so fully to the Department by telegram that I can add little information; but between ourselves, if I were betting, I should consider that the odds were sixty against and forty in favor of general war this year. I don't believe that Hitler will make war in cold blood without the stimulus of some sort of a bloody incident in the Sudeten regions. But I feel sure that the Sudeten will regard the concessions that the Czechs will offer as grossly inadequate, and I fear greatly that the Sudeten will start some sort of physical action which the Czechs will feel that they have to put down by force. If a considerable number of Sudeten should be killed, I think Hitler would march in. He might take over the whole of Czechoslovakia at once — and he could occupy the whole country within three weeks at the outside — or he might just occupy the Sudeten regions and then offer peace.

To say that peace is at the mercy of an incident was never more true than today, and the question of whether the incident will come or not is on the knees of the gods. As a result, I don't expect to leave Paris at all this summer, except perhaps for a two-day visit to John Cudahy in Dublin.

The purpose of that visit will appeal to you as a good Virginian. Mr. William Nelson Cromwell has offered to give Anne a really good riding horse and Cudahy has discovered one that he thinks she will like. So we are planning to fly to Dublin about the 29th or 30th of this month to look at horses. This trip will undoubtedly be filled with diplomatic significance but I can assure you that it has no meaning aside from the oat bin.

From this side of the ocean the economic improvement at home looks real, and my guess is that if it should continue the elections in November would turn out well. What is your opinion? Please write to me.

I really miss you and miss your letters.

Every possible good wish to you and to all the family.

Yours affectionately,

Bill

Bill's trip to Ireland was widely publicized in the local papers. He had been a friend of long standing of Eamon De Valera, the leader of Southern Ireland. It is difficult for most of us to realize the aura that surrounded an American Ambassador, with every nation wanting our country's assistance. Flattery, pomp, and special privileges were commonplace in his treatment by other governments. We had a taste of it. My wife and I, her mother, and two of our children motored in Ireland shortly after Bill's visit. When we arrived at a hotel the manager would meet us and show us to his best rooms and the following morning we would receive a visit from the American consul. I told our chauffeur that we did not like such attentions and did he know why it happened. "Sure and I just telephone ahead and tell them you are your brother." There was no more telephoning, but we did use the subterfuge once. We wanted to drive the children in the country in a pony cart but could not find one. Our chauffeur scoured the countryside and came back one day to say he could get us a pony if I would be my brother. We could not miss the opportunity, so for one afternoon I was the American Ambassador to France.

Strictly Confidential   Paris
                                                       August 8, 1938
Dear Mr. President:
    From a multitude of reliable sources, I have been informed during the past two months that the Chinese will be at the end of their financial resources by the first of next January, unless they can obtain credits abroad. Chiang Kai-shek's will to fight and the courage of the Chinese people remain unbroken; but there will be just no money to buy anything. I have had this information in a series of messages from Chiang Kai-shek, T. V. Soong, and Doctor Kung transmitted to me by the Chinese Ambassador here, and I have had the same information from a horde of detached observers.
    As you will recall, some months ago Bonnet said to me that he hoped it might be possible for the United States to extend some sort of credit or loan to China and that he was certain that if we should be willing to act, both France and Great Britain would act simultaneously though not jointly. Two days ago, Bonnet reiterated this to me. He added that he was certain that either England, France, or the United States could give credits to China without provoking any

serious Japanese reaction. The Japanese were too involved in China and were too fearful of Russian attack to dare to act against either England, France, or the United States.

This reasoning seems to me sound. I believe we should, however, avoid putting ourselves out on any long limb. I do not think we should sell the Chinese arms or munitions on credit, but I believe we should give the Chinese Government a credit of one hundred million dollars for the purchase of flour and gray goods in the United States . . .

I have talked over this idea with Henry Morgenthau and find that he is entirely in accord with me. As you know, he suggested to the Chinese Ambassador in Paris that the Chinese Government should send K. P. Chen to Washington and I have just received information that Chen will reach Washington about the same time that Henry returns.

If you should approve of this proposal, I suggest that you should let me know in advance so that I could try to push Bonnet into making good his statements to me with regard to the readiness of the French Government to take simultaneous and similar action.

I have thought about this a lot and I feel certain that we ought to do it. I hope you will too.

Love and good luck.

Yours affectionately,
William C. Bullitt

Personal and Strictly Confidential   Paris

August 17, 1938

Dear Mr. President:

The French Government is now convinced that there will be another crisis during the first weeks of September. If it should appear that war is imminent, you will be urged to take all sorts of actions by all sorts of people. I have two suggestions to make — the objections to which will be as obvious to you as they are to me so that I need not detail them.

Fear of the United States is unquestionably a large factor in Hitler's hesitation to start a war. If, in September, Europe should again appear to be on the verge of war, a quiet conversation between you and the German Ambassador in the White House might have more effect in deterring Germany from acting against Czechoslovakia with armed force than all the public speeches you or anyone else could make. You would not have to say anything except recite a few facts.

Suppose you were to say that you hoped Germany was not about to place you in the same position in which President Wilson was placed in 1914. Suppose you should add that he must be as aware as you were that although public opinion in America before the commencement of the war in 1914 had been very favorable to Germany, public opinion in America was now most hostile to Germany; and that he must be as aware as you were that if war should begin between England and France on one side and Germany on the other, there was a possibility that the United States would be drawn in.

You might add that you would be glad if he would transmit what you had said to Hitler and bid him good-bye.

You would have done nothing except call his attention to certain facts which are public property and you would have committed yourself to nothing. I think the effect of such a conversation in Germany would be immense.

If events should go further and the mobilization stage should be reached or even hostilities commenced, I think you should propose at once a conference of the sort that I suggested to you before the crisis of last May 21st. You will recall that at that time I wrote that if the worst should come to the worst, you should make a public appeal for an immediate conference at The Hague of representatives of England, France, Germany, and Italy to find ways and means of settling the dispute between Czechoslovakia and Germany; adding that a representative of the United States would participate in the conference if the four Powers should desire.

I think you should not take either of these steps unless Runciman should fail and war appear to be imminent. I will let you know at once if I think that moment has come. Meanwhile, I should appreciate it if you would let me have a line to tell me whether or not you consider these ideas cockeyed and if you have any alternatives in mind.

Blessings.

Yours affectionately,
William C. Bullitt

Lord Runciman had been sent to Czechoslovakia early in August by Prime Minister Chamberlain to attempt to mediate between the Czech Government and Henlein, leader of the Sudeten movement. William L. Shirer commented that: "The Czechs knew perfectly well that Runciman had been sent by Chamberlain to pave the way for the handing over of the Sudetenland to Hitler. It was a shabby diplomatic trick." [8]

Runciman returned to England and recommended the transfer of predominantly German districts to Germany. Chamberlain was impressed that this surrender of Czech territory was the only means of stopping Hitler from war and the invasion of Czechoslovakia. All that was accomplished was a postponement of Hitler's invasion by seven months.

One evening when my wife and I were staying at Chantilly, Bill invited Léon Blum, former Prime Minister; Paul Reynaud, future Prime Minister and Minister of Finance at that time; and Yvon Delbos, former Foreign Minister; to dine. These men all had brilliant minds. We were particularly struck by the reasoning and philosophical approach to problems by Blum and the quick, keen, and analytical insight of Reynaud. What shocked us in the conversation, which was very frank and open, was the freedom with which they discussed France's unpreparedness for war. Three men were serving dinner and there was always one in the room. The talk turned to the lack of airplanes or any protection against attacks on Paris. Figures were given as to the number of French planes and antiaircraft artillery and I remember the statement by one of them that the Germans would be able to bomb Paris at will. After they had gone I told Bill of my surprise that they should talk so openly with others present. His reply was that his servants were carefully passed upon by the French Secret Service and could be depended on, and there was nothing that he could do about it. I still feel that within twenty-four hours the Germans were in full possession of all the figures that passed across the dinner table.

Another evening Georges Bonnet, the then Foreign Minister, and his assistant Jules Henry dined at Chantilly with us, and made a completely different impression. It was at this dinner that we first met M. and Mme. Guy La Chambre, he then being Minister of Air.

Lukasiewicz had this to say about Bonnet: "Cooperation with M. Bonnet is really extremely difficult at times; none of us diplomats are ever sure how to evaluate the information we get from him, how much truth there is in it, and how much is missing from it." Daladier told Lukasiewicz: "Bonnet is very difficult and I can not have full confidence in him either." [9]

Personal and Private   Paris

August 31, 1938

Dear Mr. President:

Before you get this letter Europe will probably be even closer to Hades than it is today, and it is close enough. As you know, the Germans have one million eight hundred thousand men mobilized. Hugh Wilson, who has just been here, informs me that under the new German system of "mobilization en-route," men join their regiments while those regiments are on their way to the frontiers. The time between Hitler's decision to make war and the firing of the first guns on the frontier will be, therefore, not more than eight hours.

If we intend to do anything at the last moment to try to stop the holocaust, we shall have an almost impossibly brief period in which to work. Hugh has promised to phone me instantly if he gets word that Hitler has made the decision. I shall phone you at once, and I hope that you will send for the German Ambassador immediately and talk to him in the manner I suggested in my letter of August 17, 1938.

Guy La Chambre, Minister for Air, explained to me last night the condition of the French frontier defenses. The Garde Mobile is now on the alert at all frontiers. In every village or hamlet close to the frontiers there is one house which has been soaked with concrete and filled with machine guns. It is expected that the Garde Mobile could hold up any surprise attack for forty minutes. At the end of 40 minutes, the first frontier guards would be in position and at the end of two hours the Maginot Line and all other defenses would be fully manned. Every road leading from every frontier is heavily mined and could be made unusable for a time.

Bonnet is inclined to believe that Germany will not risk war with France and England in the month of September, but many other Ministers believe that Hitler has already decided to strike in September.

My guess is that Hitler stands such a chance of drawing Hungary into the Nazi ranks before the first of January, 1939, that he will not make war in September. But the German mobilization has produced such excitement in Czechoslovakia that a false report may make the Czechs strike first and give the German Army an opportunity to strike back. If I were betting today, I should bet that there were fifty-five chances that there would not be war in September against forty-five that there would be.

If war should begin, the result would be such a devastation of Europe that it would make small difference which side should emerge the ostensible victor. I am more convinced than ever that we should attempt to stay out and be ready to reconstruct whatever pieces may be left of European civilization.

I remember that I promised you to be in Washington again by September 25th at the latest. I want to come home very much as I am extremely tired and need a holiday and want to see you all; but I do not see the slightest possibility of leaving Paris at the moment. If there should be a settlement of the Sudeten dispute I would jump on the first boat, and I have engaged passage on both the *Normandie* sailing September 21st, and the *Manhattan* sailing September 23rd. Anne must take one or the other to get back to school in time. If I feel it would not be a neglect of duty, I shall leave with her on one or the other; but the chances look black at the moment.

Love and good luck.

Yours affectionately,
Bill

Berchtesgaden

SEPTEMBER — OCTOBER 1938

Chamberlain Meets Hitler
French Partial Mobilization
Chamberlain Meets Hitler at Godesberg
British Fleet Mobilized
Munich Four-Power Agreement
French Airplane Weakness
Poles Occupy Part of Czechoslovakia
President Aids Airplane Production

BULLITT COMES BACK FREQUENTLY to the theme that America must stay out of the threatened war, and his constant assurances to the French Government that it can not expect the United States to send an army to Europe in case of war. The statements by the French statesmen bear out the fact that he continually warned them not to look to America. Bullitt was also constantly trying to bring about a better understanding and rapprochement between France and Germany in the thought that this was the only way in which Europe could live at peace.

Georges Bonnet, French Ambassador in Washington in 1936 and Minister of Foreign Affairs in 1938, wrote: "My ambassadorship in Washington and my conversations with President Roosevelt had apprised me that it would be vain to count on immediate military aid from the United States." [1] And also: "At the moment of the Munich crisis, Ambassador Bullitt told me that the United States could not sell us the airplanes which we had asked them for." [2]

On September 4, 1938, a ceremony was held at the Pointe de Grave, Bordeaux, where the first Americans had landed in World

War I. The French had erected a monument to commemorate this event and Bonnet wished to make the unveiling the occasion of an important speech by Bullitt, which would notify the world of the support of France by the United States. Bonnet gave an account of his efforts to have Bullitt make a speech assuring France of United States support but did not succeed in getting all that he wanted.[3] Bullitt consulted with Washington, which opposed any such statement. Bonnet kept insisting and by September 2 the most he was able to obtain was this paragraph in Bullitt's speech: "The people of the United States, like the people of France, ardently desire peace. We pray, as we hope, to remain at peace with each and every other nation. But, as I said on February 22, 1937, if war breaks out in Europe, no one can say or predict whether the United States would be drawn into such a war."[4] A few days later the President stated to the press that "Ambassador Bullitt's speech does not constitute a moral engagement on the part of the United States toward the democracies . . . To include the United States in an alliance [with] France–Great Britain against Hitler is an interpretation by the political analysts one hundred percent false."

Bonnet's comments on Bullitt at this time reflect the opinion of the government officials: "Full of spirit and imagination, pleasant and gay companion, he had rapidly conquered the city of Paris. At his Embassy he gave receptions and fetes which were among the most picturesque and pretentious of this pre-war era. He had profound confidence in the strength of the French Army. Therefore he found the defeat of 1940 a bitter disillusionment, because he loved our country and considered it somewhat as his second fatherland."[5]

This letter from Judge Moore indicates the care with which an Ambassador's speeches are edited by the State Department and refers to the speech made by Bullitt at Bordeaux.

August 31, 1938

Dear Bill:

. . . I read all of your cables and have frequently commented to friends that it would not be possible for anyone except you to have so many important contacts that enable you to furnish information and opinion of the highest value. I have read the speech you expect to make soon and hope very much that this Department will not advise any substantial changes in what you have written, but this is perhaps too much to expect. While I am dead against the idea of the United States becoming involved in war, on the other hand I am satisfied that we should be very frank and emphatic in stating our conception of the value of the democratic principle and the dangerous character of the attack on that principle expressed by the policies of the totalitarian nations. We do not intend to engage in forcible measures to support our theories but we are at least entitled to make very clear what those theories are and perhaps the constant reiteration of our attitude will have the same result as the constant dripping of water on a solid surface which is after a while worn away. You remember the Latin words that convey this idea . . .

Affectionately your friend,
R. Walton Moore

Conditions had now become so alarming that Chamberlain on his own initiative telegraphed Hitler stating his desire to have a personal conversation with him. Chamberlain arrived in Berchtesgaden on September 16 and was greeted with the news that the Germans in the Sudetenland had demanded that the area be annexed to Germany. This demand had evidently been arranged by Hitler to precede his talks with Chamberlain. The conference with Hitler lasted one day and Chamberlain immediately returned to London, where he recommended that districts largely populated by Germans in Czechoslovakia be turned over to Germany. The French and British governments forthwith notified the Czech Government that it should cede to Germany all districts where more than half the inhabitants were German. In connection with the French-British talks on this question Mr. Churchill said: "Many of us, even outside Cabinet circles, had the sensation that Bonnet represented the quintessence of defeatism, and that all his clever verbal maneuvres had the aim of 'peace at any price.' " [6]

On September 22 Chamberlain again went to meet Hitler, this time at Godesberg. On presenting to Hitler the Czech acceptance of Hitler's Berchtesgaden terms, Chamberlain was shocked to hear Hitler make further demands which were not negotiable and had a time limit of October 1. Chamberlain was finally convinced of Hitler's perfidy and warned him of its consequences. He returned to London on the twenty-fourth. Meanwhile the Czechs were mobilizing and had 1,500,000 men under arms. The French partly mobilized. On September 28 the British fleet mobilized.

Hitler again invited Chamberlain to meet him together with Daladier and Mussolini on the following day in Munich. The Czechs were not invited to attend but were in Munich to learn their fate. Hitler's continual and unceasing pressure on France and England was shown by the length of this one-day meeting. It began at noon and lasted until 2 A.M. of September 30, when the humiliating agreement accepting the Godesberg terms was signed. The feelings of Chamberlain and Daladier may be best understood by Chamberlain's return to England and his famous announcement: "This is the second time there has come back from Germany to Downing Street peace with honor. I believe it is peace in our time."

Daladier, on the other hand, showed apprehension of the hostile attitude that would greet his return to France. President Beneš, after receiving the terms, resigned on October 5.

Bullitt telegraphed home on October 3 that "Daladier sees the situation entirely, clearly, realizes fully that the meeting in Munich was an immense diplomatic defeat for France and England, and recognizes that unless France can recover a united national spirit to confront the future, a fatal situation will arise within a year."

Personal and Confidential Paris
September 20, 1938

Dear Mr. President:

I write you this while the Czech Government is considering what reply to make to the British-French proposal. It seems to me that the French and British Governments have mishandled the matter abominably. They have acted like little boys doing dirty things behind the barn.

You may be sure that I will come home as soon as I feel I can, as I am dead tired. Meanwhile the prospects for Europe are so foul that the further we keep out of the mess the better.

The moral is: If you have enough airplanes you don't have to go to Berchtesgaden.

Good luck.

Yours affectionately,

Bill

THE WHITE HOUSE
WASHINGTON

September 23, 1938

Bill Bullitt just telephoned the following which he thinks you should have during Cabinet meeting in order to telephone him back immediately.

He has just been informed by the British Ambassador that Chamberlain is having conversation with Hitler and is returning to London. The news is very bad. He and all of his party are returning by airplane tomorrow morning. It is the belief that this ends the negotiation but this is not certain. It is said that Hitler wishes his troops to occupy the Sudeten. Resistance and war will follow. It is also certain that the Polish troops will march at the same moment. That may happen tonight and it is now 9:15 here. It may happen after Chamberlain sees Hitler this evening. Bullitt believes that the subject you and he have talked and written about should not be delayed. It should be accompanied by a statement about no troops crossing frontiers.

Bullitt believes that this should be seen by you immediately in Cabinet meeting and asks you please to call back immediately. I have given Hack the telephone number.

[Unsigned memorandum to the President.]

During this crisis Bullitt was in constant communication with the President and the State Department by telephone. There were sometimes several calls in one day. What follows is a transcript of one of these calls, from Bullitt to the White House. The transcriber is identified only by the initial K.

THE WHITE HOUSE
WASHINGTON

9/23-4/50 P

Bullitt:

"This is what I wanted to say [to the President]:

"The British Ambassador has now communicated to me a telegram which he has just received from Chamberlain.

"This telegram shows that the situation is not so hopeless as it appeared to be from the communication that the British Ambassador here rec'd from the foreign office in London.

"It appears that there will *not* be an entry of German troops immediately into Czechoslovakia. The dispute is on the question of how soon those troops should enter and how far they should enter and on the withdrawal of Czech police from the Sudeten regions.

"Chamberlain will return to London tomorrow morning, arriving about Noon in London and he will have with him at that time written statements of Hitler with regard to exactly what he wants, with respect to the Questions I have just given you.

"The result is that the situation, as shown by this communication from Chamberlain, is not so desperate as the situation previously shown by the communication from the foreign office in London.

"Therefore please say to the President right away that I do not feel that, in the light of this latter communication direct from Chamberlain, war is likely to break out within the next 24 hours. I think there [is] still a breathing space and therefore feel that he still has time to consider things."

K

TELEGRAM RECEIVED

This telegram must be closely paraphrased before being communicated to anyone.

Secretary of State	Paris
Washington	Dated September 26, 1938
1601, September 26, 8 P.M.	Rec'd 5:30 P.M.

Strictly Confidential for the Secretary

I have just talked with Bonnet. He said that the conversations with the British had been most satisfactory. The French had taken the line that if German troops should cross the Czechoslovak border France would fulfill her obligations. The British had not attempted to combat this position and had indicated that they would support France immediately with their fleet and air force . . .

I asked if the French Ministers and the British Cabinet had agreed to make counterproposals to Hitler. Bonnet replied that a most peculiar thing had happened in this regard. Chamberlain had said to the French Ministers that he desired to send a personal communication to Hitler suggesting alterations in the demands contained in the note which Hitler had presented to him at Godesberg. He requested permission of the French Government to send this letter as a personal message to Hitler without revealing its contents to the French Ministers.

Bonnet asserted that he and Daladier had agreed to this procedure. Three times I returned to this point and each time Bonnet insisted that he had no knowledge whatsoever of the actual contents of the personal letter which Chamberlain had sent by the hand of Horace Wilson today to Hitler. He said that Chamberlain had felt that he had established a personal relationship with Hitler and it would be better for all concerned if he should continue to handle the matter on the basis of personal and confidential communications and the French Government had accepted blindly Chamberlain's leadership . . .

BULLITT

TELEGRAM RECEIVED

This telegram must be closely paraphrased before being communicated to anyone.

Secretary of State   Paris
Washington   Dated September 26, 1938
1602, September 26, 10 P.M.   Rec'd 9:10 P.M.
Secret and Strictly Confidential for the Secretary

Just after seeing Bonnet this evening I saw Daladier. If Bonnet was devious and weak Daladier was sure of himself and strong.

He said that he had been delighted by the President's message and hoped that the President had been pleased with his reply. Since I had spoken with the Undersecretary over the telephone I was able to assure him that the President had been most pleased by his answer.

Daladier went on to say that shortly after his arrival in London Chamberlain had said to him that he wished to speak to him alone without Bonnet or anyone else. Chamberlain had then read to him a personal letter which he had prepared to send to Hitler. This letter suggested that there should be a series of modifications in the demands in the note which Hitler had handed to him at Godesberg and had contained the statement that Hitler's demands were totally impossible of acceptance by the British Government. It had also contained assurances to Hitler that there would be no delay in handing over the Sudeten regions to Hitler.

In addition to this communication Chamberlain had sent a handwritten letter to Hitler. At this point Daladier hesitated and finally said, "I will show you this as a personal friend, not as an Ambassador." He then drew from his wallet a handwritten copy of Chamberlain's second letter to Hitler.

In this letter Chamberlain stated that he had just been informed by Daladier that if German troops should cross the frontier of Czechoslovakia the French Army would attack Germany at once. He was certain that this was true. He desired to state to Hitler that in case this should occur Great Britain would enter the war at once on the side of France with all her forces.

Daladier asked that the existence of this Note be kept as a complete secret and I trust that you will be careful to avoid any possible leakage.

Daladier commented that his impression of Chamberlain was that in spite of his being a cold and limited man when he shook hands with you and said he was with you, you could count on him.

Daladier went on to say that he did not know what Hitler would say in his speech tonight. If Hitler should order general German mobilization he would order general French mobilization at 10 o'clock this evening. If Hitler should send one soldier across the Czechoslovak frontier he would attack Germany at once. Hitler's latest note to Chamberlain had been an attempt not simply to achieve the aims of Germany in Czechoslovakia but also to humiliate England and France. To fight and die was better than to submit to such an humiliation.

People had doubted the spirit of France for the past few years. The spirit of France during the past few days had shown itself to be the same old spirit which had meant so much to the world. The war would be long and terrible but whatever the cost in the end France would win.

We then referred to the general position and especially that of Poland. Daladier said that he considered that Poland was playing the part of a vulture. I referred to the demands of Poland for a common undertaking with Hungary. Daladier said that so long as he was Prime Minister he would never assent to any such dismemberment of Czechoslovakia; and finally with a twinkle in his eye said that he hoped to live long enough to pay Poland for her cormorant attitude in the present crisis by proposing a new partition of Poland to Czechoslovakia.

In the course of the conversation a member of Daladier's cabinet, whose voice I recognized as that of Patenôtre, telephoned and referred to the activities of Malvy and others, attempting to prove that Daladier was trying to drive France into war. Daladier replied, "Please say to Malvy and the rest of his friends that I have only two sons who will go to the front at once when war breaks out. I am of course hoping to produce the butchery of French youth. I am hoping that war will begin at once as that will give me the opportunity to place him and his associates in a concentration camp where they will have outlet for their venom in breaking rocks" . . .

BULLITT

TELEGRAM RECEIVED

This message must be closely paraphrased before being communicated to anyone.

Secretary of State	Paris
Washington	Dated September 27, 1938
Rush	Rec'd 11:10 A.M.

1607, September 27, 1 P.M.
Strictly Confidential for the Secretary

Chautemps has just informed me that since the French Cabinet this morning had no knowledge of the nature of Hitler's reply to the messages from Chamberlain transmitted yesterday by Sir Horace Wilson it had been impossible to come to any definite conclusions as to what policy should be followed. Daladier and Bonnet had been instructed to maintain firmly the French point of view but to attempt to continue negotiations.

Bullitt

TELEGRAM RECEIVED

This message must be closely paraphrased before being communicated to anyone.

Secretary of State	Paris
Washington	Dated September 27, 1938
Rush	Rec'd 9:46 P.M.

1620, September 27, 11 P.M.
To the Secretary

In accordance with the instructions by telephone of the Undersecretary I called on Daladier this evening, the delay in my seeing him being due to the fact that he was asleep in bed when I received my instructions . . .

He said that some time ago Beneš had communicated to him that he would be ready to hand over at once to Germany those portions of the Sudeten regions lying outside the Czechoslovak Maginot Line. He had therefore suggested to Beneš this afternoon at 3 o'clock and the British had made the same suggestion at 6 or 7 o'clock that the Czechoslovak army should be withdrawn as far as the vital line of the Czechoslovak fortifications and that the German army should be permitted to enter that portion of the Sudeten regions which lie outside the Czech Maginot Line leaving a no man's land between the two armies. He had not yet heard from Beneš; but he believed that Beneš would accept this proposal tomorrow morning . . .

Daladier then said that he felt a conference composed of England, France, Germany, Poland and Czechoslovakia might really work out the basis for peace in Eastern Europe. His basic thought, however, was that Hitler at the present time would accept nothing except the absolute humiliation of every nation on earth. He desired by such humiliation to make his wish law in Europe. In spite of every effort that he and the President might make he believed that the chance today of preserving peace in the world was not more than one in a thousand. He went on to say that Hitler's present attitude was perhaps the greatest example of folly in modern history. Germany would be defeated in the war. France would win; but the only gainers would be the Bolsheviks as there would be social revolutions in every country of Europe and [the] Communist regimes. The prediction which Napoleon had made at St. Helena was about to come true: "Cossacks will rule Europe" . . .

Bullitt

DEPARTMENT OF STATE

Memorandum of Conversation Date: September 27, 1938
Subject: Telephone conversation 9:45 A.M.
Participants: Ambassador Bullitt; Under Secretary Welles

MR. BULLITT: Have you read Hitler's reply to the President? It was sent to you last night.
MR. WELLES: I have read it. Have you read it?
MR. BULLITT: Yes. It is, of course . . . ultimatum. Have you heard yet that Chamberlain is to speak tonight?
MR. WELLES: Yes.

MR. BULLITT: The time is getting shorter and shorter and therefore any action to be taken will have to be thought about with great speed. I am thinking of an alternative which I should like to suggest to you to get your reaction.

MR. WELLES: Please do.

MR. BULLITT: In the first place I believe that the French Government this afternoon will issue a statement on all points of Chamberlain's statement of last night in which he said that the British Government would guarantee that the Czechs would carry this out rapidly and fairly. There is also discussion going on here of an attempt to appoint an international commission at once. I doubt if this can be done today. It will possibly take until tomorrow. Meanwhile time presses. I have the following — that the President might very well reply to the Chancellor's note saying that he thanks him for his reply but everyone must recognize by this time that the conditions of peace laid down in 1919 did not produce happiness and tranquillity on the Continent. Many things have changed already and remain to be changed . . . The French and British Governments have promised to see they are handed over expeditiously and fairly. The Chancellor takes the position that this handing over can take place at only the time and in exactly the manner which he himself orders, of one man deciding what appears to plunge the entire continent into war. The President suggests that a conference should be held to settle this and correlated questions. He suggests that on the 29th there should meet representatives of England, France, Germany, Poland, Czechoslovakia and Hungary. I have thought very carefully about this. Italy is left out, Russia is left out.

MR. WELLES: Give me the list again.

MR. BULLITT: France, England, Germany, Poland, Czechoslovakia and Hungary and a representative of the United States, if these powers so desire, will also be present. We suggest such a meeting at The Hague on the 29th. Such a meeting would mean that no troops would cross the border. We should be very glad to receive the Chancellor's reply if such a conference would be acceptable to him. He would immediately get great pressure from Poland and Hungary to accept it which would put him in a bad spot. Have you received all the telegrams sent last night?

MR. WELLES: I have read them all very carefully. The second one is extraordinarily interesting.

MR. BULLITT: Daladier is perfectly magnificent. I am sending a telegram almost at once incorporating these ideas. I have just formu-

lated them because I have just seen and been able to digest Hitler's
message. I don't know whether this line of thought appeals to you.
The only other line for the President would be to deliver in his
reply to Hitler a terrific statement of what the consequences will be
and where the responsibility will lie. I do not think this would be
desirable. It would drive Hitler into immediate action.

MR. WELLES: I think it is out of the question. It is not constructive.
More than that it puts this Government definitely in a position of
partiality which we don't want to take.

MR. BULLITT: At the time the President considers appealing for a
conference he might send for the German Ambassador and say to
the Ambassador some very simple things, cite some facts well known
to him — Germany's popularity in the United States in 1914, their
popularity at [the] moment well known to him, firmly trusts that
Herr Hitler will not place him in the same position that Woodrow
Wilson was placed in and with circumstances much more difficult
today than they were at that time. I think a simple statement like
that to the German Ambassador might have a very great effect. Any
further conversation I think might suggest a modification of the
Neutrality Act.

MR. WELLES: That cannot be undertaken at this moment. I am convinced of that. If you were here you would agree with me. Your
first suggestion is in entire accord with my own inclination. I will
take them up at once. I haven't seen the Secretary this morning. I
will see the President in the next hour. I will take this up with him
and see where we get.

MR. BULLITT: He may wish to wait for Chamberlain's statement tonight at eight o'clock. I think this is the only line of action which
gives a further chance for peace. If Chamberlain speaks at eight
o'clock tonight here — that will be three o'clock in the afternoon
with you — there will be plenty of time tonight after that to decide
and get something out.

MR. WELLES: If anything is to be done it will have to be done in
[the] next twenty-four hours.

MR. BULLITT: It will also have to ask representatives of those six
powers to be present on the morning of the 29th of September.
Acceptance of this conference would of course mean that troops
wouldn't cross the frontier. I have talked with Kennedy in London
and there they are thinking about nothing except how fast they can
get ready for war. He hasn't been able to see anyone of importance.

MR. WELLES: The only two people mentioned in his cable were

Oliver Stanley and someone else — no one of importance.

MR. BULLITT: Here there is still some slight hope that by pushing this matter of a statement to guarantee to Hitler . . . I doubt very much if it will be effective. I believe the chances are about ninety-five in a hundred of war beginning midnight Friday. I should appreciate it if you will call me back giving some inkling of the way your thoughts are running.

MR. WELLES: I will naturally call you back.

MR. BULLITT: Thank you very much.

On September 24 Bullitt telegraphed Secretary Hull and suggested an appeal by the President to the British, French, Italian, German, and Polish chiefs of state to send representatives to The Hague. He said that the United States should also be willing to go. Mr. Hull did not entirely agree with this but, "The President, however, believed with Bullitt that something should be done, even if it were not successful." [7] On the twenty-fifth Bullitt telephoned the State Department and reported Bonnet's suggestion that the President should offer to arbitrate. Neither the President nor Secretary Hull would accept this proposal.

On the morning of the twenty-sixth Roosevelt wired a request to the European governments that they continue negotiations. England, France, and Czechoslovakia accepted immediately and Hitler's negative reply arrived that night. Bullitt again cabled Hull urging a general conference and on September 27 Roosevelt cabled Hitler suggesting an immediate conference in some neutral spot in Europe. Hitler was not amenable.

Secret and Personal   Paris
                                            September 28, 1938
Dear Mr. President:

The enclosed telegram I was about to send to you when the news came that Hitler had invited Chamberlain, Daladier, and Mussolini to meet him in Munich tomorrow at two o'clock. Inasmuch as the message contains military secrets of the highest importance, I felt that it was desirable, in view of the change in the situation, to send it to you by mail rather than by telegraph. Please keep it for your *most private eye,* and please give me an immediate reply — I mean *immediate* — to the question with regard to how far it might be possible to export parts of planes and motors and machine tools from the United States to Canada in time of war.

It is just as vital to have this information immediately now as it was when it seemed that war was certain; because it remains vital for France to start building planes on this scale at once. Unless France and England can manufacture in this way and on this scale, the time will soon come again when Hitler will issue a ukase, and make war when it is not obeyed by France and England.

I am so relieved this evening that I feel like embracing everyone and wish I were in the White House to give you a large kiss on your bald spot.

Love, good luck, and hurrah.

Bill

Secstate
Washington
Rush — September 28, 3 P.M.

The following message is to be decoded by Mr. Salmon or the Acting Chief of the Code Room and carried to the President by him, and no copy made under any circumstances.

Secret and Personal for the President

Guy La Chambre, Minister for Air, has just given me the actual figures on the aviation situation.

If war should begin on the first of October, the French would have six hundred battle planes. This includes pursuit planes and bombers.

The British have agreed to send to France to support the French Army one hundred and twenty light bombing planes at the end of the first week, and one hundred and twenty more at the end of four weeks.

To the certain knowledge of the French Military Intelligence, the Germans have ready for battle at this moment six thousand five hundred planes of the very latest types. The division of these planes is believed to be two-thirds bombers and one-third pursuit planes.

The Italians have of the very latest types eight hundred pursuit planes and twelve hundred bombers. Both the Germans and Italians have large quantities of planes, not of the latest types.

The Soviet Government was asked recently by the French Government if Soviet planes could fly to France in case of need. The reply was that no Soviet plane had sufficient radius of action to fly to France.

The Minister for Air said that it was certain that the German planes would be able to bomb Paris at will. The French pursuit planes were so insufficient in numbers that they would all have to be assigned to protecting the observation planes of the Army. There would be no planes for the defense of Paris.

Anti-aircraft artillery was also most inadequate in quantity. There would be a certain amount of anti-aircraft artillery available for the defense of Paris but almost none for the defense of other points and none to protect French troop concentrations.

The Minister for Air felt certain that the destruction in Paris would pass all imagination. He said that he had sent his wife and child to Brittany already, and he believed that every woman and child who could leave Paris should do so at once and every man who had no urgent reason to be here should do likewise.

The Minister for Air went on to say that there was no protection whatsoever against the large-sized German bombs except a shelter covered by at least fifteen feet of reinforced concrete. It was obviously impossible to create many such shelters. There were, however, comparatively few German or Italian bombing planes which could carry bombs of the largest size. Most of the German bombing, he expected to be done with small incendiary bombs weighing about twenty pounds. It would, therefore, be useful to have plenty of sand in houses since these bombs could be put out by two shovelfuls of sand but an unconquerable fire would result if water was spread on them.

The Minister for Air went on to say that the safest place for the next two years in France would be a trench provided one was equipped with a gas mask; that we should provide ourselves with gas masks immediately and we should dig trenches in whatever gardens might be available. A trench would be a sufficient protection except in case of a direct hit and in case of a direct hit, there would be no protection. He advised me urgently to have American women and children sent out of Paris at the earliest possible moment.

I have accordingly today given instructions to Murphy to inform each member of the staff personally and quietly that I believe he should send his wife and children out of Paris at the earliest possible moment.

The Minister for Air went on to say that the estimates of the General Staff of the French Air Force were that, at the end of a month under the present circumstances, France could not have more than three hundred planes and that if good weather should continue for very long, a time might come when the number of French planes would be altogether negligible.

He felt personally that the General Staff of the Army was underestimating the importance of the air factor and he thought that it would be most dangerous to add another frontier by an attack on Spain, even though this frontier might be in existence for only a brief period because Franco had many planes.

We then discussed at length the problem of producing a sufficient number of planes to overcome German and Italian superiority in the air. The Minister for Air was of the opinion that such planes could only be produced on the continent of North America and by American manufacturers. Since the Neutrality Act would prevent the manufacture of such planes in the United States, he proposed at once to attempt to build huge factories for planes in Canada, possibly just opposite Detroit and Buffalo, so that American workmen living at home could be utilized readily. He asked me for suggestions as to the persons to take in hand this immense program of plane construction on the success or failure of which, in his opinion, the outcome of the war would depend. He added that it was, of course, vital that it should be possible to ship machine tools and plane parts and instruments from the United States to these Canadian factories.

La Chambre asked me if I could obtain in strictest confidence information for him if and to what extent it might be possible to export parts of planes and motors and machine tools from the United States to Canada without violating the Neutrality Act.

I believe that we should go to the extreme limit compatible with a reasonable interpretation of the law to permit such exports to Canada.

Will you please have someone study this question with the idea in mind that it may affect the whole future of freedom in the world.

Please give me an answer on this point at the earliest possible moment as no plans can be carried further until La Chambre knows the answer to this question.

La Chambre continued our discussion by asking me for my opinion as to the men best qualified to organize this effort on behalf of France. I suggested Jean Monnet (not repeat not Monick) who, as you know, has been an intimate friend of mine for many years, whom I trust as a brother. Monnet organized and directed the Inter-Allied Maritime Transport Council; the wheat and shipping pool and all the vast other Inter-allied organizations during the war when he was only a man of twenty-eight. He then became Under Secretary of the League of Nations and for many years has been engaged in private business.

Guy La Chambre was pleased by this idea and I suggested that Lindbergh, who is an intimate friend of Monnet's, should be associated with Monnet in this work. I suggested further that a French airplane constructor or expert should be added to Monnet and Lindbergh with Monnet as absolute boss. La Chambre was pleased by this idea and asked me to get in touch with Monnet and Lindbergh at once.

La Chambre also said that he had an option on one hundred more P-36s for delivery next spring and asked me if I thought he should exercise it in view of the terms of the Neutrality Act. I told him that I could make no predictions as to what would happen to the Neutrality Act, but I advised him to take his chance and put in the order.

I realize that at the present moment it may be impossible to modify the Neutrality Act in any way; but my personal feeling is that the horror and hatred evoked by German bombings will be so great that the people of the United States by next spring will not feel inclined to prevent planes purchased before the outbreak of war from being sent to defend whatever may be left of France from further German bombings.

I realize how carefully it is necessary to tread in this matter, but my personal feeling is that if war should break out this week, we should at the earliest possible moment permit the French and British to purchase for cash in our ports and carry in their own ships as many planes, munitions, and guns as they have money to pay for.

I thank you for your personal message which I received this morning. I was a great deal prouder of you today. Your second telegram to Hitler was a masterpiece. Congratulations and love to you all.

Bullitt

Dr. Eduard Beneš, President of Czechoslovakia, gave a different picture of Bullitt at this time. He said: "The United States Ambassador in Paris, William Bullitt, did not at first express himself publicly in favor of appeasement like Joseph Kennedy, but he worked for it incessantly. His attitude towards us during the crisis of September 1938 was wholly negative. He did not hide this. Daladier clearly hinted on many occasions that his policy of appeasement had the support of the American Ambassador and therefore also of the United States. *Bullitt himself did all he could to prevent a new great war.* He made it clear though with reservations (thus providing himself with an alibi) that in his view Prague was not behaving with sufficient circumspection towards the German minority and that President Beneš was a dyed-in-the-wool anti-German chauvinist whose policy was endangering European peace.

"Bullitt's own policy at that time was mainly dictated by his dislike — his personal dislike — of the Soviet Union which he acquired while he was Ambassador in Moscow." [8]

Having seen what success Hitler had with his threats, it was now Poland's turn to seek a piece of the spoils. Early in October, after the terms of the Munich agreement were known and the Czech Government had resigned, the Poles, in spite of the plebiscites called for at Munich, gave the Czechs twenty-four hours in which to turn over to them the district of Teschen. Teschen bordered on Poland and they claimed that its population was largely Polish. There was now no way that Czechoslovakia could resist this demand, as they already had a bitter taste of the lack of help which they could expect from their ally, France, or from Britain.

It was next the turn of Hungary to make a claim for part of Czechoslovakia, and it was not long in acting. By November 2, after meetings in Vienna, Hungary had obtained southern Slovakia and part of Ruthenia from hapless Czechoslovakia. It had been a sordid display of timidity on the part of the great powers, and a particularly disgraceful act by France, who had been Czechoslovakia's friend and ally and had a treaty to come to her aid if she were attacked by Germany.

In November of 1938 Hitler began a new and systematic persecution of the Jews. Roosevelt had worried about this problem for some time and in September he ordered four of his Ambassadors to meet in Paris to try to find a means whereby the condition of the Jews in Germany could be alleviated and a way for the United States to be of assistance to them. On September 28, Ambassadors Joseph P. Kennedy from London, Hugh R. Wilson from Berlin, and Myron C. Taylor, future Ambassador to the Vatican, all met at Bullitt's house in Paris at dinner. A discussion took place late into the night, but few suggestions of a practical nature could be developed.

Bullitt returned to America in October 1938, and immediately reported at the White House on October 13. There is no direct record of his talk with Roosevelt, but it was publicly mentioned by more than one writer. A report on the *The United States Army in World War II,* published by the War Department, says: "The first evidence of acute White House concern over the mounting powers of the Axis as a substantial threat to the security of the United States . . . reached the War Department after the return to Washington on 13 October 1938 of William C. Bullitt, then U.S. Ambassador to France. On the following day, Mr. Roosevelt announced that, after having sat up late the night before to hear the report from Ambassador Bullitt, he could not comment on current budget planning because new world conditions had compelled him and his assistants to re-check defense preparedness carefully . . . Through Mr. Bullitt's recital of French fears and desires, duplicated to a degree by reports of similar anxieties in Great Britain, President Roosevelt became convinced for the first time that American airplane production should be greatly stimulated with all possible speed.

". . . within a week of the Bullitt report to Mr. Roosevelt there was marked activity in planning." [9]

Bullitt also persuaded the President to accept Daladier's proposal of a French mission, headed by Jean Monnet, coming to America to endeavor to enlist the services of the American aviation industry in aid to France.

On October 16 Bullitt went to Hyde Park with the President and others, where the topic was the increase of aircraft production and the sale of airplanes to Britain and France. Henry Morgenthau, Jr., Secretary of the Treasury, opposed the sale to France on the basis that it would weaken the French foreign exchange position. Foreign exchange must have appeared to them as of little importance with the immediate threat of war. Jean Monnet arrived on October 18 and the President immediately discussed with him the building of aviation plants in Canada. This would be necessary, as the Neutrality Act, in case of war, would only have allowed the United States to provide basic materials and not finished products. The British had sent Arthur C. Murray, later Lord Elibank, to Hyde Park, but Chamberlain showed little interest in such plans. Monnet vigorously followed up Roosevelt's suggestion and returned promptly to France to report to Daladier.[10]

In November Bullitt went to Cuba for a month's holiday and after spending some time in Washington returned to France in January 1939.

Historian John Haight has a vivid account of part of Bullitt's activity in Washington in January 1939: "Following this staff conference (in Secretary of the Treasury Morgenthau's office), Morgenthau proceeded to the White House for a meeting with Woodring, Arnold, Louis Johnson, Charles Edison, Admiral Peoples, Collins and Kraus. Ambassador Bullitt sat at the President's side. Roosevelt reiterated his wish that every effort be made to assist France. Bullitt spoke of time running out and repeated the President's wish. He specifically called for release of the Douglas bomber. Secretary Woodring replied that the plane included many secret elements and was constructed partially at the cost of the government. The President retorted that he was determined to have the Douglas plane released. It was a tense meeting and Roosevelt had his dander up.

"When the conference broke up, Secretary Morgenthau, referring to Roosevelt's verbal order to release the plane, said, 'Mr. President, I want this in writing.' Then, with the help of his assistants, Morgenthau drafted letters to the Secretaries of War, the Navy and the Treasury, in which he wrote, 'you are directed,' and implied they had a choice between compliance and resignation. When the White House returned the letters unsigned, however, Ambassador Bullitt used his influence and within three days the letters were signed and forwarded." [11]

The Fatal Year — The Need for Planes

JANUARY 1939—MARCH 1939

French-Italian Relations
Airplane Problems
French Offer United States Island Possessions
Germans Occupy Prague
Polish Problems
A King's Visit

BULLITT RETURNED TO PARIS in January 1939 and one of his first appointments was with the Polish Ambassador, Lukasiewicz, who reported to his government: "Bullitt said, 'Should war break out, likely we shall not take part in it at the beginning, but we shall finish it.'" Further: "Ambassador Bullitt, while stating the rumor according to which President Roosevelt was to have stated that 'the frontier of the United States lies in France' was false, expressed the conviction that the President might certainly have said that he sold airplanes to France because the French Army was the first line of defense of the United States, this being in complete accord with the President's view . . .[1] Ambassador Bullitt is of the opinion that pressure exerted by the United States simultaneously on Italy and Germany on the one side and England on the other could contribute considerably toward preventing the outbreak of an armed conflict . . . I must add that Ambassador Bullitt seems to be completely sure of France's unconditional resistance to Italian demands and that he consequently excludes any possibility of British or British-German mediation with the object of finding a compromise at the expense of France."[2]

Mr. Chamberlain was still following his policy of personal, face-to-face diplomacy and in January went to Italy to talk with Mussolini. Count Galeazzo Ciano, Mussolini's son-in-law and Foreign Minister of Italy, has a revealing account of this meeting in his diary: "How far apart we are from these people! It is another world . . . 'These men,' said Mussolini, 'are not made of the same stuff as Francis Drake and the other magnificent adventurers who created the Empire. They are after all the tired sons of a long line of rich men.' The British do not want to fight. They try to draw back as slowly as possible, but they do not want to fight . . . Nothing was accomplished." [3]

Later Chamberlain took the demeaning step of submitting to Mussolini for approval a speech he was to make in the House of Commons.

The occupation of Czechoslovakia by German troops on March 15, 1939, Hitler's triumphant entry into Prague, and his proclamation of a German Protectorate was a complete surprise to the British and the deed that finally opened Chamberlain's eyes to the imminent danger. Although England had given a guarantee to Czechoslovakia, she took no action.

Hitler had not only flaunted the Munich agreement made six months previously but had also violated his personal word. He had told Chamberlain, "This is the last territorial claim which I have to make in Europe," and, "I shall not be interested in the Czech State anymore, and I can guarantee it. We do not want any Czechs anymore." [4]

Thus fell, without a shot being fired, one of the strongest armies on the continent in the defense of freedom. Not only did Czechoslovakia have over thirty mobilized divisions, but the great Skoda works was one of the finest armament factories in the world. All of this became Hitler's, and among the most amazed groups were his own generals.

Personal and Confidential   Paris
                                                    February 1, 1939

Dear Mr. President:

Here are the latest figures on plane production of the French Secret Service. The French managed to produce in the month of December ninety-four planes. The British produced between two hundred and fifty and three hundred. In addition, the British produced about one hundred training planes. La Chambre states that the French production is now rising steadily and that it will reach two hundred per month in June, and two hundred and fifty next July. By the end of the year, he expects it to be about four hundred per month.

La Chambre said that the latest information brought in by the French Secret Service indicates that although the Germans produced about one thousand planes a month in September and October last, they were unable to keep up this tempo, and in November and December produced only between six and seven hundred planes per month.

Your personal connection with the Deity continues to manifest itself in an astonishing manner. I told you that it probably would be impossible for me to bring to pass your wish that Saint-Quentin might be translated to a happier sphere. Today Guy La Chambre told me that he wants to quit as Minister for Air and wants to go to Washington as French Ambassador. He asked me if I would tell Daladier to send him to Washington as Ambassador. I replied that I would not be so impertinent and, of course, would not make any comments on my vis-à-vis in Washington, but if Daladier himself should ask my opinion, I should feel obliged to give it to him. As a result, I expect Daladier to ask me whether or not I think La Chambre would do in Washington. I think he would be bully. He is very much of a gentleman; very gay and alive; with a charming wife who used to be one of the leading actresses of France. I am sure you would like him and inasmuch as he is Daladier's most intimate friend, you would have a real Ambassador . . .

Jules Henry came up from Spain last night and told me that he personally had gone out to find the lines defending Barcelona — where he was until the very day Franco's troops entered. He asserted that the lines defending Barcelona were there but that there was not one single defender in them. He said that Barcelona just blew up and he looks for the total collapse of resistance in Catalonia within ten days and the total collapse of the Valencia and Madrid areas inside three weeks. He believes that Mussolini will follow Franco's triumphs by immediate demands on France which will have to be refused and that we shall be close to war by the end of February.

I am not so sure — because the speech made last night by that neurotic Austrian house-painter has me puzzled. I listened to it on the radio. It was unquestionably the dullest and most disorderly speech he has made and it showed, I thought, a definite hesitation about provoking war due to fear of the hostility of the United States. On the other hand, I think it showed what all the information from Germany indicates; to wit: if Mussolini goes to war for any reason whatever, Germany will have to support Italy because Germany can not afford to see Italy defeated.

Italy has the ball and I hope that you have invented some act to impress Benito if he begins to start the rumpus. It is unquestionable that your acts have had a cooling effect on Hitler and I think they might have a similar effect on Benito, who is the bad boy of the moment. Don't forget that your last communication to him was the letter telling him that he was the white-haired boy. At the moment, he thinks that you think he is grand.

There is another possible line of evolution about which I spoke to the British Ambassador today. I think there are signs that Chamberlain is preparing to act vis-à-vis France precisely the way he acted toward Czechoslovakia. I suspect that you may have Chamberlain getting together with Hitler and telling France that after all, there is much virtue in the Italian claims and that France had better give up at least half what Mussolini will demand. The British Ambassador quite violently denied that Chamberlain would take this course but I suspect that the violence of his denial meant that it is the course that will be taken. A few minutes later he said that since war would mean the triumph of the forces of Bolshevism on the Continent, any sacrifice necessary to avoid war must be made. The British have always found it easy to sacrifice the interests of other people and you may find yourself, before another couple of months have passed, wishing to request Mr. Chamberlain quietly not to behave like a S.O.B.

Léon Blum is walking into the house at this moment so that I must stop dictating.

Love to you all.

Yours affectionately,
Bill

P.S. Blum is extremely gloomy. He believes that Mussolini will make absolutely inacceptable demands just as soon as resistance to Franco collapses completely. He believes that Hitler can not avoid supporting Mussolini if Mussolini goes to war and he believes that Chamberlain at the last minute will try to sell out France in the manner that I suggested would be British policy to the British Ambassador. Blum doesn't think that there will be war before April at the earliest and may come to the United States for a brief visit the end of February. He is in fine form personally and seems to have recovered entirely from the death of his wife.

WCB

There are over thirty pages of telegrams between Bullitt and the Secretary of State at this time dealing with the purchase of airplanes or the construction of factories in the United States to make planes for France. In every instance the Secretary of State gives exact instructions to the Ambassador as to how far he may go and what he is to say. In fact, in all important negotiations with the French, Secretary Hull was kept fully informed and he in turn gave Bullitt the latest policy decisions. For the interested reader this correspondence is contained in *Foreign Relations of the United States, Diplomatic Papers, 1939* and is printed by the United States Government Printing Office.

TELEGRAM RECEIVED

This telegram must be closely paraphrased before being communicated to anyone.

Secretary of State   Paris
Washington   Dated February 6, 1939
222, February 6, 5 P.M.   Rec'd 5:11 P.M.
Strictly Confidential for the Secretary

Daladier lunched with me alone today and we discussed a number of subjects.

The Pope had sent a Dominican to him recently to say to him in the utmost confidence that in case Italy should declare war on France, he the Pope would desire to leave Italian soil at once and establish himself in France. Daladier said he had replied that he would be most happy to welcome the Pope in France. I asked where he was going to establish the Holy Father and Daladier replied that he had suggested the Château de Chambord. I said that I should be glad to have the Pope in the opposite end of my garden at Chantilly and he said that indeed the Château de Chantilly would be much more appropriate and if the event should come he would suggest that the Pope should be established there.

Daladier said that he believed the zeal of the Senators who had seen the President had so upset Mussolini that he would not announce his demands against France immediately. He believed, however, that after a certain delay Mussolini would make demands which would be totally inacceptable. Indeed so far as France was concerned the answer to any demand whatsoever on the part of Italy would be, "There is nothing to discuss." He had every reason to believe that Germany did not desire to go to war with France in support of Italy. Goering not only during their personal conversations at Munich but lately had been communicating with him in a rather surprising manner. Goering had said to him personally and had followed it up: "Why should France continue to tie herself to a decayed old nation like England — a rouged old maid trying to pretend that she is still young and vigorous and capable of being a satisfactory partner to anyone." Goering had then proposed that France should join Germany in finishing off England and that the British Empire should be divided between France and Germany.

Daladier said he had replied that this sounded very pleasant but the moment the British Empire was finished France would be the next morsel for Germany and that France could not be detached from England by any such proposal. He said that Goering had continued to talk about the folly of hostilities between France and Germany. Daladier concluded his remarks about Goering by saying that Goering had all the qualities and defects of a Nero but that at the moment he seemed genuinely friendly to France because he knew that the French army was the only real force on the continent of Europe today opposed to Germany. Daladier finally said that he thought he might invite Goering soon to make a visit to Paris.

Daladier said that in case Italy should make war on France he believed that Germany would propose to England that both states should remain neutral and then Germany employing the technique which had been used in Spain would send "volunteers," arms and munitions to Italy to make war on France. Meanwhile Great Britain would do nothing to help France.

Daladier added that at the moment Great Britain was a most weak reed on which to lean. His most recent conversations with the British with regard to possible military assistance in case of war had achieved the result that the British had promised to send to France 140 airplanes and two divisions approximating 20,000 men without any equipment except rifles and machine guns. The British had nothing more to offer in the way of support for the French army and the British Admiralty had demanded that in case of war at sea with Germany the fast French battle cruisers *Dunkerque* and *Strasbourg* should be attached to the British fleet in the Channel because the British had no ships fast enough to catch up with the German pocket battleships. I asked Daladier what the British had offered to send to the Mediterranean in recompense and he replied "nothing that wouldn't sink of its own accord."

Daladier said that he had been unable to get any exact information as to what had happened while Chamberlain was in Rome. He had only Bonnet's reports on the subject and he could not trust Bonnet too.

Daladier was of the opinion that Chamberlain in Rome had promised the Italians that he would use his good offices to obtain concessions from France to Italy. He said that the British had denied emphatically that this was the case but that he did not believe the British. He said that he anticipated that if Italy should make demands and France should refuse them, the British would suggest to the Germans that they and the Germans should intervene and settle the matter by a compromise. Daladier said that he fully expected to be betrayed by the British and added that this was the customary fate of allies of the British.

Daladier went on to say that he considered Chamberlain a dessicated stick; the King a moron; and the Queen an excessively ambitious woman who would be ready to sacrifice every other country in the world in order that she might remain Queen Elizabeth of England. He added that he considered Eden a young idiot and did not know for discussion one single Englishman for whose intellectual equipment and character he had respect. He felt that England had become so feeble and senile that the British would give away every possession of their friends rather than stand up to Germany and Italy.

On commenting on the feebleness of British policy at the moment Daladier gave the following example:

He said that some weeks ago the British had become very fearful that Germany might attack the Netherlands and seize the Netherlands as a base for attack against England. Chamberlain had therefore made an official inquiry of the French Government as to the attitude of the French Government in case of a German attack on the Netherlands. Daladier said that he had replied by a question, "What will you do?" The British Government had then answered that in case German troops should cross the frontier of the Netherlands Great Britain would suggest a committee of three to arbitrate the point in dispute! And had repeated the inquiry as to what France would do. Daladier said that he had replied that although France had no obligations vis-à-vis the Netherlands he would consider a German attack on the Netherlands as an immediate *casus belli* and would at once attack Germany. Daladier said that the British had appeared to be much gratified by this reply but that it had evoked no (repeat no) similar statement on the part of the British Government . . .

Daladier was of course intensely grateful to the President for the permission accorded to France to buy planes in the United States. He said that he intended to order at once in the United States an additional 100 Douglas planes and an additional 120 Martins.

In this connection he said that he would like to send Guy La Chambre, Minister for Air, to Washington as Ambassador. He asked me if I thought that La Chambre would be a good Ambassador in Washington and I said that I did. He then went on to say that he considered the present French Ambassador in Washington an idiot. I replied that I did not (repeat not) agree with this opinion.

Daladier said that he felt that in the interests of France both Saint-Quentin and François-Poncet must be relieved by men who were less dried up and had more contact with French life today. He finally admitted that his statement that Saint-Quentin was an idiot was exaggerated but indicated that he was dissatisfied with his service in America . . .

(END OF MESSAGE)

Bullitt

U.S.S. HOUSTON

FROM: MR. EARLY   [Undated.]
TO: THE PRESIDENT

OO 23 FROM HULL: BULLITT TELEGRAPHS HAD CONVERSATIONS DURING PAST TWENTY-FOUR HOURS WITH DALADIER, CHIEF OF THE GENERAL STAFF, SEVERAL CABINET MEMBERS, AND BLUM. ALL CONSIDER PRESENT SITUATION AT LEAST AS SERIOUS AS LAST AUGUST ON BASIS OF FOLLOWING INFORMATION:

REINFORCEMENTS GOING TO ITALIAN ARMY IN LIBYA DAILY, GERMANS SENDING AIRPLANES IN CRATES TO LIBYA EVERY DAY.

THOSE MENTIONED ABOVE BELIEVE UNACCEPTABLE DEMANDS WILL BE MADE BY MUSSOLINI BETWEEN TENTH AND END OF MARCH AND ALSO THEIR BELIEF THAT FRANCE MAY EXPECT MUSSOLINI TO MAKE WAR UPON IT ANY TIME AFTER THE MIDDLE OF MARCH, PROBABLY ATTACKING DJIBOUTI FIRST. THEY STATE ITALY HAS NOW ONE HUNDRED THOUSAND TROOPS IN LIBYA AND ABOUT TO ADD THIRTY THOUSAND. DALADIER AND GAMELIN BELIEVE THAT FRENCH CAN DEFEND TUNISIA, BUT THAT ITALY MAY ATTACK EGYPT, WHICH, ACCORDING TO FRENCH INFORMATION, IS NOT IN AS STRONG DEFENSIVE POSITION. ALL MEN ABOVE MENTIONED BE-

LIEVE THAT ALTHOUGH GERMANY DOES NOT WISH TO GO TO WAR WITH FRANCE, IT WILL GO TO WAR IN SUPPORT OF ITALY IN CASE LATTER ATTACKS FRANCE. FRENCH GOVERNMENT BELIEVES POSSIBLE AND ADVISABLE TO MAKE BROAD, COMPREHENSIVE COMMERCIAL AGREEMENT WITH GERMANY IN ORDER TO OFFER POSSIBILITY OF GOOD FRANCO GERMAN RELATIONS, IN ORDER THAT GERMANY MIGHT HESITATE TO GO TO WAR AND THUS LOSE SUCH BENEFITS. DALADIER PERSONALLY BELIEVES FRENCH NEGOTIATIONS WITH SPAIN ARE MEETING WITH SUCCESS. DALADIER AND GAMELIN ACTUALLY DISCUSSED WITH BULLITT MEASURES TO BE TAKEN IN PARIS IN THE NEXT TWO WEEKS IN THE EVENT OF AN ATTACK BY GERMANY AND ITALY. THOSE TWO OFFICIALS CONSIDER BRITISH POSITION IN THE FAR EAST EXTREMELY GRAVE, AS GREAT BRITAIN HELPLESS TO DEFEND AUSTRALIA, NEW ZEALAND, SINGAPORE, HONG KONG, OR THE DUTCH EAST INDIES AGAINST JAPANESE ATTACK. THEY SEE SOME CONNECTION BETWEEN POSSIBLE ATTACK BY ITALIANS IN LIBYA AGAINST EGYPT AND MOVEMENT AGAINST BRITISH NOT ONLY IN EASTERN MEDITERRANEAN, BUT IN THE INDIAN OCEAN AND FAR EAST. BLUM CONSIDERS SITUATION SO SERIOUS HAS DECIDED NOT TO UNDERTAKE PLANNED TRIP TO AMERICA AT THIS TIME 1900.

DISTRIBUTION: PRESIDENT, NAVAID, ADMIRAL LEAHY, COLONEL WATSON

Italy had, by conquest, formed Libya in 1912. The country stretches for almost one thousand miles along the north shore of Africa between Tunisia and Egypt, and was soon to become the scene of savage fighting between the British and Germans, in their effort to capture Egypt. In June 1940, the Italians had 200,000 troops stationed in Libya. Mussolini had built a highway from Tripoli in the west, paralleling the coast to the border of Egypt. Strung along this road were Italian garrisons and at the frontier of Egypt some 70,000 men had been assembled. None of this great force proved of value against the British, and it was not until the arrival of the Germans that Egypt was seriously in danger.

Personal and Secret   Paris
February 21, 1939

Dear Mr. President:

This letter is for you alone and I hope you will answer it by cable immediately.

About the 5th of February, Guy La Chambre said to me that Lindbergh had informed him that on a recent trip to Germany, he had ascertained that the German Government would be glad to sell Benz motors of about 1050 horsepower to France. La Chambre said that he was thinking of purchasing three of these motors to try. He asked me if I thought there would be any hostile reaction in the United States, if it should become known that the French Government had purchased *three* German Benz motors in Germany. I replied that I did not think there would be any hostile reaction; in fact, people would consider it rather clever of the French to have got examples of the best German airplane motors for thorough inspection.

Last evening Guy La Chambre called on me and said that he had just had a most important conversation with Daladier and that Daladier had asked him to speak to me, and that no one else in the French Government had or would have any knowledge of the matter that he was about to bring up. Daladier especially did not wish Bonnet and the other members of the Quai d'Orsay to know about it as they were thoroughly unreliable.

Guy La Chambre then said that the French Air Attaché in Berlin had just returned to Paris and had reported as follows: General Udet had sent for him and had stated that Lindbergh had said to General Milch that the French might like to purchase some German airplane motors for which they would be prepared to pay cash in free exchange, quite aside from any compensation agreements. Udet then said that General Milch had spoken to Goering; that Goering had spoken to Hitler who had approved the transaction; and that Goering had directed him (Udet) to inform the French Air Attaché in Berlin that the German Government would be glad to sell to the French Government three hundred Benz motors for delivery about December 1939 or January 1940.

Guy La Chambre said that the French Air Attaché was now in Paris waiting for a message to carry back to the German Government. The first observation that he, La Chambre, had made was that delay in delivery of these motors made any such proposal of doubtful value; second, that if any such proposal went through, the French must have ten of these motors for immediate inspection; third, that the entire matter would have to be considered most carefully before a decision should be made. He had, therefore, ordered the French Air Attaché to remain in Paris for the moment and he and Daladier had consulted.

Their decision was that it would be desirable to order these three hundred motors not because of the addition that they would make to France's air strength — there would be too few of them to make much difference and in case of war it would be impossible to get parts to repair any of them — but because of the improvement that might be produced by such an order in the diplomatic relations between France and Germany, and because news of such a deal would tend to make the Italians less sure of German support.

The question that Daladier wished to put up to me was whether or not the news of the purchase of three hundred airplane motors by France from Germany would produce an unfortunate effect on public opinion in the United States.

I replied that I could not answer such a question.

La Chambre said that he and Daladier had expected me to make just this reply and what Daladier wanted was for me to communicate with you personally and ask your personal opinion of the deal.

I said that I considered the question filled with high explosive and did not believe that it should be handled by telegraph; that you were at the moment on a cruiser in the Caribbean and would not return until the fourth of March; and that I believed that if Daladier wished to get your reaction to this proposal, he could not obtain it until after March fourth at the earliest.

La Chambre said that he would delay replying to the Germans until after your return.

I don't know whether or not you will care to express any opinion whatsoever; but even if you want to refuse to reply, please send me *immediately a telegram to that effect*. Guy La Chambre said that a mere indication from you that the reaction in America would be unfortunate, would be sufficient to kill the deal.

Personally, I don't like the smell of it. I do not believe that there is any real approach by Germany toward friendship with France. It seems to me that the test should be: Will Germany agree to deliver three hundred motors *next month* to France? They have plenty in stock to spare.

You know all about the possible reaction in America and I know little, so I wish you would let me know exactly what you think. I do believe that whatever indication you tell me to give to Daladier will be decisive. I shall, of course, merely mention the matter verbally. *Please telegraph at once*.

Guy La Chambre also said to me that during the same conversation in which he had talked over this matter with Daladier, he had had two shocks. He had understood, as I had from our last conversation with Daladier and Paul Reynaud, that it had been decided to exercise the options for the additional one hundred twenty Martins and an additional one hundred Douglases. Daladier now appeared to be doubtful because of the size of the expenditures in foreign aircraft — the decision having been made to buy a large quantity of Rolls-Royce Merlin motors and this German order being in prospect . . .

The second shock was that although he thought it was all fixed for him to go as Ambassador to Washington, Daladier had said to him that Georges Bonnet had just about persuaded him that Jules Henry should be sent as French Ambassador to Washington and asked him if he wanted another diplomatic post. He had said that he did not want any other diplomatic post and if Daladier should decide to send Henry instead of himself to Washington, he would prefer to remain as Minister for Air.

Please cable me as cryptically as you like. I shall understand.

Love and a lot of it.

Bill

MEMORANDUM

Paris, March 14, 1939

I spoke to the Minister for Air at his house this afternoon at 6:30, about the President's opinion. He said that so far as he was concerned, the fact that the President was unable to predict the effect on American public opinion of the purchase of three hundred Daimler-Benz airplane motors from Germany was decisive. He would leave the matter in suspense and let it die from inanition.

WCB

Personal and Secret Paris
February 22, 1939

Dear Mr. President:

This is another letter for your most private eye. And as you read it, you will chortle, remembering the day when we cooked up the Johnson Act and predicted that we would make those chickens come home to roost.

Paul Reynaud, Minister of Finance, telephoned yesterday and said that he had a matter of the utmost importance about which he wished to speak to me at once. He came in today. He said that he had become convinced that France must make immediately a settlement of her debt to the United States. No such obstacle to perfect relations between France and the United States could be permitted to exist any longer. (You will recall my telegram No. 276 of February 13, 10 P.M.)

Reynaud went on to say that France at the present time had eighty-seven billion francs in gold. He would be prepared to hand over to the United States ten billion francs in gold at once with the statement that whereas France, during a period of great economic and financial stress had been unable to make payments on her debt to the United States, now that the financial situation had improved, France desired to resume payments. He added that he did not propose that this should be a final settlement of the debt, but only that such payment in a lump sum should be accepted by the Government of the United States as sufficient evidence of good faith to relieve France from the restrictions of the Johnson Act.

He went on to say that he knew that ten billion francs, which was an enormous sum for France, representing as it did about fifteen percent of the French war chest, was a small sum for the United States, representing as it did only about three hundred million dollars. The sacrifice from the French point of view, however, when France was threatened by war, was enormous. He hoped that this would be appreciated in the United States and that such a payment might be considered sufficient to lift the restrictions of the Johnson Act.

I replied that I thanked him most heartily for what he had said; that I was certain that you would be most happy to hear of this honorable proposal; but I added that Congress controlled completely any debt settlements and that Congress was most loath to deal with the matter. I pointed out that the Hungarians had made an offer which had been buried in committee, and that a French offer of three hundred million dollars in gold to settle a debt of many billions would probably not be regarded as good business by the Congress.

Reynaud said that he understood this, but he felt that you might be able to put the question on the basis of fairness to an honorable, democratic and friendly nation which desired to do what it could and could not do more.

I then suggested that although the ten billion francs in gold alone probably would not be acceptable to the American Congress; ten billion francs plus X might possibly be acceptable; X to represent French possessions which we might desire for strategic reasons.

Reynaud replied that in addition to the ten billion francs, he felt it would be possible for France to throw in Clipperton Island (Pacific Ocean West of Central America); the French interests in the New Hebrides which they hold under a condominium with the British, and any other French possessions we might fancy in either the Caribbean or the Pacific — provided that such possessions did not have either a large population or a great sentimental value to France. As an example of islands to be excluded because of their sentimental value, he cited St. Pierre and Miquelon (south of Newfoundland).

Since you collect stamps, you don't need to look at the map: and you can count in your mind any islands or other territories that France possesses anywhere. I happen to recall a discussion we had in the White House not long ago about the need for an American base somewhere in the region of Venezuela and it occurs to me that you might fancy French Guiana.

In any event, will you please get your imagination to work furiously on this subject. I wish to God that I could be with you in the White House for one evening. Our inventions would be terrific! As it is, I can only say that if you want any French territory, plus ten billion francs in gold, in return for releasing France from the operations of the Johnson Act, it looks as if you might be able to get it.

Let me have a letter about this just as soon as you possibly can. I do not believe that you should telegraph with regard to it. Reynaud is extremely skeptical with regard to the discretion of the French Foreign Office and our Department of State, to say nothing of the privacy of our telegraphic communications. He asked me especially to refer this to you alone and to avoid absolutely official communications at this stage.

Speed is of the essence. If war should begin, the French *couldn't* make a payment.

Don't you feel rather proud of the achievements of our offspring? The carrot and the club is, after all, not a bad formula in international dealings.

A large embrace and good luck.

Bill

In March 1939, Paul Reynaud wrote of his extreme concern about a coming war, and that in the event of war, France might find herself without allies. He wished to do everything possible to have closer ties to the United States, as, in the last analysis, it could only be America which could strengthen France. A large amount of gold had accumulated in France and he hoped, by using some of this, to alleviate feeling against France in the United States on account of her failure to pay her debt to America. His offer of 300 million dollars was about ten per cent of the gold reserve of the Bank of France. He spoke of numerous discussions with Bullitt, Daladier, and Jean Monnet. As a result Monnet went to America and talked at length with President Roosevelt on May 3. The President's response was: "I do not want to take money out of France at this time." Secretary of the Treasury Morgenthau told Monnet that whereas the United States appreciated the offer, it did not want payment at that time, and that public opinion could not be more favorable to France.[5]

Personal and Secret   Paris
                                              February 23, 1939
Dear Mr. President:

A few days ago while talking with Mandel about the situation in French Indo-China and the possibility of a Japanese attack on the French railroad to stop the transit of supplies to China, a curious thought struck me.

There is an Emperor of Annam. The Emperor of Annam is not in default on any debt to the Government of the United States. The Emperor of Annam needs airplanes to defend his kingdom. Suppose the Emperor of Annam should wish to buy three or four or five hundred airplanes in the United States. Suppose either the Export-Import Bank or private bankers should wish to give credits of five years to the manufacturers of the planes in order that the business might be obtained. Would either the Export-Import Bank or any private banker or group of bankers be forbidden to offer such a credit to the manufacturer by the Johnson Act? I think not.

Would you like to have the Emperor of Annam buy a few hundred planes in the United States? And would this sort of financing be possible?

Please let me know the answer as soon as you can. If the answer should be yes, you may count on seeing a representative of the Emperor of Annam arrive incognito in the United States for the purchase of planes.

Blessings.

                                                     Bill

MEMORANDUM

                                                      Paris
                                              March 14, 1939
I spoke to Georges Mandel tonight and told him that the idea of

using the Emperor of Annam and the King of Cambodia appeared to us to be too transparent for use in time of peace.

WCB

At this time Bullitt was also engaged in the negotiations for recognition of Franco's government in Spain. Some sixteen governments had already recognized Franco and on February 28 Secretary Hull had cabled Bullitt to talk informally to Franco's representative in Paris and tell him that the American Government was considering recognition. He first wanted assurance that there would be no reprisals and that Americans and their property would be protected. Bullitt reported that the Franco representative gave absolute promises of protection of Americans but could give no promise in the matter of reprisals. In Secretary Hull's words: "The Spanish representative gave Bullitt a declaration that had been sent to the British Government, containing a weasel-worded assurance." [6] The new Spanish Government was finally recognized on April 3.

In early March the French were discussing with Bullitt the building of a factory in New Orleans to manufacture light bombers. The machinery for the factory was to be sent from France in order that the parts made would conform to those made in France. On March 7, 1939, Secretary Hull wired Bullitt to advise the French Government that the United States was strongly opposed to such a project and that the President had seen and approved his telegram.[7]

TELEGRAM RECEIVED *

A portion of this telegram must be closely paraphrased before being communicated to anyone.

Secretary of State	Paris
Washington	Dated September 19, 1939
2050, September 19, noon	Rec'd 9:40 A.M.

Secret and Personal for the President

I now have in written form the report made in Vienna on March 12th last by two leading Nazis, Secretary of State Wilhelm Keppler

---

* See Bullitt's letter of September 16, 1939, to FDR, pp. 372–374.

and Director General Vogl, to which I referred in my telegram No. 565, March 25, 1 P.M. The report reads as follows:

"On Wednesday March 8th a conference was held at the Fuehrer's which was attended by personalities from the army, economic circles and the party. 'Austria' was represented by Gauleiter Buerkel in addition to those mentioned above.

"Certain economic and labor problems were discussed first. Then the Fuehrer spoke. First he declared that the four year plan was a last resort. The real problem for the German people was to assure for itself the sources from which could be obtained the raw materials necessary for its well-being. In addition in order to enjoy this well-being enemies of the German people must be exterminated radically: Jews, democracies and the 'international powers.' As long as those enemies had the least vestige of power left anywhere in the world they would be a menace to the peace of the German people.

"In this connection the situation in Prague was becoming intolerable. In addition Prague was needed as a means of access to those raw materials. Consequently orders have been issued to the effect that in a few days not later than the 15th of March Czechoslovakia is to be occupied militarily.

"Poland will follow. We will not have to count on a strong resistance from that quarter. German domination over Poland is necessary in order to assure for Germany Polish supplies of agricultural products and coal.

"As far as Hungary and Rumania are concerned they belong without question to Germany's vital space. The fall of Poland and adequate pressure will undoubtedly bring them to terms. We will then have absolute control over their vast agricultural and petroleum resources. The same may be said for Yugoslavia.

"This is the plan which will be realized until 1940. Even then Germany will be unbeatable.

"In 1940 and 1941 Germany will settle accounts once and for all with her hereditary enemy: France. That country will be obliterated from the map of Europe. England is an old and feeble country weakened by democracy. With France vanquished Germany will dominate England easily and will then have at its disposition England's riches and domains throughout the world.

"Thus having for the first time unified the continent of Europe according to a new conception Germany will undertake the greatest operation in all history: with British and French possessions in America as a base we will settle accounts with the 'Jews of the dollar' (dollar jüden) in the United States. We will exterminate this Jewish democracy and Jewish blood will mix itself with the dollars. Even today Americans can insult our people, but the day will come when, too late, they will bitterly regret every word they said against us.

"Among those present, some were very enthusiastic while others seemed much less so."

Bullitt

TELEGRAM RECEIVED

This telegram must be closely paraphrased before being communicated to anyone.

Secretary of State	Paris
Washington	. Dated September 19, 1939
2050, September 19, noon	Rec'd 12:58 P.M.

I feel certain of the authenticity of this report which you will note was made before the invasion of Czechoslovakia. Countless other pieces of evidence indicate with equal certainty that Hitler intends first to defeat France and England, then to take their fleets and to attack the Americas in conjunction with Japan.

I am entirely certain that if France and England should be unable to defeat Hitler in Europe American soldiers will have to fight his forces in the Americas.

The opinion of our military and naval officers at this mission as well as the opinion of leading men and British military men with whom I have talked is that an embargo by the United States against shipments of airplanes and war materials to France and England will mean inevitably the defeat of France and England.

I therefore consider those who advocate today the maintenance of this embargo not only ignorant allies [of] Hitler but also war mongers for America since if they should be able to maintain the embargo they would make it certain that American soldiers would have to meet Hitler's armies in the Americas.

It is the opinion of the same military men that I have cited above that if the embargo on supplies to France and England should be lifted immediately France and England would have a 60% chance of winning the war without the participation of a single American soldier.

Bullitt

On March 14, Bullitt telephoned the President asking him to denounce Nazi aggression and asking for the repeal of the Neutrality Act.

The Germans had occupied Prague, Czechoslovakia, on March 15 and Ambassador Lukasiewicz of Poland had several talks with Bullitt about the Polish situation. He believed that there would be further aggression by Hitler and that the next problem to be solved would be the Polish city of Danzig. He wished to advise his government as to the extent of French political and military assistance in case such an attack was imminent. Although this was completely outside Bullitt's duties as American Ambassador, nevertheless Bullitt, on account of their intimacy, talked with Daladier. He reported back to Lukasiewicz that Daladier said Poland could count on French military assistance in a conflict over Danzig.[8] Lukasiewicz went on to discuss the necessity of France and England letting Germany know that: "The two powers were ready to react to fresh acts of expansion with all the might at their disposal. Knowing what friendly relations existed between Ambassador Bullitt and M. Daladier, I knew that at least part of my remarks would be repeated to the Premier." [9] It is quite extraordinary to read of the Polish Ambassador to France, in such a tense situation as then existed, turning to the Ambassador of the United States to plead his cause with Poland's ally. Lukasiewicz goes on to say: "It is childishly naive, and at the same time dishonest . . . to expose the world to the catastrophe of another war solely to satisfy the needs of the domestic politics of Chamberlain's government." [10] Evidently others agreed with Bullitt in his judgment of the motivation of the British.

Bullitt's position as more than Roosevelt's representative in France was disclosed by a statement by Lukasiewicz at that time: "He [Bullitt] informed me that, adopting my views and exercising the authority he was accorded, he had instructed the American Ambassador in London, Joseph Kennedy, to call today, Saturday, on Prime Minister Chamberlain at his residence and repeat everything to him, emphasizing categorically, the responsibility of the British Government. On Sunday, Ambassador Bullitt received in my presence a telephone call from Ambassador Kennedy regarding the conversation held with Chamberlain . . . He

[Chamberlain] manifested this [the gravity of the situation] by telling Kennedy on his own initiative that, if Hitler provoked a conflict with Poland over Danzig, England would stand by Poland and would defend it." [11]

TELEGRAM RECEIVED

This telegram must be closely paraphrased before being communicated to anyone.

Secretary of State   Paris
Washington   Dated March 18, 1939
513, March 18, 3 P.M.   Rec'd 1:40 P.M.
Secret and Personal for the President
and Acting Secretary Only

Daladier lunched with me alone today and we discussed the entire situation.

He said that he was intensely grateful for the declaration with regard to the invasion of Czechoslovakia which had been made by the Acting Secretary of State and for the statement of the President that the Neutrality Act should be changed. He considered that a change in the Neutrality Act which would permit the export in time of war of arms, munitions and aeroplanes to France would be of basic importance in the present situation.

Daladier stated also that he was delighted by the action of the American Government in continuing to recognize the Minister of Czechoslovakia in Washington as the Minister of Czechoslovakia. He had given orders that Osusky, the Czechoslovak Minister in Paris, should continue to be recognized as Minister of Czechoslovakia and had posted policemen at the Legation to prevent the entry of Germans. He did not know, however, how long Osusky would be able to continue to hold out because the Germans had already informed all officers of the Legation and the staff that reprisals would be taken against their families and relatives in Czechoslovakia if they should continue to work at the Legation.

Daladier said that he felt certain that he would receive the full powers which he had asked. He expected to use them in the first instance to mobilize at once two classes. The Germans had quietly drawn into their fifty-four active divisions 20% more men to bring them up to war strength. He felt that under the circumstances he must mobilize at least two classes.

Daladier then went on to say that he had a number of intimate personal questions he would like to ask me which he would ask as a close personal friend and not as a Prime Minister to the Ambassador of the United States. He had said to his children (he is a widower) that he expected war in the near future. He might soon be killed by a bomb or otherwise. In case of his death he advised them to consult me and take my advice as to their future. He asked me if I would object to giving them such advice and looking out for them. I replied that of course I should be most honored to do so.

Daladier then said that his next question was equally intimate. A member of the Montalembert family resident in Rome had come to see him yesterday stating that he had had conversations recently with Mussolini and Ciano and that both Mussolini and Ciano as well as the King and all other members of the Italian royal family were intensely disturbed by the increasing German powers. They desired sincerely to come to an understanding with France. They had authorized Stefani, of the Italian agency Stefani in Paris, to call on him, Daladier, to let him know exactly the terms which Mussolini was ready to accept for a complete reconciliation with France. They had added that if this preliminary conversation should result in negotiations they felt that it would be advisable to send to Rome to conduct such negotiations Pierre Laval, in whom both Mussolini and Ciano had the greatest confidence.

Daladier then said that he had no confidence whatsoever in Bonnet and did not wish to consult him with regard to this communication. He desired to consult me as an individual and not as American Ambassador and asked me to give him my personal opinion. I replied that I could give no opinion as American Ambassador; but that if a similar proposal had been made to me and I were in his place I should reply that there was an Italian Ambassador in Paris, that I would be glad to receive at any time, and if the Italian Government had any communication to make it should be made through this official and authorized channel. I felt personally that the sending of Laval to Rome would destroy the confidence in his, Daladier's, will to resist absolutely all demands against France which was the basis of his strength throughout the country. It might destroy French morale. A proposal which did not come through the Italian Ambassador must be regarded as a ruse and not as a serious act in the direction of rapprochement between France and Italy.

Daladier said that he would reply in this sense.

He then went on to say that he wished to ask me as a friend for my advice on another proposal. Herriot had talked with Litvinov and was very anxious to be empowered to go to Moscow to negotiate a firm and absolute military understanding with the Soviet Union. He asked me again as a friend and not as American Ambassador to say what I thought of this proposal.

I replied that it had been our experience that no promises made by the Soviet Union could be relied on. Nevertheless in the present situation I felt that no stone should be left unturned even though one might expect to find vermin under it. I felt, however, that Herriot whose amiable and generous qualities were deeply appreciated in the United States was too honest and sincere a person to be able to deal successfully with the Bolsheviks. I believed that if he should be sent to Moscow he should be accompanied by someone who would examine every Russian proposal with a microscope and was as unscrupulous as the Bolsheviks themselves . . .

Bullitt

Personal and Confidential Paris

March 18, 1939

Dear Mr. President:

I thank you profoundly for having had Welles make that statement about Czechoslovakia. My feeling that we had to say a word for human decency increased in intensity every hour that the word remained unsaid. It was splendidly done and, coupled with your brief indication with regard to the need for a change in the Neutrality Act, will have some effect at least in Europe.

I like also your action in continuing to recognize the Minister of Czechoslovakia as the representative of his country. I remember telling you some years ago one of the few facts that I have ever been able to tell you that you did not know already, to wit: that, during all the years when Poland had ceased to exist as a sovereign state, the Turkish Sultans invariably invited the Polish Ambassador, who did not exist, to every Court function, and at the beginning of each Court function, in the presence of the Ambassadors of Germany, Austria, and Russia, the Court Chamberlain announced to His Imperial Majesty the Sultan: "The Polish Ambassador begs to be excused as he is slightly indisposed."

That always seemed to me one of the really gentlemanly gestures in human history, and I am glad that, at least for the moment, we are following this example of the Osmanlis.

Henceforth in Europe diplomatic action will be almost impossible. A minimum of good faith is necessary for civilized intercourse, and Hitler has proved sevenfold that he is an unscrupulous liar.

My guess is that by this time next year you will wish that you had an American Army of two million men ready for action. I hope that does not prove to be true; but I fear it will. The War Department today is perhaps even more important than the Navy Department because in the Navy what needs to be done has been done, and in the War Department nearly everything remains to be done.

Blessings and good luck.

Yours affectionately,

Bill

TELEGRAM RECEIVED

This telegram must be	Paris
closely paraphrased before	Dated March 23, 1939
being communicated to anyone.	Rec'd 4:30 P.M.

Secretary of State	March 24, 1939
Washington	Copy to the President
552, March 23, 5 P.M.	Via Miss LeHand
Personal and Secret for the President	At 10:15 A.M.

Daladier spoke to me today with regard to the matter discussed in my letter of February 22. He said that he himself had initiated the proposal and that he was determined to push it through. Since he has the power to govern by decree at the present time this means something.

He was not at all horrified by the idea of X (French overseas possessions). He said that he considered it entirely reasonable and added that there were approximately fifty points where it might apply. He believed that no one was so well qualified as Jean Monnet to handle this matter and he would send Monnet a personal telegram today asking him to return to Paris from New York for a few days to discuss the matter and to return immediately to America.

Daladier added that on Monnet's arrival in Paris he would wish to have a discussion with Monnet and myself.

If you have any ideas that you think I ought to have in mind during such a discussion, you might transmit them to me by letter in the confidential pouch immediately. Don't send me your views unless you think I need them. If you could give me some personal indication for my information but not repetition as to the direction in which my geography is wrong I should be obliged. To be of use, this would have to reach me by the first pouch.

Bullitt

Mr. Ickes's diary, full of interesting sidelights on the President, contains the following in March: "The President also told an interesting story about a telephone conversation with Bill Bullitt. It seems that Bullitt called him from Paris and began by saying: 'Mr. President, of course the English Foreign Office is listening in to this conversation and we will have to be careful what we say. You and I know that they are a bunch of pusillanimous, double crossing, tricky people over there who can't be relied upon even to carry out their own undertakings. And undoubtedly the French Foreign Office is listening in too and having our conversation transcribed. But you know that bunch too. They are just as bad as the English,' etc. The President said that he listened to Bill Bullitt sounding off and concluded the conversation by saying: 'Well, Bill, I agree with you in everything you have said.' " [12]

An Ambassador's duties were varied and even with the clouds of war threatening Europe the social amenities had to be observed.

THE WHITE HOUSE
WASHINGTON

Memorandum for Mrs. Helm   April 1, 1939

The President asks that you show the enclosed to Mrs. Roosevelt and tell her it is confidential.

G. G. T.
[Grace G. Tully]

Letter from Ambassador Bullitt in re recommendations as to the personal needs of Their Royal Majesties.

See office of the chief of social entertainments.

Paris
March 23, 1939

Dear Mr. President:

I have the honor to submit herewith to the Chief of State in accordance with his request made to me at Warm Springs, Georgia, the recommendations as to the personal needs of Their Royal Majesties, George VI and Elizabeth, King and Queen, By the Grace of God, of Great Britain, Ireland and of the British Dominions Beyond the Seas, King and Queen Defender of the Faith, Emperor and Empress of India.

I may add that my most onerous diplomatic labor since reaching Paris has been the extraction of these recommendations and that I expect you to decorate me at once with the Order of the Royal Bathtub . . .

I may add that it has been indicated to me by the Government of the French Republic that the preferences of Their Majesties in the way of wines do not go beyond Veuve Clicquot and Pommery-Greno champagne of the best years. I have, therefore, prepared against the arrival of Their Majesties in Washington, one hundred bottles of Pommery-Greno, 1928, which I shall be glad to place at your disposal provided the situation in Europe should seem to indicate that there may be some chance of Their Royal Majesties going to America. My parsimony is motivated by the fact that the grand smash seems fairly imminent. I prefer, therefore, to restrain the departure of these bottles until my next departure for the United States in the hope that we may drink them together.

With my profound obeisances, I am,

Your humble and obedient servant,
William C. Bullitt

SUGGESTIONS FOR THE FURNISHING OF HIS MAJESTY'S ROOM

Large bed "de milieu" (in center of panel) with the head against the wall (never with the side along the wall).

No bolster — two pillows.

Special bolster supplied by His Majesty's valet.

Warm, but light, blankets, with a silk cover.

Very soft eider down quilt, which can be accordion-pleated at the foot of the bed.

On each side of the bed a bedside table with a lamp.

In the bathroom or bedroom (according to possibility) and preferably in a window recess on account of light, a dressing table with a triple mirror, high enough to enable contemplating oneself when standing.

Very comfortable settee.

Ash trays, matches, cigars, and cigarettes for the guests, His Majesty having his own cigarettes.

Great number of hangers: some of them very wide with the back
slightly curved; others with a double bar for trousers; no special
clip hangers for trousers.

On the desk an inkstand with two inkwells: one full of blue-black,
the other of red ink.

No toweled bathrobe. His Majesty prefers large bath towels.

To be ready to supply, if requested, garnet-red and white carnations
for boutonnieres.

SUGGESTIONS FOR THE FURNISHING OF HER MAJESTY'S ROOM

Large bed.

No bolster — two pillows.

Bed cushion supplied by Her Majesty's maid.

Light, but warm, blankets with a silk cover.

No eider down coverlet — a soft silk cover folded in four on the foot
of the bed, with one corner turned up.

Bedside table with lamp.

Bathroom

A large dressing table, or a table for the bottles.

Four glasses, one of which is graduated.

Bathrobe type of bath towel.

Quantities of hand towels.

Basket for putting linen after use.

Bath thermometer.

Several spoons, large and small.

Dressing Room or Boudoir

Dressing table perfectly lighted day and night, with armchair of cor-
responding height.

Near the dressing table a small table with drawers for hairdressing
and toilet articles. This table should be easily removable.

Very comfortable settee with soft linen blanket.

One or two ash trays and matches for the King. The Queen does
not smoke.

On the desk:

  inkstand with blue ink

  thin penholder with "J" pen (or similar make) of medium size

  red pencil

  blue pencil

  ordinary black pencils with very sharp points

  ordinary, and typewriter erasers

Breakfast and Refreshments

His Majesty

8:00 A.M. plain tea

9:15 A.M. complete breakfast with tea, toast, fruit, bacon and eggs

Her Majesty

8:00 A.M. plain tea

9:15 A.M. complete breakfast with tea, toast, and fruit

Service is always made separately, on trays, the latter prepared by the private servants of Their Majesties.

Whenever Their Majesties come home, tea should always be kept ready for them. Moreover, when they come back about midnight, ham sandwiches should be prepared.

The King generally brings his own liquor and spirits. His footman will need a tray with sets of glasses, lump and crushed ice, decanters of lemon and orange juice, and everything necessary for the preparation of cocktails and various drinks.

In all the rooms a tray with mineral water in ice, and glasses, should be constantly renewed.

Fruit is not kept in the apartments, but is often asked for during the day.

THE WHITE HOUSE
WASHINGTON

April 24, 1939

Dear Bill:

All your letters have been grand and I hope you will keep on writing to me.

We all love the list of orders for the Royal guests and only wish you were going to be here to help us out. We are also amused at the thought of the eider-down comforter in Washington on June eighth, to say nothing of the hot water bottles for the ladies in waiting!

I like the picture you sent and I do hope you are taking my conversation seriously!

My affectionate good wishes.

As always,
Franklin D. Roosevelt

Honorable William C. Bullitt
Ambassador Extraordinary and Plenipotentiary
Paris, France

19

Hitler Will Not Stop

MARCH 1939—APRIL 1939

Germans Occupy Memel
Britain and France Guarantee Poland
Italy Occupies Albania
British-French-Russian Talks
U.S. Army Inadequate

MEMEL, A PORT on the Baltic, had been part of Germany until the end of the First World War, but under the terms of the Treaty of Versailles it was ceded to Lithuania. In October 1938, Hitler had informed his generals that they must prepare for its capture. On March 22, 1939, Hitler boarded the battleship *Deutschland* on his way to Memel. He had sent an ultimatum to the Lithuanians on the day before, telling them that they must cede Memel to Germany. Shortly after midnight on March 23, Ribbentrop sent word that the Lithuanians had surrendered and signed the documents. Without firing a shot from his ship Hitler entered the port of Memel the same afternoon and accomplished his final bloodless victory.

Hitler continued his march toward war and on April 28, 1939, he made one of his lengthy speeches to the Reichstag. The speech was broadcast internationally and carried inflammatory statements against England and Poland. He denounced the Anglo-German naval treaty on account of England's new policy of encirclement. In denouncing the Polish-German nonaggression pact he said that Germany had not called up a single soldier and had not thought of any aggression against Poland; in fact such rumors were only inventions of the international press. Actually he had already given orders to his generals that Poland was to be destroyed before September 1.

Private and Confidential   Paris

March 23, 1939

Dear Mr. President:

Tonight Hitler is on his way to Memel. He will soon be making plans to visit other spots in Europe. Some day someone will have enough guts to pull a trigger and the affair will begin. The British seem to be awake at last and the French definitely are awake.

I wish you could have been here during the past few days to see how a nation should react to a tragic situation.

As you know, in the past three days the French have mobilized two classes and an extra hundred thousand specialists — including one of my kitchen boys. Everyone believes that war is inevitable and that it will come quickly. Every soldier has gone with a quiet resolution that is beyond praise and the wives and mothers and children have been just as calm.

Hitler's invasion of Bohemia and Moravia produced a curious result. It convinced every French man and every French woman that no promise of the dictators was to be relied on; that words were useless; and that Hitler could be stopped by nothing but force. As a result, there is a curious *serenity* from one end of France to the other. There is no vacillation or mourning. The spirit of the people is incomparably better than in 1914 and far better even than the spirit last September. The quiet courage and serenity in France today is the only manifestation in a long time that has made me proud to be a member of the human race.

The German game is obvious and is based on the elementary principle of military strategy that it is wise to strike where your opponents are weakest and defeat them in detail before their forces can be concentrated. Czechoslovakia has gone. Memel has gone, and an effort will be made to establish a virtual protectorate over Lithuania. The Poles then will have three German fronts to defend. They may not be the next on the list because Hungary, Rumania and Yugoslavia may be disintegrated by the pressure and threats which were used in the case of Czechoslovakia and Memel.

If those countries go, the pressure on Poland will be terrific, since the Poles will be able to look forward only to the horror of being once again the battleground for Germans and Russians.

If the Poles should cave in without fighting, the next turn would doubtless be that of France. If there were no friends or allies to the eastward, there would be a terrible temptation to France to make huge concessions to buy off Italy. That obviously would only delay the day of attack on France — and who can say that under those circumstances, Great Britain would not prefer to make her peace with Germany at the expense of France rather than risk an almost certain defeat.

The above is, I believe, the German reasoning. The moral for us is that unless some nation in Europe stands up to Germany quickly, France and England may face defeat and such defeat would mean the French and British fleets in the hands of the Germans and the Italians. We should then have the Japs in the Pacific and an overwhelming fleet against us in the Atlantic.

You know this already and I apologize for repeating it. The important thing is that the people of the United States don't yet know it.

If European war should begin, I believe the American people unanimously would say, "Send supplies to the allies but never, never, never an American soldier." I believe that even though the countries of Europe should fall under German domination, one by one, and even though it should seem that France and England were going to be defeated, the American people would not desire to declare war on Germany unless Germany had committed direct acts of aggression against the United States or American citizens.

I believe, however, that such acts of aggression would be committed and that after not more than a year of European war, the American people would desire to declare war on Germany.

At this point, it seems to me worthwhile to enter the realm of pure imagination. Here are my imaginings.

The only great army on the side of decency is the French Army; the British have even less of an army than we have and it is even worse in all respects than our own. If the French Army should be licked because it simply did not have enough men to put in line against three times the number of Italians and Germans, that would be the end of England also — in spite of the British fleet. The vital point, therefore, if war starts, will become the maintenance of the strength of the French Army.

Americans will begin to realize that fact and will begin to wish to strengthen the French Army — when it will be too late to create an American Army to intervene in time.

We ought to create that army now.

I know from our conversations of last October that you are working on the question of industrial preparation for war all the way from the production of powder down. I think we should start to produce soldiers as well . . .

You may have some General at the present time in the Army that

I know nothing about, but it occurs to me that unless you should have someone who could see this point, it might be worthwhile to bring back Douglas MacArthur, who would have to accept any conditions in advance that you might care to impose on him, and send him to direct our activities in France.

A letter of this sort may make you think that I am already marching into Berlin. I am not, and I hope to God that the whole train of events listed above as a possibility — by no means a certainty — which I have predicted, may never come to pass. I do feel sure, however, that it is essential that we should begin instantly to train a great Army. It is equally essential that we should know that if we should be drawn in, we would want to send as many men as possible to be brigaded with the French.

I wish I could talk this over with you because in order to avoid making this letter endless, I am obliged to state everything baldly and crudely. You will make your own rectifications and you will know anyhow that I am not quite so dumb as I may sound.

Love and good luck.

Yours affectionately,
Bill

Personal and Private　　　　　　　　　　　　　　　　　　　Paris
April 4, 1939

Dear Mr. President:

I lunched today with Daladier, Paul Reynaud and Jean Monnet. Daladier and Reynaud related what they had said to me about the French debt, and all four of us then discussed every aspect of the question.

Daladier said that, since he had the power to govern by decree, he could do anything he pleased about the debt, and stated that he did not care how many islands it might be necessary to turn over to the United States if only the question could be settled.

Reynaud, on the other hand, pointed out that, at a moment when Daladier had reiterated his determination not to give up one inch of French soil to Italy or any other country, it would be a bit inconsistent to hand over French territory to the United States and suggested that if we wanted some islands they might be given to us on the basis of a 99-year concession without transfer of sovereignty or a perpetual lease of bases or some other legal formula. Daladier seemed untroubled by this argument.

The upshot of the discussion was this: Two proposals were approved:

The first, that the French Government should pay at once to the Government of the United States either ten or fifteen percent of the gold reserve of the Banque de France — (the figure of ten billion francs was suggested by Reynaud) — as a gesture of good will, with the explanation that France, now that there was some improvement in the French financial position, desired to recognize in this concrete form the obligation of France to pay its debt to the Government of the United States.

It was clearly understood that this proposal could not relieve France from the operation of the Johnson Act. It was believed, however, that such a payment might remove soreness in America caused by the default.

The second proposal was that an attempt should be made through a payment of ten billion francs plus X, representing an unspecified number of unspecified islands, which might be useful to the United States as naval or airplane bases, to settle the entire question of the debt . . .

I said and repeated that, even though you might consider one of these proposals desirable, you would wish to be extremely careful about the timing of any such proposal. Public opinion in the United States at the moment was so aroused, emotional, and at once sympathetic and suspicious, that a proposal which might not be acceptable one week might be acceptable the next week.

It was finally agreed that Monnet should return to the United States in the near future, carrying a personal letter from Daladier to you empowering him to negotiate. It was understood that if you and he should work out a proposal that seemed satisfactory, the French Government would agree to make such a proposal at such moment as you might indicate.

Both Daladier and Paul Reynaud are convinced that Germany will precipitate general war in Europe before the 15th of May. (I think this is possible but by no means certain.) They are, therefore, most anxious to act quickly. They both said that they wished I would return to the United States with Monnet to try to work out the matter. I replied that I did not see how I could leave Paris at the present time. Both Daladier and Reynaud insisted, saying that I understood the French point of view completely and that it would be worthwhile for me to go home for a short time to work out this question.

Monnet's father has just had a stroke of apoplexy and Monnet left Paris this afternoon to spend two or three days in Cognac. He promised Daladier to see him the moment he returned to Paris.

I anticipate, therefore, the following development. Monnet will arrive in Washington soon after your return from Warm Springs armed with a letter from Daladier. I hope that you will have him come over to the White House some evening alone. It makes no difference whether you invite him to come for dinner or after dinner, because he is one person who has no false pride.

You will find him, as usual, utterly honest-minded and utterly discreet. I think you ought to see him alone and explore all the possibilities, knowing that you can talk with him as indiscreetly as you like, and that there will be no indiscretions. If you can work out something with him, he ought to write Daladier exactly what you think should be done, and if Daladier agrees, the formal proposal should be made to me here. Then you should pick your moment. Don't have Henry the Morgue in on your first conversation. The *Saturday Evening Post* article of April 8, 1939, has made everyone believe that even the most confidential communications with Henry will be published by him.

Reynaud, toward the close of our conversation, brought up the point that the French Government had agreed to make a settlement with the British Government on all fours with any settlement of its debt to the Government of the United States. He added that he was confident that the British Government would waive this right, if the French Government should ask to have it waived. It was agreed that nothing should be said to the British Government about the proposed negotiation with you unless and until you and Monnet should have reached agreement as to the desirable procedure.

Both Daladier and Paul Reynaud are genuinely enthusiastic about the idea. Just to test them out, I threw a bit of cold water, and Monnet poured a lot more. They were unquenched.

Congress might be willing to accept a debt settlement on the "plus X" basis, if you could present it personally to the chief leaders as a great piece of business: i.e., before the cataclysm, you had been able to hornswaggle something of real value to the United States out of France in exchange for debts about to become worthless.

Monnet understands so well both American and French opinion that I feel I could not be of much use during your discussions with him. However, I have no objections to hopping the *Yankee Clipper* if you want me.

Love and good luck.

Yours affectionately,
William C. Bullitt

In April Bullitt apparently told the British Ambassador in Paris that Mr. Roosevelt felt it important for the British to begin conscription of men into the army. For this, he received a telegram from the State Department saying that the President wished him to know that: "The question of conscription in England must be regarded as purely a question of British internal policy involving British decisions as to British national defense, and that for that reason he does not consider it possible for him to express any opinion with regard thereto." [1] Such are the ways of diplomacy that this wire was sent, although Langer and Gleason in *The Challenge to Isolation* say that Bullitt stated to them that the initiative came from the President. (My guess would be that Mr. Roosevelt told Bill on the telephone not to bother too much about the telegram. Bill also was in constant touch by telephone with Ambassador Kennedy in London at this time.)

On March 31 a provisional Anglo-French guarantee of Poland was announced.

Ambassador Lukasiewicz reported on this alliance in the following words: "On Friday, April 7, I went to Boulogne-sur-Mer with Bullitt to meet with Beck who was on his way back to Warsaw from his London visit . . . For the Poles a meeting of our Minister of Foreign Affairs, immediately after discussions with the British Government, and the American Ambassador in Paris, who was known to be President Roosevelt's right-hand man in the field of foreign affairs, was, from the point of view of British and American public opinion, undoubtedly a most desirable event." [2]

Hitler's reaction was prompt and on April 1 he delivered a belligerent speech at Wilhelmshaven. The British Ambassador in Washington, Lord Halifax, told the President that the Germans were planning a surprise attack on the British fleet, and Bullitt reported that Daladier expected war by May 1.

Italy occupied Albania on April 7 and on April 13 the British and French guaranteed the security of Greece and Rumania.

TELEGRAM

This telegram must be closely paraphrased before being communicated to anyone.

Secretary of State   Paris
Washington   Dated April 10, 1939
693, April 10, 7 P.M. (SECTION ONE)   Rec'd 7 P.M.
Personal and Strictly Confidential
for the President and the Secretary

At this moment words no matter how wise have small effect on Hitler and Mussolini. They are still sensitive to acts. I realize fully that public opinion in the United States is not yet acutely aware of the ultimate menace to the American continents involved in the present activities of Germany, Italy and Japan. I venture to suggest for your consideration nevertheless the following unless [sic] this — with the full realization that at this distance I cannot judge whether or not they are within the realm of political possibility:

1. I trust that you will put into effect immediately the measure designed to prevent all payments to Italy which we discussed in draft form when last I was in Washington.

2. I believe that in considering the question of the defense of the United States and the Americas it would be extremely unwise to eliminate from consideration the possibility that Germany, Italy, and Japan may win a comparatively speedy victory over France and England. Under those circumstances the British and French fleets might fall into the hands of our enemies. If in view of this possibility you are thinking of asking Congress to increase either the army or the navy, or both, I believe that such a request at this moment would have an immediate chilling effect on Hitler and Mussolini.

(END SECTION ONE)

                                                            Bullitt

This telegram must be closely paraphrased before being communicated to anyone.

Secretary of State   Paris
Washington   Dated April 10, 1939
693, April 10, 7 P.M. (SECTION TWO)   Rec'd 6:35 P.M.

3. I am entirely uninformed as to your strategic plans for our fleet but I venture to suggest that if the fleet should be sent now either to Honolulu or the Philippines the Japanese would not dare to send an expedition against Singapore.

4. The influence of the United States in Bulgaria is I believe still strong. I believe it might be most important if you should instruct

Atherton to say to the Bulgarian Government, and keep on saying, that we, as friends of the Bulgarian people, hope that the Bulgarian Government will not again choose the side of early victories and ultimate defeat in a great international conflict.

5. I believe the British are digging their own grave by refusing to introduce conscription and by continuing to count on the good faith of Mussolini. If you agree with this opinion I think it might be most helpful if you should ask the British Ambassador in Washington why the British Government has not introduced conscription and why it has not sent ships to Corfu.

(END OF MESSAGE)

Bullitt

Under date of April 10, 1939, Mr. Roosevelt sent Bullitt a memo with a clipping from the New York *Post* attached and asked him, "Anything in this?" The Germans had begun an attack in a Paris newspaper, *Je Suis Partout,* on the Americans and the control exercised by gangsters in the United States. Some headlines were: THE IMBECILITY OF DEMOCRACY, THE PHILOSEMITE ROOSEVELT, etc. The correspondent of the *Post* had done considerable investigation and found that *Je Suis Partout* had been a dying publication and the staff had been laid off. It suddenly sprang to life with a vicious anti-American campaign. He reported that each week when the first copy of *Je Suis Partout* came from the press it was sent to the German Embassy for approval before being issued. It was entirely subsidized with German money.

758, April 17, 5 P.M.
Personal and Confidential for the Secretary

I trust that the usual routine communication of felicitations will not be sent to Hitler on the occasion of his 50th birthday. Such a communication at the present time would diminish greatly the effect of the President's magnificent appeal.

Bullitt

Paris
May 9, 1939

Dear Mr. President:

I believe that the enclosed article from the New York *Post,* which you sent to me recently, is not to be taken too seriously.

The headlines of the article, about the German Embassy in Paris leading "attacks on U.S.," seem to be based upon the statement in the body of the article that the French publication, *Je Suis Partout,* sends its first copy hot off the press to the German Embassy and waits before continuing with the publication of the issue until it gets an O.K., from the Embassy. This is absurd.

Je Suis Partout is generally believed to have been on the German payroll for the past two or three years. It has no influence whatsoever.

Yours always,
Bill

Enclosure.

On April 16 the Soviet Union made a formal offer of a three-power alliance with France and England. The British, unaccountably, delayed accepting the proposal. One result of the failure to accept Russia's proposal was the dismissal of Litvinov as Commissar for Foreign Affairs and the appointment on May 3 of Molotov to succeed him.

Charles C. Tansill in *Back Door to War* gives an excellent account of these negotiations: "In London, Sir Robert Vansittart, the chief diplomatic adviser to the Government, expressed to Bullitt his fears that the dismissal of Litvinov meant the adoption by the Soviet Government of a policy of isolation. If this were true it soon led to the 'collapse of resistance to Hitler in Western Europe and the Balkans.' When Bullitt inquired if Litvinov's resignation had been occasioned by the dilatory and almost insulting policy which the British Government had pursued vis-à-vis the Soviet Union since Hitler's invasion of Czechoslovakia, Vansittart answered that he 'feared that British policy might have contributed to Stalin's attitude.' "

Tansill goes on to say that when Bullitt asked "why the British Government had refused to accept the French proposals relative to action in concert with Russia, Vansittart frankly replied that 'no French proposals had yet reached the British Government.' Sir Eric Phipps, in Paris, had apparently not considered them important enough to rush to the Foreign Office . . . Bullitt now hurried to Paris and persuaded Daladier to telephone to Ambassador Corbin, in London, and direct him to present the French proposals to the British Foreign Office." [3] Unfortunately the British paid little attention to Daladier and made substitute proposals to the Russians. This was the beginning of the end of any possibility of a tripartite alliance against Germany. Litvinov, a Jew and, therefore, anathema to the Nazis, had pursued a policy of collective security with the West, whereas Molotov had always been desirous of a closer entente with Hitler. Russia lost faith in the possibility of England and France's joining in opposition to Germany.

By the end of June the British had changed their tactics and Daladier told Bullitt the British were doing everything possible to accept Russia's demands. It was too late. The Russians had already turned to Germany. The final result did not take place until a week before Hitler invaded Poland, September 1, 1939. With the signing of the Soviet-German pact on August 23 the Nazis felt secure on their eastern front and could avoid the dangers of a war on both east and west frontiers.

849, April 28, 9 P.M.
Personal for the President

Daladier was utterly delighted by his conversation on the telephone with you this evening. He said that he had gotten a better idea of your personality by hearing your voice than from all the photographs of you he had ever seen and all the writings and utterances of yours that he had ever read. His bewitchment was so complete that he assured me your French was impeccable and in the best classic tradition. I replied: "Of course."

Bullitt

Personal and Confidential   Paris
April 18, 1939
Dear Mr. President:
A few weeks ago I asked your old friend and mine, General Réquin, who is now a member of the Supreme War Council, to give me his views on the American Army. Réquin replied that he would prefer to give me his views in writing. He expressed the opinion that in view of world conditions, it might be desirable to bring up

the American Army to the figure of five hundred thousand men.

I have now received a memorandum from him which discusses both the weak points of the American Army and methods of increasing its peace-time strength.

You will remember that it was Réquin who was sent to the United States in 1917 to organize the cooperation between the military forces of the United States and France. If the opinions of anyone in France on our Army are worth anything, his are. Needless to say, no reference should be made to the source from which this memorandum emanates.

Yours affectionately,
William C. Bullitt

THE WHITE HOUSE
WASHINGTON

Confidential   May 3, 1939
Memorandum for General Craig, General Marshall

The enclosed is for your own eyes only. Please read and return.

FDR

WAR DEPARTMENT
OFFICE OF THE CHIEF OF STAFF
WASHINGTON, D.C.

Memorandum for General Watson: May 8, 1939

Herewith is a memorandum from the President enclosing a personal and confidential report. I have naturally carried out the instructions. No one has seen this paper, and I have read it and studied it carefully.

I know General Réquin personally and there is little doubt that his remarks and report were very nearly correct about eighteen months ago. Since then matters have improved materially and within another year with funds now available I believe the deficiencies will be well on the way to being wiped out.

Respectfully,
Malin Craig
Chief of Staff

Enclosure.

General Réquin's voluminous report is of interest in showing our lack of preparedness. In summary, he found that our Army, including the Air Corps, consisted of 178,000 men. The National Guard units were incomplete and in general, ineffective. There were no reserves whatsoever and it was hoped to recruit 75,000 by 1942. Antitank equipment was almost totally lacking. Howitzers of 105, cannons of 155 were available only as prototypes. The antiaircraft had only a small amount of equipment. There were three to four hundred tanks, weakly armored. The organization of the division was antiquated and at least 30,000 officers needed to be trained. Stocks of munitions were small.

General Réquin concluded with several pages of recommendations for modernizing the Army.

Hitler knew that he had little to fear in the immediate future from such an armed force and the report lends additional proof of the impossibility of the United States's taking any active part militarily, if war were to break out.

20

Horses, Israel, and a Queen

APRIL 1939—AUGUST 1939

The Palestine Problem
New Neutrality Act Defeated
Airplane Difficulties
A German Spy
Hitler Refuses to Negotiate

ALTHOUGH WAR APPEARED to be imminent, Bullitt did not overlook various minor matters in his letters to the President, and the following is but one example. That the President was equally interested is shown by the memorandum at the top of the page reminding the President to discuss it at the next meeting of his Cabinet.

Paris
April 19, 1939
Mohler — See Secy. next week.
Send memo on requirements for
registration in English,
American and French

Memorandum for the President
To Take Up at the Cabinet Meeting on Friday
Personal

Dear Mr. President:

Amid the bayings, brayings and barks of Hitler and Mussolini, it is difficult to turn one's mind to other animals; but I want you to know that I have not forgotten the bar sinister which stands in the British and French Studbooks against Man o' War, Gallant Fox and all other American thoroughbreds.

I talked with Boussac, who controls the French Studbook, recently. He, together with Goubert, has been empowered to go to London to attempt to persuade the British Studbook, which is controlled by Lord Roscbery, to admit certain horses bred in France which have American blood lines, but by historical accident are admitted to the French Studbook. Boussac expressed the opinion that Rosebery would continue to refuse to admit American thoroughbreds to the British Studbook because he and other British breeders feared the competition of American breeders . . .

A club probably will have to be used . . .

In case of war, both the British and French will desire to sell large quantities of thoroughbreds to the United States. Such sales would not be prevented by a duty of 17%, and I do not think it would be advisable to try to change this rate, which is bound under our treaty with Canada.

The club I have to suggest would have only slight physical repercussions; but its moral repercussions might be enormous. Suppose William Woodward's horse, Foxbrough II, should win the Derby this year, or suppose his horse Flares should win the Gold Cup. Both of these horses are classified in England as half-breeds. If, after such a win, the Secretary of Agriculture should announce that, since American horses had proved that they were superior to British horses, he must consider that the judgment of the British Studbook as to what constitutes a thoroughbred could no longer be accepted as intelligent or authoritative, but must be considered a judgment based on pecuniary rather than sporting and breeding principles; and that until the British Studbook could prove the contrary by admitting American thoroughbreds to its record, he would be unable to receive any certificate from the British Studbook as evidence that a horse was a thoroughbred and should be admitted free of duty.

Enough people in England know that Rosebery's attitude is ridiculous, and influenced solely by cash considerations, to make the combination of American victory in the Derby or the Gold Cup, plus such a declaration by the Secretary of Agriculture, a real weapon.

The combined brains of yourself, Henry Wallace, Henry Morgenthau and Harry Hopkins will doubtless be able to invent something better than this. Anyhow, I hope you will pass this suggestion along to those who do not care to have our distinguished equines classified as bastards.

Yours affectionately,
William C. Bullitt

Meanwhile Bullitt was reporting to the State Department on developments in Italy. The British Ambassador in Rome had reported to his French colleague that Mussolini wanted the most friendly relations with England and intended to respect the Anglo-Italian pact with regard to the Mediterranean. He further said that Ciano had promised him Italy would not attack Greece and would withdraw from Spain after May 2. Bullitt's comments on all of this were that the British Ambassador was "just as great an ass as he had been all his life and that Mussolini was playing the British for suckers." [1]

For the President's Personal Files Paris
Personal May 4, 1939

Dear Mr. President:
I know that you intervened effectively in London through Joe Kennedy once in this matter. I think you will be interested, therefore, in this letter from Weizmann.*
Good luck.

Yours always,
Bill

Enclosure: 1 letter.

THE DANIEL SIEFF
RESEARCH INSTITUTE
REHOVOTH, PALESTINE

April 23, 1939
My dear Mr. Bullitt:
I arrived here just three weeks ago after an absence of nearly a year and I feel very much impelled to write you of some first impressions insofar as they bear on the subject of our recent talks in Paris.
I have come to Palestine on many occasions during the past 20 years, in times of growth and stagnation, of trouble and of prosperity. Never before, however, have I been made so intensely aware of the extraordinary transformation that has been wrought here in the character and outlook of the Jews. This is no longer a colony or a settlement. It is a real people in the most integral sense of the term . . . Last week the Jewish Labour Party, which represents the

* Chaim Weizmann was President of the World Zionist Organization.

largest force in the Jewish community and, incidentally, one of its most constructive elements, had a memorable conference in which it was decided that no sacrifice would be too heavy if thereby the paralysis of Jewish immigration, the closing of any part of the country to Jewish settlement, and the subjection of the National Home to Arab domination could be prevented. In a resolution which had the austere moral ring of the great historical declarations of the 16th and 17th centuries, it was affirmed that by abandoning its obligation to promote the development of the Jewish National Home, for which essentially the Mandate was entrusted to the British Government, the latter would divest itself of the moral and legal title by which it governs this country and reduce itself to a mere agency of coercion. You know well what the aftermath of such a declaration has been in the past. In the present case it would be fraught with supreme tragedy.

I have conveyed all this in a telegram to the Prime Minister and warned him, in as restrained language as I could use in such circumstances, of what was here at stake. I made it clear to him that the Jews were determined to make the supreme sacrifice rather than submit to such a regime. Their position is so desperate that they have little to lose . . . At a time when millions of Jews are undergoing a sadistic persecution such as the world has not known since the darkest ages, the Jews of Palestine will not put up with the land in which a National Home was solemnly promised to them by the civilised world being closed to their harassed brethren. Immigration will continue with or without Government permission as it is continuing in these days despite the Procrustean restrictions imposed upon it. Tragedies of which the world hears very little are being enacted every day along the coast of Palestine. Boats, overloaded with refugees from German concentration camps, are floating about for weeks on end in the Mediterranean, their passengers starved and afflicted with the diseases of hunger and exhaustion, among them women and children of tender age. Some of these boats have been caught by British patrol vessels and dragged to the coast then to be pushed out again into the open sea with their human cargo. Can you visualize the feelings of the Jews of this country in witnessing these ghastly spectacles, when they know all the time that these unfortunate people could be productively absorbed in Palestine without any harm being done to the Arabs?

What makes the policy of the Government so utterly amazing is the complete ignorance which it betrays of the realities of the situation in this part of the world. Every day the Arab press of the neighbouring countries reveals the fear of war that is shaking the Arab world. Their only hope is that the Western democratic powers may protect them against the onslaught of the totalitarian regimes. Never before has the British army been so popular in Egypt as it is these days. In Syria the French meet with a sympathy from the nationalist extremists such as would have been inconceivable a year ago. And at this moment when the Arabs are so evidently dependent on British help and are so conscious of it, the British Government embarks on a policy which can only be explained, if at all, by their fear that the Arabs would turn against them in case of war. For this policy the Government is prepared to sacrifice the Jews who could be of real help to them in an international conflict and whose loyalty is beyond any shadow of doubt. As the ancient Latin has it, it is sometimes "difficult not to write a satire."

I am sorry to trouble you with all this, but as I know how interested you are in the problem I trust you will forgive me for expatiating on it at such length. Perhaps you may find it possible to convey some of this to your Government. It is the only one which may conceivably still be able to prevail upon the British Government to desist from a course which, I am convinced, can only end in disaster. But it would have to be done most speedily and with more than ordinary emphasis.

> With cordial regards,
> Yours very sincerely,
> Ch. Weizmann

Personal and Secret   Paris
April 28, 1939

Dear Mr. President:

I wish I could telegraph this piece of news to you today; but Léger gave it to me on condition that it positively should not be sent by telegraph.

Gafencu, while passing through Poland, came to an understanding with Beck that, in case of an attack on Poland by Germany, Rumania would declare war at once on the side of Poland; and in case of an attack on Rumania by Germany, Poland would declare war at once on Germany.

This secret agreement was communicated orally to Chamberlain and Daladier by Gafencu. It has been concealed with extreme care from Berlin, and for obvious reasons must continue to be concealed.

Daladier stated to Gafencu today that it was absolutely essential, however, that the Rumanian Government should inform the Turkish Government that this agreement had been reached, so that the Anglo-Turkish and Franco-Turkish agreements might enter into effect at once.

Gafencu implored Daladier not to say a word about the agreement to the Turks; but promised that he would send a personal emissary to communicate the fact of the existence of this agreement to Ismet Inönü in Ankara.

Please hold this piece of information for your most secret ear. Just as soon as it ceases to be so utterly secret, I will send a telegram to the Department on the subject.

Yours affectionately,

Bill

Personal and Secret   Paris

May 4, 1939

Dear Mr. President:

Otto of Hapsburg * came to see me . . . this morning. He had lots of information which appeared to be reliable.

The most lurid bit which I pass to you for your private ear only, since he pledged me to secrecy, is the following:

On the morning when Mussolini decided to make war on Albania, he called on the King to inform him that in spite of his promises to the Albanian Government and in spite of his assurances to England, he intended to take over Albania by force.

The King stated to Mussolini that he would not be party to such an action which would bring dishonor to his name. He would resign at once in favor of the Prince of Piedmont. Mussolini then stated that in case the King should resign, the Fascist Grand Council would not permit the Prince of Piedmont to accede to the Throne, but would choose the Duke of Aosta.

Marshal Badoglio was then drawn into the conversation. He supported the King and stated that if Mussolini should attempt to have the Duke of Aosta take the Throne in place of the Prince of Piedmont, the Army would support the Prince of Piedmont. The conversation was excessively stormy and it was finally decided to call in the Prince of Piedmont.

The Prince persuaded his father not to abdicate.

* Otto of Hapsburg is the eldest son of Charles, the last Emperor of Austria. Otto later came to Philadelphia as Bullitt's guest.

Otto expressed the opinion that Badoglio, Balbo, the Army officers and the Royal House would soon see to it that Mussolini should meet an early death. The King would abdicate, the Prince of Piedmont would succeed him, and would issue a new constitution which would be somewhat similar to the present Serbian constitution. The chief men in the new regime would be Grandi and Balbo.

From the details given by Otto, I am inclined to believe that there was a very stormy scene between the King and Mussolini, but I am naturally inclined to doubt that Mussolini will shortly be translated into another sphere.

Good luck.

Yours affectionately,
William C. Bullitt

Personal   Paris
                                                          May 9, 1939
Dear Mr. President:

In spite of Daladier's insistence that your French is impeccable, you didn't seem particularly quick on the uptake when he asked you if he could appoint me French Minister for Foreign Affairs!

Nevertheless, he was bowled over by the sound of your voice.

On account of that or for some other reason, he asked me at once to draft for him a law to increase the French birth rate which he would promulgate by decree! I do not know quite what to suggest unless it is to have Joe Kennedy transferred to Paris!

The . . . Queen is now on her way to you together with the . . . King . . .

When she touched the subject of royal presents, I suggested that you would be touched close to the heart, at least as close as the stomach, by a Stilton cheese. If she brings it, you can blame and excuse me.

The . . . King is beginning to feel his oats . . . Joe Kennedy gave the Queen Virginia Ham and Pickled Peaches. She ate vast quantities, and expressed a royal desire to become more closely acquainted with the dish when in America.

I have no other tips to give you except the obvious one that it is well not to mention the Duke and Duchess of Windsor unless the King brings up the subject. He probably won't . . .

The only low news from Paris this week concerns —————— six feet five, Germanophile, and ex Minister. He has faded quickly from the political picture due to the event which occurred about two weeks ago. Daladier is my authority for this. He said that ——— called on a young lady who lives near me and was in bed with her when her *amant de coeur* broke into the apartment; beat up ——— and drove him into the street half-clothed, minus his watch, wallet, and trousers! Daladier does not expect any serious opposition from ——— in the near future.

Good luck and may you have a good time as sovereign to sovereign over my Pommery.

Yours affectionately,

Bill

Personal and Secret   Paris

May 9, 1939

Dear Mr. President:

I enclose herewith a secret report of the French General Staff which has been compiled from information gathered by the French Secret Service and is the basis on which the French General Staff has prepared its plans for coping with the German Air Force. I thought you would rather have it in extenso rather than in summary. Please note that it is *absolutely secret*.

A few days ago, La Chambre, Minister for Air, said to me that owing to the failure of the Bloch prototype which the French had expected to be as good or better than the Amiot, he had become sincerely interested in the possibility of manufacturing the Amiot plane in the United States. At the same time I received a memorandum prepared by Joseph C. Green of the Department of State which had been seen and approved by the Assistant Secretary of War, dated April 20th, reporting a conversation between these two representatives of our Government and Mr. Sol Rosenblatt on the subject of the proposed company to manufacture Amiot planes in the United States.* In that memorandum our Government representatives expressed the opinion that they "did not believe that it would be opportune for the proposed company to incorporate and begin operations *at this time.*"

The purport of the memorandum was that the project as described by Rosenblatt differed materially from the project described previously; and it was intimated that at a later date, the De-

* Sol Rosenblatt, a New York lawyer and a personal friend of Pierre Wertheimer, head of the company manufacturing the Amiot airplanes.

partment of State and the War Department might look upon it with approval.

In view of Guy La Chambre's remarks to me, I wonder if it might not be possible for you to have either the War Department or the Department of State take up the matter again with the aforementioned Rosenblatt.

Yours affectionately,
William C. Bullitt

Enclosure: Report.

THE WHITE HOUSE
WASHINGTON

May 24, 1939

Dear Bill:

On receipt of your letter of May 9 in regard to the Rosenblatt project, I took the matter up with the War Department and the Department of State. The question has been fully reconsidered. I agree however, with the two Departments that it would be very inadvisable from our point of view for Rosenblatt to go ahead with his project at this time. If he wishes to take it up again two or three months from now, the Departments will be glad to review the question in the light of the circumstances then existing, and it is possible that the situation might by that time have changed sufficiently so that we would be prepared to reverse our present position.

Affectionately yours,
FDR

The Honorable William C. Bullitt
American Ambassador
Paris

In May the Neutrality Act was coming under more and more pressure and a bill was introduced in the House of Representatives to modify it to permit purchases in the United States by England and France. On May 10, Bullitt had cabled Hull that both the French and British felt that the passage of the bill would be a strong deterrent to Hitler's going to war. The bill was defeated, and the reaction from American embassies and ministries throughout Europe was that the European countries regarded it as a blow to England and France. The Germans were, of course, delighted. In July, Bullitt wired to Hull, for the President, that with the failure of the bill in the opinion of the British and the French the chances of Hitler's going to war in August had been increased.

In a spur-of-the-moment decision Mussolini decided to enter into a military alliance with Hitler, and, as a result, the so-called Pact of Steel was signed between Germany and Italy in Berlin on May 22, 1939.

THE WHITE HOUSE

WASHINGTON

May 16, 1939

Dear Bill:

Thank you for the several documents this morning. I have not forgotten George [Earle] but, as you know, it will be a bit easier to fit him in somewhere in a month or two than just at this minute. I will try to see Henry Grady.

I had a nice talk with M. [Monnet] and since then he has seen Morgenthau twice. The gist of it is that we are all agreed that a somewhat elastic formula holds out some hope in the future but that the present time is inopportune. I told him frankly that I thought it would be a mistake for his government to deplete a bettering cash condition for a little while.

As to X, I explained to him that one or two of the larger localities would be a headache to us if we had to run them and that the money value of two or three smaller places would amount to a sum so small that even if they were of some military use to us the amount worth paying would be a drop in the bucket compared with the total owed or compared with the total of a settlement. I think he is entirely satisfied with the friendly and practical approach and also with the thought that this is not a good time to push it to any publicity stage.

It is grand of you to send the Champagne and I do wish you could be here at the time of the visit.

By the way, in regard to Reed, apparently Bill Phillips and the people here feel he has been doing a good job in Rome . . .

My best to you,

As ever yours,

FDR

Honorable William C. Bullitt
American Embassy
Paris, France

THE WHITE HOUSE
WASHINGTON

May 16, 1939

Dear Bill:

I am told that the pouch leaves today and I want to get this letter off to you to thank you for all that champagne. I really do not see why you should do this, but I know we are all going to enjoy it very much although I assure you I am not using all of it even on the Royal visitors.

I only wish you could be here with us the time of the Royal visit. At any rate I will quietly drink to your good health at the dinner.

Your letter of the ninth has just arrived and is a joy. I know you will do a good job on the French Birth Rate Law!

The little Queen has acquired a great reputation over here. It may be a difficult one to live up to. Needless to say, there is great excitement here. However, I think we will all heave a great sigh of relief once they cross the Canadian border safely on their way home.

I loved the story of —————. It is a joy.

Do write me again very soon.

As ever,

FDR

Honorable William C. Bullitt
American Extraordinary and Plenipotentiary
Paris, France

Early in June Bullitt returned to the United States, again to see a Philadelphia doctor about an injury to his shoulder which was bothering him. He only remained a week, but during that time received a letter from Alfred Harcourt of Harcourt, Brace and Company, publishers, attempting to revive in him an interest in writing an account of his career. Harcourt said, "An important book for the American public now would be one which your success in Russia and France is clear evidence of your ability to write." Unfortunately, Bullitt could never be persuaded to write about his own career, although he wrote many articles for *Life* in later years, and his writings also appeared in the *Reader's Digest* and other periodicals. In 1946 his book *The Great Globe Itself* was published. It treated of the machinations of Stalin and the Soviet Government and the failure of the American postwar foreign policy. He summarized what our policy should be and made a number of prophetic statements. In his last years many pleaded, often and unsuccessfully, that he should write at least one book on his experiences as Ambassador to Russia and to France. This book, which is his and Roosevelt's, in a small way replaces what he might have written.

While he was in Philadelphia I had told him he had some stock in two airplane companies and I received a letter from him saying he was "surprised and somewhat shocked . . . I feel that since I am a government employee at the present time, I should not hold stock in any company making munitions or implements of war." I sold the stocks.

Personal and Secret   Paris
                                                      June 1, 1939
Dear Mr. President:

You had better keep this one for your own eye and ear and for yours alone.

Daladier told me in great confidence a few days ago that a French inventor had brought to him a bag of pellets about half the size of confetti with the statement that the stuff, strewn on crops or forests, would set a fire which could not be put out. The inventor claimed, moreover, that he had the stuff in three forms: one to start an immediate fire; another to start a fire after a week; and a third to start a fire in two weeks. The French Army tried out the invention under most secret conditions and found out that his claims were true!

Daladier naturally is, to put it mildly, somewhat reluctant to consider using the stuff. I thought you would be interested, however, to know it exists. The Germans must have inventions that are equally diabolical, and contemplation of the possibilities gives one some idea of what the next war will be like.

Daladier also said that another French inventor had developed a very fine dust to be sprayed in the air from airplanes which would stop instantly any airplane motor that attempted to fly through the area containing it.

Monnet let me know that you had talked with him about the matter of attempting to talk to the German people in order to separate them, if possible, from their leaders. I asked Daladier if he had been thinking of doing anything on this line. He said that he had and that he was contemplating setting up a private radio station in Alsace to broadcast in German for this purpose.

You will remember that during the last war, it was my job to prepare the memoranda for the propaganda designed to destroy the confidence of the German people in their government. I forget if I ever told you the method I used which proved to be most effective. I used to have telegraphed to me every day — by Hugh Wilson and Allen Dulles in Bern, by John Wiley and Aleck Kirk in The Hague, and by Lithgow Osborne in Copenhagen — every criticism of the Kaiser's regime that appeared in Germany. At that time, there were about a dozen German and Austrian Socialist and Radical papers that were permitted to criticize by the relatively liberal regime that existed in Germany and Austria-Hungary. The result was that the Left in Germany heard its own words coming back from President Wilson's mouth or other sources within a week.

Unfortunately, there is no longer any free press in Germany or Italy; but much information is smuggled out. Furthermore, Hitler's answer to a repetition of this maneuver by the United States would be too easy. He can kill anything that you or any American may say by merely repeating to the German people, "Here is the old Wilson tactic again." That is enough to nullify the effect of anything from American sources. I feel, therefore, that both the British and the French are in a much better position to pursue such tactics than we are.

When I went to London for Joe Kennedy's dinner for the King and Queen, I saw Vansittart who is in charge of British propaganda and put him in touch with the one German who can handle such propaganda most effectively. I hope that may produce some action from the British end, and I will do what I can to see that the French get on the job.

Much as I dislike to refrain from trying my own hand at the job once more, I feel that it would be folly for us to try to repeat . . .

While we are on Embassies, I think I ought to tell you that Joe Kennedy phones several times a week to say that he is about to resign. I don't believe for one minute that he will. If he does, for Gawd's sake, don't appoint Mrs. Davies Ambassador to the Court of St. James's. That would break the bull's neck! . . .

Brother Hitler and the Gauleiter of Italy seem not to be contemplating starting a war in June so that I am hopeful that I may see you on the 12th. I shall leave again for Paris on the 21st.

Love and good luck.

Bill

Enclosure.

Admiral Roscoe H. Hillenkoetter, who was Naval Attaché at the Embassy in Paris, has written the following account of the thoroughly unorthodox way in which Bullitt acted as an Ambassador.

3 Kingswood Road
Weehawken, N.J. 07087
19 October 1970

Dear Orville:

. . . In the late spring of 1939, the F.B.I. here turned up evidence indicating a blonde German beauty parlor operator, female, was doing espionage for the Nazis. A warrant was issued for her, but before she could be arrested she fled to one of the German transatlantic passenger steamers which was just sailing for Europe and she got away on the liner. The papers were filled with reports of the beautiful (exaggerated) German beautician and how she had made her escape.

The ship was scheduled to stop at Cherbourg, the first port after New York. Bill called me down to his office a day or so after the German ship left N. Y. and said he was going to make up a warrant for her arrest and that I was to carry it to Cherbourg, board the German ship on its arrival, arrest this "blonde beautician," and return her to the U.S. Our new ship, the *United States,* would even delay her sailing from Le Havre in order to take this female aboard and return her to New York.

I told the Ambassador that he ought to know any warrants issued by him didn't amount to anything in France and had no legal force or standing. He said of course he knew that, but try and see what could be done anyway.

In the Embassy we fixed up an imposing looking document, with lots of seals, etc., and I started off to Cherbourg with it. When I got to Cherbourg I went to the French police, told them the story, showed them the warrant and asked their help to go aboard the German ship when it arrived and remove the spy.

As I had thought, the French immediately said that the warrant wasn't worth anything (which was correct) and the state of feeling between France and Germany at that time was a little too tense for them to permit going aboard and taking off any passengers or crew members. The French police did make one concession, however. If our blonde disembarked at all in Cherbourg, even if only for a walk around town, they would take her, turn her over to me on Bill's

warrant and I could drive her up to Le Havre and put her aboard
the *United States*. Then, by the time anybody, meaning the Germans, complained, she would be on her way back to the United
States.

Well, to sum up, the woman in question did not leave the ship in
Cherbourg, so all the above steps went for naught. But we got "A"
for effort and it was so characteristic of Bill to try and get the right
solution in a difficult and involved situation . . .

Sincerely,
Hilly

By July the German Army was sufficiently on a war footing that
they could attack Poland without warning, and without disclosing
their plans by calling for a general mobilization of troops. The
French, however, were not fully mobilized, and the general feeling was that if Hitler were going to strike he would wait until
September. By that time, snow beginning to fall in the Alps
would help to protect Italy from any attack on the part of the
French. The French were pursuing a purely defensive plan, with
the expectation that Germany, being the aggressor, would have to
attack what the French believed to be almost impregnable positions. We now know that Hitler was determined to attack Poland
and was prepared for the consequences. Bullitt had wired Secretary Hull on June 28 that Poland believed the chances of war
with Germany by the middle of August were eighty out of one
hundred. They were only two weeks early in their estimate. [2]

As in the case of Czechoslovakia, Hitler had made his plans far
in advance. While continuing diplomatic pressure on Poland
about Danzig and the Polish corridor, he gave orders to his generals on April 3, 1939, to prepare for an attack and set the date for
action as September 1, the day on which his armies crossed the
border.

Saul Friedlander in *Prelude to Downfall* describes the situation
in July in these terms: "William Bullitt, in the chaotic situation
then existing in France, was one of the most active instigators of
resistance to Hitler, and his influence was far greater than that of
any other ambassador. Moreover, he enjoyed the full confidence
of the President. On July 4, 1939, the Italian Ambassador to Paris

denounced Bullitt at the Chigi Palace as 'the most relentless adversary of Hitler'!" [3]

THE WHITE HOUSE

WASHINGTON

Confidential   July 28, 1939
Memorandum for Ambassador Bullitt, Ambassador Kennedy

I have been asked if there is any objection to private purchasing agencies being set up in this country by certain European powers, in order to centralize purchases of various kinds which they may wish to make over here. It seems to me that we should remember that these nations and the United States are at peace with the world, and that there can be no objection to the setting up of such purchasing agencies provided (a) their operations do not violate the Johnson Act, and (b) that in the event they become involved in war, their operations will not violate Section #1 of the Neutrality Law, commonly referred to as the Embargo Clause.

FDR

Done August 3rd
12:00 Noon
C.O.

THE WHITE HOUSE

WASHINGTON

July 28, 1939

Dear Bill:

I enclose a number of documents, together with an explanatory note to my Mother. Will you do the necessary about getting her signature to the deed and the proper acknowledgments, etc., in order that all the papers, including the deed from Mrs. F. D. Roosevelt and myself, for the transfer of the Library site to the United States Government may be filed and the building started?

As ever,
Franklin D. Roosevelt

Honorable William C. Bullitt
American Embassy
Paris, France
Enclosures.

THE WHITE HOUSE
WASHINGTON

August 25, 1939

Memorandum of President's Telephone Conversation with Ambassador Bullitt

This is the gist of the message sent by the President of Poland to the President of the United States in answer to his proposal sent the day before.

Thanks you profoundly and accepts direct negotiation or conciliation by any power which is an honorable neutral. He passes over in silence the question of arbitration. He expresses the hope that the note will produce the results desired. Poland is demanding nothing of Germany anywhere. They might be thinking of negotiations.

1619, August 27, midnight
Strictly Confidential

Daladier read to me this evening at 8:30 the text of the message which he received at 8 o'clock from Hitler . . .

Hitler then confirmed his refusal to enter into direct negotiations with Poland, concerning Danzig, and thought that Danzig must be returned to the Reich without negotiations.

Hitler then said that if there were war, the country which would suffer the most would be Poland, because Poland would be utterly crushed, and nobody would ever think of reconstructing Poland in its present boundaries. At this point Daladier commented that Hitler was in a sense right since Poland would be reconstructed with larger boundaries and no Germans within those boundaries.

This extremely brief summary gives the gist of a great mass of argumentation.

Daladier further stated that so far as he was concerned, there was no further question of policy to be settled. His sister today had put in two bags all the personal keepsakes and belongings that he really cared about, and was prepared to leave for a secure spot at any moment. France intended to stand by the Poles, and if Hitler should refuse to negotiate with the Poles about Danzig, and should make war on Poland, France would fight at once.

Daladier said that the British Government had not yet informed him what line it intended to take in reply to Hitler's communication to Henderson, and the subsequent message sent by airplane this afternoon. All that he had was a statement from Corbin, French Ambassador in London, that he believed that the British reply to Hitler would resemble his, Daladier's reply . . .

Bullitt

Personal and Strictly Confidential   Paris

August 29, 1939

Dear Mr. President:

Throughout the past few weeks, I have done a great many things that I have not put in the cables.

I haven't time to report, and you would not have time to read, a full list of performances . . .

I have seen Daladier constantly and intimately throughout this crisis. I do not telegraph half what he says to me for the simple reason that there is nothing he doesn't say and some of his remarks would raise hell if they should be known. He is a fine fellow and I am very fond of him and he has an altogether too-exalted idea of my own value. In consequence, he asks my judgment about nearly everything of great importance not only in the field of foreign affairs but also in the field of domestic policy, and what's more, he is apt to do what I advise.

Last Friday when he lunched with me alone at the house in town, he told me with tears in his eyes that he had said to General Gamelin that morning that the recovery of France was not due to him, but to me, and added that he didn't know whether there was a God or not, but if there was, and I ever faced Him, I need only say: "I stand on what I did for decency in the world when I was Ambassador in Paris." !!!!

The truth is that he doesn't completely trust any French politician and he needs someone to talk to that will not repeat what he says and can give him disinterested advice. He is trying now to get the house next to mine at Chantilly.

If you have any advice to give Daladier, please write me. He will take it seriously.

Love and good luck.

Bill

FOUR

War in France
1939 – 1940

21

War

British and French Failure in Russia
German-Russian Pact
War Begins
Poland's Defeat
United States's Help Needed
French Fears

WAR WAS NOW inevitable. In early August both the British and French had missions in Moscow endeavoring to come to an understanding with Russia, but it was too late. The opportunity had been lost when Russia was rebuffed in April, and the Russians had now agreed to receive a German envoy in Moscow. In 1942 Stalin told Churchill that the Russians had formed the impression that the British and the French would not go to war if Poland was attacked. Stalin understood the French could mobilize one hundred divisions and the British would at once send two, with two more to follow. Stalin said that the Russians could oppose the Germans with over three hundred divisions. On August 19, Stalin told the Politburo he intended to sign an agreement with Germany. On August 22 Ribbentrop, the German Foreign Minister, arrived in Moscow. When he met with Stalin and presented a pact the same day, Stalin insisted he remove a reference to friendly German-Soviet relations on the grounds that a sudden declaration of friendship, after the Germans had covered them with pails of manure for six years, was impossible. The pact was signed the next day and Germany was free to face France without fear of a Russian attack in the rear.

On August 16 our Ambassador in Moscow, Laurence Steinhardt, had cabled Hull that German-Russian negotiations were taking place and that he believed the British and French had not been informed of them.[1] Bullitt had wired Hull that his information was that Hitler had decided to attack Poland before August 30. Hull noted that Bullitt was frequently on the telephone to the White House and the State Department in these tragic days.[2] At three o'clock in the morning of September 1 Bullitt telephoned the sleeping President. Hitler was advancing on Poland. War had begun.

Two days later Britain and France declared war.

Acting Secretary of the Navy Charles Edison made a memorandum of what Roosevelt said to the Cabinet that afternoon. "Friday at ten minutes of three o'clock in the morning Ambassador Bullitt telephoned me from Paris the tragic news that hostilities had commenced in earnest, that bombs were falling on Polish cities. Within a few minutes I had reached Secretary Hull, Secretary Woodring and Acting Secretary Edison — State, War and Navy. Lights soon were burning in many offices. The machinery of democratic government moved swiftly and moved efficiently.

"An unknown and unknowable destiny yawned before mankind that morning. Yet, I was almost startled by a strange feeling of familiarity — a feeling that I had been through it all before. But after all it was not strange. During the long years of the World War the telephone at my bedside with a direct wire to the Navy Department had time and again brought me other tragic messages in the night — the same rush messages were sent around — the same lights snapped on in the nerve centers of government. I had in fact been thru it all before. It was not strange to me but more like picking up again an interrupted routine.

"Unless some miracle beyond our present grasp changes the hearts of men the days ahead will be crowded days — crowded with the same problems, the same anxieties that filled to the brim those September days of 1914. For history does in fact repeat." [3]

Secretary Hull provided an even more dramatic account: "The telephone rang stridently beside my bed. Tense from days of preparing and waiting, I wakened and turned on the light. It was almost three o'clock in the morning of Friday, September 1, 1939. I picked up the receiver.

" 'Cordell,' came the President's voice, 'Bullitt has just been on the phone. The Germans have invaded Poland.'

"The moment I recognized the President's voice I guessed the rest. But the news, though expected, was nonetheless a shock . . . I said to the President I intended going to my office at once. After hastily dressing and telling Mrs. Hull what had happened, I drove to the State Department and walked through the deserted corridors to my office at about 3:30.

"I asked that my principal assistants come to my office immediately. Soon I was joined by Welles, whom the President had telephoned directly. One by one the others came in, their faces alert and anxious . . .

"From my office I telephoned to Bullitt in Paris and Kennedy in London, asking for their news and appraisal . . . As reports came in later of German bombing of Warsaw and other Polish cities, I also sought confirmation.

"Exactly one week before, Ambassador Bullitt had sent the President, through me, a personal message suggesting that immediately after the first shot the President should issue to all nations concerned an appeal to refrain from bombing civilian populations . . . The President and I agreed that the appeal should be made, and Welles drafted it and had it ready. Bullitt now telephoned me, confirmed reports of the bombing of Warsaw and urged that the appeal be sent at once. We accordingly dispatched it immediately to Britain, Germany, France, Poland and Italy." [4]

The story of the German Blitzkrieg has often been told. In two days the Nazis practically wiped out the Polish Air Force. The Poles were a gallant, brave people, but in many instances they were fighting with outdated armament and methods. Photographs exist of Polish cavalry, armed with lances and galloping on superb white horses, attacking German tanks. At the end of two weeks the Polish Army of two million men had almost ceased to exist and Warsaw was being defended by its citizens. On September 17 the Russian vulture swooped down on the Polish rear and by the end of the month all resistance had disappeared. On September 29 Germany and Russia formally divided Poland.

The Russian history books carry this account of the treacherous attack on a defenseless state. "After Germany's attack on Poland and the collapse of the Polish Bourgeois-Landowner state, the Soviet Government issued an order to the Red Army (September 17, 1939) to cross the frontier and take under its protection the lives and property of the population of Western Ukraine and Western Byelorussia . . .

"The Fifth Session of the Supreme Soviet of the U.S.S.R. (November 1–2, 1939) at the request of the peoples of Western Ukraine and Western Byelorussia accepted them into the U.S.S.R. (a population of 10,000,000)." [5]

There is a dearth of letters at this time about the vital events which were occurring. This was due to the fact that Roosevelt and Bullitt were in constant touch by telephone, sometimes more than once a day and in the words of Robert Murphy, at that time Counselor of Embassy in Paris, "The two men threshed out matters of policy with no correspondence to record their discussions." [6]

Personal and Confidential   Paris
                                                        September 8, 1939

Dear Mr. President:

Daladier said to me this afternoon, "If we are to win this war, we shall have to win it on supplies of every kind from the United States. We can hold for a time without such supplies; but England and ourselves can not possibly build up sufficient production of munitions and planes to make a successful offensive possible." That statement is true.

Our military men in Paris are apt to go a step further and say that they are not sure that the British and French can hold out until transatlantic production can be brought into the struggle. There is a chance that Hitler may defeat France and England quickly. The German planes have completely disorganized the Polish defense, and they may do as much when they are turned loose on France and England this autumn. By next Spring the French and British aviation and anti-aircraft guns will be able to hold the balance.

Thus far, in France, there is a curious unreality about the war. The whole mobilization was carried out in absolute quiet. The men left in silence. There were no bands, no songs. There were no shouts of "On To Berlin" and "Down with Hitler" to match the shouts of, "On To Berlin" and "Down with the Kaiser!" as in 1914. There was no hysterical weeping of mothers, and sisters and children. The self-control and quiet courage has been so far beyond the usual standard of the human race that it has had a dream quality.

I expect the Germans to complete soon their destruction of Poland; then to offer peace to France and England. The French and British will reject this proposal and go on fighting. Then the Germans will turn loose on France and England their full air force with everything, including gas and bacteria.

I do not exclude altogether the possibility that Germany may be able to break the French line, but I do not believe that this will happen.

It is, of course, obvious that if the Neutrality Act remains in its present form, France and England will be defeated rapidly.

My work here has nearly ended. Even the problem of Americans stranded in France has been handled insofar as it can be handled on this shore. Very few Americans are coming now to the Embassy, because we have them all planted at safe places in western France waiting for boats. The usual diplomatic work has stopped since the Generals and their cannons have now taken the place of the politicians and their notes. I pick up the customary quantities of information, military and political, but I don't dare to send it by cable for fear that it may be of use to the Germans. As a result, I'm feeling rather useless.

I should like to stay in Paris through the period when the Germans turn loose their air bombardment of the city. We shall get the worst of that during the latter part of this month and in the month of October.

By November, the war will, in the customary manner, hibernate. If I'm still alive, that will be about the time for you to set me to work in the United States of America. Tony Biddle won't have a country anymore, and you can make him Ambassador in Paris.

You can put me in the Cabinet.

Otherwise, everything is all right.

Love and good luck.

Yours affectionately.

Bill

The Polish Ambassador in Paris, Lukasiewicz, gave an account at this time, September 10, 1939, of the effort of the Poles to bring the French and British air forces into action against Germany. He asked Premier Daladier to give the order and Daladier told him that the French Air Force had been ready for four days to bomb military objectives in Germany, but the British had refused. In answer to Lukasiewicz's question as to the British unwillingness to act, Daladier replied that such bombing might entail civilian losses and the British feared this might offend American public opinion. Daladier then told him to see Bullitt. Bullitt came in at once from Chantilly and, when Lukasiewicz explained the situation, told him "in no uncertain terms, that he considered such an eventuality to be absolutely impossible." Two hours later Bullitt told the Polish Ambassador that after talking with President Roosevelt and Ambassador Kennedy he was certain that nothing had been said to the British and that the bombing of German military targets would have no adverse effect on American opinion. Bullitt also gave this information to Premier Daladier. Lukasiewicz's comment was: "No one could understand the peculiar method by which the Allies fulfilled their alliance obligations toward Poland and conducted a war without fighting." [7]

Personal and Strictly Confidential   Paris
                                                    September 13, 1939
Dear Mr. President:

As I have stopped cabling the lowdown because I do not wish to risk communicating anything to the Boches, I am supplementing my cable of today by this brief word.

Daladier said to me today that when he talked to Chamberlain yesterday, he found himself in the presence of a man who seemed to him broken. He said that Chamberlain had aged terribly since last he had seen him, and had made the impression of a man who had passed from middle age into decrepitude.

He added that he felt that Chamberlain had a virtue for Great Britain at the moment. He was as typical an Englishman as anyone in the pages of Dickens and he might be, therefore, very useful for a while; but before the war should be won he would have to be replaced by a more vigorous man.

Daladier was really shocked by the cynical selfishness of Chamberlain's attitude toward the bombardment of Poland and his refusal to use the modern, excellent and numerous English bombing planes for the bombardment of military objectives in Germany.

On the other hand, he was pleased by certain aspects of their conversation. He proposed to Chamberlain the setting up of a complete organization for purchases of France and England in the United States during the war, and Chamberlain accepted this proposal.

As you may remember, it was Jean Monnet who, during the last war, set up the interallied purchasing agency and also the interallied shipping pool. Daladier intends to try to have Monnet appointed as the representative of both the French and British Governments for purchases in the United States.

I do not consider that it is impossible that the British will accept this proposal. So many Britishers know what Monnet did during the last war for the common cause, and so many others know how superbly efficient he was as the first Under Secretary of the League of Nations, that he may be accepted even by our British brethren.

Daladier said that if the British should reject Monnet to head this agency, he would like to appoint Monnet French Ambassador in Washington.

I expressed the opinion that while Monnet would do excellently in Washington, he could be much more useful if he were relieved from the polite duties of an Ambassador and charged with nothing but the serious business of supply.

You will have had from my telegram the news of the change that Daladier is contemplating making in his Cabinet long before this letter reaches you. I did not say in the telegram that Daladier had remarked that at all costs he must get rid of Bonnet, who would otherwise continue to conspire with Flandin, Pietri and other defeatists.

Daladier is in fine form, immensely burdened, of course, by the terrible responsibility that is on his shoulders; but carrying it like a man and by no means broken by it.

Most important! Daladier and I discussed the general question of the blockade. You will recall that from 1914 until the entry of the United States into the war in 1917, the Government of the United States hampered greatly the British and French blockade of Germany by maintaining a series of positions which were abandoned the moment the United States entered the war.

I believe that there is no way that we can help more at the present time than by taking at once the position vis-à-vis the blockade which we finally took after the entry into war of the United States in 1917. I believe that we should accept *in toto* the rules which we ourselves accepted then — some of which we invented. You will not need to take any affirmative action, but you will need to instruct the Department of State not to protest in any way when the French and British begin to turn the screws.

So far as I am concerned, I hope the screws will be turned quickly and completely. This, I hope, in our national interest as well as in the interest of decency in Europe. It is absolutely certain that if France and England should be unable to defeat Hitler in Europe, we shall have to fight him some day in the Americas. Please instruct the Department to get out our own blockade rules of 1918 and let the French and British apply them. You will have probably done this already, so I apologize for an unnecessary reminder.

Love and good luck.

Bill

Personal and Confidential   Paris
September 16, 1939

Dear Mr. President:

I sent a telegram today which you have probably seen, describing the manner in which the German Air Force destroyed nine-tenths of the Polish Air Force at noon on the first of September. My informant was the French Minister for Air . . .

In the course of our conversation, La Chambre added a number of facts about air fighting on the western front which I did not consider it wise to put in my cable. He said that there had been a number of air engagements between the Curtiss pursuit planes, which the French bought last year in the United States, and the German Messerschmidts . . .

La Chambre said that he feared that the German espionage service was as well organized in France as it had been in Poland. The French, therefore, had to fear that at some given moment the German bombardment planes flying so high as to be out of sight would suddenly descend on the French air fields in an attempt to destroy the French air force before it could take the air. He had, therefore, taken the utmost precautions to distribute and conceal the French planes.

He felt that as long as the French pursuit planes should remain in existence, which would not be very long, they could prevent German bombardment, by day, of Paris and other vital centers. The truth was, however, that the French did not have sufficient planes to hold the air for more than a couple of months at the outside, and he feared that the British could not be counted on for any effective action . . .

La Chambre added that he now had the exact figures with regard to the number of planes that the British could put in the air at this moment. The British had told tall stories about their production. The truth was that the British had today of the most modern types only 480 pursuit planes and 500 bombers . . .

There were two vital questions for French aviation. First, whether or not the French pursuit planes could prevent the bombardment of French plane factories; second, whether or not the French could produce sufficient motors. He was doubtful about both points.

Daladier, a couple of days ago, expressed a much more pessimistic view to me. He said that he felt that his political life and probably his personal life as well could not last more than three months. He expected Hitler, as soon as the Polish attack should have been completed, to launch the entire German Air Force against France. The bombardments of France would be so terrible that the French people would blame him for the lack of French planes and would drive him from political life and indeed would probably kill him. He did not consider that the lack of planes was his fault but he would be blamed for it . . .

Under the circumstances, I think you ought to have studied now in all its aspects the military and naval problem that will face the United States in case France and England should be defeated during the next eight months. I am convinced that if Hitler should be able to win during this period, he would be able to obtain the support of the Italians and the Japanese and would be in a position to make the attack on South America which he announced to the leaders that he convoked on the eighth of March last. I now have in written form the statement which I telegraphed to you on that subject some months ago . . .

I realize that it will probably be impossible for you to convince the people of the United States that they are menaced by Hitler. I can not express to you too strongly my conviction that we are menaced in the most terrible manner by Hitler. If we do not change at once the Neutrality Act and supply France and England immediately with all the weapons of war that we can produce, we shall be insane. It is the considered opinion not only of our own Military and Naval Attachés in Paris, but also of the French General Staff that if the United States should continue to refuse to supply airplanes, arms, and ammunition to France and England, France and England unquestionably would be defeated. It would be our turn next . . .

Love to you all and good luck.

Bill

Personal and Confidential   Paris
September 13, 1939

Dear Mr. President:

I enclose herewith a document for your stamp book, or, if you prefer, a double-sided picture frame.

On one side you will see the label of a bottle of wine such as does not exist any longer in the world, because the label comes from the last bottle in existence which Daladier and I drank at lunch at my house today.

On the back of the label you will find two unimportant signatures which convey at any rate a lot of admiration and, from the nether, a lot of affection.*

Good luck!

Bill

THE WHITE HOUSE
WASHINGTON

Memorandum for WCB   September 28, 1939

Tell the delightful gentleman who signed that label with you that if any similar bottle survives to keep it until he, you and I can partake of it together as soon as the survival of democracies is again assured.

FDR

Personal and Confidential   Paris
September 16, 1939

Dear Mr. President:

As you know, Beneš arrived in Europe intending to set up a "provisional government of Czechoslovakia." He naturally ran into a series of snags.

In the first place, both the French and British took the position

* This was probably a bottle of Fourcaud Laussac Cheval Blanc and on the back of the label was, in Daladier's writing, "Hommage Au President Roosevelt 13 7 BRE 1939" and it was signed Ed. Daladier, William C. Bullitt.
The front of the label is in such bad condition and so old that it is not possible to find the year.

that they had refused to admit that Czechoslovakia had ceased to exist as an independent state, and were still recognizing the competence of the Ministers of Czechoslovakia in both Paris and London. They desired to continue to recognize these Ministers as representing the Czechoslovak State until it should be possible to re-create a Czechoslovak State. They could see no basis for a Beneš provisional government, except Beneš's desire to place himself at the head of something again.

Moreover, nearly everyone in political life in both France and England considers that Beneš is an utterly selfish small person who, through his cheap smartness in little things and his complete lack of wisdom in large things, permitted the disintegration of his country.

I have been told that Beneš has the Czechoslovak Minister in Washington more or less in his pocket, and I am writing you this letter because I think it is important that our Government should take the same line as the French and British Governments.

There will be a Czech Army formed in France. All the agreements necessary for the setting up of this army will be made and signed by Osusky, the Czech Minister in Paris, who will continue to be recognized as the representative of Czechoslovakia on the principle that Czechoslovakia "is not dead but sleepeth."

I think our Government should take the same line. You will get into endless embarrassment, if you try to recognize a provisional government which has no existence and no authority anywhere. We can and should keep up the fiction that the Czech Minister in Washington represents the Czechoslovak State. If he asks for advice, he should be told that he should cooperate fully with the Czech Minister in France who is organizing the Czech Army and is recognized by the French Government as the sole representative of the Czechoslovak State.

Incidentally, the Czech Minister in Paris, Osusky, was for seventeen years an American citizen, a highly successful lawyer in Chicago, and during the war, one of my hired men when I was running the information on the enemy in the State Department. Indeed, the reputation I then acquired as a prophet was largely due to my use of Osusky's brains.

Our Military Attaché in Prague used to say that all Czechs could be divided into two classes: 1. Masaryk. 2. Just Czechs. Osusky has the advantage of being a Slovak!

Good luck.

William C. Bullitt

22

Supplies to the Allies

OCTOBER 1939—DECEMBER 1939

Cash and Carry
Franco-British Purchasing Agency in United States
Situation on French Front
Russia Attacks Finland
Russia Expelled from League of Nations

ON MONDAY, September 21, 1939, the President addressed a special session of Congress to ask for the repeal of the arms embargo. He said: "By the repeal of the embargo the United States will more probably remain at peace than if the law remains as it stands today. I say this because with the repeal of the embargo this Government clearly and definitely will insist that American citizens and American ships keep away from the immediate perils of the actual zones of conflict." [1]

On September 20, Bullitt had cabled Hull that Daladier, Gamelin, Léger, and others felt that Germany would win if the embargo continued.

The new bill was signed on November 4. It approved cash-and-carry so that England and France could now buy war goods. American ships could not go to the continent of Europe with the exception of the Mediterranean and the Black Sea. The Pacific and Indian oceans, and all ports in Africa south of the Canary Islands, remained open. The shipment of arms, ammunition, and implements of war on American ships to belligerent ports in the Pacific was prohibited. The act forbade travel by Americans on ships of belligerents, the arming of American merchant ships, and loans to belligerents.

One immediate subterfuge was the sale by the United States

Lines, which was controlled by the government Maritime Commission, of merchant ships to a private corporation in Belgium, which in turn could sell them to a belligerent government if they so desired.

Personal and Secret   Paris
                                                October 4, 1939

Dear Mr. President:

I enclose herewith three documents that will interest you.

The long one beginning, "Dear Sir Edward" is the communication on behalf of the French Government, written by Jean Monnet, to the British Government, in the person of Sir Edward Bridges, Secretary of the War Cabinet, concerning the organization for practical collaboration between the French and British Governments.

You will note that it follows the lines established in 1918. It is entirely sensible, I think; and I plead guilty to getting the idea started and to getting Daladier to put the matter in Monnet's hands.

Monnet accompanied Daladier to England for his conferences with Chamberlain last week, and has spent the days since talking with all the Cabinet Ministers in England. He is confident that the British will accept the organization as outlined by him in this letter. I thought you would be interested in having it in advance.

So far as the organization in the United States is concerned, the present plan is to set up a joint Franco-British purchasing agency, and not make purchases through Morgan and Company or through any other bank or agent.

I have had a large enough finger in all this business to be able to steer it, in case you have any definite ideas as to what you want or do not want. Just let me know.

The second and third documents have to do with airplane orders in the United States. They were handed to me tonight by Guy La Chambre.

The airplane situation is approximately the following: The French produced in the month of September 1939, 319 war planes. The British produced approximately 450 war planes. In addition, both the French and British produced a considerable number of training planes.

The French and British believe that the Germans can produce approximately fifteen hundred planes per month but can not go above that figure; and that the Germans are now producing one thousand planes a month.

The French and British hope that their combined production of war planes will amount to approximately twelve hundred a month by next Spring. It is obvious to everyone that if France and England are to obtain, first, equality in the air, and then dominance in the air, the productive capacity of the United States must be called into play to a much larger degree than at present . . .

The present plan is to send to the United States, as soon as the Neutrality Act shall have been changed, persons competent to carry through the business of enlarging existing plants and placing of orders.

The French Air Ministry, and Daladier as well, have great confidence in Colonel Jacquin who is now in Washington; but business on the scale contemplated — which will probably amount to a billion dollars — will probably be placed in the hands of Monnet. Nothing of course will be done until the embargo provisions of the Neutrality Act shall have been eliminated . . .

There is another enormous hole in the French defense against the German bombardment planes. The French have practically no modern "projectors," that is to say, searchlights for use against German bombardment planes that arrive at night. The French searchlights are too slow in action to follow the modern bombing planes and there is an intense fear here that night bombing of Paris and other vital centers may be most terrible . . .

My own view of the future is the following: France and England will not accept the "peace ultimatum" that Germany is contemplating. It may indeed never be launched. Germany then will attack France with all the force that she possesses or can acquire from the Soviet Union and Italy.

The attack against France may be successful. I do not believe that it will be.

If American production of airplane motors and bodies can be trebled in eight months, dominance in the air should be in the hands of the French and British by August or September of next year. This dominance could be increased greatly by the spring of 1941, and at that time France and England might hope to defeat Germany.

Germany's obvious avenue of escape then would be to go Bolshevik and summon the Soviet armies. If French and British dominance in the air should be sufficient at that time, the Soviet Union would not dare to march and France and England could impose a peace that would prevent the destruction of everything civilized on the continent of Europe by the Bolsheviks.

It is clear that the small nations of the world — and that includes every nation as small or smaller than Poland — will no longer be able to exist unless at the end of this war there can be established such a dominance in the air of the United States, England and France that the small nations can be protected without vast losses of infantrymen.

The productive capacity of France and England in airplanes is too small to achieve such dominance. The future, therefore, will depend on the production of an overwhelming number of planes in the United States.

I realize that France and England may be defeated and destroyed before our American production can be raised to a sufficient point to save them, but I hope that will not be.

I am certain that there is no single problem confronting you at the moment which is more important than the problem of increasing our production of motors and planes.

I think that the French and British will have sense enough to be ready to pay cash for the extension of existing facilities for production in the United States and for the purchase of all the production of those increased facilities, but it is obvious that such an increase in production can be carried out only with the fullest cooperation of our government and it is also obvious that such cooperation will depend entirely on yourself in the first instance.

I am sending this letter to you by special courier on the Clipper, and I hope that it will reach you in less than a week. If you have any comment or suggestions to make, will you please send me back a word by the same route . . .

We are expecting the bombs to begin falling on this house in about a week; but nobody either here or anywhere else in France is disturbed by the prospect. This people remains an example of what a nation should be when faced by the ultimate realities.

Love and good luck.

Bill

Personal and Strictly Confidential   Paris
October 18, 1939

Dear Mr. President:

I enclose herewith the agreement drawn up by the British Government and Jean Monnet covering economic cooperation. Personally, I think Monnet should head the Committee in London, and I should like to see Bob Brand at the head of the Joint Purchasing Commission in the United States.

In any event, I hope that Monnet will go to Washington to put through the business of enlarging the productive capacity of our airplane industry. The experience he had last winter has given him a knowledge of the possibilities of our industry that no one else in either France or England possesses — and every day will count.

I don't like to say so in a telegram, but I really believe that there is an enormous danger that the German Air Force will be able to win this war for Germany before the planes can begin to come out of our plants in quantity. I think we should encourage the French and British in every way possible to place the largest conceivable orders. If, before those orders are completed, the French and British shall have been defeated, we shall need the planes for our own defense.

You may still be interested in that island; but our Navy doesn't seem to be so much interested. I had my Naval Attaché telegraph to the Navy Department the text of the contract that the French Government is prepared to sign, more than ten days ago; and in spite of another telegram from the Naval Attaché asking whether the Navy Department wants to sign this contract, we have had no reply!

There has never been any question about the readiness of the French Government to let us have the island; but it was very difficult to find a legal adviser of the French Government who had not been mobilized or was not snowed under with war work to go over the contract. I had to push hard. Before you get this letter, the matter probably will be settled. If not, I shall probably send you a telegram couched in diplomatic language expressing the thought — What the Hell!

Everyone in Paris is expecting a major German attack to break the moment the present rains stop. Our preparations are superb. I have converted a wine cellar in the basement of the Embassy Residence, under the front steps, into an *abri*. It is not in the least bombproof; but I have hung in it the Turkish and Bokharan embroideries that I used to have in my house on the Bosphorus, and it is the last word in Oriental style and comfort, so that when the bombs begin to drop you may imagine Offie and myself tucked away in a Selamlik!

Our motto is: "We don't mind being killed, but we won't be annoyed."

Love and good luck.

Yours always,
Bill

A new development had arisen in the crisis of French aircraft production. Their whole program depended on the ability to acquire large amounts of the metal Duralumin from the United States. They had just been advised that they could only acquire fifty tons a month, whereas they needed at least a thousand tons to keep up with the plans for production which they had made. La Chambre pleaded fervently for the metal, suspecting that either the Germans or the Russians had cornered the market in America. Bullitt asked Roosevelt to intercede personally in the matter in order to secure their requirements.

Bullitt again expressed his fear of telegraphing information to Secretary Hull, as he felt it was almost a certainty that the Germans were decoding his telegrams. In this we now know he was right. He said to Secretary Hull: "So long as the French continue to let me have all the information that they received, and continue to talk to me about their policies with the extreme frankness that they do, I feel that it is not fair to jeopardize their position by handing information to the Germans . . .

"François-Poncet's telegram could have been made good use of by the Germans to influence adversely the rapidly improving relations between France and Italy."

Bullitt did not confine himself to his office in Paris but took any opportunity to learn at first hand about conditions in the French Army and the French plans for defense, as the following letter will show.

Personal and Secret   Paris
                                                        November 1, 1939
Dear Mr. President:

I hope you gathered from one of the discreet and dull cables to which I confine myself nowadays, that I had been at Field Headquarters with the Chief of the General Staff and his officers. The Chief of the General Staff, knowing that General Réquin was an intimate friend of mine, had brought him from his command at the front. Since Réquin has conducted all the operations against Germany in the region from Nancy to the Saar, it was possible, therefore, to get a view of the war from the front as well as from behind the lines. I have never talked with a lot of men who were more intelligent, confident or calm.

Réquin reported that the rains had been so heavy that all the trenches at the front were completely flooded and unusable. Moreover, it was impossible to construct new concrete works because the concrete was washed away by the rain at once. Furthermore, all boat bridges across streams had been swept away. In his opinion, it would be totally impossible for the Germans to launch a major offensive for at least a week. Their airplanes could not get off the ground and their tanks could not cross the fields, and even infantrymen became bogged down in the mud. All the officers were of the opinion that November 15th was the last date on which the Germans could launch an offensive before the onset of winter. They, therefore, thought that even slight rains the end of this week or next week would compel the Germans to postpone any major offensive until next March.

There is one peculiar element in the situation which no one can quite understand. The German Messerschmidts, though fast, are so stiff and clumsy in maneuvering compared to the Curtisses and French Moranes that the Messerschmidts now — apparently acting on orders — run away instantly from individual combats with the French pursuit planes.

(The British have almost nothing in the way of pursuit planes in France and there is not sufficient data for a comparison between British and German planes. Incidentally, the first two planes shot down over Paris by the French anti-aircraft were British planes that had lost their way and wandered at great height over the city! When the French General Staff expressed regrets about this incident, the British General Staff had the admirable courtesy to reply by a letter to the French General Staff expressing congratulations on the accuracy of the French D. C. A.!! You can tell Missy that the piece of anti-aircraft shell that Offie sent to her was from one of the shells that produced this incident!)

The morale of the French Army is superb but the soldiers are suffering somewhat from the cold weather because the army stock of blankets and warm clothing was used to care for the five hundred thousand Spanish refugees that poured into France after the defeat of the Republican Government in Spain, and there is a genuine shortage of blankets and warm clothing of all kinds.

The French are working hard on second, third and fourth lines of defense to back up the Maginot Line. For example, a whole series of concrete pillboxes to shelter anti-tank guns and machine guns is being built in my garden at Chantilly and all along the course of the little river, "La Nonette," which runs through it.

It is the opinion of the French General Staff that whichever army attacks first the lines of fortifications that now divide France and Germany will be defeated. Réquin, for example, sincerely regrets that the Germans have not launched an attack on the front which he commands since he is absolutely certain that he can defeat any such attack and that the German losses will be terrible.

As a result — on the old principle of strategy that you have to have a solid base and a quick moving mobile arm to swing around your enemy to smash his communications — the French Staff believes that the only way the war can be won in the field will be by a combination of air attack supplemented by tanks. That requires a sufficient number of planes to destroy the communications of an enemy army and a sufficient number of tanks to smash through the army whose communications have been cut. The French heavy tanks, as you know, are the best in Europe at the moment, and at the front have shown that their armor is not pierced but only dented by the German anti-tank guns.

The General Staff therefore feels that the missing element is an overwhelming superiority in the air. In consequence, the Staff, as well as Daladier and Guy La Chambre, have arrived at the conclusion that while France and England must produce every plane possible, the decisive weapon must be obtained by colossal purchases of planes in the United States.

Monnet is to leave for London tomorrow to have himself appointed head of the Joint French-British organization to handle all war supplies, shipping, etc.; and later to visit the United States, accompanied by some Englishman who will head the Joint Purchasing organization in the United States.

Meanwhile, as you know, the French have ordered everything that can be found in the way of Curtisses, Douglases and Martins, to say nothing of Pratt-Whitney and Curtiss-Wright engines. The total to be found is altogether insufficient.

The French and British figure roughly that by January or February, they will be producing as many planes as the Germans. To catch up with the number of planes that the Germans already have, to say nothing of establishing dominance in the air, they must count on new production from fresh sources in the United States . . .

Daladier and Guy La Chambre and Monnet and all the Generals have implored me to go to the United States to help put through this program. Since the job will be one which will take months rather than weeks, and since we ought to have an Ambassador continuously in Paris while this war is on, if only for show purposes, and since I don't quite see how I can be on both sides of the Atlantic at the same time; the question naturally arises of where I can be most useful. I believe that Ambassadors should not go home on vacation in war time.

I hope that there is no longer any question in your mind as to what you have to do. Whether you like it or not, you must remain President of the United States throughout this war.

I think you know from experience that one of the few principles that I live up to is Montesquieu's statement: "A flatterer is a dangerous servant for any master." I am not flattering when I say that there is no other man in the United States who can conduct the affairs of the country with one-half as much intelligence as yourself during this war, and there is no other man who can begin to handle the colossal problems which will arise at the end of the war.

Even though we should be able to remain neutral, as I hope we can, our influence at the end of the war would be enormous.

Our policy will be decisive in determining the kind of peace which will be made and the kind of reconstruction of the world which will be begun. I should despair of bringing any constructive results out of this war if you should leave the White House. I believe, therefore, that it is vital not only for the United States of America, but also for the rest of the world that you should run again and that you should be elected.

I should like to do anything I can to help in a pre-Convention campaign for your nomination and then in the campaign for your election. That also would mean many months at home.

As you know, I have no objection whatsoever to staying in France. I am treated here by everyone from the top to the bottom with the greatest possible kindness and, indeed, with affection; and you may be certain that I have no intention of running out of this job. But I honestly believe that I may be able to be of much more use in America during the next two years.

If you agree, the job in which I think I would be useful would be that of Secretary of War. If you do not intend to change the present set-up in the War Department, which incidentally is giving all the Army officers the jitters, you might put me in as midship-mite, otherwise known as Secretary of the Navy.

Incidentally, I believe that Tony and Margaret Biddle could handle the present job in France perfectly. They have been living in my house now for six weeks and I have introduced them to everyone from Daladier down, and they have made the most excellent impression . . .

Love to you all.

Yours always,
Bill

In regard to Bullitt's statement that the President might appoint him Secretary of War or of the Navy, they had apparently discussed these possibilities. Harold Ickes says that he proposed to Mr. Roosevelt that he make Bullitt Secretary of War and the President replied that he had thought of it. Ickes also thought of Bullitt as Secretary of State, but Roosevelt told him that he could not make such an appointment.[2] In March 1940, Mr. Roosevelt offered Bullitt the Secretaryship of the Navy and Bullitt accepted. Roosevelt had offered the position some months previously to Colonel Frank Knox, an ardent Republican, who had refused. Just after Bullitt accepted the post Colonel Knox wrote to the President that he had reconsidered in order to promote national unity. Colonel Knox was appointed Secretary of the Navy on June 19, 1940, together with another distinguished Republican as Secretary of War, Henry L. Stimson, thus in effect forming a coalition Cabinet.[3]

American Embassy   November 15, 1939
Paris
Strictly Confidential and Personal for the Ambassador
from the President

QUOTE with reference to your telegram 2739, November 13, 6 P.M. and previous telegrams on the same subject, I believe that because of the changes in the general situation since you first took up this question with the French Government, it would be wiser to abandon any idea of a lease or contract. Please suggest consequently to Daladier that the matter be handled by a mere exchange of confidential letters between him and yourself. The first letter might be from you inquiring whether the French Government would agree that the United States for training purposes and in connection with peace time maneuvers, might be enabled to utilize the atoll and lagoon for naval vessels and for planes. Daladier's reply might state that the French Government is willing to give the permission requested, with the understanding that such permission in no way affected French sovereignty over the island and its territorial waters. The third and final letter would be your confirmation of this understanding that French sovereignty would not be affected. Telegraph me what the result of your suggestion in this sense may be. UNQUOTE.

Personal and Confidential   Paris
                                                 November 15, 1939
Sir:

As you may have gathered, the only pleasure in life in this place now is doing your work well, and when I get prevented from doing work at all because I am ashamed to go to anyone in the Foreign Office, except Champetier de Ribes who knows nothing about the matter, because your damned Navy Department, after getting me to horn-swaggle an island out of the French Government, doesn't have the decency to reply for five weeks; and when I am under the illusion that I am doing what you want done, which illusion is based on a definite telegram telling me definitely that you want it done, and I get the French Government to embark on a definite policy and you kill that policy by a communication to the British Government reversing yourself, without letting me know that you have done so; and when I can't get answers to a lot of questions of the first importance, I recur to the opposite side of that quotation from Montesquieu in my last letter to you, and tell you that Fritz Kuhn and Lindbergh have become my ticket! Hurrah for fascism! What the hell!

                                                 Yours furiously,
                                                 William C. Bullitt

                                            Warm Springs, Georgia
                                                 November 23, 1939
Dear Bill:

It is a long time since I have written you but don't think you have been entirely abandoned to fate. All that you have done has been excellent and explicit and the only trouble is that the dear British and French Governments are failing, as usual, to be definite between themselves and to be definite to me. They shifted back and forth a dozen times on their relationship with the Federal Reserve Bank in New York; on their purchase methods and finally got everyone so disgusted that we had to tell them what to do. I hope they will understand it now as it is a perfectly practical thing.

While dictating the above yours of November twenty-third, No. 2813, has come in and I have talked with the Secretary on the telephone. We both feel certain that it would be a mistake for you to come over here on any such mission because it would be sure to leak out and it is not the duty of an Ambassador — even though I see no reason why, if things are really settling down to a Winter calm, you should not come over for a week or ten days and let us have a chance to see you. Incidentally, it would do you lots of good.

In regard to purchasing, I am ready to handle the whole matter over here if we only knew whom we were talking to. Our objective is the practical one of not interfering with our own military and naval program and, secondly, to prevent prices from rising in this country.

What is really needed is one Frenchman and one Britisher in Washington who will have complete and final say for their Governments. They would have to meet once a day, put all the cards on the table, stop crossing their own wires, and give us a chance to know just what they want and when they want it.

The French Government should realize that the present situation is not satisfactory either from their point of view or from ours. What we want is that perfectly possible combination of two head men — one French and one British — who will sleep in the same bed and lay all their cards on the table to prevent crossing wires.

You can tell the Prime Minister that the Government here will give every facility to the export of all types of American products, agricultural and industrial, and that the Interdepartmental Committee is ready to give all proper assistance just so long as no wires are crossed.

I hope you will follow my practice of getting away for a few weeks for a short holiday. It saves my life. If you cannot fly over here, I do hope you will go down to the south of France, or even to North Africa for a really good place away from the telephone. I am absolutely certain that you are hounded to death on a million little things.

I am wiring you today what we used to call in the old days a "tickler."

As ever yours,
FDR

Hon. William C. Bullitt
American Embassy
Paris, France

November 28, 1939

My dear Mr. President:

In compliance with your memorandum of November 25th I have repeated to Bill Bullitt your message suggesting that he come home for Christmas, or, alternatively, go to Algiers and Tunis for a couple of weeks.

Faithfully yours,
Cordell Hull

Bullitt accepted this advice and went to Africa for his holiday.

On November 28 Bullitt telephoned Secretary Hull that the Soviet Union had denounced its nonaggression pact with Finland and would shortly attack. Hull immediately sent messages to Finland and Russia offering the services of the United States in composing any differences between the two countries. Finland accepted at once, but Russia declined and attacked Finland on the following day.[4] Bullitt asked Hull to urge Britain and France to condemn Russia at Geneva, but after consultation with the President, Hull replied that not being a member of the League of Nations, we could not pursue such a course.[5] Russia was expelled from the League on December 14. No mention of this is made in the Russian history books.

For generations the Russians had feared the vulnerability of Leningrad to attack from Germany by way of the Gulf of Finland, the Baltic, and overland through Finland. By threats they obtained the right to place troops in Estonia, Latvia, and Lithuania, leaving only Finland to be dealt with. The Finns were strong in their opposition to giving or leasing strategic territory to Russia. On November 13, discussions came to an end and Finland mobilized. Denouncing the Russo-Finnish nonaggression pact, the Russians attacked on the thousand-mile frontier on November 28, 1939, at the same time bombing the open capital, Helsinki. The Russians did not have the easy task that they had anticipated and it took almost four months for the Russian bear to subdue its small neighbor. Finnish defense ended on March 12, 1940.

The Russian report of this act is: "In November, 1939, the militarists in Finland, on the orders of Fascist Germany and reactionary forces in other countries, provoked a war with the Soviet

Union. In response to this the Soviet Union was compelled to
launch operations in order to protect its northwestern frontiers.
Soviet troops broke through a powerful line of defenses and forced
Finland to capitulate." [6]

Personal and Secret   Paris
                                                        December 11, 1939

Dear Mr. President:

At lunch today at my house Daladier asked Guy La Chambre if
he had been able to get the exact figures of British airplane production. La Chambre said that, thanks to Monnet, he had at last gotten the true figures. They showed a startling difference from the figures that had been given him previously.

La Chambre said that, at the present moment, the British per
month are producing two hundred bombing planes and one
hundred eighty-five pursuit planes. In addition to these war planes
for use on land, the British are producing approximately five
hundred planes for naval use, training, and use in the colonies.

The actual figures, therefore, for the British production of land
battle planes per month are 385. The French production per month
of the same sort of planes is 350.

Daladier at great length described a diplomatic maneuver which
gave him great personal satisfaction. It appears that until about a
week ago the German Government had been sending him regularly
emissaries with peace proposals. All the proposals involved absolute
German domination of Poland and Czechoslovakia. He had been
absolutely determined not to accept any of these proposals but, in
order to stave off a German attack this autumn, he had wished to
make the Germans continue to believe that he might accept one or
another of these proposals. He, therefore, had taken all the proposals under consideration and considered each one for as many days or
weeks as possible, and then invariably had replied by some question
which enabled him to string out the conversations.

The German proposals had all come from Goering. A little more
than a week ago, Daladier had put the question to the gentleman
who had been running back and forth between Paris and Berlin:
"What proof have I that Goering is prepared to throw out Hitler?"
This question apparently had been a difficult one to answer and he
now felt that he could no longer string the Germans.

He was convinced that his pretense of readiness to consider German proposals had been the main factor in keeping the Germans

from attacking this autumn. He was thoroughly pleased with himself since he felt that France and Great Britain would be in a much better position to receive a German attack next Spring.

He said that he was absolutely convinced that such an attack would be made next Spring by way of Holland and Belgium. He thought that the attack would be made in the month of March. He went on to say that he had kept Bonnet, whom he described as a coward, and several worse things connected with rear ends, in his Government in order to encourage the Germans to believe that there was a possibility of a French surrender. He did not know now how long he would keep either Bonnet or de Monzie in his Government.

Good luck.

> Yours affectionately,
> Bill

Personal and Strictly Confidential Paris

December 11, 1939

Dear Mr. President:

At my house today from one until four, Daladier, Guy La Chambre, Jean Monnet and René Pleven discussed the problem of winning the war.

Pleven is leaving Paris tonight to take the Clipper that will bring you this letter by the hand of my Counselor of Embassy, Robert Murphy. I have not time to give you the three hours of conversation which was as interesting as any three hours that I have ever spent. I must, however, give you before the train leaves Paris as much as I can.

Pleven is Jean Monnet's right-hand man, and at the moment, enjoys the title of Assistant to the President of the French-British Committee of Coordination, in London.

He is an old and close friend of mine. I consider him one of the most subtly intelligent and reliable human beings that I have ever known. You can talk to him with absolute certainty that what you say will not be repeated. If you would enjoy a quiet evening with a French gentleman who has a profound knowledge of what is happening in Europe and speaks English perfectly, you might invite Pleven to have a quiet evening meal with you at the White House. This is not at all necessary, however, since although he would enjoy deeply a talk with you, and I am equally certain that you would enjoy him, he is not a person who cares *per se* about being invited by the great.

It is, however, vitally important that you should help him to carry out the mission on which Daladier is sending him to Washington.

Daladier, today at luncheon, repeated what I have communicated to you before: He believes that the war can not be won unless France and England can obtain in the United States ten thousand airplanes with engines during the year 1940. He is sending Pleven to Washington to see if it may be possible to organize such a production.

Personally, I agree with Daladier that the war can not be won unless France and England can obtain absolute domination in the air. Approximately ten thousand planes from the United States during the year 1940 will be necessary to obtain such domination.

I believe that this question at the moment surpasses all others in importance. I believe that if the United States can produce these planes for sale to France and England, the French and British will win the war; and I believe that our Government should do everything that it can reasonably to facilitate the production of this number of planes . . .

I do not consider that the problem of obtaining ten thousand planes in the United States in the year 1940, in addition to those already contracted for, is unsolvable. It will require an immense amount of organization, and also quiet assistance on the part of our Government.

Pleven will reach Washington at the same time as this letter. I am giving him a little personal note to Miss LeHand. I am also giving him a brief personal note to Henry Morgenthau. Will you please, as soon as you have read this letter, pick up your telephone and tell Henry Morgenthau to put Pleven into touch with Captain Collins of the Procurement Division immediately? If Henry wants the order in writing, please give it to him in writing. I should like to stress again that Pleven wishes to see Captain Collins *not* to ask him at this time to assist in making any purchases for the French Government, but purely in order to make use of the knowledge of the Procurement Division for his preliminary inquiry as to the possibility of producing ten thousand additional planes and engines in the United States in 1940.

Since various telegrams from the Department of State have authorized me to say that the cooperation of our Government and the

Procurement Division would be given to the French Government, I assume that there will be no difficulty about putting Pleven in touch with Captain Collins immediately. If there should be any difficulty, I hope that you will steam-roller it at once.

I can not exaggerate the importance that Daladier attaches to this mission of Pleven's. His entire attitude toward the war will be influenced profoundly, or even decided, thereby.

Daladier said to me at lunch today: "At this moment, it is of no importance for you to be Ambassador in Paris. Our relations are such that any Secretary of Embassy can carry out the daily business satisfactorily. The one vital problem today is the production of planes in the United States. I implore you to leave for the United States as soon as possible to work out this problem."

Your nice cable of November 28 sent from Warm Springs gives me a free hand to come home for a brief holiday if I consider it wise; but I foresee on this plane business tasks which will require pertinacious and constant attention over a large number of weeks — if not months. We shall run up against the same difficulties that we ran up against last December and January when Monnet was purchasing the planes which are now proving to be so useful at the front. There will be all sorts of personal fears and hesitancies to be overcome. I want, therefore, to know that I can stay at home until the job is done.

If you have any intention of doing what I suggested in my letter of November 1st, I wish you would inform me of the intention in order to give me time to take the Clipper which would put me in Washington by the first of January. If you haven't any such intention, I wish you would order me to be at home for consultation on the first of January.

I have spent the past few days down by the Italian front trying to get some perspective on this war. The more I think about it, the more convinced I am that the only road to salvation lies through a quadrupled production of planes in the United States.

I want very much to talk with you about all the things that I do not dare to put in black and white, and I want to work on the problems that seem to me the real problems.

Now please pick up your telephone and tell Henry Morgenthau to put Pleven in touch with Captain Collins immediately!

Merry Christmas and a Happy New Year.

Yours affectionately,
Bill

To this letter Roosevelt replied that he could not order Bullitt home and that it might react against the very purpose Daladier had in mind. In a handwritten postscript to the telegram Roosevelt said that he would not do it "at this time but will do so when Kennedy returns to London."

TELEGRAM SENT

DEPARTMENT OF STATE
WASHINGTON

December 22, 1939

Amembassy
Paris (France)
Your 3023, December 21, 8 P.M.
Secret for the Ambassador from the President and the Secretary

Daladier is asking us to assume greater responsibility than is possible. Practically speaking it might well react against the very purpose he had in mind. Please make this clear to him and explain why we cannot order you home at this time but will do so when Kennedy returns to London.

Hull

Personal and Confidential   Paris
December 19, 1939

Dear Mr. President:

This letter should probably be addressed to the Secretary of Commerce since it concerns oysters — particularly *huîtres de pleine mer,* the saltiest of the tribe. But as a sea-going man, you ought to be interested in oysters that are fished up in the open by the Bretons. So here is the story.

On November 22nd, Royall Tyler, who is an old friend of mine, as he doubtless is of yours, called on me and said that Avenol, Secretary General of the League of Nations, was most anxious to see me since he felt that I did not like him and he wished me to like him. I replied that he could tell Avenol that I had never liked him. He was a *Maréchal de Pompes Funèbres,* and there was no reason why I should see him. Royall Tyler persisted, however, and asked me to have luncheon with him and Avenol. I accepted on condition that we should eat at the Fontaine Gaillon and should start with *huîtres de pêche*. At least the food would be good even though the conversation might be bad.

We had the luncheon on the 29th of November and Avenol was just as dead a dog as usual. I began to make fun of him about the League and especially the pleasure of working with his Soviet associates. He seemed to have plenty of hatred for his Russian colleagues, so I asked him why he didn't get rid of them by having the Soviet Union expelled from the League because of its aggression against Finland. He replied that the League was so dead that it would certainly be impossible to get any action by the League on the Soviet aggression against Finland.

Thereupon, I delivered an oration on morality in the world which was very nearly as good as yours when you shook your finger at Litvinov and announced: "You will believe in God."

Avenol, in self-defense, said that so far as he was concerned, he would be delighted to see the Soviet Union expelled from the League and regretted that it would be impossible to obtain such action. Whereupon, I told him that if he would carry through the matter, I would undertake to get into motion within two hours the energies necessary to throw the Soviet Union out of the League.

I emphasized that I had no instructions from my Government; that anything which I did get started would be the result of William C. Bullitt and not American Government action; that I happened to have appointments after luncheon with Rochat and the Finnish Minister; and one the next morning with Champetier de Ribes. I thought that would suffice.

Avenol was gloomily skeptical, but at least seemed interested in the idea that he might not have to work with a Bolshevik any longer in his Secretariat.

After lunch I saw Rochat at the Quai d'Orsay. He was even more negative than Avenol. He said that he was certain that any action by the League was out of the question; no nation would have the courage to take up the matter; that Finland would not appeal to the League, etc., etc. Whereupon, I gave him a lecture also on human morality and left to receive the Finnish Minister at my house.

He is a nice, timid, little fellow and when I asked him why Finland did not appeal to the League, he replied that he felt certain that the League would not dare to take up the aggression against Finland any more than it had dared to take up the aggression against Poland. He thought an appeal to the League by Finland might embarrass France and England. I told him that I felt there could be no disadvantage to Finland in making the attempt to get the support of the League, there might be a great advantage to Finland. If France and England should be embarrassed by being asked to fulfill their most solemn pledges, I thought it was time that they should be embarrassed.

The Finnish Minister asked me if he could telegraph his Government what I had said, and I told him that, provided he made it entirely clear that I was speaking as an individual and not in any way as the representative of the Government of the United States, he could telegraph anything he liked to his Government . . .

I picked up my telephone and told Avenol that the Finnish Minister was with me; that I was insisting with *force majeure* that they should have an immediate conversation; that I was sending the Finnish Minister to his office in my car; and that he would arrive in two minutes . . .

I had too many other engagements that day to bother about the Finnish business any more. But the next morning I had an appointment with Champetier de Ribes. I told Champetier exactly what I had said to Avenol, the Finnish Minister, and Rochat, again stressing the fact that my remarks were entirely personal and had nothing whatsoever to do with the views of the Government of the United States. Immediately after our conversation, Champetier de Ribes had his regular morning conference with Daladier. He repeated to Daladier what I had said and to everyone's astonishment — except my own — Daladier said that I was entirely right; that Finland should be supported to the limit and every effort should be made to throw the Soviet Union out of the League.

Daladier went so far as to give immediate orders that the French Government should get in touch with the British Government and say to the British Government that this was going to be the French line of policy whether the British Government liked it or not. The British objected; but Daladier went right ahead and called a Cabinet meeting the same afternoon and had the policy approved . . .

Avenol went back to Geneva knowing that he had the full support of the French Government. The Finnish Government replied to the Finnish Minister in Paris that it thought the idea of an appeal to the League a good one. Avenol, on returning to Geneva for the first time in all the years that he has been Secretary General of the League, began to dash around like a young colt. The Finns made their appeal and the Soviet Union got the boot.

You will remember that in the year 1934, after the Bolsheviks had broken all the promises which Litvinov gave us, you instructed me to do what I could to make it clear that it was better for any nation to have really friendly relations with the United States rather than unfriendly relations. Since you put no time limit on this instruction, I consider that my activities on the afternoon of November 29th and the morning of November 30th fall within the scope of your instruction. Whether they do or not, I know that you will like them anyhow.

The moral is: Eat oysters!

Love and good luck.

Yours affectionately,
William C. Bullitt

P.S. I enclose a document which I have just received from the League of Nations. I wish you would keep it for me as it will be the only record of the connection between a peaceable luncheon at the Fontaine Gaillon and the exit of the Bolshies.

WCB

Société des Nations   League of Nations

To see the vacant chair, and think,
'How good, how kind, and he is gone.'

In Memoriam
XX, st. 5
Tennyson

Fontaine Gaillon, November 29th
Geneva, December 14th, 1939

In an effort to secure peace in Europe the French Foreign Minister, Barthou, was able to achieve the admission of Russia to the League of Nations in September 1934. On December 14, 1939, the League expelled the Soviet Union.

23

Hitler Attacks

JANUARY 1940—MAY 1940

Welles's Trip
Reynaud Premier
Norway and Denmark Invaded
Belgium and Holland Invaded
Churchill Prime Minister
Dunkirk Evacuated
Belgium Surrenders
French Gold to America

AT THIS TIME Bullitt was being consulted in Paris by prominent Frenchmen as to the advisability of seeking a compromise peace with Germany. In the words of Robert Murphy, then Counselor of Embassy in Paris: "They esteemed Bullitt for one thing only; his formidable criticism of the Soviet system, based upon his experiences as the first American Ambassador to the U.S.S.R. Because his hostility to communism was so well known, the American Ambassador could argue more persuasively than anybody else in Paris that winter against suggestions that Europe could tolerate any kind of peace which would leave Hitler dominant." [1]

Early in December the question of Allied purchases in America, to which there are so many references in the letters, was finally resolved. An Anglo-French Coordinating Committee was established with Jean Monnet as chairman. The President appointed a committee consisting of a representative from each of the Treasury, War, and Navy Departments to act as liaison between their orders and American procurement.

Bullitt spent Christmas in Philippeville in Africa and returned to the United States in February. He reported to the President on his visit to the French front and stressed his fears of the power of the German Air Force against France. He consistently urged the President to increase the production of airplanes, both in order to supply France and England and, in case of their defeat, to have the United States in a formidable position to oppose any German threat. It was not until the spring that Roosevelt was finally persuaded, and he then asked for the production of 50,000 planes a year.

On this trip to America Bullitt had dinner one night in February at the White House, an account of which has been given me by one of Bullitt's closest associates: "I was in Washington with him on consultation, as he came back to report orally to Mr. Roosevelt on the extremely pessimistic outlook on the war; i.e., the French expected the Germans to invade Norway and Denmark, to clear the northern flank before attacking Holland, Belgium and France . . . at dinner in the White House with only the President and Miss LeHand present. They had the usual badly prepared cocktail which Mr. Roosevelt made and then dinner was served. At the dinner table Mr. Roosevelt collapsed and Dr. McIntire was called and took over. Miss LeHand and Mr. Bullitt left matters to Dr. McIntire, who described it as a 'very slight heart attack' . . . He [Mr. Bullitt] did see the President a few days later prior to going back to France, at which time Mr. Roosevelt told him he wished him to plan to come back for good in the spring to become Secretary of the Navy."

Bullitt made a brief visit to Rome in January 1940, and had an audience with Pius XII, at which they discussed the possibilities of peace. Part of a long telegram on this subject reads:

"He hoped that at some future day he and the President in collaboration could help establish peace on earth. I asked him how he felt about the cooperation of Mussolini in such a collaboration. A shadow crossed his face as if I had said something slightly indecent and he said: 'Your President is disinterested and a genuine lover of humanity. I care about nothing except bringing souls to God and relieving the sufferings of humanity. These are my sole concerns on earth. The Italian Government has its own selfish political entanglements and its own selfish political aims.'

"The Pope went on to say that he felt that both sides were much too far apart for there to be any hope at all of stopping the war in the near future. He thought it would be unwise to make any attempt now to mediate or appeal for peace. He had no intention of making such an appeal or offering mediation."

A report on the Pope's views was not sufficient for Bullitt in one message and he continued at length about Finland. A portion of this reads:

"At the present moment Daladier desires to send divisions of French Chasseurs Alpins to Finland but neither Norway nor Sweden will permit their passage and Great Britain will not agree to a naval descent on Petsamo or Murmansk. Daladier's personal feelings with regard to the Russian attack on Finland are so strong that he may be able to drive the British into agreement for a French attack on Petsamo."

He next touched on Russia and reveals possible action against the Soviet in these terms:

"I believe that the project of an attack by the French and British fleets on Batum and an airplane attack on Baku to deprive Russia of oil supplies will not be pushed at the moment. It is by general agreement the most effective manner to injure the Soviet Union; but is opposed by the British admiralty. Winston Churchill himself is strongly opposed to any hostile activity directed against the Soviet Union. Moreover Turkey is opposed to the passage of the British and French fleets into the Black Sea for the purpose of attacking the Soviet Union."

Just for good measure Bullitt concluded the telegram with the following, and the State Department must have felt that for the moment it had ample information to digest.

"In reply to your letter of November 24 received recently in which you indicate that you would like to have my personal opinions.

"1. I have no doubt about the determination of either France or England to go on fighting until the Nazi regime in Germany shall have been destroyed. Daladier and Chamberlain are preparing for a three year war. The political position of both Prime Ministers at the moment is strong. It will probably remain strong unless there should be severe military reverses.

"2. The allies will not attack this year either on the western front or in the Near East.

"The Germans may attack on the western front." 2

TELEGRAM RECEIVED

This telegram must be closely paraphrased before being communicated to anyone.

Secretary of State   Paris
Washington   Dated January 15, 1940
80, January 15, 9 P.M.   Rec'd 7:45 P.M.
Strictly Confidential

Léger said to me this afternoon that in his opinion there were at least 75 chances in a 100 that Hitler would attack the Netherlands and Belgium in the very near future.

He said that until about two weeks ago Hitler had believed that Mussolini could procure him a good German peace by playing on the tender heart strings of the Pope and President Roosevelt and the weak stomachs of the King of the Belgians and the Queen of the Netherlands.

He thought that Hitler now knew that neither the Pope nor the President was likely to be led into attempting to bring about a peace which would leave Germany in possession of Poland and Czechoslovakia and the Nazi party undefeated.

He felt that Hitler now knew he would have to fight. There was evidence increasing hourly that Hitler had decided to attack Belgium and the Netherlands at once. The German General Staff was still opposed to such an attack but could no longer resist the pressure from Hitler. Both the Dutch and the Belgians were fully prepared to fight and they would have the full support of the French Army.

(In this connection I may add that military men in Paris [*] the Dutch army relatively valueless but on the other hand hold a high opinion of the fighting ability of the Belgian army. In case of German attack therefore they believe that Dutch resistance north and east of the Rhine will be overcome fairly quickly by the Germans but that resistance of the Dutch, Belgians and French south and west of the Rhine will be prolonged indefinitely.)

* Apparent omission.

Léger went on to say that although the probable attack on the Netherlands and Belgium dominated the situation at the moment the French Government had by no means forgotten the power of the Finns. He was happy to say that the first 30 planes sent to Finland (see my No. 3062, December 30, 6 P.M.) had already arrived and had taken the air today.

The question of aid to Finland was becoming more and more complicated. The French Government had offered to send an army to Finland either by way of Norway and Sweden or by way of Petsamo. The Norwegians and the Swedes had refused to permit the passage of a French army to Finland and the British had refused to permit any expedition against Petsamo.

The French had gone so far as to propose that if the British would release the three Polish destroyers which are now with the British fleet they would add sufficient French cruisers to them to make a strong Polish fleet and the Polish fleet would cover the landing of the French army at Petsamo.

The British first had stated that the Poles were absolutely opposed to any such action. General Sikorski, Polish Prime Minister, in the presence of himself and Daladier had stated flatly that he would be delighted to have a Polish fleet attack Petsamo and cover the landing of the French army. Confronted with this statement of General Sikorski's the British had finally taken refuge in a simple negative stating that they controlled the allied effort at sea; that the Polish fleet would have to be based on British ports and that they would not do anything which could be construed by the Bolsheviks as a hostile British act against the Soviet Union.

Léger expressed the opinion that the British were entirely idiotic in believing that they could detach the Russians from the Germans and that they could finally obtain the support of the Soviet Union against Germany.

He went on to say that the French Government had proposed to the British Government that the British and French fleets both should enter the Black Sea and bombard Batum and send airplanes to bomb Baku and thus cut off both Germany and the Soviet Union from supplies of oil. The British Government had replied that no British ship would be fitted for any action in the Black Sea hostile to the Soviet Union. Léger added that the Turkish Government also was opposed to permitting the passage of the French and British fleets to the Black Sea and a bombardment of the Russian coast.

Léger said that he really could not understand the attitude of the

British with regard to support to Finland and hostility to the Soviet Union at the present time. He asked me if I had any information on this subject and I replied that I had none. I should be grateful if you have anything of interest that you may care to communicate to me.

The French position is that France will not break diplomatic relations with the Soviet Union or declare war on the Soviet Union but will if possible destroy the Soviet Union — using cannon if necessary.

Bullitt

PARIS
JANUARY 30 1940

MARGUERITE LEHAND
THE WHITE HOUSE

PLEASE PAT GOD FIFTY-EIGHT TIMES ON HIS BALD SPOT FOR ME AND GET HIM TO ISSUE THAT SUMMONS WHICH HAS NOT YET ARRIVED. LOVE.

BILL

[Roosevelt's birthday.]

The Jupiter Island Club
Hobe Sound, Florida

20 March 1940

Dear Mr. President:

You should never read thank you notes; but I am very thankful to you for a lot of things besides having Anne and myself at the White House. That was a joy to us both. However, I want to thank you more for that little radio address which put the moral case perfectly. And for the private thing you said to me. It meant much to me, and it has changed in the happiest way Anne's entire view of the future. I did not realize until we were here together how lonely she felt, alone in America. And I am deeply grateful that she will not be.

If your cold doesn't improve, why not come down here? I can get you a house easily from almost any rich Republican. You won't I am almost sure — so that I shall see you Monday in Washington.

Thanks especially for just being yourself.

Yours affectionately,
Bill

The "private thing" is doubtless Roosevelt's offer of the post of Secretary of the Navy and Bullitt's return to America.

In February Harold Ickes reported that the President informed the Cabinet that he was sending Sumner Welles, Under Secretary of State, to talk with the foreign officers of France, England, Germany, Italy, and perhaps some of the neutral countries. The President made it clear that these talks would not be reported to the Cabinet. Ickes's comment was: "My guess was that the proposal had emanated from Welles, who saw an opportunity to step out more toward the center of the stage." [3] In retrospect it seems an extraordinary mission. The United States had able ambassadors in all these posts and it is easy to understand the feelings that Kennedy and Bullitt must have had in respect to Welles's trip. What could Welles accomplish in an interview with Chamberlain, to whom Kennedy was so close, or Daladier, whose feelings for Bullitt were so well known? No good came of the trip.

Robert Murphy, Counselor of Embassy in Paris, received Mr. Welles in Paris in Bullitt's absence and comments: "I knew that Bullitt had not been consulted about this abrupt move, and that his pride would be wounded. I knew that the Ambassador felt he had an understanding with President Roosevelt which made him the principal White House adviser on European affairs . . . When Roosevelt sent Welles to Europe without even informing Bullitt, the latter understandably concluded that Welles had violated an agreed division of functions, and a bitterness developed which, in my opinion, was a severe blow to American wartime policy making . . . I shall always regret that efforts to resolve their private differences were unsuccessful. I am convinced that if the President had kept the ardent support of these two positive personalities during his last two years, when his health declined so disastrously, American postwar policies would have been shaped much more realistically. Bullitt, in particular possessed a cool, clear awareness of Russian aims which might have proved invaluable to Roosevelt at Teheran and Yalta, and later to President Truman at the Potsdam Conference." [4]

Mr. Murphy goes on to say that in his papers he had a copy of a petition brought to him while Welles was in Paris. It summarized the views of several former French Premiers and Foreign

Ministers. They urged that Bullitt not return to Paris unless he could persuade the President to side openly with the Allies. Otherwise, Welles's visit would appear to repudiate Bullitt. If Roosevelt was taking the initiative toward a compromise peace then American policy would be the reverse of that advocated by Bullitt. Murphy expresses the opinion that on this occasion Roosevelt was probably using foreign policy for domestic political purposes.

In Mr. Hull's account of this trip he said that the President had told him that Welles had asked several times to be sent on special missions and Mr. Hull felt that any such trip would hold out false hopes, that rumors would arise as to the purpose of the trip and that it would create confusion in Europe and the United States.[5] Welles was not authorized to make any proposals on behalf of the United States.

Documents from the government files in London give a vivid picture of the British reaction to Welles's visit. Sir Robert G. Vansittart, chief diplomatic adviser to the government, wrote the following memorandum on March 18, 1940:

"Mr. Sumner Welles emerges more and more clearly as an international danger. His idea of security via disarmament first is nonsense, and I am glad that the Prime Minister dealt with him so firmly on all grounds, though I regret that he [the Prime Minister] even contemplated the possibility of gradual disarmament with this Germany, for until the Germany not only of Hitler but of the military caste has been disposed of, disarmament is not only a delusion but a deathtrap.

"But Mr. Sumner Welles' chief crime towards common sense and humanity is that he has now gone so far as to want us to make peace with Hitler. That surely is lunacy for which both he and his chief, President Roosevelt deserve the highest condemnation. It is now pretty clear, as the Prime Minister says in these minutes, that President Roosevelt is ready to play a dirty trick on the world and risk the ultimate destruction of the Western Democracies in order to secure the re-election of a democratic candidate in the United States. It is not only the Prime Minister who has drawn this deduction; it is the general expectation of everybody that I know who also knows anything of the American situation. It may well be that this criminal manoeuvre may be set in train before we have a chance of getting it stopped, but I feel strongly that we should exert the greatest and most immediate pressure on President Roosevelt to prevent him from selling the world for his own particular mess of pottage. I suggest that we should tell him plainly and in time that we are horrified at Mr. Welles' idea of making peace with Hitler, that we take it for granted that it is in no way shared by the President and wish to warn him in time that should he sponsor any such move it would be immediately rejected by ourselves and by France. There is nothing like heading off a dangerous move in time, and if we do not take this action we shall soon be invited to commit suicide to secure office for the Democratic Party in the United States. That will mean a permanent breach in Anglo-American relations. We ought to get off the mark quickly with this action, for it is of course certain that the meeting between Hitler and Mussolini is the first step towards getting us to accept either impossible proposals touched up a little bit speciously on paper and on paper only, or else getting us into the dock. And if we do not act promptly we shall find the Pope and Roosevelt backing the Italo-German booby-trap.

"P.S. Mr. Sumner Welles of course knows perfectly well that any peace proposals on the part of Hitler are pure eyewash and he means to restart the march to world conquest after a short breathing space. Welles was in fact explicitly warned of this fact by his compatriot, Mr. Jordan, who is at present in Germany." [6]

The files of the Foreign Office in London show that the Prime Minister, Mr. Chamberlain, gave the Cabinet a lengthy account of his talk with Welles. There are also records of Welles's talks with the First Lord of the Admiralty, the Chancellor of the Exchequer, and the Secretary of State for Foreign Affairs. They all made it clear to Welles that his proposals were unrealistic and unacceptable.

The finale of this escapade was contained in a visit to Mr. Hull by Lord Lothian, the British Ambassador, on March 22, 1940. He called to express the thanks of the British for the promptness with which our government had acted to stop the "peace at any price" talk, based upon what Welles might be doing in Europe.

Personal   April 1, 1940

Dear Mr. President:

I noticed that Representative Hamilton Fish and Senator Reynolds have stated that they would like to have an inquiry into the
outburst of German propaganda designed to prove that not Hitler,
but Roosevelt, through his Ambassadors in Europe started the present war! As you know, for some time I have had arrangements
made to return to Paris by the Clipper leaving the day after tomorrow. Under the circumstances, it may be desirable for me to delay
my departure and appear before the Foreign Relations Committee
of the Senate, although I could add nothing to the denial that I
have already issued.

Very sincerely yours,
William C. Bullitt

As early as October 1939, Hitler had begun to plan his next
move, the occupation of Norway. The importance of this action
lay in the shipments of Swedish ore to Germany. In the summer
months the iron was shipped by boat from the mines in the north
of Sweden and through the Baltic. In winter this route, because
of ice, became impracticable and the ore was sent by rail to Narvik in Norway. The Norwegian traitor Major Quisling first met
Hitler in Berlin in the middle of December. Quisling proposed a
plan for his followers to seize strategic points in Norway, especially Oslo, the capital. Quisling had certain connections in the
army and assured Hitler he could take over the government with
German help. By the first of March, 1940, Hitler issued an order
for the occupation of Denmark and Norway in a simultaneous operation.

Both the Danish and Norwegian governments were warned, on
good authority, of the approaching invasion, and also had evidence of German naval and military activity to show that attack
was imminent, but neither of them awoke to the danger or took
the news seriously. After the German ships had already put to
sea, Chamberlain made his famous speech that Hitler had "missed
the bus" because he had failed to attack France.

At half past four in the morning of April 9, the German Ambassadors in Oslo and Copenhagen demanded that the two countries accept the protection of Germany. Denmark was in no position to defend itself, but the Norwegians put up a gallant and hopeless resistance. In spite of British and French attempts to oust them, the Nazis soon held the territory of both these neutral countries.

Personal and Confidential   Paris
                                                            April 12, 1940
Dear Mr. President:

Since my return to Paris, I haven't been asked a question by anyone about the German White Book. It fell completely flat here.

Daladier, however, did an extremely nice thing. I enclose a letter which he wrote personally with his own hand to you, dated April 4th and sent to the Embassy for forwarding.

In case you have difficulty with his handwriting, I enclose a typewritten copy which I have had made, and a translation in case you ever wish to publish it.

Daladier's idea was that the Germans might continue to attack you and me and that their attacks might be taken up during the campaign by the Republicans. He wished, therefore, to put a letter in your hands that you could publish at any moment you might see fit. I think his idea was a good one and it was certainly a gentlemanly and generous one.

If the Germans should make any further allegations and Senator Reynolds and Ham Fish or others should become annoying, the publication of Daladier's letter ought to smash the propaganda.

Good luck and every good wish.

Yours affectionately,

Bill

Enclosures: Original of Daladier's letter.
French typewritten copy of Daladier's letter.
English translation of Daladier's letter.

MINISTRY OF WAR
FRENCH REPUBLIC

Office of the Minister   Paris
                                                            April 4, 1940
My dear President:

I have just read the allegations of the Nazi Government on the subject of pretended declarations of Ambassador Bullitt.

No one can foresee to what limits German propaganda will carry its lies. Also I feel I should tell you that during the past two years when I was Prime Minister, Ambassador Bullitt always said to me that in case of a European conflict, France should make her decisions knowing that, according to the opinion of Ambassador Bullitt, the United States of America would not enter the war.

I have learned with keen regret that you have been suffering from a severe grippe. I hope that this letter will find you completely recovered and I send you my best regards.

Edouard Daladier

THE WHITE HOUSE
WASHINGTON

Dear Bill:

I have been very much pleased with Daladier's letter of April 4. As you say, it was a very generous gesture on his part. I am enclosing my reply to him which I wish you would hand him and tell him personally how much I appreciated his thinking of writing.

Believe me

Yours very sincerely,

FDR

The Honorable William C. Bullitt
American Ambassador
Paris

My dear Mr. President:

Ambassador Bullitt has sent to me the letter which you were good enough to address to me on April 4. I have read your letter with much appreciation and I am grateful to you for your thought in sending it to me.

I hope that you have now fully recovered from the effects of your accident last winter.

I send you the assurances of my highest regard, and believe me

Yours very sincerely,

Franklin D. Roosevelt

His Excellency Monsieur Edouard Daladier
Minister of War
Paris

Not all historians agree on Bullitt's ability to keep the French and American governments properly informed, and the following quotation from Alistair Horne's *To Lose a Battle* gives the other side of the picture: "In harbouring any anticipation whatever that the United States would instantaneously send him 'clouds of planes' or ever declare war on Hitler, Reynaud was under a hopeless delusion." A footnote referring to this sentence says: "For this, the American Ambassador in Paris, William Bullitt, must be held greatly to blame. In an age when ambassadors carried weight and were more than merely the post office clerks they tend to be today, Bullitt appears to have sinned by misleading both his own country and France as to the true situation in the other; Washington was persuaded by Bullitt that France's fighting capacity was much greater than it was, while through him the French Government was led to expect far greater aid than could possibly have been forthcoming from the United States at that time." [7] Having read the documents in this book, the reader may determine for himself the accuracy of this statement.

Personal and Confidential   Paris

April 18, 1940

Dear Mr. President:

The war is so completely in the hands of the soldiers and so completely out of the hands of the diplomats that I have sent you few telegrams.

The German attack on Denmark and Norway; plus the fact that the harvest this year in Germany, Hungary, Rumania and Poland will be short; plus the concentration of 155 German divisions close to the French, Belgian, and Dutch frontiers; plus German actions which seem to indicate a menace to Sweden, the Netherlands, Belgium, Hungary and Yugoslavia has convinced everyone here that Germany in the near future will launch new attacks. No one pretends to know where the first blow will fall but everyone expects action. The French General Staff expects an attack on the western front before the first of May. The Swiss remain confident that Germany will not attack Switzerland.

The belief is general that Mussolini is about to make a move against either Yugoslavia or Greece. His complete approval of the German invasion of Denmark and Norway; plus further troop concentrations at Brindisi and in Albania; has made Reynaud, Daladier and the rest conclude that he will either seize Corfu or attempt to take the whole of Dalmatia.

I had hoped that the repercussions caused here by Welles' trip would have died down completely before my return; but Reynaud, Daladier, Chautemps, Blum and all the rest of the French politicians, to say nothing of all the diplomats here have insisted on talking about the trip. They have all said the same thing; to wit: that Welles "eulogized" Mussolini to everyone and in discussing Germany, produced the impression that Germany could not be beaten. Daladier used the word "eulogy"; Reynaud used the word "commendation"; Chautemps used the word "praises," etc. The meaning was the same.

Daladier said that the impression Welles produced was that you thought Germany was invincible and that France and England ought to try to get a peace of compromise which would leave Germany in control of Central and Eastern Europe by using the good offices of a great man — Mussolini. Daladier was a bit shocked and sore; Chautemps went so far as to say that he was much too intimate a friend of mine not to let me know that the visit had been exceedingly damaging both to your influence in France and to my influence, since the impression had been produced either that you were unaware of Mussolini's real character and intentions or that I was unaware of what was in your mind.

I replied in the same tone to everyone; that I was entirely certain that neither you nor Welles had had the slightest intention of using Welles' visit to persuade the French and British to stop fighting and leave the fate of Europe to Mussolini as arbiter. I added that I could not believe that Welles had praised Mussolini in any terms which would suggest that you thought Mussolini should be entrusted with the peace-making.

There are, of course, a lot of defeatists in this country, including Bonnet, who attempted to make great use of Sumner's praise of Mussolini, but their campaign was cut short by Mussolini's approval of the German invasion of Denmark and Norway.

The present fighting will soon wash out the memory of that visit. But for Heaven's sake, don't again let a Mussolini lemon be sold to you or anyone else.

I have been highly restrained in this report since certain of the remarks which have been made to me have been violent in the extreme. Now let's forget the matter for good.

Yours affectionately,
William C. Bullitt

Personal and Confidential   Paris
                                                    April 28, 1940

Dear Mr. President:

A letter, ready to go forward to you tonight, predicting what
would happen in Norway, has been overtaken by the event. There
is no point in burdening you with a lot of words just to prove that I
am a prophet. So I have burned up the letter, and instead will send
you this line by the hand of Freeman Matthews, First Secretary of
this Embassy, who will carry in the other hand five pâtés de foie
gras.

In summary, the situation seems to be the following:

The Germans will be able to drive the Allies out of all positions
in Norway except Narvik. Both Reynaud and Daladier are bitter
about the manner in which the Norwegian affair has been handled.
They both favored the idea; but insist that the British made no
proper preparations and have handled and are handling the expedition with complete lack of intelligence, although with courage.
Reynaud is violent on the subject of lack of brains in the British
Government and the British High Command. Daladier, who was
not present at the meeting in England at which the Norwegian decision was taken, blames Reynaud as well as the British for not fore-
seeing the German riposte, and preparing adequately to meet it.

If the fighting in Norway should go as badly as Reynaud and
Daladier expect, they believe that the neutrals of Central and Southern Europe will be so impressed by the superiority of the German
Army that they will fall into the maw of Germany and Italy almost
without resistance.

Both expect Mussolini to attack Yugoslavia. Reynaud is apparently opposed to making war on Italy, even though Italy should attempt to seize Dalmatia. Daladier, on the other hand, favors war in
support of Yugoslavia.

Both Reynaud and Daladier expect defeat in Norway to produce
most serious repercussions in France. Reynaud foresees his own fall
and Daladier thinks that he as well as Reynaud will be completely
discredited and that a defeatist government of Flandin, Laval and
Bonnet will come in, with a program of peace at almost any price.

I think that is much too gloomy a view. The fighting spirit of
the French people is untouched and one defeat will not damage it
greatly. Moreover, defeat in Norway would, I think, merely awaken
the English. It is incredible, but everyone coming to Paris from
London tells me that the British have not yet realized that they are
engaged in a life and death struggle.

In any event, the immediate prospects are unpleasant and it is clear that the United States has to be ready to meet the consequences of a defeat of France and England. You and I agree on what that would mean. I find myself thinking about the security of our communications through the Panama Canal. I remember a talk we had in 1932 about a Nicaraguan ditch.

The gloom at the top here — Herriot and Chautemps are as pessimistic as Reynaud and Daladier — is thick. I spend my time reminding people that the worst usually doesn't happen. But I am being careful to avoid expressing any opinions on what should or should not be done.

If by chance both Daladier and Reynaud should be discredited, it would be difficult to find an adequate replacement. The chief deficiency in France and England, as usual in most countries at most times, seems to be lack of really first-rate men at the top.

The only particularly cheerful news that I have to give you is that Offie is catching bigger and better brochet [pike].

Love to you all.

Yours affectionately,

Bill

That Mr. Roosevelt was feeling the strain of his seven years in office is contained in a note in Louis B. Wehle's file in his own handwriting. It is dated April 1940 and marked "WCB." "That FDR is tired out and has no more enjoyment out of the Presidency, and doesn't want to run; that he is going to back Hull; that he still hangs on so as not to throw away all chances for himself, but WCB thinks he will not run."

From this time on Bullitt deluged Washington with telegrams, sometimes several in one day, and in addition was of course talking to the President constantly by telephone. These messages, too numerous to quote, told of the impending withdrawal of British troops from Norway, and of Reynaud's conviction that the Italians would attack France when they could obtain the maximum gain with the minimum expense. The British Ambassador in Rome told him that even if Italy attacked Yugoslavia, Great Britain would not attack or blockade Italy. He advised Mr. Roosevelt that the French told him that any peace proposal from the President at this time would have a disastrous effect on French and British morale. He told of the possibility of the fall of Reynaud's government, but that any new government would push the war vigorously.[8]

The fatal tenth of May again brought the unleashing of the German Blitzkrieg. Without any warning or pretext the Nazi armies attacked two more neutral countries, Belgium and Holland. The Dutch opened their dikes in a vain attempt to stem the German tide, but they were in no position to face the might of German arms and were forced to give up the struggle in five days. The Belgians were better prepared and faced the Nazis with courage and determination. However, on the morning of May 28 King Leopold III of Belgium, who had sought the help of the British and the French, surrendered without consulting his allies and without the advice of his Cabinet. The British had between three and four hundred thousand men in their expeditionary force and there were over two million Frenchmen under arms.

This same May 10 was for the English a day of far-reaching and paramount importance. It brought to the leadership of the British Empire a man who will live in history as the probable savior of England and who will rank among the world's greatest and most courageous statesmen of all time. Chamberlain resigned and Churchill became Prime Minister. His thoughts at this time give profound insight into the character of this great man: "I can not conceal from the reader of this truthful account that as I went to bed at about 3 A.M. I was conscious of a profound sense of relief. At last I had the authority to give directions over the whole scene. I felt as if I were walking with Destiny, and that all my past life had been but a preparation for this hour and for this trial . . . I thought I knew a good deal about it all, and I was sure I should not fail. Therefore, although impatient for the morning, I slept soundly and had no need for cheering dreams. Facts are better than dreams." [9]

It was on May 13 that Churchill made his famous speech, saying: "I have nothing to offer but blood, toil, tears and sweat." There is a remarkable resemblance between these words and those of Garibaldi almost one hundred years earlier, who, when addressing his men, said: "I offer neither pay, nor quarters, nor provisions; I offer hunger, thirst, forced marches, battles and death." Both men were facing insuperable odds with indomitable courage.

On May 15 Churchill asked Roosevelt for the loan of forty or fifty old destroyers from the United States Navy. He also asked for airplanes and antiaircraft artillery. The transfer of these destroyers did not take place until August and was made in consideration of Great Britain leasing certain naval bases in the West Indies to the United States. According to historian James V. Compton, the so-called destroyer deal made "a considerable impression" and apparently persuaded Hitler that America had become a virtual belligerent in the Allied cause.[10]

Bullitt's messages continued to pour into Washington in Personal and Secret telegrams to the President and on May 13, he asked the President's opinion and urged his approval, of the desire of the French to send aviators to be trained in the United States as the French schools were inadequate. In reply to this the President suggested that American instructors train the pilots in Canada. The French requested permission for the sending of an aircraft carrier to pick up one hundred Curtiss P-36 airplanes in New York, or have American pilots fly the planes over. On the same day Bullitt wired about the fighting in Belgium and said: "In addition to its work at the front, the German air force has bombarded at will every aviation field in France and, for example, at Orléans has destroyed many planes on the ground. However great the courage of an army or a civilian population, dominance of the air appears today to be decisive."

On May 13 Bullitt suggested that opinion in Italy would be so aroused if the Holy Father were to leave Rome that, "If you have not already done so, I hope that you will invite the Pope to take refuge as your guest in the United States in case of necessity. It occurs to me that the place to offer him as a residence is the ancestral home of Charles Carroll of Carrollton."

The next day he reported that there were no French planes available to face an Italian attack and asked for a number of old American destroyers to be used by the French in the Mediterranean against Italian submarines.[11]

In other telegrams of this day Bullitt suggested letting Mussolini know that if Italy entered the war the United States would cut off all remittances from Americans to Italy, and that no government official believed that France could resist an attack from Italy, with all its army occupied with combating the German attack.

TELEGRAM

This telegram must be closely paraphrased before being communicated to anyone.

Secretary of State	Paris
Washington	Dated May 14, 1940
Rush	Rec'd 6:55 P.M.

659, May 14, 7 P.M. (SECTION ONE)
Personal and Secret for the President

I received from Rome at 7 o'clock this evening Ambassador Phillips' rush 341, May 14, noon.

I felt that it was my duty to communicate the information it contained immediately to the Prime Minister. He was in a meeting of the War Cabinet but came out and I communicated the information to him at 7:10 P.M.

He said that the British Ambassador in Paris had just given him the same news. He expressed the opinion that Italy certainly would enter the war on the side of Germany and might even attack France tonight.

I asked where he expected the attack. He said that it might come in Tunis or might be begun by bombardments of the Riviera and Marseilles by Italian planes.

The Prime Minister went on to say that he felt Mussolini had decided to act at this moment because of the appalling success which the German army had had in the sector Montmédy-Sedan. He said that the Germans had attacked with colossal tanks and at the same time with a totally overwhelming mass of bombardment planes and pursuit planes.

(END SECTION ONE)

Bullitt

TELEGRAM

This telegram must be closely paraphrased before being communicated to anyone.

Secretary of State   Paris
Washington   Dated May 14, 1940
Rush   Rec'd 6:40 P.M.
659, May 14, 7 P.M. (SECTION TWO)

The German tanks had crossed the River Meuse as if it did not exist. They had run through the French anti-tank defenses which consisted of railroad rails sunk deep in concrete and protruding from ground as if the rails were straw. They had crossed the anti-tank traps and had completely demolished the concrete fortifications by which the Maginot Line had been extended in that region since the beginning of the war.

Reynaud then said "at this moment there is nothing between those German tanks and Paris."

He stated that the French were attempting a counterattack to cut off the raids made by this German tank advance but he did not know what hope of success remained. Even without the participation of Italy, France faced one of the gravest and most terrible moments in her history. With the participation of Italy the result would be tragic not only for France and England but for every country in the world including the United States.

(END SECTION TWO)

Bullitt

TELEGRAM

This telegram must be closely paraphrased before being communicated to anyone.

Secretary of State   Paris
Washington   Dated May 14, 1940
Rush   Rec'd 6:43 P.M.
659, May 14, 7 P.M. (SECTION THREE)

We were at one of the most terrible moments in human history. France would fight on but the French soldiers, brave as they were, could not stand against simultaneous attacks by tanks on the ground and bombs and machine gun bullets from the air.

Reynaud then implored me to obtain additional aeroplanes from the United States. I told him I feared there were none to be had.

He then said that the war with Italy would involve Italian submarine attacks on all shipping in the Mediterranean. The British and French had an inadequate number of destroyers. He knew that the United States had a large number of old destroyers which could be used effectively against submarines. He implored me if possible to have the Government of the United States declare these destroyers to be without military value and sell them to the French and British Governments.

(END SECTION THREE)

Bullitt

TELEGRAM

This telegram must be closely paraphrased before being communicated to anyone.

Secretary of State	Paris
Washington	Dated May 14, 1940
Rush	Rec'd 8:10 P.M.
659, May 14, 7 P.M. (SECTION FOUR)	

He then went on to say that he had just talked with the British Prime Minister on the telephone. The British had been obsessed by the idea that the seizure of Belgium and the Netherlands was merely a preparation for air attacks on England. He had convinced Churchill at last that the real objective of the German army was the destruction of the French army and Churchill had agreed to send all the British planes available to assist the French in the Montmédy-Sedan sector.

Reynaud again referred to the overwhelming effect of the attack of heavy tanks combined with incessant bombing from the air.

In conclusion he thanked me with genuine gratitude for having given him the information I had communicated and said once more that at this moment we faced the enslavement not only of Europe and of Africa, but also the rest of the world by a barbarism which would crush twenty centuries of Christian civilization.

(END OF MESSAGE)

Bullitt

On May 15 Reynaud advised Churchill that the Germans had broken through into open country and that the war would be lost in a few days unless the British would send their planes. "Churchill, Reynaud said, had screamed at him that there was no chance of the war being lost and he, Reynaud, had replied that Churchill knew as well as he knew him that so long as he, Reynaud, should remain Prime Minister France would fight to the bitter end." Reynaud advised Bullitt on this day that the French were outnumbered ten to one in planes.

Bullitt now turned from the battle to advising the President to warn American insurance companies not to insure Italian vessels.

On May 16 Bullitt sent the wives and children of the Embassy staff to Bordeaux and also agreed, at the request of the British Ambassador, to take charge of Great Britain's interests in Paris. The British Embassy was now burning its documents and the American Embassy destroyed all codes, with two exceptions. This was done at the urging of Reynaud.

This same day the Dutch Minister of Foreign Affairs told Bullitt that if England became unsafe the Queen would like to come to America.

In spite of these frequent and voluminous telegrams there is mention of constant telephone calls to the President in Bullitt's files.[12]

On May 17, 1940, Guy La Chambre was replaced as Minister of Air by Captain Laurent Eynac.

TELEGRAM RECEIVED

This telegram must be closely paraphrased before being communicated to anyone.

Sent to White House 5/15/40 — 11:55 A.M.   Paris
Secretary of State   Dated May 15, 1940
Washington   Rec'd 10 A.M.
Rush
665, May 15, noon
Personal and Secret for the President

Paul Reynaud asked me to come to the Foreign Office this morning at 10:15. When I called he said that he wished to keep me and through me you fully informed personally as to the developments at the front. The situation continued to be one of the utmost gravity. The greatest battle in history was in progress in the region of Sedan. The Germans had crossed the Meuse at many points north of Sedan.

This morning at 6 o'clock Daladier had telephoned to him and had stated that the French troops positively could not hold out today against the masses of tanks and airplanes which were being launched against them and that the battle certainly would be lost quickly unless the troops could be protected from German attacks from the air.

He, Reynaud, had telephoned immediately to Churchill in London and had stated that since the Germans had broken through into open country where there were no fortifications whatever on the most direct route to Paris and since there was nothing to oppose the floods of German planes and tanks except ordinary infantrymen and artillery the war might be lost in the course of a few days and in his opinion would be lost unless the British should send their airplanes from England at once.

Churchill, Reynaud said, had screamed at him that there was no chance of the war being lost and he, Reynaud, had replied that Churchill knew as well as he knew him that so long as he, Reynaud, should remain Prime Minister France would fight to the bitter end. It was his duty however to tell Churchill the facts. Churchill thereupon promised to call together at the earliest possible moment the War Cabinet and attempt to persuade the War Cabinet to promise to send the British pursuit planes which were being kept in England for the protection of factories to be sent at once to France to join in the battle of the Meuse.

Reynaud added that General Giraud had been recalled from Antwerp to take command of the French troops in the Sedan sector.

Reynaud said that the French planes were outnumbered almost ten to one and he implored me once more to ask you if it might not be possible by any means whatsoever to obtain new supplies of planes from the United States. I answered that you were as aware of the need as he was and that it was no lack of desire to help but simply the fact that the planes did not exist.

He then suggested that the planes of other types than those which the French had bought hitherto might be available in small quantities and asked if it might not be possible to obtain such planes. I replied that his own representative in Washington Colonel Jacquin knew better than anyone else what could be bought in America and that he had only to order Jacquin to act in order to obtain every plane available. He said that the difficulty was that Jacquin was not aware of the extreme gravity of the situation. I said that he should be informed.

Reynaud went on to say that the information from Italy indicated that Mussolini was preparing to attack almost immediately.

He repeated his request for old American destroyers. Will you please let me know if you can do anything about this matter?

I communicated to Reynaud your views that aviators should be trained in Canada and not in the United States. I added that you would be glad to keep in close touch with the matter and suggested that since the training was to be carried out in Canada the best way to organize it would probably be to have Lord Lothian call on you to make certain that nothing was done which would conflict with your desires.

I assume that when you said to me over the telephone yesterday that "the boat was all right" you meant that there was no objection to sending an aircraft carrier to take planes which had already been set up. Please cable me a confirmation of this immediately.

In concluding our conversation Reynaud said that the French counterattacks against the German "hernia" in the Sedan region had not been successful either in cutting it off or reducing it. On the contrary the "hernia" was growing hour by hour.

The situation could not be more grave.

(END OF MESSAGE)

Bullitt

TELEGRAM SENT

DEPARTMENT OF STATE
WASHINGTON

American Embassy   May 15, 1940
Paris (France)
Your 665, May 15, noon

With regard to sending an aircraft carrier to carry planes which have already been set up, it would not seem possible to load the planes in New York as, under international law and American statute, a vessel of war cannot increase its armed strength in neutral ports. However, there would seem to be no difficulties if the French desired to have the planes set up in the United States, flown to Canada, and thence by Allied pilots to some port on the east coast of Canada, possibly Halifax, where an aircraft carrier could load them.

Colonel Jacquin should naturally receive immediate instructions and adequate authority.

Hull

The French were obsessed with the numbers and power of the German Air Force and, as the correspondence shows, kept pressing Bullitt to help them obtain American planes for France.

The most misguided estimates were made of the quantity of planes available to Germany, and of her monthly production. The Germans had been able to deceive completely her enemies and there are even stories of their showing visitors a field filled with planes and then flying these planes to the next field to be inspected. Up to the very end of the fighting the French believed in the great numerical superiority of the German fighters, and as late as June 11, 1940, General Weygand, then in command of the French Army, vainly urged Churchill to send every British fighter squadron to France.[13]

Although the Germans did have more bombers, France far outnumbered her in fighting planes which were of such value in defense. The German Stuka dive bombers were so slow that in the Battle of Britain German losses were painfully high.

Figures now available from the German Military History Research Bureau, Specialty Group VI, Air Force and Aerial Warfare History, show that on May 10, 1940, the day the attack on France began, the Germans had 1711 bombers, 414 dive bombers, 354 escort fighters, 1356 fighters, 830 reconnaissance and other planes, or a total of 4665.

A Commission was appointed in 1947 by the French National Assembly to inquire into the events which took place in France from 1933 to 1945. Testimony before this Commission stated that on this same date (May 10, 1940) the French had 461 bombers, 429 reconnaissance, 277 observation, and 2122 fighter planes. A total of 3289.

However, on neither side were all these planes immediately available for combat.

General Arnold, Chief of Staff of the United States Air Force, estimated that in 1938 Germany had 10,000 planes.[14]

Charles A. Lindbergh, who visited Germany and was shown her air force, reported in September 1938: "The French situation is desperate. Impossible to catch up to Germany for years, if at all. France is producing about forty-five or fifty warplanes per month. Germany is building from 500 to 800 per month, according to the best estimates. England is building in the vicinity of seventy per month." Later, in October, he wrote: "The French estimates of German production facilities indicate that Germany can build 24,000 planes per year. French Intelligence places the existing German air fleet at 6000 modern planes . . ." In June he had written that in case of war the Germans would immediately have supremacy in the air, as they had developed a huge air force.[15]

Albert Speer, German Minister of Armaments and War Production, states without qualification: "The troops . . . had started the war in 1939 with only 771 fighter planes." [16] According to the figures of the German Military History Research Bureau, when the Germans began their lightning attack on France they had in combat 1076 fighter (Jäger) planes, 345 dive bombers, and 246 escort fighter planes.[17]

In a German diary of the war, showing the daily disposition of units, the terminology differs somewhat, but the figures for May 10 show 1016 fighter planes, 42 pursuit, and 248 destroyer planes. In addition there were in the Netherlands 35 pursuit planes and 23 destroyers.[18]

On the production side, Germany was turning out approximately 125 fighter planes per month in the beginning of 1940.[19] The British produced 325 planes in May 1940,[20] and the French delivered over 600 to the Air Force.[21] They had previously purchased 544 American planes.[22]

The testimony at the French Commission hearing shows that when the fighting began on May 10, 1940, the French had, in opposition to the 1300 to 1400 German fighters, 2122 fighters (Chasse), but only 790 were in service.[23] The British had, in France, 474 of all types.[24] According to the same French testimony, in the following thirty days 668 fighter planes were added to the French Air Force.

The Germans, far better informed than the Allies, were fully aware of the numbers of planes opposed to them and estimated 764 French fighters and 456 British aircraft, of which 261 were fighters.[25] General Adolf Galland, Commander in Chief of German Fighter Forces, stated: "Our numerical inferiority was roughly balanced by our technical superiority." [26]

The mystery of Germany's overwhelming victory in the air is perhaps explained by testimony before the Commission of the French National Assembly. Included in this testimony at the official hearing, and documented by figures, were statements by the following Generals:

General Vuillemin, Chief of the General Staff of the Air Force, stated on July 29, 1940, that: "The French aviation remained, at the armistice, ready to continue the fight with first line effective planes greater [in number] than it had on May 10th." [27]

General d'Astier de la Vigerie commanded the aviation in the northern zone. He stated to the Minister of Air that: "Almost every evening I had to lift up my telephone and take the initiative to inform the commanders of the army and of the group of armies that I had, for the following day, a certain number of formations without missions, adding, 'Have you any to give them?' Their reply was invariably the same: 'We thank you very much but we do not have use for them.' General d'Astier added that a mixed group of fighters and bombers attached to an army corps did nothing during ten to fifteen days. [28]

General Massenet de Marancour gave an equally remarkable account of the French failure to use the planes available to them. [He said: "I was commandant of the Third Air Region which extended from Brittany to the Pyrenees . . . I was in very frequent communication with General Redempt [commander of aviation depots] on the subject of the excessive quantities of war planes which remained, in my schools, without surface covering and I frequently heard his complaints on the subject of the planes which he did not know what to do with and that the General Air Staff did not take from him. I know that, every evening, General Redempt sent to the Headquarters for Air, the list of all the planes which they could have delivered and this list was long.

. . . On the ground at Tours, for example, more than 200 war planes were stationed at the disposition of Air Headquarters. Of this number, 150 were single seated fighters, Bloch 151 . . . In the month of January 1940 I asked for authorization to take twenty to form, with my pupils, fighting patrols for the defense of cities . . . General Picard wrote me, in his own hand, that he regretted but that headquarters had put an embargo on all airplanes in the depots and refused to disturb one . . .

The 10th of May 1940, the 150 Bloch 151 were still at Tours." [29]

It is apparent that the Germans did not have greatly superior numbers of fighter planes, and in fact the combined forces of Britain and France, had the planes been used, were greater than those of her enemy. From the testimony it is very evident that the French did not use the planes which they had available and this opinion is confirmed by the statement of General Gamelin, the Commanding General of the French Army. At the committee hearing he testified, under oath: "M. Guy La Chambre will tell you that there were, the 10th of May, about two thousand fighter planes of recent model. But of these 2000 planes, there were only with the armies, equipped, but 900, and of these 900, only 418 were engaged in the battle, this is at least, the figure given by General d' Harcourt, Superior Commander of fighters, in his testimony at the inquiry of Riom June 15, 1942." [30]

General Gamelin did not attempt to justify his failure to use his planes and gave no explanation of why only 418 were engaged. He closed this part of his testimony with the words: "What is the mystery which exists in this domain of aviation? I humbly admit to you that I know nothing. [Je n'en sais rien.]" [31]

Guy La Chambre has written me his thoughts on the possible failure to use the air force. "It would appear that the High Command of the French, haunted by the remembrance of the war of 1914–18, which was a long war, had thought the war of 1939 would have the duration of the former one, hence the relatively considerable number of new airplanes held in reserve . . . in particular the number of fighting planes, which, not engaged in the course of the Battle of France, reached North Africa to continue the war and became relatively important . . . In conclusion one could not pretend that the principal cause of the defeat of 1940 rested in the numerical inferiority of the French aviation, given the fact that General Vuillemin, Commander in Chief of these forces, had, himself, declared that these even continued at the moment of the armistice of 1940 'to continue the battle with forces superior in number to those which she had available at the moment of entering the war.' The truth is that in my eyes — but this is a personal opinion — what gave the victory to Germany on the Meuse was the combined action of aviation and tanks, a use which had not been foreseen by the Allied Command."

TELEGRAM RECEIVED

This telegram must be closely paraphrased before being communicated to anyone.

Sent to President 9:35 A.M. May 16th

Secretary of State	Paris
Washington	Dated May 16, 1940
Rush	Rec'd 7:21 A.M.
692, May 16, 11 A.M.	

Personal and Secret for the President

Paul Reynaud said to me at 10:20 this morning that the news which I did not dare to put in frank form in my telegram No. 690 of last night to you recounting my conversation with Daladier while Gamelin telephoned was true.

The Belgian army south of Namur had collapsed completely. The Germans had poured through this gap motorized units. These motorized units had now reached the region of Laon and Reims.

The hole made by the collapse of the Belgian army had not been filled to the slightest degree and the German army was pouring through it all its motorized and mechanized divisions.

The final and most horrible and incredible blow was that all the railroad workers of Belgium had gone on strike and were refusing to transport French troops.

In consequence it appeared to be impossible to hope that the hole could be stopped.

Reynaud concluded his statements to me by the words "I am sorry for the democracies."

Bullitt

TELEGRAM RECEIVED
This telegram must be closely paraphrased before being communicated to anyone.

Secretary of State	Paris
Washington	Dated May 17, 1940
720, May 17, 3 P.M.	Rec'd 1:30 P.M.

Personal and Secret for the President

Reynaud and the Minister for Air and Mandel have all spoken to me unofficially about the need to obtain American pilots as soon as possible.

I am told that if the Government of the United States would permit reserve pilots to resign their reserve commissions with the understanding that if they should survive the present war they would be reinstated and if the French should establish at Windsor, Ontario, a recruiting bureau which would offer the franc equivalent of 400 dollars per month per pilot plus expenses it is almost certain that a thousand pilots would desire to enlist in the French Army at once.

Would you have any objection to such procedure? This question is entirely personal, unofficial and off the record.

Bullitt

TELEGRAM

736, May 18, noon
Personal and Secret for the President

. . . I happened to be with Daladier at 8:40 in the evening of Wednesday, May 15, when Gamelin telephoned to give him the first information that anyone had about the collapse of the Belgian Army holding the line of the Meuse south of Namur and the success of the Germans in pouring motorized, mechanized and armored divisions through the large hole.

Daladier was totally incredulous and stupefied. As the information came over the wire from Gamelin, he kept exclaiming, "It cannot be true," "Impossible," and when Gamelin told him there were German troops in armored cars already in front of Laon and Reims, the moment was terrific.

He urged Gamelin to make an immediate counterattack and Gamelin said he did not have enough men. I cannot describe the scene in a telegram at this moment, but after fifteen minutes of conversation Daladier hung up the telephone and we went together to look at the big general staff map on his wall for a little village called, — if I remember correctly, Liesse — on the road to Laon to which the German armored cars had returned after being at Laon. It was hard to find the village and harder to find anything to say, so that he simply said that this swift German advance gave the Germans a great opportunity to surge in from both sides of the tremendous salient and capture the tanks and leave Daladier, who was convinced that the army he had himself built up was about to be destroyed.

Since I was the only civilian besides Daladier and certainly the only foreigner who had this information, I felt that I had no right to send you a frank telegram at that time, but I hope you were able to read between the lines of the one I did send you . . .

Bullitt

The arms embargo had been lifted in November 1939 and America afforded Britain and France every facility for securing American military supplies. The French placed sizable orders, but British orders were very few. By May 1940, however, the President and Secretary Hull had become thoroughly aroused, and when Bullitt cabled Hull on May 13 and suggested that France would send an aircraft carrier to load planes, Hull replied at once that the planes would have to be flown to Canada and loaded there. They could not be shipped from the United States. The planes were sent, arriving too late to help the French. The President also offered to release to France two thousand 75 millimeter guns from the First World War.[32]

TELEGRAM RECEIVED
This telegram must be closely paraphrased before being communicated to anyone.

Secretary of State   Paris
Washington   Dated May 16, 1940
706, May 16, 6 P.M.   Rec'd 5:05 P.M.
Personal and Secret for the President

I should like to speak what follows into your most private ear at the White House and to have no record of it. It is the sort of hypothesis that we often discuss but never put on paper. However, I cannot talk with you so here goes.

It seem obvious that unless God grants a miracle as at the time of the battle of the Marne, the French army will be crushed utterly. The British, who have not yet sent to France the quantities of pursuit planes that they have in England to protect their factories (they have exactly two squadrons in France), are already beginning to be critical and contemptuous of the French. That was the tone of the British Ambassador when he spoke to me this morning.

I think that it may possibly be of the utmost importance for the future of the United States that you should have in mind the hypothesis that, in order to excape from the ultimate consequences of absolute defeat, the British may install a government of Oswald Mosley and the union of British fascists which would cooperate fully with Hitler. That would mean that the British navy would be against us.

I think that, perhaps by way of a conversation with Mackenzie King [Prime Minister of Canada] or some direct arrangement with the officers of the British fleet, you ought to try to make certain that in case the war goes as badly as it may, the British fleet would base itself on Canada for the defense of the dominion which might become the refuge of the British crown.

Bullitt

Bullitt's doubts about the British were still in his mind, but this attitude gradually changed to one of admiration.

On March 21, 1940, Paul Reynaud had become Premier and Minister of Foreign Affairs, with Daladier remaining as Minister for National Defense and Minister of War. On May 18, Reynaud took over these two posts. Reynaud was to remain in office until June 16, 1940.

TELEGRAM

Secretary of State	Paris
Washington	Dated May 20, 1940
Rush	Rec'd 2:20 P.M.
772, May 20, 5 P.M. (SECTION ONE)	

. . . Last night by chance I met the wife of the Minister of Blockade Madame Georges Monnet who had been at Soissons attempting to evacuate small children. They were walking on the road toward Paris since they had no means of transportation and she was trying to keep them singing to help their little feet to move. Two German aeroplanes came down and machine gunned them and the road was filled with little bodies.

The same story I have from fifty witnesses French and American. (END SECTION ONE)

Bullitt

[Section two omitted.]

TELEGRAM

Secretary of State   Paris
Washington   Dated May 20, 1940
Rush   Rec'd 1:55 P.M.
772, May 20, 5 P.M. (SECTION THREE)

I talked with Wayne Taylor, representative of the Red Cross in Paris, and he stated that what I have reported above did not give one-tenth of the truth. The barbarities of the Germans and the sufferings of the French were ten times more horrible. He estimated that there were at least five million persons on the road and that a vast number of these would die of starvation and illness unless they could be cared for by American help.

I asked you over the telephone to try to get Congress to vote today twenty million dollars for the succor of these refugees. In the opinion of Wayne Taylor this sum would not be sufficient. He believes that whatever should be given could be expended more efficiently through the French Red Cross.

(END SECTION THREE)

Bullitt

SECRET SECRET

FROM: STATE DEPARTMENT   19 MAY 1940
  TO: PRESIDENT U.S.
 VIA: NAVAL RADIO WASHINGTON

AMBASSADOR BULLITT SAYS REGARDING A CONVERSATION HE HAD LAST NIGHT WITH PREMIER REYNAUD THAT THE PREMIER FEELS THAT THE SITUATION IS EXTREMELY SERIOUS. GERMAN DRIVE IS DIRECTED TOWARDS CHANNEL PORTS TO INTERCEPT FRENCH TROOPS IN BELGIUM AND TO SECURE BASES FOR ATTACKS ON GREAT BRITAIN. IF GERMANY IS SUCCESSFUL, BECAUSE OF HER GREATER IMMEDIATE STRENGTH, AND GAINS THESE OBJECTIVES, THE ALLIES MIGHT BE BEATEN INSIDE OF SIXTY DAYS. PREMIER REYNAUD WANTS THE PRESIDENT TO MAKE A DECLARATION THAT THIS COUNTRY'S INTERESTS WILL NOT ALLOW IT TO PERMIT THE ALLIES TO BE DEFEATED. BULLITT TOLD HIM THAT SUCH A DECLARATION WOULD HAVE NO GREAT VALUE BECAUSE OF CONGRESS. REYNAUD SAID HE COULD NOT UNDERSTAND ATTITUDE OF CONGRESS WHEN ULTIMATE DEFEAT OF U.S. IS AT STAKE. BULLITT REAFFIRMED THAT PUBLIC OPINION IN AMERICA IS NOT READY FOR SUCH A STEP. REYNAUD REPLIED THAT IT AT LEAST WOULD ENCOURAGE ALLIES AND DISCOURAGE THE ENEMIES.

AMBASSADOR BULLITT IS TRANSMITTING REQUEST FOR PREMIER WHO WANTS AN EARLY REPLY TO HIS PLEA.

AMBASSADOR AGREES WITH ESTIMATE OF GRAVITY OF SITUATION BUT DOESN'T BELIEVE SUCH A STATEMENT WOULD HAVE THE DESIRED EFFECT.

TELEGRAM

This telegram must be closely paraphrased before being communicated to anyone.

Secretary of State   Paris
Washington   Dated May 22, 1940
Rush   Rec'd 3:05 P.M.
823, May 22, 6 P.M.
Personal and Secret for the President

   Take the shortest line from 1914 angels [Mons] to a shelled cathedral [Reims] and remember taxicabs [reserves sent from Paris] and hope.

Bullitt

TELEGRAM

888, May 26, 1 P.M.
Personal and Secret for the President Only

   I should like to give you my most private opinion on the present military situation for your most private ear. I believe that the British, Belgian and French armies in Flanders will be obliged to surrender within two or three days and that there is no hope that they may be able to cut through to join the main body of the French Army.

   Within five or six days the German mechanized divisions will have marked [sic] up the remains of these allied armies and have been reformed for the march on Paris. The Germans meanwhile are concentrating huge masses of infantry just to the North and South of Laon. When the German mechanized divisions are ready to advance, they will sweep easily to the Seine at Havre and Rouen. If the French should send the full reinforcements they have to meet this threat of envelopment of Paris from the Northwest the striking force now being concentrated in the Laon area will break through on the direct road to Paris by Soissons, Compiègne, Senlis, Chantilly

and Meaux. It appears, therefore, that Paris will be in danger of occupation in about ten days and, however bravely the French army
may fight, it is difficult to imagine circumstances which will enable
Paris to be defended successfully. I regret deeply to feel obliged to
express such an opinion but I think you ought to know just how serious the situation is.

Bullitt

The courageous and magnificently executed withdrawal of the
British Army from Dunkirk was ordered on May 28, all shipping
and small craft having been assembled in readiness since the twentieth. Churchill paid tribute to the gallant assistance of the
French, telling how they had withstood the attacks of seven German divisions for four days and thus kept them from reaching the
beachhead. The French fought until they had exhausted their
ammunition and 50,000 men were captured.

On May 29, Secretary Hull amended the Neutrality Act regulations so that American pilots could deliver planes to the Maritime
Provinces of Canada for shipment to Europe.

Washington
May 26, 1940
4 P.M.

The Secretary of State to the Ambassador in France [Bullitt]

The President desires that you communicate immediately the
sense of the following to Reynaud and to Daladier:

While we still hope the invasion will be checked, if the worst
comes to the worst, we regard the retention of the French fleet as a
force in being as vital to the reconstitution of France and of the
French colonies and to the ultimate control of the Atlantic and
other oceans and as a vital influence towards getting less harsh terms
of peace. That means that the French fleet must not get caught bot-
tled up in the Mediterranean. Those ships in the east Mediterranean
must be in a position to exit through the Suez Canal. Those at
Toulouse, Tunis, and Algiers must be able to exit past Gibraltar
and be in a position, if the worst comes, to retire to the West Indies
or to safe ports in the West African possessions.

The same thought is being conveyed in the strictest confidence to the British regarding the British fleet.

Finally, if the Germans hold out alluring offers to France based on surrender of the fleet, it should be remembered that these offers are of no ultimate value and that the condition of France could be no worse, but in fact would be far stronger, if the fleet were removed as a whole to safe places.

Hull

Two days after this telegram the tragic surrender of the Belgian Army took place and the feelings of the Belgian Government are vividly shown in the ensuing messages.

TELEGRAM

899, May 27, 9 P.M.
Personal and Secret for the President

Daladier has just had luncheon with me alone and has expressed his most intimate opinions.

In somewhat more tragic form, he expressed the terms contained in my 888, May 26, 1 P.M. He added, however, that he felt sure that, if the Germans could force the French Government to evacuate Paris, they would not enter at once but would permit Paris to fall into the hands of a communistic mob for several days: a communistic mob which would burn, pillage and murder everyone decent who might remain in the City. He was, therefore, in favor of the Government remaining in Paris even though the Government should be captured in Paris.

In this connection, he expressed the opinion that, while no German general would order his soldiers to pillage the American Embassy and murder the members of the staff, Goebbels would arrange for the French Communists to carry out this task before entry of the German troops. This may be possible, but I have no intention of leaving Paris and neither have the other members of the staff. Such happening would be unpleasant, but brief, and no one here would have any great objection to anything except being treated like Schuschnigg and fed atropine and bromides in order to disintegrate. In such case anyone would count on you for immediate action. Personally, I do not think there is any chance of the Germans risking this sort of behavior.

Bullitt

TELEGRAM

This telegram must be closely paraphrased before being communicated to anyone.

Secretary of State	Paris
Washington	Dated May 28, 1940
Rush	Rec'd 8:30 A.M.
912, May 28, 11 A.M.	

Personal and Secret for the President

The Belgian Ambassador called on me this morning at 9:30 a completely broken man. He said that the King's action in ordering the entire Belgian army to surrender, without consulting either General Gort or General Blanchard or informing the Belgian Government, was an act of dishonor without parallel in history. Since a King without honor was nothing, the King no longer existed. The Prime Minister of Belgium would denounce the King's action this morning on the radio and would announce that it was illegal since such acts had to be countersigned by the Prime Minister and would call on all Belgians to go on fighting.

The Belgian Ambassador went on to say that he had come to ask me whether in view of the treachery and dishonor of the King the invitation of the President to the Royal children still stood.

I replied that I had of course had no communication with you on this subject; but that I felt that you would not wish to visit the sins of the father on the children and that your invitation would stand.

I went on to say that on the other hand several serious problems now arose. If the King had ordered his army to betray its Allies he doubtless had done so after previous agreement with the Germans with regard to his personal life. The King might now be on his way back to his Palace in Brussels and might desire to have his children join him and although he had forfeited by his action of treason all rights as a King he still had humane rights as a father.

At this point the Belgian Ambassador interrupted me to say that yesterday evening shortly before the news had arrived of the King's order to his army to surrender he had received a telegram from the King stating that he was most grateful [*] and to me and that he desired his children to proceed immediately to Lisbon and to leave for the United States . . .

Bullitt

* Apparent omission.

The Ambassador in France [Bullitt]   Paris
to the Secretary of State   May 28, 1940
           1 P.M.

Personal for the President Only

During the course of our conversation this morning, Reynaud's remarks about the American Fleet enabled me to bring up the question of the French Fleet. It took very little conversation to convince him of the truth of the arguments which you advanced in your 943, May 26, 4 P.M. I believe as strongly as I have ever believed anything that you will be unable to protect the United States from German attack unless you have the cooperation of the French and British fleets. I believe that one of the surest ways to obtain such cooperation would be by sending our Atlantic Fleet to the Mediterranean.

In any event I ask you solemnly and urgently to send immediately a cruiser to Bordeaux for two purposes: First, to bring to Bordeaux immediately from 5 to 10,000 Thompson submachine guns caliber .45, model 1928 A-1, and one million rounds of ammunition; and second, to carry away from Bordeaux the entire French and Belgian gold reserve. The French reserve is 550 tons. The Belgian 100 tons.

The reason for the request for these arms is that both Reynaud and Mandel now expect a Communist uprising and butcheries in the city of Paris and other industrial centers as the German Army draws near. The Paris police have no weapons except antiquated single shot rifles.

Mandel appealed to me personally this morning to obtain the submachine guns at the earliest possible moment.

I told him to have orders sent to Purvis at once in Washington to purchase these weapons and munitions on behalf of the French Ministry of the Interior for the use of the French police. Please ask Henry Morgenthau to round up every available weapon of this kind he can to the number of 10,000 and please put them on cruiser tomorrow. Take them from Navy stock if you have to and replace them. Incidentally, we have exactly two revolvers in this entire Mission with only 40 bullets and I should like a few for ourselves . . .

The French have no ships available on which to send their gold reserve. I know where it is and it is out of harm's way for the moment. Please tell this to Henry Morgenthau. If you cannot send a cruiser of the San Francisco class at once to Bordeaux please order the *Trenton* at Lisbon to take on fuel and supplies at once for a trip to America and order her today to Bordeaux.

Reynaud has just said to me that if we can send a cruiser to Bordeaux or to any other port he will put the entire gold reserve on it and send it to the United States.

Bullitt

On May 29, the cruiser *Vincennes* and two destroyers were sent to Casablanca, returning to America with $250,000,000 in gold.

TELEGRAM

This telegram must be closely paraphrased before being communicated to anyone.

Secretary of State	Paris
Washington	Dated May 28, 1940
929, May 28, 10 P.M. (SECTION ONE)	Rec'd 7:17 P.M.
Personal and Secret for the President	

Spaak, Minister for Foreign Affairs of Belgium, asked to see me this evening and I received him at 7 o'clock.

He said that he wished to thank me for the statements that I had made this morning to the Belgian Ambassador with regard to the Royal children. (See telegram No. 912 of May 28, 11 A.M.).

He went on to say that since the King had committed an act which dishonored not only himself but also the entire Belgian nation from which the honor of Belgium could not recover for a hundred years it was impossible for anyone to expect you to receive the Royal children at the request of a man whose name would go down in history as the synonym of dishonor.

It was his present opinion and that of the Belgian Government that you should not be asked to receive the Royal children. They should be kept in France in the horrible and remote château where they are now lodged. He trusted that if you should receive a further appeal from the traitorous King Leopold you would ignore it.

(END SECTION ONE)

Bullitt

TELEGRAM

This telegram must be closely paraphrased before being communicated to anyone.

Secretary of State   Paris
Washington   Dated May 28, 1940
929, May 28, 10 P.M. (SECTION TWO)   Rec'd 7:22 P.M.

Since this is the position of the Belgian Government the question of the opinion of the French Government does not arise and the children will remain in France.

In discussing the action of the King, Spaak said that since the beginning of the war the Belgian Ministers had been shocked to perceive on many occasions that the King had no sense of loyalty whatsoever to his Allies. They had tried to impress on him the fact that since he had appealed to the British and French for aid, he was obliged to give every help in his power to the French and British. He had said if the Germans asked him to do anything against the French and British he would abdicate at once. The fact was that he had committed the most terrible act of treachery and a crime against the French and British and apparently was so without moral sense that he did not realize the depth of his infamy.

(END MESSAGE)

Bullitt

Late in May Bullitt was consulted about the difficulties the British were experiencing with Ambassador Joseph P. Kennedy's defeatist talk. In the files of the British Foreign Office there are some remarkable records of these troubles. British dislike of Mr. Kennedy reached its climax in May 1940 when M. Roche of the French Embassy complained to Mr. John Balfour, Head of the American Department, about Mr. Kennedy's remarks and his attitude toward the war. (The file memorandum says, "He thinks and hopes that we shall be defeated." [33]) The suggestion by the Foreign Office was that the right way to treat the situation was "to get the French Government to complain to Mr. Bullitt of the specific remarks of Mr. Kennedy . . . We could authorize the French to tell Mr. Bullitt, for the President's private information, that we have much regretted the campaign in which Mr. Kennedy has seen fit to indulge by spreading stories of England can't win and (more recently) doesn't deserve to win both here and in the United States."

The memorandum, all written in longhand, also has comments written by Sir David Scott, Assistant Under Secretary of State, Sir

Alexander Cadogan, Permanent Under Secretary of State, and Lord Halifax, Secretary of State for Foreign Affairs.

One reason for asking Bullitt to intervene is that "for us to speak to the United States Embassy direct would only make matters more difficult for us at a difficult moment. Mr. Bullitt has wholeheartedly espoused the French cause, which Mr. Kennedy is very far from having done, and is on better and more intimate terms with the President." [34]

The Foreign Office file on Mr. Kennedy's anti-British statements is full of memorandums, newspaper articles, and even Kennedy's private telegrams. In approving the above-suggested action, Mr. Balfour noted: "We consider that he is undoubtedly a coward . . . we would certainly welcome a somewhat stiffly worded remonstrance by the French Government . . . addressed to Mr. Bullitt." [35] The final summing up of British opinion of Ambassador Kennedy is contained in a short paragraph: "Mr. Kennedy is a very foul specimen of double crosser and defeatist. He thinks of nothing but his own pocket. I hope that this war will at least see the elimination of this type." [36]

(Initiated and written by Vansittart and initialed by Lord Halifax.)

TELEGRAM

920, May 28, 4 P.M.
Strictly Confidential for the Secretary

Charvériat read to me this morning a telegram from Poncet in Rome reporting a conversation that he had had with Ciano [Mussolini's son-in-law] in the course of which Ciano said that he could guarantee Italy would not go to war before the first of June. He declined, however, to make a similar remark about the first of July and added that the decision was entirely in the hands of Mussolini and that no one knew when he would make the decision. There is no doubt whatever in Poncet's mind that unless some new factor intervenes Italy will enter the war, probably during the first week in June.

I still believe that the only new factor which might prevent Italian action and prevent it entirely without risk to the United States would be an order to our Atlantic Fleet to proceed to Lisbon. On the subject of the President's démarche of Sunday, Ciano said to

Poncet that the President's line of approach was an entirely inspiring, fruitful one and that Mussolini was merely irritated by the acts of the President to prevent him making whatever decision he chose about entering the war.

Bullitt

TELEGRAM

921, May 28, 5 P.M.
Personal and Secret for the President

If you will carefully consider from the point of view of the defense of the United States the consequences of permitting France and England to be defeated without establishing Fleet co-operation, I think you will feel that the risk involved in sending the Atlantic Fleet to Lisbon is entirely outweighed by the benefits to be gained.

Bullitt

24

The Swastika in Paris

JUNE 1940—JULY 1940

Rout of French Army
Italy Enters War
Reynaud's Mistress
Germans Enter Paris
French Government in Bordeaux
Bullitt Leaves Paris
British Attack French Fleet
Death of French Republic
Vichy

BY THE END OF MAY the advance of the Germans had turned the fighting into a rout of the French Army and it was apparent that they would shortly reach Paris. Bullitt's thoughts were turned now to what he could do by remaining in Paris to save the city from destruction, riots, and pillaging. The time for buying airplanes (although hundreds of French planes were still available and unused) had passed. It was a question of supporting those in the French Government with the will to carry on the war and of giving help to civilians.

TELEGRAM

948, May 29, 10 P.M.
Strictly Confidential for the President and the Secretary

Reynaud has just read to me a telegram containing the text of the report of Sir Percy Lorraine, British Ambassador in Rome, on his conversation with Ciano yesterday. Ciano said to the British Ambassador that he had promised that he would keep him informed if there were any great change in Italian policy. He had sent for him to say to him that Mussolini had decided to go to war in the immediate future. The delay before Italy should enter the war would be measured not in weeks, but in days. Ciano went on to say that even if France should offer Italy today Tunis, Morocco and Algeria, that would not be enough. Mussolini had decided on May 8th to go to war and had merely been waiting for the most favorable moment. The efforts of the Allies to buy him off with concessions and the efforts of President Roosevelt, he considered indecent and immoral attempts to persuade him to break his pledged word. A Fascist never breaks his word (see promises in regard to Ethiopia, Albania, etc.).

Sir Percy Lorraine replied that if Italy went to war against France and England, he hoped that Count Ciano understood that Great Britain would make war on Italy with all her force. Ciano replied that he expected nothing else from a nation which had fought so bravely in the past, but that this would make no difference whatever in Mussolini's decision.

Reynaud expressed the opinion that Italy might make war within the next two or three days.

I replied that it was difficult for me to believe that after the promise that the Italian Government had made to the American Government that the *Manhattan* would be permitted to leave Italy in safety, Mussolini would dare make war until the *Manhattan* had passed the Straits of Gibraltar. The *Manhattan* presumably would leave Genoa on June 1st and would pass the Straits of Gibraltar on June 3rd. I, therefore, considered that June 3rd or June 4th was the more likely date for an attack than in the next three days.

Bullitt

Personal and Confidential   Paris
                                                              May 30, 1940
Dear Mr. President:

This may be the last letter that I shall have a chance to send you before communications are cut.

The morale both of the French Army and the civilian population is a vast credit to the human race; but there are four German soldiers to every one French, and there is no longer either a British or Belgian Army, and supplies of material on this side are already running low.

When the Germans strike on the Somme and Aisne, therefore, in spite of all the courage and character that will go into stopping them, the Germans may reach Paris very soon.

Everyone here believes — and by everyone I mean the hardboiled like Mandel as well as the softboiled like Herriot — that the moment the French Government leaves Paris the Communists of the industrial suburbs will seize the city, and will be permitted to murder, loot and burn for several days before the Germans come in.

Since I am not *persona grata* either to the Communists or to the Nazis, I do not expect to have much influence with either regime which may be set up, but I shall do my best to save as many lives as possible and to keep the flag flying.

My guess is that, shortly after the first shock and disorder, a stern, cruel, but orderly German regime will be installed, which will in one way or another prevent me from having contact with anyone. Probably I shall have to transact all business through Bob Murphy, the Counselor of Embassy, who is a corker. Under those circumstances, I could certainly be of more practical use running that Department in Washington than here.

No American Ambassador in Paris has ever run away from anything, and that I think is the best tradition that we have in the American diplomatic service. But if the calm of death descends on Paris, I should like to be in very active life trying to prepare the USA for Hitler's attack on the Americas which I consider absolutely certain.

If that silence of death descends for a couple of weeks, I think the wisest course would be for you simply to announce my appointment, and inform the German Government that you desired my return to the United States to be facilitated.

Since Italy — unless you can throw fear into Mussolini now — will be in the war, I should probably have to travel through Germany and the Baltic States to Finland, and take a boat from Petsamo to the United States. The Finns are, I understand, about to start a line by that route.

It is curious, but, if Italy should come into the war, there would be no other way to get home except via Siberia; and while I don't mind in the least facing German bombs, I should not like again to have to face those Siberian lice!

In case I should get blown up before I see you again, I want you to know that it has been marvelous to work for you and that I thank you from the bottom of my heart for your friendship.

Yours affectionately,

Bill

Secretary of State   Paris

Washington   Dated May 31, 1940

Rush   Rec'd 10:45 A.M.

973, May 31, 1 P.M

Strictly Confidential for the President and the Secretary

The magnificent resistance of the French and British armies at Dunkirk during the past two days has been of a quality that astounded even the leading members of the French Government.

Moreover, the German aviation in the Dunkirk area during the past 24 hours has definitely been dominated by French and British aviation.

During the French retreat of yesterday the Germans did not succeed in dropping a bomb on the French army.

The French are under the impression that the Germans have lost their 3000 best pilots and that although they still have vast masses of machines they no longer have men who compare in quality to the French aviators.

Moreover, not only in the Dunkirk district but in the region of Rethel the German infantry have made attacks in the most crude mass manner as if their junior officers could not be compared to the junior officers of the Kaiser's army. The French 75's have inflicted tremendous casualties on the Germans in the past two days.

I cannot express to you the gratitude with which the information contained in your 535, May 30, 4 P.M. was received in Paris today when I communicated it and I should like to add that no one was more grateful than myself.

That is an act of vital importance.

Bullitt

On the 31st of May, 1940, Mr. Churchill and Mr. Clement Attlee, leader of the Labour party and now a member of Churchill's War Cabinet, flew to Paris where they attended a meeting of the Supreme War Council, which was held in Paul Reynaud's office at the War Department. The only French ministers present were Reynaud and Marshal Pétain, who attended for the first time. The discussion ranged from Norway and Dunkirk to Italy and

Spain. Bullitt's unusual position with the French Government is shown in the following telegram:

TELEGRAM RECEIVED

This telegram must be closely paraphrased before being communicated to anyone.

Secretary of State   Paris
Washington   Dated May 31, 1940
Rush   Rec'd 2:40 P.M.
979, May 31, 6 P.M.
Personal and Secret for the President

When I called on Paul Reynaud by appointment this afternoon at 4:30 he had in conference in the next room Churchill, Attlee, various British generals and admirals, Weygand and Darlan. He said that Churchill wanted to speak to me so that after I had talked briefly with Reynaud I joined the group in the conference room.

The news is encouraging. As a result of the superb courage of the troops in the Dunkirk area it has been possible to save already 150,000 British troops and 15,000 French troops. The French with their customary spirit are holding the lines to enable the British to leave first.

Reynaud said that it was now hoped that many more thousand men could be embarked — they would of course lose all their materials. Reynaud added that this comparatively favorable turn in the situation had been due to two factors: 1. The incredible courage of the French and British troops. 2. The new British planes which had swept the Germans out of the air. He stated that the fighting on the Somme also had been going well. The French had captured the German bridgehead at Abbeville.

Churchill said to me that the British aviation operating from its home bases as it could in the Dunkirk area had been able to clean the air of German planes. He was extremely encouraged by this since it demonstrated clearly that the British planes and pilots were superior to their enemies.

Churchill asked me to transmit a single message to you. There had been serious destroyer losses in removing the troops from Dunkirk. Now that it was almost certain that unless you could frighten Mussolini, Italy would declare war on France, the need for destroyers for France was enormous and vital. He asked me please to impress on you this fact with all possible urgency.

In this connection, I hope you will consider the formula suggested in my telegram No. 963 of this morning and that you will be able to turn over 24 old destroyers immediately to the French navy . . .

Everyone present at the meeting was full of fight and determination.

I shall say no more about it, but merely repeat that this war is not (repeat not) lost.

Bullitt

TELEGRAM

966, May 31, 11 A.M.
Secretary of State

The calm of the people of Paris, who realize fully that they may be killed within a few days, is as extraordinary as it is noble. I think the President and the Postmaster General will be especially interested to know that the outdoor stamp market in Champs Élysées is still functioning calmly. Children are still riding the same eight old donkeys in the Champs Élysées and others sit daily in the sunshine watching the Punch and Judy Show.

The French at this moment do honor to the human race.

Bullitt

TELEGRAM

This telegram must be closely paraphrased before being communicated to anyone.

Secretary of State   Paris
Washington   Dated May 31, 1940
Rush   Rec'd 6:42 A.M.
962, May 31, noon (SECTION ONE)
For the President and the Secretary
Your 534, May 30, 3 P.M.

The French Government is fully aware of the vitally useful part that our fleet is playing in the Pacific.

Reynaud in appealing to me to request you to send the Atlantic fleet to the Mediterranean said, "We are most grateful for the presence of your fleet in the Pacific. Without firing a shot it is keeping the war from spreading to the French and British Empires in the

Far East. We hope it will stay there. Your Atlantic fleet can play exactly the same role in the Mediterranean."

(END SECTION ONE)

Bullitt

TELEGRAM

This telegram must be closely paraphrased before being communicated to anyone.

Secretary of State   Paris
Washington   Dated May 31, 1940
Rush   Rec'd 7:25 A.M.
962, May 31, noon (SECTION TWO)

I believe that if we had sent the Atlantic fleet on a visit either to Greece or Tangier when first I made the recommendation more than two weeks ago Mussolini would not have dared to treat pressure of our Government to keep him out of war in the manner that he has.

I gather from your telegram under reference that you now consider inevitable the entrance of Italy into the war.

I feel sure that you realize the consequences that a stab in the back by Italy at this moment may have for France and England as well as the consequences it may have later this year for South America and the United States. I trust that no member of the American Government is still cherishing in the words of Reynaud "fatuous and naive illusions as to the virtues of Mussolini" and that the moment he stabs you will take every economic and financial measure that constructive imagination can devise to weaken Italy.

(END SECTION TWO)

Bullitt

TELEGRAM

This telegram must be closely paraphrased before being communicated to anyone.

Secretary of State   Paris
Washington   Dated May 31, 1940
Rush   Rec'd 6:45 A.M.
962, May 31, noon (SECTION THREE)

To believe that the Government of the United States will be able ever to cooperate with Mussolini is as dangerous to the future of

America as would have been the belief that our Government could cooperate with Al Capone.

The latest information of the French Government indicates that Mussolini will make war on France on June 4.

I am sure you realize the bitterness that such a blow will produce.

May I inform the French Government when stating — as I must in view of your telegram under reference — that there is no hope whatsoever the Atlantic fleet will come to Tangier, that the moment Mussolini strikes economic and financial measures will be taken at once by our Government to make the lot of the aggressor hard?

Anything you can do now will leave Mussolini less strength with which to cooperate with Hitler in attacking the Americas.

At this moment words are not enough. Indeed unaccompanied by acts they are rather sickening.

(END MESSAGE)

Bullitt

TELEGRAM SENT

DEPARTMENT OF STATE
WASHINGTON

American Embassy   May 30, 1940
Paris
Strictly Confidential for the Ambassador
Your 916, May 28, 1 P.M.

The President desires me to let you know that it is absolutely impossible to consider sending the fleet to the Mediterranean. The presence of the fleet in the Pacific at this time is a very practical contribution to the maintenance of peace in the Pacific. The value of this contribution is fully appreciated by the British Government and, it is assumed, by the French Government as well.

What vessels we have in the Atlantic are required under present circumstances either for patrol duty or for special service in South and Central American waters.

From the strictly practical aspect, the presence of an American fleet at this time in the Mediterranean would result in very serious risks and hazards and it would be impossible, for reasons which are, of course, apparent, for the fleet to base itself on any ports in or near the Mediterranean should Italy enter the war. Finally as you will recognize, unless any fleet sent were sufficiently large to be effective the impression created would be the reverse of that desired.

Hull

Approved by the President 11 P.M. — May 29, 1940 [In Secretary Hull's writing.]

THE WHITE HOUSE

WASHINGTON

May 31, 1940

Bullitt:

I am sorry you keep referring to the Atlantic fleet because such talk reminds me of mother Alice who met a rabbit.

I cannot of course give you a list of the disposition of our ships but if you knew it you would not continue fantasies.

Incidentally, further strong steps were taken yesterday by me in regard to the Mediterranean threat.

Roosevelt

[A handwritten note.]

Actually there was no Atlantic fleet available for European service. What ships there were, were concentrated in Central and South American waters and the United States was obligated by the Declaration of Panama to have ships in this area.

Paul Reynaud speaks of seeing Bullitt almost every day,[1] of Bullitt having told him that there were ninety chances out of one hundred that Italy would enter the war. This information also came from a talk Bullitt had with Ciano.[2]

THE WHITE HOUSE

June 1, 1940

Memorandum for the Under-Secretary of State:

In reply to Bullitt's No. 963, Paris, May 31st, 9 A.M., I suggest the following:

I regard suggestion for building destroyers here most inadvisable because it takes about two and a half years to complete them. Any exchange for American destroyers probably inacceptable because of enormous sea area which must be patrolled by us and would require Congressional action which might be very difficult to get. Our old destroyers cannot be sold as obsolete as is proved by fact. All of them are now in commission and in use or are in process of being commissioned for actual use.

Several American Republics have destroyers which they might be willing to sell and could sell under their laws.

FDR

On May 14, French Premier Paul Reynaud had broached the idea of the sale or lease of old destroyers, and on May 15, Churchill had asked for a loan of forty or fifty. FDR had cabled Churchill that he could not take such a step without authorization from Congress, and added that we needed the destroyers for our own defense. Reynaud renewed his request on May 31.

William L. Shirer comments on Bullitt's dislike of the Communists, which showed itself strongly during the battle of France: "Bullitt's hysteria about Communism, which stemmed no doubt from his years as Ambassador to Russia, led to some fanciful reporting." Bullitt had cabled home that Reynaud had told him that the railroads in Belgium were on strike and refused to transport French troops, and the next day he said the strike was organized by Communists on orders from Moscow, but it had been broken by the shooting of the Communist ringleaders. Shirer made a careful investigation and could find no evidence of the strike. Shirer goes on: "But to the excitable American Ambassador in Paris, the Communists were responsible for a great deal that was going wrong."

He goes on to cite a message from Bullitt that the French heavy tanks were manned by Communists who refused to advance and sabotaged their machines; also an account from Bullitt of a Communist regiment's revolting. Of these messages Shirer has this to say: "These two horrendous tales appear to have been made up out of the whole cloth by Bullitt's informants . . . and swallowed by the Ambassador, who was prone to believe any tall tale about Communists." [3]

TELEGRAM

1006, June 3, 3 P.M.
Rush

The City of Paris was bombed heavily today. I can as yet give no extent of the dead and wounded.

I was at a luncheon given by the Minister of Air at the Ministry of Air in honor of the Paul Ward Aviation Mission. There were present a number of leading figures in the French Aviation industry. The reception hall and dining room of the Ministry of Air are on the roof and with a balcony outside the reception room.

We were having sherry and biscuits before luncheon when the air raid siren sounded, but since it seemed highly improbable that the Germans had bombarded the center of the City of Paris, instead of seeking the air raid shelter, we went on the balcony to see the planes. A minute later a bomb dropped in a large field adjacent to the Air Ministry about a hundred yards from us. Another bomb dropped exactly on the roof of the reception room of the Ministry of Air to which we had withdrawn — obviously it did not explode. It is now being rendered harmless. Heavy bombs fell on all sides of the Ministry of Air and we went down to the Air Raid Shelter amid flying glass and plaster. We were obliged to remain in the shelter for a period of one hour.

Two cars of guests at the luncheon were struck and burned up in the courtyard at the entrance to the Ministry.

My own car was untouched and I am entirely uninjured and lost only my hat and gloves, which are sitting at this moment close to the unexploded bomb.

TELEGRAM RECEIVED
This telegram must be closely paraphrased before being communicated to anyone.

Secretary of State	Paris
Washington	Dated June 4, 1940
1022, June 4, 4 P.M.	Rec'd 1:52 P.M.

Personal and Secret for the President

Marshal Pétain lunched with me alone today. After luncheon, talking in the garden, he said that he wondered if the French Government had ever given you a completely frank view of the present situation. I replied that I feel that both Reynaud and Daladier talked with me with entire frankness. He went on to say that nevertheless he would like to let you know how he personally viewed the situation.

The threefold superiority of the Germans in manpower was accompanied by a much greater superiority in aeroplanes and in tanks.

The airplane had proved to be the decisive weapon in this war. France was hopelessly outnumbered in the air.

Against the German attack which would be made before the end of this week on the Somme and in the region of Laon and the region of Reims the French had nothing to oppose but their courage. In all forms of material they were now desperately outclassed . . .

It was certain that Italy would enter the war. There were no planes to combat the Italian planes and the destruction which the Italian planes might inflict on the southern portions of France would be terrible. Moreover the Italians might land troops from parachutes and take the entire French Alps region from the rear . . .

Since all the British had been embarked the British had ceased to send their planes in anything like the numbers they had employed so long as the British Expeditionary force was at Dunkirk.

Furthermore, at this moment when the French had almost no reserves and were facing the greatest attack in human history the British were pretending that they could send no reserves from England. There was actually now one British division in France and the British were asserting that they could send no more.

Moreover they had refused to send over the British aviation, which alone could combat the German air force, to support the French army. Moreover, they had refused to agree to unified command in the Mediterranean when it was obvious that only a unified command and a joint attack of the British and French forces in the Mediterranean the moment Mussolini should declare war could give hope of eliminating Italy from the conflict.

Under the circumstances, he was obliged to feel that the British intended to permit the French to fight without help until the last available drop of French blood should have been shed and that then with quantities of troops on British soil and plenty of planes and a dominant fleet the British after a very brief resistance, or even without resistance would make a peace of compromise with Hitler, which might even involve a British Government under a British Fascist leader.

The Marshal added that he intended to make statements in line with the above at the meeting of the War Council tomorrow. He felt that unless the British Government should send to France to engage in the battle which was imminent both its air force and reserve divisions the French Government would do its utmost to come to terms immediately with Germany whatever might happen to England. He added that it was not fair for any French Government to permit the British to behave in a totally callous and selfish manner while demanding the sacrifice of every able-bodied Frenchman.

Bullitt

TELEGRAM RECEIVED

This telegram must be closely paraphrased before being communicated to anyone.

Secretary of State   Paris
Washington   Dated June 5, 1940
Rush   Rec'd 6:30 A.M. 6th
1047, June 5, midnight
Personal and Secret for the President

Reynaud was enormously pleased by his conversation with you on the telephone this evening. As he told you the fighting is going well. The French infantry have held all the German attacks in spite of German superiority in material and especially in planes. I had a long talk with Reynaud this afternoon in the course of which he said to me that he had sent this morning the stiffest note that he could compose to Winston Churchill on the subject of the withdrawal of the British pursuit planes from France.

He added that a number of British bombardment planes were still operating in France but the British had withdrawn their entire pursuit force. This made it easy for the German bombers to drop as many bombs as they could carry on the French troops.

Reynaud said that he considered it utterly shocking that the British should withdraw these planes and added that Churchill gave as an excuse the conviction that British pursuit planes must be based on British bases, that it was unwise to base them on French flying fields, and that since they could not operate in the present battle except from French flying fields they should not operate at all.

Reynaud was expecting a reply from Churchill to be delivered shortly after I left him tonight. He said to me, before I left, that if Churchill's reply should be in the negative he would attack Churchill tomorrow as violently as he could. Either the British were allies or they were not. If they were allies, they could not, with honor, withdraw their planes from the crucial battle of the war any more than King Leopold with honor could withdraw his soldiers . . .

Reynaud added that he intended to keep both the portfolio of Foreign Affairs and the portfolio of War. He intended to direct the

Ministry for Foreign Affairs himself and to let General de Gaulle run the Ministry of War.

Two weeks ago this General was a Colonel in the tank corps. He showed great initiative and courage in stemming the German advance on Paris. One day last week when I was talking to Reynaud he called him in to introduce him to me. He is a young man who appears to be vigorous and intelligent . . .

Bullitt

FROM: AMBASSADOR BULLITT   6 JUNE 1940
TO: THE PRESIDENT OF THE USA   RESTRICTED CABLE

I THINK YOU WOULD LIKE TO KNOW THAT THIS MORNING THE PISTOLS WHICH GEORGE WASHINGTON GAVE TO LAFAYETTE WERE PRESENTED TO ME IN THANKS STOP THEY WERE LEFT BY LAFAYETTE TO HIS AIDE DE CAMP JOLLAND STOP

Personal and Confidential   Paris
                                              June 6, 1940
Dear Mr. President:

I am glad you approved my Jeanne d'Arc speech. I shall make it Sunday, the Lord willing, and it will help.

The French troops have held again magnificently today, and only in the region of the lower Somme where the British collapsed have they had to retreat. Everyone is full of fighting spirit and hope.

While the French soldiers and civilians are displaying a courage and character beyond praise, strange things are still going on at the top. Paul Reynaud, who has great personal qualities, is completely dominated by his mistress, the Comtesse de Portes, who has the virtue of being sincerely fond of him.

The changes in the French Cabinet yesterday were dictated by her. She hates Daladier; therefore Daladier has disappeared in disgrace, and Baudouin, of whom she is fond, becomes Undersecretary of the Foreign Office. He is the official of the Banque de l'Indo-Chine who conducted, with invariable success and without a single loss, speculations against the franc on information received from various Ministers of Finance whose duty it was to support the franc with the money of the French taxpayer. Henry Morgenthau has full information with regard to this matter.

Bouthillier, whom the Comtesse de Portes has had appointed Minister of Finance, is a stupid functionary who will do anything that he is told to do. The day of his appointment Reynaud said to me, "He is intolerable," but the Comtesse de Portes said to me that night: "He is so fond of Paul!" That was decisive!

. . . I doubt, however, that even the Countess will be able to drive him into giving an important appointment to de la Grange, although she will undoubtedly ask for one because the Baroness de la Grange invites her for dinner, whereas no other lady does. Reynaud can't very well after what he said to me.

The people of France who are fighting with an absolute selflessness deserve better at this moment than to be ruled by a Prime Minister's mistress — not even a King's! In the end she will be shot. Meanwhile, she will rule the roost.

As I telegraphed you through the Navy, Reynaud forbade her to come in the room when he went to talk to you on the telephone; but she came right in and when he ordered her out of the room, refused to go. As I suggested, I think you should avoid such conversations in the future since the lady in question will repeat them all over town in exaggerated form . . .

Needless to say, Offie enjoys the most intimate relations with the Comtesse de Portes, as with everyone else. She summons him for intimate conversations to her "love nest" almost daily; and he keeps her within reasonable bounds. I have less patience than he with lack of character so that more than ever, Offie is the power behind the throne . . . A few days ago, the Comtesse de Portes said to him that if the American Embassy had any difficulty with any department of the French Government or the French Army, he had only to let her know and the matter would be settled to our satisfaction at once. He tried it once and it worked!

I am dictating the foregoing to Offie and he objects to my sending it to you, but I am insisting on exercising the sole shred of authority that I still possess.

I trust that this sort of gossip will not seem to you unworthy of the tragic days through which we are passing. I thought that you would like to know that there is still some continuity in French life, and that the mistress of the ruler again directs the State as she has since time immemorial.

We had another air raid at five o'clock this morning, and I was delighted to find that I could sleep peaceably in my sumptuous wine cellar.

Good luck and love to you all.

Yours affectionately,
William C. Bullitt

Paris

June 7, 1940

Personal and Confidential

Dear Mr. President:

I do not want you to conclude from a letter I wrote you this morning that Offie is indispensable in Paris. Tony Biddle will do just as well. In fact, the Comtesse de Portes already has had her eye on him and has done everything possible to introduce him and Margaret into the select circle which gathers nightly in her apartment.

Seriously, the job to be done here now consists in part in flattering the King's mistress. At that, I am rotten; so that I have no compunctions about saying that when Edison goes out on the twenty-fourth of June, I want to come in on the twenty-fifth. Something may arise here which may make it advisable for me to stay a bit longer, so that you had better phone me or give me some indication before making any announcement.

Tony is just as eager to get to work in Paris as I am to get to work in the United States, and I can promise you with my customary modesty that from my experience here, I now know more about how to get ready for war than anyone except yourself.

I have just heard that the British have decided to send their pursuit planes to join in the battle now in progress. I assume that this is because you were as nasty on this subject as I was. I congratulate you.

As you will have learned from the telegrams, the Minister of Armament personally brought to me the secret plans, specifications and working drawings for the production of the French 47 millimeter anti-tank gun which is a wonder; and I received from him fifteen minutes ago the same documents for the production of the Saumur thirty-ton tank which has proved to be definitely superior in battle to the German tanks.

If there is anything that you want for either our army, navy, or air force, I will guarantee to get it at once and bring it home with me.

Love and good luck and may we drink a toast together on the Fourth of July.

Yours affectionately,

Bill

TELEGRAM RECEIVED

This telegram must be closely paraphrased before being communicated to anyone.

Secretary of State   Paris
Washington   Dated June 8, 1940
1098, June 8, 9 P.M.   Rec'd 7:50 P.M.
Personal and Secret for the President

Will you please have put on the next Clipper twelve Thompson submachine guns with ammunition, addressed to me for the use of this Embassy. I am fully prepared to pay for them myself.

There is every reason to expect that if the French Government should be forced to leave Paris, its place would be taken by a communist mob.

Bullitt

TELEGRAM SENT

DEPARTMENT OF STATE
WASHINGTON

American Embassy   June 9, 1940
Paris
Strictly Confidential for the Ambassador
Your 1098, June 8, 9 P.M., and your telephone conversation with the President of yesterday

Instructions have been sent to the Commanding Officer of the U.S.S. *Trenton* now at Lisbon to make available the material you require. I suggest that you send a trustworthy representative immediately to Lisbon to contact the Commanding Officer of the *Trenton* and to receive the material as official supplies for the use of the American Embassy in Paris. Every precaution should be taken to avoid publicity.

Hull

With the Germans outside the gates of Paris and the French Government fleeing the city, Bullitt took a trip to the east of France on June 9. In the village of Domrémy-la-Pucelle, the birthplace of Jeanne d'Arc, he attended a ceremony held in the garden of her house to dedicate an altar donated by Americans in the local church, where she had worshiped five centuries previously. Placing a white rose on her statue in the name of President Roosevelt, he said in part: "Americans know on which side stand right, justice and Christian decency and on which side are wrong, cruelty and bestiality . . . From one end of this earth to the other every civilized man is praying, after his fashion, for the victory of France . . . Guard France! In the service of God and man let your spirit lead to Christian victory." [4] The Germans occupied Domrémy-la-Pucelle the following day.

The President, by virtue of a 1917 statute, never repealed, now allowed Army and Navy airplanes to be returned to the manufacturers for resale to Britain and France. He also sent half a million rifles, eight hundred field artillery guns, and several hundred planes and machine guns to Britain.

TELEGRAM RECEIVED

This telegram must be closely paraphrased before being communicated to anyone.

Secretary of State   Paris
Washington   Dated June 9, 1940
Rush   Rec'd 8:56 P.M.
1109, June 9, midnight
Strictly Confidential for the President and the Secretary

I have just had a long conversation with Reynaud whom I saw five minutes after he left the Council of Ministers at the Élysée.

He said that it has been decided to remove from out of Paris at once all ministries and services that were not directly involved in the prosecution of the war.

He would remain in Paris until the last possible minute and would keep with him the Minister of Marine, the Minister of Armament and the Minister for Air.

All other Ministries including the Foreign Office would be evacuated to Touraine. He asked me especially to emphasize in any communication that I might make to you that this measure was not a measure taken with a view to surrender but a measure taken with a view to prosecuting the war to the bitter end. Neither he nor any Frenchman had the slightest intention of giving up the fight.

He then said that he felt that he himself and the remaining ministers might be compelled to leave Paris in the immediate future and added that he was intensely desirous that I should accompany him — plus a series of compliments which I shall refrain from transmitting.

I said to Reynaud that no American Ambassador in history had

ever left Paris and that I had no intention of leaving Paris and positively would not so long as I thought I could be of use here. He
protested that he would have no real means of communicating with
you.

I then stated to him in absolute confidence that if I should be cut
off from communications with him by the capture of Paris by the
Germans Ambassador Biddle would be named as my deputy. He replied that this gratified him extremely. If I could not be with him
there was no one in the world that he would so gladly have as Ambassador Biddle for whom he had the greatest liking and respect.
He suggested that I should send to Ambassador Biddle immediately
such members of the Embassy staff as might be useful to him, and I
shall do so at once.

We discussed the military situation and he called in General de
Gaulle, the Undersecretary for War, who in reality is now directing
the Ministry of War . . .

Reynaud then stated that in spite of eleven telegrams and seven
personal telephone conversations he had been unable to persuade
Churchill to put into the present battle more than one fourth of the
British pursuit planes.

I informed Reynaud that today General Smuts had sent to the
British Government an urgent telegram stating that he considered
that it was the duty of the British Government to the British Empire to put into the present battle every plane and every man that
might be available. I have the text of this telegram which is worded
superbly and states that it is the duty of the British Government not
only to the people of Great Britain but also to all the peoples of the
Empire to put into the present battle every resource of the Empire
without selfishness.

Reynaud who had not yet been informed of this action of General Smuts said that he obviously could not complain to you about
the conduct of his ally but he would be intensely grateful if you
could, through the British Ambassador in Washington, express your
bewilderment at the refusal of the British Government to put into
the battle more than one fourth of the British pursuit planes at a
time when the French soldier was bearing the entire brunt of the attack without British assistance and when all the blood that was flowing to protect the civilized sections of the earth was French blood.

I replied that I would gladly communicate this message to you.

Reynaud then said that he would like to talk to you once more
from Paris before he should be obliged to leave and said that he

thought he would like to put through such a telephone call tomorrow for the purpose of assuring you that it was his intention and that of every Frenchman to fight to the last drop of blood. Whether or not you accept such a call is entirely up to you . . .

Bullitt

TELEGRAM

Secretary of State   Paris
Washington   Dated June 9, 1940
Rush   Rec'd 4:06 P.M.
1106, June 9, 7 P.M.

Hoppenot advises us that the Ministry of Foreign Affairs is addressing letters to all missions advising them of the imminent departure of the Government from Paris. The letters are not yet signed and he could only say that the Ministry of Foreign Affairs will be based at Langeais in the Touraine. Departure of the competent officials is now under way. According to unconfirmed reports some of the German forces are approximately 25 miles from Paris.

Bullitt

TELEGRAM SENT

DEPARTMENT OF STATE
WASHINGTON

NO DISTRIBUTION   June 9, 1940

American Embassy
Paris (France)
Rush
Your 1106, June 9, 7 P.M.
For Bullitt from the President

On the assumption that all or most of the foreign chiefs of Mission follow the French Government to its temporary capital, I have reached the conclusion that it would be preferable to alter the plans we had previously agreed upon, and have you do likewise. In the first place I doubt if the German military officials would cooperate with you in trying to ease the general situation. More important, however, I consider it highly desirable that you be in direct contact with the French Government in the event of certain contingencies arising. In order to forestall any possible criticism of a last minute change in your announced plans, you may inform the French Government that you are leaving Paris with the other Chiefs of Mission at my express request.

Not Sent

FDR

[This is handwritten by FDR.]

On June 10, 1940, at four in the afternoon, the Italian Foreign Minister notified the British Ambassador in Rome that on the following day at 1:00 P.M. the Italian Government would be at war with Great Britain. The attack on France took place on June 10. At that moment the stab in the back appeared easy and potentially profitable to Mussolini. He had five years of glory and agony before his assassination on April 28, 1945, when he and his mistress ended a life of deceit, ignominiously hanging by their heels from lampposts in Milan.

11 June 1940

Dear Mr. President:

Please keep this for me — or for yourself if I don't turn up. Note the promise about fighting even in the possessions in America.

You know who dictated that.

Love to you all,

Bill

[A handwritten letter.]

Enclosed with this letter was a letter from Paul Reynaud to the President, signed and dated by Reynaud June 10, 1940, and inscribed "To my dear friend Wm. C. Bullitt, great Ambassador of a great country."

Bullitt immediately telegraphed the letter as follows:

For the Press
Immediate Release

Secretary of State	June 13, 1940
Washington	Paris
Rush	Dated June 10, 1940
June 10, 6 P.M.	Rec'd 10:13 P.M.
Personal for the President	

I have just received from Paul Reynaud, President of the Council of Ministers, the following message to you. He telephoned to me and asked me to transmit it immediately since his own code clerks could not possibly do the work. This is the full text of the message referred to in my telegram earlier today.

"Mr. President: I wish first to express to you my gratitude for the generous aid that you have decided to give us in aviation and armament.

"For six days and six nights our divisions have been fighting without one hour of rest against an army which has a crushing superiority in numbers and material. Today the enemy is almost at the gates of Paris.

"We shall fight in front of Paris; we shall fight behind Paris; we shall close ourselves in one of our provinces to fight and if we should be driven out of it we shall establish ourselves in North Africa to continue the fight and if necessary in our American possessions.

"A portion of the government has already left Paris. I am making ready to leave for the front. That will be to intensify the struggle with all the forces which we still have and not to abandon the struggle.

"May I ask you, Mr. President, to explain all this yourself to your people to all the citizens of the United States saying to them that we are determined to sacrifice ourselves in the struggle that we are carrying on for all free men.

"This very hour another dictatorship has stabbed France in the back. Another frontier is threatened. A naval war will begin.

"You have replied generously to the appeal which I made to you a few days ago across the Atlantic. Today this 10th of June 1940 it is my duty to ask you for new and even larger assistance.

"At the same time that you explain this situation to the men and women of America, I beseech you to declare publicly that the United States will give the Allies aid and material support by all means 'short of an expeditionary force.' I beseech you to do this before it is too late. I know the gravity of such a gesture. Its very gravity demands that it should not be made too late.

"You said to us yourself on the 5th of October 1937: 'I am compelled and you are compelled to look ahead. The peace, the freedom and the security of 90% of the population of the world is being jeopardized by the remaining 10% who are threatening a breakdown of all international order and law.

" 'Surely the 90% who want to live in peace under law and in accordance with moral standards that have received almost trusty acceptance through the centuries, can and must find some way to make their will prevail!'

"The hour has now come for these. Paul Reynaud."

Bullitt

This letter Premier Reynaud described as his last act before leaving Paris. He went on to say: "Mr. Bullitt, whom I had seen almost every day since my arrival in power, came to say good-bye and asked me to put my signature on the message that I had given him in the afternoon. He stays in Paris. It is the tradition of the Ambassadors of his great country." [5]

On June 4 Churchill had made one of his greatest speeches in the House of Commons and part of it is given here to show the similarity of his views with those of Reynaud, who also would not accept defeat:

"We shall go on to the end, we shall fight in France, we shall fight on the seas and oceans, we shall fight with growing confidence and growing strength in the air, we shall defend our Island, whatever the cost may be, we shall fight on the beaches, we shall fight on the landing grounds, we shall fight in the fields and in the streets, we shall fight in the hills, we shall never surrender, and even if, which I do not for a moment believe, this Island or a large part of it were subjugated and starving, then our Empire beyond the seas, armed and guarded by the British Fleet, would carry on the struggles, until in God's good time, the New World, with all its power and might steps forth to the rescue and the liberation of the Old." [6]

TELEGRAM

Personal and Secret for the President
1142, June 11, 10 A.M.

In order to receive messages from the United States after occupation of Paris and possible destruction of our official radio receiving set at the Chancery, it is suggested that commercial radio stations broadcasting shortwave programs to Europe broadcast such message at the end of their normal broadcasts. To let us understand that the message is designated for us have the announcer broadcast: the following is from Pearl Smith to her mother, father, etc. The employment of any girl's name will signify that the message is intended for Paris and of course the same message should be broadcast several times at different hours to ensure reception on our ordinary radio sets.

1140, June 11, noon

I have talked with the Provisional Governor of Paris, who is the single governmental official remaining, and it may be that at a given moment I, as the only representative of the Diplomatic Corps remaining in Paris, will be obliged in the interest of public safety to take control of the City pending arrival of the German Army. I believe there are many precedents for such action by American Representatives: for example, Smirna.

I shall, of course, refrain from any proposals to do this unless it should prove to be absolutely necessary in the interests of saving human lives. Incidentally, Reynaud and Mandel just before their departure requested me to do this, if necessary.

Bullitt

TELEGRAM

This telegram must be closely paraphrased before being communicated to anyone.

Secretary of State   Paris
Washington   Dated June 11, 1940
Rush   Rec'd 6:10 P.M., 12th
1149, June 11, 3 P.M. (SECTION ONE)
Personal and Secret for the President

The evacuation of Paris has added a million to the number of men, women, and children who are moving into southwestern France whose lives can be saved only by American aid.

You will recall that when I described to you over the telephone about 3 weeks ago the condition of the refugees from Belgium and northern France you said that you would ask Congress immediately for $20,000,000 to keep them alive.

Later I was informed that at the request of the Red Cross which was putting on a drive for funds you would not ask for this sum or any other from the Congress until the conclusion of the Red Cross drive.

I was furthermore informed by you over the telephone that

within three days a ship entirely filled with Red Cross supplies would leave the United States for Bordeaux.

(END SECTION ONE)

Bullitt

TELEGRAM

This telegram must be closely paraphrased before being communicated to anyone.

Secretary of State   Paris
Washington   Dated June 11, 1940
Rush   Rec'd 11:35 A.M.
1149, June 11 (SECTION TWO)

Since I was under the illusion that the Red Cross would handle this matter with the urgency and efficiency demanded by the sufferings of the refugees I did not suggest that you ignore the Red Cross and have recourse to the Congress.

The ship whose sailing you promised in three days has not yet left the United States. This ship the *McKeesport* I am authoritatively informed is the only ship which has been chartered by the Red Cross. There are now six million persons in southwestern France who will die unless American aid for them is organized immediately with the utmost efficiency.

(END SECTION TWO)

Bullitt

TELEGRAM

This telegram must be closely paraphrased before being communicated to anyone.

Secretary of State   Paris
Washington   Dated June 11, 1940
Rush   Rec'd 10:18 A.M., 12th
1149, June 11 (SECTION THREE)

This is no time to be a respecter of persons. I consider criminal the negligence of the Red Cross in failing to organize a regular supply line to Bordeaux three weeks ago. I am now convinced that the officials of the Red Cross are incompetent to organize relief on the scale demanded. The problem is as great as the problem of feeding and supplying the entire French Army.

I suggest that today you take the organization of a supply line to Bordeaux out of the hands of the Red Cross and place it in the hands of the most competent Admiral of the United States Navy. Or you might place an Admiral in the Red Cross with complete power to act.

At least two ships a week should reach Bordeaux from this moment on.

You cannot tolerate today the incompetence of any individual or organization which is preventing supplies from reaching dying French men, women and children.

(END SECTION THREE)

Bullitt

TELEGRAM

This telegram must be closely paraphrased before being communicated to anyone.

Secretary of State	Paris
Washington	Dated June 11, 1940
Rush	Rec'd 12:25 P.M.
1149, June 11 (SECTION FOUR)	

Harry Hopkins telephoned to me about a week ago to ask me the amount I estimated would be needed for the maintenance of life in southwestern France this year. As he doubtless told you I stated that I thought at least $100,000,000 would be needed.

I have discussed this question fully with Wayne Taylor and he agrees with me that this sum is not an overestimate. Two ships a week, $1,000,000 a ship.

Please take action today and do not tolerate for personal or any other reasons continued incompetence in saving lives.

The mere fact that the ship which you promised would arrive on May 30 will not reach France before June 30 should be sufficient evidence to justify your acting in the most drastic manner.

(END MESSAGE)

Bullitt

June 11, 1940

Memorandum for the Secretary of State

I suggest the following telegram to Bullitt which, if you O.K., should go out tonight. We may not be able to reach him tomorrow.

Rush
American Embassy
Paris, France
For: Bullitt
From: The President
June 11, 10 P.M.

It is strongly recommended that if all foreign chiefs of mission fol-low French Government to its temporary Capital, you should do likewise. Because it is impossible here to know last minute develop-ments or the wishes of the French Government, I must rely on your discretion and assume you will make your decision in the best inter-ests of the United States and of humanity.

As long as you are in communication with French Government you remain in full charge of relations between the two Govern-ments. If in Paris or elsewhere you are cut off from access to French Government, Biddle will temporarily act as representative of United States.

No authority can be given to you to act as a representative of the French Government or local government but, again, being on the spot, you will, as a red-blooded American, do what you can to save human life.

We are doing everything possible in regard to your dispatches about Red Cross arrangements.

On behalf of the Government of the United States I salute you in this hour of crisis and personally you have my ever affectionate re-gards.

Franklin D. Roosevelt

TELEGRAM

Secretary of State   Paris
Washington   Dated June 12, 1940
Rush   Rec'd 5:08 P.M.
1157, June 12, 11 A.M.
Personal and Secret for the President

I was and am deeply grateful for your telegram triple priority 648, June 11, 9 P.M.

I remember an evening with you in the White House about two

years and a half ago when I said to you that I felt sure there would be war while I was Ambassador in Paris and that the Germans probably would reach Paris and that since there would be danger that the Department of State would wish to order me to leave Paris and that I would not leave and therefore would prefer not to receive such an order since I should have to disobey it. You said you would see to it that I should not receive such order and I am grateful to you for remembering and handling this matter just the way you have handled it.

As I said to you when you telephoned me the night of Sunday the 9th my deepest personal reason for staying in Paris is that whatever I have as character, good or bad, is based on the fact that since the age of four I have never run away from anything however painful or dangerous when I thought it was my duty to take a stand. If I should leave Paris now I would be no longer myself.

(END SECTION ONE)

Bullitt

TELEGRAM

Secretary of State   Paris
Washington   Dated June 11, 1940
Rush   Rec'd 2:33 P.M., 12th
1157, June 11 (SECTION TWO)

I am certain it is my duty to stay here.

This Embassy is the only official organization still functioning in the City of Paris except the Headquarters of the military forces, Governor and the Prefecture of Police.

Thousands of people of all nationalities, French, Canadian, English, Belgian, Rumanian and even Italian are turning to us in despair for advice and comfort. The fact that I am here is a strong element in preventing a fatal panic.

Furthermore, a moment will come soon when I hope to be of even more use. The military Governor of Paris, General Hering, has just repeated to me the request previously made by Reynaud, Mandel and Langeron, the Prefect of Police.

(END SECTION TWO)

Bullitt

TELEGRAM

Secretary of State   Paris
Washington   Dated June 12, 1940
Rush   Rec'd 5:10 P.M.
1157, June 12, 11 A.M. (SECTION THREE)

The Military Governor, with his army, will at a given moment leave Paris in retreat. He will leave in Paris General Dentz as Commander of the Paris region. Owing to danger of fires and mobs, they have decided to leave the police and the firemen of the city at their posts until the Germans shall have occupied the city fully. They have stated to me that at a given moment — not far off — they will ask me in writing, as representative of the diplomatic corps in Paris, to act as guardian of the civil authority of this community during the transition from French Government to German military occupation, and to treat the General commanding the German forces for the orderly occupation of the city.

I propose therefore at the appropriate moment to have broadcast a radio message stating that at a given time an automobile of the American Embassy in Paris properly marked will move slowly along the road to Chantilly to the German line.

(END SECTION THREE)

                                                   Bullitt

TELEGRAM

Secretary of State   Paris
Washington   Dated June 12, 1940
Rush   Rec'd 11:55 A.M.
1157, June 12 (SECTION FOUR)

I propose to send my Military Attaché and my Naval Attaché to the German General commanding the forces in the Paris area to explain the situation and return with the suggestions of the German command as to methods of facilitating the orderly transition of government. I believe that this procedure may save thousands of lives and I hope that you will not object to it.

The French are still holding the line of the Nonette in my garden at Chantilly but the Germans have crossed the little river near Senlis and the position is difficult. The French all along the line are fighting with the same incredible courage in the face of four times their numbers. The Germans have crossed the Seine in force and are approaching Evreux.

There was a little shooting in the streets of Paris last night but not much.

(END SECTION FOUR)

Bullitt

TELEGRAM

Secretary of State   Paris
Washington   Dated June 11, 1940
Rush   Rec'd 3:56 P.M., 12th
1157, June 11 (SECTION FIVE)

In conclusion I am absolutely confident of the ability of Tony Biddle to handle the contacts with the French Government which is dispersed throughout Touraine. I have sent him a strong staff and he has promised me to make H. Freeman Matthews, who is one of the ablest and finest foreign service officers, his chief adviser.

I have said nothing in this cable about the tradition that the American Ambassador does not leave Paris. Remember Gouverneur Morris and his wooden leg in the terror, Washburne in the Commune, Herrick. It will mean something always to the French and the Foreign Service to remember that we do not leave though others do.

FOLLOWING IN FRENCH. (J'y suis. J'y reste.) END FRENCH.

Love to you all.

(END MESSAGE)

Bullitt

TELEGRAM

1145, June 11, noon

We are entirely cut off from official information. Ask for the truth about rumor that Turkey or Soviet Union have declared War on Italy.

Bullitt

TELEGRAM

1159, June 12, 4 P.M.

I have just learned that you were asked at a recent Press Conference whether or not it was true that I had attended the last meeting of the French Cabinet and that you replied that you did not know. I should be grateful if you should inform the Press at your next Press Conference that I did not actually attend the last Cabinet Meeting and that I never attended any Cabinet Meetings. As I reported in a cable last Sunday night, I saw Paul Reynaud and some of his colleagues at the Ministry of War shortly after they left the meeting of the Cabinet at Élysée.

Bullitt

Admiral Roscoe H. Hillenkoetter (Naval Attaché at that time in Paris) has kindly written to me the following account of the German occupation of the city.

"The Germans entered Paris early in the morning of 14 June 1940. The night before the Ambassador had all the remaining Embassy staff sleep in the Embassy, because of rumors of what might happen, etc. The majority of the Embassy personnel together with families had left several weeks earlier for Tours.

"Contrary to rumors, the night passed quietly, although artillery firing could be seen and heard to the northwest.

"On reaching the Place de la Concorde, the Germans took over the Hotel Crillon and made it their military headquarters. About 10:00 on June 14 the Ambassador called Colonel Fuller, the Military Attaché, and myself, to his office and told us to go over to the Crillon, make the preliminary calls, and arrange for the German general to call on the Ambassador (sticking strictly to protocol).

"Fuller and I went across the street to the Crillon, identified ourselves, and were immediately shown into the German general's office and sitting room. We were received most graciously and affably, and although it was only about 10:30 A.M., were offered a glass of what the General said was the very best brandy in the Crillon.

"He was most happy to make his call on the Ambassador at 1:30 P.M. as the Ambassador wished — assured us that all American property would be protected, and that we could count on the best of cooperation as far as the German military were concerned. (In general, this turned out to be true; it was with the German *civil* administration that we had all our trouble.)

"Before leaving the General, Fuller and I were invited by him to assist him in the review of the Green Heart Division which he had previously commanded, and which was to march through the Place de la Concorde at 3:30 that day. There being no easy way to decline, Fuller and I accepted.

"The call on the Ambassador went off in the most 'correct' fashion. The Ambassador was assured that all American interests would be respected, etc., etc., and after about ten minutes of correctness, the General left. Fuller and I accompanied the Ambassador on his return call to the General at about 2:30 which also lasted just about ten minutes.

"At 3:30, Colonel Fuller and I met the General in the middle of the Place de la Concorde, and the General asked us to stand on the reviewing line with him to watch his erstwhile division pass. Both Colonel Fuller and I could easily see how that would look in newsreels, photos, etc. — two American officers taking a review with a German general. So we hastily, but firmly, declined, saying that we didn't feel worthy to share the General's honor; that it was his division and his glory; and that it would be a shame to deprive him of even a share of the glory. Colonel Fuller and I then moved back into the crowd of civilians watching the 'march-past.'

"The next day, 15 June, the Ambassador sent me over to see the General and get permission for the Ambassador and party to drive out to Chantilly to see how the Ambassador's house had fared during the invasion. The General was very perturbed and said, that 'of course, the Ambassador could go,' but then he asked me to ask the Ambassador to wait until the next day. The General explained to me that there had been some fighting around Chantilly, and he wanted to check to see that the house was all O.K. It turned out that there was only very minor damage to the house at Chantilly — an artillery shell had knocked off a portion of an upper corner of the house. Otherwise, nothing else was damaged, and nothing inside had been disturbed, looted or whatnot.

"So, the next day, 16 June, about 11 A.M. the General sent over a motorcycle platoon as an escort, and the Ambassador and his party got in his car. Accompanied by the motorcycles the trip to

Chantilly was uneventful as was the return. Everything at Chantilly was found undisturbed, except for one corner as noted above."

Berlin
June 13, 1940
4 P.M.

The Chargé in Germany [Heath] to the Secretary of State

The American Minister at Bern telephoned the Embassy at 2:15 this afternoon that he had received the following telephone message from Ambassador Bullitt at 11:30 A.M. Swiss time with the request to transmit it to this Embassy for immediate communication to the German Government:

"Paris has been declared an open city. General Hering, Military Commander of the Paris District is withdrawing his army which has been defending Paris. All possible measures are being taken to assure a security of life and property in the city. The gendarmerie and police are remaining and the firemen are also remaining to prevent fire. General Dentz is remaining as Commander of the Paris area but without troops simply with the gendarmerie and the police.

"Ambassador Bullitt is remaining in Paris with the gendarmerie, Military and Naval Attachés, the Counselor of Embassy and six Secretaries of Embassy as the representative of the Diplomatic Corps. Mr. Bullitt hopes to be of any assistance possible in seeing to it that the transfer of the government of the city takes place without loss of human lives. This entire communication is made at the personal request of General Dentz."

Since dictating the foregoing, I have received another telephone call from the American Legation in Bern which stated that Mr. Bullitt had said that he was without radio or cable communication with the United States.

Heath

On June 14, 1940, Premier Reynaud addressed a handwritten letter to President Roosevelt in which he said: "I thank you for having published in America the message which I addressed to you the tenth of June. I can also tell you that for six days and six nights our troops have fought, without one hour of rest, one against three, with armament five times less powerful . . . Our army is now cut into many pieces. Our divisions are decimated. Generals are commanding battalions. The Reichswehr have arrived in Paris . . . At the most tragic hour of its history, France must make a choice. Should she continue to immolate her youth in a combat without hope? Shall her Government leave the national territory in order not to surrender to the enemy and to continue the fight on the sea and in North Africa? . . . We can not choose this way, that of resistance, unless a chance of victory appears in the distance or if a light shines at the end of the tunnel . . . Therefore, France can not continue the battle unless American intervention will reverse the situation by rendering the victory of the Allies certain. The only chance of saving the French nation . . . is today to throw in the balance the weight of the power of America. It is also the only chance to avoid, after having destroyed France and then England, Hitler attacking America . . . if you can not give to France, in the coming hours, the certainty that the United States will enter the war with very brief delay, the destiny of the world will change. You see, then, France sinks like a drowning man, and disappears, after having thrown a last look at the land of liberty from whom she awaits salvation." [7]

On June 14 the newspapers reported that Bullitt had been placed in protective custody by the German military authorities in Paris. Mr. Roosevelt characteristically asked: "Could the Ambassador be protected against what and whom?" Of course the report was untrue.

In Bordeaux on Sunday, June 16, the French Cabinet spent a long day of bitter arguments. Reynaud was being vehemently urged to seek an armistice by General Weygand and several members of his government. This he refused to do, only agreeing to a cease-fire, which would allow the government to go to Algeria and continue the war from there. The discussions were acrimonious, even being participated in by Madame de Portes, who urged her lover to accept an armistice. There are frequent references to her intruding on the meetings. There was, however, one interruption of great historical importance. De Gaulle was now with Churchill in London and telephoned to Reynaud the British

offer of a union with France. After giving him the text, Churchill talked the terms over with Reynaud, who agreed enthusiastically. He little knew the temper of his Cabinet, which refused to
consider such a proposal, and thus the last hope of saving the situation was gone. President Lebrun now exercised his constitutional duty and asked Reynaud to form a new Cabinet on condition that he ask for an armistice. This Reynaud refused to do
and Lebrun called on Marshal Pétain to form a new government.
General Weygand, who had accepted defeat, became Minister of
Defense, and Admiral Darlan, Minister of Marine.

By June 19 the government in Bordeaux had decided to move
its headquarters to Morocco and sail the next day. Pétain was to remain in Bordeaux and had delegated his powers to Chautemps.

By trickery and forgery on the part of Raphael Alibert, an adviser to Pétain, the departure was delayed and only thirty members of Parlement left France, but unfortunately many of these
were men such as Daladier, Mandel, who was later murdered by
Pétain's government, Mendes-France and Delbos, who were devoted
to resistance to the Germans.

The Senate, suspecting a trap, voted not to leave France. It
was against this background of deceit and intrigue that Bullitt re-
joined the French Government.

THE WHITE HOUSE
WASHINGTON

June 20, 1940

Memorandum for the Secretary of State

Just before leaving, I note the enclosed from the *New York Times*
and the Washington *Post*. Don't you think, in fairness to Bullitt, that
you should say something, calling the newspapers by their right
name. It is, after all, only fair to Bullitt.

FDR

Enclosures: Two clippings in regard to Mr. Bullitt's
remaining in Paris, which is reported to have
annoyed the Secretary of State.

Bullitt's decision to remain in Paris was entirely in keeping
with his character, his sense of chivalry, and his feeling for the

dramatic. However, he came under considerable criticism in the United States for his action. Secretary Hull in his *Memoirs* spoke of it thus: "Ambassador Bullitt acted with the military governor in turning the undefended city over to the Germans without loss of life. Bullitt, at his own wish, had remained behind rather than accompany the French Government to Tours and then to Bordeaux . . . The decision, in my opinion, was unfortunate. It deprived Bullitt of all contact with the French Government during the crucial week between June 10, when it left Paris, and June 17, when it asked for an armistice . . . Bullitt explained to me later that three years before this event, he had discussed this very possibility with Mr. Roosevelt, and they agreed that Bullitt should remain in Paris if the Germans were about to occupy it . . . In any event, as the Germans approached Paris, Bullitt communicated to the President direct that he knew the State Department would oppose the proposal he was about to make, hence he was approaching him personally . . . When I became aware of Bullitt's proposal I went to see the President. I said I opposed this project and thought our Ambassador should go with the French Government . . . The President himself then telephoned Bullitt and said that he and I thought the Ambassador ought to leave Paris with the Government . . . Bullitt said he could not run away from danger, and argued the President out of his opposition . . . Nevertheless, to my mind Bullitt was both capable and sincere. And, having the courage of his convictions, he naturally did not hesitate to proclaim and pursue them." [8]

Bullitt's comment on these paragraphs from Secretary Hull's book was contained in a long letter to the *New York Times* on February 16, 1948, shortly after the publication of Hull's *Memoirs*. He first spoke of his code messages to Roosevelt being necessary on account of the lack of security in the State Department of which Secretary Hull was aware, and the probability that these codes were known to the totalitarian powers. He speaks of Mr. Hull as "one of the most discreet of men" for whom he had always "had high respect." He goes on to say that his remaining in Paris was not any disrespect to Mr. Hull but was the result of his talks with the President, who agreed to his remaining. This decision was tacitly confirmed by telegrams from Hull. The

British had asked Bullitt to take charge of their affairs in Paris and in asking Secretary Hull for permission to do so, Bullitt said: "Hull approved taking over the British interests." On May 23, 1940, Bullitt wired Hull suggesting that if the French Government left Paris, Ambassador Anthony J. D. Biddle should go with them as a special representative. On May 27, Secretary Hull replied: "The President is happy to approve your suggestion that if the French Government should leave Paris, it might be advisable to have at its temporary residence a high ranking official and that Ambassador Biddle should take over this duty."

In this same letter Bullitt refers to the fact that Roosevelt had asked him to be Secretary of the Navy on or about June 24, 1940, and that he had accepted.

Robert Murphy, Counselor of Embassy, has written about these last hectic days in Paris, and Bullitt's decision to remain in the city: "I reflect with satisfaction upon one contribution which Bullitt and his staff were able to make in 1940 by remaining in the city. That Paris survives in all its glory today seems a miracle when I recall how we in the embassy assumed that the capital would be ground to rubble when the German armies were approaching, and Reynaud proclaimed that the French would fight from street to street and house to house. It was only at the very last moment that Reynaud asked the American embassy's intervention in making Paris an open city. Bullitt was in constant touch with the French Premier and doubtless had some influence in his decision." [9]

Although Bullitt had been asked to remain in Paris by the French Government, not all of the French agreed with this action. Premier Reynaud felt that in entrusting the city to Bullitt's hands he might be able to convince the Germans that no pillage or destruction would occur. Paris was not harmed in any way, and it will never be known whether Bullitt influenced the German action in sparing the city. General de Gaulle felt, however, that his remaining was a mistake. He said: "Shortly afterwards [on June 10, 1940], when I went to see M. Paul Reynaud, I found Mr. William Bullitt there. I supposed that the United States Ambassador was bringing some encouragement for the future from Washington. But no! He had come to say good-bye.

The ambassador was remaining in Paris with the intention of intervening, if need be, to protect the capital. But, praiseworthy as was the motive which inspired Mr. Bullitt, the fact remained that during the supreme days of crisis there would be no American ambassador to the French government. The presence of Mr. A. J. Drexel Biddle . . . would not, whatever the qualities of this excellent diplomat, remove the impression on our officials that the United States no longer had much use for France." [10] This is a perfect example of the continuous division of opinion in French government circles. On the one hand, the head of the government asked Bullitt to stay in Paris, and on the other the man who was later to lead France was opposed.

After the war Bullitt became a warm friend of de Gaulle's and spent many hours, as a private citizen, with the general at the Élysée Palace.

Roger Langeron, prefect of police in Paris, wrote an account of these tragic days, and in the book which he gave to Bullitt he wrote: "For my eminent friend, His Excellency Ambassador Bullitt, who represented with so much 'éclat' at Paris the great American Republic, this book which recalls some of the moving hours which we lived together."

A few of his remarks about Bullitt are: "Towards evening, a visit from William Bullitt. He has decided to remain in our occupied capital and to contribute to the protection of the population. We are bound by friendship. Cordial, courageous, intelligent, a man of great heart. We will work together very affectionately." [11] On June 12 Bullitt telephoned Langeron to express his admiration for the conduct of the police, and Langeron notes: "He knows that nothing is more precious to me than his approval." [12]

On June 14, when Langeron learned that one of his principal assistants had been summoned by the Germans, he went immediately to seek the aid of Bullitt to protest this violation of promises given to him that same morning. "Bullitt did not hesitate a second." He sent Robert Murphy immediately to the German general, to say that no one would be able to answer for the security of Paris. By eleven that evening the assistant was freed.[13]

Langeron gives a vivid account of Bullitt in these first days of the occupation. The Germans had immediately begun installing telephone wires to the Hotel Crillon, their headquarters, which adjoins the American Embassy. "Last night they began to work on the roof of the Embassy. The Ambassador immediately sent word to the General that, if everything was not removed in one hour, he would consider it an inroad on American soil, and that he, personally, would open fire on all Germans who were still there . . . The Germans took everything away immediately." [14]

On July 4 Langeron noted: "Bullitt has gone . . . He is a great friend that I lose . . . He will be a great friend of France which has real need for it." [15]

Bullitt stayed in Paris until June 30 in order to help any remaining Americans, and some British, to leave the country. The Germans were so confident that the war was over that they interposed few objections to this exodus. The Germans also gave him a great deal of information on their plans to finish up in France and then proceed with their attack against England.

On June 30, 1940, Bullitt left Paris with quite a cavalcade, consisting of Robert Murphy, Admiral Hillenkoetter, Colonel Fuller, Offie, and two old friends, Mr. and Mrs. Dudley C. Gilroy. Mr. Gilroy was a retired major in the British Army, and Mrs. Gilroy's friendship with Bullitt dated from their childhood in Philadelphia. Mr. Gilroy managed a large racing stable at Chantilly near Bullitt's house. They were issued American passports and Gilroy was told not to talk. They crossed the German lines without incident and proceeded to Vichy. Here he met Guy and Madame La Chambre, whom he persuaded to accompany him to America to give our aviation authorities the benefit of his advice and experience as Minister of Air.

The final word on the question of Bullitt's remaining in Paris was written by the President. In a letter dated October 29, 1943, to the publisher of the Philadelphia *Record,* he said: "In the case of the fall of Paris, communications with the United States were practically broken off. He did the obvious and right thing to do — use every effort to save Paris and its civilian population from destruction and death. He followed the action of the American Ambassador in 1914, Honorable Myron Herrick, who received great applause from all parties in this country because he did not go with the French Government to Bordeaux when Paris was threatened by the Germans, who got to within a few miles of it.

This attack on Bullitt is another piece of dirty political falsification."

17, July 4

Your 683 June 29. I beg again to refer to facilities granted me at Paris. German authorities permitted freedom of movement in the Paris area for me and my staff, its local telephone and postal services. But at the time of my departure there was no long distance or telegraph service and no mail service outside the occupied territory. The Minister in charge of the reopened German Embassy informed me that he would accept for transmission via Berlin a limited number of clear telegrams, but that courier service could not be permitted. The German Embassy requested that we communicate with the German authorities through its medium. The German Embassy also agreed to accept letters to our Embassy in Berlin containing whereabouts and welfare telegrams for transmission to the Department. A number of such letters were handed the German Embassy. We do not know whether they were ever received by our Embassy in Berlin.

Every facility was granted to American citizens in the Paris region. American property has been respected and our citizenship not molested. The Embassy has issued approximately seven hundred certificates which have been affixed to business and residential properties owned or controlled by our nationals. So far as we are able to ascertain, these have been respected by the German military.

Bullitt

Memorandum for the Secretary   Washington
                                                   July 31, 1940

My dear Mr. Secretary:

A mutual friend of ours told me that you were in some doubt as to the circumstances of my remaining in Paris after the arrival of the Germans. I feel that no doubt should exist on this point in your mind or anyone else's, either now or hereafter, and wish, therefore, to give you this written memorandum.

The President and I had discussed the possibility of the occupation of Paris by the German troops as far back as three years ago, and had agreed that I should carry on the tradition of Gouverneur Morris, who stayed in Paris even throughout The Terror; Washburne, who stayed in Paris through the siege of Paris and the Commune in 1870; and Herrick. Last February when I was at home, we discussed the matter again, and the President agreed that I should stay in Paris under any and all circumstances. You will recall that, in telegrams about arrangements in Paris, I stated that of course I should remain in the city.

About a week before the French Government left Paris, the Prime Minister, Paul Reynaud, said to me that he understood that I intended to remain in Paris even if the Germans should take the city, and that he hoped I would, since he felt that I might be able to perform a service of inestimable value in preventing the destruction of the city by the Germans.

Before the departure of the Government from Paris, Reynaud and Mandel, the Minister of the Interior, both asked me if I would get in contact with the German authorities before the German Army should reach Paris and attempt to make certain that the occupation should take place without disorder or bloodshed. At that time, the French were most apprehensive also about the four hundred thousand Communists of the industrial suburbs. For a week a secret communist radio station in the Paris region had been urging the workmen to revolt and kill all members of the Government and the bourgeoisie.

Reynaud and Mandel stated to me, however, that they intended to withdraw from Paris all the French police and firemen. I replied that while I might be able to do something to preserve order if the policemen and firemen should remain, I could do nothing if the police and firemen should be withdrawn. Thereupon, they agreed to leave the police and firemen.

It was at this juncture that the President telephoned to me and, to my great surprise, said that you and he thought that I ought to leave Paris. I asked why, and he replied that you both felt that I would be murdered either by the Communists or by the Nazis since I was acutely disliked by both Communists and Nazis. I answered that it seemed to me that the question of my personal safety was one which concerned me, and that I would no longer be myself if I should run away from danger.

I reminded the President of our previous conversations on this point and he did not urge me to leave, nor did he advance any other reason for my leaving except that he said he did not want me to be killed since I could be more useful in the United States, and moreover he feared that if the Germans once got me in their hands they would not let me go.

We then agreed that there was a certain action which he intended to take which would make certain my release by the Germans. In conclusion, I thanked the President for telephoning me and handling the matter as he did.

Strictly between ourselves, immediately after hanging up the telephone, the President said that he really could not urge me to leave because he himself would have taken exactly the same attitude that I had taken.

I am preparing for you a full report on our activities in Paris before and after the German occupation of the city. In this memorandum I merely wish to make clear that at no time did I receive any order either by telegram or telephone to leave Paris.

Respectfully yours,
William C. Bullitt

The British, fearing that the French fleet might fall into German hands, had dispatched their ships to Africa, where some of the French fleet was stationed at Oran, Dakar, Mers-El-Kébir, and Alexandria. The French were asked to either join the British fleet, sail to a British port, sail to a French port in the West Indies and be demilitarized, or sink their own ships.

If none of these terms was complied with, the British admirals were instructed to attack and sink the French ships. The action against the French, with such tragic results and loss of life for them, took place between July 3 and July 8, 1940. At Oran one battleship was blown up, two ran aground, and one escaped, although damaged. At Alexandria the French ships removed their gun mechanisms, discharged their oil, and sent their crews back to France. At Dakar the battleship *Richelieu* was torpedoed.

Bullitt had then arrived in Vichy and saw Pétain the day after the attack. He cabled Hull that several Cabinet members advised immediate acts of war against the British, but Pétain insisted on confining their action to breaking off diplomatic relations.

TELEGRAM

359, July 12, 2 P.M. from Madrid
Strictly Confidential for the President and the Secretary

The intense anger caused in France by the British attacks on the French Navy is so universal at Vichy even among the French who have been intensely pro-British that little stands between French acts of war against the British except the good sense of Marshal Pétain. During the last week I have said to each member of the French Cabinet that in my opinion he must realize that only a British victory can restore the independence of France. In each case the member of the Cabinet in question has agreed but Baudouin is apparently anxious to bring France into war on the side of Germany and alleges that as an ally of Germany, France could obtain much better terms than as a defeated enemy. Laval is not very far from acceptance of this point of view. If the British should continue acts of aggression against France which should further arouse French opinion, I am not sure that Laval and Pétain would be able to hold back the tide.

B.

Bullitt talked with various members of the French Government when he reached Clermont-Ferrand about the first of July, 1940, and cabled home his impressions.

TELEGRAM

La Bourboule
July 1, 1940
9 P.M.

The Ambassador in France [Bullitt] to the Secretary of State
Personal for the Secretary and the President

I had long conversations today with Lebrun, Pétain, Darlan, and Chautemps; and also spoke briefly with Weygand. The impression which emerges from these conversations is the extraordinary one that the French leaders desire to cut loose from all that France has represented during the past two generations, that their physical and moral defeat has been so absolute that they have accepted completely for France the fate of becoming a province of Nazi Germany. Moreover, in order that they may have as many companions in misery as possible they hope that England will be rapidly and completely defeated by Germany and that the Italians will suffer the same fate. Their hope is that France may become Germany's favorite province — a new Gau which will develop into a new Gaul.

This mental disorder yesterday was accompanied by a physical disorder in living conditions and office arrangements which was fantastic. As you know the French Government arrived in Clermont-

Ferrand yesterday. Displeased by living arrangements it left today for Vichy. In view of the disorder none of the statements which were made to me today should be taken as indicating any fixed line of policy or opinion. The truth is that the French are so completely crushed and so without hope for the future that they are likely to say or do almost anything.

I called on Lebrun at 11:30. When he entered the room he had a telegram from the United States (Atlanta, Georgia) imploring him not to surrender the French Fleet to Germany. He said that he had received hundreds of such telegrams. I replied that these telegrams unquestionably had shown him the terrible shock to American public opinion that had been produced by the idea that France could deliver into the hands of her enemy a weapon with which to cut the throat of her ally, England. He immediately became very excited and said that the French positively would not deliver the fleet to Germany for the Germans intended to carry out the clauses of the armistice and that he was certain that they would not take and employ these warships.

He then said that the United States had done nothing to help France which had been fighting the battle of all the democracies and that criticisms from the United States were in extremely bad taste.

I replied that we had done all that we could; that we had made it clear to France from the beginning that we would not enter the war; that the people of the United States could understand that the French Army had been obliged to surrender and that this action was considered as bad as the action of the King of the Belgians in withdrawing his army from the battle at Dunkirk which had been vigorously condemned as an act of treachery by the French. The permitting the fleet to fall into German hands was, however, much more serious. It meant providing means to destroy an ally.

Lebrun flew into a passion and said that the British had given almost no help whatsoever to the French. They had sent 10 divisions incompetently officered which had proved to be deficient in fighting spirit. They had run from the Somme and the British Government had withdrawn the British pursuit planes from the battle of the Somme. The British would soon suffer the same fate that the French had suffered. It would then be the turn of the United States and he would like to see whether either Great Britain or the United States would stand up to the Germans as well as France.

He then suddenly, without mental continuity, stated that in his belief the British would be able to beat off the German attack and that he heartily hoped they would be able to. He then launched into a description of the pitiable plight of the refugees, which is indeed horrible, and stated that if the fleet had been sent to England the Germans unquestionably in retaliation would have destroyed Paris, Lyon, and every other city in France.

I have never seen Lebrun in such a state of nervous excitement and it was obviously wearisome to carry the conversation further.

I then called on Marshal Pétain who was calm, serious and altogether dignified . . . After I talked for an hour the Marshal asked me to take luncheon with him and as a result I talked with him for 3 hours.

The Marshal first asked me about conditions in Paris which I described in great detail and made a number of recommendations all of which he noted. He then said that he desired to thank me most profoundly for having remained in Paris and for having arranged the orderly occupation of the city. He said that he personally and all other Frenchmen owed me a deep debt of gratitude for this act. He then said that he felt that the main outlines of the future were clear. The Germans would attempt to reduce France to a province of Germany by obtaining complete control of the economic life of France and by maintaining France in a condition of permanent military impotence. It had been obvious to him when he had returned from his Embassy in Spain that the war was lost. He had attempted to persuade Reynaud to ask for an armistice the moment the British had refused to send their pursuit planes to participate in the fighting on the Somme. The truth was that the British had scarcely participated in that decisive battle of the war. Their troops had run, and although they had had 40 squadrons of pursuit planes in England they had sent only 5 to participate in the battle. French losses of material in Belgium and on the French frontier had been such that the French troops outnumbered 4 and 5 to 1 had finally been without munitions. The French Army had disintegrated and there was nothing to do except to make peace.

The Marshal then went on to say that the question of the fleet had been a terribly difficult one. He himself had taken the position that the French Fleet would never be surrendered to Germany and he wished to tell me that orders had been given to every captain of the French Fleet to sink his ship rather than permit his ship to fall into German hands.

He thought that German conduct in France indicated a desire to obtain the collaboration of the French as the chief conquered province of Germany. He did not believe that the Germans would break the terms of the armistice and he thought that they would on the contrary do everything to obtain the good will of the people of France and their cooperation in a subordinate role . . .

Marshal Pétain went on to say that he expected Germany to crush England rapidly and he believed that Germany would make her chief demands at the expense of England. Germany probably would annex certain portions of France and would probably control the whole of France through economic arrangements but he felt that England would be destroyed by Germany and that while Germany would take French Morocco and other French possessions on the Atlantic coast of Africa she would also take South Africa, India, and Canada if the United States should be defeated. He believed that the Italians would take Tunisia, Egypt, and Syria and perhaps some portion of continental France. He felt that Algeria would be permitted to remain in French hands. He expressed great bitterness against Churchill and General de Gaulle.

Pétain added that he had just asked the German Government to permit the French Government to establish a sort of Vatican City at Versailles from which France could be governed much more efficiently than from Vichy.

Admiral Darlan was intensely bitter against Great Britain. He said he felt that the British Fleet had proved to be as great a disappointment as the French Army. It was directed not by a man, but by a board of directors who could never make up their minds about anything until it was too late. He had spent a month trying to discover who was responsible for the fiasco of the Norwegian expedition and he was unable to pin the responsibility on any single Englishman since the board of directors had taken the responsibility collectively . . .

Darlan went on to say that he felt absolutely certain that Great Britain would be completely conquered by Germany within 5 weeks unless Great Britain should surrender sooner. It would in his opinion be entirely impossible for the British to send a single ship into the port of London or into the ports of Plymouth, Southampton, and Portsmouth. The Germans could take Ireland easily and close the ports of Glasgow, Liverpool, Cardiff, and Bristol. Great Britain would die of asphyxiation even without a German invasion. For his part, he did not believe that the British Government or people would have the courage to stand against serious German air bombardments and he expected a surrender after a few heavy air attacks.

I remarked that he seemed to regard this prospect with considerable pleasure and when he did not deny this remark but smiled I said that it seemed to me that I had observed that the French would like to have England conquered in order that Germany might have as many conquered provinces to control as possible and that France might become the favorite province. He smiled again and nodded.

I then asked Darlan if he expected an attack on the United States. He said that he felt certain that Hitler would attack the United States shortly after disposing of England and equally certain that the defenses of the United States would prove to be as vulnerable as those of England. He then said that he felt that the President of the United States had made a great mistake in criticizing the French Government's agreements with regard to the fleet. He, Darlan, had sent word to the officers of the fleet before the armistice negotiations that he would take one of two courses. If the Germans should demand the fleet and insisted on the demand they would be ordered to leave at once for Martinique and Guantanamo to place the fleet in the hands of the United States. If on the other hand it should be possible to keep the fleet out of the hands of the Germans and in French hands he would prefer such a solution. Under no conditions would he send the fleet to England since he was certain that the British would never return a single vessel of the fleet to France and that if Great Britain should win the war the treatment which would be accorded to France by Great Britain would be no more generous than the treatment accorded by Germany.

He added that he had given absolute orders to the officers of his fleet to sink immediately any ship that the Germans should attempt to seize. He said that preparations for the sinking of the ships had been made on every French vessel.

I said to him that I did not see how the French could have any control over any French vessel which might return to French ports under German control. He replied that there would always be aboard the vessels sufficient Frenchmen to sink them and that they would be on the alert.

I asked what vessels he expected to send back to Toulon. He replied that he expected to send both the *Dunkerque* and *Strasbourg* to Toulon. I expressed the opinion that this means that the two most valuable units of the French fleet would soon be in German hands since the Germans could always say that one term of the Armistice or another had not been carried out and that they were justified therefore in disregarding the other terms of the Armistice.

Darlan replied that he had just as little confidence as I had in any German promise. But all the behavior of the Germans since their conquest of France had indicated that Germany desired to make France a willing vassal of Germany. It was in his opinion certain that Hitler intended to bring the entire continent of Europe including England into a single customs union and that he desired to make France his leading vassal state. France could do nothing but accept such a position at the moment. Hitler might spread his empire from one end of the earth to the other including the United States but all such empires eventually broke up because the masters in each subordinate country began eventually to sympathize with the country in which they were resident. He did not believe, therefore, that German domination of the earth would be permanent although it might be long. However disagreeable this prospect was it had to be faced.

Darlan then went on to say that the British Government was refusing to permit a French cruiser and two torpedo boats which were in the harbor of Alexandria to leave for French ports. He added that he intended to give immediate orders to these ships to shoot their way out if necessary.

He commented that he felt that when England should be forced to submit to Germany's will we should find the British eager to see the United States in the same subordinate position.

Darlan then said that the French army had not only been defeated but completely disintegrated. The French fleet had not been defeated and its spirit remained intact and he hoped and believed that the officers' corps of the French navy would play a great role in rebuilding France. Every report from the front since May 10 indicated that the French soldier still had all the courage and ability that he had ever had. In his opinion the soldiers of 1940 were fully equal to the soldiers of 1914. But the entire system of parliamentary government in France had been rotten and the high commander of the army had proved to be equally rotten. A complete change in French ways of life was needed . . .

Chautemps and Senator Henry-Haye gave me a concrete description of the present plan to change the French Constitution. Chautemps said that Pétain had asked him to join his Government and he had done so but he was gradually being shoved aside as an adviser of Pétain by Laval. He said that Pétain, Weygand and Laval intended to abolish the present French Constitution and to introduce a semi-dictatorial state in which Parlement would play a small role. The model would be probably the German Constitution when Hindenburg had been President and Hitler Chancellor. Pétain would be Hindenburg and Laval would be Hitler. Pétain, Weygand and Laval all believed that if a dictatorship of this kind should be introduced in France before the peace France would obtain much better terms than could be obtained under a parliamentary regime.

Henry-Haye said that all the senators and deputies would be summoned to a constitutional convention to establish this new form of government . . .

I received a long letter tonight from General Réquin who commanded at the end the superb French resistance at Rethel where his troops stood until they had not one cartridge left.

It gives the same impression. I have talked with many soldiers who fought until they were totally without munitions and then charged with the bayonet.

The simple people of the country are as fine as they have ever been. The upper classes have failed completely.

Bullitt

William L. Shirer says of this report: "Bullitt's report gives better than any contemporary record I have seen the state of mind and heart and soul of the tattered men who controlled the French government at this hour of adversity and trial . . . One gets the impression that it was the most disillusioning day of his life. But it produced what must be by far the most enlightening diplomatic dispatch he ever wrote . . . No better account of the muddled thoughts of the old man who now presided over the destiny of France was ever given." [16]

In the south of France near Sète on June 28, 1940, the automobile containing the Comtesse de Portes and Paul Reynaud met an accident in which she was killed and he was gravely injured. In Bullitt's files is a tragic letter of grief from Reynaud written from the hospital in Montpellier on July 3. It is difficult to decipher and must have caused him much pain in writing, but it shows his deep friendship for Bullitt. He speaks of his approaching marriage with the Comtesse and her desire that he continue the struggle for France. He said: "I will carry out her wish. But how

greatly I have need of friends such as you — so few — to help me!
. . . I tried to carry out my policies, and did not renounce them
until I found I was in an impossible position to do it. I will tell
you all of that when I see you, but when? . . . When will I be
able again to serve my country? In what way? I know nothing.
. . . Ah, if you could come here . . . I have never had such need
of my friends of the first rank, such as you." All during these ca-
lamitous days Bullitt was reporting, often several times a day, to
Washington.

On July 5, Bullitt wired from La Bourboule further talks:

TELEGRAM

La Bourboule
July 5, 1940
11 A.M.

The Ambassador in France [Bullitt] to the Secretary of State

I had long conversations with Pétain, Laval, Chautemps, Baudouin, General Réquin, and others yesterday. Pétain was engaged
in preparing a message to you stating the facts from the French
point of view with regard to the British attack on the French
Fleet . . .

The reaction produced by the news of the British attack on the
French Fleet was, of course, violent in the extreme. Several members of the present Cabinet advocated immediate acts of war against
England. Baudouin stated to me that he had led the fight in the
Cabinet to prevent any act of war; but I learned later from three of
his colleagues that he had advocated an act of war. Pétain was resolutely opposed to anything more than a break in diplomatic relations with England. Orders have been sent recalling the French
Chargé d'Affaires in London.

The Germans and Italians were quick to try to take advantage of
the violent wave of anti-British feeling. They lifted the armistice
clauses with regard to the French Fleet and the French Air Force
and also permitted the French to stop demobilization of that portion of the French Army still remaining intact on the Italian frontier. Moreover, Pétain informed me that the clause forbidding
him and the Government to use the radio for broadcasts had been
lifted . . .

Pétain recognizes that only a defeat of Hitler by some other
power can restore independence to France. He is, therefore, sin-

cerely desirous of a British victory. Pétain was inclined to minimize "breach" by attributing it to Churchill's personal lack of balance. Incidentally, Darlan was opposed to acts of war against England on the ground that the French Fleet could not now fight except by receiving its supplies entirely from German and Italian hands and he was unwilling to take any such assistance . . .

Bullitt

Bullitt was in constant touch with the French officials and cabled daily to Washington.

The President of the French Council of Ministers [Pétain] to President Roosevelt

. . . Since I came to power, setting it as my aim first to assess the inescapable consequences of a hopeless military situation, then to put to work all those elements of recovery which France is fortunate enough to possess, I have constantly striven to reconcile the situation into which I had been forced, by circumstances well known to the British Government, with the maintenance of normal and friendly relations between France and Great Britain. I have on many occasions charged our Ambassador in Washington to express to your Government my intention in that regard.

It was no fault of mine that this was not accomplished. In view of a coup de force for which there was no excuse and which threatens to leave me without means for attaining my aim of equitable mutual understanding, I felt that I should establish the responsibilities for a situation which I deplore, and it is with confidence that I lay the case before you, Mr. President, whose active friendship for France will not, I am sure, fail my country in the cruel misfortune from which I have undertaken to extricate it.

Marshal Pétain

TELEGRAM RECEIVED

Secretary of State · Barcelona
Washington · Dated July 12, 1940
Rush · Rec'd 1:05 P.M.
47, July 12, 1 P.M.
Strictly Confidential for the President and Secretary

Following from Ambassador Bullitt:
One of the highest officials of the French Government who is on such terms of intimate friendship with me that I cannot doubt the

authenticity of his information or the disinterestedness of his advice, advised me to cease telegraphing any messages of importance from the Vichy area and to advise you to refrain from sending me messages of importance. He stated that certain persons in authority unfriendly to the United States had decided to use them between you and me in as unpleasant a manner as [*].

Since I felt obliged to communicate with you frankly at once, I left La Bourboule yesterday morning, reached Barcelona at four this morning, and shall proceed to Madrid by airplane this afternoon. From Madrid I shall telegraph you: but there are certain matters that I do not dare trust to cables, which may be decoded.

Bullitt

TELEGRAM

363, July 13, 11 A.M.
From Madrid — Strictly Confidential

At five o'clock in the evening on July 10th, Jeanneney announced the vote which terminated the existence of the French Republic. I left the next morning for Madrid.

For reasons explained in my previous telegrams from Barcelona and Madrid I can no longer communicate with you confidentially from Vichy.

I left immediately after the abolition of the Republic because I considered that in the absence of instructions and the impossibility of receiving any for many days, the American Ambassador accredited to the President of the French Republic should avoid official visits to the representatives of the new fascist state.

The death of the French Republic was drab, undignified and painful. The deputies and senators met in the theater of the Casino at Vichy at 12 o'clock in the afternoon and immediately a screaming squabble arose over methods of procedure. Herriot's brief speech was the single example of courage and dignity during the dreary afternoon. He pointed out that the French Government had decided to go to North Africa; that Daladier, Campinchi and others who had boarded the *Massilia* which had been placed at their disposal by the French Government, had done so thinking that the Government was going to North Africa to continue the war, and insisted that they should not be treated as men who had run away. His words made such a deep impression that Laval immediately took

* Omission.

the platform and admitted that everything that Herriot had said was absolutely true. The deputies and senators voted, deposited their ballots, then walked out of the theater. It took an hour and a half to count the ballots and when Jeanneney arose to announce the result just before seven o'clock, there were not more than 50 senators and deputies in their seats and perhaps 200 spectators in the galleries.

Jeanneney read the fatal figures and declared the session of the National Assembly closed. As he pronounced the word, "Closed," a voice, strangled with emotion, cried, "Vive la République, quand même!" Those who desired the death of the Republic were taken aback and ten seconds passed before a few of them remembered that it was their duty to cry, "Vive la France."

If the French, even those who now control, should be permitted to act freely they would establish a fascist state that would be as far superior in decency and humanity to the totalitarian states set up by the Russians, Germans and Italians as the French themselves are superior to those races in humanity and decency; but the knowledge which is at the bottom of the mind of every Frenchman in search [sic] is the knowledge that the Germans control France absolutely and that no government set up in fascist form or any other form will be able to wriggle out of their grip until they have done what they wish with France.

The single reality on the Continent of Europe today is Hitler's will.

The last scene of the tragedy of the death of the French Republic was well placed in a theater.

Bullitt

TELEGRAM
364, July 13, 12 noon
Strictly Confidential — From B. in Madrid

Both Blum and Reynaud had the courage to come to Vichy for the National Assembly in spite of real danger involved. I called on them both. Blum was full of courage and despair. Reynaud, his head bandaged and one eye still bloody from the automobile accident in which his fiancée, the Countess de Portes, was killed, was a broken man. He said that he thought he might soon be in prison because of the arrest of his two private secretaries who were stopped as you know at the Spanish frontier carrying a large suitcase filled with twenty million francs in paper; a considerable quantity of gold, jewels, and Reynaud's most private personal files, including all his correspondence with General Gamelin.

Reynaud said that when he had become Prime Minister he had not had time to attend to the secret funds of the Prime Minister personally and had turned them over to his private secretary, Lecas. He feared that the money in the suitcase had been taken from the secret funds. He feared, moreover, that the gold and the jewels had belonged to his fiancée. The papers had been from his most personal files. He swore to me that he had given no orders to Lecas to take any of these things. He said that at the moment when Lecas attempted to cross the Spanish frontier, he, Reynaud, had expected to leave France to become French Ambassador in Washington and no doubt Lecas thought he was doing a service in attempting to get to Lisbon with the articles in his suitcase. The situation was horrifying since it would be most difficult for him to prove that he had not given Lecas orders to do what he had done.

Bullitt

The Soviet, during these days when both German and French forces were fully occupied, made additional bloodless extensions of its territory. The Soviet account reads: "June 26, 1940, the Soviet Government proposed to Rumania that she return to the U.S.S.R. the territory of Bessarabia that had been seized in 1918 and hand over the northern part of Bukovina that was inhabited by Ukrainians. On June 28, Rumania accepted the proposal. The family of Soviet peoples was joined by 3,700,000 new citizens." [17]

In July the Soviet absorbed three more small and defenseless states and explained the acquisitions in these terms: "The Lithuanian, Latvian and Estonian peoples re-established Soviet power in their countries. The Latvian, Lithuanian and Estonian and Soviet Socialist Republics were founded and voluntarily entered the Soviet Union in August 1940." [18]

After the fall of France, the Vichy Government arrested many of the former leaders. Among these officials were Premiers Léon Blum, Daladier, and Reynaud, as well as Cabinet officers Guy La Chambre, Pierre Cot, Mandel, and others. In Bullitt's files are letters from some of these prisoners which were smuggled out and mailed to him in America. They are heartbreaking documents from men who had stood to the last against surrender to the Germans.

Blum was in prison at Portalet and Suzanne Blum wrote to Bullitt that this prison was almost inaccessible in winter and that "in spite of their courage it is not certain that they can survive. The sun never shines, they are not authorized to receive food from the outside, hence they will receive nothing. Imagine what that can be for men of more than sixty, already weakened by a year in prison. Can you help them and send them some food? As Offie is not here I can prepare everything myself and send it to you or whoever you name . . . I am very anxious about those I love and I hope that once more your friendship will know how to do miracles."

Bullitt and his party left Lisbon on July 15, 1940.

FIVE

Special Assignments
1940–1942

25

Warning America

AUGUST 1940—MAY 1941

Bullitt Speaks at Independence Hall
Britain Receives American Destroyers
Daladier Writes from Prison
Bullitt Resigns
Lend-Lease Bill
Sumner Welles

IN MY WIFE'S DIARY there is the following under date of July 20, 1940: "Anne, Orville and I took 7 A.M. train to New York to meet Bill coming in on Dixie Clipper. A marvelously interesting and exciting experience. Nine of us for supper."

It was indeed exciting, with dozens of reporters and cameramen trying to obtain a firsthand account of all that was happening in France. Bill naturally said little of what is in these letters, wanting first to talk with Mr. Roosevelt, as he had been virtually cut off from any contact for over a month. On the plane with him was former Empress Zita of Austria and her daughter the Princess Elizabeth. The ride from La Guardia Airport to the Pennsylvania Railroad Station was too exciting for us. Bill had a police escort of motorcycles and we left the airport with sirens blowing and flags flying, plunging through all the red lights of the city streets at about fifty miles an hour. In our taxi we soon realized how ridiculous it all was, and much to the disgust of escorting police and our chauffeur we told him to pull out of the cavalcade. We arrived at the station about five minutes after Bill and with half an hour to wait for the train. Bill and Anne spent the weekend with us and left for Washington on Monday, where he reported to the President, going with him a few days later to the President's home at Hyde Park.

In May 1940, Churchill broached the question of the loan to Britain of American destroyers. In July and August Churchill carried on lengthy negotiations with Roosevelt, hoping to obtain from the United States some of the old but reconditioned destroyers which were in the East Coast Navy yards. He asked for fifty or sixty, as the British losses were very heavy; four had been sunk and seven damaged in ten days, largely by air bombing. The island and the Atlantic convoys could not be protected for long with such results, and the British position was becoming desperate. On both sides the question had to be handled with great caution. Churchill had to consider the feelings of Parliament and the overseas possessions when he offered to lease bases in the Western Hemisphere to the United States, and Roosevelt had to take into account public opinion and various factions in the Congress.

Langer and Gleason in *The Challenge to Isolation* say of the situation at this time: "There is no evidence that it [the destroyer exchange] appealed to the President, who, so far as one can determine, was at a complete loss how to proceed. In the quiet of Hyde Park he arranged with Ambassador Bullitt to have the latter deliver an important address to test the strength of popular sentiment. In a speech to the American Philosophical Society in Philadelphia on August 18, 1940, Bullitt developed the theme that the country was in great danger. The Nazi machine was one that could not be stopped. If Britain went under, the United States would inevitably be the next Nazi target, and the Atlantic, he warned, might serve as a highway rather than a barrier: 'The truth is that the destruction of the British Navy would be the turning of our Atlantic Maginot Line . . . The soothing words "Atlantic Ocean" are being used now by the propagandists of the dictators in the hope that they become the lullaby of death for the United States . . . It is as clear as anything on this earth that the United States will not go to war, but it is equally clear that war is coming towards the Americas . . . I am certain that if Great Britain is defeated, the attack will come.' " [1]

DEPARTMENT OF STATE

WASHINGTON

Personal   August 13, 1940

Dear Mr. President:

This is the address to be delivered at the invitation of the American Philosophical Society in Independence Square by Thomas Jefferson on his return from his Embassy in France during the French Revolution.

You will note that this is Jefferson's first rough draft and that he has promised that while it will not be expanded, it will be reduced in girth.

Blessings, dear George, and may your cherry trees flourish.

> Yours very respectfully,
>
> T. Jefferson
>
> per WCB

P.S. Incidentally, one of my great-grandfathers was the boy's guardian.

> WCB

[Address returned to Ambassador Bullitt on August 15, 1940.]

DEPARTMENT OF STATE

WASHINGTON

Memorandum   August 12, 1940

The Acting Secretary of State, Mr. Sumner Welles, read the address which I propose to deliver on the evening of August 18 at Independence Square, Philadelphia, at luncheon today in the Mayflower Hotel, and stated that he approved every word of it.

> WCB

P.S. The President read and approved the address in bed at 9:45 the next morning.

> WCB

This speech, delivered with the approval of the President and the State Department, was probably the most outstanding one of Bullitt's career. It was a fervent appeal to America to wake up and realize the peril it faced. Wendell L. Willkie had accepted the Republican nomination for President the previous day. A very large segment of the American people were isolationists and wanted no part in European disputes, feeling that the Atlantic Ocean would fully protect our country. It was in opposition to this opinion that Bullitt spoke, hoping to arouse America to its danger. The *New York Times,* August 20, 1940, said editorially: "He had a message that needed to be delivered. The American people should be grateful to him for letting them hear it . . . Our own history in the next few years will be happier if our people act now, in the spirit of Mr. Bullitt's warning."

In 1789, Thomas Jefferson, Minister to France, having just witnessed the beginning of the French Revolution, as Bullitt had seen the fall of France, stood on the steps of Independence Hall and addressed his fellow countrymen.

On Sunday, August 18, 1940, with the glow of the setting sun casting a soft light over the audience gathered in Independence Square, Bullitt spoke. The rostrum was erected on the south side of Independence Hall. The door behind the speaker's desk, thrown wide to show the Liberty Bell, was flanked by two armed bluejackets. To add to the drama of the occasion a detachment of sailors from a French cruiser faced the audience, and a Marine band provided entertainment prior to the exercises.

The speech was made under the auspices of the American Philosophical Society, whose home adjoins Independence Hall. The society was founded by Benjamin Franklin and among its early members were Thomas Jefferson, George Washington, James Madison, and Alexander Hamilton.

As one journal described the speech, which was to cause a furor in the Congress: "No one doubted that his words had first been well weighed by Mr. Roosevelt. But never before had a United States Ambassador, a member of the Administration, been permitted to talk on international affairs with such undiplomatic, brutal bluntness. Mr. Bullitt minced no monosyllables." Bullitt quoted Hitler's strategy: "Each country will imagine that it alone will escape. I shall not even need to destroy them one by one. Selfishness and lack of foresight will prevent each one fighting until it is too late." Bullitt had seen Hitler succeed with this plan against France and his speech was a deliberate challenge to the pacifists in the United States. He told them they completely misunderstood the Nazi system and that by their failure to arm they were deliberately playing into the hands of the dictators in their plans for an assault on America, once Great Britain was defeated. He bitterly denounced the Communists and Nazis in America and said: "Why are we sleeping, Americans? . . . When are we going to let legislators in Washington know that we don't want any more politicians who are afraid of the next election and scared to ask us to make the sacrifices that we know are necessary? . . . Demand the privilege of being called into the service of the nation. Tell them [the Congress] that we want conscription." The newspaper accounts said that the cheering was so recurrent and prolonged that Bullitt had to stop frequently with unfinished sentences hanging in the air. "His address was devoid of oratorical flourishes. His demeanor was one of frank sincerity and high patriotism, a clear premonition of danger to the United States."

It was evident that the speech was made on behalf of President Roosevelt, who was in no position to make such statements. His official blessing was further confirmed by those who surrounded Bullitt on the platform; included were former Ambassador to Poland Anthony J. D. Biddle; John Cudahy, Ambassador to Belgium; the Polish Ambassador to the United States; Francis Biddle, Solicitor General of the United States; Rear Admiral Watson, Commandant of the Navy yard; and numerous others.

Many newspapers carried the speech in full, with much editorial comment. One editorial stated: "If Bullitt is 'alarmist' enough to alarm us into action he will have saved his country. We can think of no higher praise for one of the great speeches of our time." [2]

The storm broke quickly in Congress and Bullitt was castigated in the Senate and House. Senator Clark (Democrat, Missouri) called for his arrest, quoting Section 201 of the Criminal Code, which provided for a fine of $500 and a year in prison. He was joined by other isolationists. In the House, Representative Schafer (Republican, Wisconsin) said that the warmonger Bullitt should be locked up. There is no question that this speech helped to awaken America to the danger which threatened, and it was of assistance to Roosevelt in determining his action on the destroyers.

At the end of July, Churchill had wired Roosevelt: "Mr. President, with great respect I must tell you that in the long history of the world this is a thing to do now." [3] By September, Britain had the fifty destroyers and offered in exchange long-term leases to the United States of bases in Newfoundland, Bermuda, and the West Indies.

Bill's superpatriotism occasionally brought a comment from others, and Bill was fond of telling a story of one conversation with the President. According to Bill, he was expatiating to the President on what a high moral basis the United States should act and kept referring to "my country." After a good deal of this the President finally interrupted with: "Bill, could I have just a little bit of your country?"

August 26, 1940

Dear Mr. President:

I don't know exactly what you want for your speech in the Great Smokies, but Steve Early has told me that you will make a long speech full of facts at Chattanooga the same day, and that your program calls for only a brief address in the Great Smokies.

So here you are — Washington and Lincoln rolled into one, with a touch of the Lord.

I am tired and I shall leave tomorrow for the West and not come back until I hear that you want me.

Good luck.

Yours always,
Bill

On September 21, 1940, the University of Pennsylvania celebrated its two-hundredth anniversary and there was considerable discussion among the trustees about giving Mr. Roosevelt an honorary degree. Most of the trustees were staunch Republicans and it was a bitter pill, for the President was thoroughly disliked. Sophistry won the day and the degree was conferred on the President of the United States. It was an extremely hot day and the trustees all wore cutaway coats made for winterwear. Had we worn the usual caps and gowns, we would have been in our shirt-sleeves under the gowns. To add to the discomfort the stage at Convention Hall was brilliantly lighted and the heat was insufferable. Mr. Roosevelt sat in the center of the stage flanked by Justice of the Supreme Court Owen J. Roberts, a trustee, and Thomas S. Gates, President of the University. Facing the trustees on the opposite side of the stage were Bill and Senator Guffey of Pennsylvania, whom the trustees disliked. I don't remember exchanging a smile with Bill, as it was all very tense. Mr. Roosevelt made what we considered a political speech, completely out of keeping with an academic celebration.

October 14, 1940

Dear Bill:

Charges are still being made in some quarters that this government assured the Government of France that if France should become engaged in war in Europe, the United States would enter the war.

I think the time has come, once and for all, when we should reveal the falsity of such statements. I am, therefore, giving you a copy of a letter which I received from Prime Minister Daladier. This letter was written by the Prime Minister to me under the date of April 4, 1940. It is taken from the official records and should be accepted as indisputable proof of the fact that no such assurances were given the French by the Government of the United States.

I understand that you are to deliver an address in Chicago on Monday, October 21st and I hope that you will use this letter as part of the remarks you will make on that occasion.

Sincerely,
FDR

Honorable William C. Bullitt
Department of State
Washington, D.C.

On October 21, 1940, Bullitt spoke before the Council of Foreign Relations in Chicago. The speech was carried throughout the country by radio. The letter to which President Roosevelt refers was the one from Premier Daladier in his own handwriting, to the President previously quoted.

Bullitt, in his speech, pointed out that the new Triple Alliance between Germany, Italy, and Japan presented a clear threat to the United States. He called for a determination to stay out of war and an increased army, and he stressed the importance of a large production of airplanes. He closed on the note that "you cannot appease the unappeasable."

Rittenhouse Club
1811 Walnut Street
25 October 1940

Dear Mr. President:

Your speech here was a masterpiece, and reaped many votes.

Unexpectedly my broadcast from Chicago seems to have been effective. I have finished New York and Philadelphia, and am ready for any work you want.

Good luck.

Bill

The President was now re-elected for his third term of office.

The Anchorage
Connecticut Ave. at Que St.
7 November 1940

Dear Mr. President:

In accordance with excellent custom I submit to you my resignation as Ambassador to France.

I need to see you as soon as possible but have just heard from the White House that you will be busy until Monday.

Whatever time you may fix, please, for many real reasons make the place the White House and not the office.

May I count on a moment Monday evening?

Yours affectionately,
Bill

THE WHITE HOUSE
WASHINGTON

November 9, 1940

Dear Bill:

1. Resignation not accepted.
2. We will talk about that and the future later.
3. Hope to see you very soon.

As ever,
FDR

Honorable William C. Bullitt
Ambassador to France
State Department Building
Washington, D.C.

The Anchorage
Connecticut Ave. at Que St.
November 9, 1940

Memorandum by Bullitt

President: Hello, Bill! How are you?

WCB: I'm sorry to bother you, Mr. President, but Henry-Haye, the French Ambassador, has just told Murphy, who is going to Vichy that Welles asked him this afternoon for the *agrément* for Admiral Leahy. I thought you said this afternoon that I was to remain as Ambassador to France and go off on a holiday until December 15th. It's known all over town now and puts me in a fine spot.

President: Bill, believe it or not, I forgot all about it. It's entirely my fault. I wouldn't blame Welles entirely. You see, they went ahead on it. I sent Pa [General Edwin] Watson last week up to see General Pershing to see if he would take the job. Pa told the State Department that Pershing was going to write me a letter saying that he couldn't do it. Welles went ahead this afternoon with it. It's all right though, Bill, because you remain as Ambassador until the appointment is made. When we hear from France, we can make the appointment but you will remain as Ambassador.

WCB: Yes, but what on earth am I going to do after you put me in that awful position? Leahy is now Ambassador — after I told the press this afternoon that I was remaining Ambassador to France. It's done now.

President: No, Bill. You remain as Ambassador until the appointment is made. You're all wrong on your protocol.

WCB: But, Mr. President. What am I going to say to the press? This is shocking.

President: Sure, I understand, Bill. Damn the press. Just say you're still Ambassador and I'll say the same thing to the press tomorrow.

WCB: You say Pa Watson went to see Pershing a week ago. It was a week ago that you wrote me that letter saying: "1. Resignation not accepted."

President: I know, Bill. But I forgot about the whole business completely. Just let it go that way for the time being.

WCB: Well, my dear fellow, I don't hold anything against you for it. I never have held anything against you in my life.

President: Of course not, Bill. I'll tell the press tomorrow you're still Ambassador to France.

WCB: Well, I had better tell the press simply that I am returning to private life.

President: No, just tell them you're still Ambassador until the appointment is made. I'll say the same thing. Don't bother about it. Damn the press.

WCB: Well, I'll just say I'm going back to private life and that's that.

President: Well, say just for a short time.

WCB: Well, this is certainly a funny one, if anything ever was funny. It certainly leaves me in a spot.

President: Sure, Bill. I understand. It must have knocked you cold. But let it go at that.

WCB: All right. But it certainly is a strange one and don't worry. I don't hold it against you. I understand how it happened. Goodbye and God bless you.

President: Thanks, Bill. Good night and take care of yourself.

At this time Bullitt mentioned to friends that Roosevelt had offered to appoint him Ambassador to Great Britain, but he had declined as he felt it high time he remained in America. His daughter was growing up and he wanted her to have friends in this country and a home in the United States. He rented a house in the country near Philadelphia about four miles from where we lived.

From November 1940 until November 1941 there are numerous telegrams between the White House and Bullitt arranging for appointments with the President, but there are few letters of importance.

Although Daladier was in prison, he was able to write to Bullitt and to receive letters from him. The position of Daladier was similar to that of Louis XVI imprisoned in the Temple before his death on the guillotine. For history's sake his letters would have made fascinating reading — as these do. On December 24, 1940, Daladier wrote:

My dear Bullitt:

I have had the pleasure sometimes of receiving news of you, but since the Presidential election, I know nothing of you. You must know of the plots which have begun against you at this time, in last October, by the Boches and by Laval, with the thought of hurting you and consequently President Roosevelt. These gentlemen sent my secretary Mlle. Mollet, whom you knew, I think, to me at the country prison of Chazeroy, where I was. They proposed to alleviate my captivity, and to end it later, if I agreed to sign a Declaration which would have been published and sent out over the radio, in which I would have stated that I would not have entered the war except under pressure from England, and from you, Bullitt, who had promised me the support of the United States. I do not have to tell you that I rejected with contempt such a Declaration. The Boches, always in agreement with the French government, during the night broke into the home of my lawyer in Paris and seized his files, with the hope of finding documents of a nature which would compromise you. Naturally, they did not find anything. Then they twice sent Mlle. Mollet to Chazeroy who returned to Paris — as she had come — nevertheless with this message of mine: that I would find the means of drinking on November 5th a glass of champagne to the health of a great heir of the Mohicans. I do not know if you were told all of that but I asked your former colleagues to tell you at the time. Since then they transferred me to the prison of Bourassol, near Riom, from which I have the pleasure of writing to you to wish you a Merry Christmas.

The government of Vichy wants the trial of Riom to begin the end of January. In spite of the regime which the French people are undergoing, they remain attached to liberty and democracy. Also throughout France, except in the government, they wish for English victory, and the hatred against Hitler and the Germans is very great. The truth is beginning to come out on the treachery of French Hitlerites before the war, and during the war. I receive every day from the common people moving testimonies of sympathy. It is why the Vichy Government wants to make short work of things and to organize as rapidly as possible a caricature of justice. If the trial took place, according to French law, either before a jury or before the High Court, I would certainly be acquitted. But by a decree which violates the Constitution, without its being officially abrogated, and without a new Constitution being submitted to the ratification of the people, the government has created what it calls a Court of Justice, for which it has, itself, chosen the judges. That has never happened in the history of France . . . They have refused to give me important documents which I have asked for, for my defense. They have brought pressure on witnesses . . . They have only given the lawyers a few days to examine an enormous brief . . . I regret that I do not know or can not reach the American journalists to inform

them of all these arbitrary measures, of this parody of justice . . .
What a shame that you have not returned to France. They would
not have dared to do all of that in your presence. But perhaps you
can help me by letting your friends know the truth. Naturally all
the French Hitlerites, supported by the Germans, are absolutely enraged against me, and Georges Bonnet is at their head, the most re-
pugnant liar in the world . . .

The truth is that the General Staff committed a formidable error
in the disposition of our forces: they massed the best and greatest
numbers of our troops on a part of the Belgian frontier, besides in
the Maginot line which was already very strong, and on the line of
the Meuse they only put a few divisions of inferior value whereas
this region served as the pivot of the movement on Belgium . . .
Since the reserves for the most part were grouped opposite the gap
at Basle, at Switzerland and the Jura, they did not arrive in time on
the Meuse or the Oise . . .

At all events they could have resisted as the Russians resisted Napoleon, by giving the order not to even defend the cities. Above all,
they could have gained North Africa with all our fleet intact, there
received your airplanes which would have arrived in quantity. If
they had done this, Italy today would be out of the war and England would have at its disposition a million tons of war ships
which would have made life hard for the Germans in the North Sea
and the Atlantic. I am in despair when I think of all that.

But, perhaps, nothing is yet lost. Shut up in this prison, where
my son Jean and my son Pierre come to see me from time to time, I
can not measure exactly the chances of England. She gives a magnificent example of courage and energy. She does honor to the human
race. But could you send to them before spring, airplanes, arms,
munitions? Will your laws allow it? Is your production already
massive? Today is truly the supreme battle between dictatorship
and democracy . . .

I am happy, my dear Bullitt, to have been able to write you this
letter. Perhaps you will find it too long, but you will excuse me in
thinking of the pleasure that I have in writing to you. I do not
know the Admiral [Leahy] who succeeded you here and naturally I
cannot enter into communication with him . . .

I do not know if I will ever see you again. But I wish to tell you
that the recollection of our friendship is one of the best of my life.

Bien à vous,

Ed. Daladier

In Bullitt's files there is also a copy of a letter which Daladier sent to Pétain. He accuses him of employing methods without example in France. Without even knowing the charges against him he is imprisoned in a fortress (prison of Bourassol). He tells Pétain that the process at Riom is to open at once by Pétain's order; he has been refused any of his papers for his defense by his lawyer. Daladier closes his letter with these words:

"I rise in indignation against these new violations of human rights which have recognized for every accused the right to defend himself. It has never been contested in any civilized nation up until now."

Derwen
Penllyn, Pa.
December 28, 1940

Dear Mr. President:

It was a joy to see you in such fine form and to work, even though briefly, on the speech.

The State Department has informed me that it can not order the shipment of my personal belongings from Paris until you have accepted my resignation in writing; the present status of the matter being that all I have is your letter of November 9th, refusing to accept my resignation! Will you please, therefore, in your best style dictate an acceptance of my resignation "effective on the date set by the Secretary of State." This phrase is for technical reasons and was given to me by the Chief of Foreign Service Administration of the Department of State.

Good luck and every good wish.

Yours affectionately,
Bill

On December 29, 1940, the President made one of his famous Fireside Chats on the radio from the White House. It shows clearly the way his mind was working and the efforts he made to arouse the American public to the danger that lay ahead. A few sentences from this address give succinctly the tone of the message:

"The Nazi masters of Germany have made it clear that they intend not only to dominate all life and thought in their own country, but also to enslave the whole of Europe, and then to use the resources of Europe to dominate the rest of the world.

"If Great Britain goes down, the Axis powers will control the continents of Europe, Asia, Africa, Australia and the high seas and they will be in a position to bring enormous military and naval resources against this hemisphere.

"There can be no appeasement with ruthlessness.

"We must be the great arsenal of democracy . . . We have furnished the British great material support and we will furnish far more in the future."

In January 1941, President Roosevelt addressed Congress on the state of the nation and said: "I find it, unhappily, necessary to report that the future and safety of our country and of our democracy are overwhelmingly involved in events far beyond our borders . . . The future of all the American Republics is in serious danger."

THE WHITE HOUSE

WASHINGTON

January 7, 1941

Dear Bill:

Your letter of resignation as Ambassador to France is before me. It is with great reluctance that I accept it and only because of the urgent personal reasons you advance which I cannot disregard; however the resignation will not be effective until the expiration of your present leave of absence.

The high measure of ability you brought to your task and the devotion with which you served your country distinguish your services as an American Ambassador and I take this occasion to convey on the part of the Government of the United States my deep appreciation for the work you have done, together with a message of warm personal regard.

Very sincerely yours,

Franklin D. Roosevelt

The Honorable William C. Bullitt
Derwen
Penllyn, Pennsylvania

On January 25, 1941, Bullitt appeared before the House Foreign Affairs Committee to testify on the Lend-Lease Bill. At this hearing the question was again raised as to whether Bullitt had assured the French that they would get assistance from the United States in case of war. Bullitt characterized the allegations against him as German propaganda and read into the record Premier Daladier's letter to Roosevelt which has been quoted on pages 407–408.

The *New York Times* on January 26 printed the charges that the United States had encouraged the French and British to fight. The *Times*'s report inferred that secret commitments or "gentlemen's agreements" had been given promising the full military aid of the United States, after an interval, as in the World War I: "Colonel Charles A. Lindbergh in his testimony brought this charge out into the open more than any other witness has done." It is difficult to understand, in view of the information now available, how such a charge could have been made.

Bullitt's testimony largely consisted of statements he had already made in his Independence Hall speech, and other speeches and articles, dwelling on the danger to the United States in case of the defeat of Britain. In part he said: "It is so greatly to the advantage of the totalitarian States to have us stay out of war while they are attempting to conquer Great Britain, Greece and China that no matter how much aid we furnish and no matter what form that aid may take, the dictators will hesitate to declare war on us unless they have first conquered Great Britain. If they declared war, they could not now get at us." The *New York Times* reported that when he had finished his testimony, "Mr. Bullitt stood up and said solemnly to the whole Committee: 'The Skipper has set the course. You Representatives are the officers, we out of office are the crew. Our cargo is America!' Resounding applause followed." The Lend-Lease Bill was passed by the Congress and became law when the President signed it on March 11, 1941. Essentially it provided for the immediate supply of arms, munitions, ships and aircraft to Great Britain with payment to be made at a later date.

Later, Mr. Bloom, the chairman of the committee, congratulated Bullitt as he left the witness stand amid loud applause and observed that he would bet the former Ambassador had never before received one like it. It was Bullitt's fiftieth birthday.

Some time later Bullitt told a friend that too much solicitude was felt at the White House about the President's health, that the main point in everyone's mind was not to help England save the world but to protect the President.

Since Bullitt was now in America, conversations, in great part, took the place of letters. Bullitt dictated the following memorandum immediately after a talk with the President on April 23, 1941.

MEMORANDUM

I saw the President at the White House offices this morning at 11:15. He first said that La Guardia had presented to him a new scheme for Home Defense . . .

I replied that I had been telling him for four months that I did not want to work on Home Defense but on licking Hitler . . .

I then said that I felt we were not handling at all the question of public opinion. I believed that it was certain that we would go to war with Germany. We no longer had an easy choice between war and peace . . .

The President added that the problem which was troubling him most was that of public opinion. He had just had an argument with Stimson on the subject. Stimson thought that we ought to go to war now. He, the President, felt that we must await an incident and was confident that the Germans would give us an incident . . .

I then said to the President that Judge Moore had sent for me on his deathbed and charged me with a duty which I could not evade, however unpleasant it was to carry out. The Judge had said to me that he could not die in peace of mind unless he knew that the President was certain to be informed with regard to a very dangerous matter. He had been resolved to call on the President and take it up with the President personally but he felt that he would never again leave his bed. The Judge had asked me, as a dying wish, to see to it that the President was informed with regard to the contents of certain papers.

I went on to say that one of these papers gave in brief form the information that the Judge desired to communicate to the President and that I would ask him to read this one paper and no more. I then handed the President the document . . .

The President read the first page of this document and looked over the other pages and finally said, "I know all about this already. I have had a full report on it. There is truth in the allegations" . . .

I . . . then said that Judge Moore had felt that the maintenance of Welles in public office was a menace to the country since he was subject to blackmail by foreign powers and that foreign powers had used crimes of this kind to get men in their power; and that the Judge was also convinced that this matter was one of the utmost danger to the President personally . . . and a terrible public scandal might arise at any time which would undermine the confidence of the country in him, the President.

The President said that he did not believe that any newspaper would publish any information about this matter. It was too scandalous for any newspaper to print. I replied that Judge Moore had thought that the scandal would not arise as a result of newspaper publication but that there would be a demand for criminal prosecution of Welles . . . The President said . . . that he thought that Welles would never be able to behave in that way again since he was having Welles watched by a guardian (under the guise of his needing a bodyguard as a public official) now day and night to see to it that Welles did not repeat such a performance. I said that the question was not one of future acts but of past crimes committed. I added that the Secretary of State had said to me after discussing this matter that he considered Welles worse than a murderer.

The President replied that he knew that this was a crime and he knew that Welles was liable to prosecution but that he did not believe that anyone would initiate prosecution.

I added that morale in the Department of State and the Foreign Service was being ruined by the knowledge that a man of the character of Welles was in control of all appointments and transfers. I repeated that blackmail of high government officials guilty of crimes of this nature had been used often by different powers to oblige such men to act as traitors . . .

The President said that he was fully aware of this danger but there was for him a different question involved and that he had not decided how to handle it. Welles was useful in the State Department and he found it convenient to have him there. The question, therefore, was of ending the utility of somebody he found useful. I replied that I questioned the utility of Mr. Welles . . . He was thinking of asking Americans to die in a crusade for all that was decent in human life. He could not have among the leaders of a crusade a criminal like Welles.

I added that I wished to make it clear that in stating to him that I wanted to work on licking Hitler I meant that I wanted to do all I could to accelerate our preparation for war but that under no circumstances would I take any position in the Department of State or in the Foreign Service until he should have dismissed Welles.

At this point the President pressed the button under his desk and summoned General Watson.

I rose and remarked that I would expect to hear from him the end of this week and took my leave.

The President, when General Watson entered the room, said: "Pa, I don't feel well. Please cancel all my appointments for the rest of the day. I want to go over to the House."

Although this meeting was the genesis, almost two years later, of the end of the close association between the two men, Roosevelt continued to see Bullitt and give him important assignments, even appointing him Ambassador to all countries as personal representative of the President, sending him to the Middle East in 1942. However, there was no regular post for him in foreign affairs; nor was he to receive the appointment to the Cabinet, which the President had frequently discussed with him.

On the fifth of May, 1943, Bullitt wrote the following memorandum.

May 5, 1943

Yesterday General Watson telephoned to me that when he had told the President yesterday morning that I wished to see him, the President had replied that before seeing me he wanted me to discuss a matter with White House Secretary Stephen Early. Later Mr. Early telephoned asking me if I would drop in at his office and I said that I would do so at 11 o'clock this morning . . .

Mr. Early then said that the President had requested him to take up a matter with me and he hoped that I would realize that he did so in the friendliest spirit and that he would have wished me to take up the matter with him if he had been in my position and I in his. He went on to say that the President had received reports that I had talked with the Secretary of State and other people about the "unfortunate weaknesses" of Sumner Welles. I replied that I had discussed this subject three times with the President himself; that I had taken a number of documents into the President's office covering the case to show the President; that the President had read one of them and had then said that he knew that Welles was guilty of the criminal behavior alleged. I said that since I had discussed this matter with the President, himself, I did not wish to discuss it with anyone else in the White House. I would discuss it with the President if he wished.

Mr. Early said that the allegation which had now come to the President's ears was that I had turned over "at a dinner" a large number of documents with regard to the Welles case to a hostile newspaper publisher. I replied that that was an absolute damned lie. Mr. Early said, "to be specific," that "the allegation was that I had turned over the documents to Cissy Patterson," publisher of the Washington *Times Herald*.

I replied that that was a complete lie. I added that I had known Mrs. Patterson for over thirty years and that we had remained on a friendly footing seeing each other three or four times a year, always disputing on political matters but remaining friends, and I called his attention to the fact that I had been attacked in a personal manner in Mrs. Patterson's paper only ten days ago.

Mr. Early said that he knew that this was my relationship with Mrs. Patterson and that it was exactly the same as his own. He said that he personally had been convinced that there was no truth in this allegation and that he was delighted to be able to return to the President and say that it was a complete falsehood. I got up to go and Mr. Early said that the Welles case was of course intensely serious and that he felt it was about to break into the open. I said that I had gone to the President in the first instance to warn him that unless he should dismiss Welles, Welles would be his Achilles Heel, and that he must dismiss him both for his own good and for the good of the country. I said that I had observed that the President had resented my remarks and that his attitude toward me had changed from that time on, and that our intimate friendship had ended. I added that I felt that no man could be a loyal servant to the President of the United States if he did not open his mind to him with absolute frankness, especially as the President had become increasingly surrounded by flatterers and "yes men" . . . He said that he knew that I had always spoken perfectly frankly to the President and that he had respected me greatly for so doing, "even though the President got angry." I said that I knew no other way to work with a man who bore the responsibilities of the President than by opening my mind to him completely so that he could read what was in it like a man who reads the pages of a book. I felt deeply that the President had gone wrong terribly in the case of Welles.

Mr. Early repeated that he believed that the Welles case was going to break; that of course he, the President and everyone else in the White House knew that the allegations were true, but the President had hoped to keep the case quiet.

We then shook hands and I left.

Mr. Hull has given a very complete account of the causes given by the President for the resignation of Under Secretary of State Sumner Welles. Before leaving for the Quebec Conference with Churchill in August 1943, the President called Mr. Welles to the White House and asked for his resignation. The causes for this action were apparently Mr. Welles's inability to accept orders and his frequent habit of acting on his own initiative without consulting the Secretary of State. Mr. Hull had authorized Mr. Welles to consult with the President provided that Mr. Hull was informed. This Mr. Welles did not do and at times attempted to obtain decisions from the President. Mr. Welles also interviewed foreign Ambassadors without keeping the Secretary informed. Mr. Hull further accused Mr. Welles of carrying on a personal correspondence with our diplomats and even with officials of other governments which should have gone through regular State Department channels. Early in 1942 Mr. Welles made two speeches on foreign affairs without the consultation or approval of the President or the Secretary. On June 20, 1942, Mr. Hull told Mr. Welles in no uncertain terms that this practice could not continue. He also spoke to him of his visits to the President without keeping the Secretary informed and said that there could not be two heads in the State Department. For a time the air was cleared and Mr. Welles conformed to Mr. Hull's orders, although he did continue to go to the President. Mr. Hull also complained of Mr. Welles's inability to work in a team, his policy disagreements, and his failure to supervise the administration of the State Department, a duty of the Under Secretary.

In the summer of 1943, Mr. Roosevelt agreed with Secretary

Hull that Mr. Welles must go, and the President offered to send him to South America as a roving Ambassador or on a special mission to Russia. This would have softened the blow of his dismissal. Mr. Welles called on Mr. Hull, told him there was no purpose to such a trip, shook hands, and left. Mr. Hull's comment is: "I have not talked with him since." [4]

President Roosevelt announced Mr. Welles's resignation as Under Secretary of State on September 25, 1943. The *New York Times* said: "The announcement of Mr. Welles' resignation came after weeks of reports, unconfirmed officially, that he had left the State Department, with the alleged reason given that he could not get along with Secretary Hull. The facts of this situation remained obscure tonight, so far as the White House statement was concerned. The President did not make public Mr. Welles' letter of resignation, nor the text of the acceptance as is generally done."

Actually, Welles had presented his letter of resignation to the President on August 16 and there is an undated memorandum in the President's handwriting: "Sumner — to break with Pearson and Allen — and let the country know. Steve [Early] to tell Pearson and Allen they are doing a disservice to nation. 3 lies in a quick row. A. Welles to me on boat the doom of Spain. B. The bills on my desk. C. The Watson-Speaker story." In a letter accompanying his resignation Welles said: "But I am positive that for me to retain temporarily my present position, and undertake the kind of Foreign Mission you suggested [a conference in Moscow], would only make possible a continuation of the existing situation, which inevitably creates embarrassment for you, and confusion with regard to your conduct of Foreign Relations at a very critical moment." On September 21 Welles asked the President, on account of his relations with Secretary Hull, to announce the acceptance of his resignation, which was done on the twenty-fifth. The President continued his personal friendship with Welles and in October wrote to him: "I do hope that when you get back to Washington you will come in to see me. There are many things I want to talk over with you." [5]

In June 1941, Bullitt suffered a loss which must have had an effect on his relations with the President. "Missy" LeHand, the

President's private secretary for over twenty years, had a stroke
and was no longer able to work. She and Bullitt had been in constant communication since 1932 and she was able to keep him
very accurately informed on the President's feelings about certain
matters and about what Bullitt was reporting.

Bullitt was now left with no close contact with the President
when he was not in Washington, and as Miss LeHand had a real
influence on the President's thoughts and his likes and dislikes,
one more cord in the intimacy with Roosevelt was cut.

26

Attack on Russia

MAY 1941—NOVEMBER 1941

London Bombed
Hitler Advances on Russia
United States Troops in Iceland
Roosevelt Meets Churchill in Newfoundland
Reynaud Writes from Prison

THE GERMAN BLITZ on England began in August 1940 and reached great intensity during the period from September to November when over two hundred bombers attacked London every night. The raids reached a climax with the attack on London on December 29.

In the spring of 1941 the Germans renewed their attacks. In March they bombed the ports, concentrating on Portsmouth — one of the main bases of the British fleet — Manchester, Liverpool, the Clyde shipbuilding works, and also, again, London. April brought the heaviest bombardment with huge attacks on Coventry, London, and the port of Plymouth.

The horror of these onslaughts made a profound impression on Bullitt and he again tried to persuade the President to move toward a positive step of help to Great Britain.

Bullitt constantly prodded the President to take action, but rarely succeeded in his efforts. Early in June, Bullitt told Harold Ickes that he had lunched with the President and urged him to declare war in order to protect America by coming to England's aid before the attacks on England precluded any effective action. The President told him he was waiting for an incident and Bullitt told him he might wait too long and that Germany would not provide an incident. The President believed in his sense of timing and also told Bullitt that, although he might carry the Senate, he was doubtful about the House. Ickes remarked: "The plain fact is that the President can always find some good reason for not moving, while uttering threats from time to time." [1]

The Carlton Hotel
Washington, D.C.
May 21, 1941

Dear Mr. President:

I have just returned from a three weeks trip to Kentucky, Tennessee, Massachusetts, New York, New Jersey and Pennsylvania in the course of which I have talked with men of all sorts and conditions.

The remark that I heard most often from high and low was "I don't know what we ought to do. It's too complicated. The President knows." There is a desire to know the facts — *from you* — and an intense desire to know what you think ought to be done, and a readiness to follow you wherever you may lead. You could, I think, even reverse your entire policy and be followed by a vast majority. In other words, your personal prestige has never been higher and you have only to lead. The moment seems to be ripe for bold action — and it is 11:59.

I have not asked to see you because I have heard that you are still in need of rest; but of course await your pleasure.

Good luck.

Yours affectionately,
Bill

In spite of the unpleasant discussion about Sumner Welles the President apparently, at that time, did not hold it against Bullitt and sent him the following invitation:

TELEGRAM
Official Business — Government Rates

June 3, 1941

Hon. William C. Bullitt
Penllyn, Pennsylvania

The President hopes you can lunch with him Executive Offices Thursday June fifth one P.M. Please confirm. Regards.

Edwin M. Watson
Secretary to the President

Hitler was now about to commit the major error which was to cost him his life and destroy Germany. On December 18, 1940, he had decided to invade Russia on May 15, 1941, even though in August 1939 his Foreign Minister Ribbentrop had flown to Moscow to sign a nonaggression pact with the Soviet. In early April the British were convinced that the Germans were planning an attack on Russia and on the nineteenth of the month a message was delivered to Stalin to this effect. The American Government also advised the Soviet of an imminent attack.

The American commercial attaché in Berlin, Sam E. Woods, had an entrée to German secret planning through a friend who was highly placed in German affairs and was privy to German plotting. As early as August 1940 Woods was informed of Hitler's secret plans for the invasion of Russia. There was a typical spy-story background. Woods would reserve two seats at a moving picture house and send one to his informer, who would pass the information to him in the darkened theater. The Germans' plans were to invade Russia in the spring of 1941. After carefully checking the accuracy of this information, Mr. Hull instructed Sumner Welles to give it to the Russian Ambassador, Oumansky, who presumably forwarded it to his government in March. Mr. Welles, in fact, twice warned the Soviet Ambassador, to no avail.

At this time German planes were flying over Soviet territory and the Russians issued a warning note. The reason for the Russian obtuseness is unknown, but with over one hundred German divisions massed on their frontier, they were still continuing to ask on June 21, through Foreign Office channels, what had brought about this situation. They were almost totally unprepared for the blow which struck on June 22. Hundreds of Russian planes were destroyed on the ground, and within a month the German armies had thrust forward three hundred miles into Russian territory.

For once the Russian account corresponds with the truth. It said: "One of the causes of the Soviet failure at the beginning of the war was the incorrect estimation of the pre-war situation made by J. V. Stalin who then stood at the head of the government. Stalin over-estimated the significance of the Soviet-German

Non-Aggression Pact and did not believe the information received [from England and America] concerning Germany's preparation for an invasion of the U.S.S.R. This was one of the reasons for the Soviet troops in the western parts of the country being taken by surprise." [2]

Meadow Farm
Penllyn, Pennsylvania
July 1, 1941

Personal

Dear Mr. President:

The line you took when Germany attacked the Soviet Union — that of giving support to anyone (even a criminal) fighting Hitler — was, of course, sound. But the emotions aroused by the spectacle of Nazis fighting Bolsheviks were so conflicting that most people needed a lot more guidance than they got. Public opinion is now befuddled. The feeling has begun to spread that we no longer need to hurry our war preparations and that the communists have become the friends of democracy.

I think you should take the first opportunity — perhaps your next press conference — to point out:

1. That the German attack on the Soviet Union makes it essential for us to produce with greater speed than ever, since Germany may soon have all the resources of the Soviet Union at her disposal and we must develop our war production faster than Germany can develop war production in Soviet territory.

2. That Communists in the United States are just as dangerous enemies as ever, and should not be allowed to crawl into our productive mechanism in order later to wreck it when they get new orders from somewhere abroad.

I find myself thinking constantly also, as you doubtless are, about the stream of German supplies going unhampered across the Mediterranean to Libya. I see nothing to stop that except British warships — released from the North Atlantic by our ships taking their place.

Incidentally, it seems to me that since the Free French forces are fighting Hitler and since we've said we'll help forces fighting Hitler, you ought to announce openly that we will supply the Free French in Equatorial Africa. It is in our interest to go on trying to stiffen

Pétain, energize Weygand and support de Gaulle. And it is not beyond the wit of man to do all three without breaking relations with Vichy.

Good luck.

Yours affectionately,

Bill

On July 7, 1941, President Roosevelt informed Congress that, in order to prevent any attack on the United States by Germany, the United States Navy had landed in Iceland and American troops had also been sent to Trinidad and British Guiana.

In the first days of August, 1941, President Roosevelt ostensibly went for a short holiday on the Presidential yacht. No announcement was made as to the length of the cruise, but as day followed day without any knowledge as to the whereabouts of the President, speculation became rife. He transferred at sea to the cruiser *Augusta,* leaving the yacht to continue the cruise as a blind. (My wife and family were sailing off the coast of Maine at the time and saw the yacht draw alongside the *Augusta* and the President change ships. They were warned off by boats from the *Augusta,* but my wife telephoned me that evening to tell me that the disappearance of the President was no longer a mystery.)

Churchill, on the new British battleship, the *Prince of Wales,* shortly to have a tragic end with the loss of half of its crew, arrived at Placentia Bay, Newfoundland, on August 9. Churchill had brought with him the First Sea Lord, the Vice-chief for Air, and other government officials. In President Roosevelt's party were the chiefs of the armed forces, Sumner Welles from the State Department, and various government officials. The meeting lasted from August 9 until August 12. The famous Atlantic Charter, largely drafted by Churchill, was the result of this conference and set forth the aims and ideals of Britain and the United States. The working out of Lend-Lease was further developed. A future postwar organization for the preservation of peace was also discussed. All the global phases of the war were explored, including the Far East, although the United States was not to be involved for another four months.

*

Although both Reynaud and Daladier were now in prison they managed to continue to communicate with Bullitt until their release by the advancing American forces.

Among the documents from Reynaud is one dated August 17, 1941; Reynaud smuggled out of prison the text of a book of his tenure of office. This text was delivered to Bullitt with an accompanying letter: "My dear friend, A true horn of plenty was thrown into the room of the prisoner: hams, chocolate, American cigarettes, altogether a pile of precious things which had disappeared from our life. Thank you for my neighbor Mandel and for myself. I was very touched to feel, by this gift, your faithful thought. The food is still acceptable here, although they serve too often beet leaves which the pigs themselves look upon without enthusiasm. I have the best room of the 'château' 1880 without running water, three windows with a passable view . . . My morale is as hard as the iron bars of my windows. One year of tête-à-tête with one's self is an admirable treatment if it is not a catastrophe. The guards are Alsatians, at heart with us . . .

"The attacks of the Paris newspapers (therefore the Germans) against 'Reynaud and Mandel' are much stronger for some time. It is we who interest them, they have told Daladier's lawyer. Very flattering. Déat demands my inculpation. It would be the honor of my lifetime to be condemned for the crime of not surrendering. You can guess the cold contempt of Mandel. We are still in the regime of the 'lettres de cachet' as in the time of Louis XV, with less taste. Condemned or not condemned I will be in prison until you again become ambassador at Paris. Therefore, hurry up.

"I send you, *confidentially,* under separate cover, the fruit of the work of the prisoner. It has to do with very freely written notes. Every day I add a few lines. You will find, I believe, things which will interest you. You can communicate it confidentially to your great leader, whom history will admire for his great psychological work and the strength of his decision in order that his people remain worthy of their great traditions . . .

"The President of the Republic had a lively repugnance in conferring power on Pétain. Also, before the coalition formed against my policy of resistance, by the Marshal [Pétain], the heads of the Army and the majority of the Ministers, wanted me to bow before the majority and demand the armistice. I refused. I believed, also, that the conditions of the armistice would be unacceptable (were they not?). In that case it was understood that I would return to power. I am told that you have been told a great deal of nonsense about that. I am the only one to know what went on because many of the members of my entourage had undergone nervous collapse due to seeing the exodus on the roads. I acted alone. Some will learn, with astonishment that I maneuvered on June 16, to have withdrawn by the British Government the authorization they gave us that morning to ask for an armistice in order to preserve against my adversaries the argument 'the word of France.'

"If I undergo the fate of Dormoy [assassinated by the Vichy police] my daughter will get in touch with you, after the war, to let you know the facts, because I count very much even beyond the tomb, on the opinion of your great people.

"I also send you two arguments which appear in my 'book of complaints' and which will give you the temperature of my relations with Vichy. As you will see, I did not collaborate. In this regard I wish to tell you that if anyone asks in Washington to intervene for me, I will disavow it. I do not want to ask anything, neither directly nor indirectly from the men of Vichy. Someday I will tell you all that they have tried against 'the man of the resistance.'

"Mandel sends you his best regards. I join in the expression of my faithful friendship."

In another letter of ten pages Reynaud replies with vigor to lies which were being published about him. In a memorandum he tells of his being accused while he was in an inaccessible prison in the Pyrenees, isolated by snow and seven hundred kilometers from the location of the trial at Riom, where all his documents were. It was not possible for him to study the charges nor to have any contact with his lawyers.

Both Daladier and Reynaud were liberated by the Allies in 1945 and both returned in 1946 to the National Assembly. Reynaud became Minister of Finance in 1948. He was extremely active and wrote copious memoirs about his part in the prewar government. He lived to be eighty-seven. Daladier was active politically until 1955 and then devoted himself to writing until his death.

Bullitt spoke to the Union League of Philadelphia at a large luncheon on October 23. The League is a Republican club founded in 1862 and its membership comprises many of the most important men in the area. It was unusual for a Democrat to address the club, and Bullitt was introduced by the President of the League with the words, "The Ambassador has come here to carry out the thought that many of your directors had in mind, that you ought to be advised of the situation." Bullitt began in a light vein by saying, "From time to time I have dared to hope that I might enter heaven, but I never dared hope that I might enter and speak in the Union League." He rapidly warmed to his theme of the danger to America and that war could come to its shores if England were defeated. In many ways the speech was a repetition of the Independence Hall address, but in this case it was also an appeal to many leaders of the Republican party to urge their representatives to strengthen America and give all-out aid to Great Britain.

27

Egypt and War with Japan

DECEMBER 1941—JANUARY 1942

Germans in Africa
Bullitt Goes to Cairo
At War with Japan
Reports from the Near East
Proposal to Invade Africa

IN FEBRUARY 1941, the first German troops appeared in North Africa to reinforce the Italian army in Tripolitania. Erwin Rommel was the German general in command of the Afrika Korps and very shortly made it clear to the Italians that he was not satisfied with only holding Tripolitania but would take the offensive. His daring leadership, his brilliant campaigns, and his notable success astonished the world, including his own countrymen. It won for him an accolade by Churchill in the House of Commons: "We have a very daring and skillful opponent against us, and may I say across the havoc of war, a great general." [1]

Rommel advanced rapidly across the desert and by the fall of 1941 had gone seventy miles beyond Tobruk, where a British garrison of 33,000 was to hold out for another eight months, finally surrendering in June 1942.

Roosevelt now wanted a clear picture of the situation in North Africa and the Middle East and sent Bullitt to Cairo to report to him. During Bullitt's flight to Egypt the Japanese attack on Pearl Harbor took place, and the telegrams that follow should be read with that in mind. The United States was now at war and Britain's ally. American forces, such as they were, could be freely used and there was no longer any question of all-out aid, or neutrality.

The great battle of Alamein did not take place until a year later on the night of October 23, 1942, and by November 4 victory had been assured. On that day Churchill wired General Alexander: "If wholesale captures of the enemy and a general retreat are apparent, I propose to ring the bells all over Britain for the first time this war." [2] The Sherman tanks and self-propelled guns given by America were all used in the battle, which resulted in the capture of thirty thousand Axis prisoners, the destruction of over two hundred German tanks, and the clearing of the skies of the German Air Force. It was now Rommel's turn to praise the British: "The British artillery demonstrated once again its well-known excellence. Especially noteworthy was its great mobility and speed of reaction to the requirements of the assault troops." [3] It was the first British victory of the war.

MEMORANDUM

Washington, D.C.
November 22, 1941

The President invited me to lunch with him on Tuesday, November 18. He said that the situation in Africa, the Near East, and the Middle East was worrying him . . . He needed a first-hand report on the whole area from French Equatorial Africa through to Iran. Indeed, he needed an equally comprehensive report on the situation in Singapore and the Dutch East Indies. He wanted the sort of report that would make him feel as though he had been there himself. He proposed that I should go as his personal representative with the rank of Ambassador to West Africa, Egypt, Libya, Palestine, Iraq, and Iran, and return by way of Karachi, India, Singapore, and the Dutch Indies. He stated that he wished this trip to be made for him and for him alone. He proposed that any telegrams I might wish to send should be sent by Naval Radio and stated that he would keep Cordell Hull informed but would not communicate my messages to anyone else in order that leaks via Drew Pearson might be prevented.

He stated flatly, and without suggestion from me, that he knew that Mr. Welles would do everything possible to knife me in the back and said that he intended to prevent any such behavior if I would undertake the trip. He went on to say that on my return from this trip he would wish me to attempt to organize in Washing-

ton with him appropriate action to carry out any of my recommendations with which he might agree.

After a discussion of this situation, which lasted an hour, I told
the President that I would consider making the trip immediately. It
was understood that if I should take the trip I should be master
completely of my own movements and should decide for myself how
long it might be desirable to remain in one place and by what route
I should return to the United States.

I informed the Secretary of State, with whom the President had
previously discussed this matter, of what the President had said to
me and suggested to the Secretary of State that, since I had absolute
confidence in Mr. Dunn and since he had also, I should arrange all
details through Mr. Dunn. The Secretary of State expressed his approval.

William C. Bullitt

THE WHITE HOUSE
WASHINGTON

November 22, 1941

My dear Mr. Bullitt:

Reposing special faith and confidence in you, I am asking you to
proceed at your earliest convenience to the Near Eastern area, there
to act as my personal representative with the rank of Ambassador.

I desire you to proceed by way of Africa and to use your own
judgment with regard to the length of your stay and the points you
visit. I further desire that you proceed from that area to India,
Burma, the Straits Settlements, and the Dutch East Indies, returning
to the United States by way of the Pacific.

If you should have urgent information to communicate to me en
route I wish you to use the Naval Radio for this purpose.

If, after making a study of the situation in the Near East, you
should consider it advisable to return to Washington by way of the
Atlantic, rather than the Pacific, you should act in accordance with
your own best judgment.

I desire you to make all your reports and recommendations personally to me.

Very sincerely yours,
Franklin D. Roosevelt

The Honorable William C. Bullitt
Washington, D.C.

November 25, 1941

American Embassy
London (England)
Secret and Personal from the President for the Former Naval Person. *

In view of growing importance of operations Middle East and Libya, I am sending my old friend Bill Bullitt as my personal representative to visit that area, to report to me and to be of what assistance he can to your supply and similar problems. He leaves by Clipper the southern route about December first.

I would be grateful if you personally would ask your civilian and military authorities out there to put at Bullitt's disposal such information as you and they think proper. If there is any person in the area whose opinions you would wish Bullitt to seek, or if there is any special problem you think Bullitt should devote special attention to, please let me know.

I am very happy at the progress of the Libyan advance. Its repercussions over here are excellent.

As you know, the coal strike is off through agreement on arbitration and I hope to mediate the proposed railroad strike in the next week.

Roosevelt

Carrying out President Roosevelt's request, "the Former Naval Person," as Roosevelt always addressed Churchill, instructed Captain Oliver Lyttelton (later Lord Chandos), who was at that time Minister of State representing the War Cabinet in the Middle East, to give Bullitt every possible bit of assistance and information. Lyttelton was more than cooperative and a friendship developed between the two men which lasted throughout their lives.

In spite of Bullitt's feeling about the British, the ensuing messages will show his admiration for them. In a letter to the President he closes with the statement: "I wish to add only that the chief asset of the British in this area is their quality of being without fear."

Much has been written about the warning that the United States had of the possibility of immediate war with Japan in December 1941. The following letter, only five days before the at-

*Churchill.

tack on Pearl Harbor, suggests that the President had no indication of any imminent danger in the Far East. The Generalissimo referred to was Chiang Kai-shek, who at that time was the Nationalist leader of the Mainland of China.

THE WHITE HOUSE
WASHINGTON

Dec. 2, 1941

Dear Bill:

I hope if you come back via the Far East you will see the Generalissimo if possible.

FDR

Hon. William C. Bullitt
[A handwritten note.]

3030 Cambridge Place N.W.
Washington, D.C.
5 December 1941

Dear Mr. President:

Two thoughts on departure.

1. Don't let Churchill get you into any more specific engagements than those in the Atlantic Charter. Try to keep him from engaging himself vis-à-vis Russia. The Treaties — if made — will be as difficult for you to handle as the secret Treaties were for Wilson.

2. If you establish a legation in Afghanistan — send someone who speaks Russian. Loy Henderson is the best man — unless you have to keep him in the Dept. of State.

Merry Xmas and Happy New Year.

Bill

Bullitt heard of the Japanese attack on December 7, on his way to Egypt. His plane had stopped at Trinidad and he wrote:

"I drove to the residence of the British Governor, Sir Hubert Young. As I entered the residence I was welcomed by the sounds of someone banging on the piano as hard as he could and shouting some kind of a song. It was the Governor who rushed forward with his hands outstretched and said, 'The Japs have attacked Pearl Harbor.' 'Allies at last,' he said and continued to burst with enthusiasm and happiness. We talked and walked in the garden under the huge trees. At the foot of the garden a band was playing hymns and patriotic airs. The Governor summoned his aide-de-camp and said most emphatically, 'I have been forbidden until this moment to have played together my national anthem and your national anthem and now I can as we are allies!' Then he gave orders to his aide-de-camp to have played 'The Star Spangled Banner' and 'God Save the King.' We stood at attention while the band played 'The Star Spangled Banner,' filled with emotion. Then the band played 'Roll Out the Barrel.' The Governor grew purple and exploded . . ." [4]

Travel in 1941 was more complicated than today's flights. Bullitt spent the nights at Miami, Trinidad, Belém, and on the plane, where he slept on the floor on the way to Khartoum and Cairo. Here he was met at the airport by Oliver Lyttelton, Air Marshal Tedder, and General Auchinleck, the Commander in Chief in the Middle East.

The British declared war on Japan on December 8. The Japanese action had taken Hitler completely by surprise but on December 8 he ordered the German Navy to attack American ships and three days later Germany declared war on the United States. The Japanese followed up their attack on Pearl Harbor by immediately seeking the two great new battleships of the British. The *Prince of Wales* and the *Repulse* had arrived at Singapore on December 2 and on December 8 left that port to oppose the Japanese attack on Malaya. By the afternoon of December 10 these magnificent fighting craft lay at the bottom of the sea, sunk by airplane action. The Commander in Chief, Admiral Phillips, went down with his ship. The Japanese aircraft which had carried out the operation had come from Saigon, four hundred miles away, a hitherto unknown range for an attack by such airplanes. Churchill noted: "The efficiency of the Japanese in air warfare was at this time greatly underestimated both by ourselves and by the Americans." [5]

With the destruction of the American fleet at Pearl Harbor and the loss of these two ships, there was nothing to oppose the Japanese in the Pacific or Indian oceans. The elimination of the German and Italian forces in North Africa became vital. William L. Langer, in *Our Vichy Gamble*, says: "The idea of an American operation against North Africa was one dear to President Roosevelt from an early date. The entire region was of obvious and vital interest to the United States and offered the possibility of establishing a base for operations on the continent of Europe. In December, 1941, the President had sent Bullitt to North Africa and the Near East as Ambassador-at-Large, and Bullitt had sent back from Cairo a plan for invasion that had been worked out by General Catroux. Since Churchill was visiting in Washington at Christmas, 1941, the two statesmen canvassed the possibility of action in North Africa in some detail and decided to go on with the scheme." [6]

Bullitt spent Christmas in Jerusalem and obtained on-the-spot briefing on the situation in that area. He returned to the United States late in January.

HOTCHKISS CAIRO
21 DECEMBER 1941
1429/21
192300 CR 0177

FOLLOWING STRICTLY CONFIDENTIAL FOR THE PRESIDENT FROM BULLITT — THE BRITISH ARE HANDLING THE SITUATION HERE BETTER THAN WAS INDICATED BY THE REPORTS RECEIVED IN WASHINGTON BEFORE MY DEPARTURE. I BELIEVE THAT LYTTELTON, AUCHINLECK AND THE REST ARE DOING AS GOOD A JOB AS CAN BE EXPECTED WITH THE INADEQUATE MEANS AT THEIR DISPOSAL AGAINST A DETERMINED ENEMY LED BY A SOLDIER OF GENIUS. ROMMEL HAS AGAIN ESCAPED AN EXCELLENT TRAP SET FOR HIM BUT THERE ARE AT THIS MOMENT NOT MORE THAN 30 GERMAN TANKS IN CONDITION TO FIGHT. IN ADDITION ROMMEL HAS APPROXIMATELY 30 ITALIAN TANKS AND A NUMBER OF ARMORED VEHICLES AND APPROXIMATELY 60,000 INFANTRY. ROMMEL'S FORCES ARE ALL ON THIS SIDE OF BENGHAZI EXCEPT ONE ITALIAN DIVISION IN TRIPOLI WHICH IS REPORTED TO BE LOW IN HEALTH AND MORALE. IF THE BRITISH CAN GET TO BENGHAZI, AS THEY EXPECT THEY HOPE TO BE ABLE TO PUSH ON TO TRIPOLI AND THE TUNISIAN FRONTIER, BUT IT IS 1450 MILES BY THE ONLY ROAD FROM THE BRITISH BASE IN CAIRO TO THE FRONTIER OF TUNISIA. 27 DIFFERENT LANGUAGES AND DIALECTS ARE USED BY THE SOLDIERS OF AUCHINLECK'S ARMY AND A BRIGADE OF FREE FRENCH FROM SYRIA IS ABOUT TO BE ADDED . . . CONTINUED

HOTCHKISS, CAIRO
DEC. 21, 1941
192300 (CONTINUED)

STRICTLY CONFIDENTIAL FOR THE PRESIDENT FROM BULLITT — AS YOU
ARE AWARE, BUT FEW PERSONS IN WASHINGTON REALIZE, THE FIGHTING
IN THIS AREA IS BEING CARRIED ON BY COMPARATIVELY TINY FIGHTING
FORCES. THEREFORE A SLIGHT INCREASE OR DIMINUTION IN THE FORCE
HERE MAKES THE DIFFERENCE BETWEEN DEFEAT AND VICTORY. IN VIEW
OF THE VITAL IMPORTANCE OF NORTH AFRICA FOR AN ULTIMATE AT-
TACK ON ITALY AND GERMANY AND IN VIEW OF THE IMPORTANCE OF
HAVING A BRITISH ARMY ON THE EASTERN BORDER OF TUNISIA RATHER
THAN A GERMAN ARMY, AND IN VIEW OF THE FACT THAT THE ENEMY
IS NOW ON THE RUN I BELIEVE THAT (1) IT WOULD BE FOLLY TO
WITHDRAW FORCES OF ANY KIND FROM THIS AREA NOW. (2) THAT THE
FORCES NOW HERE SHOULD BE STRENGTHENED IN ANY WAY THAT WILL
NOT REDUCE FORCES WHICH ARE VITALLY NEEDED AT OTHER POINTS. IT
IS ESSENTIAL THAT THE ESTABLISHED PROGRAM FOR DELIVERIES HERE OF
AIRCRAFT, AIRCRAFT EQUIPMENT, .30 AND .50 AMMUNITION, 250-LB
BOMBS AND 500-LB BOMBS AND MOTOR TRANSPORT SHOULD BE
MAINTAINED AND THAT THERE SHOULD BE NO DIVERSION TO OTHER
AREAS. IT IS VITAL THAT THE PROJECTS WHICH WERE STARTED BY GEN-
ERAL BRETT SHOULD BE CARRIED THROUGH. IN VIEW OF SERIOUS GERMAN
ATTEMPTS TO REINFORCE THIS THEATRE OF WAR NOTABLY BY THE
TRANSFER OF THE ENTIRE 2ND GERMAN AIR CORPS FROM THE MOSCOW
FRONT TO ITALY AND FLIGHTS OF PLANES OF THIS AIR CORPS TO LIBYA,
IT IS MY BELIEF THAT THE SUCCESS OF THE BRITISH PLANS TO PUSH ON
TO THE FRONTIER OF TUNISIA DEPENDS ON THE PROMPT IMPROVEMENT
OF BRITISH TRANSPORT AND COMMUNICATIONS. THE BRITISH ARE SHOCK-
INGLY SHORT OF COMPETENT TRUCK DRIVERS. THEIR SYSTEM OF TELE-
GRAPH AND TELEPHONE COMMUNICATION HAS BEEN STRETCHED TO THE
BREAKING POINT. AS AN EXAMPLE, WHEN I ATTENDED WITH LYTTELTON
AND AUCHINLECK A MEETING OF ALL THE STAFFS YESTERDAY FOR THE
EXCHANGE OF INFO, NO NEWS HAD COME FOR 24 HOURS FROM THE
FIGHTING FRONT. LYTTELTON, AUCHINLECK, AND AIR MARSHAL TEDDER
HAVE ALL PROPOSED TO ME IN WRITING THAT WE SHOULD TAKE OVER
WITH OUR OWN ARMY UNITS UNDER COMMANDS OF GEN. MAXWELL
CERTAIN PORTION OF THE TRANSPORTATION BURDEN AS WELL AS THE
INSTALLATION, MAINTENANCE, AND OPERATION OF A SYSTEM OF TELE-
PHONE AND TELEGRAPH COMMUNICATIONS. I AM SENDING IN AMERICAN
EQUIVALENTS THE WRITTEN REQUESTS PRESENTED TO ME BY THE BRIT.

YESTERDAY BY A SEPARATE MESSAGE THROUGH GEN. MAXWELL TO THE WAR DEPT. I HOPE THAT YOU WILL BE ABLE TO SEND AT LEAST THE TRUCK DRIVERS IMMEDIATELY. COOPERATION BETWEEN THE BRITISH AND GEN. MAXWELL IS EXCELLENT AND HE CONCURS IN MY OPINION THAT THE BRITISH ARE DOING AS GOOD A JOB AS THE INADEQUATE MEANS AND THE IMMENSE TERRAIN WILL PERMIT. PLEASE SHOW THIS MESSAGE TO MARSHALL, STIMSON, AND HOPKINS

(END)

CAIRO

23 DEC 1941
PART ONE 202300 CR 0677

FOLLOWING FOR THE PRESIDENT FROM BULLITT, STRICTLY CONFIDENTIAL — THE BRITISH BOTH ON THE WEST COAST OF AFRICA WHERE I CONFERRED WITH GENERAL GIFFARD AND HIS STAFF AND IN CAIRO BELIEVE THAT THEY HAVE ABSOLUTE INFORMATION WITH REGARD TO THE FOLLOWING POINTS. (1) THERE ARE ONLY TWO GERMAN DIVISIONS ON THE SPANISH FRONTIER OF THE PYRENEES. (2) ALL BRITISH INFORMATION INDICATES THAT THERE ARE NO GERMAN AIRCRAFT IN EITHER MOROCCO, ALGIERS, TUNIS, OR THE DAKAR REGION. MOREOVER THERE ARE NO GERMAN SUBMARINES BASED AT DAKAR OR ON THE PORTUGUESE POSSESSIONS ON THE WEST COAST OF AFRICA. GENERAL GIFFARD STATED THAT HE HAD A CAREFUL INVESTIGATION MADE OF THE ENTIRE COAST AND ES [enemy ships?] OPERATING IN THE SOUTH ATLANTIC ARE REFUELED BY SUPPLY SHIPS AND NOT FROM SHORE BASES. (3) THE BRITISH HERE BELIEVE THAT THE WEATHER AND THE CONCENTRATION OF TURKISH TROOPS IN THRACE WILL CAUSE THE GERMANS TO PUT OFF ANY POSSIBLE ATTACK AGAINST TURKEY UNTIL THE EARLY SPRING

(PART TWO 202300 CR 0678) MY 202300 FOR THE PRESIDENT FROM BULLITT CONTINUES — THE BRITISH AIR MARSHAL IN CAIRO TEDDER DESIRED ME TO CALL TO YOUR ATTENTION THAT THE GERMAN FAILURE TO GET THROUGH TO THE OIL WELLS OF THE CAUCASUS HAS MADE THE OIL WELLS OF THE PLOESTI REGION IN RUMANIA VITAL TO GERMANY. HE BELIEVES THAT THREE SQUADRONS OF LIBERATORS BASED IN CAIRO COULD DESTROY THIS OIL FIELD IN AN ATTACK TO BE SUSTAINED OVER A PERIOD OF TWO MONTHS. I TOLD THE AIR MARSHAL AND GENERAL AUCHINLECK THAT WE WERE EXTREMELY SHORT OF LIBERATORS AND THAT I FELT ALMOST CERTAIN THAT WE SHOULD HAVE NONE TO SPARE FOR THIS PURPOSE. HE WAS NEVERTHELESS MOST INSISTENT THAT I SHOULD PRESENT THIS POSSIBILITY TO YOU AS THE VITAL LINK IN THE WHOLE STRATEGIC PICTURE.

(PART THREE 202330 CR 0676) MY 202315 FOR THE PRESIDENT FROM
BULLITT CONTINUES — THE BRITISH AIR FORCE OPERATING IN LIBYA IS
STILL STRONGER THAN THE GERMAN. THIS IS DUE TO SHORTAGE ON THE
GERMAN SIDE OF AVIATION GASOLINE AND MAINTENANCE FACILITIES.
THE GERMANS SAID ITALIANS ARE MAKING MOST DETERMINED EFFORTS
TO GET THROUGH GASOLINE AND OIL AND TANKS AS WELL AS AIRPLANES
TO LIBYA. IF THEY SHOULD SUCCEED IN DELIVERING A FEW LARGE CAR-
GOES THE ENTIRE PICTURE IN THIS AREA WOULD CHANGE AT ONCE.
SPEED IS THEREFORE ESSENTIAL. LYTTELTON HAS INFORMED ME THAT
AUCHINLECK IS TO BE GIVEN COMMAND NOT ONLY OVER NORTH AFRICA,
PALESTINE, AND SYRIA BUT ALSO OVER IRAQ AND IRAN. WAVELL IS TO
COMMAND IN INDIA AND BURMA. GENERAL WHEELER'S MISSION IN IRAQ
AND IRAN WILL THEREFORE IN THE NEAR FUTURE BE OPERATING IN AN
AREA COMMANDED NOT FROM DELHI BUT FROM CAIRO. BULLITT

The air battles over Ploesti were to prove the supreme daring
and courage of the United States Air Force. Shortly after the preceding telegram, plans were made to bomb this reservoir of Nazi
aviation fuel. The Ploesti refineries were situated thirty-five
miles from Bucharest in Rumania and refined about one third of
Germany's output of aviation gas and tank fuel. They were also
supplying one half of Rommel's need for oil. In May of 1942
twenty-three Consolidated Liberator (B-24) bombers left Florida
to fly to Africa. Lacking the range of present-day planes, they
went by way of Brazil to West Africa. They landed on a civilian
air base at Accra, the navigators having no directional aids and
taking their course from National Geographic Society maps. From
here they took off for the Nile, which they managed to reach
without serious mishap.

On June 11 the first American bombers flew on a mission of attack in Europe. It was an extraordinary flight. They could not
fly in formation at night so each pilot and navigator was on his
own. The distance was 2600 miles round trip, an impossible
task for these heavily loaded planes. They had no fighter escort
and Ploesti was the most heavily defended target in the Reich.
They were still using National Geographic maps and neither the
pilots or their crews had any previous experience or even training
in a bombing mission at night. Permission to land in Russia did
not arrive until after the planes left Egypt.

Thirteen planes took off, each with a ton of bombs, and twelve of them reached the Ploesti area. Not a plane or a man was lost but none of them returned to base, landing instead in Syria, Turkey, and Iraq. The raid caused no damage but it did prove that American aviation could achieve what seemed impossible.

Plans for destroying the Nazis' fuel continued to be of prime importance in the minds of the leaders, but it was not until August 1, 1943, that the next mission took off to Ploesti. This was on a far different scale and 178 planes were assigned to the task. They were equipped with all of the then existing aids to navigation and bombing. It was to be a daylight raid with the planes flying as close to the ground as possible in order to escape radar; some flew as low as fifty feet. One plane removed the top of a haystack. By now the Germans had over two hundred antiaircraft guns around the refineries and hundreds of machine guns. They even had an armored train which ran parallel to the attacking American planes, shelling them as they passed. There were countless German and Rumanian fighter planes to pick off the Liberators. The bravery of the crews was beyond words. With planes on fire they dived into blazing refineries, ran straight at the antiaircraft batteries machine-gunning the gunners, and turned for home on two or three engines. Of the approximately 1600 men who reached the target area, 446 were officially reported as killed or missing, and fifty-three Liberators were lost, including eight that landed in Turkey.

In spite of the amazing courage and recklessness of the American aviators, the Germans were able to restore production at Ploesti in a few weeks.

TELEGRAM

[Undated.]

Secret for the President

When I first reached Cairo, I suggested to Lyttelton that it ought not to be impossible to get the French Fleet in Alexandria (one battleship, three heavy cruisers, one light cruiser, four destroyers, and one submarine) to come over to our side. He stated that the difficulty was that the French officers and men were much too hostile both to the British and the Free French to be willing to join either the British Fleet or the forces of de Gaulle. I suggested that they might perhaps be ready to join the American Fleet. Lyttelton was struck by the idea and telegraphed to Churchill but as yet has had no reply.

On my return to Cairo yesterday I discussed this matter again with Lyttelton. He still believes it can be put through if you and Churchill want it put through.

I should like to explore the possibilities minutely, and suggest that you and I use as a private code word for this matter "John Paul Jones," and refer to it in future communications merely by the word John or Paul or Jones.

The French ships are in bad condition, moreover, I may find difficulties that would make any action undesirable.

It is obvious that if the French Fleet in Alexandria should join our cause, there would be danger of an eruption from Darlan and the Germans. I should be inclined to take a chance on that. How do you feel about it? Would you have any objection to the French Fleet here running up the American flag? I shall do nothing until I hear from you.

Bullitt

TELEGRAM

[Undated.]

Secret for the President

The British here are confident that they will be able to push into Tripoli so rapidly that it is not impossible that they may reach the frontier of Tunisia in about six weeks.

It is obvious that at such a distance from their Cairo base the British can not hope to take Tunisia by force of arms if opposed by the French forces there. Conversations which I have had with General Catroux and many other Frenchmen and with Lyttelton and others here who have the usual sources of information lead me to believe that it may not be impossible to establish such an organization of Frenchmen within Tunisia so that there would be sufficient cooperation to enable the British to seize the vital port of Bizerta. I believe that I should go into this question minutely and that we should do whatever is possible to bring about such a result if at the last moment you and Churchill wish to have the attempt made.

My conversations in Egypt, Syria, the Lebanon, and Palestine have convinced me that our country has a unique position in that we are not hated by the Vichy French or the Free French or the British; whereas they are not fond of each other. I think that the presence of even one American company with our flag on the Tunisian frontier even though it might be a transport company would be of real value. In this connection, I should like to have, if possible, a reply to my message to you of December 20 and my message through General Maxwell to the War Department on the same subject.

Bullitt

TELEGRAM

[Undated.]

Secret for the President

1. Lyttelton has asked me to join him in a statement of our views, which are in agreement, on the possibility of an invasion of Tunisia in case Auchinleck's forces should reach the Tunisian frontier. As his means of communication and codes are much more rapid than our own, he is telegraphing tonight to the British Ambassador for you and Churchill a draft which we have prepared together.

2. I consider it important that you should give the orders requested in my telegram of December 20th and in the telegram I sent on the same date through General Maxwell to the War Department. The problem of transport, and telegraph and telephone communications, in this area is becoming more serious with each step that the British advance.

Bullitt

Personal and Confidential

Cairo
December 27, 1941

Dear Mr. President:

The British are confident that they will be able to reach the border of Tunisia in about six weeks. In consequence, Lyttelton and all the British Generals, General Catroux and all the French officers talk to me constantly about the problem of getting Tunisia and all the rest of French North Africa to side with us at the moment of the arrival of the British forces on the Tunisian frontier.

It will be impossible for the British to maintain a force of more than one division of the Tunisian frontier due to the length of the

1450-mile line of communications from Cairo. It is, therefore, clear that Tunisia can not be taken by force in the face of resistance by the Vichy French troops now in Tunisia.

It might conceivably be possible to send a surprise expedition to land to the south of Bizerta and seize the base but I believe that Bizerta could not possibly be held against the French troops which would be brought rapidly from Tunisia, Algeria and Morocco.

The problem is, therefore, the old one of obtaining the voluntary cooperation of the French in North Africa.

The Frenchmen with whom I have talked agree that there will be no chance of getting the French in North Africa to come over to our side unless we can send an American Expeditionary Force to Casablanca. We should probably have to send one hundred thousand men — to be safe against German attack through Spanish Morocco — and we should have to take the Azores, Madeira and the Canaries and maintain a large naval force and air force for the protection of transport.

I assume that the fighting in the Far East has drained our resources to such an extent that, at this moment, it is impossible for us to consider any such expedition however desirable it might be. If I am mistaken in this assumption and if you can even consider sending such a force, I hope that you will cable me at once just two words: "Can consider."

I assume that any such reply from you is out of the question. If it is out of the question, we can do something to prepare the way for the moment when we shall be able to send such an expedition. Both the British and Free French feel certain that the Vichy French forces on the frontier of Tunisia will be most hostile to them and that it will be difficult for them to avoid frontier incidents if they should reach the Tunisian border. They are most anxious to have some sort of an American force on that border, as they say — truly, I think — that the French have only the friendliest feelings toward Americans.

Two suggestions have been made to me:

1. We have in Egypt now a large number of American planes. If we could send over sufficient American pilots and officers to establish a Lafayette Escadrille which would use these American planes, and operate against the Germans and Italians as they retreat toward the Tunisian frontier, a great effect would be produced on the French in Tunisia. This ought to be possible.

2. There are still a large number of American tanks ready for ac-

tion in Egypt. If we could send over sufficient personnel and officers to make up one tank unit, the presence of such a unit would
have a great effect on the French on the Tunisian frontier.

I have not the slightest doubt that the presence of American
troops on the Tunisian frontier would be most valuable especially
if a considerable number of men or officers should be able to speak
French. If our men could establish the first contacts on the frontier of Tunisia, it might be possible for them to oil the way for the
British and Free French — who should be able to send a vast
number of agents into North Africa.

All this is in the realm of hypothesis, and I am writing this letter merely because I am certain that I shall have — and you, perhaps, will have — dozens of appeals from the Free French and
British to do something immediately about North Africa.

I returned to Cairo yesterday from Syria, the Lebanon, and Palestine. In those countries all is quiet on the surface but seething
underneath. There is no sign whatsoever of reconciliation between
the Arabs and Jews in Palestine. The British Generals, officers and
colonial officials in those areas are not only anti–Vichy French but
also anti–de Gaulle French, and say perfectly frankly that they think
the French ought to be kicked out of the Near East permanently
and that Great Britain should take over the Near East permanently. I am not sure that they are wrong; but they are carrying
their hostility to the French to stupid lengths. Everyone for the
moment loves us. And I think that our policy in this area ought to
be the simple one of keeping the French and British pulling together until the end of the war.

The British have 84,000 Australians in Syria, the Lebanon and
Palestine. They spend their time running trucks off roads, getting
drunk and smashing up bars. Indeed, the British Command in
these regions under General "Jumbo" Wilson still seems to be imbued
with the idea that war is a polo game in which personal courage
and individual heroism will counterbalance lack of preparedness
and supplies. For example, the vital link from Haifa to Beirut
which the British have said they were going to get finished in six
months is being worked on at the moment by 150 native laborers
equipped with the most primitive tools!

The question of transport and communications in this area is
vital and I hope that before this letter reaches you, you will have
ordered to this area the transport units and signal units requested
in my telegram to you of December 20, and in the supplementary

telegram which I sent through General Maxwell to the War Department.

Christmas in Bethlehem was a beautiful experience.

Bless you.

Yours affectionately,
William C. Bullitt

TELEGRAM

Rush   [Undated.]
Secret for the President

I hope that you and Churchill in your planning are keeping in mind the vital need to retain Egypt as a secure base not only for operations in Libya, Tunisia, Palestine, the Lebanon, Syria and Turkey but also for transit of planes to India and the Far East.

As I have noted in previous messages the distances in this area are so immense and the forces engaged so small relatively that a comparatively slight increase in force on the German side might entirely change the picture.

For example, one large convoy from Italy to Tripoli with sufficient aviation gasoline to furnish the German Second Flying Corps, now waiting in Sicily and Italy, would enable that Corps to operate in Libya and take control of the air from the British. In view of the present condition of the British Naval forces based on Alexandria, of which Churchill has certainly informed you, the stopping of convoys to Tripoli will not be easy.

To draw forces away from this area or to fail to reinforce this area because of demands from the Far East might lead to a repetition of events in Libya when forces were withdrawn to go to Greece. The successes which the British have gained in Libya have been dearly bought and will lead to no decisive result unless Tripoli should be occupied.

Some days ago I was shown the telegram in which the British Command here stated its requirements. Churchill doubtless has already communicated this to you. I wish to add only that the chief asset of the British in this area is their quality of being without fear. I think they need in addition at this moment reinforcements in naval vessels, aircraft, tanks, and transport and signal units.

Bullitt

Telegram from Cairo, dated December 31st, 1941
Most Secret
Following from Mr. Bullitt and Minister of State [Lyttelton]

Please convey simultaneously to President Roosevelt and the Prime Minister personally.

1. This telegram represents the agreed views of Mr. Bullitt and myself on the subject of possible invasion of Tunisia if and when all Tripolitania should be occupied by His Majesty's Forces. We have had the advantage of a general discussion with Catroux, particularly upon the French officers in Tunisia, but we could not carry on the discussion very far for obvious reasons.

2. We assume the following premise applies today:

(A) That some resistance by the French in Tunisia is certain and that French blood would be shed.

(B) That the strain on shipping and Naval escorts would preclude the immediate supply of substantial forces in Tunisia from Alexandria and that, therefore, the bulk of any supplies for these forces must come through the Western Mediterranean.

(C) That it would be impossible to supply forces through the Western Mediterranean if the French in Algeria and Morocco should be engaged in hostilities against us. We must count on the probability that German Air reinforcements would cross to Algeria and Morocco and operate against our shipping from those bases. We must also count on the probability that the Vichy French fleet would operate against us.

3. The Commanders-in-Chief have not yet completed their study of the problem and the above premises may consequently be qualified, but we do not think they can be materially changed.

4. Catroux put the minimum force necessary to invade Tunisia from the South at six Divisions. We think this should be accepted with reserve but taking into account the possibility of large reinforcements being brought from Algeria and Morocco we consider the force must be substantial.

5. We consider that in view of 2 (C) above operation would not be sound unless simultaneously with the invasion of Tunisia United States Forces should seize Casablanca or possibly Agadir. Such an operation would seem to involve preliminary seizure or control of Canaries, the Azores and Madeira; we think invasion of Tunisia must not be considered in isolation from the problem or of reactions of all French North African Colonies. We believe there would be

French resistance to landing of American forces unless careful preparations should have been made within French North African Colonies. We think it may be possible to have American forces welcomed in French North African Colonies provided certain French leaders can be approached and informed that an American landing in force at either Casablanca or possibly Agadir is to be expected.

6. Above opinions are based on the present situation remaining unaltered. We believe the Germans may take action which would bring the majority of the French in North Africa over to our side if we should be in a position to give them effective and immediate aid.

7. We therefore recommend that if resources permit:

(A) British forces in Middle East which are already estimated to be considerably short of minimum required for defense of two fronts, should be reinforced.

(B) U.S.A. should immediately start preparations for Casablancan expedition.

(C) propaganda and subversive activities in all French North African Colonies should be immediately concerted between the United States and Great Britain.

8. With regard to 7 (A) considerable supply problems will be involved in employing forces in Tripolitania and if premise 7 (B) is correct we must look to supplies and reinforcements for Tunisia after its occupation being shipped through Western Mediterranean.

9. With regard to 7 (C) the nature of the propaganda is one of nice judgement and Bullitt and I propose to sketch tentative plan for submission to you.

10. We would emphasize that this is a preliminary telegram which is sent by us to reach you while the Prime Minister is still in Washington and that it is sent without full consultation between Commanders-in-Chief. It appears however to us that if resources are available in the near future the planning must start at once in order that we may either be ready to undertake invasion by force at a later date or reach the highest possible state of preparations to take advantage of any favorable opportunity produced by German action against France.

JAN 14 1942

FROM BULLITT
ACTION THE PRESIDENT

I HAVE STUDIED THE SITUATION IN IRAQ, IRAN, SYRIA, THE LEBANON, PALESTINE AND EGYPT. UNLESS YOU HAVE WORK FOR ME TO DO IN INDIA

OR CHINA OR SOME OTHER COUNTRY IN THIS AREA, I BELIEVE THAT I
SHOULD RETURN TO WASHINGTON AT ONCE TO REPORT TO YOU ON THE
PRESENT FACTS AND FUTURE PROSPECTS IN THIS AREA AS THE ENTIRE
WORLD SITUATION HAS CHANGED SINCE MY LEAVING. PLEASE REPLY AS
SOON AS POSSIBLE AS IT IS DIFFICULT TO MAKE TRAVEL ARRANGEMENTS.

28

The Middle East and Local Politics

FEBRUARY 1942—MARCH 1942

Pennsylvania Governorship
Plans for the Middle East

IN THE MIDST OF PLANNING global strategy and landings in Africa, Mr. Roosevelt never forgot the local political scene.

MEMORANDUM

Washington, D.C.
February 21, 1942

Dear Mr. President:

I don't know which Joe the Guff* may be playing for a sucker — yourself or myself — or the Democratic Party in Pennsylvania.

At any rate, he said to Dave Stern* that you had told him that you wanted me to run for the Governorship.

Then the story was broken in the worst possible way.

Then Joe announced that he intended to back Judge Ralph Smith and at the same time stated to the press that I would be one of four candidates in an open primary!

He has since been telling everybody that labor would be opposed to me "because I had no labor record," and using the names of Phil Murray and Tom Kennedy.* According to Dave Stern, who has had

* Joe the Guff was Joseph F. Guffey, United States Senator from Pennsylvania, and a power in Democratic politics. David Stern was publisher of the Philadelphia *Record* — a morning newspaper — and an ardent supporter of President Roosevelt. Phillip Murray and Thomas Kennedy were leaders of organized labor.

Charley Ervin canvass the labor leaders, they want me and say that I am the only person who stands a chance of winning.

Dave Stern says that as things stand we are in for a certain defeat. He is very eager to see you for a few minutes, and if you have a moment after your speech, I think you ought to see him at the *House*, not the office.

Personally, all this gives me no pain at all, because as I said to you, I would a thousand times rather work with you on the job of defeating Hitler and the Japanese rather than take on the relatively minor problems of Pennsylvania.

I am sending you this memorandum therefore merely to let you know that the situation is lousy, so that if you want to do anything about it you can.

Bill

OFFICE OF THE ATTORNEY GENERAL
WASHINGTON, D.C.

Personal and Confidential   February 23, 1942
Memorandum for the President

Re: Pennsylvania Politics

I think you should see David Stern, of the Philadelphia *Record*, as soon as possible; and then probably talk to some of the Pennsylvania leaders together — David Lawrence and Meredith Meyers, John Kane from Pittsburgh, and Jim Clark (who took Jack Kelly's place) of Philadelphia.*

We are headed, in my opinion, for certain defeat unless complete unity is worked out before the primaries. All of the candidates must retire except the one agreed on. I believe that the only man with a chance for success is Billy Bullitt. I do not think he wants it much, but with your support and harmony he would have a fair chance. I have talked to the labor people and believe that labor, at least in the Eastern end of the State, are for him. The Archbishop has intimated that he will oppose Bill as he has been twice divorced, and has written a dirty book!

I am of the opinion that Joe Guffey would rather take a chance of defeat than have Bullitt elected. Joe should be "persuaded"; or, if

* David Lawrence, mayor of Pittsburgh, Meredith Meyers, John Kane, and James Clark were leading Democratic politicians in Pennsylvania. John B. Kelly had led the party in Philadelphia, was an Olympic oarsman and the father of the future Princess Grace of Monaco.

he does not go along, disregarded. I suggest, however, that the first thing is to see Stern, which should be done within the next three days. This should be arranged so that reporters will not see him.

Respectfully,

Francis Biddle

Bullitt, not enthusiastic about leaving foreign affairs but willing to do as the President wished in the matter, did not run for governor. He was, however, an unsuccessful candidate for mayor of Philadelphia in 1943.

3030 Cambridge Place, N.W.
Washington, D.C.
4 March 1942

Dear Franklin:

When I saw you at the service in St. John's Church this morning, I wanted deeply to shake your hand and say, God bless you.

Since I could not, I do it now.

May God be with you.

Bill

[This is the only letter (handwritten) in which Bullitt calls the President by his first name. He was careful to always address him as Mr. President, but when they were alone together the intimacy was greater.]

MEMORANDUM

Washington, D.C.
March 13, 1942

My dear Mr. President:

I feel that I should repeat to you once more that the entire area south of Turkey remains a vacuum in respect of air force.

As you know, the British have promised to take care of the air for Turkey, if Hitler should attack Turkey. They have no planes closer to Turkey than the Libyan front, where Rommel's air force is now nearly the equal of the British air force.

If Hitler should threaten Turkey, the British would be obliged either to withdraw their entire air force from the Libyan front and send it to the Turkish frontier — or default on their promise to Turkey.

We are not certain that Turkey will fight against German invasion even if backed up by a British or an American air force. We are almost certain that if no such air force is ready for action, Turkey will submit and permit German troops to pass through into the Lebanon, Syria and Iraq. You know the weakness of the British forces now in that area.

A small German army diverted by Hitler from the Russian front to the Turkish border could, therefore, put in desperate danger not only the east coast of the Mediterranean, the oil wells of Mosul, the Persian oil fields, and the refineries at Abadan and Bahrein, but — in cooperation with Rommel — the entire Red Sea and Persian Gulf areas.

If we should send American air units under American command to Egypt immediately, they could enter the fighting on the Libyan front at once and be ready for immediate transfer to the southern Turkish frontier. They would not be stationed somewhere awaiting a possible attack. They would be in battle from the day they should arrive.

I find that almost everyone concerned with military matters in Washington is convinced intellectually that we must reinforce the air arm in the Near East; but I can not find the will to divert aircraft from other points.

It seems to me urgent that this question should be re-examined and that we should make every effort to get into the Near East at the earliest possible moment three hundred pursuit planes and one hundred bombers with full supplies, equipment and ground units. It may already be too late.

If neither the British nor ourselves are prepared *now* to send such an air force into the area, we should at once re-examine the construction projects under the Maxwell and Wheeler Missions. Why use shipping to construct ports, docks, assembly plants and railroads for eventual use not by the British but by the Germans?

Bill

THE WHITE HOUSE
WASHINGTON

March 17, 1942

Memorandum for General Marshall

Will you speak to me about this [above memo] at your convenience?

FDR

WAR DEPARTMENT
OFFICE OF THE CHIEF OF STAFF
WASHINGTON

Memorandum for the President   March 18, 1942

The urgency of Ambassador Bullitt's concern as to the *Middle East* is justified. From a military viewpoint, the region invites attack, and its loss would permit junction by sea between the Japanese and the Germans with the disastrous consequences for the United Nations implied by such an eventuality.

Agreements with the British, prior to December 7, have always placed the Middle East in the sphere of exclusive British responsibility. However, the critical nature of the present situation is such that I have already informed Sir John Dill that the War Department stood ready to assist, in every practicable way, in improving Middle East defenses.

The principal need is for air units. Air Marshal Portal has asked General Arnold for 3 bomber groups and 2 pursuit groups. The Combined Chiefs of Staff have communicated to London a plan (attached), developed by General Arnold, for the transfer to that region of two U. S. pursuit groups, two light groups, and one medium group — the airplanes to come from numbers already allotted to the British in this country. Should it develop that the British requirement in the Middle East involves planes rather than operating personnel, I doubt that we can do much to help. However, we are making every possible effort to meet this situation.

Of course, the meat of the situation for us is the urgent necessity of meeting our responsibilities in the Southwest Pacific, the reinforcement of Alaskan defenses, and, above all, the gathering of air power in England. A few minutes ago I received from Admiral King a list of army planes and anti-aircraft guns guarding the fleet base at Pearl Harbor, with the statement that "the picture is not any too encouraging." The Secretary of War has found the need for additional planes in Panama. I will not elaborate on the State Department's desires for planes for South America.

Marshall
Chief of Staff

Enclosures: Proposal for Estab. of U.S. Air Units in Cairo
Memo. for Pres. from Mr. Bullitt with memo. from President

29

Out of a Job

MARCH 1942—JUNE 1942

The Near East
Views on Stalin
Bullitt Seeks New Work

MEMORANDUM

8 April 1942

As soon as I entered the President's office at one o'clock today he began by saying: "Bill: Is there anything so dumb and pigheaded as a 76 year old man?" and went on to say that Secretary Stimson had argued with him that owing to the decision not to send the necessary support in planes, shipping, etc., to the Near East, I should not return to that area since I would have to tell General Auchinleck, Air Marshal Tedder and Admiral Cunningham that they were going to get no additional help and that indeed they were going to get far less than the inadequate amount they had been promised.

I replied that in my opinion Secretary Stimson was absolutely right. I said that the only effect that could be produced by my returning to the Near East now would be despair on the part of everyone and since I could state only that the area was being abandoned to Hitler if Hitler should choose to take it. I reminded the President that ever since my return I had done everything I could to obtain reinforcements for the area, that the reinforcements had been refused and that I considered the decision not to reinforce the Near East a terrible mistake.

The President continued to argue that I should leave for the Near East next week and again referred to Secretary Stimson in an uncomplimentary way and I replied that I thought Stimson had done a better job than any man in the Cabinet and the President admitted that Secretary Stimson had done an exceedingly good job.

The President then said that he wanted me to go out to the Near East anyhow, adding that he had had no real idea of the situation from the West Coast of Africa through to Teheran until I had returned and reported to him. He said that I had made him feel as if he had seen the entire area with his own eyes and he wanted me to go out there and be his eyes again. I said that information was coming in daily from that area from his diplomatic representatives and army officers and that I could tell him exactly what the situation was without making another such trip. The President said that his diplomats were worthless, he thought they made no sense and neither did the army officers out there. He didn't want their opinion. He wanted mine. He said, "For example, I want to know exactly what the situation is in Iran. How the Persians, the British and the Russians are getting along together." I replied that he could get that immediately by telegraphing to his Minister in Teheran. He answered that his Minister in Teheran was worthless and added that he couldn't even remember his name.

I said that I was fully in accord with Secretary Stimson. I certainly would not go out to the Near East and lie either to the military or civilian leaders in that area and if I told them the truth they would be plunged into despair. The President then said that I could go out and refuse absolutely to discuss any military or naval question. I could just say that I knew nothing about the military plans of the British and American Governments. I laughed quite sincerely at this and said that any such idea was simply idiotic; that no one in the entire Near East ever discussed anything except the military situation and that it was just as impossible to have any conversation on the Near East without discussing military and naval questions as it was in Australia and Bataan. The only thing people were interested in was whether or not they could preserve their lives and the countries they were living in from Hitler's domination. If I should be so silly as to go out to that area in which I had established very close relations with a large number of British and French officials, to say nothing of certain local leaders my refusal to discuss the military and naval situation would produce an even worse result than my discussing it honestly. The President then said he was trying to send me out to buy him a pair of pants and I was trying to say to him that I had to go for a fur coat. He wanted to know how the whole thing looked there since the two months I had returned.

I then said to the President that I positively would not go on a mission in which I did not believe, based on a policy that I thought disastrously mistaken, but added that if the policy should be changed in the immediate future and immediate support sent to the Near East, especially plane support, it might make sense for me to go out, flying first to London to talk with Lyttelton and the British authorities about planes for the defense of the area.

I then said to the President that I had no desire to continue to have a high paid job with a large title and have no work to do; that I had completed today all the tasks that had developed out of my recent mission and that I wished to know what, if anything, he wanted me to do. The President said that he had been thinking of me lately entirely in connection with the Near East and that he would have to turn his mind on where he wanted me to work if I would not go to the Near East at this time under present conditions.

We then discussed a number of posts that I might occupy. In the course of the conversation, the President said that of course I could do almost any cabinet job better than the man now in it.

By this time the servants had entered the room bringing the President's luncheon to him and I said to the President that I would not telephone to him asking for any appointment but that I would leave the matter up to him and that he could summon me if he should so desire.

The President said that he would send for me in the immediate future.

WCB

THE WHITE HOUSE
WASHINGTON

April 13, 1942

Memorandum for the President

Last week when you saw Bill Bullitt you only had about three minutes to give him as you were far behind on your appointments and he had a very unsatisfactory visit. I hate bothering you with this but, as he mentioned in his memorandum, he has to give up his Philadelphia house and is in a quandary as to where to move and what to do for the future.

You said you were going to try to think up some position for

him. Have you any thoughts on this? What can I tell Bill and may
he come in and see you for at least a fifteen-minute appointment
without interruption?

G. [Grace G. Tully]

On April 20, Bullitt wrote to Secretary of War Henry L. Stimson offering his services for active military duty in the Commandos, but his request was denied.

Bullitt and Roosevelt were at opposite poles in their views of Stalin and had many heated arguments about his trustworthiness. Neither was able to persuade the other and their differences are brought out in an account by a French author, Laslo Havas, in *Assassinat au Sommet*. Unfortunately he does not give the source of his authority but does give a picture of the way Roosevelt and Bullitt were divided in their opinion. Havas cites a letter from Roosevelt to Stalin asking for a meeting with no staff present, only Harry Hopkins, an interpreter, and a stenographer. He says that Ambassador Davies took this letter to Moscow and that Churchill was not told of it.

A free translation of Havas's story is: "Naturally, even that was not entirely true. Besides the Russian Ambassador, Harry Hopkins, adviser of the President, was au courant with the letter — he was also au courant with everything — also was William Bullitt, former Ambassador in France. In the course of a three-hour conversation, Mr. Bullitt had attempted to convince the President that the attitude which he had with regard to the Russians, in being ready to make almost any concession, would have catastrophic consequences. But in vain.

"Roosevelt did not attempt to refute the arguments of Bullitt. He felt, he said, that Stalin was not the man that one thought him. He was persuaded, he added, that if he gave Stalin all that it was possible to give him, without asking anything in return, 'noblesse oblige,' he would not even come to the idea of Russia's annexing a single country or a single province.

"Such logic made Bullitt lose his sang-froid and he said to Roosevelt that the man with whom he dealt was not the Duke of Norfolk, but 'a Caucasian bandit.' Roosevelt felt deeply offended by this description of a man whom he considered the greatest of his contemporaries." [1]

In an article Bullitt wrote for *Life,* August 30, 1948, he presented much the same picture of this interview, using many of the identical words.

3030 Cambridge Place, N.W.
Washington, D.C.

Personal June 13, 1942

Dear Mr. President:

I am doing nothing in this war.

I do not care about anything except helping to beat Hitler and the Japanese. If there is anything I can do with you or for you, I want to do it. If there is nothing, I must try to serve in other ways.

Please let me know — and soon.

Yours affectionately,
Bill

THE WHITE HOUSE
WASHINGTON

June 17, 1942

Dear Bill:

You may not realize it but I have really been trying to work out something definite and useful for you to get to work at. I fully realize how you must feel but I don't want to put you in as a Second Lieutenant and things have got to the point that people who are specialists are scarce, whereas people like you and me, who are jacks of all trades, have a hard time!

My best to you,

As ever yours,
FDR

Honorable William C. Bullitt,
3030 Cambridge Place, N.W.
Washington, D.C.

THE WHITE HOUSE
WASHINGTON

Later June 17, 1942

Dear Bill:

This moment has come something where you can be of real service. Cordell Hull tells me that it seems advisable for many reasons to bring Johnson home from Australia. As you know, he was very successful in China as Ambassador, but I would rather have a little more active fighting type of person in Australia today. I realize this is not an Embassy, but it is far more important in wartime than almost any Embassy in peacetime. I spoke to Cordell about your going and he is really enthusiastic at the idea, and I hope, and he hopes, that you will agree to do it.

If you do accede, I would want to give you a certain amount of background in regard to Curtin, Evatt and General MacArthur and I feel very sure that you would do a difficult job extremely well. Let me know what you think.

Always sincerely,
FDR

Honorable William C. Bullitt
3030 Cambridge Place, N.W.
Washington, D.C.

30

In the Navy

JUNE 1942—NOVEMBER 1942

Bullitt Appointed Assistant to Secretary of Navy
London Conference on War Plans
Eisenhower's Thoughts
Submarine Menace
Landings in Africa
Unifying the French Forces
Casablanca Conference

IT BECAME increasingly evident to Bullitt that the President did not have any work for him along the one line in which he was interested, the defeat of the Germans and the restoration of France. In spite of the Vichy Government he still believed in the resurrection of France, and it was to this end that he wished to devote all his efforts. He accepted a new position, which within a month was to take him to England and involve him in the plans for the landings in Africa and later in France.

Meadow Farm
Penllyn, Pennsylvania
June 18, 1942

Personal

My dear Mr. President:
   Secretary Knox has proposed to me that I should become a Special Assistant to the Secretary of the Navy, and I have accepted, and agreed to go to work in the Navy Department on Monday, June 22. Knox has outlined the work he wishes me to do and I find it of great interest.

For this reason — and others — I cannot accept the post which you kindly suggested in your second letter of yesterday.

As I shall go on the Navy payroll on June 22nd, I should be grateful if you would accept my resignation as your Personal Representative with the rank of ambassador which I sent you on April 20th. I can't be on two Government payrolls at once!

I am most happy to have found a spot — however minor — in which I can render real war service.

If ever you feel like havin a swim, ask Grace * to phone me.

As ever yours,

Bill

THE WHITE HOUSE
WASHINGTON

June 22, 1942

Dear Bill:

It is with great regret that I accept your resignation as my Personal Representative with the rank of Ambassador. I can well understand your desire to get into active service, and you can be quite sure that I will call on you at any time in the future when the occasion arises.

I am delighted that you are continuing in the Government and I know you will do a grand job for the Navy. My best wishes and appreciation for your loyalty and devotion to your country.

As ever yours,

FDR

In the summer of 1942 a divergence of opinion developed between the British and the Americans as to future attacks on Germany. The Americans themselves were divided. General Marshall favored an attack on the continent. Admiral King felt that concentration should be in the Pacific. Neither was enthusiastic about a landing in North Africa, which the British favored. The President was attracted to the British plan and wrote a memorandum for the representatives he sent to England for a conference. In this memorandum he stated, among other instructions: "I am opposed to an American all-out effort in the Pacific against Japan with a view to her defeat as quickly as possible . . .

* Grace G. Tully, the President's secretary.

Defeat of Germany means the defeat of Japan, probably without firing a shot or losing a life." [1] On July 16, 1942, General Marshall, Admiral King, and Harry Hopkins flew to England. Bullitt accompanied them, representing the Secretary of the Navy. Before his departure the President gave him a brief note to Churchill saying: "My old friend, Bill Bullitt, will arrive in London the latter part of this week. As you know each other I need only say that I am sure he will receive every co-operation and facility."

A deadlock developed in the meetings with the British and it was only after instructions were received from the President that agreement was reached to abandon a landing in France in 1942 and to press forward for an attack on North Africa in the fall of that year.

On July 17, 1942, Bullitt lunched at 10 Downing Street with Mr. and Mrs. Churchill. Bullitt noted that Churchill was in fine physical and mental shape. They discussed the German submarine sinkings of Allied ships and "Churchill seemed absolutely and genuinely convinced that an invasion of France would result in complete annihilation of the troops involved." Churchill showed great interest in having Bullitt recount to him the entry of the Germans into Paris.

On July 20 Bullitt dined with General de Gaulle and René Pleven, his Minister of Finance.

In a brief meeting between Bullitt and General Eisenhower on July 31, Eisenhower said: "The whole picture was now so mixed up that he thought it was just a God damned mess." Bullitt saw General Eisenhower again on August 13, and discussed the invasion of Africa. Here is Bullitt's record of the conversation:

Conversation with General Eisenhower

The General said that he would appreciate it greatly if immediately on arriving in Washington I would see General Marshall and would say to him:

1. That he, Eisenhower, didn't like his revised plans any more than General Marshall liked them. He was simply obliged to do what he could with the forces, military, air and naval, which would

be available. So far as he was concerned, he had received the order to try to carry out the operation and he would carry it out even if he had to go in himself with only two squadrons. He was keenly aware that the abandonment of the idea of a landing simultaneously on the West greatly increased the risks but there simply were not enough forces available to land simultaneously. He expected, after landing in the north, to move overland to the west. When I expressed doubt as to the feasibility of this he said that in any event there would be small temptation for the forces on the west to come eastward to attack him.

2. Eisenhower asked me expressly to impress on Marshall the need for the most careful preliminary preparation in the area and then for the setting up immediately of a civil administration which would have to be headed by an "F" [Frenchman]. He said that he had not worked out a mechanism for this in his own mind but that he thought he ought to have a civil administration section of his staff and that at the earliest possible moment the actual administration should be placed in the hands of an "F." He asked me what I would do if the President should order me to take charge of the civil administration — what person I would get. I replied that I would immediately get M. [perhaps Monnet] and build up the entire organization on the basis of his advice and assistance. General Eisenhower said that it was obviously totally impossible for him to organize the administration in an area which contained so many different races of such different (diverse) and peculiar habits. Gave habits of its inhabitants. He was also certain that the President could not possibly organize such an administration effectively because of his inclination to treat everyone outside the British Isles as natives.

3. Eisenhower asked me also to stress to Marshall that it was absolutely necessary for supplies for the civilian population to be brought in as soon as our troops should land. If we could at once improve the food situation with especial attention to peculiar wants such as sugar and butter, we might rapidly overcome any feeling of bitterness. He was keenly aware the problem was not that of seizing and holding a hostile country but of obtaining the maximum support of populations that might be turned into active sympathizers.

4. General Eisenhower said that he would like, if possible, to make the eastern end of the operations American in order that the troops approaching and occupying Bizerte should be American since he realized that the British were suspected acutely of desiring to capture

and hold Bizerte permanently, and that there would be intense hostility to British troops entering that region.

5. General Eisenhower said that he hoped I could impress on Admiral King and everyone in the Navy Department the need to regard this operation as a continuous amphibious operation in which the Navy would have a continuing role to play with considerable forces. The only way he could be sure of getting rapidly to his objectives would be if he had plenty of craft to use along the coast under air cover. He had been astonished to find that the Navy had been regarding this operation as one in which the Navy would have merely a temporary escort duty. That was not true. The Navy would have a continuous combat duty.

General Eisenhower said that he hoped I would explain the entire internal problem in the area as fully as possible not only to General Marshall but also to all the leading officials of the War Department and to the President. So far as he was concerned, he had such absolute confidence in General Marshall that he was ready to take blindly any orders from Marshall and he hoped that I would talk with Marshall before seeing anyone else.

(Under occupying Bizerte, add) Eisenhower said that he would like to have some American troops as a spearhead in the region of Bizerte and if he should be obliged, because of shortage of Americans, to hand over the Bizerte position to the British, he would insist on having an F. civil governor . . .

Bullitt's acquaintances in London were varied. He lunched or dined with many people, among them George Bernard Shaw and the King of Norway. He wrote Secretary of the Navy Knox an account of this lunch:

Personal and Secret   London
                                              August 13, 1942
Dear Frank:

Yesterday I lunched with King Haakon of Norway and he told me the following story.

He had been at lunch with the King of England at Buckingham Palace, and George VI had teased him about the unreadiness of his guards in Oslo when the Germans had attacked.

King Haakon said that in reply he had asked King George if he was so very sure that there would be an immediate response in London in case of sudden assault on Buckingham Palace, and the King of England had said that he was certain that the arrangements for his protection were perfect.

King Haakon said that he had then suggested that they should stroll in the garden and that King George should call his equerry and tell him to inform the Guard that German parachutists had dropped in the Palace Garden, and see just how long it would take for troops to arrive.

King George called his equerry and gave the order and the equerry immediately informed the Guard by telephone.

King Haakon said that while they had stood in the garden awaiting the arrival of the British troops, he had kept his wrist watch in full view to time the exact moment of arrival.

After two minutes, when nothing had happened, he had said to his younger relative: "Well, I am dead now and I am not so sure you aren't."

They had waited until five minutes had elapsed. No guards had appeared. The King of England again had summoned his equerry and asked what the devil had happened and why there had been no response to his alarm order. The equerry had gone again to the telephone and had come back with the reply that the Guard on duty had replied that he was certain that there must be some mistake; there couldn't be parachutists in the garden of Buckingham Palace because there had been no air raid warning! . . .

William C. Bullitt

Secretary of War Henry L. Stimson made a memorandum of a conversation with Bullitt on September 1 in which Bullitt outlined the progress of the submarine war. Bullitt gave him a very somber picture of the submarine condition as he had gathered it from the air forces and submarine fighting forces in Great Britain. Bullitt reported that the Germans had 300 submarines of which 120 were at sea, and in addition there were 150 training in the Baltic. She was building from 20 to 28 per month, and in the first thirty months of the war had lost 100. He suggested that our bombing be confined to the submarine dockyards. His figures on the shortage of escort vessels were disheartening — the United States was short 792 and the United Kingdom, 600. Bullitt also suggested that we use our old B-24s for submarine patrol work.[2]

The information on German submarines proved to be more accurate than the estimates of German airplane production.

Albert Speer reported that in 1942 they were producing 20 small (about 800 tons) vessels per month.[3]

DEPARTMENT OF THE NAVY

OFFICE OF THE SECRETARY

WASHINGTON

October 15, 1942

Dear Mr. President:

Since you are handling certain matters personally, I think you ought to know the following!

André Philip, a French Socialist Deputy, who was intensely opposed to the Armistice and is now one of General de Gaulle's leading supporters, has arrived in this country. Yesterday I listened while Philip answered the questions of another Frenchman.

Philip stated that he had spent the night secretly with Herriot early in August, having visited Herriot for the purpose of inviting him to leave France and join the de Gaulle movement.

Herriot, Philip asserted, stated to him that he would be glad to leave France and join de Gaulle, as soon as he should have published his letter of protest dated August 31, 1942.

Philip said that, recently, after the publication of Herriot's letter, Herriot had sent him word that since their talk in August he had received 19 invitations to leave France, two from persons alleging that they were representatives of the American Government, several from persons alleging that they were representatives of General de Gaulle, several from persons alleging that they were representatives of the British Government, the Czech Government, etc., etc. Herriot had added that he felt certain that some of these men must be stool-pigeons either of the Vichy Government or the German Gestapo. He had, therefore, refused to budge and was awaiting a word from someone in whom he had confidence and knew to be the representative of some genuine governmental authority.

Philip stated that he was absolutely sure that Herriot still could be got out of France. He said that Herriot's present guards merely went to sleep in Herriot's barn at night. He added that General de Gaulle was most anxious to have Herriot out, since Herriot had stated to him (Philip), "I am at General de Gaulle's orders."

Philip praised the military abilities of General Giraud and said that he had controlling influence in the existing French Army; but insisted that Giraud was politically nothing more or less than Action Française.

In accordance with your instructions, I have not discussed the matter of which we spoke on Friday last, October 9th, with anyone. I am, therefore, entirely without information as to the contacts that you may have established with Herriot.

Nevertheless, for what it may be worth, I should like to give you my opinion on the desirability of getting Herriot out of France immediately. To control the French Generals and other leaders, you will need intensely a French political figure of world reputation on our side in North Africa. Herriot, as you know, is my oldest political friend in France and my judgment with regard to his availability may be warped by this fact; but I can not honestly think of anyone so good in the present circumstances. He would be more acceptable than any other political leader to General de Gaulle, and probably not unacceptable to General Giraud.

Jeanneney might serve if Herriot should be unobtainable. Jeanneney was, as you know, President of the French Senate until the Republic was abolished. He is an old man but still full of spirit and character — an old war horse of French democracy. In default of Herriot, he might do. If you desire me to do anything about Herriot or about Jeanneney, please let me know, as I shall not mention the matter to anyone unless I hear from you.

When last we talked, you asked me to prepare a draft of a more or less formal proclamation, and a draft of an informal statement. Both documents must be prepared at the last moment, on the basis of the latest information. For example, if Herriot should be here in America or in London, or on board ship, your statements would be couched in different terms than if you should have no one of stature as a French leader.

In any event, however, I think you ought to put somewhere in your Proclamation the following thoughts:

American forces have landed in North Africa. They are an Army not of Occupation, but of Liberation. Their task is to help the French to free all French territory from Nazi domination. Every inch of ground they take will be restored to France.

They will be reinforced in every possible way until all Axis forces shall have been driven from Africa. A service of supply for them and for their French allies, both military and civilian, has been organized on a scale which will relieve the distress and increase the welfare of the populations of North Africa.

Frenchmen! The young Americans who have crossed the Atlantic to help you drive out your enemies are the sons of the Americans who fought for the freedom of France in 1917 and 1918. Like their fathers, and like yourselves, they believe in liberty, democracy and peace. Like all Americans, they wish to see France once more free and strong.

They know that although the body of France is in chains the soul of France has never surrendered to the Nazis. They know that their place is beside you and your place is beside them in war and in peace.

Together with the youth of all the United Nations, you have the world to remake. The order of the day is the text of the *Marseillaise:*

"ALLONS, ENFANTS DE LA PATRIE!"

Whenever you get ready to do something final on this, remember that literal translations are no good. I'll be glad if you want, to put whatever you want into French that rings.

Yours very sincerely,
William C. Bullitt

P.S. A simultaneous message to French Veterans from Pershing might be useful.

WCB

None of what Bullitt suggested was included in the President's message to the French people.

General Henri Giraud was one of the heroes of the First World War who had been captured by the Germans in both 1914 and 1940. He made daring escapes from his prisons and became one of the leading French military figures, ranking above General de Gaulle. Robert Murphy, who had had a long and intimate knowledge of the French Government, was assigned in 1941 to Algiers as our representative in French Africa, which was still under the Vichy regime. It was Murphy's difficult task to prepare the way for the American landings which were to take place November 8, 1942. The French command in Africa was in the hands of Admiral Michelier, who was violently opposed to any American action, and one French general, when Murphy put forth a suppositious case of American aid, said: "I will meet you with all the fire power I possess."[4] During the spring and summer Admiral Darlan (Minister of Marine, Vice President of the State Council, in command of the French fleet and the overall direction of French Africa), becoming convinced of Allied victory, had discussed with Murphy the participation by the French in the African attack. Darlan had also agreed to defend the French fleet from the Germans.

On D-day the situation with the French was tense. Giraud, who arrived from France by submarine (he insisted on an American submarine, but since there was none available, an American officer was placed in technical command of a British submarine at Gibraltar, from whence Giraud sailed), was insisting that both French and American armies be under his command. Darlan, who represented the Vichy Government and had full authority from it as commander, also arrived in Africa purely by chance to visit his son, who was ill in Algiers. De Gaulle had not been given any advance notice of the landing because both Roosevelt and Churchill feared his indiscretion.

There was much opposition to de Gaulle on the part of many of the French in Africa, and he did not take part in any of the early activities. He proposed to General Giraud on December 27, 1942, after Darlan's assassination, that he come to Africa to discuss grouping under one authority all French forces. He arrived at the Casablanca Conference on January 22, 1943. He was more than difficult, even refusing for a time to meet General Giraud.

It was against the possibilities of all these difficulties that Bullitt wrote the President suggesting that Herriot be brought from France as the man with the stature and authority to bring together all the different French factions, and the individual who would represent the civil authority over the military. Herriot was not included.

In November 1942, Roosevelt and Churchill endeavored to arrange a meeting with Stalin, with no success. Although Stalin replied that he welcomed the idea of such a meeting, he was not in a position to leave the Soviet Union even for a day. In the same message he asked Churchill for a reply to his demand for a second front early in 1943 and added: "In the Stalingrad area we are keeping a large group of the German troops surrounded, and we hope to annihilate them completely." His hope was more than fulfilled.

In Stalin's reply to Roosevelt he touched on the subject of Darlan. There had been much criticism of the Allies' dealing with Darlan, a member of the Vichy Government, and many said it would alienate the Russians on account of the Communists' hatred of all Fascists. Stalin wired Roosevelt: "In my opinion, as well as in that of my colleagues, Eisenhower's policy with regard to Darlan, Boisson, Giraud and others is perfectly correct. I think it a great achievement that you succeeded in bringing Darlan and others into the waterway of the Allies fighting Hitler."

Roosevelt and Churchill proceeded with plans to meet in North Africa to confer with the military top men, both British and American. Roosevelt suggested "some possible tourist oasis . . . One of the dictionaries says 'an oasis is never wholly dry.' Good old dictionary!"[5] The President arrived in Casablanca on January 14, 1943, and found Churchill awaiting him. Meanwhile the British advance across the African desert had begun with great success.

The conference began January 15 and at the conference between Roosevelt and Churchill were the chiefs of staff of both nations. General Alexander was present to report on the victories of his Desert Army, which was advancing rapidly. General Eisenhower also attended, conferring frequently with General Alexander.

It was at this conference that the fateful words "unconditional surrender" were first used by the President, who reported to Hopkins, "Suddenly the Press Conference was on, and Winston and I had had no time to prepare for it, and the thought popped into my mind that they had called Grant 'Old Unconditional Surrender,' and the next thing I knew I had said it."[6] The principal decisions taken at the conference included the defeat of the German submarines, aid to Russia, the defeat of Germany in 1943, the occupation of Sicily, and increased air activity over Germany. Operations against Japan were not to be undertaken on a large scale until Germany was defeated. It was not until January 24 that the press learned that the President and Churchill had been meeting.

The results of the conference were decisions to demand the unconditional surrender of Germany, Italy, and Japan; to capture Tunis; to occupy Sicily; to enlist Turkey as an ally; to continue the heaviest possible air offensive against Germany; and to continue pressure on Japan with a full offensive after the fall of Germany.

This meeting was one of the best-kept secrets of the war, and when it ended and its conclusions were given to the press, the reporters could not believe that Roosevelt and Churchill had been together in Africa for two weeks without their knowledge.

Meadow Farm
Penllyn, Pennsylvania
February 14, 1943

Jean Monnet said to me last night that he had had a conversation with Harry Hopkins about the behavior of General de Gaulle at the Casablanca Conference.

Hopkins said that de Gaulle three times had refused to come to Casablanca and had imposed all sorts of conditions for coming. Finally Churchill had sent de Gaulle a telegram stating that unless de Gaulle came at once to Casablanca the British Government would stop all supplies of money to de Gaulle. De Gaulle had then come at once.

De Gaulle had been very cordial and correct in his personal approach to the President and had said that he conceived his role to be that of Jeanne d'Arc. It was his mission in life to resurrect France. After de Gaulle had talked with Giraud, he had talked again with the President and had said, "I must state to you frankly that I am no longer a military leader. I am the leader of a great political movement. I am today in the position of Clemenceau." The President laughingly had replied, "General, you told me the other day you were Jeanne d'Arc and now you say you are Clemenceau. Which are you?" De Gaulle replied, "I am both."

WCB

SIX

Postwar Plans
The French Army
1942 – 1945

31

Accurate Forecasts—A Plan for Europe

NOVEMBER 1942—AUGUST 1943

Administration of Occupied Territories
Casablanca Conference
United States Political-Military Strategy
Quebec Conference
How to Deal with Stalin

MR. ROOSEVELT WAS still calling on Bullitt for help and advice in the conduct of the war. He now asked Bullitt to give him his views in an entirely different field. Bullitt plunged into this new project and in a very short time gave the President his recommendations.

November 19, 1942

Dear Bill:

I wish that in your spare time you would give me your personal views on the machinery of preparation for civil administration in occupied territories.

We must remember that the cardinal principle is twofold — that in the first instance, occupation is wholly a military matter and that only when the military authorities are ready to turn over, civilian authority should be put into operation.

The second rule is that just as much civilian authority should remain in the hands of local existing government as possible or, failing that, all possible civilian authority should be exercised by local civilians.

This problem involves the Army school or schools of administration, the Department of the Interior as our principal agency for governing territories — Puerto Rico, etc. — and the State Department.

I realize that there can be no general rule because every occupation brings in different problems.

What I should like to have you do is to make a personal study of this and let me have some kind of a broad outline for my information.

I am sure all the existing agencies of the Government will do all they can to help you.

As ever yours,
Franklin D. Roosevelt

Honorable William C. Bullitt
Navy Department
Washington, D.C.

The following letters are extraordinarily prophetic documents. The reader will immediately recognize how many of Bullitt's forecasts concerning Stalin's actions were to come true. These predictions may be compared with the advice he had given Woodrow Wilson at the Versailles Peace Conference in 1919. Had either Wilson or Roosevelt heeded his opinions it is entirely possible that the whole future history of Europe and the world would have been affected. At this time Stalin was constantly urging the Allies to deliver an increasing amount of supplies to Russia and to open a second front on the continent of Europe. The landings in Normandy were not to take place until June 6, 1944, but British convoys had begun delivering supplies to Russia on August 12, 1941. When the United States entered the war American ships and supplies joined the British in the perilous trip around the north of Norway to Archangel and Murmansk. These convoys were continuously attacked by the German aircraft and navy, often with great success. The loss of life and of ships was heavy in the bitterly cold waters of the northern seas. Stalin never expressed appreciation for this major and costly help, but unceasingly kept demanding more.

In retrospect it would appear that had Bullitt accompanied Roosevelt, and later President Truman, the meetings with Stalin might have been on a more realistic basis and might have saved the world untold misery.

The only comment in the correspondence about this letter is a note by the President, "File-confidential," but the matter was fully discussed with Bullitt at a later date at the White House.

My dear Mr. President:

I thank you for your letter of November 19, 1942, asking me to give you my "views on the machinery of preparation for civil administration in occupied territories." Since receiving it, I have discussed the question with the Secretaries of State, War, Navy and Interior and some of their subordinates.

The problems of civil administration in different countries and areas are so diverse that few, if any, general rules can be laid down except the two you stated in your letter. Each nation presents an individual problem requiring special treatment. I shall, therefore, attempt to deal with each country or area separately, and, at the end, try to draw some general conclusions and make some recommendations.

You are already *in* the civil administration of North Africa and the question is no longer entire [sic]. Nevertheless, I should like to make some practical suggestions.

I think you should at once get going the production of North African iron ore and phosphates. Aside from other advantages, the result would be a great gain in shipping . . .

Food production in North Africa can be increased greatly. Food grown on the spot for our army and the British will not have to be imported. Again shipping will be gained. I think you ought to send at once to North Africa not men to gather agricultural statistics — the French in North Africa already have more statistics than anyone can use — but practical men to tell you within two weeks what to have planted at once.

Our objective is to get the maximum French military assistance against Germany — first in North Africa, then in continental France. To that end we should equip as fast as possible Giraud's troops with modern arms, planes, uniforms, shoes — everything. You should agree now with the British that the French Army is to be equipped entirely from the United States. The advantages to us, military and political, are so obvious that I need not enumerate them.

I still believe, as I said to you long ago, that the best means to get all France into the war wholeheartedly on our side is to set up as head of the French civil administration in North Africa, a French democratic statesman known for his unrelenting opposition to Germany, and to subordinate all Generals and Admirals to him. But since you have not been able to get either Herriot or Jeanneney to

North Africa — and they are the only ones who could rally all the forces of French democracy — I think you should bring Giraud forward. Indeed, as his army grows he will come into the spotlight naturally. Giraud is a good General who has never been criticized except for being too intrepid — too much of a warrior — and he is a hero in France today because of his escape from Germany. He is a good Gallic symbol . . .

Darlan unquestionably has rendered our occupation of French Africa much easier. But each gift that he brings us diminishes his utility, since he has that much less to bring. His acts as head of Pétain's governing apparatus hung an albatross around his neck. He cannot get it off. To continue to use him as the Top Frenchman would be to alienate most of the strong and decent elements in France . . .

Your statement indicating the temporary nature of our relationship with Darlan took the right line; and to those who may advise you to retain Darlan, I think you should say, "Who ever heard of calling Judas and saying, 'On this rock I found my Church.' "

As I said to you often from 1933 to 1940, brains in public life in France are as numerous as leaves on the trees but there is almost no character. To get the national revival we need in France, both for the war and the peace, we have to choose a French leader of character. Herriot, Jeanneney and Giraud have character. Darlan should be eased gradually into a comfortable villa in Africa — or perhaps Palm Beach! — with a good chef and a good cellar and nothing to do — and forgotten. By coming over to our side he has saved his life. That's all he deserves.

I shall visit the Army and Navy schools of civil administration this week and report to you as soon as possible.

Yours very sincerely,
William C. Bullitt

DEPARTMENT OF THE NAVY
OFFICE OF THE SECRETARY
WASHINGTON

December 17, 1942

Dear Mr. President:

I submit installment number 2 of my answer to your order of November 19, 1942 . . .

Interior is interested in becoming residuary legatee of Pacific islands captured by the Army and Navy. Mr. E. D. Hester, Economic Adviser to the U.S. High Commissioner to the Philippine Islands, has drawn up a comprehensive plan for administration by civilians of such islands as we may acquire in Polynesia, Micronesia and Melanesia.

Rightly he begins his paper with the statement, "Were it not for the strategy of defense and communication, the Pacific Islands would be of minor material importance to the United States." All government departments agree that our primary interest in acquiring the islands is strategic. (Incidentally, I think we should grab as many as possible, since every island large enough to hold an air field is today an unsinkable aircraft carrier.) . . .

I believe that full control of the Pacific islands should be given to Navy until the end of the war, and that full control by the Navy should continue after the war until such time as the President may consider it in the public interest to transfer control of certain islands to Interior.

It is highly improbable that the Navy will wish to continue to govern *all* the islands. But islands which contain important naval bases and air fields probably should remain under Navy control. The Navy probably will wish to divest itself of administration of hundreds of islands . . .

The problems of administration raised by occupation or liberation of European countries are so complex that I reserve them for the next installment of this report.

Yours very sincerely,
William C. Bullitt

On Christmas Eve 1942 Bill had joined the rest of our family for dinner. In the middle of the meal the telephone rang. It was the President calling Bill to tell him that Admiral Darlan, who had taken command of the French forces in Africa on November 10, had been assassinated. The President wanted to discuss with Bill what steps the United States should take, as the situation, politically, in North Africa was extremely tense at that time. The conversation continued for fifteen or twenty minutes.

DEPARTMENT OF THE NAVY
OFFICE OF THE SECRETARY
WASHINGTON

January 29, 1943

Dear Mr. President:

The appended will take thirty minutes of your time.

It is as serious a document as any I have ever sent you. I hope you will read it.

I warn you its conclusion is that you ought to talk with Stalin as soon as possible.

Good luck,
William C. Bullitt

Washington, D.C.
January 29, 1943

Dear Mr. President:

I submit installment number three of my answer to your order of November 19, 1942.

It is based on two assumptions: 1. That we shall continue to fight until Germany, Italy and Japan are utterly defeated and physically occupied by our troops and those of the other United Nations. 2. That our aim is to establish a world of liberty, democracy and peace.

In your letter of November 19, 1942, you said that, in preparing for civil administrations in occupied territories in Europe, "There can be no general rule because every one brings in different problems."

Nevertheless, it is possible, I think, to lay down two general policies that are sound:

1. To refuse to recognize as a de jure government any de facto regime set up by us in any occupied or liberated country until the people of such country shall have had a chance to express their will . . .

2. To choose to head de facto administrations in countries which we liberate or occupy, men who will (a) give us immediately maximum possible military assistance; (b) favor the major policies of the United States . . .

In what countries in Europe may we reasonably hope to set up de facto administrations, followed by de jure governments, that will work for a world of liberty, democracy and peace?

The answer to this question lies largely in Stalin's hands. He may set up Soviet governments in many of the countries in which we now expect to set up democratic governments.

We have little firsthand, detailed information about Stalin's views and aims. We have only statements by Molotov and Lozovsky, and the impressions of travelers, like Willkie. Many people, including President Hoover, have said lately that Stalin has changed his political philosophy. He is said to share your views expressed in the Atlantic Charter, and to favor the Four Freedoms. It is stated that he has abandoned all idea of world communism and is ready to dissolve the Comintern. He is said to want no annexations but to be interested only in security. He is reported to be determined to have the Soviet Union evolve in the direction of liberty and democracy, freedom of speech and freedom of religion.

We ought to pray God that this is so; for if it is so, the road to a world of liberty, democracy and peace will be relatively easy — and if it is not so, the road will be uphill all the way.

If Stalin is for our war aims, no power on earth will be able to prevent the establishment of a good peace.

It is, therefore, in our national interest, to attempt to draw Stalin into cooperation with the United States and Great Britain, for the establishment of an Atlantic Charter peace. We ought to try to accomplish this feat, however improbable success may seem.

It may be that Stalin, having "liquidated" the old communists to whom Communism was a religion, having been shocked by the consequences of his own collaboration with Hitler, having probed (as we can not) the depth of the wound inflicted on the Soviet Union by Hitler's armies, having remembered that the Tsar's armies, after two years of war, drove back the Austrians and the Germans 350 miles and then collapsed — it may be that Stalin, chastened, has changed.

The persons who hold this to be true say that we can obtain Stalin's full and frank cooperation, if only we will overcome his distrust of the United States and Great Britain by increasing our war aid to the Soviet Union, establishing a second front in western Europe, and promising help to rebuild the devastated areas of the Soviet Union after the war. They say that Stalin will trust us and work with us hand-in-hand, if we trust him and give him these things.

This view of Stalin is not only the view of several recent travelers in the Soviet Union but also the view being propagated by the Comintern. It is the communist party line in Great Britain, the United States and all other countries where there are communist parties. It is the line of the fellow travelers and many "liberals." Since Stalin personally sets the party line, it is what Stalin wants us to believe about him. Is it what he is? Or only what he wants us to think he is?

The most careful search for factual evidence to support the thesis that Stalin is a changed man reveals none. And since the thesis implies a conversion of Stalin as striking as the conversion of Saul on the road to Damascus, we have to keep our fingers crossed, and approach the question of Stalin's intentions with the same admirable realism with which Stalin approaches all questions affecting the Soviet Union.

We have to remember that what we are now asked to believe is just what we were asked to believe when the United Front policy was adopted by the Comintern Congress of 1935 — and that it was stated frankly in the proceedings of that Congress (which records we have), that this was merely a method of hoodwinking the world outside the Soviet Union. We have also to remember that all the things we are asked to give and do in order to make Stalin lose "distrust of us" will be of the greatest concrete benefit to the Soviet Union whether Stalin is for us or against us. We have to look for evidence of conversion.

We find no evidence; but we find in all democratic countries an intense wish to believe that Stalin has changed — a wish we share. Therefore, we have to suspect that this view is a product of the fatal vice in foreign affairs — the vice of wishful thinking.

In point of fact, the extraordinary valor with which the peoples of the Soviet Union have fought against the Nazis has rendered the Russians so popular in both the United States and Great Britain that all possible virtues are being attributed to the Soviet Government, and both basic Russian Nationalist policy and Soviet Communist policy are being overlooked in a warm sentimental wave of enthusiasm. Wishful thinking has produced the following logic: Because the Red Army has fought magnificently, the Soviet Union is a democratic state which desires no annexations and is devoted to the Four Freedoms; because Stalingrad has been defended with superb heroism, there is no O.G.P.U. (Secret Police).

The reality is that the Soviet Union, up to the present time, has been a totalitarian dictatorship in which there has been no freedom of speech, no freedom of the press, and a travesty of freedom of religion; in which there has been universal fear of the O.G.P.U. and Freedom from Want has been subordinated always to the policy of guns instead of butter.

Again and again our diplomatic representatives in Moscow have been assured by the Soviet Government that the absolute monopoly of foreign trade will not be abandoned because its abandonment would mean the collapse of the whole Soviet system of State-directed economy. We know, therefore, that areas annexed by the Soviet Union, will be withdrawn, as heretofore, from the area of normal trade between nations, which it is our policy to extend.

Stalin has subordinated "world revolution" to the interests of the Soviet State; but he still maintains in each country in the world, either openly or secretly, a 5th column for the Soviet agents — in the form of public or underground Communist Parties. Stalin directs their activities in the interests of the Soviet State, using them for espionage, propaganda, character assassination of opponents, and political influence through fellow travelers or dupes.

Stalin places first the welfare of the Soviet State, and treads softly, therefore, in extending communism to other countries; but there is no evidence that he has abandoned either the policy of extending communism or the policy of controlling all foreign communist parties. Under Lenin the primary task of each national communist party was to foment world revolution. Under Stalin the primary task of each national communist party is to serve as 5th column for the Soviet State. World revolution is a secondary objective.

Stalin lets no ideological motives influence his actions. He is highly intelligent. He weighs with suspicious realism all factors involved in advancing the interests or boundaries of the Soviet Union. He moves where opposition is weak. He stops where opposition is strong. He puts out pseudopodia like an amoeba rather than leaping like a tiger. If the pseudopodia meet no obstacle, the Soviet Union flows on.

Even if Stalin has not changed, as we pray he has — if we can play on this characteristic behavior pattern of his with sufficient skill and force, we may be able to set up throughout Europe the sort of democratic administrations we want. We have to demonstrate to Stalin — and mean it — that while we genuinely want to cooperate with the Soviet Union, we will not permit our war to prevent Nazi domination of Europe to be turned into a war to establish Soviet domination of Europe. We have to back democracy in Europe to the limit, and prove to Stalin that, while we have intense admiration for the Russian people and will collaborate fully with a pacific Soviet State, we will resist a predatory Soviet State just as fiercely as we are now resisting a predatory Nazi State.

The wishful thinkers just now are fond of arguing that "Stalin has become a Russian nationalist, interested only in security for his country, therefore, the Soviet Union will become pacific." They forget conveniently that the Russian nationalist State was never pacific. Tsarist Russia was, and the Soviet Union today is, an agglomeration of conquered peoples. Since the time of Peter the Great, the Russians have extended their rule ruthlessly over one people after another. Primary school books in the Soviet Union are issued in 156 different languages and dialects.

The Russians are an immensely endowed people, physically strong, intellectually gifted, emotionally rich. The Ukrainians are even more gifted than the Russians. They were overcome by the Russians by force of numbers. The Russians win their battles both in the field and in bed. No race on earth, not even the German, has shown such burgeoning energy as the Russian during the past hundred years. They have conquered one sixth of the earth's surface. They are still bursting with expansive energy.

Even their unsuccessful wars point the moral. They fought the Crimean war to get Constantinople, the Bosphorus and the Dardanelles. They fought the Russo-Japanese war to get Manchuria and Korea. The world war of 1914 grew out of the clash of Russian and German power politics in the *Western* Balkans. And the Tzar wanted Narvik!

Even if Stalin had become a mere Russian nationalist — which he has not — that would be no guarantee of pacific behavior; indeed, it would be a guarantee of aggressive imperialism.

What are Stalin's present aims? He has avowed, through Molotov, Lozovsky and others, the following:

1. To annex Bessarabia. (We can not object to this.)

2. To annex Bukowina and the heights of the Carpathians. (This would give the Soviet Union easy military access to the Hungarian plain and to southern Poland.)

3. To annex an undefined area in Eastern Poland. (This in spite of the fact that the attempt of the Red Army to stand on the line of the Bug against the Nazi Army brought disaster.)

4. To annex Lithuania. (And thus extinguish the liberty of a brave and fine Catholic people.)

5. To annex Latvia. (And destroy a heroic small people of Western civilization.)

6. To annex Estonia. (" " " ")

7. To reoccupy the areas seized from Finland after the Soviet Union's aggression in 1939. To acquire Petsamo. To demilitarize Finnish Karelia: thus making it possible for the Soviet Union to invade Finland with ease at any time. (Lozovsky has gone as far as to state to members of our Embassy that the Soviet Union will annex all Finland.)

These are Stalin's minimum aims in Europe; the aims he considers respectable enough to avow: the aims for which he will struggle fiercely.

The ground is being prepared by familiar Soviet tactics for the achievement of further aims, if and when the right moment comes:

A. *Rumania* — Soviet officials have not bothered to conceal their intention to use the defeat of Rumania and the suffering of the Rumanians to install a Soviet Government in Rumania . . .

B. *Bulgaria* — Great popular enthusiasm for Russia, plus defeat, is counted on to pave the way for the inclusion of Bulgaria in the Soviet Union by the Anschluss methods used in 1940 against Estonia, Latvia and Lithuania — a combination of 5th column communist activity and Soviet threats.

C. *Yugo-Slavia* — The "partizans" now fighting, plus the familiar methods, will it is hoped prepare the way for the setting up of a Soviet Government in Yugo-Slavia.

D. *Czecho-Slovakia* — Beneš has made a deal with the Soviet Union, said to be based on a Soviet promise to let Czecho-Slovakia have the Ruthenian tip of Slovakia (now in Hungary's possession), in return for a promise by Beneš to do nothing in foreign relations without previous consultation with the Soviet Government and consent of the Soviet Government. Beneš now is behaving as if he were a Soviet agent, just as, in Moscow the Czechoslovak Minister acts as an agent of the O.G.P.U.

E. *France* — Stalin's present policy is to set up a de Gaulle government based on support of certain elements of the Right and the Communists; to crush the democratic elements between; and eventually to have the French communists dominate de Gaulle. Stalin and de Gaulle have made a deal, and de Gaulle has announced officially the adherence of the French Communist Party to his "National Committee."

F. *Germany* — Stalin in both public and private utterances has made clear his policy towards Germany. In his speech of November 6, 1942, Stalin said:

"We have no such task as the annihilation of Germany. Our first task is precisely this — to annihilate the Hitlerite State and its instigators. We have no such task as the annihilation of every organized military force in Germany, because any literate man will understand that this is not only impossible in respect to Germany, as also in respect to Russia, but also inexpedient from the point of view of the victor."

By making a distinction between the Hitlerite State and Germany, Stalin is following the tactics used so successfully on German public opinion in 1918 by Woodrow Wilson. Just as Wilson's objective was to set up a democratic government in Germany which would cooperate with the Western democracies, so Stalin's objective is to set up a Soviet Quisling government in Germany (which at the outset probably would not be totally communist), which will cooperate with the Soviet Union. The Communist organization in Germany is strong; and strong is the propaganda appeal of the statement: "We Germans can save ourselves and our country by embracing communism."

G. *Poland* — The eventual reduction of Poland to the status of a small Soviet Republic is another bit of the Soviet picture.

H. The Bosphorus and Dardanelles, Northern Iran, etc., are remoter aims.

All these aims, from A to H, are desiderata *not musts* on Stalin's program. If any one of them can be achieved without provoking too much opposition, the amoeba will flow in. If strong opposition should be met, which might be injurious to the Soviet Union, the aim would be shelved. That there will be no strong opposition, is the view now held widely among Governments in Exile in London, among many groups in England, and among a great number of men of all nationalities who know Europe . . .

The argument for this view is the following:

When Germany surrenders, the United States and Great Britain will still have on their hands a war with Japan, which may be long. There will be no single power or coalition in Europe to counterbalance the Soviet Union. The Soviet Union will be in a position to devote all its strength to overrunning Europe because the Soviet Union will not be at war with Japan. Moreover, the United States and Great Britain will be able to shorten their war with Japan greatly, if the Soviet Union will accord them use of Soviet airfields in Siberia for bombing Japan . . .

Under these circumstances the United States and Great Britain will not have enough physical force or enough psychological preparation to resist the Soviet Union in order to establish a democratic order in Europe or even to get a compromise agreement from the Soviet Union.

While the United States and Great Britain are engaged in defeating Japan, the Red Army, accompanied by a mob of fraternizing common soldiers from the German and all other Axis armies, and a swarm of propagandists, now ready in Moscow, will sweep through Europe from east to west, being welcomed by the Soviet 5th columns already organized in every European country. Then will follow the familiar comedy. There will be no talk of "annexation by the Soviet

Union." There will be a "freely chosen form of government" (Soviet); "free expression of the people's will" (under occupation by the Red Army); and out will be trotted again all the obscene lies that accompanied the "freely expressed desire of the Baltic Republics, to be received into the Soviet Union" . . .

If this prognosis should be justified by the event, we should not have to develop many "views on the machinery of preparation for civil administration in occupied territories." There would be few occupied territories in Europe in which we would have anything to say about "civil administration."

How can we make sure that this will not happen — and achieve our own aim of peace in a world of freedom and democracy?

When Germany collapses we must (1) be in position to prevent, by one method or another, the flow of the Red amoeba into Europe; (2) set up in occupied or liberated countries in Europe democratic administrations which, working together, will be strong enough to provide the requisite defense against invasion by the Soviet Union.

No single state in Eastern Europe can be made strong enough to resist the flow of the Soviet Union without the support of other states. A combination of feeble states will be inadequate. An agglomeration of weaknesses is not strength.

We are obliged, therefore, in setting up administrations in occupied and liberated countries, not only to set up democratic administrations but also to lay the ground work for a combination of democratic governments in Europe strong enough to preserve democracy in Europe and keep the Bolsheviks from replacing the Nazis as masters of Europe.

This task is an enormously difficult one, which will demand not only the united and directed efforts of all agencies of the American Government but also the full cooperation of the British Government.

The British unfortunately — as well as some Americans — are in the grip of an idea which, if adopted as a policy, would result in such enfeeblement and enragement of Europe that Soviet domination would be easy. Many British officials are saying now that they intend to disarm totally every nation on the Continent of Europe, keep this disarmed Europe disunited, and maintain peace in Europe by having Europe guaranteed by the United States, Great Britain and the Soviet Union — all fully armed.

This is not the old British policy of the Balance of Power in Europe but a new one of the Balance of Impotence . . .

Since the fall of France in 1940, the people of the United States have learned that we cannot afford to let Great Britain and the British Empire be conquered by a foreign enemy. It is not too much to say that, tacitly and unconsciously, the people of the United States have accepted the policy that in the forseeable future we will not let Great Britain be conquered without fighting to prevent her defeat. We have, therefore, a duty to oppose, in the name of closest friendship, any policy that will endanger Great Britain, and eventually ourselves, even if the British Government unwisely should consider it in the interest of Great Britain.

Control of the Continent of Europe by the Soviet Government would be no less dangerous to Great Britain than control of the Continent of Europe by the German Government, and the policy of the Balance of Impotence would promote rather than prevent control of the Continent of Europe by the Soviet Government for the following reasons:

A guarantee of Europe by the Soviet Government would have practical value only if adequate force should stand behind the eastern frontier of Europe ready to resist the Red Army. The onward flow of the Soviet Union has never been impeded by any written agreement — from the early days of the Bolshevik revolution, to the days of the non-aggression Treaties with Finland and Poland, broken by Stalin in 1939, and the non-aggression Treaties with Estonia, Latvia and Lithuania, broken by Stalin in 1940. Soviet invasion finds barriers in armed strength, not in Soviet promises.

Indeed, the Baltic States, Finland and Poland knew so well that a Soviet guarantee would serve merely to open their frontiers to the Red Army, that they repeatedly rejected proposals of guarantees by the Soviet Union. The event proved they were right . . .

In addition, the Balance of Impotence policy would produce a moral revolt against the British and ourselves throughout Europe. Laval has been saying for months that this was the "peace" the United States, Great Britain and the Soviet Union intended to impose on Europe. This has been denied by every man in Europe who is on the side of the Western Democracies in this war. If we reveal that we intend to disarm Europe and leave the Soviet Union armed, we shall wreck any reputation for decency or common sense that we have in Europe. We cannot in honor place Christian civilization in Europe at the mercy of communist dictatorship.

The final answer to the Balance of Impotence Policy is that it is too disreputable to be avowed in time of war, and no policy too disreputable to be brought into light of day and exposed to public discussion can acquire the support of world public opinion or form the basis for world peace.

If the Soviet Union as well as Europe could be disarmed, an argument might be made (an unwise argument at best), for establishing an Anglo-Saxon armed dictatorship over all the earth. But the Soviet Union can not be disarmed. Since this is so, Europe cannot be made a military vacuum for the Soviet Union to flow into. Europe must be made not a military cipher but a large digit capable of defending itself against the Soviet Union.

Since it is our policy — and rightly our policy — to disarm and keep disarmed completely both Germany and Italy and to destroy their war industries, the two most populous nations of Europe will be withdrawn from the total of military strength in Europe. It is doubtful that a combination of all the other nations of Continental Europe can be made strong enough to withstand assault by the Soviet Union without British support. The balance of power which it is the interest of Great Britain and ourselves to seek is the balance between an integrated Europe (with Germany and Italy disarmed) and the Soviet Union.

An integrated democratic Europe, pacific but armed, is a vital element for the creation of world peace. How can such a Europe be achieved?

The first prerequisite is complete agreement between Churchill and yourself that it is desirable to create such a Europe. If you should have persuaded yourself that to adopt the Balance of Impotence policy is merely to adopt Soviet dictatorship over Europe, it ought not to be difficult for you to persuade Churchill.

If you can not get Churchill to work for an integrated Europe, there will be no integrated Europe. We are not strong enough in force or brains to achieve such an aim against the will of the British. The most intimate cooperation between ourselves and the British is, indeed, the sine qua non of every step towards peace. We shall, of course, compete in trade; but competition between us in major policies will be fatal to us both, and fatal to liberty and democracy in the world . . .

Europe, integrated and democratic is an essential element for the construction of durable peace. If such a Europe can be achieved, it should become — as a unit — one of the Powers which unites with the United States, Great Britain, the Soviet Union, China, etc., in worldwide agreements for the maintenance of peace.

These world agreements will be futile unless the substructure is sound — just as the League of Nations and the Kellogg-Briand Pact were futile because the substructure provided by the Treaty of Versailles was unsound.* It was obvious when that Treaty was signed that the Treaty was the dog and the League of Nations the tail, and that the tail would not wag the dog.

World-wide peace agreements or mechanisms will always be futile unless the substructure is sound. They will always acquire applause for their authors because mankind longs for peace — Mr. Kellogg and Mr. Briand were once considered great men — but they will evaporate into nothing under the stresses and strains set up by a bad basic settlement . . .

If it is agreed that it is in the interests of the United States, Great Britain — and peace — to establish an integrated, democratic Europe strong enough to defend itself against the Soviet Union, with the aid of Great Britain, and more remotely the United States, we should agree then as quickly as possible with the British on the strategy and tactics necessary to achieve our aims.

We should do this quickly. In the battle for peace time is running against us.

We shall never again have as much influence on Great Britain and the Soviet Union as we have today. Today they are dependent on us for their lives. We are the lady bountiful. They are the beggars. Our influence over Great Britain and the Soviet Union will decrease in direct proportion to our approach to victory over Germany. On the day Germany surrenders, our influence over the Soviet Union will reach zero — unless the Soviet Union should be in war with Japan.

The first aim of our peace strategy should be to get the Soviet Union to go to war with Japan.

Soviet Policy in the Far East is firmly based on the conclusion that it is contrary to Soviet interests to be at war on two fronts.

The Soviet Government today would prefer not even to discuss the use of Soviet fields in the Maritime Provinces of Siberia by American bombers. We should have to take a strong position on future aid to the Soviet Union even to compel the opening of discussions. If we should force the opening of discussions — which we should do in our national interest — the Soviet Government probably would try to drag out the talks, and ask us to create the right

* The Kellogg-Briand Pact, signed in August 1928, was an agreement to outlaw war eventually acceded to by sixty-three nations including, among others, the United States, Great Britain, France, Germany, the Soviet Union, Italy, and Japan.

atmosphere by accepting Soviet aims in Europe. The Soviet Government, indeed, probably would try to string out the talks until it had taken what it wanted in Europe and until we had reduced the Japanese fleet and air force to impotence.

The objective of the Soviet Government would be to weaken our resistance to the sovietizing of Europe by compelling us to defeat Japan the hard way — by direct naval assault, island by island through the Pacific . . .

If we continue our present policy of giving Stalin all possible aid while asking nothing from him in return, we shall probably find ourselves in this position in the Far East just as we shall probably find ourselves in the European position previously described.

Our bargaining position will be hopeless after the defeat of Germany; but it is still good. While it is still good, I think, you should invite Stalin to visit you in Washington. If he will not come to Washington, you should invite him to meet you in Alaska. Weather conditions probably would make early June the earliest practicable date for a meeting in Alaska. The earlier the date, the stronger will be your bargaining power.

I am certain that you yourself should handle this negotiation with Stalin. No other American could make the impression on him that needs to be made. And Stalin must be the negotiator on the other side. No Soviet official, not even Molotov, dares to commit his boss on anything important, and the negotiation must be for high stakes.

By using the old technique of the donkey, the carrot and the club you might be able to make Stalin move in the direction in which we want him to move.

You would have a substantial carrot: War aid of all sorts to the Soviet Union; post-war aid for rebuilding the Soviet Union; genuine security for the Soviet Union through agreements to maintain peace between the United States, the Soviet Union, Great Britain, Integrated Europe, China, etc.

Your club would have lead in it, not cotton: You could intimate that you might have to turn our major war effort against Japan instead of Germany; intimate a possible diminution or cessation of war aid to the Soviet Union at the end of the present protocol; intimate that you would find it too difficult from the point of view of domestic politics to agree to post-war aid for rebuilding the Soviet Union; intimate, also, full opposition to predatory Soviet policy in Europe and Asia.

Speed, in beginning these negotiations with Stalin, is of the essence. Your carrots and your club will slip gradually out of your hands.

Men, at some times are masters of their fate. You have your power now — and while you have it you must use it. You will lose it the day Germany collapses. Wilson could have written his own ticket before the Armistice of 1918. You may be able to write yours — now.

If you can get Stalin to agree (1) to make war on Japan, or let us use the air fields of the Maritime Provinces, (2) to promise in writing not to annex (by the familiar process) any European country, (3) to dissolve the Comintern, you will have delivered a greater stroke for liberty, democracy and peace than any you have yet struck.

But even if Stalin rejects your proposals, you will have gained much for yourself and future Presidents. The Communists of the United States and the world, and their fellow travelers and dupes, will never be able to use as propaganda against democracy the argument that the Soviet Union was never offered full friendship and cooperation by the United States. That will be a powerful argument against the Government of the United States unless you see Stalin and make your proposal . . .

Whether you succeed or fail to get an agreement from Stalin, therefore, we should not supinely accept as inevitable the irruption of the Red Army into Europe. And we should define as Europe the Europe of *1938*, minus Bessarabia which should go to the Soviet Union.

There is only one sure guarantee that the Red Army will not cross into Europe — the prior arrival of American and British Armies in the eastern frontiers of Europe. To state this is to state what appears to be an absurdity, if the assumption is made that we can reach the eastern frontiers of Europe only by marching through France, Italy and Germany. It may, however, be possible to reach this frontier before the Red Army, if we make our attack on the Axis not by way of France and Italy but by way of Salonika and Constantinople.

The worst basis for military decisions is political expediency. Certainly no sound strategic conception should be altered for political reasons. But there is a large body of military opinion in Washington that favors — on purely military grounds — striking at the Axis by way of Greece, Turkey, Bulgaria and Rumania rather than by way of France and Italy. And if military considerations are equal, the strategic plan that promises political success is to be preferred to the strategic plan that promises political disaster.

This is a question for you and Churchill, and your military advisors to decide . . .

On these problems (and a host of others), you will need the united labors of the best brains you have in the military, political, economic, and relief fields. I think you should order the study to be made at once.

To win the peace at the close of this war will be at least as difficult as to win the war. The hardest thinking, the most careful planning, and most concentrated efforts are necessary *now* if we are to establish a world of liberty, democracy and peace. We must define our aim, plan our work and work our plan, by unified and directed activity on the part of every agency of the Government that has a contribution to make to our total effort.

Wisely you have asked many departments of the Government and many agencies and private organizations and individuals to study the problems of peace. But today in the field of peace it is as if, in the field of war, the War and Navy Departments should be attempting to run the fight against the Axis with no General Staff, no Joint Staff, no Combined Staff, leaving every difficult decision, even of detail, to you.

The Department of State, to be sure, has been entrusted with the duty of making plans for peace — and rightly. Hull has an old line American wisdom which is so great that I have not known him to go wrong once in the past ten years on a fundamental decision. Moreover, his prestige in the nation is unique. He is far more trusted than any other member of your administration. And he has an influence with the Senate which is very great and will be vital in obtaining the consent of the Senate to postwar agreements.

But Hull's authority in his own Department has been nibbled at so long by various subordinates that there are within the Department of State four mutually antagonistic organizations functioning in semi-independence. The first step toward getting the same drive into our fight for peace that we now have in our fight for victory is to give Hull orders to dismiss any and every member of his Department or the Foreign Service that he chooses to get rid of and to strengthen his Department in every possible way; and to take on his own shoulders — with responsibility to you alone — the fight for peace. There are plenty of good men in the Department and the Foreign Service, and in other government departments and the country, to form a really great staff. It is late in the day to do this. It is not yet too late. It soon will be too late . . .

My recommendations therefore are:

1. Agreement with Churchill that the Balance of Impotency Policy for Europe is contrary to the interests of both the United States and Great Britain.

2. Agreement with Churchill to adopt the policy of an integrated, democratic Europe.

3. Conversations between you and Stalin.

4. Immediate study of attack on the Axis by way of Greece, Turkey, Bulgaria and Rumania.

5. Immediate order to Hull to reorganize the Department of State.

Detailed recommendations for setting up machinery for installing democratic administrations in countries in Europe which we may occupy or liberate, I reserve for the next installment of my answer to your letter of November 19, 1942.

Very sincerely yours,
William C. Bullitt

Fleet Admiral William D. Leahy, Chief of Staff to the President and later Ambassador to the Vichy Government in France, wrote in his book *I Was There:* "Bill Bullitt, who was always well informed on European politics and who had spent much time in Russia, had me to lunch at his residence on March 4 [1943], and we discussed his ideas on problems that seemed likely to face us in the immediate postwar period. Bullitt said that America then had sufficient power to force upon the Allies a policy to govern postwar international relations in Europe similar to the power possessed by Woodrow Wilson prior to the armistice that ended the last war in 1918.

"He was convinced that immediately upon the collapse of Germany this power would pass from America to Soviet Russia, which latter nation would impose the peace terms and the geographical distribution of territory. This would inevitably result in Soviet ascendancy throughout Europe.

"He believed that the Department of State should be reorganized into a dynamic peace staff provided with a national postwar policy, and directed to work at once toward a successful accomplishment of that policy, using every power available to us, and before our influence would be destroyed by a collapse of Germany. He thought the Department at that time was completely disorganized and inefficient even in its routine peace time activities." [1]

Later in the book Admiral Leahy says that Bullitt made a prediction to him that it would be necessary for the United States to accept General de Gaulle.

Churchill arrived at the White House on May 12, 1943. He remained for two weeks, spending the weekend at Shangri-La, the President's camp, within easy reach of Washington. During this visit Churchill addressed the Congress and the speech was broadcast throughout the world.

DEPARTMENT OF THE NAVY
OFFICE OF THE SECRETARY
WASHINGTON

May 12, 1943

Dear Mr. President:

Herewith a memorandum on our major political-military strategy.

I feel deeply that Churchill's visit gives you an opportunity to take the world leadership that at this moment should belong to the President of the United States.

Yours very sincerely,
William C. Bullitt

MEMORANDUM

Our national interests in this war are: (1) to defeat Japan, Germany, Italy, and their allies, as quickly as possible with as small American losses as possible; (2) to achieve a world settlement that will give us additional physical security, and give the entire world a possibility of enduring peace.

Our major military strategy to achieve those aims is based on the following theorem:

The basic strategy of the United Nations aims to hold Japan in check so that she cannot overwhelm the Chinese or launch an offensive against Russia, India, or Australia; and, while doing this with the minimum forces required, to concentrate all remaining forces for the destruction of the armed power of Germany. This strategy is dictated by the fact that the largest single land force on the side of the United Nations — the Red Army — is committed to the struggle against Germany and cannot be shifted elsewhere. Sound military judgment therefore demands that all additional strength be concentrated to bring the fight with Germany to a conclusion, leaving Japan to be dealt with later by the full strength of the United Nations.

This theorem is based on *two false assumptions:* (1) that, after the defeat of Germany, the Soviet Union and Great Britain will turn all their strength immediately against Japan; (2) that the war aims of the Soviet Union, Great Britain and the United States are identical.

Unfortunately, the probability is that, after the defeat of Germany, we shall get no help from the Soviet Union and only conservative assistance from Great Britain in our war against Japan. (When Japan is on her last legs the Soviet Union will probably invade and annex Manchuria.)

Furthermore, it is certain that, if we have a hard war to fight against Japan while the Soviet Union is at peace and Great Britain fighting only conservatively, we shall have no decisive voice in the settlement in Europe. (We shall be asking the Soviet Union for support against Japan, and the whip in all negotiations will be in the hand of Stalin.) Europe will be divided into Soviet and British spheres of influence — according to present Soviet and British plans — and further wars in the near future will be rendered inevitable.

Therefore if we fail to get pledges now from both Great Britain and the Soviet Union that they will (a) go to war with all their forces against Japan as soon as Germany is defeated; and (b) establish a united democratic Europe, we shall lose all possibility of achieving an enduring peace; and — after having sacrificed the flower of our army and air force in combat against Germany — we shall face without much support a Japan that will have had two more years in which to increase her strength by organizing for war purposes the territories she has captured. This she is doing rapidly. Thus we shall achieve the maximum of American losses and the minimum of satisfactory settlements.

In view of these facts and probabilities, we must ask ourselves if there is not a major political-military strategy which might produce results more in accord with our national interests than the major strategy now envisaged — and at less expense in American blood.

We are pledged to clean out the Mediterranean by wiping the enemy from North Africa and such islands as are deemed necessary to ensure relatively safe passage of merchant shipping from Gibraltar to Port Said. We have no other outstanding promises or commitments. After opening the Mediterranean we shall be free in honor to turn the major portion of our war effort against either Germany or Japan.

We know that in all human probability: (1) Germany, whose inferiority in the air is now marked, cannot knock out either the Soviet Union or Great Britain even though we turn away from Europe to the Far East a sufficient proportion of our strength to defeat Japan — without of course withdrawing essential minimum support from Great Britain and Russia. (2) As soon as we shall have cleaned out the Mediterranean we can use that sea for a movement from west to east. We and the British can attack the Japanese in Burma next October with forces sufficient to reestablish minimum essential communications with China. At the same time — in fact right now — we can establish a strong American air force in China for the bombing of Japanese shipping in Chinese ports and along the Chinese coast. We can, in cooperation with the Chinese, Australians, New Zealanders and British, defeat Japan, and then turn our full strength to the task of assisting the British and the Russians to finish the Germans — who would be far weaker than this autumn.

In view of these facts and possibilities, it would be in line with American interests to put our position to Churchill in the following manner:

1. If we are to continue the policy of turning our major forces against Germany, he *and Stalin* must agree explicitly: (A) That after the defeat of Germany, Great Britain and the Soviet Union will immediately turn their full strength against Japan. (Churchill will be glad to agree. Stalin is the question). (B) That Europe is to be organized as a democratic unit which will take its place along with the United States, Great Britain, the Soviet Union and China as one of the great guarantors of world peace, and that the states of Europe are not to be over-run and are not to be placed in tutelage in British and Soviet spheres of influence.

2. If we cannot obtain explicit engagements from Churchill and from Stalin on these points, we shall be obliged to turn our major offensive effort against Japan although continuing essential minimum support to the Soviet Union and Great Britain.

3. If, after the defeat of Japan, Great Britain and the Soviet Union should still be at war with Germany, we, of course, would turn all American forces immediately against Germany.

If this line should be followed in conversations with Churchill, and later with Stalin, either we would get explicit promises of British and Soviet support against Japan and promises with regard to a settlement in Europe which might make peace conceivable, or we would be free to turn against Japan our full military strength unimpaired by the grave losses which would be incurred if we should first attack Germany — and on returning to the European theater with all our forces we would have a decisive voice in the European settlement.

You will recall that in the long memorandum I sent you on January 29th, 1943, which we discussed later at luncheon, I suggested that, *after* getting satisfactory promises from Churchill and Stalin with regard to European settlements, you should consider the advisability of invading Europe by way of Turkey, Thrace, Bulgaria and Rumania in order to make it difficult for Stalin to break his promise and over-run Central Europe. I still believe that this suggestion merits serious consideration; but it should be adopted only *after* you have prior agreements with Churchill and Stalin on Europe and the Far East — otherwise every American interest demands the defeat of Japan before the defeat of Germany. Indeed, it is so clearly in our national interest to attack and defeat Japan before attacking on the continent of Europe that political considerations alone justify giving Churchill and Stalin a chance to meet our Terms for attacking first in Europe.

The most curious phenomenon of the present period is the fact that at a time when our military strength is increasing prodigiously our world political leadership is disappearing. You remember Napoleon's remark that Wellington won at Waterloo because he did not realize he was beaten. We are in the opposite case. We are losing our world leadership because we do not realize that we have won power over the world. We are not exerting *our* will to achieve *our* aims — which happen to give the world a better chance of peace than the aims of any of our Allies. We can achieve *our* aims in *our* way — if *you will.*

WCB

In the *Life of Lord Halifax* by the Earl of Birkenhead, the wide divergence of opinion between the British Ambassador and Bullitt is shown by the following:

"Some time before, William Bullitt and Edward [Halifax] had walked for half an hour in the Observatory Garden discussing the enigma of Russia's secret intentions:

" 'I found Bullitt in a great state of excitement about the Soviet and very anti-Russian. He thinks we and his own Government are completely blind to the kind of thing he anticipates Stalin will want to do. As he sees it he will seek to dominate and control all Central and South-Eastern European Governments . . . and one of these days we shall all wake up to find Russia a great menace to our free democracies. I told him that this was not the impression gathered by those who had had to do with Stalin, but this naturally made no impression on him. He is a strange fellow, and I don't think judgement is his strongest quality.' "

Lord Halifax's biographer notes that: "It is not hindsight to say that Edward showed a certain obtuseness and lack of vision in the views he held at the time on this all important issue." [2]

The conference in Quebec with Churchill began on August 19, and prior to the meeting Churchill made a brief visit to Hyde Park. The conference convened with the knowledge of the approaching Italian surrender, which took place on September 3, 1943, and on October 13 the Royal Italian Government declared war on its former Axis partner, Germany.

Washington, D.C.
August 10, 1943

My dear Mr. President:

The impending visit of Mr. Churchill offers a chance — perhaps the last chance — to initiate with regard to the problems of Europe a policy in accord with the vital interests of the United States and Great Britain.

The chief of these interests is a lasting peace. And the objective of our policy toward Europe must be the creation of conditions that will offer some possibility of establishing lasting peace.

Domination of Europe by Hitler's Nazi dictatorship has been judged rightly to be an intolerable menace to Great Britain and the United States and their free institutions. Domination of Europe by Stalin's Communist dictatorship would be as great a threat to Great Britain and to the United States.

If Germany is to be defeated without such cost in American and British lives that victory might well prove to be a concealed defeat (like the French victory in the war of 1914), the continued participation of the Red Army in the war against Germany is essential.

The problem presented today to American and British statesmanship is, therefore, the problem of preventing the domination of Europe by the Moscow dictatorship without losing the participation of the Red Army in the war against the Nazi dictatorship.

In frankness, we must admit that we have not given this urgent political problem the attention it deserves and have not worked out with the British and the Russians any common plan for its solution. To delay further is to risk political catastrophe in Europe.

We can no longer reasonably hope to come to an agreed and honorable solution with the Soviet Union. Stalin again has avoided meeting you and it is difficult to believe that in his evasion there is not a desire to avoid being obliged to answer direct questions as to his intentions in Europe. For six weeks he has refused to receive either the American Ambassador or the British Ambassador in Moscow. And he has caused his Ambassadors to Washington and London to absent themselves from their posts, so that serious discussion of serious questions between Washington and Moscow, and London and Moscow, at this moment is impossible.

Stalin, however, without committing himself directly, has indicated in various ways his intentions with regard to various European countries.

In considering his intentions it is well to remember that he has three distinct methods of bringing peoples under his authority: (1) Invasion by the Red Army; (2) threat of invasion by the Red Army; (3) Communist revolution. It is also well to remember that he has his fifth columns in every country of Europe and that he has in Moscow organized groups or committees ready to operate in every country in Europe.

Stalin's intentions with regard to Europe seem to fall into the following pattern:

1. He has declared the Baltic States, Eastern Poland, the Bukovina, and Bessarabia to be integral parts of the Soviet Union.

2. The terms for peace with Finland which he gave us — especially the impossible demand that Finland must pay half the cost of the war — seem to indicate that he does not desire peace with an independent Finland but the total defeat of Finland and its annexation.

3. Stalin's intentions with regard to Poland seem fairly clear. The setting up of the communist "Free Polish Committee" in Mos-

cow, the creation of a communist "Free Polish Army" in the Soviet Union, and the secret activities of Soviet agents in Poland (with regard to which we have full information), add up to an intention to establish a Polish state controlled from Moscow either by the establishment of a Soviet Quisling Government in Poland or by the inclusion of Poland as a state in the Soviet Union.

4. We have less evidence with regard to Stalin's intentions concerning Rumania but there are numerous small pointers which indicate that he intends to bring Rumania under his authority by communist revolution coupled with an advance of the Red Army.

5. Stalin's interest in the Yugoslav Partisans, his strong position in Bulgaria, his relations with Beneš and the Czech underground, and his interest in seeing to it that any Government set up in France should be based in part on communist elements, are too well known to require discussion. Less well known are reports from Hungary and Austria indicating intense communist activity.

6. The Manifesto of the "Free German Committee" in Moscow has clarified Stalin's policy with regard to Germany. Conditions in Moscow are such that this Manifesto could not have been prepared or issued except on Stalin's order. It does not bind Stalin but it indicates the development of events in Germany that he hopes for: The overthrow of Hitler and the Nazis; the establishment of a "strong democratic power that will be implacable, that will ruthlessly suppress any attempt at new plots against the rights of free people or against European peace"; immediate cessation of military operations; recall of troops to the frontiers of Germany without their being disarmed; a request for peace negotiations. The Manifesto contains also the statement: "In this manner it [i.e., the new German Government] will attain peace and again place Germany on an equal footing with other nations."

The catch in this proposal is, of course, in the use of the word "democratic." To the communists the word democratic means the exact reverse of its meaning to us. To us it connotes freedom, the Bill of Rights, "government of the people, by the people, and for the people." To the communists it means a totalitarian dictatorship of the Soviet type — a government of the people, by the dictator, for the people. To the communists, our democracy is a government of the people, by the capitalists, for the capitalists. It is an extraordinary fact that we have let the communists steal our best word and give it a new meaning in the minds of the masses of Europe.

This is not to say that Stalin desires to set up a communist regime in Germany immediately after the defeat of Germany. On the contrary, he seems to wish to set up, in the first instance, a sort of Kerensky regime to bear the onus of the surrender — a government sufficiently controlled by communists to guarantee its failure, and the eventual installation of a frankly communist government controlled by Moscow.

It should be clear even to the most wishful thinker that, if Moscow-controlled governments should be installed in Germany and in central and eastern Europe, any serious attempt by Great Britain to keep the Soviet Union from controlling the remainder of Europe would lead either to collapse into communism of the remaining capitalist countries of Europe or to war between the Soviet Union and Great Britain.

A Europe divided into a Soviet sphere of influence, which would be communist, and a British sphere of influence, which would be capitalist, would produce at best an uneasy armistice but no peace. Europe would be another "house divided against itself " . . .

If, therefore, the British and American armies get into eastern and central Europe and establish themselves there before the Red Army gets in, and handle the situation firmly and intelligently, there is small chance that the Red Army will attempt to get in.

War is an attempt to achieve political objectives by fighting; and political objectives must be kept in mind in planning operations. Our political objectives require the establishment of British and American forces in the Balkans and eastern and central Europe. Their first objective should be the defeat of Germany, their second, the barring to the Red Army of the way into Europe . . .

It is not inconceivable that if we should have occupied Hungary and Rumania and should be advancing into Southern Poland, Slovakia and Austria, and if Hitler should be overthrown, the German Army leaders would prefer to hold on the eastern front, north of the Pripet Marshes, as they did in 1918 and 1919, and fall back rapidly before us until we should have occupied a line all the way to the Baltic . . .

The first step toward preventing Soviet domination of Europe is the creation of a British-American line in Eastern Europe. The second is the setting up of democratic governments behind our lines and the prevention of communist revolts. We should decide as rapidly as possible what men we can count on to set up such governments, and we must keep in mind that all governments we set up must be progressive governments with the most advanced programs

of social justice. We shall find our strongest supporters among be-
lievers of all the Christian Churches.

We must also make clear our position toward the whole problem
of Europe. No one in Europe today has the slightest idea what our
program is. This is natural since we have no program. Stalin has a
clear program and a vast organization working day and night to
carry it out.

. We cannot beat something with nothing. We must state our case.
And we should state it in words that will echo in the hearts of those
who may support us. The situation in Italy demands an early statement of our intentions. We should make our statement to Italy, a
statement to all the peoples of Europe.

This statement should be made to the peoples of Europe by yourself, on behalf of the people of the United States. Its effect would be
enhanced if in one way or another Mr. Churchill should endorse
it . . .

Yours very sincerely,
Bill

The year 1943 was filled with disillusionment and disappointment for Bullitt. The President paid no attention to his long,
carefully reasoned and documented reports on how to secure a
just and lasting peace for the peoples of Europe, and remembering the results of the Peace of Versailles in 1919, Bullitt was filled
with gloom and foreboding. He had accurately fathomed the future policy of Russia and felt that every day that passed without
some action being taken by the President to thwart Russia's aims
made it more certain that all of Eastern Europe would fall under
the domination of the Soviet. He was frustrated over his inability
to persuade President Roosevelt.

On November 23, 1943, the President met with Mr. Churchill
and Chiang Kai-shek for the conference at Cairo, Egypt. Several
questions were discussed, among them the problem of a Supreme
Commander. The Americans wanted a Commander of northwest
European operations, a Commander of the forces in the Mediterranean, and a Supreme Commander over both. Mr. Roosevelt
also spent considerable time with Chiang Kai-shek, much to Mr.
Churchill's displeasure.

Churchill and Roosevelt went on to Teheran, where the first

session of the meetings with Stalin took place on November 28. This was the first time that all three had met together to discuss the prosecution of the war. The meetings were followed by small luncheons and dinners which gave them better opportunities for informal talks with one another.

The conference ended with an agreement that the invasion of France should take place in May 1944, that the partisans in Yugoslavia would be supported, that further attempts should be made to bring Turkey into the war, and that the military staffs of the three countries should keep in close touch.

32

Victory and Death

JANUARY 1944—JULY 1945

Final Break Between Roosevelt and Bullitt
Bullitt Joins de Gaulle
With the French Army
Roosevelt's Death
Victory Parade in Paris

ALTHOUGH 1943 HAD ENDED so dismally for Bullitt, the year 1944 was to prove one of the happiest and most exciting of his career.

MEMORANDUM

January 16, 1944

Otto [of Hapsburg] called on me this afternoon at four o'clock to give me an account of the conversation he had just had with the President. He said that they had talked for an hour and a half and the President could not have been more cordial. He said the President had told him that he positively had not promised the Russians that they could occupy Hungary. The President had indicated that the countries he had told the Russians they could take over and control completely as their sphere — so completely that the United States could from this moment on have no further policies with regard to them were: Rumania, Bulgaria, Bukovina, Eastern Poland, Lithuania, Estonia, Latvia, and Finland. He said that the President had told him that Stalin had insisted that his Rumanian annexation should include a portion of Transylvania now held by Rumania.

He said that contrary to the general impression, the President had seemed to be just as fond of Churchill as ever and not to have been captivated personally by Stalin . . .

Otto said the President had said in so many words that he believed the Russians ought to have Eastern Poland.

Otto also said that the President had told him flatly that Rumania had offered him, the President, unconditional surrender recently but that he had been unable to do anything about the unconditional surrender of Rumania since he had promised Stalin that Rumania was entirely a Russian problem to be dealt with as the Russians might wish.

WCB

MEMORANDUM

February 1, 1944

I called on the Secretary of State at 10:30 this morning at his request. He said that yesterday in the course of a conversation with the President, he had said to the President . . . that I should be used in a position of real importance at the present time.

Hull said that the President had then said that he had not liked the way I had acted in the Welles affair. Hull said that he had replied that if I had done anything to help get Welles out of the picture, he, the President, should be most grateful to me; that he and himself, Hull, had been sitting on a keg of dynamite for two years and that anyone who had helped get Welles out of the picture had performed a great public service. He said, "I told the President that it was criminal for a man of Welles' habits to hang himself around our necks and hang on when he knew that the exposure of his behavior would blow the Administration into the air."

He said that the President had then said, "Well, what kind of a job can we put Bill on?" and that he had then suggested that as Ambassador-at-Large, I should be put in charge of all our relations from Dakar and Casablanca through the Mediterranean to Teheran. He said that the President had said that he would think it over.

I asked Hull what he thought that meant, adding that I could not say even if such a job were offered to me that I would wish to take it. Hull said that he thought that it meant that the President had gotten over the top of the hill of his rage at me arising from the Welles case and he asked me if I would not wait for another week or ten days before definitely going into private life. I said that I would . . .

I then asked Hull if he had taken up with the President the suggestion that I had made to him, Hull, on Sunday that the President should send a strong personal appeal to Stalin stating that after their conversations in Teheran he had hoped that a close cooperation and collaboration could be established between the United States and the Soviet Union not only during the war but after the war; that the action of the Soviet Union against Poland had aroused grave doubts in public opinion in the United States, and that if the Soviet Union should continue this policy it would be most difficult for him, the President, to continue this policy of cooperation. Hull said that he had made this suggestion to the President strongly yesterday and that the President had taken it under favorable consideration but that he did not yet know whether or not the President would act on it.

WCB

MEMORANDUM

March 11, 1944

I called on Cordell Hull at 3:30 this afternoon . . .

I then asked Cordell what the substance of his conversation had been with the President just before his departure. He said that he had taken to the President a memorandum for the President's O.K., saying that I was to be appointed Ambassador-at-Large to function in the area of West Africa, North Africa, and the Near and Middle East and to serve as American Political Adviser on the staff of the Commander-in-Chief of the Mediterranean area. Hull said that when he had submitted this to the President, he had been of course certain that the President would concur since the President had already told him twice that this was O.K. He said that he did not know what had happened but it was evident that the President had changed his mind completely. He said that he, Hull, had argued with him, the President, for about five minutes and had gotten no answer and that the President had finally written on the memorandum, "Why not Minister to Saudi Arabia?" Hull then said, "You know I don't keep any secrets from you, Bill, and I'll show it to you." He searched in his desk for a minute and drew out the memorandum which was worded exactly as he had stated. It was with the words penciled at the bottom of the page with the President's handwriting: "Why not Minister to Saudi Arabia?"

Hull went on to say that he had the impression definitely that the President knew perfectly well that I would not accept such a post and that his act in proposing that it should be offered to me was merely a stall . . .

We then went on to discuss the general international political situation. Hull said that he was at his wit's end and wished that he could get out of the State Department but added quickly that he had so few months to remain that he thought he would stay and try to keep things running. He said that he was trying to make a good record of friendliness toward the Russians for future use; that he was trying to get some sort of cooperation with the Senate; and that he was trying under terrible difficulties to keep some hand on our larger international policies. He added that he still did not know what had happened at Teheran and that he had no knowledge whatsoever of the constant stream of communications that was being exchanged between the President and Churchill and Stalin. He added that the President seemed to be cut off from advisers of all kinds of international affairs. He certainly was not consulting him, Hull; Hopkins had been ill for some time and he was so ill that he might never come back to work and the President was apparently just making decisions without consulting anyone. He said that while Stettinius was a very decent fellow he was entirely inexperienced in foreign affairs except in the domain of Lend-Lease and could not be expected to advise the President.

Hull said that he had never known the President to be so aloof and he thought this might be due to the fact that the President was complaining of constant headaches.

WCB

On several occasions Bullitt, restive with his Washington duties, applied directly to Secretary of War Stimson for active duty with the army. These offers were declined and he promptly wrote to General de Gaulle offering to join the Free French Army, which was to land on the south coast of France on August 15, 1944, promptly capturing the two great ports of Toulon and Marseille on August 28. General de Gaulle in a handwritten letter from Algiers replied in the following terms:

Mr. William C. Bullitt   Algiers
                                                        25 May 1944
My dear Ambassador,
    There are some consolations. Your letter, for me, is one. It will be for all the French. Come now! Good and dear American friend. Our ranks are open to you. You will return with us into wounded

Paris. Together, we will see your bestarred flags mingled with our tricolors.

I send you, my dear Ambassador, my warmest regards.

C. de Gaulle

[A handwritten letter.]

Thus began one of the best years of Bill's life. He was in action, he was part of the French Army, and above all his deep sense of the romantic and dramatic finally could dominate his daily life and thoughts.

Late in May 1944, Bill stayed with us to say good-bye, and in June sailed for Europe. He joined General (later Marshal) de Lattre de Tassigny, who was in command of the First French Army. Bill received a commission as a Commandant (Major) in the French infantry and became an aide to General de Lattre, going with him on all occasions and living in his quarters. General de Gaulle has described de Lattre as "emotional, flexible, farsighted and widely curious, influencing the minds around him by the ardor of his spirit and winning loyalty by the exertions of his soul, heading towards his goal by sudden and unexpected leaps, although often well calculated ones." [1]

De Lattre was without doubt one of the ablest of the French generals in their best fighting tradition. He was well loved by all ranks and admired for his boldness and strategy by French and Americans alike. Bill described him as "taut, intense, intuitive, with the eye of a wary eagle above a jutting beak of a nose, de Lattre is an embodied will to victory . . . From himself, his officers and men, he demands perfection. He feels no patience with anything less than faultless conduct, and he breaks a general as ruthlessly as a corporal. Quick to anger, equally quick to sympathy, he is at the same time admired, loved, feared and hated. Yet he is always respected because he is a genius as a strategist and tactician, and he is harder on himself than on anyone under his command." Bill had the greatest affection for him, which almost amounted to hero worship.

The French Army landed at two small towns in the south of France and after driving the Germans out of Marseilles advanced northward along the Rhône River. By September they had reached the Vosges Mountains, but were held up at Colmar after breaking through the Belfort Gap. In December they were still in the Vosges and the winter was a particularly harsh one. By the middle of December 1944, the morale of the army was low. The reason, according to General de Lattre, was: "From one end of the hierarchy to the other, particularly among the officers, the general impression is that the nation has neglected, has abandoned us . . . The real source of this problem is the nation's non-participation in the war." [2]

It was not until January 19, 1945, that the advance began again, and in February drove the Germans from Colmar. Strasbourg had fallen and in February all of Alsace had been liberated. On March 30 the Rhine was crossed and on April 20 Württemberg was captured and the Danube was behind the French. Germany had now collapsed and the surrender was signed at Reims on May 7, 1945.

Bill's letters to me tell of his life during this fighting. The first account of it is dated October 14, 1944:

> I am in Paris on a mission for two days and return to the front tomorrow. Nothing since 1919 has given me so much satisfaction as the job I am doing now, and I haven't felt so well in twenty years. I weigh 160!
>
> We crossed from Italy in an infantry landing craft — two nights in the hold with eighty others, quite comfortable and I joined General de Lattre de Tassigny at his first headquarters at Pierrefeu. Since then I have spent about twenty hours a day with him — as he doesn't care for sleep and I go along wherever he goes. As you know he is Commander-in-Chief of the First French Army — the only French Army. He is a great fellow — with many of General MacArthur's characteristics, plus the dash of a French cavalry leader. He goes into the front line constantly with your humble brother along — so that I have a chance to be in the scrap both at the planning end and the execution. We were in the middle of the battle at Toulon and Marseille — and a lot of village and mountain attacks.
>
> I have been able to be of some real service at various times — and I do jobs for him from the highest level to the lowest, including the interpreting when General Marshall or other big fish come along. The hours are long and the discipline absolute and the physical life

hard. We have no heat or hot water and I get a bath when we visit American headquarters! But his chef is superb and I picked up a lot of the best wines in Burgundy for de Lattre's "popote."

My house at Chantilly is intact and my servants still there. The apartment in Paris is dirty but o.k. Nearly all my close friends have survived and I have been kissed more times than I shall ever be again. You'll be glad to know that both Guy La Chambre and his wife are well and happy. Even old Hortense [Anne's nurse] has survived. Daladier's son Jean — twice wounded in the Maquis — told me last night that his father is still o.k. in Germany — or rather a prison in the Tyrol — and that when the Germans took him out of France he left clutching a large package of pipe tobacco I had got through to him. Apparently every package to prisoners that I sent was delivered.

Paris is a bit sad as there are no lights and no restaurants except in a few hotels — but the French are as delightful as ever and the young men of the F.F.I. who volunteer for the Army are filled with a spirit that passes belief . . .

I don't need anything, and I don't know any way you could send me anything if I did need it. The standard of living and communications of the French Army is not exactly that of the American! Everyone, French and American alike, has been angelic to me and you may be sure that if I do have any needs they will be filled somehow over here.

Please give my love to Anne, Susy and Rita and Louisa. As I do not know when I shall have a chance to send a letter again I'll also say Merry Xmas and a Happy New Year.

I hope you can read this in spite of my effort to write as small as possible with a scratchy French pen. This decision to go into the French Army was good. Indeed, I don't see why I never thought of becoming an army officer.

Love and good luck,
Bill

It was undoubtedly on this trip to Paris that Bill was able to make a dramatic gesture, dear to his heart and in keeping with his nature. He had left the Embassy in Paris over four years before and he was now able to return and personally unlock the gates which had been closed for so long. Moreover, he was in a French uniform.

7 November 1944

Dear Babe,

I have not had a single letter and I wish you would send me a lot of family news. I suspect that you have written but the letters have been lost somewhere in the French P.O. which is not too efficient. If you want to send me anything you can by way of a package addressed to Colonel Strohm, 46th General Hospital. I don't need anything but I could consume some chocolates and some nuts — and lots of news. Will you do all the usual Xmas presents for me and some small thing for Anne?

Love,

Bill

26 November 1944

Dear Orville,

I was utterly delighted to hear from you. Now that you are free from the War Production Board, why don't you come over and do some work in France? You can have my apartment in Paris and the Château de St. Firmin for weekends. Paris is far from gay but it would do you good to see how persistently the French are working at the job of pulling themselves together . . . I am sure you followed the French offensive in Alsace. It was a miracle of doing much with small means — a complete strategic and tactical surprise to the Germans. The French troops and Generals had all the intelligence and guts of 1914.

As usual I went everywhere with de Lattre and saw a lot of the real thing at distances of a few yards. Incidentally in addition to being a member of de Lattre's military Cabinet, I am now serving on the General Staff as "Chef de la Section d'Action sur le Morale de l'Ennemi." So I have plenty of work to do and at least the illusion that I am being of some real service. Also when the great arrive — Churchill, de Gaulle, Eisenhower, etc., I usually have some interpreting to do.

We have had rain every day except three since September 26 — two months solid — and need gills rather than a nose through which to breathe; but I have not even had a cold and am in full health.

I don't know what on earth to tell you about money [this was not unusual, as over the years his bank would call me to say he was overdrawn] because I get no mail and haven't the slightest idea what my obligations may be. Over here I have almost no expenses while at the front — which is nearly all the time — and I get paid 4000 francs a month by the French. I do need money when in Paris and prices there are atrocious. I shall try and put $2000 in my dollar account at Morgan & Cie. I assume there is plenty in my account at the Girard Trust.

I approve everything you do in advance.

God bless you all,

Love,
Bill

Paris
13 December 1944

Dear Babe,

. . . de Lattre has said to me that I am to be made a Lt. Colonel at Xmas. We have been cold and dirty for three weeks and had no water to drink — and I have been cleaning my teeth in Corton Charlemagne 1941 at 250 francs a bottle! It all seems to agree with me and I am in fine health.

God bless you and keep you well,
Bill

At Christmas I received a letter from Douglas MacArthur II from Paris, saying he had seen Bill, who was in grand form and looked fit despite the hard and rugged life he had been leading at the front.

18 December 1944

Dear Orville,

I shall think of you all at Xmas and wish I could be with you, but don't imagine I shall be doing any suffering. We have water now and plenty to eat — cooked in the best French manner, and I am thriving. What's more I have now lots of good friends here — all the way from the C. in C. in soldiers 2ième Classe, and the work is both interesting and exciting. Why don't you get a job in France? Why not come over for Will Clayton [Assistant Secretary of State]? The General who is living in the Château will probably get out of it by February 1st, and you would like it. Did I tell you it is not only intact but also furnished as that S.O.B. Abetz [Otto Abetz, German Ambassador to Paris] who occupied it for four years had to run so fast that he didn't have time to take away his furniture!

Most of it is ugly — but it is pleasant to have captured something from one of the slimy Boches, and there is one good rug.

All your news of the family delighted me. I shall write John tonight — but it seems impossible to send a letter that far.*

The Boches are still fighting like tigers and will have to be beaten in field after field, and that will not be a short job, but I think that six or eight months ought to cover it — unless there is some sort of catastrophe. I have rarely had a more interesting work than during the past few days — at the top — and the little section of the General Staff which I run is also going well. When I was in Paris last week I was given so many Xmas presents that I shall feel as if I was a small boy again on Xmas day.

Most of my French friends are back in their houses and I have three rooms always open to me, at Dr. Roussi's — he is again Rector of the University of Paris — Senator Cuttoli's and Guy La Chambre's, and the director of the Ritz has offered me his own rooms — so that even in Paris I have plenty of warmth.

God bless you all and give you a Happy New Year.

Love,
Bill

While Bullitt was with the French Army the famous conference at Yalta took place in February 1945.

Bullitt's lengthy memorandums to the President of January 29 and August 10, 1943, preceded this conference by two years. The President did not accept the advice offered to him and preferred to believe that he could deal with Stalin and have confidence in his promises. Bullitt had correctly predicted that, unless Roosevelt could obtain written assurances from the Soviet on the future of Europe while Russia needed the help of the United States and Great Britain, Stalin would work his will after victory over Germany was obtained. Bullitt predicted the annexation by Russia of Bessarabia, Bukowina, part of Poland, Lithuania, Latvia, Estonia, and certain areas of Finland. He also believed that Rumania and Bulgaria would enter the Soviet Union and that Czechoslovakia would do nothing in foreign relations without Russian approval. He felt sure that Stalin's aim was to set up a

* Our youngest son, John, was a sergeant in the infantry in the Pacific.

partially Communist government in Germany and to make Poland a small Soviet Republic.

Russia was able to carry out most of this program, perhaps largely owing to the failure of the President to heed this warning, and the result has been the division of Europe with a vast Communist sphere of influence.

My brother's letters to me contain no mention of Yalta and it is highly doubtful that he had any knowledge of what took place.

Mr. Offie has written this recollection of the President at the time of the Yalta Conference:

"I saw Mr. Roosevelt the last time personally on board the S.S. *Quincy* in Algiers Harbor. He received me flanked by his daughter, Anna. He looked ghastly, sort of dead and dug up. The same reaction was had by Doug MacArthur, who had come down from Paris with his chief at that time, Mr. Caffery, as well as by Kirk, our Ambassador in Rome, who knew Mr. Roosevelt well from college days. Harry Hopkins was carried off the S. S. *Quincy* on a stretcher and, accompanied by Chip Bohlen, was flown to Marrakech to get strength enough to be flown to the United States. Pa Watson, who died en route to the United States, was under an oxygen tent, and another principal aide was in the sick bay with a bad case of influenza. As Kirk said, 'C.O., this is really a ship of death and everyone responsible in encouraging that man [FDR] to go to Yalta has done a disservice to the United States and ought to be shot.' "

President Roosevelt died of a massive cerebral hemorrhage at Warm Springs on April 12, 1945.

9 January 1945

Dear Orville,

. . . I would enjoy some peppermints and chocolates and a case of whiskey and a box of cigars and shall put the request on a separate piece of paper, as per your order. I had a fine Xmas at the front — plenty of snow — and a bully New Year's Eve in Paris at Guy La Chambre's.

Work continues to be interesting as you may imagine in view of events. Don't let anyone fool you — the Germans are still very tough and we shall be lucky if we finish them by next Xmas.

Love and good luck to you all.

Bill

P.S. Why not get a job over here?

On January 19 I received a letter from Mr. Offie, who was now United States Deputy Political Adviser at Allied Force Headquarters in Italy, reporting that he saw Bill in Paris and that Bill was finally getting my letters. He asked me to send Bill some books on foreign affairs and history and assumed I was taking care of his income tax and any other bills. "I can tell you from experience that it is no good sending him bills. He just doesn't open them."

73 Rue de la Tour
Paris
20 February 1945

Dear Orville,

About six weeks ago I was hit by a car in Alsace and my left leg, hip, back and ribs were somewhat damaged. Like a fool — because I was busy with the preparations for the attack on the pocket in Alsace — I said nothing to anyone and went on with very tough days at the front in very cold weather. The result was that after about nine days I was totally unable to stand up. I spent about a week on my back at Headquarters and then was moved to the American 46th General Hospital where I was on my back for nearly three weeks. Your box of nuts and chocolates reached me there and were marvelous. They turned me out about ten days ago and I went up again to the Rhine — but after doing Alsace with de Gaulle and de Lattre my leg went bad again and I was sent to Paris for treatment at the American Hospital. [While Ambassador Bill was president of the hospital.] My leg is much better and I am living at Douglas MacArthur II's house and spending the mornings at the hospital having treatment. The pain in my back and hip is almost gone and otherwise I am in wonderfully good shape. Every organ examined to the limit and certified perfect — blood pressure 130 over 80. [This injury was to plague Bill for the rest of his life. He walked with a cane and in his later years had difficulty in walking.]

I am extremely anxious to get back to the front and shall not stay in Paris one day more than necessary . . . De Gaulle asked me if I didn't want to fly home to get fixed up; but I told him I wanted to visit Berlin first. Everyone has been angelic to me — French and American alike. Incidentally, the work that is being done by the American doctors and nurses is superb beyond all praise. The wounded are as well taken care of as if they were at home.

I don't need an earthly thing, but it is always good to get chocolates . . . The way things are going I have some hope of seeing you again before October — and perhaps very much sooner.

Don't worry about me. I am absolutely o.k. and Paris is as lovely as ever. Spring is beginning. On the way up here the fields were beginning to show wild flowers and the air was full of larks.

Best love to you and Susy and all the children.

Bill

Bill remained with General de Lattre until the end of the war, when the French Army was on the Danube, returning home in July. He received the Croix de Guerre with palm and the Legion of Honor. Mme. La Maréchale de Lattre de Tassigny has kindly permitted me to quote from an article that she wrote about Bill for a French journal. She tells of a visit which General de Gaulle made to General de Lattre at Besançon. De Gaulle was on his way to Nancy and Bill said to him, "General, you should really pay a visit to Domrémy." To which the reply was, "Jeanne d'Arc, yes, I will go, she has well merited it." De Gaulle made a detour of several kilometers and on reaching the home of Jeanne d'Arc he knelt on the threshold and prayed for the French Army and its protection by the saint.

Another day a delegation of Russian generals arrived for lunch at General de Lattre's headquarters and Bill, knowing how the Russians felt toward him, asked to be put at the foot of the table. At the end of lunch his Russian neighbor, turning to him, said, "Without doubt you rose from the ranks." At least he was sure he had not been recognized! On the day that the French entered Baden-Baden, General de Lattre jokingly spoke at dinner of appointing Bill as governor of the city. This was taken seriously by the American press, which announced the appointment, and it created quite a tempest in a teapot. When General de Lattre left the troops of occupation Bill gave him a sword cane inscribed with the words, "For my friend Jean, whom I will never forget."

In these months, Bill had had all the exciting and romantic experiences which his sentimental and idealistic nature forever craved, but the apogee was to come in a final blaze of French emotional outpouring. On July 14, 1945, the French national holiday celebrating the fall of the Bastille, the French Army held a victory parade in Paris which was reviewed by General de Gaulle as it marched up the Champs Élysées. It was one of the hottest days of the summer, with brilliant sunlight, and along the entire line of march the pavements were packed with deliriously shouting crowds. I am indebted to M. André Chamson, former member of the Académie Française and now Director General of the Archives de France, for an account of this day. M. Chamson, like Bill, was a Commandant and an aide to General de Lattre. He has written to me, "A few days before the fourteenth of July we had received the order to make ourselves as neat as possible — which was not without creating grave problems for us — we were soldiers at the end of a campaign, and it was not without some difficulty that we were able to make ourselves presentable. I see very exactly the order of march, from the Place de la Bastille to the Arc de Triomphe de l'Étoile, passing by the Place de la République, the Grands Boulevards, the Rue de la Madeleine and the Place de la Concorde.

"At the head of this parade was a jeep in which a non-commissioned officer held aloft the flag of the General, commander of the First French Army. Behind this jeep at fifty metres, came a command car in which rode General de Lattre. At a few metres behind him three command cars drove abreast carrying the officers who had been personally chosen by General de Lattre, and in the car on the right were, side by side, with arms folded, the Commandant Bullitt and the Commandant Chamson.

"I think that for the former Ambassador of the United States in France, this passage across Paris in all the intoxication of a victory which wiped out four years of servitude, was a thrilling adventure. It was for me, and after a quarter of a century, it remains so; and I still hear, in the roar of the tanks, the immense ovation of the people of Paris who celebrated through the victory of the Allies, the victory and the liberation of France."

LE JOUR DE GLOIRE EST ARRIVÉ!

References

Bibliography

References

BIOGRAPHICAL FOREWORD (*pages xxxv–xlvi*)

1. Bullitt file.
2. British Foreign Office, 4954 FO 371/16599, 1668 3/4/33 372.
3. Ibid., 4954 FO 371/17255, 8689 12/6/33 253.
4. *Evening Bulletin,* February 26–27, 1967.

CHAPTER 1 State Department and Versailles Conference 1917–1932 (*pages 3–14*)

1. William C. Bullitt, *The Bullitt Mission to Russia* (New York: B. W. H. Huebsch, 1919), p. 33.
2. Ibid., pp. 63–64.
3. Ibid., p. 40.
4. George F. Kennan, *Memoirs, 1925–1950* (Boston: Little, Brown, 1967), p. 80.
5. Beatrice Farnsworth, *William C. Bullitt and the Soviet Union* (Bloomington, Ind.: Indiana University Press, 1967), p. 54.
6. Louis Fischer, *Men and Politics: An Autobiography* (New York: Duell, Sloan and Pearce, 1941), p. 132.
7. George Goldberg, *The Peace to End Peace: The Paris Peace Conference of 1919* (New York: Harcourt Brace, 1969), p. 93.
8. Ibid.
9. John M. Thompson, *Russia, Bolshevism, and the Versailles Peace* (Princeton, N.J.: Princeton University Press, 1966), pp. 167, 379.
10. Bullitt, *Mission to Russia,* p. 66.
11. Ibid., p. 94.
12. Ibid., p. 93.
13. Winston S. Churchill, *World Crisis, 1918–1928: The Aftermath* (New York: Scribner, 1929), p. 179.
14. *The Observer,* October 25, 1970.
15. British Foreign Office, 4954 FO 371/4001, 54942 4/9/19.
16. Ibid., 4954 FO 371/4002A, 105169 7/21/19.
17. Ibid., 4954 FO 371/4002A, 105159 7/21/19, 108759 7/28/19.
18. Ibid., 4954 FO 371/4003, 146853 10/10/19.

618 : *References*

19. Bullitt, *Mission to Russia,* p. 96.
20. Farnsworth, p. 67.
21. Bullitt file.

CHAPTER 2   Introduction to the Governor 1932–1933 (*pages 15–33*)

1. Eugene Lyons, *Assignment in Utopia* (New York: Harcourt Brace, 1937), p. 500.
2. Louis B. Wehle, *Hidden Threads of History* (New York: Macmillan, 1953), p. 113.
3. William E. Dodd, Jr., and Martha Dodd, eds., *Ambassador Dodd's Diary 1933–1938* (New York: Harcourt Brace, 1941), p. 278.
4. Wehle, p. 118.
5. Ibid., p. 119.
6. Ibid.
7. Philadelphia *Inquirer,* February 3, 1933.
8. British Foreign Office, 4954 FO 371/16666, 117, C845 1/31/33.
9. Harold L. Ickes, *The Secret Diary of Harold L. Ickes* (New York: Simon and Schuster, 1954), vol. 1, p. 658.

CHAPTER 3   Assistant to Secretary of State 1933 (*pages 34–53*)

1. Cordell Hull, *The Memoirs of Cordell Hull* (New York: Macmillan, 1948), vol. 1, p. 260.
2. Ibid., p. 267.
3. Ibid., p. 296.

CHAPTER 4   Ambassador to the Soviet Union 1933 (*pages 57–75*)

1. William Phillips, *Ventures in Diplomacy* (Boston: Beacon Press, 1952), p. 158.
2. British Foreign Office, FO 371/16599, A1668 4954 372 3/4/33.
3. Ibid., FO N8689, FO 311/17255, 4954 254 12/6/33.
4. Cordell Hull, *The Memoirs of Cordell Hull* (New York: Macmillan, 1948), vol. 1, p. 200.
5. Louis B. Wehle, *Hidden Threads of History* (New York: Macmillan, 1953), p. 115.

CHAPTER 5   The Beginning of Disillusionment 1934 (*pages 76–89*)

1. Cordell Hull, *The Memoirs of Cordell Hull* (New York: Macmillan, 1948), vol. 1, p. 303.
2. U.S. Foreign Relations, telegram 9/19/35, 124.611/274A275.
3. U.S. Foreign Relations, telegram 4/9/34, Soviet Union 1934, 800.51 W89 USSR/28.

CHAPTER 6   Attempts at Friendship 1934 (*pages 90–100*)

1. Hull's letters 123, Bullitt/179, State Department, Department of Communications and Records, 1/8/35.

CHAPTER 7   Inside European Diplomacy 1935 (*pages 101–114*)

1. Winston S. Churchill, *The Second World War* (Boston: Houghton Mifflin, 1948–1953), vol. 1, p. 123.
2. Ibid., p. 129.

CHAPTER 9   The Third International Congress and Disappointment 1935 (*pages 129–142*)

1. British Foreign Office, N6058 4783, FO 371/19449 11/23/35.
2. U.S. Foreign Relations, Soviet Union 1934, 811.003/1543A.
3. Charles E. Bohlen, *The Transformation of American Foreign Policy* (New York: W. W. Norton, 1969), p. 57.
4. William Phillips, *Ventures in Diplomacy* (Boston: Beacon Press, 1952), p. 163.
5. U.S. Foreign Relations, Soviet Union 1935, Bullitt to Hull telegram 711.61/573, 11/9/35.
6. Ibid.
7. Winston S. Churchill, *The Second World War* (Boston: Houghton Mifflin, 1948–1953), vol. 1, p. 133.
8. John Morton Blum, *Roosevelt and Morgenthau* (Boston: Houghton Mifflin, 1970), p. 134.

CHAPTER 10   Leaving Russia 1936 (*pages 143–163*)

1. Bullitt to Hull, Berlin 5/18/36, State Department 740.00/52.
2. British Foreign Office, 371/20349 4783, N2609 344 5/15/36.
3. Ibid.
4. George F. Kennan, *Memoirs, 1925–1950* (Boston: Little, Brown, 1967), p. 80.
5. Ibid., p. 79.

CHAPTER 11   Paris at Last 1936 (*pages 167–193*)

1. James A. Farley, *Jim Farley's Story, the Roosevelt Years* (New York: McGraw Hill, 1948), p. 194.
2. Juliusz Lukasiewicz, *Diplomat in Paris 1936–1939*, ed. Waclaw Jedrzejewicz (New York: Columbia University Press, 1970), p. 303.
3. Robert Murphy, *Diplomat Among Warriors* (New York: Doubleday, 1964), p. 29.
4. Ibid., p. 30.
5. Ibid., p. 32.
6. Harold L. Ickes, *The Secret Diary of Harold L. Ickes* (New York: Simon and Schuster, 1954), vol. 3, p. 124.
7. Ibid., p. 136.
8. Paul Reynaud, *La France A Sauvé l'Europe* (Paris: Flammarion, 1963), p. 505.
9. Chautemps to Fitzgibbons, April 2, 1958, a personal letter.
10. Forrest Davis and Ernest K. Lindley, *How War Came: An American*

White Paper: From the Fall of France to Pearl Harbor (New York: Simon and Schuster, 1942), p. 45.

CHAPTER 13 The Tension Tightens 1937 (*pages 203–220*)

1. British Foreign Office, C1533 4786 2/24/37, FO 371/22909.

CHAPTER 14 Personal Diplomacy 1937 (*pages 221–244*)

1. Telegram, Bullitt to Hull, 7/30/37, 793.94/9098.
2. Bullitt file.
3. Bullitt to Hull, 11/23/37, 1267 123/382, State Department, Department of Communications and Records.

CHAPTER 15 Reconciling France and Germany of No Avail 1938 (*pages 245–265*)

1. Gordon A. Craig and Felix Gilbert, eds., *The Diplomats 1919–1939* (Princeton, N.J.: Princeton University Press, 1953), vol. 1, p. 656.
2. Ibid., p. 657.
3. Winston S. Churchill, *The Second World War* (Boston: Houghton Mifflin, 1948–1953), vol. 1, p. 28.
4. Charles Callan Tansill, *Back Door to War* (Chicago: Henry Regnery, 1952), p. 321.
5. William L. Shirer, *The Rise and Fall of the Third Reich: A History of Nazi Germany* (New York: Simon and Schuster, 1960), p. 298.
6. Harold L. Ickes, *The Secret Diary of Harold L. Ickes* (New York: Simon and Schuster, 1954), vol. 2, p. 381.
7. George H. Hanna, *Outline History of the U.S.S.R.*, trans. by author (Moscow: Foreign Languages Publishing House, 1960), p. 315.
8. Churchill, *Second World War*, vol. 1, p. 254.

CHAPTER 16 France Awakens 1938 (*pages 266–283*)

1. Gordon A. Craig and Felix Gilbert, eds., *The Diplomats 1919–1939* (Princeton, N.J.: Princeton University Press, 1953), p. 662.
2. William L. Langer and S. Everett Gleason, *The Challenge to Isolation, 1937–1940* (New York: Harper and Brothers, 1952), p. 123.
3. Juliusz Lukasiewicz, *Diplomat in Paris 1936–1939*, ed. Waclaw Jedrzejewicz (New York: Columbia University Press, 1970), p. 98.
4. Charles A. Lindbergh, *The Wartime Journals of Charles A. Lindbergh* (New York: Harcourt Brace, 1970), p. 36.
5. Ibid., p. 70.
6. Ibid., p. 81.
7. Ibid., p. 82.
8. William L. Shirer, *The Rise and Fall of the Third Reich: A History of Nazi Germany* (New York: Simon and Schuster, 1960), pp. 376–377.
9. Lukasiewicz, *Diplomat in Paris*, p. xix.

CHAPTER 17   Berchtesgaden 1938 *(pages 284–303)*

1. Georges Bonnet, *Défense de la Paix: De Washington au Quai d'Orsay* (Geneva: Les Éditions du Cheval Aile, 1946), p. 205.
2. Georges Bonnet, *Vingt Ans de Vie Politique 1918–1938* (Paris: Fayard, 1969), p. 261.
3. Bonnet, *Quai d'Orsay*, p. 205.
4. Ibid., p. 207.
5. Ibid., p. 206.
6. Winston S. Churchill, *The Second World War* (Boston: Houghton Mifflin, 1948–1953), vol. 1, p. 301.
7. Cordell Hull, *The Memoirs of Cordell Hull* (New York: Macmillan, 1948), vol. 1, p. 591.
8. Eduard Beneš, *Memoirs of Dr. Eduard Beneš: From Munich to New War and New Victory*, trans. by Godfrey Lias (Boston: Houghton Mifflin, 1928), p. 173.
9. Mark S. Watson, *United States Army in World War II: The War Department, Chief of Staff Pre-War Plans and Preparations* (Washington: Historical Division, Department of the Army, 1950), p. 131.
10. John McVickar Haight, Jr., *American Aid to France: 1938–1940* (New York: Atheneum, 1970), pp. 28–35.
11. Ibid., pp. 91–92.

CHAPTER 18   The Fatal Year — The Need for Planes 1939
    (pages 304–330)

1. Juliusz Lukasiewicz, *Diplomat in Paris 1936–1939*, ed. Waclaw Jedrzejewicz (New York: Columbia University Press, 1970), pp. 168–169.
2. Ibid., p. 170.
3. Galeazzo Ciano, *The Ciano Diaries* (New York: Doubleday, 1946), pp. 9–10.
4. Winston S. Churchill, *The Second World War* (Boston: Houghton Mifflin, 1948–1953), vol. 1, p. 345.
5. Paul Reynaud, *Mémoires — 1936–1940* (Paris: Flammarion, 1963), p. 265.
6. Cordell Hull, *The Memoirs of Cordell Hull* (New York: Macmillan, 1948), vol. 1, pp. 616–617.
7. U.S. Foreign Relations, France 1939, 851.248/154 3/7/39 138.
8. Lukasiewicz, *Diplomat in Paris*, p. 174.
9. Ibid., p. 175.
10. Ibid., p. 180.
11. Ibid., pp. 182–183.
12. Harold L. Ickes, *The Secret Diary of Harold L. Ickes* (New York: Simon and Schuster, 1954), vol. 2, p. 602.

CHAPTER 19   Hitler Will Not Stop 1939 *(pages 331–343)*

1. William L. Langer and S. Everett Gleason, *The Challenge to Isolation 1937–1940* (New York: Harper and Brothers, 1952), p. 126.

2. Juliusz Lukasiewicz, *Diplomat in Paris 1936–1939,* ed. Waclaw Jedrze-jewicz (New York: Columbia University Press, 1970), p. 185.
3. Charles Callan Tansill, *Back Door to War* (Chicago: Henry Regnery, 1952), pp. 528–529.

CHAPTER 20   Horses, Israel, and a Queen 1939 *(pages 344–361)*

1. Telegram Bullitt to Hull, 4/12/39 740.787.
2. Cordell Hull, *The Memoirs of Cordell Hull* (New York: Macmillan, 1948), vol. 1, p. 652.
3. Saul Friedlander, *Prelude to Downfall: Hitler and the United States, 1939–1941* (New York: Viking Press, 1966), pp. 73–74.

CHAPTER 21   War 1939 *(pages 365–375)*

1. Cordell Hull, *The Memoirs of Cordell Hull* (New York: Macmillan, 1948), vol. 1, p. 656.
2. Ibid., p. 660.
3. Franklin D. Roosevelt, *F. D. R., His Personal Letters, 1928–1945,* ed. Elliott Roosevelt (New York: Duell, Sloan and Pearce, 1950), vol. 2, p. 915.
4. Hull, *Memoirs,* vol. 1, pp. 671–672.
5. George H. Hanna, *Outline History of the U.S.S.R.,* trans. by author (Moscow: Foreign Languages Publishing House, 1960), p. 316.
6. Robert Murphy, *Diplomat Among Warriors* (New York: Doubleday, 1964), p. 33.
7. Juliusz Lukasiewicz, *Diplomat in Paris 1936–1939,* ed. Waclaw Jedrze-jewicz (New York: Columbia University Press, 1970), pp. 302–305.

CHAPTER 22   Supplies to the Allies 1939 *(pages 376–396)*

1. Cordell Hull, *The Memoirs of Cordell Hull* (New York: Macmillan, 1948), vol. 1, p. 683.
2. Harold L. Ickes, *The Secret Diary of Harold L. Ickes* (New York: Simon and Schuster, 1954), vol. 3, pp. 136, 230.
3. William L. Langer and S. Everett Gleason, *The Challenge to Isolation 1937–1940* (New York: Harper and Brothers, 1952), pp. 509–510.
4. Hull, *Memoirs,* vol. 1, pp. 705–706.
5. Ibid., pp. 709–710.
6. George H. Hanna, *Outline History of the U.S.S.R.,* trans. by author (Moscow: Foreign Languages Publishing House, 1960), p. 317.

CHAPTER 23   Hitler Attacks 1940 *(pages 397–438)*

1. Robert Murphy, *Diplomat Among Warriors* (New York: Doubleday, 1964), p. 34.
2. State Department, 1/25/40 740.00119 EW.
3. Harold L. Ickes, *The Secret Diary of Harold L. Ickes* (New York: Simon and Schuster, 1954), vol. 3, p. 138.

4. Murphy, *Diplomat*, p. 35.
5. Cordell Hull, *The Memoirs of Cordell Hull* (New York: Macmillan. 1948), vol. 1, pp. 737–738.
6. British Foreign Office, 117 FO 371/24406, 1807 3/18/40.
7. Alistair Horne, *To Lose a Battle: France 1940* (Boston: Little, Brown, 1969), p. 573.
8. Telegrams to State Dept., 563, 5/2/40; 571, 5/3/40; 594, 5/8/40.
9. Winston S. Churchill, *The Second World War* (Boston: Houghton Mifflin, 1948–1953), vol. 1, p. 667.
10. James V. Compton, *The Swastika and the Eagle* (Boston: Houghton Mifflin, 1967), p. 91.
11. Telegrams to State Dept., 639, 5/13/40; 640, 5/13/40; 642, 5/13/40; 646, 5/13/40; 657, 5/14/40.
12. Telegrams to State Dept., 665, 5/15/40; 686, 5/15/40; 696, 5/15/40; 697, 5/16/40; 709, 5/16/40.
13. Churchill, *Second World War*, vol. 2, p. 154.
14. John McVickar Haight, Jr., *American Aid to France: 1938–1940* (New York: Atheneum, 1970), pp. 54–55.
15. Charles A. Lindbergh, *The Wartime Journals of Charles A. Lindbergh* (New York: Harcourt Brace, 1970), pp. 35–36, 70, 82–83.
16. Albert Speer, *Inside the Third Reich*, trans. Richard and Clara Winston (New York: Macmillan, 1970), p. 407.
17. Bundesarciv/Militararciv (BA-MA) RL 2/1737, vol. 8, V. 4.5–29.6 1940.
18. Andreas Hillgruber and Gerhard Hümmelchen, *Chronik des Zweiten Weltkrieges* (Frankfurt am Main: Bernard and Graefe Verlag für Wehrwesen), pp. 9, 10.
19. Adolf Galland, *The First and the Last: The Rise and Fall of German Fighter Forces, 1938–1945*, trans. Mervyn Savill (New York: Henry Holt, 1954), p. 14.
20. Churchill, *Second World War*, vol. 2, p. 715.
21. Assemblée Nationale, *Commission of Inquiry on Events in France, 1933 to 1945* (Paris: Presses Universitaires de France, 1951), no. 2344, vol. 2, p. 343.
22. Assemblée Nationale, *Commission of Inquiry*, vol. 2, p. 337.
23. Ibid., p. 343.
24. Churchill, *Second World War*, vol. 2, p. 41.
25. Hillgruber and Hümmelchen, *Chronik*, p. 10.
26. Galland, *The First and the Last*, p. 13.
27. Assemblée Nationale, *Commission of Inquiry*, vol. 2, p. 343.
28. Ibid., p. 353.
29. Ibid., pp. 354–355.
30. Ibid., p. 388.
31. Ibid.
32. Hull, *Memoirs*, vol. 1, p. 766.
33. British Foreign Office, A 1945 FO 371/24251 1807, 187 5/22/40.
34. Ibid., A1945 FO 371/24251 1807, 188 5/22/40.
35. Ibid., A1945 FO 371/24251 1807, 186 5/23/40.
36. Ibid., A605 FO 371/24251 1807, 163 1/25/40.

CHAPTER 24   The Swastika in Paris 1940 (*pages 439–493*)

1. Raul Reynaud, *Mémoires — 1936–1940* (Paris: Flammarion, 1963), p. 395.
2. Paul Reynaud, *La France A Sauvé l'Europe* (Paris: Flammarion, 1947), p. 198.
3. William L. Shirer, *The Collapse of the Third Republic* (New York: Simon and Schuster, 1969), pp. 681–682.
4. *New York Times*, June 10, 1940.
5. Reynaud, *La France*, p. 296.
6. Winston S. Churchill, *The Second World War* (Boston: Houghton Mifflin, 1948–1953), vol. 2, p. 118.
7. Bullitt file.
8. Cordell Hull, *The Memoirs of Cordell Hull* (New York: Macmillan, 1948), vol. 1, pp. 789–790.
9. Robert Murphy, *Diplomat Among Warriors* (New York: Doubleday, 1964), p. 41.
10. Charles de Gaulle, *The War Memoirs of Charles de Gaulle* (New York: Viking Press, 1955), vol. 1, p. 61.
11. Roger Langeron, *Paris, Juin 40* (Paris: Flammarion, 1946), p. 26.
12. Ibid., p. 31.
13. Ibid., p. 54.
14. Ibid., p. 65.
15. Ibid., p. 108.
16. Shirer, *Third Republic*, p. 905.
17. George H. Hanna, *Outline History of the U.S.S.R.*, trans. by author (Moscow: Foreign Languages Publishing House, 1960), p. 317.
18. Ibid., p. 316.

CHAPTER 25   Warning America 1940–1941 (*pages 497–518*)

1. William L. Langer and S. Everett Gleason, *The Challenge to Isolation 1937–1940* (New York: Harper and Brothers, 1952), p. 756.
2. Philadelphia *Record*, August 19, 1940.
3. Winston S. Churchill, *The Second World War* (Boston: Houghton Mifflin, 1948–1953), vol. 2, p. 402.
4. Cordell Hull, *The Memoirs of Cordell Hull* (New York: Macmillan, 1948), vol. 1, p. 1231.
5. Welles file, Hyde Park Library.

CHAPTER 26   Attack on Russia 1941 (*pages 519–526*)

1. Harold L. Ickes, *The Secret Diary of Harold L. Ickes* (New York: Simon and Schuster, 1954), vol. 3, pp. 538–539.
2. George H. Hanna, *Outline History of the U.S.S.R.*, trans. by author (Moscow: Foreign Languages Publishing House, 1960), p. 319.

CHAPTER 27   Egypt and War with Japan 1941–1942
(*pages 527–545*)

1. Winston S. Churchill, *The Second World War* (Boston: Houghton Mifflin, 1948–1953), vol. 3, p. 200.
2. Ibid., vol. 4, p. 600.
3. Ibid., vol. 4, p. 601.
4. Bullitt file.
5. Churchill, *Second World War*, vol. 3, p. 619.
6. William L. Langer, *Our Vichy Gamble* (New York: Knopf, 1947), p. 285.

CHAPTER 29   Out of a Job 1942 (*pages 551–556*)

1. Laslo Havas, *Assassinat au Sommet* (Paris: B. Arthaud, 1968), pp. 100–101.

CHAPTER 30   In the Navy 1942 (*pages 557–568*)

1. Winston S. Churchill, *The Second World War* (Boston: Houghton Mifflin, 1948–1953), vol. 4, p. 443.
2. Stimson papers, Yale University Library.
3. Albert Speer, *Inside the Third Reich*, trans. Richard and Clara Winston (New York: Macmillan, 1970), p. 273.
4. Robert Murphy, *Diplomat Among Warriors* (New York: Doubleday, 1964), p. 112.
5. Churchill, *Second World War*, vol. 4, p. 687.
6. Ibid., vol. 4, pp. 666, 667, 668.

CHAPTER 31   Accurate Forecasts — A Plan for Europe 1942–1943
(*pages 571–600*)

1. William D. Leahy, *I Was There* (New York: McGraw Hill, 1950), pp. 148–149.
2. Birkenhead, Earl of, *Life of Lord Halifax* (Boston: Houghton Mifflin, 1966), p. 548.

CHAPTER 32   Victory and Death 1944–1945 (*pages 601–614*)

1. Charles de Gaulle, *The War Memoirs of Charles de Gaulle* (New York: Viking Press, 1955), vol. 2, p. 299.
2. Ibid., vol. 3, p. 160.

Bibliography

1. Barros, James. *Betrayal from Within*. New Haven: Yale University Press, 1969.
2. Bendiner, Robert. *The Riddle of the State Department*. New York: Farrar & Rinehart, Inc., 1942.
3. Beneš, Eduard. *Memoirs of Dr. Eduard Beneš: From Munich to New War and New Victory*. Translated by Godfrey Lias. Boston: Houghton Mifflin, 1928.
4. Berzins, Alfreds. *The Two Faces of Co-Existence*. New York: Robert Speller and Sons, 1967.
5. Birkenhead, Earl of. *Life of Lord Halifax*. Boston: Houghton Mifflin, 1966.
6. Blum, John Morton. *Roosevelt and Morgenthau*. Boston: Houghton Mifflin, 1970.
7. Bohlen, Charles E. *The Transformation of American Foreign Policy*. New York: W. W. Norton, 1969.
8. Bonnet, Georges. *Défense de la Paix*. Geneva: Les Éditions du Cheval Aile, 1946.
   ————. *Vingt Ans de Vie Politique: 1918–1938*. Paris: Fayard, 1969.
9. Bullitt, A. Ernesta. *An Uncensored Diary from the Central Empires*. New York: Doubleday, 1917.
10. Bullitt, William C. *The Bullitt Mission to Russia*. New York: B. W. Huebsch, 1919.
    ————. *It's Not Done*. New York: Harcourt Brace, 1926.
    ————. *Report to the American People*. Boston: Houghton Mifflin, 1940.
    ————. *The Great Globe Itself*. New York: Scribner, 1946.
    ————. *Report to the Joint Committee on Foreign Economic Cooperation Concerning China*. Washington: U.S. Government Printing Office, 1948.
    ————. Sundry magazine articles.
11. Burns, James MacGregor. *Roosevelt: The Soldier of Freedom*. New York: Harcourt Brace, 1970.
12. Chandos, Lord. *Memoirs: An Unexpected View from the Summit*. London: Bodley Head, 1962.
13. Churchill, Winston S. *World Crisis, 1918–1928: The Aftermath*. New York: Scribner, 1929.

————. *The Second World War.* 6 vols. Boston: Houghton Mifflin, 1948–1953.

14. Ciano, Galeazzo. *The Ciano Diaries.* New York: Doubleday, 1946.

15. Compton, James V. *The Swastika and the Eagle.* Boston: Houghton Mifflin, 1967.

16. Craig, Gordon A., and Gilbert, Felix, eds. *The Diplomats: 1919–1939.* 2 vols. Princeton: Princeton University Press, 1953.

17. Davis, Forrest, and Lindley, Ernest K. *How War Came: An American White Paper: From the Fall of France to Pearl Harbor.* New York: Simon and Schuster, 1942.

18. Deane, John R. *The Strange Alliance.* New York: Viking Press, 1947.

19. de Gaulle, Charles. *The War Memoirs of Charles de Gaulle.* 3 vols. New York: Viking Press, 1955.

20. Dodd, William E., Jr., and Dodd, Martha, eds. *Ambassador Dodd's Diary 1933–1938.* New York: Harcourt Brace, 1941.

21. Dugan, James, and Stewart, Carroll. *Ploesti: Great Ground-Air Battle, 1 August 1943.* New York: Random House, 1962.

22. Farley, James A. *Jim Farley's Story, the Roosevelt Years.* New York: McGraw Hill, 1948.

23. Farnsworth, Beatrice. *William C. Bullitt and the Soviet Union.* Bloomington: Indiana University Press, 1967.

24. Fischer, Louis. *Men and Politics: An Autobiography.* New York: Duell, Sloan and Pearce, 1941.

25. Forrestal, James. *The Forrestal Diaries.* Edited by Walter Millis and E. S. Duffield. New York: Viking Press, 1966.

26. Friedlander, Saul. *Prelude to Downfall: Hitler and the United States, 1939–1941.* Translated from the French by Aline B. and Alexander Werth. New York: Knopf, 1967.

27. Galland, Adolf. *The First and the Last: The Rise and Fall of the German Fighter Forces, 1938–1945.* Translated by Mervyn Savill. New York: Ballantine Books, 1965.

28. Gamelin, Maurice G. *Servir La Guerre: Septembre 1939–19 Mai 1940.* Paris: Librairie Plon, 1946.

29. Gardner, Lloyd C. *Architects of Illusion: Men and Ideas in American Foreign Policy.* Chicago: Quadrangle Books, 1970.

30. Goldberg, George. *The Peace to End Peace: The Paris Peace Conference of 1919.* New York: Harcourt Brace, 1969.

31. Grew, Joseph C. *Turbulent Era.* Boston: Houghton Mifflin, 1952.

32. Haight, John McVickar, Jr. *American Aid to France: 1938–1940.* New York: Atheneum, 1970.

33. Hanna, George H. *Outline History of the U.S.S.R.* Translated by the author. Moscow: Foreign Languages Publishing House, 1960.

34. Hart, B. H. Liddell. *History of the Second World War.* New York: Putnam, 1971.

35. Havas, Laslo. *Assassinat au Sommet.* Paris: B. Arthaud, 1968.

36. Hillgruber, Andreas, and Hümmelchen, Gerhard. *Chronik des Zweiten Weltkrieges.* Frankfurt am Main: Bernard and Graefe Verlag für Wehrwesen, 1966.

37. Horne, Alistair. *To Lose a Battle: France 1940.* Boston: Little, Brown, 1969.

38. Hull, Cordell. *The Memoirs of Cordell Hull.* 2 vols. New York: Macmillan, 1948.
39. Ickes, Harold L. *The Secret Diary of Harold L. Ickes.* New York: Simon and Schuster, 1954.
40. Kennan, George F. *Memoirs, 1925–1950.* Boston: Little, Brown, 1967.
    ———. *Russia Leaves the War: The Americans in Petrograd and the Bolshevik Revolution.* Princeton: Princeton University Press, 1956.
41. Langer, William L. *Our Vichy Gamble.* New York: Knopf, 1947.
42. ——— and S. Everett Gleason. *The Challenge to Isolation, 1937–1940.* New York: Harper and Brothers, 1952.
43. Langeron, Roger. *Paris, Juin 40.* Paris: Flammarion, 1946.
44. Leahy, William D. *I Was There.* New York: McGraw Hill, 1950.
45. Leuchtenburg, William E. *Franklin D. Roosevelt and the New Deal.* New York: Harper and Row, 1963.
46. Lindbergh, Charles A. *The Wartime Journals of Charles A. Lindbergh.* New York: Harcourt Brace, 1970.
47. Lukasiewicz, Juliusz. *Diplomat in Paris 1936–1939.* Edited by Waclaw Jedrzejewicz. New York: Columbia University Press, 1970.
48. Lyons, Eugene. *Assignment in Utopia.* New York: Harcourt Brace, 1937.
49. Murphy, Robert. *Diplomat Among Warriors.* New York: Doubleday, 1964.
50. Phillips, William. *Ventures in Diplomacy.* Boston: Beacon Press, 1952.
51. Rauch, Basil. *Roosevelt from Munich to Pearl Harbor.* New York: Creative Age Press, 1950.
52. Reynaud, Paul. *Mémoires — 1936–1940.* Paris: Flammarion, 1963.
    ———. *La France A Sauvé l'Europe.* Paris: Flammarion, 1947.
53. Roosevelt, Franklin D. *F.D.R., His Personal Letters.* 4 vols. Edited by Elliott Roosevelt. New York: Duell, Sloan and Pearce, 1950.
    ———. *The Public Papers and Addresses of Franklin D. Roosevelt.* 13 vols. Edited by Samuel I. Rosenman. New York and London: Macmillan, 1938–1950.
54. Shirer, William L. *The Rise and Fall of the Third Reich: A History of Nazi Germany.* New York: Simon and Schuster, 1960.
    ———. *The Collapse of the Third Republic.* New York: Simon and Schuster, 1969.
55. Sims, Edward H. *The Greatest Aces.* New York: Harper and Row, 1968.
56. Spears, Edward L. *Assignment to Catastrophe.* 2 vols. New York: A. A. Wyn, Inc., 1955.
57. Speer, Albert. *Inside the Third Reich: Memoirs.* Translated by Richard and Clara Winston. New York: Macmillan, 1970.
58. Steffens, Lincoln. *Autobiography of Lincoln Steffens.* New York: Harcourt Brace, 1931.
59. Sulzberger, C. L. *A Long Row of Candles.* New York: Macmillan, 1969.
60. Tansill, Charles Callan. *Back Door to War.* Chicago: Henry Regnery, 1952.
61. Thayer, Charles W. *Bears in the Caviar.* Philadelphia: Lippincott, 1950.
62. Thompson, John M. *Russia, Bolshevism, and the Versailles Peace.* Princeton: Princeton University Press, 1966.
63. Thompson, Laurence. *The Greatest Treason: The Untold Story of Munich.* New York: William Morrow, 1968.

64. Thorne, Christopher. *The Approach of War, 1938–1939*. New York: St. Martin's Press, 1967.
65. Walsh, Warren Bartlett. *Russia and the Soviet Union*. Ann Arbor: University of Michigan Press, 1958.
66. Watson, Mark S. *United States Army in World War II: The War Department, Chief of Staff Pre-War Plans and Preparations*. Washington: Historical Division, Department of the Army, 1950.
67. Wehle, Louis B. *Hidden Threads of History: Wilson Through Roosevelt*. New York: Macmillan, 1953.
68. Williams, John. *The Ides of May*. London: Constable, 1968.

Index

Index